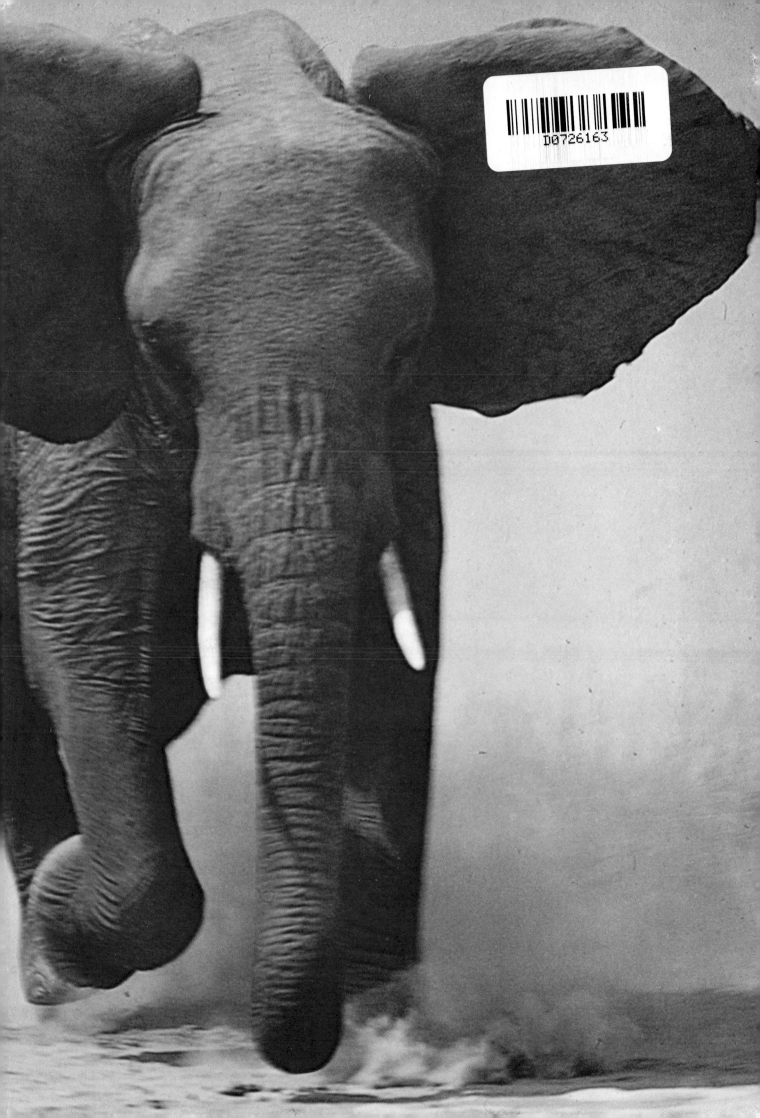

ENCYCLOPAEDIA
OF ANIMALS
IN COLOUR

Edited by Dr Maurice Burton

ENCYCLOPAEDIA OF ANIMALS IN COLOUR

Foreword by Lord Zuckerman FRS

OCTOPUS

ACKNOWLEDGMENTS

The Publishers would like to thank the following individuals and organizations for their kind permission to reproduce the illustrations in this book.

Photographers are listed alphabetically with their agent's initials, where applicable, abbreviated as follows:

(AFA)   Associated Freelance Artists Ltd
(Ardea)   Ardea Photographics
(NSP)   Natural Science Photos
(Res)   Bruce Coleman Ltd

H. Albrecht (Res) 74
Australian News & Information Bureau 59(t)
M.E. Bacchus (NSP) 170
Des Bartlett (Res) 17, 18(b), 37(t), 52, 60(b), 93, 112, 140(r), 176(b), 187(t), 215(b), 232(b), 234, 275
P. Boston (NSP) 151(t)
P.A. Bowman (NSP) 101(l)
J.D. Bradley (NSP) 60(t)
T.R.M. Brosset (NSP) 213
J. Brownlie (Res) 31, 54, 279
Jane Burton (Res) 22, 23, 57(t), 72(br), 80(t), 82, 104, 114, 116(b), 138(b), 146(b), 164(t), 166(b), 171(b), 173(b), 191, 192, 194(b), 196(b), 197, 204(tl,tr), 208(t), 214(b), 218(t,b), 226(t), 237(t), 241, 254(b), 271(b)
P.J.K. Burton (NSP) 148, 195(b), 263
R.W. Burton 27
B. Campbell (Res) 72(tl), 103(tr), 161, 206(b)
M.J. Coe (NSP) 62, 142
Bruce Coleman (Res) 182(b), 272, 288
P.R. Colston (NSP) 115
D. Corke 128, 132(b), 169(r)
W. Curth (Ardea) 124(t)
J. Dermid (Res) 208(b)
M. Desfayes 229(t)
Nicole Duplaix 44, 103(tl)
A.W. Engman (Res) 66(b)
A. Foley (AFA) 168(t)
Dr J.B. Free 26(br), 131(b), 151(b), 152, 153, 215(t), 276(t)
C. Frith (NSP) 107, 118
Dr C.H. Fry 45, 46(t)
Mrs H. Gauthier-Pilters 67
Sven Gillsater (Res) 163(b), 250
J.A. Grant (NSP) 51
A. Gray (NSP) 53
C.A. Guggisberg (Res) 203(b), 242
G. Hakansson (Res) 32
J.A. Hancock (Res) 110(t)

Dr M.P. Harris 96, 119, 121(t), 202
W. Harstrick (Res) 29(l)
E.H. Herbert (AFA) 85, 210
Udo Hirsch 50, 81(t), 144(tr), 169(l), 277
Dr C.M. Hladik 68, 130, 181(t), 185, 220(t), 294
Eric Hosking 1, 49, 78(b), 81(b), 83(t), 92, 98(b), 133(t,b), 136(t), 139, 174(t), 175, 194(t), 196(t), 200, 206(t), 219, 228, 229(b), 244, 293(t)
D. Hughes (Res) 20(t), 95(r)
Peter Jackson (Res) 33, 58(b), 90, 109(t), 193(t)
Russ Kinne (Res) 37(b), 40(bl,br), 46(b), 78(t), 84(b), 88(t), 100(b), 113, 144(tc), 188, 204(b), 262(t), 280
Geoffrey Kinns (AFA) 87, 129(b), 134, 149, 150(t), 183(b), 214(t), 236, 266
Leonard Lee Rue (Res) 125, 286
D.B. Lewis (NSP) 232(t), 235(t), 293(b)
D. MacCaskill (AFA) 147(b)
John Markham 159, 172, 178, 205, 292, 296
Dr R.D. Martin 176(t), 260
J.H. Mehrtens 29(r)
Dr P.A. Morris 17, 26(t), 55, 56, 75, 80(b), 100(t), 127(t), 138(t), 158(b), 198, 220(b), 222, 224(tr), 243, 256(l,r), 262(b), 290(t)
W.J.C. Murray (Res) 240
R.K. Murton (Res) 102(b), 150(b)
Norman Myers (Res) 66(t), 257, 270
E.G. Neal (Res) 34(b)
John Norris-Wood (NSP) 193(b), 230(bl)
Charles Ott (Res) 69, 226(b)
L.E. Perkins (NSP) 105
R.T. Peterson (Res) 19(br)
Graham Pizzey (Res) 38, 97, 122, 183(t), 186, 225, 274(b)
H.J. Pollock (Res) 79
J. Pope (NSP) 77, 132(t)
Dr D. Pye 41(b), 42(t)
Masood Quarishy (Res) 165, 207(b)
D. Robinson (Res) 43, 230(t)
T.W. Roth (Res) 187(b)

Arne Schmitz (Res) 63
Vincent Serventy (Res) 58(t)
Heinz Sielmann 47(t,b)
Sher Jang Singh (Res) 89(b), 199, 278
H. Silvester (Res) 156
James Simon (Res) 48(b), 166(t), 273
M.F. Soper (Res) 168(b)
Simon Trevor (Res) 35, 72(cr), 111, 179
A. van den Nieuwenhuizen 6, 16, 20(b), 21, 24, 25, 28, 34(t), 41(t), 48(t), 59(b), 61, 65, 70(t,b), 71, 73, 76, 84(tl), 89(t), 91, 98(t), 103(bl,br), 108, 116(t), 120(t,b), 121(b), 124(b), 126, 127(b), 129(t), 131(t), 135(t,b), 136(b), 137, 141(b), 143, 144(tl), 144(b), 146(t), 147(tr), 155, 157(t), 162, 163(t), 164(b), 171(t), 174(b), 177(x3), 180, 181(b), 184, 189, 195(t), 201, 203(t), 207(tr), 209(l,r), 212, 217, 221, 223(b), 224(tl), 224(b), 230(br), 231, 235(b), 238, 248, 254(t), 258(t), 259, 261, 265, 267, 269, 271(t), 274(t), 282, 284, 287, 291, 298
Drs A.A.M. van der Heyden 109(b), 110(b), 157(b), 207(tl), 239, 276(b), 300
A. van der Werken 268
J. van Wormer (Res) 86, 147(tl), 190
R.W. Vaughan 19(t), 19(bl), 216(l,r), 255
P.H. Ward (NSP) 26(bl), 36, 64, 88(b), 102(tx3), 140(l), 160, 173(t), 246, 247, 283, 290(b)
Philip Wayre 39, 42(b)
J.S. Wightman (Ardea) 223(t), 233, 289, 297
Dr D.P. Wilson 2, 3, 18(t), 30, 40(t), 57(b), 83(b), 84(tr,tc), 94, 95(l), 99, 101(r), 141(t), 158(t), 182(t), 237(b), 249, 251, 253, 285(t,b)

Planned for Octopus Books Limited by
Elsevier International Projects Ltd, London
© Elsevier Sequoia SA, Lausanne

English version first published 1972 by
Octopus Books Limited
59 Grosvenor Street, London W1
Translation © 1972 Octopus Books Limited

Reprinted 1974, 1976, 1977

ISBN 0 7064 0168 9

Printed in Czechoslovakia by Polygrafia
50 335/2

FOREWORD

One would be able to read about lions, vampire bats and zebras in any ordinary encyclopaedia. So too one would about Henry VIII, printing presses and railway engines. In the days when one man could comprehend, or pretend to comprehend, all existing knowledge, a comprehensive encyclopaedia could also be written by one man. This long ago became impossible. Today we therefore have encyclopaedias on a single broad subject written by a team of experts each versed in one or other of its aspects.

This is a foreword to no ordinary encyclopaedia. First it is a work which deals with only a single branch of knowledge—zoology. But it is more than that. It is an abridged version of a much larger work, compiled by some two hundred authorities from all parts of the world, which will appear as several volumes under the editorship of Dr Burton, long a friend of The Zoological Society of London. In order that it could become available to a far wider readership, he and the publishers have wisely decided to condense the best of the full work into a relatively small volume.

One of the pleasing aspects of present-day publishing is the increasing use of colour. The first printed books on natural history were, of course, in black-and-white, and the pictures far from accurate. Colour was laborious and costly. Today it is a commonplace, and no-one wishing to give the general reader any sense of the richness of the world of living creatures would fail to take advantage of the methods of colour photography and printing which are now available. In this respect this present encyclopaedia, even if circumscribed in its text matter, sets a high standard. For this reason alone the book is to be welcomed. But above all it can be welcomed because it makes available in very handy form a reference guide to the changing animal world of which our own species, Man, provides only a single example of the richness of life.

5

The White-faced or Moustached tamarin, one of the South American marmosets. It lives in the vast upper Amazon basin from the lowlands to 600ft.

INTRODUCTION

The theory of evolution, the idea that life began in a very simple form and that the incalculable millions of plant and animal species evolved as the product of sequences of small changes, was taking shape in the minds of biologists long before Darwin. It is a popular misconception, which dies hard, that Darwin 'invented' the theory of evolution, and without belittling his achievements it must be recognized that he did no more than suggest a method by which it takes place. For it is only against the background of such an idea that the known facts of biology can be reasonably interpreted or make sense.

We can go further and say that even if the concept of evolution were false something comparable with it would need to be assumed in order to produce a logical classification of living organisms. And without such a classification the massive number of known species would be unmanageable.

In this encyclopaedia the customary method is used of arranging the subjects alphabetically, but each species or group of species described is also given a classification, of no more than family, order, class and phylum, these main taxa (a taxon is a major grouping) indicating its position in the animal kingdom. To anyone not fully versed in the subject these details have a limited value, so an overall view of the animal kingdom must be included.

The simplest animals now living are similar to the simplest whose fossils are known, scattered through the rocks for hundreds of millions of years past. They are the Protozoa, single-celled and microscopic. Although there is more than one opinion as to how the rest of the animal kingdom, of multicellular animals, arose from them, the easiest thing to visualize is that groups of single cells came to live together in loose colonies.

Some of the present-day Protozoa live in colonies, and sponges, in which the tissues are ill-defined, are little better than large and elaborate colonies of single cells which to a degree still retain individual autonomy. The sponges do not, however, indicate a main line of evolution; they are aberrant from it, a group of animals that went out on a limb. The big advance was made when the cells formed themselves into well-defined tissues, as they do in the Cnidaria (formerly known as the Coelenterata), which include the Sea anemones, hydra, jellyfishes and corals, also called stinging or nettle animals because they possess stinging cells, or nematocysts. In these the body is made up of two layers, an outer ectoderm or skin, and an inner endoderm, or digestive layer, with a gelatinous layer,

There are four groups of Protozoa, those which, like amoeba, move about by pseudopodia, or false feet, which are blunt or filamentous extensions of the protoplasm, often root-like, so the group is named Rhizopoda. It includes: 1. Amoeba; 2. *Difflugia*, which covers itself with sand-grains; 3. Foraminifera, with a calcareous shell, and 4. Radiolaria, with a siliceous skeleton. The next group, Flagellata or Mastigophora, has one or more flagella, and includes: 5. *Noctiluca*, a marine, luminescent member of the plankton, and 6. *Euglena*, and 7. *Volvox*, two of the so-called plant animals. The third group, Sporozoa, not represented in this diagram, are parasitic in the bodies of plants and animals. The fourth group, Ciliata or Ciliophora, bear cilia, either all over the body, as in 8. *Paramecium,* in a ring at one end, as in 9. *Stentor* or 10. *Vorticella,* or partly forming distinct organs of locomotion, so that the animal appears to walk with legs, as in 11. *Stylonichia*.

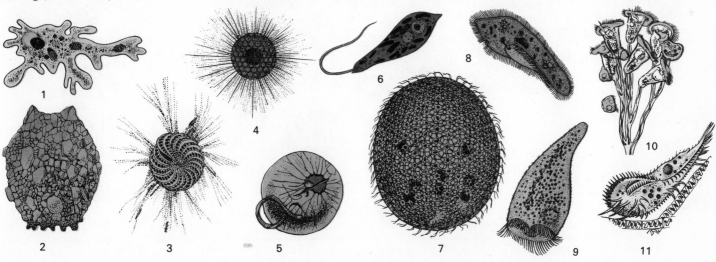

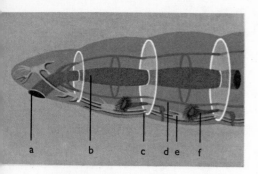

Head end of an earthworm to show the first few segments and their contained organs: a. mouth, b. gullet, c. nerve-cord, d. blood vessel, e. nerve ganglion, f. nephridium (excretory organ).

1. Life-history of a fly: a. egg, b. larva, c. pupa, d. adult leaving pupal case, e. its wings still crumpled, f. wings fully expanded and dried.

2. External features of a typical four-winged insect: a. antenna, b. compound eye, c. spiracle, d-h. parts of an insect's leg; d. coxa, e. trochanter, f. femur, g. tibia, h. tarsus.

3. Anatomy of a typical four-winged insect: a. brain, b. ocellus, c. gut, d. Malpighian tubule, e. gonad or reproductive organ, f. main blood vessel, g. main nerve cord.

or mesogloea, between. The body of a Sea anemone is, therefore, a hollow two-layered bag, a jellyfish being the same but with the mesogloea enormously increased.

All the rest of the animal kingdom, other than the Protozoa, sponges and Cnidaria, are three-layered, the third layer, or mesoderm, being the one that gives rise to the system of muscles. There are muscle fibrils in the Cnidaria, but they are not true muscle, and there is true muscle in a few sponges, but they do not compare with the muscle system of other animals.

The next big evolutionary step forward came when the muscle system became broken up into blocks so that the body was segmented. This is best seen in an earthworm (although there are a number of smaller groups, less specialized, for example the flatworms, which illustrate better how this probably came about). In an earthworm the body is ringed externally and each ring represents a segment.

From an earthworm-like ancestor sprang most of the invertebrate groups and also the vertebrates, by elaboration of the body tissues and an increase in the number of organs, as well as by the increasing specialization or organization of these organs. All the steps in the sequence took place long ago, in animals lost forever by decay or at best preserved as fossils. It is the hard parts, the skeletons, mainly that are preserved, although sometimes portions of the soft parts are also preserved. By deduction and analogy from such material as is available, however, a fairly clear picture can be built, enough to enable us to work out the broad lines of what took place. Even so there are gaps, small and large. One very large gap is that which we have already seen, between the Protozoa and the rest of the animal kingdom. Another will be encountered later.

Early in the study of zoology, it became apparent that there are three distinguishable large groupings: the Protozoa, the invertebrates and the vertebrates. At one time it was customary to speak of these as three sub-kingdoms of the animal kingdom. The three are of unequal value and size. The vertebrates include the well-known and familiar animals, the fishes, amphibians, reptiles, birds and mammals. The number of known

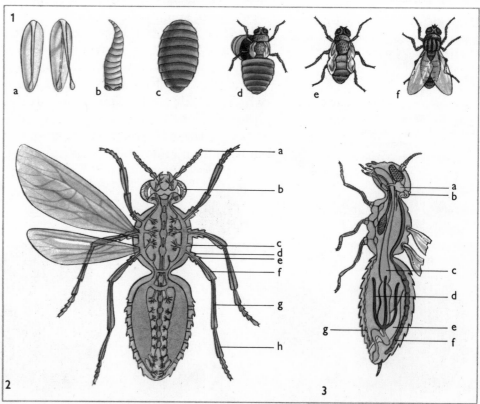

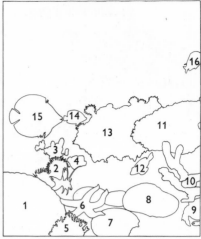

Undersea reefs, in warm seas, bear rich aggregations of many species: 1. Brain coral; 2. Hermit crab with Sea anemones on its shell; 3. Sea fans; 4. Sea mat or Moss animal; 5. Stag's horn coral; 6. Starfish; 7. mushroom-shaped solitary coral (*Fungia*); 8. Bath sponge; 9. Sponge crab (carrying a sponge on its back for camouflage); 10. Red or Precious coral (*Corallium rubrum*); 11. Organ pipe coral; 12. Sea perch (*Hypoplectus unicolor*); 13. Sea anemone (*Tealia*); 14. marine angelfish (*Pomacanthus arcuatus*); 15. Imperial angelfish (*P. imperator*), 16. porkfish (*Anisotremus virginicus*).

species currently estimated for the Protozoa is 50,000, that for the vertebrates is even less, at 43,300, while for the invertebrates (other than Protozoa, which should properly be included as invertebrate, or without backbone) is 1,200,000, of which 852,000 are insects. These figures are subject to wide fluctuations, according to who is making the account and also in time, because new species are constantly being described. Moreover, it is axiomatic that there are many new species yet to be discovered, particularly in the seas, among small parasites and in Protozoa. Consequently, the grand total quoted for living species may fluctuate from one to ten million, according to which book is consulted. The figures given here are conservative and they represent at least an approximate ratio between invertebrates and vertebrates of 30:1. Furthermore, the invertebrates, in strong contrast to the vertebrates, are diverse in appearance, structure and organization. This is emphasized when we consider the next level of grouping, the phyla (singular phylum).

The Protozoa form one phylum, the vertebrates are all included in another phylum, the Chordata, but the invertebrates are represented by 20 phyla, one of which is the enormous phylum Arthropoda, or jointed-legs, which embraces not only all the insects but also the crustaceans, spiders, ticks, mites, millipedes, centipedes and a few other groups.

This gives us the clue to visualizing the evolution of the animal kingdom in graphic form. Starting with the earliest forms of life 1,500,000,000 to 2,000,000,000 years ago (this estimate is still a matter for conjecture), the invertebrates proliferated along many lines (or phyla), which can be visualized as a leafless shrub. Some branches died out, others remained alive but threw out few twigs, others were long but without side-shoots, but one (the Arthropoda) threw out masses of twiggy shoots and tended

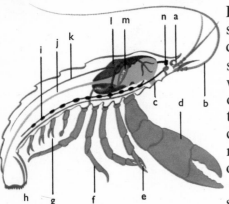

Anatomy of the crayfish: a. eye, b. antenna, c. mouth, d. chela or large claw, e. small claw on first pair of walking legs, f. walking leg, g. swimmeret on underside of abdomen, h. telson, or tail, i. central nerve cord, j. intestine, k. dorsal blood vessel, l. heart, m. gonad or reproductive organ, n. green gland or excretory organ.

Basically, the mammalian skull differs little from one order to another. The same bones are present although they differ in their proportions. The most obvious differences are in the teeth: 1. order Cetacea (dolphin), fish-eating, small conical teeth all of similar size; 2. order Primates (chimpanzee), fruit-eater or, at times, omnivorous; 3. order Carnivora (cat), with shearing molars, for cutting flesh; 4. order Artiodactyla (cow), herbivorous without upper incisors, the lower incisors cutting against a hard pad in the upper jaw, no canines, and crushing and grinding molars; 5. order Insectivora (shrew), insectivorous, small sharp teeth, molars with small sharp cusps; 6. order Rodentia (squirrel), gnawing teeth, chisel-like incisors.

to overshadow the rest of the shrub. Then, at a geologically very recent date, only 450,000,000 years ago, a lusty new branch arose, which gave rise to the vertebrates.

Any attempt at visualization must be an over-simplification, because we are dealing with a sequence that in its immensity in time, space and detail baffles the imagination and may not logically be reduced to such simple terms. Confronted with the sequence even the most eminent scientist has relatively the mind of a child, and can only command language that is severely restricted, and must use simple demonstrations like this to grasp the problem for himself or expound it to others.

Let us go back now to the stream of animal evolution itself, from the single cell to the group or colony of cells, through the two-layered or diploblastic Cnidaria, to the three-layered or triploblastic animal with its segmented body, as represented by the earthworm. From the earthworm, with its rings or annuli, representing the segments, and its bristles (setae or chaetae) along each side of the body, we can move forward to a crustacean, like the woodlouse, in which the setae are replaced by legs. If we can imagine the body of the woodlouse marked off into three distinct regions, giving a head, a thorax and an abdomen, with all but three pairs of legs lost and some wings added, we have an insect.

This is a crude example of how comparisons can be made and transitions imagined from one animal to another to fill in the gaps lost in the fossil record. Sometimes a lucky find helps even more. For example, the Mollusca include snails and slugs, oysters and mussels, and limpets, none of which shows a segmentation of the body. Yet for other reasons it was assumed that molluscs must have had ancestors with segmented bodies. It is not many years ago, in 1952, that a kind of limpet was dredged from the sea, off the Pacific coast of America, in waters 3,570 m deep. It was named *Neopilina*. Its shell is like that of a limpet but its soft parts show pairs of muscles, pairs of nerves and pairs of gills, as in a truly segmented invertebrate. *Neopilina* is a living fossil and a missing link. Since 1952 other specimens have been taken, in depths between 2,000 and 6,500 m, in the Pacific and in other tropical seas. This suggests *Neopilina* is widespread, yet has been missed until twenty years ago, in spite of the thousands of deep-sea dredgings that have been made.

There are many groups of animals, such as the lampshells (Brachiopoda), Moss animals (Bryozoa), Horseshoe worms (Phoronida) and others, whose relationship with other animals are obscure. There is always the hope that one day missing links for these will come to light.

To illustrate further that the bottom of the zoological barrel has not yet been scraped, mention may be made of the phylum Pogonophora. Two species were discovered in the first half of this century and cursorily dismissed as some kind of marine worm. Pogonophora are worm-like but 500 times as long as they are broad and they live in tubes on the sea-bed. Collected in dredges they look like tangles of fibre and were either shot overboard again as rubbish or put in jars with other specimens and forgotten. Today over 100 species have been described from all over the world. Although they look like elongated marine worms—and some scientists would classify them as such—the structure of their internal organs strongly recalls that of primitive vertebrates. The Pogonophora may yet give a clue to the ancestry of the vertebrates. If they do they will have helped to close the most refractory gap in the animal sequence, that between the invertebrate and vertebrate.

Many painstaking efforts have been made to close this gap. The size of the problem involved can be gauged more especially by the differences in the nervous system and main blood vessels of the two groups. In the invertebrates the main nerve cord lies under the digestive tube: i.e. it is ventral. The main blood vessel lies above the tube: i.e. it is dorsal to it. In vertebrates the positions are reversed. One theory elaborated in the early part of this century had it that an invertebrate turned and swam on its back to become the ancestor of the vertebrates. Invertebrates also lack a notochord, a stiff cellular rod laid down in the embryo around which the vertebral column, or backbone, of vertebrates develops. Then came the discovery of several unusual marine animals which either had a notochord, as in the lancelet, or had what appeared to be the beginnings of a notochord, as in the Acorn worms, Sea squirts, salps and others. These all look like invertebrates, but have a dorsal nerve cord and a ventral main blood vessel in addition to the notochord. They seemed to form an acceptable series linking the two main groups. Moreover, some of them have peculiar free-swimming larvae which are like the larvae of another well-known phylum of invertebrates, the Echinodermata, which include starfishes, Sea urchins, brittlestars and others. These had always been regarded as lower invertebrates, about on a level with earthworms. Now they were elevated to higher invertebrates, especially when it was discovered that they have the same serum as vertebrates, quite different from that of all other invertebrates.

Unfortunately, more recently, doubt has been cast on the significance of some of the strands that were supposedly combining to join vertebrate with invertebrate. Nevertheless, for the moment, except for the echinoderms, these creatures are retained in the subphylum Protochordata (i.e. forerunners of the chordates) and with the subphylum Vertebrata comprise the phylum Chordata.

Once we get to the Vertebrata everything is plain sailing. There is an almost perfect series of transitions among the fossils between fishes and amphibians (newts, salamanders, frogs and toads), and between the amphibians and reptiles. Also, there are many clues among the fossils indicating that birds and mammals had reptilian ancestors. Perhaps the most striking is the fossil of what was essentially a flying lizard covered with feathers. It is known as *Archaeopteryx*, and its remains were found in a limestone at Solenhofen, in Bavaria. This, the most primitive of known birds, was about the size of a pigeon. It had a long tail supported by a string of bones, as in a lizard's tail, its beak was equipped with teeth, there were claws on its wings and scales on its head as well as its legs and feet.

There is a similar, though less obvious, link between the most primitive living mammals, the monotremes, and the reptiles. The monotremes include the echidna and platypus of Australia. The first looks superficially like a hedgehog, the second looks like almost any other aquatic mammal apart from its 'duck-bill'. In both, the skeleton has many small details found only in reptiles and several important features of the soft internal organs are reptilian. Unfortunately, to date there is virtually no fossil material for the monotremes.

When it is realized the vital part the internal structure of an animal can play in deciding its relationships, the handicaps under which the early zoologists worked become readily apparent. At first only the crudest groupings had to serve as classification. Birds were obviously a natural group. Fishes were less so because they were used to include whales, dolphins and porpoises, which are now known to be warm-blooded mammals. Otters were also accepted as fish, but less on zoological grounds than to satisfy a religious dogma. Reptiles were apt to embrace almost anything of moderate size that crawled, not surprisingly since the name is derived from the Latin *reptere*, meaning to creep; but smaller creeping

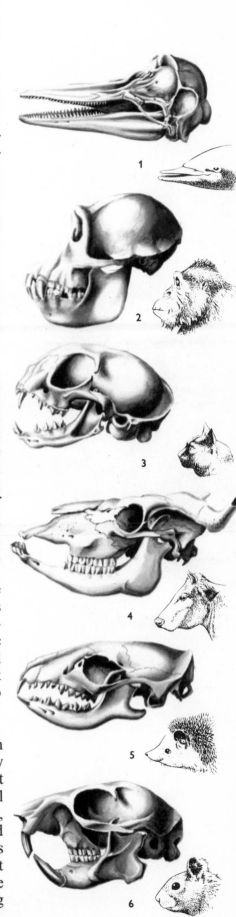

animals were worms, whether they were earthworms, threadworms, insects or even some reptiles—hence, glow-worm (an insect) and slow-worm (a reptile). Other groupings of the invertebrates were even more crude and often equally fallacious.

Since zoology was only for the savants, and savants of different nationalities, Latin was the language used in describing animals, and plants also. It was often dog-Latin, at times untranslatable or nearly so. But, as always, when a situation begins to show signs of lapsing into chaos, somebody is at hand to try to bring it into order. In England, John Ray (1627–1705), author of many books on plants and animals, was already germinating ideas which were to lead to a stable method of classification. It was, however, left to a Swedish botanist, Karl von Linné (1707–1778), or Carolus Linnaeus as he preferred to be known, to take a revolutionary step. Linnaeus suggested that each species should be known by two names, a generic name and a specific name. Thus, the domestic dog is *Canis* (name of genus) *familiaris* (name of species). Linnaeus also established Ordines, or as we call them today, orders. He placed dogs, wolves, cats, seals and others, in the order Ferae, the equivalent today being the order Carnivora. These and other orders, the Bruta, Primates, Glires and so forth being placed in the Class Mammalia.

In his *Systema Naturae*, Linnaeus proposed a complete classification of the then-known animal species. The work ran into several editions, and the tenth edition, published in 1758, is the one now accepted by international consent as the starting point for the binomial system, by which every species is known by two names.

The only major addition came in 1876 when the word 'phylum' was proposed for a main division of the animal kingdom. The complete tabulation for a dog now reads as the chart (*left*).

Kingdom	Animalia
Phylum	Chordata
Class	Mammalia
Order	Carnivora
Family	Canidae
Genus	*Canis*
Species	*familiaris*

A person studying the *Systema Naturae* can be excused for wondering how anyone could have made sense of it. The relationships of the animals themselves are badly confused: for example, in the order Bruta, the elephants, sea-cows, sloths, anteaters and pangolins are embraced as close relatives, and in the order Primates the bats rub shoulders with man, the apes, monkeys and lemurs. Nevertheless, it was the springboard from which the more refined classification of modern times was to emerge, by one change after another, one adjustment after another. The process is not yet finished, for the classification of the animal kingdom still differs from book to book, author to author, and will continue to change. The one solid and persistent feature is that every animal is known primarily by a generic and a specific name.

Linnaeus' action in grouping the bats with man and the apes has more to recommend it than appears to be the case at first sight, as subsequent history shows. In the *Systema Naturae* the classification starts with man, in the order Primates, the first in rank and importance. Zoologists after Linnaeus put the matter right by relegating bats to a subordinate position and placing the rest of the primates at the head of the table, with man as the topmost evolutionary pinnacle. This was epitomized by the architectural decoration on the Natural History Museum in London. The terracotta walls, outside and inside the building, are adorned with representations of all manner of animals. On the top of the pointed arch, high above the large and ornate main entrance, the architect placed the naked figure of Adam. Since this figure was 90–100 feet above ground level, its nakedness was unobtrusive to passers-by in the prudish Victorian era when the building was completed.

Human conceit had taken a knock with the publication of Darwin's *Origin of Species* and *Descent of Man*, in 1858 and subsequent years. In the debates that followed there was a feeling of shock that man (i.e.

Western man) should be classified with the animals, even shown to be descended from animal stock. It seems to have passed quite unnoticed that Linnaeus had done the same thing a century earlier. Nevertheless, the building completed in 1881 in South Kensington to house the natural history collections from the overcrowded British Museum at Bloomsbury had in its decor somewhat restored the balance. Man, in the shape of Adam, was on the apex.

In 1939, three events occurred which were curiously linked. Dr George Gaylord Simpson, of the United States, was busy compiling a new and comprehensive classification of mammals, which was subsequently published in 1945. In this, he demoted the Primates (Man included) from the summit of animal classification to a subordinate position—alongside the bats. He seemed to infer that apart from the large size of his brain man was primitive: i.e. zoologically he is unspecialized, compared with rodents, carnivores, whales and the hoofed animals.

Even if it had been generally known that Simpson was planning to topple the human race from its exalted and self-imposed position, few would have given it a second thought. In 1939 events were fast moving towards a global catastrophe that seemed to contemporary witnesses likely to result in the downfall of Western civilization, if not the human race itself.

It is probably no more than a coincidence that the figure of Adam should have toppled, at about this same time, for no obvious reason or cause, from its position on the apex over the main entrance to the Natural History Museum, onto the courtyard below.

It may be that these few paragraphs of history have little to do with Linnaeus or zoological classification. At worst, they will draw attention to the position of the order Primates, and to the reasons for it, in the current classification of the Mammalia, which is as follows (starting with the lowest):

CLASS: Mammalia (mammals)
  SUBCLASS: Protheria (monotremes)
  SUBCLASS: Theria (marsupials and placental mammals)

The placental or true mammals are further subdivided into:
  ORDER: Insectivora (moles, shrews, hedgehogs)
  ORDER: Tupaioidea (Tree shrews)
  ORDER: Dermoptera (Flying lemurs)
  ORDER: Chiroptera (bats)
  ORDER: Primates (lemurs, monkeys, apes, man)
  ORDER: Edentata (anteaters, sloths, armadillos)
  ORDER: Pholidota (pangolins)
  ORDER: Lagomorpha (pikas, rabbits, hares)
  ORDER: Rodentia (squirrels, rats, mice, porcupines, beavers)
  ORDER: Cetacea (whales, dolphins, porpoises)
  ORDER: Carnivora (dogs, cats, weasels, hyaenas, bears)
  ORDER: Pinnipedia (seals, sealions, walruses)
  ORDER: Tubulidentata (aardvark)
  ORDER: Proboscidea (elephants)
  ORDER: Hyracoidea (hyraxes)
  ORDER: Sirenia (sea-cows)
  ORDER: Perissodactyla (horses, zebras, asses, tapirs, rhinoceros)
  ORDER: Artiodactyla (pigs, hippopotomus, peccaries, camels, giraffe, deer, antelopes, cattle)

Probably it would be more true to say that man has been dragged down to this subordinate position in the scale of mammals by his relatives and especially the lemurs. There can be no doubt that the lemurs, monkeys and apes represent close relatives of man and must be grouped together in one order. Some of the lemurs are very close to the kind of mammal whose fossils are found in the Jurassic rocks, and must be very near to the ancestral mammalian stock. Perhaps the outstanding feature which marks the primates as primitive is the retention, almost in its original form, of the pentadactyl limb.

Studies in comparative anatomy indicate that the first fishes to venture on land had modified paired fins which foreshadowed the limbs of the tailed amphibians, to which the fishes gave rise. These amphibians had five toes on each foot, hence pentadactyl limb. Except where the limb has become modified, this is generally the pattern also of the reptilian limb; in birds it has generally been transformed into a leg with three toes pointing forwards and one pointing backwards, the forelimb having been modified almost beyond recognition into a wing.

If we take the sequence of mammalian orders listed above to represent an ascending scale from the Insectivora to the Artiodactyla, this is based very largely on what has happened to the pentadactyl limb, the extreme modification being in the limbs of the hoofed animals (Perissodactyla and Artiodactyla), in which the toes have been mainly reduced to one or two, and the remaining bones very much elongated to give the running limb that has been the secret of their success. One has only to look at the tremendous herds of hoofed animals which, until the end of the 19th century, ranged over Africa, and to compare this with the continents of Europe, Asia and North America, to be able to picture how 10,000 years or more ago, when the human race consisted of very small populations, these lands must have been teeming with hoofed animals. They had other specializations, in the teeth and in the digestive system, which contributed to their success, but however we look at it there can be no denying that the hoofed animals have been enormously successful and much of this must have been owed to their anatomical specialization.

Any attempt to expound the theory of evolution or any of its implications within a few pages must lead to over-simplification from which many important details must be missing. At best, what has been said here can serve only as a rough guide. The same can be said of any attempt to set forth a scheme of classification. Nevertheless, the abridged table that follows may be of some value. Schemes of classification of the animal kingdom change, in one or other important respect, almost yearly, if not more often. The one set forth here is as up-to-date as it is possible to be.

Perhaps one important caution should be given. A phylum is a major taxon, as we have seen. Yet some phyla contain only a few species and others, for example, Arthropoda (see below), contain the insects and other large groups, together totalling over a million species. As a rule, the fewer the species in a phylum the more certain it is that they represent a dying race: the greater proportion of the species in that phylum will be extinct.

Simplified scheme of classification of the Animal Kingdom

PHYLUM Protozoa: single-celled animals.

PHYLUM Mesozoa: containing a few species only which may link the Protozoa with the rest.

PHYLUM Parazoa or Porifera: sponges.

PHYLUM Cnidaria: Sea anemones, jellyfishes, corals, Sea pens, hydra.

PHYLUM Ctenophora: Sea gooseberries or combjellies (formerly joined with the Cnidaria in the phylum Coelenterata).

PHYLUM Platyhelminthes: flatworms.

PHYLUM Nemertinea: Ribbon worms.

PHYLUM Aschelminthes: rotifers, roundworms.

PHYLUM Acanthocephala: Thorny-headed worms.

PHYLUM Entoprocta: formerly included with the Moss animals or Bryozoa.

PHYLUM Bryozoa (=Polyzoa, Ectoprocta): Moss animals.

PHYLUM Phoronida: Horseshoe worms.

PHYLUM Brachiopoda: lampshells.

PHYLUM Mollusca: molluscs, including chitons, mussels, oysters, clams, snails, slugs, octopus, cuttlefish, squid.

PHYLUM Echiuroidea: (no common name).

PHYLUM Annelida: Ringed worms, including earthworms.

PHYLUM Arthropoda: Jointed-legged animals.
  SUBPHYLUM Onychophora: peripatus.
  SUBPHYLUM Tardigrada: bear-animalcules.
  SUBPHYLUM Chelicerata: spiders, mites, ticks, scorpions, harvest-men, horseshoe crabs.
  SUBPHYLUM Mandibulata: millipedes, centipedes, insects, crustaceans.

PHYLUM Chaetognatha: arrow-worms.

PHYLUM Pogonophora: (no common name).

PHYLUM Echinodermata: starfishes, Sea urchins, brittlestars, Sea cucumbers, Sea lilies.

PHYLUM Chordata.
  SUBPHYLUM Hemichordata: Acorn worms.
  SUBPHYLUM Urochordata: Sea squirts, salps.
  SUBPHYLUM Cephalochordata: lancelet.
  SUBPHYLUM Vertebrata.
    CLASS Agnatha: lampreys, hagfishes.
    CLASS Chondrichthyes: sharks, rays, skates.
    CLASS Osteichthyes (=Pisces): bony fishes.
    CLASS Amphibia: salamanders, newts, frogs, toads.
    CLASS Reptilia: reptiles.
    CLASS Aves: birds.
    CLASS Mammalia: mammals.
      SUBCLASS Protheria: monotremes.
      SUBCLASS Theria: marsupials and placental mammals.

Bearded lizard of Australia in threat posture, with mouth open and throat pouch inflated, displaying its 'beard'.

AARDVARK *Orycteropus afer*, large African burrowing mammal with no close living relatives, placed by itself in the order Tubulidentata (the tube-toothed) so called because of the fine tubes radiating through each tooth. The teeth themselves are singular in having no roots or enamel.

The aardvark (Afrikaans for 'earth-pig'), has a sturdy body, 6 ft (180 cm) long including a 2 ft (60 cm) tail and stands 2 ft (60 cm) high at the shoulder. The tough grey skin is very sparsely covered with hair. The head is long and narrow with a snout bearing a round pig-like muzzle and small mouth. The ears are large, resembling those of a donkey. The limbs are very powerful with four strong claws on the front feet and five on the hind feet.

Aardvarks excavate burrows, 3–4 yd (3 m) long with their powerful limbs and sharp claws, working with incredible speed. In midsummer the female gives birth in her burrow to a single young, occasionally twins. After two weeks the young aardvark is strong enough to come out from the burrow and go foraging with its mother. At six months it is able to dig its own burrow and fend for itself.

The aardvark feeds mainly on termites. It can rip a small hole in the rock-hard walls of the nests with its powerful claws, insert its muzzle and then pick out the swarming termites with its 18 in (45 cm) long, slender, sticky tongue. FAMILY: Orycteropidae, ORDER: Tubulidentata, CLASS: Mammalia.

AARDWOLF *Proteles cristatus*, African relative of the hyaenas, is somewhat larger than a fox, weighing 50–60 lb (22–27 kg) with a yellow-grey coat with black stripes and black legs below the knee. The muzzle is black and hairless, the tail bushy and black-tipped. The hair along the neck and back is long and may be erected when the animal is frightened. It is found throughout southern and eastern Africa as far north as Somalia, in sandy plains or bushy country. It is rarely seen, being solitary and nocturnal, spending the day in rock crevices or burrows.

It differs in form from true hyaenas in having five instead of four toes on the front

feet, larger ears and a narrower muzzle with weaker jaws and teeth. It feeds, therefore, almost entirely on termites although, lacking strong claws to tear open the termite nests, it has to be satisfied with taking the insects from the surface or digging them out of soft soil. It sweeps up the termites in hundreds with amazing speed with its long sticky tongue.

After a gestation of 90–110 days, a single litter of two to four blind young ones is born each year. FAMILY: Protelidae, ORDER: Carnivora, CLASS: Mammalia.

ABALONE *Haliotis*, American name for a large Pacific ormer or Ear shell, a gastropod mollusc with a single flat shell beautifully iridescent on both surfaces. There is usually a line of perforations near the edge of the shell through which water is expelled after passing over the gills. The largest, the Red abalone

H. rufescens, is up to 10 in (25·4 cm) across. The flesh from the large muscular foot of the mollusc may sometimes be eaten as a delicacy. FAMILY: Fissurellidae, ORDER: Archaeogastropoda, CLASS: Gastropoda, PHYLUM: Mollusca.

ACORN BARNACLES, large barnacles without a stalk so that the chalky box that surrounds the body is seated direct on the substratum. They are extremely numerous between tide marks. See barnacles.

ACORN WORMS, sluggish worm-like marine animals with the body in three clearly distinguishable parts: an anterior proboscis, shaped like a very elongate acorn, leading by a narrow neck to a 'collar', commonly wider than the third and main part, the 'trunk', which tapers gradually towards its rear end.

The extraordinary aardvark or 'earth-pig' of Africa, one of several kinds of animals specialized for living exclusively on ants and termites. (Inset) Looking down on the crown of one of its teeth showing the tubular structure, which determines the name of the order, Tubulidentata, in which it is placed.

Addax

Paired gill slits or pores open from the pharynx, the front part of the gut, through the body wall of the trunk just behind the base of the collar. These are numerous and their number increases with age. Externally, they appear as small pores, but internally they have the elongate U-shaped slit with a tongue bar in the middle reminiscent of the gills of the *lancelet.

Most Acorn worms are 4 in (10 cm) in length, but *Balanoglossus gigas*, of Brazil, may be more than 3 ft (1 m) long. All are burrowers and *B. gigas* makes a burrow several metres in length. Acorn worms live in soft sand or muddy sand between tidemarks or just below low tide level. For the most part they feed on sand, digesting the minute organisms living on or between the sand grains. They make a U-shaped burrow, eating the surface sand or mud which is richest in nutrients. Like lugworms they form coiled castings on the surface. CLASS: Enteropneusta, SUBPHYLUM: Hemichordata, PHYLUM: Chordata.

ADDAX *Addax nasomaculatus*, a medium-sized desert-living antelope, 42 in (107 cm) high, with spiral horns up to 36 in (90 cm) long; in males the horns may form 2½–3 spiral turns; in females, only 1½–2. Addax normally weigh 265–300 lb (120–150 kg) but a big male in good condition will weigh as much as 440 lb (200 kg). It has big, splayed hoofs; in summer it is white with a grey-brown tinge; in winter, grey-brown. Calves are red. Like the oryx, it has a remarkable ability to tolerate high temperature without significant water-loss.

The addax is found in the whole desert region between the Nile and the Atlantic Ocean. Formerly its range extended to the Mediterranean coast in Libya and Egypt, and the Atlas range in the Mahgreb, and south into northern Nigeria and northern Cameroun. In the summer rainy season (July to September) it goes south to the southern Sahara and the Sudan savannah; in the winter rains (November to March), it returns north. Only 5,000 addax remain in the wild; fortunately it breeds well in zoos. One young is born at a time, in winter or early spring.

Normally, addax are found in areas with large sand dunes and hard desert ground. They live in family groups of 5–15, of one male with several females and calves; other males live solitarily or associate with herds of Addra gazelle, *Gazella dama*. During the cold weather, they dig small holes in the sand with their hoofs, for shelter against the wind. FAMILY: Bovidae, ORDER: Artiodactyla, CLASS: Mammalia.

ADDER *Vipera berus*, or Northern viper, is variable in colour and pattern but is most commonly cream, yellowish or reddish-brown with black or brown markings. It nearly always has a dark zigzag pattern down

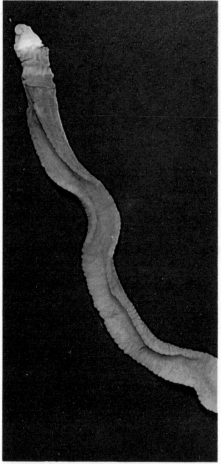

Acorn worms burrow in the sandy bed of the sea.

the middle of the back. These markings and the short, thick body, together with the copper coloured iris and vertical pupil make this snake easy to recognize, at close quarters. The adder occurs farther north than any other snake in Europe and Asia. It occurs within the Arctic Circle and ranges well into southern Europe, where dry, open moorlands and heaths, sunny hillsides and open wood-

land are its preferred habitats. Adders mate in April and May, and the young are born in August and September. They hibernate but may emerge early to bask in sunshine on warm days in February and March. They cannot tolerate very hot sun and retreat into shade during the hottest part of summer days. They hunt lizards and small mammals mainly in the evening and at night. Adder venom is dangerously toxic to humans, especially small children. FAMILY: Viperidae, ORDER: Squamata, CLASS: Reptilia.

AESCULAPIAN SNAKE *Elaphe longissima*, a long non-venomous snake of central and southern Europe and Asia Minor, about 5 ft (1·5 m) long. It is named after Aesculapius, mythical founder of the science of medicine who is usually represented with a large snake coiled round his staff. FAMILY: Colubridae, ORDER: Squamata, CLASS: Reptilia.

AFRICAN EYE WORM *Loa loa*, a parasitic worm infecting man. It does not live permanently in one site of the body, but wanders through various tissues and organs and so causes considerable damage and discomfort to the host. It is transmitted from person to person by the bite of a blood-sucking fly (*Chrysops*). The adult female worms, living in the subcutaneous tissue of man, liberate microfilariae (larvae), which are carried around the body in the blood stream. During the day, when the flies are actively feeding, the microfilariae are to be found in large numbers in the superficial blood vessels of the body, but at night they retreat to deeper vessels. Larvae are taken up by the flies as they suck blood and undergo development in the body of the insect. When infective to the human host, the larvae escape from the proboscis of the fly during feeding.

The adult worms are 1–3 in (2·5–7·5 cm)

The aardwolf, although related to hyaenas, lacks their powerful teeth and jaws.

long and move about just below the surface of the skin. They cause irritating swellings, but these usually subside fairly quickly. More painful sensations arise when they are in the area of the eyes, their movement across the surface of the eyeball causing irritation, soreness, excessive watering and disturbed vision. ORDER: Spirurida, CLASS: Nematoda, PHYLUM: Aschelminthes.

AGAMIDS, a large family of lizards living in the Old World, differ from most lizard families in their teeth, which are fixed by their bases on the summit of the ridge of the jaw. The tongue is short, thick and slightly forked. Agamids are small to medium-sized lizards with powerful claws. They live on the ground, in rocks or in trees. The scaly skin often consists of small spines, mainly on head and tail. The ability to change colour depending on temperature and emotional changes is well developed. Most agamids feed on insects and other small invertebrates. A few are omnivorous, others mainly herbivorous. Nearly all agamids lay eggs, only a few bearing live young.

There are 300 species mainly in the oriental region, Africa, the Indo-Australian Archipelago and Australia. The hardun *Agama stellio* lives in the southern part of the Balkans and a few species are found in central Asia.

With their flattened heads and strong limbs the medium sized agamas look like typical lizards. They live on the ground, among rocks or on thick tree trunks. Some of the rock dwellers have taken to living in the walls of houses, like the African *Agama agama*. FAMILY: Agamidae, ORDER: Squamata, CLASS: Reptilia.

AGOUTIS, almost tailless rodents, about the size of a large rabbit but with rather long slender legs. They live in a variety of habitats, but are found especially in forest, from southern Mexico to southern Brazil, where they feed on leaves and fruit. Agoutis usually have rather speckled coats. FAMILY: Dasyproctidae, ORDER: Rodentia, CLASS: Mammalia.

Black-browed albatross on nest.

Wandering albatross incubating.

AJOLOTE *Bipes biporus*, one of three species of worm-lizard of Mexico and southern Baja California. The soft skin of its body is folded into numerous rings and this, with its cylindrical body, gives it a close resemblance to an earthworm. Its eyes are covered with skin but it has two forelimbs each with five toes well equipped with claws. FAMILY: Amphisbaenidae, ORDER: Squamata, CLASS: Reptilia.

ALBATROSSES, 14 species of large, longwinged, gliding seabirds comprising the Diomedeidae, one of the families of tubenosed birds. They vary in length from 28–53 in (17–135 cm) and have a broad wing-span, the largest being 11½ ft (3·5 m).

Albatrosses are stoutly-built with a white or brown plumage. The head is large and carries a strong, hooked bill, with nostrils opening through horny tubes. The legs are short, the hind toe is rudimentary or missing, and the other three toes are webbed. The sexes are similar, except in the Wandering albatross *Diomedea exulans*.

There are only two genera of albatrosses: *Diomedea* with 12 species, and *Phoebetria* the Sooty albatrosses with two. All albatrosses except four breed south of the equator.

When not on the breeding grounds they spend most of their time in the air. They eat most kinds of marine animal which can be found at the surface.

The *Diomedea* albatrosses breed in colonies of many hundreds, mostly on remote oceanic islands. Nests vary from a simple scrape to a conical mound 1 ft (30 cm) or more high made of turf or soil and lined with feathers and grasses. There is one egg, white often speckled with red-brown. The sexes share incubation which lasts from about 65 days in the smaller species to 70–80 days in the larger

species. Albatrosses have elaborate courtship displays involving, in the various species, a wide variety of calls. All the albatrosses lay their eggs between September and January, except the Waved albatross *Diomedea irrorata* which lays during May and June.

The nestling period of the albatross is very extended, so much so that the larger species are not able to breed every year. Both sexes feed the chick, by regurgitation, regularly for the first week or so, then with decreasing frequency. The greatest danger the albatross chick has to face is predation by skuas.

The two species of *Phoebetria* do not breed in large colonies. They are found in the temperate subantarctic latitudes of the South Atlantic and Indian Oceans. Unlike other albatrosses they build their nests on inaccessible cliff shelves, and are more manoeuvrable and generally lighter on the wing.

Albatrosses have a unique faculty of sustained sailing, gliding flight. This is dependent on a high air speed. Albatrosses' wings have the highest aspect ratio (proportion of length to breadth) of any bird, from 20 to 25. This is the shape which is pre-eminently adapted to gliding. The albatross is in fact admirably adapted for 'dynamic soaring', which is the method of flight evolved for making use of the difference in speed of winds at sea-level and those at some height, normally up to 50 ft. In this way the albatross can travel for miles with never a wingbeat.

Albatrosses have suffered considerably over the years as a result of human activities. They have always been used for food, and in the late 19th century suffered severely when their plumage came much into demand for women's hats. The Second World War was a great threat to albatross colonies in the Pacific. Many have been killed on Midway Atoll, on which was once a thriving albatross colony.

When molested, albatrosses eject the contents of their stomach with some force and accuracy. This is an effective deterrent for most animals, but not for humans. FAMILY: Diomedeidae, ORDER: Procellariiformes, CLASS: Aves.

Laysan albatross chick, born to a life of danger from the advances of human technology.

Alder flies

ALDER FLIES, four-winged insects of the order Neuroptera, represented in Britain by only two species, *Sialis lutaria* in ponds and lakes and *Sialis fuliginosa* in running water. They are stout-bodied, brown, have long filamentous antennae and fold their wings along the back in the form of a ridged roof. The adults live among aquatic vegetation and reeds in May and early June. They are weak fliers and frequently fall onto the water surface where they form food for fishes. The fisherman's artificial fly, the 'alder', is modelled on them. The eggs are laid in large batches on reeds and other emergent water vegetation. The larvae on hatching crawl or fall into the water where they live at the bottom feeding on worms, other insect larvae and small molluscs. The larvae of the British species grow to about 1½ in (4 cm) in length but those of the American Dobson fly *Corydalis* are commonly over 3 in (7½ cm) long and have enormous scissor-like mandibles which are retained by the adult male. FAMILY: Sialidae, SUBORDER: Megaloptera, ORDER: Neuroptera, CLASS: Insecta, PHYLUM: Arthropoda.

ALEWIFE *Alosa pseudoharengus*, a herring-like fish of the western north Atlantic and related to the shads of Europe. Its common name may be a 17th century corruption of the American Indian name for the fish *Aloofe*, or it may be derived from the French *Alose* meaning a shad. The alewife is a silvery fish with marked striations radiating across the gill cover. It rarely reaches 12 in (30 cm) in length. It is found both in the sea and in freshwaters, the populations often migrating back and forth. Normally they live in deep water but in June or July they come into the shallows or feeder streams to breed. The alewife plays a fairly important part in fisheries along the Atlantic coast of the United States and in the Great Lakes. FAMILY: Clupeidae, ORDER: Clupeiformes, CLASS: Pisces.

ALFONSINOS, are ocean-living fishes of waters down to 2,500 ft (750 m) in the Atlantic and Indo-Pacific regions. *Beryx splendens* is world-wide and *B. decadactylus* is not uncommon off the continental shelf of the North Atlantic. Both have silvery bodies with reddish fins and forked tails. The first ray of the pelvic fins is spiny. The body is deep and compressed and the eyes large. They are rarely used for food except in Japan where *B. splendens*, which reaches 2 ft (60 cm) in length, is a popular table fish. FAMILY: Berycidae, ORDER: Beryciformes, CLASS: Pisces.

ALLIGATOR SNAPPING TURTLE *Macroclemys temmincki*, the largest freshwater turtle in the United States and one of the largest in the world. Reaching a weight in excess of 200 lb (90 kg) it is sluggish and

American alligators, less aggressive than crocodiles, tend to run away from man.

heavily armoured, frequenting the bottoms of lakes and rivers. It is unique in possessing a built-in fishing lure: a fleshy appendage on the floor of the mouth that resembles a twitching worm. Fishes, attracted by this lure enter the mouth and are swallowed. The ruse is enhanced by the dull coloration and rough shell, which is usually heavily covered with algae, rendering the turtle invisible. FAMILY: Chelydridae, ORDER: Testudines, CLASS: Reptilia.

Young alligators look almost benign.

ALLIGATORS, two species of crocodilians distinguished by the pattern and arrangement of the teeth. In the alligator the lower row of teeth project upwards into a series of pockets in the upper jaw so that when the mouth is closed, the only teeth exposed to view are the upper teeth. This gives the alligator an appearance of 'smiling' when viewed from the side. The crocodile, on the other hand, normally has both rows of teeth exposed when the jaws are closed, and these intermesh with one another. Particularly prominent is the enlarged tooth fourth from the front which may even extend above the line of the upper jaw giving a constricted appearance immediately behind the nostrils. So the crocodile's 'smile' resembles a toothy leer.

Alligators are found only in two widely separated parts of the world: the upper Yangste River valley in China and the south-eastern United States.

Alligators construct underground dens, portions of which are filled with water. One method used by collectors for locating alligators is to probe with a long pole into the soft earth along a river bank. At egg-laying time in the spring, a female American alligator constructs a large mound of mud and vegetation about 5–7 ft (1·5–2·5 m) wide at the base. 20–70 hard-shelled eggs 3⅓ in (8·5 cm) by 2½ in (6·5 cm) are laid in a cavity in this, and are then covered with more debris and sealed in by the mother. The peeping of hatching young after 10 weeks of natural incubation encourages the female to tear open the nest and help release the eight-inch (20 cm), brightly coloured black and yellow young which then make for the nearest water and are given some protection by the female for the next few months. They grow by about 12 in (30 cm) a year during their first few years.

Alligators have been known to attain in the past over 20 ft (6 m) in length and such individuals probably weighed well over half a ton. A 19 ft (5·8 m) specimen was shot in Louisiana a generation ago. Today, 10 ft (3 m) specimens are a rarity, and 8ft (2·4 m) individuals are hard to find in the wild. FAMILY: Alligatoridae, ORDER: Crocodylia, CLASS: Reptilia.

ALPACA *Lama pacos*, a camel-like domesticated animal of the high Andes. It stands 3 ft (90 cm) at the shoulder, its long fleece, often reaching the ground, is of uniform black, reddish-brown or even white, as well as mixed colours, but piebalds are much rarer than in llamas. There is a tuft of hair on the forehead. The alpaca inhabits the high plateaux of Bolivia and, particularly, Peru. The principal centre of breeding from time immemorial has been on the high plateau of Lake Titicaca in the Departments of Puno, Cuzco and Arequipa. The alpaca thrives best at altitudes between 13,000 and 16,000 feet (4,300–5,300 m) with low air humidity, except in the rainy season. At lower altitudes the animals are often rachitic and their wool is poorer. The alpaca has very sensitive feet and prefers the soft moist ground with tender grasses of the 'bofedales', where there are many pools and puddles in which they like to wallow. Alpacas are more fastidious feeders than llamas.

Gestation is 11 months. The mares foal in the rainy season. From the age of seven onwards alpacas are used only for meat production. At the present time the quality of alpaca wool is only slightly lower than that of the vicuña and is being even further refined by crossing with vicuñas. The suri, a breed of alpaca with finer, thicker and longer hair, provides up to 11 lb (5 kg) of wool per annum, but shows a greater susceptibility to parasitic diseases. Shearing takes place every 2 years before the rainy season in November or December, when temperatures are fairly uniform. It is done with ordinary knives or with shears. The Indian women can divide the wool into seven classes just by feeling it. Black alpacas are particularly in demand owing to the heavy coat of hair. There are numerous large commercial farms, but most of the

alpacas are owned by Indians. In Peru the number of alpacas is estimated at over 2 million and in Bolivia at about 50,000. FAMILY: Camelidae, SUBORDER: Tylopoda, ORDER: Artiodactyla, CLASS: Mammalia.

AMBYSTOMATIDS, North American Mole salamanders, are sturdily built broadheaded, medium-sized salamanders. They include the Marbled salamander *Ambystoma opacum* which may attain a length of 5 in (12·5 cm) and is terrestrial. It lives on hillsides near streams from New England to Northern Florida and westwards to Texas. Breeding takes place in autumn, fertilization is internal and the eggs are laid in shallow depressions on land, usually guarded by the female until the next heavy rain, when they hatch. In very dry conditions they may not hatch until the following spring. In most other ambystomatids, such as the Spotted salamander *Ambystoma maculatum*, which has the same range as the Marbled salamander, courtship takes place in water with an elaborate ritual. The sperm are released in a packet, or spermatophore, which the female picks up with her cloaca. The Spotted salamander breeds in the early spring when it may be seen in fairly large numbers making its way to the breeding ponds. After breeding they return into 'hiding' until the next spring and for the rest of the year they are secretive and rarely seen. The eggs hatch in 30–54 days releasing larvae of ½ in (1.25 cm) long. After 60–110 days the external gills are resorbed, metamorphosis is complete and the animal becomes terrestrial at a length of 2–3 in (5–7·5 cm). Adults grow to a length of 9 in (22·5 cm).

The Tiger salamander *A. tigrinum* may grow to 13 in (32·5 cm) which makes it amongst the largest of the terrestrial salamanders. It derives its name from the yellow or light olive bars on its upper surface. It has a similar distribution to the Marbled and Spotted salamanders except that it is a lowland form. Its eggs are laid in deep-water ponds, metamorphosis is completed quickly.

Another familiar Mole salamander is the Frosted flatwood salamander *A. cingulatum*,

American Wood warblers

The alpaca, a relative of the South American llama, has been domesticated for its wool since about 200 BC. This is the more remarkable when we recall that at the time of the conquest of South America by the Spanish and Portuguese the only other animals domesticated there were the llama, another humpless camel, and the Guinea pig.

4½ in (11·25 cm) long, named for the greyish dorsal markings on a black background which suggest frost on leaves. The second part of the name refers to distribution of the species in the wire-grass flatwoods between North Carolina and northeast Florida.

The Ringed salamander *A. annulatum* is generally only found in the mating season after heavy rain when it may be seen in shallow pools, from Central Missouri to West Arkansas and Eastern Oklahoma. For the rest of the year it is difficult to find despite its comparatively large size of 8 in (20 cm).

The majority of salamanders, including the ambystomatids, are usually voiceless. A notable exception is the Pacific 'giant' salamander *Dicamptodon ensatus*, which occurs in the moist coastal forests from British Columbia to Northern California and may reach a length of 12 in (30 cm). It makes a low-pitched bark or scream, especially when disturbed. As its name suggests this is a large species. In contrast to the slender, graceful appearance of the other ambystomatids this form has a clumsy build, yet it can apparently climb well and has been found several feet above the ground in small bushes or on sloping tree trunks. Almost all ambystomatids have well developed lungs but the Olympic salamander *Rhyacotriton olympicus*, 4 in (10 cm) long, has extremely small lungs. It inhabits mountain streams of the coastal forests of Oregon and Washington.

The genus *Rhyacosiredon* is known from four species which occur at the southern edge of the Mexican plateau.

Neoteny (breeding in the larval state) is not uncommon in the Ambystomatidae, the best known example being the axolotl, the permanent larva of *Ambystoma mexicanum*. It is found around Mexico city and keeps well in captivity. Some species of salamander are habitually neotenous in one part of their range and not in another. For example, in the eastern subspecies of the Tiger salamander metamorphosis takes place within a few months, but in the western subspecies metamorphosis often fails to take place, the animals breeding as larvae. The major factor which contributes to the neoteny is a lack of iodine in the water. FAMILY: Ambystomatidae, ORDER: Caudata, CLASS: Amphibia.

AMERICAN WOOD WARBLERS, a New World family of small perching birds, with nine primary wing-feathers, which includes the tanagers, troupials etc. There are about

Amoebae

113 species, varying from 4–7 in (10–18 cm) long, found from Alaska and northern Canada south to southern South America. They are brightly coloured with striking patterns of orange, yellow, black and white plumage. Some, however, have dull, uniform grey or brown plumage while others have bright plumage with blue or red markings. Sexual and seasonal differences in plumage-pattern are common in the more brightly coloured of the northern species, but in many of the tropical ones females are also brightly coloured and they keep their bright plumage all the year round.

The majority of the Wood warblers inhabit areas of woodland or scrub, but some have adapted to marshes and swamps and even to open fields and the sparse vegetation of the edges of deserts. Most of the species live in trees and vegetation and feed on insects caught among the foliage. Some that have developed wide, flat bills and pronounced bristles around the gape live by hawking flies and other airborne insects from a perch, as do the European flycatchers. A few species, including the North American Black-and-white warbler *Mniotilta varia*, creep up tree trunks and boughs, picking food from the bark like tree-creepers.

Most Wood warblers build cup-shaped or domed nests in bushes or trees, or on the ground concealed by vegetation. The oven-bird *Seiurus aurocapillus*, and some of the other terrestrial members of the family, build large dome-shaped nests on the ground with small side-entrances. They lay two to five eggs, incubated by the female alone, but both parents feed the young until after they fledge. The eggs of most species are white with brown or grey spots, but some tropical species have immaculate white eggs. FAMILY: Parulidae, ORDER: Passeriformes, CLASS: Aves.

AMOEBAE, single-celled animals which move by means of pseudopodia—out-pushings of cytoplasm. The amoeba pushes out a broad tongue of cytoplasm and then flows into it, a process known as amoeboid movement. The amoebae have been recognized since 1755. The amoeba seen in 1755 by Rosel von Rosenhof was a large freshwater form which was first called 'der kleine *Proteus*' and later a variety of names including *Chaos* and *Proteus*. Whatever this organism was it was not the organism known today as *Amoeba proteus* which was described in 1878. The problem is that there are a number of large freshwater amoebae which differ considerably from one another but these differences were not recognized a century ago. Any historical review is clouded with confusion and it is best to begin with the situation as it exists today. The best known of the large freshwater amoebae is *Amoeba proteus*, 0·5 mm long, the protozoan commonly studied in schools. *Amoeba proteus* lives in bodies of

permanent water and occupying similar habitats are two other amoebae, *A. discoides* and *A. dubia*. All three possess a single nucleus. There are also a number of large amoebae which possess numerous nuclei, for example *Pelomyxa*. As well as these large freshwater amoebae there are also a number of smaller amoebae which occur in ponds and streams.

An amoeba reproduces by dividing into two equal parts. It begins by becoming spherical, then the nucleus divides into two. The two halves of the nucleus move apart, the cell then splits down the middle giving two separate amoebae each with a nucleus. This process is known as binary fission and it takes less than an hour to complete. ORDER: Amoebida, CLASS: Sarcodina, PHYLUM: Protozoa.

AMOEBAE, TESTATE, bottom-dwelling single-celled animals found in freshwater and in damp places such as sphagnum moss. A few are marine. They divide asexually and form cysts under adverse conditions, which allow them to survive periods of drought. They possess a shell, consisting of a single chamber, which distinguishes it from the shells of the Foraminifera which typically have several chambers. Some shells consist of a pseudochitin secreted by the amoeba itself, as in *Arcella*, but in others the substance produced by the amoeba may be impregnated with foreign substances such as sand grains or other similar particles, as in *Difflugia*. In one genus, *Euglypha*, the shell consists of siliceous plates secreted by the animal itself. ORDER: Testacida, CLASS: Sarcodina, PHYLUM: Protozoa.

AMPHIOXUS, another name for the *lancelet.

AMPHIPODA, with over 3,600 species from the seas and fresh waters of the world, the order is one of the most successful and dominant of the Crustacea.

The suborder Gammaridea contains over 3,000 species distributed over 57 families. They are regarded as the typical amphipods.

The sandhopper *Orchestria gammarella*, nearly twice natural size, lives among small red sandweeds and tiny pebbles.

The body which is without a carapace, shows the usual division into head, thorax and abdomen. The legs hang vertically downwards and give no stability for a vertical stance. Thus amphipods lie on their sides and drag themselves over the substratum by the last five pairs of legs assisted in water by the pleopods of the abdomen.

The feeding methods of amphipods show great variety. They are scavengers, either vegetarian or omnivorous.

When breeding the male lies across the female and passes sperm into her brood-pouch. The pair separate and the female immediately lays her eggs in her brood-pouch. The number of eggs in each brood varies from two to 750 and there is usually more than one brood each year.

The suborder Hyperiidea containing 300 species are characterized by the extensive development of the eyes which take up the sides of the head. The Caprellidea contain the caprellids and the cyamids, often referred to as the Skeleton or Ghost shrimps. See sandhoppers. CLASS: Crustacea, PHYLUM: Arthropoda.

AMPHISBAENIDS, or worm-lizards represented by some 125 species in Africa, South America and Mexico, in Europe, one in the United States and several in the West Indies. Three species have small but well developed forelegs. With this exception they closely resemble earthworms. Their movement, unlike that of snakes or legless lizards, is in a straight line and they can move backwards or forwards with equal ease. There are no external ear openings, the eyes are covered with scales and, when visible, appear as dark spots. Only the left lung is present. There is considerable doubt whether they are lizards or even reptiles.

Amphisbaenids live in underground burrows, beneath forest litter or in the nests of ants and termites. In parts of South America, the local peoples (which believe the animal to be a venomous snake) refer to it as 'mother of ants'. Examination of the stomach contents reveals little other than ants and termites. FAMILY: Amphisbaenidae, ORDER: Squamata, CLASS: Reptilia.

AMPHIUMAS, are elongated salamanders averaging about 24 in (60 cm) and may reach 46 in (116 cm). The tail, if undamaged, is approximately ¼ the total length and tapers to a point. The most distinctive anatomical feature is the presence of two pairs of small legs, with 1–3 toes according to species, totally useless for propulsion. The head is long, pointed and compressed from the top. The colour is dark, uniformly brownish grey or slate grey above and lighter below. There are no gill openings or fins behind the head, and no external gills. The eyes are very small.

Amphiumas are found in warm, weedy, waters in the lowlands of southeastern and

Anglerfishes

Angel fishes from the Amazon are among the
easiest to keep in captivity and have
become a familiar sight in home aquaria.
They seem to do little more than hang
motionless in the water.

ANGEL FISHES, members of the freshwater genus *Pterophyllum* of the family
Cichlidae. These are highly compressed,
deep-bodied fishes with slender, filamentous
pelvic rays. When seen head-on through a
growth of water plants, the extreme narrow-
ness of the body makes the fish look like just
another plant stem. The light brown flanks
are marked with four darker vertical bars, so
that even from the side the fish blends with
its surroundings.

Three species are usually recognized, *P.
eimeki*, *P. altum* and *P. scalare*. Hybrids between *P. eimeki* and *P. scalare* are commonly
sold. *P. altum* is imported less often than the
other two species.

P. scalare is the largest of the three species
in the Amazon, grows to a total length of 6 in
(15 cm) and has a body height (including fins)
of 10¼ in (26 cm). They spawn on broad-
leaved plants which have previously been
cleaned by the fishes themselves. After the
eggs have been deposited, the parents continually fan them and at 86°F (30°C) the
young hatch in about 30 hours. The parents
assist the young to hatch by chewing at the
eggs and spitting the young onto leaves.
There they hang suspended from short
threads until the parents remove them to a
shallow depression or nest in the sand. After
four to five days the young, who may number
as many as a thousand, are able to swim and
the parents lead their brood out of the nest.
FAMILY: Cichlidae, ORDER: Perciformes,
CLASS: Pisces.

ANGEL SHARKS or monkfishes, sharks
whose large pectoral fins give them a 'hybrid'
appearance between a shark and a ray.
Unlike the rays, the pectoral fins of Angel
sharks are not joined to the head. There
are two dorsal fins, no anal fin and the
nostrils have two barbels that extend into the
mouth. The latter is almost terminal and not
underslung as in most sharks. Angel sharks
are found principally in temperate waters
and they feed mainly on fishes. The monkfish
Squatina squatina of European waters is the
largest, reaching 8 ft (2·4 m) in length and
weighing 160 lb (73 kg). FAMILY: Squati-
nidae, ORDER: Pleurotremata, CLASS: Chondrichthyes.

ANGLERFISHES, highly specialized marine
fishes found in all oceans from shallow waters
down to the abyssal trenches. They are
divided into the Lophioidea, Antennarioidea
and Ceratioidea. Their most outstanding
feature is the tendency for the first ray of the
dorsal fin to be long with a lure at its tip with
which the anglerfish 'angles' for its prey. In

gulf-coastal plains of the United States and
into the Mississippi Valley as far north as
Missouri. They are mostly active at night
searching for small aquatic animals. Besides
soft-bodied prey like worms and insect
nymphs, their powerful jaws enable them to
crush snails and subdue crayfish. An occasional frog or fish is caught with a surprisingly fast strike. They may occasionally
come out on land on wet nights.

Fertilization is internal. In the Two-toed
amphiuma *Amphiuma means* fairly large
elliptical eggs, ⅓ in (8 mm) in diameter, are
extruded like a row of beads connected by a
continuous gelatinous string. The eggs may
number 48 or more and are sometimes
guarded by the female who stays with them in
a sheltered hollow during the long incubation
period of several months. The eggs hatch in
about five months into 2 in (5 cm) long larvae
which metamorphose and lose their external
gills when 3 in (7·5 cm). During growth the
legs, which start off well developed, fail to
keep pace with the rest of the body. FAMILY:
Amphiumidae, ORDER: Caudata, CLASS:
Amphibia.

ANACONDA *Eunectes murinus*, the largest
of the non-venomous boas, inhabits swamps
and slow moving rivers in the northern parts
of South America to the east of the Andes.
It is the largest of living snakes, for although
its length is a little less than that of the
Reticulated python of Asia it is proportionately much thicker. Even a relatively small
snake seems almost unending as it crawls
through undergrowth so with a little em-

broidery about adventures in remote corners
of the earth the record length claimed for an
anaconda attained 140 ft (42 m). The current
record for anacondas seems to be 37½ ft
(11·4 m) placing the anaconda just ahead of
the Reticulated python in record length.

Its reputation as a man-eater is largely
undeserved. A large anaconda may be capable of devouring a child but such occur-
rences are rare. It generally shuns human
habitations and preys chiefly on birds and
small or medium-sized mammals such as
rodents and peccaries. Fish and caimans are
also included in its diet.

The female gives birth to up to 72 living
young, each about 3 ft (1 m) in length. FAMILY:
Boidae, ORDER: Squamata, CLASS: Reptilia.

ANCHOVIES, small and silvery fishes found
in temperate and especially tropical seas with
a few species passing into freshwater or with
permanent populations in rivers. Anchovies
can be distinguished from any small herring-
like fishes by the pointed snout that overhangs the mouth. The body is slender, more
or less compressed depending on the species,
there is a single soft-rayed dorsal and anal fin
and the tail is forked. The silvery scales are
often easily shed. The majority of the hundred species grow to 4–6 in (10–15 cm), but a
few may reach 12 in (30 cm). The best known
is the European anchovy *Engraulis encrasi-
colus* that forms large shoals and is found
from Norway to the Mediterranean and the
west coast of Africa and forms the basis for
large fisheries. FAMILY: Engraulidae, ORDER:
Clupeiformes, CLASS: Pisces.

An anglerfish *Antennarius*, lies in wait on the sea-bed to catch passing prey.

addition, the pectoral fins in many species are borne on fleshy limbs, which adds to their bizarre appearance.

The Lophioidea are large shallow water fishes up to 4 ft (120 cm) long. The Common anglerfish *Lophius piscatorius*, or Fishing frog, is found around European and American coasts. It is greatly flattened, lying like a huge disc on the sea bottom. The mouth is enormous and the jaws are lined with sharp, needle-like teeth. The eyes are on the top of the head and the brown body is fringed with small flaps of skin so that its outline is broken rendering the fish inconspicuous. The eggs of the anglerfish are contained in a long ribbon of mucus 1–3 ft (30–90 cm) wide and up to 50 ft (16 m) long, often reported floating at the surface.

The Antennarioidea include two important families. The family Antennariidae are flattened from side to side. One of the best known members is the Sargassum weed fish *Histrio* spp. The second family is the Ogcocephalidae, often called the batfishes. They are flattened like the lophioids and have large heads and fairly small bodies. The most striking feature is the limb-like pectoral fins which are muscular and are used to crawl about the bottom with a slow, deliberate

waddle. The lure is hidden in a tube above the mouth and it can be projected out when the fish is hungry. Batfishes grow to about 15 in (38 cm) and are found in both the Atlantic and Pacific Oceans.

The Ceratioidea or Deep-sea anglers, are essentially midwater fishes of the deep seas. The body is rounded, not flattened, but the characteristic fishing lure is present. *Ceratias holboelli* is a species that grows to 36 in (90 cm). Most of the ceratioids, however, are only a few inches long. They are usually dark brown or black, without scales and with a fragile, velvety skin, although some have warty projections on the body. The lure is luminescent.

The male Deep-sea anglerfishes are parasitic on the female. ORDER: Lophiiformes, CLASS: Pisces.

ANGWANTIBO *Arctocebus calabarensis*, a small, golden brown mammal related to lorises and monkeys, with forward-directed, large eyes and a pointed snout. Its head and body measure 9 in (22·5 cm) with a 2 in (5 cm) tail almost hidden in the fur. Each hand has a widely opposed thumb, a very small nailless index finger and a short third finger. The big toe is widely opposed to the other

toes. These grasping extremities are very powerful, and it is said that the angwantibo spends most of its time hanging upside-down from branches. Like the potto and the loris it is very slow-moving and walks with a deliberate, clasping pace, its hands and feet acting like pincers.

The angwantibo lives high up in the trees in the tropical forest of West Africa from the Niger to the Congo, but is rarely seen, so little is known about it. It probably sleeps clasped to a fork of a tree, like the potto. The main item of diet is probably insects, supplemented by soft fruits, this being reflected in its long, pointed canines and well-developed sharp cusps on the cheekteeth.

There is only one baby at a birth, after a gestation of about 4 months, and it climbs directly onto the mother's fur. Thereafter, it is carried around by the mother until reaching independence. There seems to be no well-defined breeding season. FAMILY: Lorisidae, ORDER: Primates, CLASS: Mammalia.

ANIS, three species of cuckoos, genus *Crotophaga* of southern USA, Central and South America, inhabiting clearings and open country of the tropical lowlands. Of medium size, they have a mainly black plumage, slightly glossed with bronze, green or blue. Their tails are long and appear to be loosely joined to the body, while the legs and wings are relatively short. The birds often look awkward and ungainly. The most conspicuous feature is the bill which on the Smooth-billed ani *Crotophaga ani* is very deep and laterally flattened, appearing large and arched in outline from the side, narrow and blade-like from in front. In the Groove-billed ani *C. sulcirostris* it is less deep and has several longitudinal grooves on each side, while in the Greater ani *C. major* the narrow flattened ridge is much reduced and confined to the basal part of the bill.

Anis are highly sociable and usually move about in small groups within a territory. Groups of Smooth-billed anis will defend their territory against intruders of their own species. They feed extensively on the ground, on insects, particularly grasshoppers, but they will take small lizards, and also berries.

A group of anis will usually nest communally. The nest, in a tree, is a cup of sticks, with an inner cup of finer material; the whole being very bulky if a number of birds are involved. Green leaves are used for the lining and both twigs and leaves may be added while incubation is in progress. Several females will lay in one nest. A single bird lays four or five eggs and up to 29 have been found in one nest, those at the bottom are not incubated sufficiently and fail to hatch. The eggs are blue-shelled, but the blue is covered with a white layer, thin enough for the blue to show when scratched during incubation. FAMILY: Cuculidae, ORDER: Cuculiformes, CLASS: Aves.

ANOA, two small species of buffalo on the island of Celebes differing from the Water buffalo and tamarao in their small size, rounded skulls, slender build and straight horns. The horns in both are back-pointing in line with the forehead. The Lowland anoa *Bubalus (Anoa) depressicornis* is 34 in (86 cm) high with horns 12 in (30 cm) long in males, 9 in (21·7 cm) in females. Both sexes are jet black with sparse hair and the legs are white below the knee and hocks. The horns in adults are strong ridged and triangular in section at the base. The Mountain anoa *B. (A.) quarlesi* is only 28 in (69 cm) high with horns 6½ in (16 cm) long in both sexes. The horns are simple, smooth and conical even in adults. Both sexes are usually black with thick woolly hair and the white on the legs is restricted to a pair of spots above the hoofs. Calves of both species are golden brown; adult Mountain anoas are sometimes brown. FAMILY: Bovidae, ORDER: Artiodactyla, CLASS: Mammalia.

ANOLE, American lizard-like reptiles of the family Iguanidae. There are 165 species, of which the best known is the Green anole *Anolis carolinensis*. Anoles, which are also known as American chamaeleons from their ability to change colour rapidly, range from 5–19 in (12·5–47·5 cm) in length. The toes of anoles are armed with small sharp claws and have adhesive pads of minute transverse ridges which enable them to cling to rough and smooth surfaces alike. The Green anole is active in daylight and moves continuously searching for insects in bushes and trees. Male anoles have a reddish throat sac which is extended to deter rival males from encroaching on another's territory. FAMILY: Iguanidae, ORDER: Squamata, CLASS: Reptilia.

ANTBIRDS, a large diverse family of small American perching birds, sometimes called 'antthrushes'. There are 223 species all less than 12 in (30 cm) long. The plumage is in shades of black, grey, brown, rufous, chestnut, olive and white, and the females often differ from the males in having black replaced by brown, rufous or chestnut. There is often a short crest, and the feathers of the back, rump and flanks are long, loose and silky. The wings are short and rounded, the bill stout and strong with a hooked upper mandible and the feet and legs strong and well developed. The voice is generally harsh and unmusical.

The family is confined to wooded areas, essentially lowland and mountain forest, in Central and South America, from southern Mexico to Argentina, extending farther south on the eastern side of the Andes than on the western side. It reaches Trinidad and Tobago, but not the Antilles.

The female angwantibo, with pincer-like hands and feet, carries her infant on her back.

Ant lions

The nest may be a woven cup suspended by the rim from a forked twig or may be a normal nest supported in a fork, but some species are said to nest in holes or on the ground. Two white eggs with blotches, spots or scrawls of brown, purple, lavender, or reddish hues, often as a zone at the larger end, seem to be the normal clutch. The incubation period is between 14 and 17 days, the nestling period between 9 and 13. The sexes share duties at the nest, and the female broods at night. FAMILY: Formicariidae, ORDER: Passeriformes, CLASS: Aves.

ANT LIONS, the larvae of insects belonging to the Neuroptera and related to the Lacewing flies. The Ant lion digs itself a small conical pit in sand or soft soil and buries itself at the bottom. Ants and other small insects fall into the pit and are seized before they can escape up the loose soil of the pit walls. Ant lions, *Myrmeleon* spp, are common in southern Europe and the family is very widely distributed in tropical and subtropical regions.

The adult Ant lion fly bears a superficial resemblance to the thin-bodied dragonflies, from which it is easily distinguished by its long clubbed antennae and two prominent parallel veins in the wings which have no cross veinlets between them. Some of the tropical species may have a wing-span of up to 4 or 5 in (10–12½ cm). Their wings are usually of equal size, translucent with mottled patches. Some tropical species have enormously elongated hindwings drawn out at the ends so that they are shaped roughly like a squash racquet. Ant lions are nocturnal and their weak flight, achieved with their seemingly oversized wings, makes them conspicuous as they fly around lights.

Army ant soldier with workers.

ant is recognizable by its 'waist' or petiole formed by a narrow segment or segments between abdomen and thorax. Females and males are winged when they leave the nest but are wingless at other times. Winged ants, which fly slowly in great clouds at certain times of the year, are not a separate species but the reproductive members of colonies which have left to swarm.

Ants are very clearly polymorphic with worker, male and female castes. Males of all species are similar being winged and having well developed eyes and long antennae. They are usually to be found only at certain times of the year, for they do not survive mating for long and are not readmitted to the nest after the nuptial flight.

With very few exceptions, all species of ants have a clearly recognizable worker caste consisting of sterile females whose function is to forage, build the nest and care for the young. They are wingless and often their eyes are small. In many species the workers do not produce eggs but in some they lay eggs which are used to feed young

larvae. These eggs, as they are not fertilized, could only give rise to males. Workers vary in size and typically those hatched from the first eggs laid by a queen establishing a new nest are smaller than those forming the bulk of the population. However, there may be a spread of size at all times in the colony, the smaller ones then seem to pass most of their time within the nest while the larger ones protect the nest and forage. But there may be two very clearly defined kinds of workers and in this case the larger ones, known as the soldiers, have very large, strongly chitinized heads and strong mandibles. One of their functions is to fight to protect the nest, but in addition they may help the smaller workers when they have found a large piece of food that needs to be broken up before it is transported to the nest.

The ant queen is solitary and not accompanied by a male when she establishes a nest. She is usually larger than males or workers but has fully functional mouthparts. After fertilization, which generally takes place in the air, the queen lands and pulls off her wings with her jaws or rubs them off against a solid object. She then begins to excavate a small chamber within which she remains until the following year. Very soon she lays a few eggs which will develop into workers. She tends these eggs and when the larvae hatch she feeds them upon salivary secretions depending, herself, solely upon nutriment from her fat body and from her flight muscles which degenerate during this period. These first workers show the effect of their reduced food supply in being small, but they can nevertheless break out of the chamber to forage and bring back food both for the queen and for the later young. Many species of ants found colonies in this way. A queen may live for as

Larva of Ant lion *Myrmeleon alternatus*.

The larvae generally have pear-shaped bodies with enormous curved mandibles. Some species in Southeast Asia have a greatly elongated prothorax which gives the impression of a very long neck. FAMILY: Myrmeleontidae, SUBORDER: Planipennia, ORDER: Neuroptera, CLASS: Insecta, PHYLUM: Arthropoda.

ANTS, of which there are 3,500 species, are social insects living in colonies, which may consist of a few individuals, as in the Ponerinae, or as many as 100,000 individuals in, for example, the Wood ant *Formica rufa*. An

Wood ant nests made of heaps of pine needles may be more than 3 ft (1 m) high.

long as 15 years and throughout this time is capable of laying eggs which are fertilized by sperm deposited in her receptaculum seminis during the mating flight.

The eggs of ants are white and not more than $\frac{1}{50}$ in (0·5 mm) long. The 'ants eggs' sold as fish food are the cocoons and not the true eggs. Workers carry the eggs about as conditions within the nest change, always maintaining them in that part of the nest where the conditions are optimal. They are licked by the workers and this keeps them free of fungal infection. The larvae are grub-like with a head and about 13 segments. They are legless but seem, in some species, to solicit food from workers by side-to-side movements of the front end of their bodies. They are kept in piles of equal size and of roughly equal age.

On the whole the larvae are fed upon regurgitated liquid material. The foragers transfer food to other workers and the same kinds of trophallactic relationships exist amongst ants as amongst honeybees. In some primitive ants (Ponerinae) insect prey is given to the larvae, which are active enough to tear it apart, and de-husked seeds are given to the larvae of Harvest ants. In due course the larvae pupate, often first spinning a cocoon around themselves. Workers aid them in breaking out of this covering when they have changed to the adult form. The caste of an ant is determined by the amount of food fed to it as a larva. Those destined to be reproductives are given a high protein diet while the future workers receive a largely carbohydrate diet.

Colonies of ants live in a great variety of structures. Many make galleries in the soil with chambers scattered through the depth of the nest. In these chambers broods are kept, or seeds stored as food, or fungus grown upon beds of macerated leaves. These fungus gardens are typical of the Leaf-cutter ants of the tropics (Attinae) which strip nearby trees to obtain the material upon which to grow their fungus. Their young are fed upon the bromatia, bodies produced by the fungus only in this underground situation.

Other species make mound nests. The Wood ant of Europe digs down a short distance and makes part of its nest below ground but above it piles pine needles, small twigs and the like between which the galleries of the nest penetrate. The entrances to the passages are closed when it is necessary to conserve heat within the mound and are re-opened if the internal temperature rises too high. Some of the smaller ants, like *Leptothorax*, which have colonies of relatively few individuals, may live under the bark of sticks lying on the ground. 'Paper' made from wood chewed by the insects themselves is another building material, while some tropical species occupy chambers within plants. The plants response to this is often to produce gall-like formations which become

Busy scene at entrance to an ant's nest. Ants have long been symbols of diligent toil.

riddled with the ants' galleries. One unusual type of nest is built by the Tailor ant *Oecophylla smaragdina*. Workers hold two leaves together, grasping one with their mandibles while gripping the other with their hindlegs. Other workers, holding larvae in their jaws, 'sew' the leaves together by moving the heads of the larvae to touch first one leaf and then the other. The larvae produce silk which holds the leaves firmly together.

The Army ants (Dorylinae) do not construct a nest. They move in long columns over the countryside clearing it of other insects and even small birds and mammals as they go.

The habit of looking after aphids to obtain food from them is widespread. Sometimes ants will protect such greenfly by building shelters over them or, in the case of *Lasius flavus*, excavating 'stables' around the rootlets upon which the aphids feed. The honeydew collected by the ants is a food surplus to the greenfly's requirements which is exuded from its anus. SUPERFAMILY: Formicoidea, ORDER: Hymenoptera, CLASS: Insecta, PHYLUM: Arthropoda.

APHIDS, greenflies or plant-lice, sap-feeding insects of the order Homoptera, which also contains cicadas, Scale insects, Spittle bugs and whiteflies.

There are about 4,000 known species of aphids. Some are restricted to specific climatic or vegetational zones, while others, such as the Peach-potato aphid *Myzus persicae* and the Cabbage aphid *Brevicoryne brassicae*, are cosmopolitan.

Aphids are small soft-bodied insects with piercing mouthparts and the tubular proboscis or rostrum usually has four evident

segments. They feed by piercing the tissues of plants with their proboscis to take up the sap. The legs, usually long and slender, end in a bi-segmented tarsus and a pair of claws. The four wings, when present, are transparent and the hindwings are narrower and smaller than the forewings. The antennae have three to six segments. Most species have paired cylindrical tubes or cones, the cornicles or siphunculi, projecting from the upper surface of the fifth or sixth abdominal segment. The last abdominal tergite is usually prolonged over the anus into a cauda.

Aphids are among the most important insect pests of plants, not only causing direct damage by feeding but indirect damage by transmitting viruses. Some, such as the Peach-potato aphid, feed on a number of different plants, but other species, such as the Sycamore aphid *Drepanosiphum platanoidis*, feed only on one kind of plant. Many species feed exclusively on leaves and young shoots, others on the branches of woody trees and shrubs, others below ground on roots, and some live in galls.

Adult males and females may be winged or wingless and the females may produce eggs or living young. Females may be sexual, requiring fertilization, or they may reproduce parthenogenetically.

Many species have a complex life-cycle, the sexual generation living on one kind of plant, the primary host, and the parthenogenetic generations living on others, the secondary hosts. In some species, however, the sexual and parthenogenetic generations occur on the same host. By contrast, some species have no sexual phase and reproduce only by parthenogenesis.

Species that alternate between hosts usually

spend the winter as eggs laid on the primary host, often a woody plant. An example is the Black bean aphid *Aphis fabae*. Its eggs are laid on the Spindle tree and on the sterile Guelder rose. They hatch in spring to produce wingless females, which reproduce parthenogenetically and viviparously. Their progeny reproduce in the same way, but in the third or later generations winged parthenogenetic viviparous females are produced. These migrate to herbaceous secondary hosts, such as beans, sugarbeet and poppies, during May and June and establish colonies. Throughout the summer new generations of winged or wingless parthenogenetic viviparous females are produced on these plants and the winged forms fly to establish colonies on other plants. Towards the end of summer or during early autumn, winged males and winged viviparous females are produced, which return to the winter hosts, and reproduce parthenogenetically to produce wingless sexual females, which mate and eggs are laid.

Others live continuously on one kind of plant, such as trees or grasses. For example, the Sycamore aphid lays eggs on the sycamore tree, *Acer pseudoplatanus*, and on related species.

Aphids are very weak fliers and the distances they migrate depend on the strength and direction of the air currents they enter. The average duration of single flights seems to be between one and three hours: distances travelled may range from a few yards to hundreds of miles.

Aphids and related insects, such as Scale insects and cicadas, excrete a clear fluid called honeydew. From very early times deposits of honeydew on or near plants have attracted interest, especially because of their large sugar content. The 'mannas' collected and consumed by peasants in the Middle East are mainly the accumulated excreta of aphids and Scale insects, the deposits hardening and crystallizing in the sun.

Many aphid species are attended by ants which collect and feed on their honeydew, the aphids often being referred to as 'antcows'. Some species are more or less adapted to live with ants and do not thrive without them. This association is termed myrmecophily. Other species are merely visited by ants on their host plants, the aphids benefit by the removal of the sticky honeydew and some by the protection afforded by the ants against parasites and predators.

Many of the subterranean aphids feed on the roots of plants penetrating ant nests and it is in this situation that aphids receive the best care and protection.

The main insect predators are ladybirds, hoverflies, lacewings and anthocorid bugs. Only the larvae of hoverflies and lacewings, but both larval and adult ladybirds and anthocorids, feed on aphids. SUPERFAMILY: Aphidoidea, ORDER: Homoptera, CLASS: Insecta, PHYLUM: Arthropoda.

APOSTLEBIRD *Struthidea cinerea*, Australian fluffy, grey birds, with short thick bills, are highly sociable, living in groups of a dozen, and are named after the 12 Apostles. When resting they huddle together and preen each other. FAMILY: Grallinidae, ORDER: Passeriformes, CLASS: Aves.

ARACARIS, small to medium-sized toucans of the forests of Central and South America, belonging to two genera, *Andigena* and *Pteroglossus*. FAMILY: Ramphastidae, ORDER: Piciformes, CLASS: Aves.

ARAPAIMA *Arapaima gigas*, a large, primitive fish of the Amazon basin, one of the largest of all freshwater fishes, reaching about 9 ft (2·8 m) in length (reports of fishes reaching 15 ft (4·3 m) are probably exaggerated). It has a long, sinuous body, with the dorsal and anal fins set far back, the scales on the body thick and large, and the mouth not protrusible.

The arapaima is an avid fish-eater and even the armoured catfishes are readily taken. The front part of the body is a bronze-green, but nearer the tail red patches appear and the tail itself can be mottled orange and green. Arapaima live in murky waters and the swimbladder has been adapted for breathing atmospheric oxygen, the adult fishes coming to the surface about once every 12 minutes to breathe.

Male arapaima guard the eggs, which are laid in holes dug out of the soft bottom of the river bed. For three months the young fishes stay with the father and during that time they remain close to his head. What keeps them there is a substance secreted by the male from glands opening from the back of the head. Should the male be killed while looking after the young, the latter will disperse until they encounter another male and will join his brood. FAMILY: Osteoglossidae, ORDER: Osteoglossiformes, CLASS: Pisces.

ARCHERFISH *Toxotes jaculatus* and related species from southeast Asian freshwaters that shoot down insects with droplets of water. The archerfishes are small, rarely reaching more than 7 in (18 cm) in length. They have deep bodies and the dorsal and anal fins are set far back. The body is generally silvery with three or four broad dark bars on the flanks.

They live in muddy water and swim just below the surface searching for insects that rest on overhanging leaves. When a suitable insect is spotted, the fish pushes its snout out of the water and squirts droplets at it until it falls into the water and can be eaten. An adult can hit a fly up to 3 ft (90 cm) away. Their aim is remarkable. Before 'shooting' an archerfish manoeuvres to place its body in as nearly a vertical line as possible, to minimize refraction. The jet of water is squirted between the tongue and the roof of the mouth, water being forced through the channel between the two emerging as a fine stream.

They usually hit with the first shot but will alter their position in the water and try again if they fail. The act of shooting seems to be induced by hunger. FAMILY: Toxotidae, ORDER: Perciformes, CLASS: Pisces.

Arapaima, largest freshwater fish.

ARCTIC FOX *Alopex lagopus*, of the arctic regions of Old and New Worlds, weighing 7–19 lb (3–9 kg), has small rounded ears and a long bushy tail. During summer the coat is a smoky grey and in winter pure white. Blue forms are sometimes found, the fur of which becomes only white-tipped during the winter, giving a silvery-grey appearance. The Arctic fox feeds mostly on lemmings but Ground squirrels, Beach flies, birds' eggs and even salmon may be taken. The litter of six or seven cubs is born in an underground burrow. FAMILY: Canidae, ORDER: Carnivora, CLASS: Mammalia.

ARMADILLO, the only armoured mammal, related to the sloths and anteaters.

Armadillo armour is remarkably modified skin in the form of horny bands and plates connected by flexible tissue that enables the animal to move and bend its body. Narrow bands across the back break the rigidity of the armour there. The underparts are covered with soft-haired skin, and in many armadillos hair projects either between the bands or from under the side plates and legs. The hairs are greyish brown to white, and the armour is brown to pinkish. Most armadillos can draw their legs and feet beneath the shell and a few can roll into a ball. The Three-banded armadillo *Tolypeutes*, of the Argentine pampas, however, is the only one that can completely close up into a perfect sphere, snapping the shell shut like a steel trap. As a result of the armour armadillos are heavy animals. They are reputed to be able to walk on the bottom of ponds and other bodies of

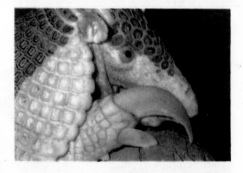

Armadillo, showing the digging claw.

water, but they are also good swimmers.

Armadillos have small ears, an extensible tongue, relatively good senses of sight, smell and hearing, and strong claws on the forefeet. They have normally 14 to 18 molars in each jaw, but the Giant armadillo *Priodontes gigas* may have 80 to 100. Armadillo teeth are among the most primitive found in mammals, being simply peg-shaped blocks of dentine without enamel, and they grow continuously at the roots.

The numerous species of armadillos range from southern Kansas and Florida to Patagonia. Most live in Brazil, Bolivia and

Wood ants 'milking' Black bean aphids.

Armyworms

Argentina. Only one, the Nine-banded armadillo *Dasypus*, reaches North America.

In the armadillos polyembryony (the production of two or more identical offspring from the division of a single fertilized ovum) commonly occurs, with as many as 12 young from a single fertilized egg, but the usual number per litter is two to four, and often only one embryo survives. The Nine-banded armadillo *Dasypus novemcinctus*, typically gives birth to quadruplets. Armadillo young at birth are covered with soft leathery skin that gradually hardens into an armour.

Powerful diggers and scratchers, armadillos forage and root for a variety of food: insects and other arthropods, worms, eggs, small reptiles and amphibians, fruits, leaves and shoots, and even carrion. They generally walk on the tips of the claws and the entire soles of the feet. Most can run rapidly. They may be nocturnal or diurnal, and their home is an underground burrow dug with their claws or one abandoned by other animals. FAMILY: Dasypodidae, ORDER: Edentata, CLASS: Mammalia.

ARMYWORMS, term given to the caterpillars of some moths, which sometimes appear in enormous numbers and, after having exhausted local food supplies, migrate in vast armies to new areas. The most important species is *Leucania unipuncta*, occurring in North America, Australia and elsewhere.

L. unipuncta feeds mainly on grasses and grain crops and the caterpillars may do enormous damage. In an outbreak in 1953 in Kentucky alone armyworms ate about $3,500,000 worth of crops. Most of this damage is done by the last stage larvae which are up to 2 in (5 cm) long. They can be controlled with insecticides and, when they are migrating, new crops can be protected by digging a ditch across their line of march. The caterpillars are unable to climb up the steep sides of the ditch and accumulate in the deeper parts. They can then be destroyed by pouring diesel oil over them.

The adult moth to which an armyworm gives rise is a pale brown insect with a wing-span of about $1\frac{1}{2}$ in (3·8 cm). The adults migrate as well as the caterpillars and their migrations, occurring unseen at night, may partly account for the sudden upsurges of armyworms in areas in which they had not previously been common. An adult female lays up to 2,000 eggs in batches of 25–100 and these hatch in a week or so. In Canada there are only two generations each year, the partly grown larvae of the second generation overwintering hidden at the bases of plants, but in the warmer south development may be continuous with five or more generations in a year. With a breeding rate as high as this plague numbers can appear in a very short time. ORDER: Lepidoptera, CLASS: Insecta, PHYLUM: Arthropoda.

ARROW-WORMS, small worm-like marine animals belonging to one genus and important because they indicate the movements of sea water. Their entire lives are spent drifting. Like all planktonic animals their swimming speed is less than the movements of the sea around them and they are transported long distances, mostly in the surface waters, though three species are carried in deep oceanic currents. Arrow-worms are torpedo-shaped and usually less than $\frac{1}{2}$ in (1 cm) long, the largest of them, *Sagitta maxima*, reaching 2 in (5 cm).

Apart from the head and the posterior reproductive region, the arrow-worm is largely transparent. The body is flattened with thin lateral extensions or fins and a horizontal tail fin. On either side of the mouth there are hook-like bristles used as jaws. The transparent body permits an all-round vision through spherical eyes, befitting an animal living in suspension and surrounded by both food and predators.

Arrow-worms feed on other animals of the plankton by suddenly darting like an arrow towards their prey with a quick up and down flip of the tail. Yet, though capable of these sudden bursts of speed, they are truly planktonic. Animals of similar size are seized with the jaws and swallowed whole. At certain times of the year arrow-worms are responsible for great mortality among developing fish fry. In their turn they are consumed by larger predators of the plankton including jellyfishes and comb-jellies, as well as by plankton-eating fishes such as herrings. PHYLUM: Chaetognatha.

ASCARIS *Ascaris lumbricoides*, a round-worm, is one of the largest and most widely distributed of human parasites. The incidence of parasitism in populations may exceed 70%; children are particularly vulnerable. The adult parasites are stout, cream-coloured worms that may reach a length of 1 ft (30 cm) or more. They live in the small intestine.

It has been estimated that one female can lay 200,000 eggs per day. These have thick, protective shells, do not develop until after they have been passed out of the intestine and for successful development of the infective larvae a warm, humid environment is necessary. The infective larva can survive in moist soil for a considerable period, protected by the shell. Man becomes infected by accidentally swallowing such eggs, often with contaminated food or from unclean hands. The eggs hatch in the small intestine and the larvae undergo an involved and an, as yet unexplained, migration around the body before returning to the intestine to mature. After penetrating the wall of the intestine the larvae enter a blood vessel and are carried in the blood-stream to the liver and thence to the heart and lungs. In the latter they break out of the blood capillaries, move through the lungs to the bronchi, are carried up the trachea, swallowed and thus return to the alimentary canal. During this migration, which may take about a week, the larvae moult twice. The final moult is completed in the intestine and the worms become mature in about two months.

An infected person may harbour one or two adults only and, as the worms feed largely on the food present in the intestine, will not be greatly troubled, unless the worms move from the intestine into other parts of the body. Large numbers of adults, however, give rise to a number of symptoms and may physically block the intestine. As in trichiniasis migration of the larvae round the body is a dangerous phase in the life-cycle and, where large numbers of eggs are swallowed, severe and possibly fatal damage to the liver

Arrow-worms *Sagitta elegans*, tiny marine animals that prey on fish fry.

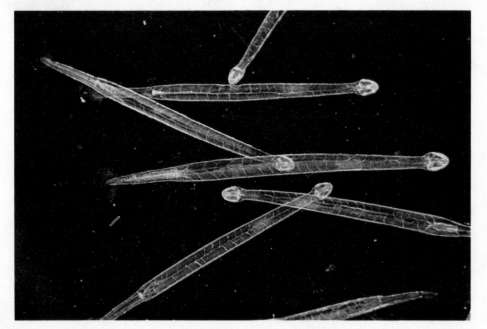

and lungs may result. Chronic infection, particularly in children may retard mental and physical development. Medication is often effective in removing the adult worms, although surgical removal may be necessary when the worms have moved into other organs. In regions where infection is common, hygienic measures, particularly with regard to treatment and disposal of nightsoil, are essential in order to prevent reinfection. FAMILY: Ascaridae, ORDER: Ascaridida, CLASS: Nematoda, PHYLUM: Aschelminthes.

ASS, a horse-like animal that existed in three subspecies in the deserts and semi-deserts of northern Africa, but has been largely exterminated by man. Their range is now restricted to the Danakil region of Ethiopia where the total population numbers an estimated two to three hundred Nubian wild asses *Equus asinus africanus* and to northern Somalia, the Somali wild ass *E. a. somalicus*. There may also be some asses left in the Tibesti mountains of the central Sahara.

African wild asses are grey or reddish-brown and have a dark cross on their withers, one line running down the back, the other at right angles down to the shoulders. They often have dark, horizontal stripes on their legs, especially on the outer side, possibly a vestigial, zebra-like stripe-pattern. They have a shoulder height of 48 in (1·2 m).

The Asiatic wild asses are better known under the vernacular names of their subspecies: the onager *E. hemionus onager* of Iran, Afghanistan, Turkmenia and Rann of Kutch, western India; the kulan *E. h. hemionus* of Mongolia, and the kiang *E. h. kiang* of Tibet and the Himalayas. A further subspecies, the Syrian wild ass *E. h. hemippus* is now extinct. The onager, shoulder height 48 in (1·2 m), is light yellowish-brown in summer, but darker in winter. Its underparts, legs and muzzle are white. The kulan, shoulder height 50 in (1·35 m), is darker and more reddish-brown. The kiang, shoulder height 54 in (1·4 m), is the tallest of the Asiatic wild asses. Its coat is pale chestnut brown in summer and more reddish in winter.

Originally, the Asiatic wild asses had a range from Arabia, Syria and Turkey to northwest India and from the southern European USSR to Tibet and Mongolia. During the last few centuries they have been persecuted by man, being competitors of domestic stock for food and water. Their range is now restricted to a few isolated areas.

All wild asses are inhabitants of steppes, semi-deserts and even deserts, but they depend on surface water as they need to drink every two or three days. The Asiatic wild asses live in groups of up to 15 head which, during seasonal migrations, may join up to form larger herds. There is no set breeding time and foals are born in any month of summer. FAMILY: Equidae, ORDER: Perissodactyla, CLASS: Mammalia.

White-backed magpie *Gymnorhina hypoleuca* from South and Central Australia and Tasmania. Unlike the European magpie the Australian magpie has a beautiful carolling song.

ASSASSIN BUGS, or Kissing bugs, Blood-sucking conenoses or Masked hunters, predacious bugs usually living on the blood of other insects, but also attacking the higher animals and man. The 3,000 species are rather flattened, roughly oval-shaped insects, with small heads bearing protruding eyes and long antennae and with a prominent snout. The wings are folded flat on the back and the six long legs give the insect a superficial spider-like appearance. Many species found in human dwellings may be from ½–1½ in (1·3–3·8 cm) long. The mouthparts, as with all members of Hemiptera, are tubular and adapted for piercing the host's body and sucking its blood. When the insect is not feeding, the mouthparts, which are termed collectively the rostrum, are carried out of sight underneath the head and body. The edges of the abdomen are flattened as thin plates visible at the sides of the closed wings and in some species the plates are brightly coloured with red, yellow or pink, although more generally the whole insect is brownish.

The majority of the Assassin bugs are found in the New World, especially Central America and northern South America. Other species occur in Europe, Africa (including Madagascar) and southern Asia.

Assassin bugs are active runners and good fliers. Most species live in the nests or burrows of rodents, armadillos and opossums. A few live in close association with man, spending the daytime in crevices in roofs and walls and feeding at night by sucking the blood of sleeping humans or domestic animals. FAMILY: Reduviidae, ORDER: Hemiptera, CLASS: Insecta, PHYLUM: Arthropoda.

AUSTRALIAN MAGPIES, birds peculiar to Australasia, having mainly black, grey and white plumage and a general resemblance to crows or large shrikes. The name is sometimes restricted to species of *Gymnorhina*. All have loud and often melodious calls. They occur wherever some trees are present, being tree-nesters. They make a typical cup-shaped nest mainly of sticks with a lining of finer material. The eggs are brown, green or bluish, patterned with dark blotches or spots.

Known as Piping crows or Bell-magpies, more often simply as magpies, they have a strikingly pied plumage, the head, wings and tail being black and normally most of the body being white. They feed mainly on the ground, walking about like crows, and take mainly insects. They nest in a communal territory but individual females make their own nests within the territory, the males helping only when the young fledge. They are generally aggressive birds. FAMILY: Cracticidae, ORDER: Passeriformes, CLASS: Aves.

AUSTRALIAN TREECREEPERS, six species of finch-sized, slender-billed, strong-footed birds unrelated to other treecreepers but resembling them in taking insects from crevices while spirally ascending vertical tree-trunks or branches. They also feed on the ground. When climbing their tails are not pressed to the tree but held away from it and they perch crossways on twigs. The plumage is grey or brown with streaked areas and light buff patches are visible on spread wings in flight. The nest is a cup built in a hole or hollow branch and the eggs are heavily spotted. FAMILY: Climacteridae, ORDER: Passeriformes, CLASS: Aves.

Australian wrens

Avocet, handsome wading bird with a turned-up bill, the victim of marsh drainage.

AUSTRALIAN WRENS, small, slender-billed insectivorous birds usually regarded as warblers. Their habitats range from forests to deserts with sparse vegetation. They build domed nests. The best known, the Blue wrens *Malurus*, have vividly-coloured males, and additional birds assist nesting pairs. FAMILY: Muscicapidae, ORDER: Passeriformes, CLASS: Aves.

AVOCETS, wading birds of the genus *Recurvirostra*. The four species are characterized by a long, slender, markedly up-curved bill and legs long in proportion to body size; the legs trail behind the tail in flight. Their plumage is chiefly black and white , though immature birds retain some brown feathers. The sexes are similar.

The avocet *R. avosetta* breeds chiefly on the coasts of the North Sea, the southern Baltic and the Mediterranean, and eastwards to Mongolia. A few breed also in South Africa. The northern populations winter mainly on the lakes of East Africa and in southeast Asia.

In Australia, the genus is represented by the Red-necked avocet *R. novaehollandiae*, which rarely moves outside that country. On the American continent there is one migrant and one resident form. The somewhat larger American avocet *R. americana* breeds as far north as southern Canada but winters in Central America. The Chilean arocet *R. andina* is found in the salty lagoons of the Andes.

Avocets nest colonially on muddy or sandy islands, and use little more than a lining of dead plants. They lay a single clutch of usually four eggs.

Avocets frequent shallow, preferably saline or brackish lakes, marshes or mudflats. They feed on small crustaceans, by sweeping the slightly open bill from side to side, sifting the first few inches of water, or the liquid top surface of muddy deposits. FAMILY: Recurvirostridae, ORDER: Charadriiformes, CLASS: Aves.

AXIS DEER, alternative name for the chital.

AYE-AYE *Daubentonia madagascariensis*, a cat-sized nocturnal mammal with coarse black hair, large membranous ears, big forward-directed eyes and a bushy tail. The head and body length is 16 in (40 cm) and the tail is 22 in (55 cm).

The aye-aye is a lemur and is restricted to Madagascar like all other lemurs. Its distribution is the northeastern coastal rainforest. However, destruction of the forest has led to the virtual extinction of this remarkable species. Recently, a dozen aye-ayes have been introduced on the island reserve of Nosy Mangabe off northeast Madagascar, in the hope of preserving the species.

Aye-ayes typically live high up in the trees. They have a mixed diet of insect and plant food. Unlike other lemurs, *Daubentonia* has two continuously-growing incisors in both upper and lower jaws. The canines are missing, and there is a gap (diastema) between the incisors and the pre-molars. The aye-aye seems to use both its sense of smell and its large, mobile ears to locate the insect grubs beneath the bark of dead branches. The incisors are then used in a rapid, intense fashion to make a hole, and the thin middle finger of one hand is used to hook out the larva.

Aye-ayes build complicated nests in bowl-like forks of trees, about 40 ft (12 m) up, consisting of a framework of thin branches interwoven with leaves. Very little is known of their reproduction except that there is one offspring at each birth, and it seems that this is carried around on the mother's back in the manner typical for the larger lemurs. When the first aye-aye was found, its squirrel-like appearance led early authors to place it in the order Rodentia. It was only when its anatomy was studied in detail that the conclusion was reached that it is an unusual lemur. FAMILY: Daubentoniidae, SUB-ORDER: Lemuriformes, ORDER: Primates, CLASS: Mammalia.

AYU *Plecoglossus altivelis*, a peculiar salmon-like fish found in Japan. Most of the salmonid fishes have pointed teeth but the ayu, amongst other anatomical peculiarities, has plate-like teeth. Because of this, it is placed in a family of its own. It grows to about 12 in (30 cm) and migrates into freshwater to spawn. During the upstream migration, Japanese fishermen used to bring their trained cormorants at night to the rivers, attach rings round the throats of the birds and then release them into the water. The ring prevented the cormorant from completely swallowing the ayu and when the bird returned the fisherman took the fish from it and sent it off on another foray. Up to 50 ayu can be caught by one cormorant in a night. Cormorant fishing is now little more than a tourist spectacle. FAMILY: Plecoglossidae, ORDER: Salmoniformes, CLASS: Pisces.

BABBLERS, noisy birds but otherwise inconspicuous inhabitants of forest and thick scrub. The majority occur in flocks, often within the mixed species flocks so characteristic of tropical forests. For the most part babblers are insectivorous, though a number, particularly among the song-babblers, supplement their diet with fruit outside the breeding season.

The jungle-babblers are nondescript brownish species which can be divided into two distinct ecological groups. Species of *Pellorneum* and *Trichastoma* are mainly terrestrial and have short wings and tails but long legs and strong feet. Species of *Malacopteron* are more arboreal, and consequently have longer wings and tails but shorter legs. Jungle-babblers occur in both the Ethiopian and Oriental regions, extending as far eastwards as the Philippines and Celebes.

Scimitar-babblers and wren-babblers, though closely related, differ considerably in appearance. Typical scimitar-babblers, such as species of *Pomatorhinus*, have long curved bills, long tails and short legs, while typical wren-babblers, such as species of *Ptilocichla* and *Napothera*, have short straight bills, short tails and long legs. Scimitar-babblers forage acrobatically around branches and

Stachyris striata, one of the tit-babblers at its nest among reeds.

creepers, probing with their long bills and using their long tails as a balance. By contrast, wren-babblers are terrestrial, as their long legs and short tail would suggest. They occur from the Himalayas to Australia.

The tit-babblers and tree-babblers, as exemplified by the genera *Macronus* and *Stachyris*, are more uniform in size and proportions than the previous groups. As their names suggest, they are mainly arboreal and they forage in an acrobatic tit-like manner. They occur mainly in the Oriental region, from India to the Philippines, Borneo and Java, though four species of *Neomixis* are confined to Madagascar.

The song-babblers range in size from about 4–12 in (10–30 cm). Species of *Turdoides* are characteristic of the Middle East and the drier areas of the Ethiopian and Oriental regions, where they occur in almost any kind of thick scrub. Most other species occur in forest, by far the majority of them in the Oriental region. They include the laughing-thrushes *Garrulax*, most of which are large and noisy, while many are beautifully patterned. A few sing particularly well and are much prized as cage-birds in China. Species of *Pteruthius*, *Myzornis* and *Leiothrix* are also prettily marked and one of the latter, the Red-billed leiothrix *L. lutea*, is a very popular cage-bird more commonly known as the Pekin robin.

The rockfowl were formerly thought to be related to starlings but are currently thought to be large and specialized babblers. The two species have heads completely devoid of feathers, hence their alternative name of Bald crows. In one species, the Grey-necked rockfowl *Picathartes gymnocephalus*, the bald head is bright yellow; in the other, the White-necked rockfowl *P. oreas*, it is pink. Both species have short rounded wings, a long tail and long legs and are said to move gracefully on the ground by means of enormous hops. They live in the forests of West Africa, in areas in which large moss-covered boulders, cliffs and caves abound.

The ground-babblers are another particularly diverse group. The group includes

among its 20 or so species the rail-babblers *Eupetes* and quail-thrushes *Cinclosoma*. The ground-babblers are confined to the Australasian region, with the exception of a rail-babbler *E. macrocercus* that lives in the forests of Malaysia.

The jungle-babblers, scimitar-babblers and wren-babblers, tit-babblers and tree-babblers, and a very few of the song-babblers and ground-babblers, build domed ball-like nests of moss and dead leaves which are well hidden on or close to the ground. The majority of the song-babblers build open cup-shaped nests which are hidden in low trees, bushes and creepers, while a few of the ground-babblers, such as the quail-thrushes, build open cup-shaped nests on the ground. The rockfowl differ from other babblers by nesting in small groups, building cup-shaped nests of mud, plastered to rock faces in caves or under overhangs. FAMILY: Muscicapidae, ORDER: Passeriformes, CLASS: Aves.

BABIRUSA *Babyrousa babyrussa*, a large almost hairless hog with a brownish-grey rough skin. The head and body length is 34–42 in (86·4–106·7 cm); height at shoulder is 10·8–12·5 in (27·4–31·7 cm). There are four toes on each foot with the centre two functional and the outer two forming dew claws. Unlike other members of the family the upper tusks in males go up through the top of the muzzle and curve slightly backwards. The lower tusks do not touch the upper tusks and extend outward.

The babirusa is limited to the Celebes and Molucca Islands.

Information on breeding is scarce. In the London Zoo captive females have given birth to single young in January, March and April following a 125–150 day gestation period.

Babirusa inhabit dense damp forests and bamboo thickets. Like most other hogs, they are social animals and travel in small groups. They feed mostly on fruits, green vegetation, roots and tubers. FAMILY: Suidae, SUBORDER: Suiformes, ORDER: Artiodactyla, CLASS: Mammalia.

Baboons

An unusual babbler, the White-necked rockfowl *Picathartes oreas* of West Africa.

BABOONS, typical open-country monkeys of Africa, distinguished by their long muzzle, especially in the male, and large size. The most widespread, *Papio hamadryas*, is distributed all over the savannah, semi-desert and lightly forested regions of Africa south of the Sahara. There are also two species in the thick forests of the Cameroun region with very short tails, brightly coloured buttocks and heavy ridges on either side of the nose. Savannah baboons are not highly coloured, have no strong ridges, and their tails curve up, back and down in an arc.

It was once thought there were five species of baboon in the savannah areas, each confined to a portion of the range; but recent studies have demonstrated the existence of inter-gradation between them, with hybrid troops and clines of colour and hair patterns through the range. To the north they are more stocky, the males have big manes, the face juts and the pointed nose extends beyond the end of the muzzle. They are light in colour the hairs being banded dark and light. To the south baboons are more long-legged and rangy, the male has little or no mane, the face is more bent downwards, and the nose does not overhang the end of the muzzle. The

colour is darker and the hair less banded. Eight sub-species are recognized:

Hamadryas, Mantled or Sacred baboon *P. hamadryas hamadryas*. Small, 2½ ft (76 cm) long, tail 2 ft (61 cm), weight up to 40 lb (18 kg); females brown, males grey; males with huge mane which ends in middle of back, very short hair on rest of body. Face pinkish, ischial callosities red. Northern Somalia, Eritrea and southwestern Arabia.

Baby baboon riding pick-a-back.

Olive baboon *P. h. anubis*. Much larger, olive-green; male with long mane. Face and ischial callosities black. Senegal east to Ethiopia and Kenya, intergrades with Hamadryas along Awash river, northern Ethiopia. Guinea baboon *P. h. papio*. Smaller, maned, reddish, with red ischial callosities. Restricted to small area of Senegal, Guinea and Gambia. Yellow baboon *P. h. cynocephalus*. Long-legged, no mane, yellowish. East Africa, from Amboseli (where intergrades with Olive baboon) to Zambezi.

Dwarf baboon *P. h. kindae*. Like Yellow baboon but much smaller and short-faced; Zambia and Katanga.

Kalahari chacma baboon *P. h. ruacana*. Variegated, brownish, long face and long crest of hair on nape and withers. Southern Angola and Southwest Africa.

Grey-footed chacma *P. h. griseipes*. Dark yellowish, larger than Kalahari chacma, otherwise similar. Rhodesia and Mozambique; intergrades with Yellow baboon in eastern Zambia.

Black-footed chacma *P. h. ursinus*. Blackish brown, with black hands and feet; largest of all baboons. South Africa, except for northern Transvaal.

Baboons, aggressive and dangerous, live in large troops whose composition and social behaviour vary from area to area. In the savannahs of East and South Africa the troops are smallish with 20–80 animals and each troop stays together all the time. However, in the desert areas of Eritrea, northern Somalia and Southwest Africa, huge troops are found, as many as 150 together, but these split up during the day into one-male units and bachelor bands. This latter type of society is typical especially of Hamadryas baboons. The more typical savannah baboons have a more or less hierarchical organization within the troop, a single male often being dominant in all respects. However, different individuals may appear to dominate in different situations and sometimes two or three of the less strong males may constantly associate together and take precedence in situations where a single stronger male would otherwise always dominate. Females are always subordinate to males, and have a kind of rank order amongst themselves, although this too may be broken: for example, a female with a young infant is treated with consideration by the rest of the troop.

Within the baboon troop the sex ratio is more or less equal; there are, however, two or three times as many adult females as there are adult males, since females mature at 4–5 years, males only after 7–10 years. The troop has a wide home range, with a core area consisting of a clump of trees. Around this, the troop wanders within a radius of a mile or more, and may travel as much as 6 miles in a day, foraging as they go. Baboons feed on seeds, tubers, grass, insects—even scorpions

The male Olive baboon with cape-like mane.

Backswimmers

Backswimmer, photographed from below, showing reflection in surface film.

common name for a group of aquatic bugs. They resemble water-boatmen, family Corixidae, in general appearance, for their body is boat-shaped and streamlined and they swim by using their long hindlegs as paddles. However, they differ from waterboatmen in swimming on their backs and are vicious predators often attacking and killing animals larger than themselves, including young fish. The sharp stylets in their mouthparts can inflict painful wounds and they should be handled carefully. FAMILY: Notonectidae, CLASS: Insecta, PHYLUM: Arthropoda.

BADGERS, medium-sized members of the weasel family Mustelidae, well known for their digging habits. Badgers comprise six genera which are distributed over North America, Eurasia and Indonesia as far as Borneo. The South African ratel is some-times included as a seventh genus. The name is derived from the French *becheur*, meaning digger or gardener. All badgers are heavily built and their muscular legs appear even shorter than they are, due to the thickness of the coarse fur. The tail is 1–8 in (2–20 cm) long. All badgers have potent anal scent glands which appear to be particularly effective in the oriental Stink badgers. Considerable size and colour variations exist. Three genera, *Meles*, *Taxidea* and *Melogale*, have distinct black and white facial 'masks' contrasting with the inconspicuous salt-and-pepper grey of the back and the black underparts and legs. Badgers usually excavate their burrows or sets where there is sufficient cover, in woodland or, in drier areas, brushland, and choose sandy limestone or clay. The European badger *Meles meles* is gregarious and the sets may become, with successive generations, an extensive maze of tunnels up to 100 ft (30 m) long, leading to chambers lined with a 'bedding' of leaves or grass. Sometimes up to ten entrances and exits can be discovered but usually only two or three are in use at one time. Small ventilation holes air the tunnels closest to the surface. Dry bundles of bedding are collected, either pushed or carried backwards into the set, clasped in the forearms, the badger shuffling along on elbows and hind-feet. Bedding may also be nosed to the surface during the night and spread around the set to air, then gathered again before daybreak. Not only do badgers keep the set clean underground but they also dig shallow pits nearby where dung is deposited.

The diet covers a wide range of vegetable and animal matter, showing great seasonal and local variations. Voles, hedgehogs, moles may be eaten as well as smaller frogs, slugs, beetles and above all, earthworms. Fruits of every kind, maize, wheat and even fungi are also taken when available.

The European badger is found in Eurasia down to southern China. Males are slightly

and snakes. Baboons have also been observed to kill and eat young gazelles; they do not stalk them with intent as chimpanzees do, however, but probably merely stumble on a baby gazelle that has been left lying in the grass by its mother.

By day a baboon troop will often associate with a herd of ungulates, especially impala. The association is mutually beneficial: the impala are alert and give warning of danger, while the baboons are powerful and fearsome, and can offer protection to the antelopes. Leopards and cheetahs are not infrequently turned away by a group of male baboons. On the other hand, a lone baboon, even a male, may be killed and eaten by a leopard.

The baboon troop is very tightly knit; an individual very rarely changes troops. A very big, unwieldy troop will split into subgroups for foraging, and gradually two independent troops will result. Dominant males and females with infants travel in the centre of a troop; younger and weaker males tend to move along the edges, and are the first to see and warn of danger. When this happens the big adult males move forward. Like Old World monkeys, a male baboon's canines are long and sharp, with a razor edge up the back.

Gestation last six months; the infant is born black, and is a focus of solicitous attention from other troop members. At first it rides on its mother's belly, later on her back. After four to six months the infant changes to the adult coloration and a little later is weaned.

Although Olive baboons penetrate far into the forests of the northeastern Congo, the real forest baboons are the Short-tailed drill *Papio leucophaeus* and the mandrill *P. sphinx*. Mandrills are even larger than most baboons, dark brown with white cheek-fringes, a yellow beard, and tuft of hair on the crown. The face is brilliantly coloured in the adult male: the nose is red, the ridges on either side of it blue. In females and young the same colours are present, but much duller. The penis is red and the scrotum is blue; the ischial callosities are red, and the buttock hair blue and white. The maxillary ridges are diagonally grooved. The drill is smaller than the mandrill, more olive in colour, with a black face and no grooves on the muzzle ridges; the chin is red; there is a white fringe all round the face.

The mandrill lives in Cameroun, Equatorial Guinea, Gabon and the Congo (Brazzaville), mainly near the coast. The drill is found in the same areas but prefers more inland forests, and extends onto Mt. Cameroun, the Cross River district of Nigeria, and the island of Fernando Po. Both live mainly on the forest floor but do not hesitate to climb trees, eating fruit and berries as well as bark and roots. The troops are large, up to 60 in number, but split into one-male parties at times (at least in the drill), which forage separately for several days. Intertroop location signals are given as they come back together again. FAMILY: Cercopithecidae, ORDER: Primates, CLASS: Mammalia.

A pair of European badgers *Meles meles* leaving their set at nightfall.

larger than females measuring 27–40 in (67–100 cm) and weighing 22–55 lb (10–25 kg), depending on the season. Large layers of fat are present in autumn. Hibernation occurs only in the colder areas of their range. Breeding usually occurs in spring or late summer, but there is delayed implantation varying from 2–10 months. The embryo develops for a few days, then lies dormant and is not implanted in the uterus until much later. The cubs are born in February or March. Numbering two to four, the blind cubs remain in a nesting chamber for several weeks.

The American badger *Taxidea taxus* occurs throughout the drier regions of the United States down to southern Mexico. Stockier than the European badger, it appears to be even more 'flattened'. The black and white facial stripes are narrower and less distinct. Measuring 21–35 in (52–87 cm) and weighing 8–22 lb (3·5–10 kg), it is usually smaller than the European badger. Unlike its European counterpart, the American badger is solitary most of the year and does not use the same burrow generation after generation. Breeding takes place in late summer and delayed implantation occurs, so that the cubs are not born until the following April. Weaned at six weeks, the young become independent by late autumn and set off on their own for the winter.

The hog-badger *Arctonyx collaris* is found from India to Sumatra and up into China. More upstanding, albeit stout, this species nevertheless retains the same stocky appearance, with formidable claws. A large hog-badger measures approximately 32 in (80 cm) overall and weighs 25 lb (11 kg). The most distinguishing characteristic is the long, mobile snout, used in foraging for grubs and insects.

The Malayan Stink badger *Mydaus javanensis* and the Palawan Stink badger *Suillotaxus marchei* are the rarest members of this group. The Malayan species which occurs also in Sumatra, Java and Borneo has an overall dark brown or black coloration.

The Bornean ferret badger *Melogale orientalis* is widespread from Nepal to Borneo

and three species are currently recognized. This is the smallest badger, measuring 19–25 in (48–63 cm), the bushy tail accounting for a third of the total length. FAMILY: Mustelidae, ORDER: Carnivora, CLASS: Mammalia.

Bald eagle, America's national emblem.

BALD EAGLE *Haliaetus leucocephalus*, a very large sea eagle confined to North American coasts, lakes and rivers, and the American national emblem. It feeds by fishing or by robbing other birds. Two races occur, one in central and southern United States, the other in Alaska and western Canada. The Florida population breeds in winter and migrates north in hot summers. The Alaskan birds feed largely on dead and dying Pacific salmon for part of the year. Formerly common, it is now much reduced in central-south USA through shooting (despite national status) and pesticide poisoning. It breeds in trees, making huge nests, laying two or three eggs and rearing one or two young per year. FAMILY: Accipitridae, ORDER: Falconiformes, CLASS: Aves.

BANANAQUIT *Coereba flaveola,* a small, 4 in (10 cm), grey and bright-yellow bird with a conspicuous white eye-stripe and a rather long decurved bill. It is widespread in tropical America from the West Indies, where it is probably the commonest bird, south to Argentina and Paraguay. The bananaquit has adjusted well to man and is

now found both in the native forests and in gardens, plantations and cleared areas. It feeds on fruit, nectar and insects. It constructs many domed nests, some of which are used for nesting and others for roosting. FAMILY: Coerebidae, ORDER: Passeriformes, CLASS: Aves.

BANDED ANT-EATER *Myrmecobius fasciatus* or numbat, a pouchless, termite-eating marsupial which lives in the fallen hollow limbs of wandoo trees *Eucalyptus redunca* in southwestern Australia. The numbat shares common features of behaviour, reproduction and chromosome cytology with the marsupial 'cats' and their allies to which it is undoubtedly closely related in spite of numerous aberrant features of dentition. Adult animals are rat-sized and weigh about 1 lb (454 gm).

The coat of the numbat is coarse but it is none the less a remarkably beautiful animal having bright rusty-red fur broken by six or seven creamy white bars across the hind part of the body. The head is flat above, the nose of the adult animals long and pointed and the tail long and wand-like especially when, as sometimes happens, it is held above the body with the hairs erect. There are five toes on the forefeet and four on the hindfeet. The skull is broad and expanded with four incisors (three in the lower jaw), a single canine and three premolar teeth on each side of the jaws. Unlike most other marsupials, however, the numbat has more than four molar teeth in each jaw and they are reduced in size and degenerate in accord with the insectivorous mode of feeding. The food is termites and ants. There may be as many as six molars in each jaw giving a total of about 50 teeth. FAMILY: Dasyuridae, ORDER: Marsupialia, CLASS: Mammalia.

BANDICOOT, a rabbit-sized marsupial, insect and small-animal eater with carnivorous dentition, as in Native cats, but with the same foot structure as in kangaroos and wallabies (syndactylous). They are perhaps most nearly related to the dasyurids (Native cats, etc). They have pointed ears and tapering snouts.

The name 'bandicoot' was apparently first applied to large rodents (genus *Bandicota*) which inhabit southern Asia. The word means 'pig-rat' in Telugu, a Dravidian language of India. The marsupial bandicoots are quadrupedal but with hindlimbs enlarged and carrying most of the body weight while the forelimbs are used for scratching and digging. The insect food is mainly taken from the top few inches of soil or from rotting wood on the surface of the ground. Bandicoots show a remarkable amount of growth after sexual maturity and the 20 or so species cannot be separated by size alone. The smallest bandicoot is *Microperoryctes* of west New Guinea Mountains, less than 1 ft (30 cm)

Bandy-bandy

The bandicoot has earned a bad name by digging on lawns in search of insects.

long, with a hindfoot length of 1·2 in (3 cm), while the largest forms of Short-nosed bandicoots genus *Isoodon* and Rabbit-eared bandicoots genus *Macrotis* are up to 2½ ft (75 cm) long and have foot lengths three times greater. The tail is much shorter than the body length in all except Rabbit-eared bandicoots. FAMILY: Peramelidae, ORDER: Marsupialia, CLASS: Mammalia.

BANDY-BANDY *Vermicella annulata*, a small venomous snake found throughout most parts of continental Australia, from the west coastal forests to the central deserts. Up to 3 ft (0·9 m) long the bandy-bandy is a slender, small-headed snake with up to 70 alternate black and white bands along its length. It is a burrowing snake which forages above ground at night, feeding on insects, small lizards and especially Blind snakes. It is, however, not regarded as dangerous to humans or domestic animals because it has small fangs and a mild venom. When threatened the bandy-bandy exhibits a distinctive behaviour pattern in which it throws its body into a series of stiffly-held loops. FAMILY: Elapidae, ORDER: Squamata, CLASS: Reptilia.

BANTENG *Bos javanicus*, species of wild ox in Southeast Asia, closely related to the gaur. Banteng are smaller than gaur, averaging a height of 5½ ft (170 cm), and longer-legged, with a smaller dorsal ridge. Like the gaur, the legs have white 'stockings' but unlike them they also have a white patch on the buttocks. The horns are more angular, averaging 24 in (60 cm) in length in bulls but only 12 in (30 cm) or so in cows. The forehead between the horns is naked and heavily keratinized. Bornean banteng are called temadau; in Burma they are called tsaine; and in Cambodia, ansong.

Unlike gaur, banteng prefer flat or undulating ground, with light forest and glades

of grass and bamboo. They are less timid than gaur, and more often enter cultivated fields. They live in herds of 10–30, but many bulls live solitary lives except in the rut. They are more or less nocturnal, feeding during the night and in the early morning, and lying up in the forest to chew the cud by day. In the monsoon season, they go up into the hills, ascending sometimes to 2,000 ft (600 m), to eat the young bamboo shoots.

In Bali, banteng have long been domesticated and form a characteristic breed, which is smaller than the true banteng with a more extensive dewlap and lower dorsal ridge; males are never quite black. In parts of Indonesia the Bali ox is extensively used as a draught animal and for milk. FAMILY: Bovidae, ORDER: Artiodactyla, CLASS: Mammalia.

BARBARY APE *Macaca sylvana*, a large terrestrial macaque monkey, tailless and long-coated living in the forests of northwest Africa. A small colony has been maintained on Gibraltar for many years. Barbary apes roam the forests in large bands feeding on leaves, fruit, insects and scorpions, often raiding crops. They are the only species of macaque outside Asia. The species once ranged across the whole of north Africa and into southwest Asia. FAMILY: Ceropithecidae, ORDER: Primates, CLASS: Mammalia.

BARBARY SHEEP *Ammotragus lervia*, a native of North Africa, inhabits the hot arid mountains from the Red Sea to Morocco. It has been successfully introduced in southwest USA. Barbary sheep have no preorbital and interdigital glands, but odoriferous glands on the naked underside of the long tail, as in goats. The long neck mane and cheek beards they share with the urials, the most primitive of sheep. Adults are rufous-grey in colour with lighter bellies, groins and rears. In their social adaptations they are

much like the primitive sheep, but with a more generalized combat behaviour. They clash in a similar way to Mountain sheep and are better horn- and shoulder-wrestlers than these. In addition, they jab with their sharply pointed horns and can inflict severe wounds. In this way they resemble neither sheep nor goats but their ancestors, the goat-antelopes. There is little difference in external appearance between adult males and females except in size. FAMILY: Bovidae, ORDER: Artiodactyla, CLASS: Mammalia.

BARBEL *Barbus barbus*, one of Europe's largest members of the carp-like family Cyprinidae. It is also the only European member of the genus *Barbus* found outside the Danube basin. Like other cyprinids, the barbel is streamlined and a good swimmer, well adapted to the swift waters near weirs and in rapid stretches of rivers. It reaches about 14 lb (over 6 kg) in weight. Its name derives from the four barbels around the mouth. FAMILY: Cyprinidae, ORDER: Cypriniformes, CLASS: Pisces.

BARBETS, stocky, powerfully built birds closely related to the honeyguides. The largest is about 12 in (30 cm) long, the smallest 3½ in (9 cm) long. The majority of barbets have relatively large heavy bills, sometimes with serrations or 'teeth' along the cutting edges of the upper mandible. These 'teeth' reach their greatest development in a number of African species, notably the Double-toothed barbet *Lybius bidentatus*, and presumably help in the plucking and manipulation of the fruits. The feet of barbets are zygodactyl (with two toes pointing forwards, two backwards), and a number of species regularly clamber about tree trunks and branches in woodpecker fashion. Many barbets are brilliantly coloured, notably the American species and the Oriental barbets, the latter being bright green, adorned with gaudy patches of blue, red, yellow and black around the head. The sexes are usually similar, though there is strong sexual dimorphism in some of the American species.

Barbets are so named because the majority have well developed chin and rictal bristles, or conspicuous tufts of feathers over their nostrils, often as long or longer than the bill.

It seems likely that they are sense organs for measuring the size of fruits, so preventing time being wasted in attempts to swallow fruits that are too large, or which might wedge in their throats.

The 76 species of barbets are found in the tropics of America, Africa and Asia as far east as Borneo and Bali. FAMILY: Capitonidae, ORDER: Piciformes, CLASS: Aves.

BARK BEETLES, a name usually reserved for the Engraver beetles but also used for other beetles that live under the bark of trees. Many are predacious, feeding on other insects living beneath the bark, but some have forsaken this habit to become vegetarians and serious pests of stored grain. ORDER: Coleoptera, CLASS: Insecta, PHYLUM: Arthropoda.

BARKING DEER *Muntiacus muntjak*, name given to Indian muntjac because of its peculiar cry, like a hoarse resonant bark. See muntjac.

BARNACLES, crustaceans of the subclass Cirripedia. They are all marine and occur in countless millions on the shore-line of almost every coast, attached to almost all floating objects and to objects on the sea-bottom. A mile-long stretch of rocky shore may have as many as 2,000 million Acorn barnacles. Like most crustaceans each individual animal goes through a series of juvenile stages before becoming an adult. Most barnacles have free-swimming larvae which pass through seven stages, six nauplius and a cypris stage, and in many places these form a notable part of the plankton at certain times of the year. Adult cirripedes are usually fixed to a solid support and they then look quite unlike other crustaceans, so much so that they used to be classified as Mollusca.

Cirripedia divides into a number of orders. The first, the Thoracica, is made up of the suborders Pedunculata and Operculata. In the Pedunculata, the most primitive, the animal is enclosed in a number of calcareous plates and borne on a stalk or peduncle. The Pedunculata include the familiar barnacle often spoken of as the Ships' barnacle.

The operculate or Acorn barnacles are common in the sublittoral and on all rocky coasts, often completely covering wide stretches of rock. They have no stalk and the calcareous plates have come together to form a chalky box containing the barnacle's body.

They are all very similar in construction and in their life cycle. *Balanus balanoides*, the common European species, is typical. Its soft parts are enclosed in a shell cemented securely to the substratum. The shell opens to the exterior at the operculum which consists of four valves on a flexible membrane under the control of the animal inside and only when these are opened can the cirri (legs) be protruded and water flow in.

The body of the animal is attached underneath the opercular membrane round and beneath the large adductor muscle by which the two halves of the operculum are brought

together. It consists of a thorax with a bag-like prosoma from which arise the cirri. The abdomen is vestigial. The mouth is situated on the prosoma. It should perhaps be emphasized that living tissue is continuous around the whole of the interior of the shell.

The cirri are pushed out and then swept downwards acting as a drag-net to capture food and at the same time driving a current of water through the mantle cavity so bringing oxygen to the body surface through which it is absorbed.

The early stages of the embryo are passed inside the parental body, at the base of the mantle cavity. Later, as larvae, they are expelled on the current of water induced by the movements of the cirri. SUBCLASS: Cirripedia, CLASS: Crustacea, PHYLUM: Arthropoda.

BARRACUDAS, tropical marine fishes related to the Grey mullet family Mugilidae. The barracudas are fierce predators which, in some areas such as the West Indies, are more feared than sharks. The body is elongated and powerful, with two dorsal fins. The jaws are lined with sharp dagger-like teeth which make a neat, clean bite. There are many records of barracudas attacking divers and they appear to be attracted to anything that makes erratic movements or is highly coloured. They feed on fishes and have been seen to herd shoals of fish, rather after the manner of sheepdogs, until they are ready to attack.

The smallest *Sphyraena borealis* grows to about 18 in (46 cm) and is found along the North American Atlantic coast. The Great barracuda *Sphyraena barracuda* which grows to 8 ft (2·4 m) in length, is found in the western Pacific and on both sides of the tropical Atlantic. A certain mystery surrounds its habits, for it is known to attack divers in the West Indies but in the Pacific region, and particularly in Hawaii, it has the reputation of being harmless to man. In the Mediterranean there is a single species, *S. sphyraena*, which reaches 5 ft (1·5 m) in length. FAMILY: Sphyraenidae, ORDER: Perciformes, CLASS: Pisces.

BASILISKS, lizards of the genus *Basiliscus* containing several species inhabiting Central America and ranging as far north as central Mexico. They live along the banks of the smaller rivers or streams where they bask during the day or sleep at night on bushes that overhang the water. Basilisks are slender lizards with long slim toes and tail and the males are often adorned with crests.

Speed is the chief means of snatching up food (insects and small rodents or birds) and escaping enemies. When attempting to escape basilisks head for water and run across it. A fringe of scales along the lengthy rear toes provides support as they dash over the surface. Basilisks are known as the Jesus Cristo lizard for the ability to 'walk on the

Barbary sheep, the only wild sheep of Africa, from Morocco to Upper Egypt, has goat-like horns.

Basket stars

A group of bass, marine fishes highly regarded by anglers. They freely take a bait.

water'. As its speed slackens, however, the lizard begins to sink and must swim.

Basilisks are normally some shade of brown with white or yellow bands or mottling. FAMILY: Iguanidae, ORDER: Squamata, CLASS: Reptilia.

BASKET STARS, brittlestars in which the simple five-armed symmetry is obscured by the numerous side branches of the arms. Up to 2 ft (61 cm) across the spread arms they are found in deep seas down to 5,000 ft (1,600 m). The curling tendril-like branches of the arms recall the Gorgon's head of Greek mythology. When feeding a Basket star clings to a rock with two arms and holds the others up, like a basket, to catch food. ORDER: Euryalae, CLASS: Ophiuroidea, PHYLUM: Echinodermata.

BASKING SHARK *Cetorhinus maximus*, second only to the Whale shark in size and immediately recognizable by its very long gill

clefts which extend from the upper to the lower surface of the body. There are two dorsal fins and one anal fin, very small teeth in the jaws, and the general body colour is a grey-brown. The maximum size is 45 ft (13·5 m) and 30 ft (9 m) is not uncommon. The Basking shark feeds by straining plankton from the water. The gill arches are equipped with rows of fine rakers (up to 4 in/10 cm long and over 1,000 in each row) and these form a fine sieve. This system can provide enough food for an animal that may weigh over 4 tons (4,000 kg). Basking sharks lacking gillrakers are sometimes found and it is thought the rakers may be shed in winter and regrown every spring. They derive their name from their habit of lying at the surface. They are not dangerous to man, except perhaps accidentally when in collision with small boats.

The Basking shark is found everywhere, but chiefly in temperate waters. ORDER: Pleurotremata, CLASS: Chondrichthyes.

A group of bass, marine fishes highly regarded by anglers. They freely take a bait.

BASS, a term used in Europe for the Sea perch *Dicentrarchus labrax* and its close relative the Black-spotted bass *D. punctatus*. The bass, considered by many to be one of the best of European angling fishes, is a coastal fish that often enters estuaries and even ascends rivers. It is found in the Mediterranean and off the coasts of Spain and Portugal but reaches the southern coasts of the British Isles. It is found off shelving sand or shingle beaches and is often fished for in the breakers, where it feeds on fishes (sandeels, sprat and herring). Specimens of 18 lb (8 kg) have been caught but fishes of 2–7 lb (0·9–3 kg) are more usual. There are two dorsal fins, the first spiny and separated from the second. The back is blue-green, the flanks silver with a black lateral line and a white belly. The Black-spotted bass is a smaller fish, reaching 2 ft (60 cm) in length and the body is speckled with black spots. This species does not reach as far north as the British Isles. See also Black bass. FAMILY: Serranidae, ORDER: Perciformes, CLASS: Pisces.

BATFISHES, common name given to two different groups of fishes. Members of the family Ogcocephalidae, a family of the anglerfishes, are sometimes referred to as batfishes although the term is more appropriately used for members of the Platacidae, a family containing marine perch-like fishes with greatly extended wing-like dorsal and anal fins. Species of *Platax* have highly compressed, almost circular bodies and their long fins give them a bat-like appearance when swimming. They grow to about 2 ft (60 cm) and are found in the Indo-Pacific region. They are red-yellow with dark vertical bands in the young which disappear with age and

The basilisk, South American reptile, named after the legendary monster of Europe, best known for its running on water.

The Great barracuda *Sphyraena barracuda*, of both sides of the Atlantic, has a reputation for ferocity.

Wing-like fins of the batfish *Platax* invite comparison with the familiar mammal.

strongly resemble floating and yellowing leaves of the Red mangrove. When chased by a predator in a mangrove swamp, the fishes stop swimming and drift motionless like leaves. They feed on small crustaceans and the general detritus of coastal and mangrove swamp. FAMILY: Platacidae, ORDER: Perciformes, CLASS: Pisces.

BATH SPONGE, the fibrous skeleton of an animal used for bathing and in a wide range of commercial purposes. In life the skeleton is covered with a yellow flesh bounded externally by a purplish-black skin which may be pale yellow when the sponge has been growing in dim light. The Bath, or Commercial, sponge lives in warm seas, from shallow waters to not more than 600 ft (200 m) and may be one of a few species, the chief of which are *Spongia officinalis*, with a fine-meshed skeleton, and *Hippospongia equina*, with a coarser skeleton. The main centres of sponge fisheries are the Mediterranean, especially the eastern half, and the Gulf of Mexico and especially around the Bahamas, Florida and Honduras. Bath sponges also occur, but in more limited numbers, in the Red Sea, Indian Ocean and on the Great Barrier Reef of Australia. FAMILY: Spongidae, ORDER: Demospongiae, CLASS: Gelatinosa, PHYLUM: Parazoa.

BATS, one of the most distinctive groups of animals. They are mammals since they are covered by fur and suckle their young, yet they can all fly in a sustained manner which no other mammal can do. They therefore form a well-defined division called the Order Chiroptera, a name meaning 'hand-wings'. Because all bats are noctural in habits, and the majority are tropical in distribution, they are relatively little known and it is seldom realized that they are both numerous and diverse, with about 800 species or about one-seventh of all mammals.

The bats belong to the basically primitive group of mammals called the Unguiculata which also includes the primates and the insectivores. Bats are probably descended from insectivores but their origins are rather obscure because they have left few fossils. The earliest known bats, from the Eocene period, are remarkably similar to present day forms. It is therefore impossible to tell how flight developed or what bats were like before they could fly. Linnaeus first classified bats with primates because their forelimbs bear 'hands' instead of paws and because the males have a free penis. These similarities now seem rather superficial, but there is little doubt that the two groups are quite closely related.

Bats are subdivided into two suborders —the Megachiroptera and the Microchiroptera. Although these names mean 'big bats' and 'small bats', there is a considerable overlap in their size ranges. The Megachiroptera vary in weight from about 1 oz (25–30 g) to 2 lb (900 g) with wingspans of 10 in (25 cm) to over 5 ft (150 cm), while adult Microchiroptera range from about ⅛ oz (3·5 g) to 6½ oz (180 g) with wingspans of 6 in (15 cm) to 3 ft (90 cm). Megachiroptera have very large eyes and nearly always have a claw on the first finger as well as on the thumb. Because most of them have dog-like faces they are often called 'flying foxes'. They are often called 'fruit bats' but not all eat fruit; the Microchiroptera are often called 'insectivorous bats' although their diets vary tremendously and some eat fruit.

The body form of bats is largely governed by the requirements of flight. The skeleton is frail and light but the fore-limbs are enormously developed. The upper arm is short and strong with a powerful shoulder joint to bear the weight of the body. In the so-called advanced families each arm has a double articulation with the shoulder blade, making a firm hinge for flapping movements. The forearm is very long with only a single bone, the radius, and bears a short, compact wrist in which many of the bones are fused together for further strength. From this projects a short thumb with a claw used for climbing or walking. In vampires which are especially agile on the ground, the thumb is well developed as a 'foot' and bears a fleshy pad that acts as a 'sole'. The fingers are all very long with extended shanks between the knuckles; the index and middle fingers are

Head of False vampire *Cardioderma cor.*

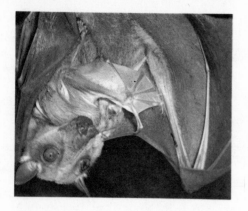

Hammer-headed bat suckling her baby.

close together at the leading edge of the wing while the ring and little fingers fan out behind to support the main wing surface. This whole arrangement gives fine control of the wing shape since all the joints can be flexed by tendons operated from muscles in the arm. Thus bats are by far the most manoeuvrable of aerial animals.

The whole of the forearm is webbed by a thin, double layer of skin which forms the wing membrane. This runs from the shoulder across the kink of the elbow to the wrist, between all the fingers (but rarely includes the thumb) and from the little finger backwards along the body to the ankle of the back leg. It contains elastic strands and fine muscle fibres within it so that it collapses when the wing is folded and does not interfere with walking. In flight it also acts as a radiator since it contains a network of fine blood vessels in which the blood is cooled to prevent the bat becoming overheated by its exertions. When the bat lands the blood supply to the wings is much reduced so that heat is then conserved.

The back legs of bats have thighs and shins of roughly equal length and a short, round foot with five small toes bearing sharp claws. The tendons in the foot prevent the toes from straightening when the leg is extended so that bats can hang from a toe-hold without effort and indeed often die without falling off. The hips are also unusual because the joints are permanently twisted so that the knees point upwards over the back instead of forwards. This position is the most convenient for hanging. It also allows the legs to kick downwards to assist the wingbeat when flying.

The tail and the flight membrane between the legs are very variable. The Megachiroptera have at most a simple flap along the inside leg and the feet are held together in flight; the tail if present is short and free. In the Microchiroptera there is generally, but not always, a large tail membrane stretched between the legs, with the actual tail incorporated in it. The trailing edge of the tail membrane is strengthened by a whip-like cartilage called the calcar which projects towards the mid-line from the ankle.

Bats give birth to well developed young, usually singly, although twins are quite common in some species. Mating occurs in the daytime roost and courtship appears to be perfunctory. Promiscuity is the rule and both pair formation and paternal care are unknown. In temperate climates the breeding cycle of Microchiroptera is interrupted by hibernation since mating occurs in the autumn. The sperm are then stored inside the female until ovulation, and fertilization occurs after she awakens in the spring. The young are born in all-female nursing colonies during early summer. The mothers have two functional teats on the sides of the chest, but some bats also have a second, non-lactating pair in the groin which the baby holds during flight. When the baby grows too heavy to be carried it is left behind in the colony while the mother is hunting.

Tropical bats under constant climatic conditions appear to breed repeatedly throughout the year. Female Molossidae are sometimes pregnant while still suckling a baby, and a young female bat may itself become pregnant before it is fully weaned.

In the Old World the Megachiroptera are completely vegetarian, mostly eating fruit, flowers or pollen. One small group in the Far East, with an isolated member in Africa, are almost exclusively nectar drinkers. They hover or perch close to night-opening flowers and sip the rich fluid with very long, rough-tipped tongues. The majority of the Old World Microchiroptera are insectivorous but a few, notably the Megadermatidae, are 'bats of prey', hunting small vertebrate animals such as mice, lizards and other bats. One or two species in Asia probably catch small fish with their back feet as they fly low over open water.

In the New World, the true vampires feed only on the blood of larger vertebrates, attacked as they sleep. They have large, sharp incisor teeth to open a wound gently, a muscular, grooved tongue for sipping the blood and secretions in their saliva which prevent the blood from clotting. They can imbibe enormous quantities of blood and excrete the excess water rapidly, and are very agile on the ground in case their host should awaken when they are so engorged that they fly only with difficulty. Finally there are two specialized New World fishing bats. Both have very large back feet which seize fish from the water during flight.

During the winter in temperate countries the food of bats becomes scarce. Unlike small insectivorous birds, bats seldom migrate for long distances. Instead most of them hibernate. During the autumn they become very fat with accumulated food reserves and sink into a dormant state that is more extreme than daily sleep. Heart-rate, breathing and all other bodily functions are greatly suppressed throughout the winter. It is not true, however, that hibernation is

uninterrupted, for bats are sometimes seen flying about in mid-winter.

The Megachiroptera all possess very large eyes, capable of superb night vision. Only one kind of megachiropteran is known to be able to fly safely in complete darkness. This is the genus *Rousettus* which has normal megachiropteran eyes on which it relies whenever the light is adequate. When vision fails these bats are able to use acoustic guidance by making short, high-pitched sounds and detecting echoes from nearby objects. The sounds are made by clicking the tongue.

Flight guidance in the Microchiroptera is quite different. Nearly a quarter of the species, from all major families, have been investigated. They emit a constant train of sound pulses during flight or even when active on the ground. These pulses differ from those of *Rousettus* in being produced vocally from the modified voice-box and in being almost entirely ultrasonic—that is, too high in pitch to be audible to man although their intensities may be very high. The actual sound frequencies range from about 15 KHz (just audible) to 150 KHz, having wavelengths of $\frac{5}{6}$ to $\frac{1}{12}$ in (2·2–0·22 cm). Insectivorous species have been shown to be capable of detecting and avoiding wires only 4 thousandths of an inch thick (0·1 mm) even in the presence of considerable background noise. Moreover they detect, locate and intercept their insect prey in mid-air by this acoustic method, a task that is apparently too difficult for even the best night vision. ORDER: Chiroptera, CLASS: Mammalia.

BEARS, characterized by their heavy build, thick limbs, diminutive tail and small ears, the members of the Ursidae comprise nine species with a wide distribution which covers the northern hemisphere and overlaps in a few places in the southern hemisphere. The fur is coarse and thick, and, with the exception of the Polar bear, dark. The tuberculous

A Brown bear of the northern hemisphere. Although given such names as Syrian, European and grizzly, according to where they live, all Brown bears belong to one species.

molars indicate an omnivorous diet while the plantigrade walk (the whole sole of the foot resting on the ground with each step) gives the bear a slow and ponderous gait but when pursuing or pursued it will gallop. Some species climb well.

The eyes and ears are small and of all the senses smell is the sharpest and vision the least acute. Usually peaceful and timid, bears may become formidable when wounded or suddenly disturbed, using their claws and teeth in conjunction with their great strength. Solitary and nocturnal, bears wander over their territory, the cubs remaining with the mother until half-grown. Species living in colder areas may become lethargic during the winter, but true hibernation does not take place, only a winter dormancy.

The cubs are very small at birth, weighing approximately 1/350th of the adult weight. Gestation varies between six to nine months long and delayed implantation occurs in most species, so the fragile young are born during 'hibernation', emerging from the den two or three months later. Sexual maturity is reached at two years for the females and up to six years for the males. The total life span can attain 40 years under ideal captive conditions, but in the wild it is less than half that.

The European Brown bear *Ursus arctos*, the most widespread, has a short neck and large dog-like head. The grizzly, an American subspecies, is the largest terrestrial member of the Carnivora, some individuals reaching 113 in (280 cm) in length and weighing over 1,700 lb (780 kg) but 80 in (200 cm) and 550 lb (250 kg) are more usual measurements. Coat colouration varies from cream to blue-black. Distributed across Alaska and Canada down to the western portion of North America, it is also found in the mountains of Europe and Asia Minor, across to the Himalayas. Once known as *Ursus horribilis*, the grizzly has the reputation of being particularly ferocious. The strength of the Brown bear is proverbial, sometimes killing an adult cow with a swipe of the forepaw and dragging the carcass back to the den. In certain areas fish are scooped out of the stream and form a large part of the diet. Fruit and grass are eaten in the spring as a laxative when the bears become active again after 'hibernating'.

The North American Black bear *Euarctos americanus* is smaller than the Brown bear, rarely measuring more than 70 in (180 cm) in length or weighing over 330 lb (150 kg). Different colorations exist: black, cinnamon and even white. The muzzle is often brown. The paws, which are less massive, make this species particularly agile and full-grown adults can still climb trees. Breeding takes place in June or July but the fertilized egg does not become implanted in the uterine wall until November. One to four cubs are then born in January or February and remain with the mother until the following autumn.

A Grizzly bear watches a puma feeding. Although they are basically vegetarian, grizzlies will readily eat flesh, either freshly killed or as carrion.

The Spectacled bear *Tremarctos ornatus* is the only South American species, living both in low forests and up to 1,000 ft (300 m) in the Andes. Measuring 60–70 in (150–180 cm), adults weigh up to 300 lb (140 kg) but the shaggy coat contributes to the bulky appearance. Some individuals have uneven white streaks circling the eyes and extending to the muzzle, down the throat to the chest, while others are completely dark brown-black.

The Polar bear *Thalarctos maritimus* is the only completely carnivorous bear. Its year-round cream colour is perfect camouflage. It has a more slender and longer neck than the Brown or Black bear. The soles of the feet are thickly haired, providing insulation and a secure grip on the ice. The forepaws are partially webbed and the neck and shoulder muscles greatly developed, making the Polar bear a tireless swimmer. Attaining occasionally 9 ft (200–280 cm) in length, the weight is from 800 to 1,550 lb (400–700 kg) depending on the season. Nomadic in the extreme, Polar bears are sometimes discovered resting on ice floes 200 miles (320 km) at sea.

Seals are the main prey. The bear waits for the seal to surface at its breathing hole in the ice then grabs it and hauls it out. 30 lb (13 kg) of seal blubber (rather than the flesh) can be eaten at one sitting. Mating occurs in mid-April or May and while tracking the solitary females over great distances, the males become extremely irascible. In winter, the females excavate a shallow den under the snow and there the cubs are born in January. Blind and helpless, they are the size of a Guinea pig at birth. The mother does not leave this makeshift shelter, living off her fat reserves, until the cubs can follow her about. When they emerge during the early summer months, the young Polar bears are weaned on berries and Arctic hares, to be initiated the following winter to seal hunting. Because the cubs stay so long with the female, breeding takes place only every other year, which accounts for the low population numbers.

Because Polar bears are such favourites as cubs, and because they breed readily in zoos, the documentation of the early life history is fairly complete. A typical cub weighs 1½ lb (648 gr) and measures 1 ft (30 cm) at birth. At the end of the month the weight will have increased to 6 lb (2·8 kg) and by the end of ten months will have reached a weight of 175 lb (80 kg). The eyes open on the 33rd day and first begin to focus on the 47th day. The ear opens on the 26th day but the cub's hearing is imperfect until the 70th day. Not until the eyes can focus does the cub begin to walk at all and is not walking really strongly until about the 70th day. From such signs as can be gleaned from the cub's behaviour the sense of smell does not function strongly until about the 50th day. In brief, therefore, a Polar bear cub is using the energy from its intake of food in bodily growth rather than in the development of the senses or in developing the muscular movements that will make it independent.

For purposes of comparison only, a human baby weighing at birth 7½ lb (3·4 kg) will have increased its weight to about 16 lb (7·2 kg) at the age of 7 months when the average Polar bear cub will have increased from 1½ lb (0·6 kg) at birth to 120 lb (54·6 kg).

The two babies are alike in at least one respect, that they tend to have individual fads and idiosyncrasies, and to react peevishly when thwarted in these.

The Himalayan bear *Selenarctos thibetanus* occurs in the elevated forests of Baluchistan, Afghanistan, westward to the Himalayas and northwards into China and Siberia. Its coat is black (or brown during the summer moult) and the white chevron stands out clearly on the chest. The tufted ears are relatively larger and the muzzle shorter than in the European Brown bear but they share common behavioural traits. 'Moon' bears or 'Blue' bears, as they are also called, descend to the valleys to spend the winter and do not

Beavers

A beaver pond formed when a stream is dammed by beavers. The dam is constructed of branches and logs floated into position by the beavers and plastered with mud.

'hibernate', becoming intermittently dormant only during the height of a monsoon or a blizzard. This heavy animal is an agile climber, building rough nests in low trees to sunbathe or nap. A den is preferred when rearing cubs. Family parties have been observed foraging together in fruit trees and the juveniles remain with the parents for at least a year, sometimes even after the next litter is born.

The Indian and Ceylonese Sloth bear *Melursus ursinus* is quite different from other Asiatic bears. The muzzle is elongated into a snout which shows great lateral mobility. Smaller and even shaggier than the Himalayan Black bear, it has a mantle of long, coarse fur on its shoulders, giving it a humped appearance. There is also a wide, often semi-circular shaped yellowish expanse of fur on the chest but the overall coloration varies from reddish-brown to black. It weighs 200–240 lb (90–110 kg) and measures 56–70 in (140–180 cm) in length. Solitary and nocturnal, it spends most of the day sleeping in jungle caves. Along with a long snout and extremely mobile lips, it has a gap in its front teeth, due to the absence of a pair of incisors in both jaws. After tearing a termite nest apart with its claws, this 'vacuum-cleaner' bear places its muzzle near the hole and sucks in the grubs with such force that the noise can be located 200 yd (180 m) away. After a seven month gestation, two or three cubs are born in the spring. Strangely enough they are carried on the mother's back during her nightly rounds and when she climbs a tree. Later, even when several months old the young, if suddenly alarmed, scramble over each other to reach this safe vantage point, now with room only for one.

The Sun bear *Helarctus malayanus* of Malaya looks like a diminutive, short-haired version of the South American Spectacled bear but the chest and eye patches when present are usually of a tan colour. This is the smallest member of the bear family, measuring 44–56 in (110–140 cm) and weighing 50–140 lb (22–65 kg) at the most. It occurs in the forests of Burma down the Malaya Peninsula to Sumatra and Borneo. The claws are used, when feeding, to scatter fruit or tear open bee hives and termite hills. Afterwards, the bear licks up the insects among the debris with its long prehensile tongue. Small rodents, birds and eggs also complement the diet. FAMILY: Ursidae, ORDER: Carnivora, CLASS: Mammalia.

BEAVERS, largest rodents in the northern hemisphere, sometimes exceeding 88 lb (40 kg). The heavy body is covered with a thick fur making a waterproof coat. The hind paws are large and webbed to the tips of the five toes. The second toe has a double nail, similar to a bird's beak, which acts as a fine comb. The hindquarters are very powerful in contrast to the small forelimbs, which barely touch the ground when it is moving along. All orifices can be closed when the beaver is under water including the cloaca, which is closed over the ano-urino-genital organs. The tail is an indispensable counterpoise on land and a horizontal rudder when the animal is in the water, with a heavy burden in its arms. The lips close behind the incisors, protecting the mucous membranes from water and from splinters of wood while the animal is working under water. The front paws, which are veritable hands, nimble and skilful, carry, push, pull, steer, scratch and groom. The beaver can remain under water

for up to 15 minutes. Finally, its brain is smooth, so the beaver is known as lissencephalic, but includes a cortex which compensates in thickness (from this aspect it is classified at the top of all rodents) for what it lacks in surface folds. That is, although the surface of the brain is smooth the beaver does not lack intelligence and is placed above all other rodents.

Scientists make a distinction between two kinds, the European *Castor fiber* and the American *C. canadensis*, but both types can be crossed and produce fertile hybrids, which, unfortunately, has happened all over Finland. The two types are known as 'geographical' types, in order to emphasize that the infinitesimal differences to be found are due to their (relatively recent) spatial separation. Since then they have become more rare, because of hunting and trapping, they have disappeared from many regions, although the total area of distribution has changed very little. Fortunately, energetic steps taken for their preservation and recolonization during the last few decades have given them back to the USA, Norway, Sweden and the USSR. They have just been reintroduced into Switzerland with some chances of success.

They have been known to live for 30 years and more in zoos. Although a beaver can breed from the age of two years, it is not at that time fully grown. A beaver and its mate seem to remain together for a long time, if not for their entire life. Both defend their common territory from outsiders of their own kind.

The mating season is in February, when the winter ice is melting; the beavers pair under water, *more humano*, or even at the edge of the water. About 100 days later young are born, fluffy and resourceful, eyes already open. A litter averages three young. The mother keeps them in the burrow for two or three weeks, together with last year's young. They are suckled during this period of confinement only, but the mother brings them tender young leaves a few days after birth. If by chance the young escape from the burrow through gaps in the walls, or even through the diving hole, the mother brings them back at once, walking semi-erect and carrying them between her chin and her arms. The young remain under their parents' tutelage, disturbing them more by their restlessness than helping by their presence. They chatter a lot, particularly inside the burrow; their cries are at first rather like those of puppies, then like human infants.

The beaver is superior to all other mammals in the efficiency and technical skill used in organizing its domain. It prefers to settle on shallow lowland streams, where there is plenty of vegetation, and by means of dams converts them into a series of water-levels, which provide protection from enemies coming from the river banks and an easy and rapid means of getting around. Furthermore, by keeping the water at a constant level, they camouflage the underwater entrance to their burrow and ensure access to their winter stores, even if the surface of the water is frozen. Although, during the summer months, beavers live on all kinds of plant life, during the hard weather they live on the bark of willows and poplars which they have collected in front of the entrance.

The beaver's shelter may be merely a cavity dug in the steep bank of the river starting from a sloping gallery which begins just below the surface of the water. If the banks are too low, the beavers build a lodge, a wooden dome consolidated with mud and having a diameter of up to 18–20 ft (6–7 m). The largest lodges may have several rooms, each having an independent gallery. Inside, the nest may be seen, provided with a bedding of dry shredded wood. Each family has several homes, inhabited successively apparently according to whim.

The most surprising piece of work is the dam, which may reach enormous widths, up to more than 1,000 yd (914 m). In spite of their size they are the work of at most two or three families living amicably together.

The communications network is almost entirely aquatic, except for a few short straight paths towards the felled trees. If it is necessary to go farther the beavers can dig long canals. FAMILY: Castoridae, ORDER: Rodentia, CLASS: Mammalia.

BED-BUGS, cosmopolitan blood-sucking insects associated with man and many animals, including birds and bats. They are true bugs, members of the order Hemiptera. The Common bed-bug *Cimex lectularius* and the Tropical bed-bug *Cimex rotundatus* (= *C. hemipterus*) commonly occur as parasites of man. The pigeon-bug *Cimex columbarius*, associated with pigeons, doves and Domestic fowl, is now considered a race of the Common bed-bug, and indeed, the two races are known to thrive on both man and birds. A similar, but smaller species in House martins' and swallows' nests will also bite man.

The adult is flat and roughly oval in shape, being about $\frac{1}{5}$ in (5 mm) long and $\frac{1}{8}$ in (3 mm) broad, covered with fine short hairs and usually mahogany brown, but it may appear more reddish if it has recently fed or purple if an older meal is still present in its gut. Immature bed-bugs (or nymphs) are paler than adults. When in need of a meal bed-bugs are paper-thin but appear much fatter, even almost globular after a large meal. They cannot fly and all that remains of the wings are a pair of short flaps on the middle segment of the thorax.

The Common bed-bug is found throughout Europe, Russia, northern India, North Africa, North and South America and Australia. It tends to be replaced in the

tropics by the Tropical bed-bug, very similar to it. The fact that several species of bed-bugs feed on birds and bats, which habitually breed in caves or rock clefts, suggests that man and the Common bed-bug may have commenced their 'partnership' when man himself inhabited caves. Most authorities consider the Middle East as the most likely area of origin, especially on the eastern Mediterranean coasts. They were known to the Romans and Ancient Greeks. Bed-bugs were recorded from the area now known as Germany in the 11th century, but apparently did not invade Britain until the early 16th century and Sweden until the 1800's.

After mating the female lays 150–200 eggs at the rate of two or three per day. Each egg is creamy white, slightly curved and elongated with a lid or operculum at one end, and is about $\frac{1}{25}$ in (1 mm) long. They are deposited in crevices and cracks, behind skirtingboards, wall paper and similar sites, each being firmly fixed in place with a glue-like secretion produced by the accessory glands of the female reproductive apparatus. The eggs require a temperature of at least 55°F (13°C) to hatch. At 82°F (28°C) they will hatch in five or six days. When fully developed the tiny nymph forces off the operculum and emerges as a miniature of the adult, about the size of a pin head. It moults and forms a new, larger skin to accommodate each of five increases in size between egg and adult. Each nymphal stage needs at least one full blood meal before proceeding to the next growth stage, but additional blood meals may occasionally be taken.

The bed-bug sucks the blood of its human host using a rostrum or jointed beak beneath its head. When not in use this is carried pointing backwards under the head, but it is swung forwards and extended when the bug feeds. It is composed of two pairs of needle-like stylets which are supported by a jointed lower lip (the labium). The two pairs of stylets when pressed together form two tubes, a larger one for sucking up blood and a smaller

Carmine bee-eater *Merops nubicus.*

one through which saliva is pumped into the wound. A hungry bed-bug penetrates the skin using the serrated tips of the stylets, so that these come to rest in a blood capillary. Saliva is pumped through the insect's mouthparts into the capillary. A mixture of blood and saliva is then sucked up the canal in the stylets and passed into the gut. The saliva prevents coagulation of the host's blood and hence clogging of the delicate stylet mechanism and the gut is avoided. The intense irritation from bed-bug bites is apparently caused by the saliva, the wound made by the stylets being a very minor puncture. Some people seem to be very much more sensitive to bug bites than others and many tend to lose their sensitivity if bitten repeatedly. A bed-bug may take up to 12 min to fully gorge itself. After feeding it has a bloated appearance, having imbibed up to six times its own weight of blood. Feeding occurs about once a week in summer, less frequently in cooler weather, and probably not at all in unheated premises in the winter in Britain.

Bed-bugs are chiefly nocturnal and only seen in broad daylight if very hungry. They are said to be most lively just before dawn and it may be supposed that those seen walking in daylight are individuals that have failed to secure a suitable blood meal in the normal hours of activity. ORDER: Hemiptera, CLASS: Insecta, PHYLUM: Arthropoda.

BEE, flying insect of the order Hymenoptera. Bees differ from other members of this order in their habit of providing nectar and pollen for their young. See bumblebees and honeybee.

BEE-EATERS, a family of insect-eating, bright-plumaged birds of the Old World; chiefly found in the tropics, with one species in Europe and one in Australia. The best known is the European bee-eater *Merops apiaster*. It is a summer visitor to the Mediterranean countries, and western Asia. It spends the winter in Africa south of the Sahara, particularly in southern Africa. Bee-eaters live on flying insects, caught in graceful pursuit flights, and have pointed decurved beaks, pointed wings and very short legs. The sexes are similar. In some species the central tail feathers are elongated.

Bee-eaters are well named, for practically all the species feed exclusively on airborne insects, with bees and their allies (Hymenoptera) comprising 80% or more of their diet. There are two principal ways of feeding; the smaller species keep watch for passing insects from a vantage-point like a bush, fence-post or telephone wire, and the larger species hunt on the wing. In either case an insect is pursued with a fast and dextrous flight and snapped up in the bill. Generally the bird returns to its perch, where it beats the prey against the perch until it is inactive.

The worker honeybees and other stinging

Bellbird

Red-throated bee-eater *Merops bullocki*.

Hymenoptera have their stings removed by an instinctive pattern of behaviour. The insect is held in the beak near the tip of its abdomen, which is rubbed against the perch so that the venom is discharged. Apart from bees, most other suitably-sized flying insects are also preyed upon: damsel-flies, termites, butterflies, bugs, beetles, grasshoppers etc. After a rainstorm in Africa, flying ants and termites emerge in great profusion and are hunted by many kinds of birds; an excited flock of wheeling bee-eaters is often in attendance. FAMILY: Meropidae, ORDER: Coraciiformes, CLASS: Aves.

BELLBIRD, name used for birds with bell-like calls. In South America it is used for several species of cotingas of the genus *Procnias* (Cotingidae). These are the size of large thrushes and may have a featherless throat or various types of vermiform wattles. Their calls consist of far-carrying notes, like the tolling of a large bell or the clang of a hammer on an anvil, and may be monotonously repeated for long periods. They can be heard up to a mile away and may be intolerably loud at close quarters. The birds are forest-dwelling, fruit-eating species and little is known of their life-histories.

In Australia the name is applied to the Crested bellbird, *Oreoica guttaralis*, a species of whistler (Pachycephalinae). This is a bird of dry regions, thrush-like and dull brown in colour with a short erectile crest. The male has a mainly black head, and is white around the bill and throat. Its bell-like call consists of two slow notes followed by three quieter ones, all uttered in a muted ringing tone which makes the call sound like a distant cattlebell. It is ventriloquial in quality, the bird being difficult to locate from the sound which seems to come from much farther off.

In New Zealand the name is used for a species of honey-eater, *Anthornis melanura*, Meliphagidae. This is again about the size of a thrush and a dull olive and yellowish green in colour, the male plumage having some iridescent purple on the head and yellow tufts at the sides of the breast. The song, which may be heard at all times of the year, is a series of up to six notes, of a liquid quality, and at a distance the louder notes sound remarkably bell-like. The female also sings, but her song is shorter and weaker.

BELUGA, derived from the Russian for 'white' is the name for two animals. The beluga *Huso huso* is the largest of the sturgeons and probably the largest of all freshwater fishes. It is found in the seas and rivers of the Soviet Union and reaches 29 ft (8·8 m). The beluga *Delphinapterus leucas*, or White whale, is a relative of the narwhal.

BHARAL or Blue sheep *Pseudois nayaur*, is not a large animal, the males rarely exceeding 150 lb (68 kg) in live weight. The head and horns resemble those of Barbary sheep, but there is no long hair on the cheeks, chin or neck. The horns are as large as those of the much larger Barbary sheep, reaching up to 31 in (88 cm) in length with a basal circumference of 13½ in (34 cm). The body is stocky and the legs are short. The ears are long, narrow and pointed and the tail is long and naked on its underside. There are no pre-orbital, inguinal or interdigital glands. These are typical goat features. Like all sheep or goats, the bharal has only two teats.

This is a strikingly coloured little goat with white margins down hind and front legs, a white rump patch and belly, the latter bordered by a dark brown flank stripe. The front of the legs, as well as the nose, neck and chest are dark brown, or even blackish in old males. The body is brown-grey in autumn. The smooth horns tend to be dark olive in colour.

Like sheep, bharal are social animals. Male and female groups range apart except in the rut which begins in late October. The large horns and sturdy skulls suggest that bharal clash forcefully. Occasionally, they fight like goats. The gestation period probably lasts six months. Twins are uncommon. The usual life expectancy is 12 to 15 years. FAMILY: Bovidae, ORDER: Artiodactyla, CLASS: Mammalia.

BICHIRS *Polypterus*, a genus of primitive freshwater fishes of Africa comprising about ten species. The name *Polypterus* signifies 'many fins', for when these fishes are alarmed or excited a row of 8–15 little finlets are erected along the back. The body is covered by thick, rhombic scales of a type known as ganoid (with a covering of ganoine as in certain extinct forms). A pair of spiracles (the vestigial first gill slits in most bony fishes) are conspicuous. In the larvae there are leaf-like external gills such as are known in the South American and African (but not Australian) lungfishes and also in amphibians but in no other bony fishes. In some species of *Polypterus* these gills later disappear. The intestine has a spiral valve which serves to increase the absorbent surface of the gut. This, too, is a primitive feature that is now found only in sharks and in such bony fishes as the sturgeons, lungfishes, the coelacanth and such fishes as the bowfin in the order Holostei. Bichirs can live out of water for a while breathing air into their lungs which are large but not quite so efficient as those of the lungfishes. The pectoral fins are similar to those of the coelacanth and its fossil relatives, with the finrays arising from a fleshy lobe. FAMILY: Polypteridae, ORDER: Polypteriformes, CLASS: Pisces.

BINTURONG *Arctictis binturong*, related to Palm civets but unlike them in appearance. It is long-bodied with short legs, 2–2½ ft (60–76 cm) long with a bushy, slightly prehensile, tail slightly less than this. Its coat is shaggy, black with brown or grey on the tips of the hairs, with long black ear-

Bearded bellbird *Procnias averano*, of South America and the island of Trinidad. The male has a metallic call which he makes from a fixed point throughout the day.

tufts and with white on the ears, face and unusually long whiskers. The binturong is nocturnal and spends the day mainly curled up in the tree-tops, sometimes coming out to bask on a branch. It is known to range from Burma to the Philippines but it may possibly live farther to the north, in Assam, Nepal and southern China. It eats mainly fruit and green shoots, its teeth being blunter than those of typical carnivores, but it also hunts small mammals and birds. FAMILY: Viverridae, ORDER: Carnivora, CLASS: Mammalia.

BIRD-EATING SPIDERS, large spiders which sometimes catch and eat birds. Very small tropical birds are sometimes caught in the strong orb webs of *Nephila* but even the giant theraphosid spiders like *Zasiodora* and *Grammostola* catch birds very rarely despite their being called Mygale or Bird spiders. ORDER: Araneae, CLASS: Arachnida, PHYLUM: Arthropoda.

BIRDS OF PARADISE, strongly-built perching birds famous for the brilliantly coloured and elaborately shaped plumes used in display. They are closely related to the bowerbirds. Birds of paradise range from 5–40 in (13–100 cm) long. Their legs and feet are rather stout and their tails vary from short and square to very long and wire-like. The bill may be fairly heavy with or without a hooked

Prince Rudolph's blue bird of paradise *Paradisea rudolphi,* displaying upside-down.

tip or long, thin and sickle-shaped. In some species the sexes are much alike but others show such marked sexual dimorphism in plumage that each sex was originally described as a separate species. Birds of paradise are found in the forests of New Guinea and nearby islands, with a few species in northern Australia and the Moluccas. They feed mainly on fruit, but also on insects, spiders, Tree frogs, lizards and other small animals.

The less ornate Birds of paradise have black plumage with little or no decoration, as in the Paradise crow or Silky crow *Lycocorax pyrrhopterus* of the Moluccas in which both male and female are blackish with no ornamental feathers. In Princess Loria's bird of paradise *Loria loria* the sexes are different; the female dull olive-brown and the male black with iridescent patches on wings and face. In the more ornate species the female remains dull brown or grey, while the male has elaborate crests or long plumes on the body or tail. One of the more ornate species is the 12-wired bird of paradise *Seleucidis melanoleuca* in which the male is black and yellow with yellow feathers on the flanks that end in 6 in (15 cm) tips that bend forwards. The King bird of paradise *Cicinnurus regius* has long curling, central tail feathers which are wire-like with 'flags' at the tips. The body is red above, white below. Another remarkable species is the King of Saxony bird of paradise *Pteridophora alberti*. Mainly black and yellow, the male has two long wire-like plumes set with small blue 'flags' trailing from the head. These are 18 in (45 cm) long, twice as long as the bird. Perhaps the most ornate, and bizarre, is the Superb bird of paradise *Lophorina superba* which is black with a bright bronze, green or mauve gloss and has an enormous 'cape' of long feathers on the nape which are raised in display.

The males of the plainly coloured species, such as the Trumpet birds or manucodes *Manucodia*, chase the females through the trees and display to them, but the ornate males usually gather to display in particular places, sometimes with several males in one tree. The combination of displays and calls of several males is probably more successful in attracting females than the same number of

Red-plumed or Count Raggi's bird of paradise *Paradisea apoda raggiana.*

Bison

isolated males. The males spread their plumes, flap the wings, sway and posture, and even display hanging upside down, as in the Greater bird of paradise *Paradisea apoda*. The King bird of paradise hangs upside down with spread wings and walks along the undersides of branches. FAMILY: Paradisaeidae, ORDER: Passeriformes, CLASS: Aves.

BISON *Bison bison*, or buffalo, the largest land animal in America, the bulls weighing up to a ton or more (907 kg) and standing 5 to 6 ft (1·5–1·8m) at the shoulder. The huge head, which appears extra large because of the long hair; the great hump on the shoulders; the dark brown woolly hair covering the forequarters; and the small naked hips are characteristic of the bull. Females are smaller and less striking. Both sexes have horns, but those of the bull are more massive. The calves are a light tawny colour in contrast to their dark brown parents.

During the breeding season from July to September, the bulls leave their male herds and mingle with the cows and calves, the strongest bulls tending individual cows until copulation is completed. Cows are sexually mature at two and a half years, and normally produce a single calf after a gestation period of about nine months.

The total population of bison was probably some 60 to 70 million animals when white man first arrived in America. Despite their great abundance, the bison probably roamed mostly in groups of 20–30 individuals and

only occasionally in herds of 100 or more, and the herds seem to have migrated only to the limited extent of perhaps 200 to 300 miles (300 to 500 km), rather than making the long northward and southward treks described in early accounts. FAMILY: Bovidae, ORDER: Artiodactyla, CLASS: Mammalia.

BITTERLING *Rhodeus sericeus*, a 3 in (8 cm) carp-like fish from lowland waters of Europe, the breeding cycle of which involves a freshwater mussel. The bitterling is normally silvery but in the breeding season the male develops violet and blue iridescence along the flanks and red on the belly, the fins becoming bright red edged with black. In colour, the female is less spectacular but develops a long pink ovipositor from the anal fin. It is this ovipositor, a 2 in (5 cm) tube for depositing the eggs, that gives a clue to the extraordinary breeding biology of the bitterling. Most carps merely scatter their eggs, but the female bitterling carefully deposits its eggs inside a freshwater mussel, hence the need for the long ovipositor. The male then sheds its milt and this is drawn in by the inhalant siphon of the mussel and the eggs are fertilized inside. Normally, one has only to touch these mussels and the two halves of the shell are snapped shut. The female bitterling, however, conditions the mussel by repeatedly nudging it with its mouth. This remarkable nursery for the eggs is clearly of great value to fishes that would otherwise lose a large percentage of the eggs through predators. In return the mussel releases its larvae while the bitterling is

A bitterling *Rhodeus sericeus*, of Europe, inspecting a freshwater mussel.

laying its eggs. These fasten onto the skin of the bitterling, which carries them around until they change into young mussels and fall to the bottom. FAMILY: Cyprinidae, ORDER: Cypriniformes, CLASS: Pisces.

BITTERNS, fairly large birds with a distinctive booming call, usually restricted to reedbeds and marshes. The cosmopolitan subfamily of bitterns comprises two genera *Botaurus* and *Ixobrychus*, the genus *Botaurus* containing the Eurasian bittern *B. stellaris*, the Australian *B. poiciloptilus*, the American *B. lentiginosus* and the South American *B. pinnatus* which replace each other and together form a superspecies. Of the genus *Ixobrychus*, the Least bittern *I. exilis* of North America, the Little bittern *I. minutus* of Europe, Asia, Africa and Australia and the Chinese little bittern *I. sinensis* form another superspecies.

The biftern *B. stellaris* is resident in British and European marshes while the smaller American bittern is a rare vagrant to Europe having been recorded in the Channel Islands, the Faeroes, Iceland, at least once in Germany and over 50 times in Britain.

The sexes of all the *Botaurus* species have similar plumage, that of the bittern *B. stellaris* being soft golden-brown and owl-like, heavily mottled with black above, longitudinally streaked below. A mane of long feathers on the neck and throat can be erected at will. Their necks and legs are shorter than those of herons. The 3 in (7·5 cm) bill is yellowish-green, the eyes yellow and the legs and feet pale green. They have powder-down patches on the breast and rump, one pair fewer than the herons, and the toothed middle claw is used to apply powder-down to the contour-feathers in preening. The finely divided particles of the disintegrating filaments of powder-down coagulate slime which coats the plumage when bitterns feed on eels. The bittern measures 30 in (76 cm) and weighs about 3 lb (1·3 kg).

Distribution is restricted by nesting requirements to reedbeds and rank vegetation

Bison bull, immediately recognizable by its heavy forequarters and low slung head.

Bittern, inhabitant of reed-beds throughout Europe, famous for the male's booming call during the breeding season.

Black bass

by sluggish water. The extensive marshes of North Jutland, the 'plassen' of Zuid-Holland and Utrecht, Austria's Neusiedler See and the Danube marshes provide typically ideal haunts for many bitterns. In Europe bitterns breed from 60°N to the Mediterranean basin and very large numbers are present in the USSR.

At any hour of the day or night from February to late June the male utters a resonant boom which may be repeated from three to six times and is notable for its carrying power, which is certainly over 1 mile (1·6 km).

The nest is built up above water level on matted roots in a reedbed and is constructed of reeds and sedge, lined with finer material. Three to six olive-brown eggs, without gloss, laid at intervals of two or three days, are incubated by the female alone. The young, too, are fed entirely by the female. Small mammals, birds (including young reedlings), water insects and crustaceans are all eaten but the principal diet appears to be fish, mainly eels, and frogs.

The protective coloration is much enhanced by the bird's habit, when disturbed, of standing rigid with bill pointed skywards, presenting to the intruder the striped undersurface which blends so well with the surrounding reeds as to render the bird virtually invisible.

The Little bittern *Ixobrychus minutus* is the only European member of a genus containing a dozen species. Sluggish rivers, backwaters, even small ponds satisfy this bird's nesting requirements and they nest practically throughout Europe, building sometimes just above water level and sometimes in willows up to 10 ft (3 m) above the water. FAMILY: Ardeidae, ORDER: Ciconiiformes, CLASS: Aves.

BLACK BASS, freshwater fishes of North America belonging to the genus *Micropterus*. The Large-mouthed black bass *M. salmoides* and the Small-mouthed black bass *M. dolomieu* both reach about 2 ft (61 cm) in length and are good sporting fishes. The two species were introduced into Europe in 1883 but neither has been particularly successful. They are most commonly found in southern Europe. In England they have not become naturalized except for a small colony of Large-mouthed black bass which is apparently thriving in Dorset. The same species was also introduced into East Africa and has done well in ponds and lakes in colder areas above 4,000 ft (1,200 m). Bass were chiefly introduced into Europe for sport but they have not found favour with European anglers because they seem to be very wary and retire to the deepest parts of lakes when they grow to any size.

Bass have strong teeth in the jaws and are predatory fishes which lurk amongst stones or weeds and pounce on their prey (fishes, frogs,

Blackheaded gull on nest with chick.

etc.) occasionally playing with their food as a cat does with a mouse. Both species are nest builders, constructing a large shallow nest which in the Small-mouthed bass is lined with leaves. FAMILY: Centrarchidae, ORDER: Perciformes, CLASS: Pisces.

BLACKBIRDS, certain dark-plumaged songbirds of the thrush family, Muscicapidae, in Europe and the oriole or troupial family, Icteridae, in North America. ORDER: Passeriformes, CLASS: Aves.

BLACKBUCK *Antilope cervicapra*, the most common Indian antelope, closely related to the gazelles. Females and young are yellow-fawn with a white belly and white eye-ring; after three years of age, the male begins to turn black. In the south of India males are usually dark brown; in all cases the true sable livery is assumed only during the rut, after the rains. Only the male has horns: these are ringed, closely spiralled, 25 in (65 cm) long in the south, shorter in the north. Blackbuck stand 32 in (80 cm) high, and weigh 90 lb (40 kg).

The blackbuck is found on all plains of peninsular India, south from Surat, and east into Bengal, west into Punjab and Rajputana. Herds number 20–30, and are led by a female; during the breeding season, the bucks split the herds up into harems; a buck struts about in front of his harem making short challenging grunts, with head thrown up so that the horns lie along the back, and the face-glands widely open. The main rut occurs in February and March, but some breeding occurs in all seasons. Gestation is 180 days.

Once there were 4 million blackbuck in India; they were hunted by Maharajahs with tame cheetahs. Now there are some thousands, but they are thin on the ground. They occur in all plains country, entering both open forests and grasslands, as well as in cultivated areas. They graze in the morning, lie up during the heat of the day, and feed again in late afternoon. Eyesight is very keen. When alarmed,

the herd moves in light leaps and bounds, like gazelles, then breaks into a gallop. FAMILY: Bovidae, ORDER: Artiodactyla, CLASS: Mammalia.

BLACK-HEADED GULL *Larus ridibundus*, found through much of Europe, is 15 in (38 cm) long and may be distinguished in flight by the white leading edge to the wings. It has a dark red bill and legs and, in summer, a chocolate brown head. In winter the head is white with a dark marking behind the eye. Young birds before their first winter are mottled grey-brown above, but have the pale leading edge to the wings. The Black-headed gull is common in many areas, in town and cities as well as open country, and inland as well as on the coast. It nests in colonies on the ground in marshes or on islands, moorland, shingle beaches, sand-dunes and other similar situations. Other features of its life-history are very similar to those of other gulls. FAMILY: Laridae, ORDER: Charadriiformes, CLASS: Aves.

BLACK WIDOW SPIDER *Latrodectus mactans*, jet black North American spider with a sinister reputation. Underneath the abdomen is a small hour-glass mark in vivid scarlet which represents warning coloration. The bite of this spider causes intense pain accompanied by symptoms of nausea, partial paralysis and difficulty in breathing and the venom is said to be 15 times as potent as that of a rattlesnake. Fortunately the quantity injected is far less than that of a snake. Death is known but this is not usual. A serum has been prepared in America but in its absence doctors usually give intravenous injections of 10 cc of 10% calcium chloride or gluconate.

The Black widow is less than ¾ in (18 mm). It lives a retiring existence and is not aggressive. Men are likely to be bitten more frequently than women because the cavity beneath the seat of earth privies is often selected by the spider to spin the strong coarse threads of its snare and anything brushing against these threads is apt to be bitten.

Most members of the genus *Latrodectus* share the same evil reputation. These include the malmignatte of southern Europe, the red-back of Australia, the katipo of New Zealand and others in Africa. These can usually be distinguished from the American Black widow by the possession of scarlet spots or bands but some have proved to be only subspecies. FAMILY: Theridiidae, ORDER: Araneae, CLASS: Arachnida, PHYLUM: Arthropoda.

BLEAK *Alburnus alburnus*, a small fresh-water carp-like fish in slow-flowing waters and large lakes in Europe north of the Alps, which has also been reported from brackish water in the Baltic. It is gregarious and frequently seen shoaling at the surface and catching insects; it will also browse on the bottom for aquatic larvae. During the breeding season of April to June the males develop a green-blue coloration on the back and the fins become orange. The sticky eggs are laid between stones in shallow running water. Lake-dwelling bleak migrate up feeder streams to breed. Large numbers of bleak were formerly caught and their silvery scales used in the manufacture of artificial pearls. Since the adults are only about 8 in (20 cm) long and are practically tasteless, bleak are rarely caught for any other purpose. FAMILY: Cyprinidae, ORDER: Cypriniformes, CLASS: Pisces.

BLESBOK, one of the subspecies, the other being the bontebok, of the hartebeest *Damaliscus dorcas* known as the Bastard hartebeest. See Bontebok.

BLIND SNAKES or Worm snakes, are among the most primitive of living snakes. The 300 species are grouped into two families, the Typhlopidae, which contains the vast majority, and the Anomalepididae. Blind snakes occur throughout the tropical and sub-tropical zones and extend also into South Africa and the southern region of Australia, but not Tasmania. Most are quite small and worm-like, though a few reach a length of 2 ft (61 cm) or more. They have poorly developed teeth, on the mobile upper jaw only. Vestiges of the hindlimbs are sometimes present. They feed on a variety of small soil animals, such as worms, termites, and ants and their eggs and larvae, are nocturnal and live underground, or under large flat stones, rotting logs or stumps, or in termite nests. The tail is very short and ends in a small, sharp spine, which is pushed into the soil and provides a purchase when the animal is moving forward.

The eyes are small and very poorly developed, and each appears as a dark spot covered over by a transparent scale. Probably they can only distinguish between light and darkness. FAMILIES: Typhlopidae, Anomalepididae, ORDER: Squamata, CLASS: Reptilia.

BLISTER BEETLES, winged true beetles with characteristically soft bodies and long legs, comprising, with the flightless Oil beetles, the family Meloidae of 2,000 species.

The Blister beetles are widespread and are particularly notable for the complex and hazardous life-history of many species. For example, in one species the larvae hatch from eggs deposited in autumn near the nests of certain bees. In spring a few only of these minute larvae out of the 2–10,000 eggs laid by each female, succeed in grasping the hairy bodies of the male bees, later transferring to female bees. The female bee constructs a nest of cells in the ground, each cell being stocked with honey, pollen and a single egg. When the bee deposits the egg the beetle larva drops on

to it and is then sealed up by the bee in the cell. The larva feeds first on the bee's egg and then on the food store of honey and pollen and after a complicated development a mature beetle emerges from the cell.

Blister beetles contain the substance cantharidin in many of their tissues and structures. Perhaps the best known in this respect is the 'Spanish fly' *Lytta vesicatoria*, a common insect in parts of southern Europe. In recent times the administration of cantharidin as an aphrodisiac by non-qualified persons has lead to deaths and during the 19th century its use as a blistering agent for many kinds of ailments caused great misery. FAMILY: Meloidae, ORDER: Coleoptera, CLASS: Insecta, PHYLUM: Arthropoda.

A blowfly *Calliphora*, also known as bluebottle, laps liquid food with its proboscis.

BLOWFLIES, large-eyed flies, with worldwide distribution, such as the bluebottles *Calliphora* and the greenbottle *Lucilia sericata*. Bluebottles and others lay their eggs in decaying meat and other foodstuffs, hence the expression 'fly-blown', but the greenbottle and *Lucilia cuprina* lay their eggs in living sheep causing a serious condition called sheep-strike. At one time blowflies were used in hospitals to clean wounds as the larvae ate rotting flesh but left healthy tissue. FAMILY: Calliphoridae, ORDER: Diptera, CLASS: Insecta, PHYLUM: Arthropoda.

BLUEBOTTLE, name given to two similar species of true flies. *Calliphora erythrocephala* and *C. vomitoria*, which are a little under ½ in (1¼ cm) long, stoutly built and of a metallic blue colour. Each female lays up to 600 eggs which hatch in about a day. These larvae are the 'gentles' used by anglers as bait but they are commonly also called maggots. Under favourable conditions the larvae pupate in about a week and emerge as adults a fortnight later.

Several other metallic blue flies occurring in the tropics are commonly called bluebottles. Among these are the Screw worms. Greenbottle refers to a number of metallic green flies, many of them closely related to

bluebottles. All have larvae which feed on decaying animal matter, but greenbottles are less prone to come indoors. Some lay their eggs in the wool of live sheep and the larvae attack the flesh causing a disease known as 'sheep strike' which is often fatal. FAMILY: Calliphoridae, ORDER: Diptera, CLASS: Insecta, PHYLUM: Arthropoda.

BLUEFISH *Pomatomus saltatrix*, a marine perch-like species amongst the most savage of all fishes. Bluefishes are deep-chested, slender-tailed and derive their name from their colour. They live in fast moving shoals in all tropical and subtropical waters except the eastern Pacific. Anglers hunt for bluefishes which may reach 30 lb (13 kg) in weight, both for sport and for food.

The large shoals of bluefishes that move up and down the American Atlantic shores principally feed on the enormous shoals of menhaden *Brevoortia*. The bluefishes have the reputation for being animated chopping machines the sole aim of which appears to be to cut to pieces, or otherwise mutilate, as many fish as possible in a short time. They have been seen to drive part of a shoal of menhaden into shallow coves from which they cannot escape. The menhaden apparently fling themselves onto the beach in an effort to escape from these savage predators. The sea is bloodstained and littered with pieces of fish after the bluefishes have eaten. As many as 1,000 million bluefishes may occur each summer season off American coasts and if each eats only ten menhaden a day and the season lasts for 120 days, then the stock of menhaden must be depleted by 1,200,000,000,000 individuals during that time. FAMILY: Pomatomidae, ORDER: Perciformes, CLASS: Pisces.

BLUE WHALE *Balaenoptera musculus*, the largest animal of all time. Prior to being over-hunted it reached a maximum size of 100 ft (33 m) and a weight of 130 tons. Another name for it is sulphur-bottom because individuals are sometimes tinged yellow on the underside due to a coating of the microscopic plants known as diatoms. See rorquals.

BOAS, non-venomous snakes that bear their young alive. They usually have hindlimbs, at least in the male, in the form of claw-like spurs. Most have two functional lungs of which the right is much larger than the left. In this respect they are intermediate between the lizards, which usually have two lungs of equal size, and the higher snakes in which the left lung has disappeared. All boas bring forth their young alive.

Probably the best known is the Boa constrictor *Boa constrictor* of Central America, tropical South America and the Lesser Antilles. Many stories have been written about the great size and prowess of the Boa constrictor but it is only the fifth

Boatbill

largest of living snakes, having a maximum length of a little over 18 ft (5·5 m). Its food consists mainly of small mammals and the occasional bird and lizard. Like most boas its prey is killed by constriction before being swallowed whole.

The habitat of the boas is varied ranging from arboreal to fossorial and semi-aquatic. Some species, such as the Boa constrictor, and the Rainbow boa *Epicrates cenehria* are surface dwellers. These tend to inhabit scrubland and wooded regions where their blotched or reticulate pattern forms an excellent camouflage. There are seven species of *Epicrates*, six of which inhabit the West Indies. The only mainland member of this genus, the Rainbow boa is primarily a surface dweller feeding on small rodents. It rarely exceeds 4 ft (122 cm) in length.

The arboreal species include the South American Tree boas *Corallus*, the Malagasy tree boa *Sanzinia madagascariensis* and the Papuan tree python *Chondropython viridis*. These are often blotched but two species, the Emerald tree boa *Corallus caninus*, of South America, and the adult of the Papuan tree python have acquired an effective camouflage in their bright green colour with whitish markings. This is an excellent example of

parallelism, where two unrelated species acquire a similar appearance as an adaptation to a similar environment. These two species are also alike inasmuch as the young differ from the adults in being yellow or pinkish brown with darker markings.

The Cuban ground boa *Tropidophis semicinctus* possesses the defensive habit of voluntarily bleeding at the mouth. At the same time the eyes become ruby red. See anaconda. FAMILY: Boidae, ORDER: Squamata, CLASS: Reptilia.

BOATBILL *Cochlearius cochlearius* or Boatbilled heron, a small, grey heron with a black crown and long, black ornamental plumes on the back of the head. The bill is broad and scoop-like. It is confined to Central and northern South America, where it inhabits mangrove swamps. It feeds at night, as its large eyes suggest, and is usually inactive by day. Little is known of its diet or how it uses the oddly-shaped bill. The clutch of two to four pale blue eggs are laid on a platform of dead sticks, built in a mangrove tree. FAMILY: Ardeidae, ORDER: Ciconiiformes, CLASS: Aves.

BOBCAT *Lynx rufus*, the wide-ranging wild cat of America, which probably got its name

from its short tail and a lolloping gait rather like that of a rabbit. Its total length is about 2½–3 ft (76–92 cm) with an average weight of 15–20 lb (7–9 kg) but it can be much larger. The colour varies with the race and habitat but in general is brown spotted with grey or white. The short tail has a black bar on the upper side fringed with white hairs and the ears are tipped with pointed tufts of hair which are said to improve the bobcat's hearing. Bobcats are found throughout most of the United States, Mexico and the south of Canada. Because of their small size and the variety of prey they feed on, ranging from small rodents to deer and domestic animals, they have largely survived the spread of agriculture. Usually two kits are born, at any time of the year, in a den or under logs, and are defended by their mother. FAMILY: Felidae, ORDER: Carnivora, CLASS: Mammalia.

BOLLWORMS, caterpillars of several species of moths which feed in cotton bolls.

BONGO *Boocerus euryceros*, close relative of the eland but lacking the dewlap and the frontal tuft, and with open-spiralled horns more like the kudu. The average height is 4 ft (120 cm), weight 480 lb (220 kg). There

A young bongo *Boocerus euryceros*. The bongo, of the tropical African forests, is probably the most handsome of antelopes.

Blue-faced booby of the tropical seas. Mariners used to find these birds easy to catch. They nicknamed them boobies, for allowing themselves to be caught.

is an erect mane from shoulder to rump. The colour is reddish, with 11–14 transverse white stripes, a white chevron between the eyes, white cheek-spots, throat-band, lips and chin, and a white stripe down the inner side of the limbs. The horns may be over 3 ft (1m).

Bongos inhabit the tropical forest belt of Africa from Sierra Leone to Togo. They occur again from Cameroun, south of the Sanaga river, across the Congo into the extreme southern Sudan, but are not found in Nigeria. East of the Congo, bongos are found only in isolated montane forests in Kenya. In these eastern forest 'islands', bongos ascend to 7–10,000 ft (2,100–3,050 m). They live in the densest parts of the forest, where they move about by day. Bulls are often solitary, but some join with the herds of cows and calves, which may number as many as 20. They are fond of wallowing. They can move very fast through the forest, slipping under obstacles with the ease of a limbo dancer, with head held low and horns laid back. Bongos feed on leaves and shoots and can rear on their hind-legs, planting the front hoofs on tree trunks, to browse. The horns are kept sharp by constant rubbing, but bongo appear to be as unaggressive and placid as eland. FAMILY: Bovidae, ORDER: Artiodactyla, CLASS: Mammalia.

BONITOS (sometimes spelt bonitas in the United States), a name for certain smaller tuna-like fishes. In Europe, *Katsuwonus pelamis* is known as the Oceanic bonito, but in the United States this species is referred to as the skipjack. The bonitos, in the broad sense, are found in both Atlantic and Indo-Pacific regions. They are highly streamlined, often with the fins folding into grooves, and the tail is crescentic. Their bodies are superbly adapted for an oceanic life. The pelamid or Belted bonito *Sarda sarda*, known in the United States as the Atlantic bonito, is found on both sides of the Atlantic as well as in the Mediterranean and sometimes reaches British coasts. It attains 3 ft (91 cm) in length and its high quality white meat is canned in the United States. The Oceanic bonito has a similar distribution and reaches about the same size. It differs from the Belted bonito in having bluish bands running horizontally along the lower part of the body instead of obliquely. It has a remarkable turn of speed, about 25 mph (40 kph) which enables it to chase flying fishes, often leaping clear out of the water to do so. FAMILY: Scombridae, ORDER: Perciformes, CLASS: Pisces.

BONTEBOK, one of the two best-known of the Bastard hartebeste, the other being the blesbok, the two forming a single species *Damaliscus dorcas*. They are both reddish, darker on the sides of the face, the neck, flanks and outside of the limbs as far as the knees and hocks. The rump, face-blaze and shanks, as well as the underside, are white. They stand 36–48 in (90–120 cm) high, and weigh 250–300 lb (114–136 kg). The two races are well-known and easy to tell apart: the bontebok *D. d. dorcas*, in which the dark areas are blackish, the white rump patch goes all round the tail-root, and the knees and hocks are white; and the blesbok *D. d.* *phillipsi*, in which the dark areas are not black, the face-blaze is divided by a dark bar above the eyes, the rump patch is small and does not go round the tail-root, and the knees and hocks are not white. The bontebok used to be found from the coast of the south-western Cape from the Bot River (near Caledon) to Mossel Bay. After severe reduction in numbers during the last century, it survived only on farms and today there are about 750.

Blesbok were found from the Cradock and Cathcart divisions of the Cape to the Orange Free State, southern Botswana and southern Transvaal, separated by 200 miles (320 km) from the nearest bontebok. It was severely overhunted and survived only on farms; it has now been reintroduced over much of its former range, and has been introduced into northern Transvaal.

Bontebok and blesbok are among the fastest antelope in all Africa. They run extended, low off the ground. When alarmed, they first stand in a stiff pose with head held high and neck up, the limbs held rigid and spread apart. The flight distance is 300 yds (274 m). FAMILY: Bovidae, ORDER: Artiodactyla, CLASS: Mammalia.

BOOBIES, fairly large seabirds related to gannets, and which they replace in tropical waters. They resemble them in general appearance, physiology and many details of their life-history, but are smaller and considerably lighter, weighing from 2–4 lb (0·9–2 kg), and have a more extensive area of bare facial skin which, together with the legs

Male Satin bowerbird of the coastal area of eastern Australia at its bower.

and feet, is more brightly coloured in some species.

There are six species. The Masked booby *Sula dactylatra*, the Red-footed booby *Sula sula* and the Brown booby *Sula leucogaster* are all 'pan-tropical'. The Peruvian booby *Sula variegata* and the Blue-footed booby *Sula nebouxii* are confined to the eastern Pacific, the former occurring in the fish-rich cold Humboldt current area off Peru and Chile. The latter occurs farther north as far as Baja, California. Finally, the Abbott's booby *Sula abbotti* breeds only on Christmas Island in the Indian Ocean. FAMILY: Sulidae, ORDER: Pelicaniformes, CLASS: Aves.

BOOKLOUSE, name given to over 1,000 very small to minute insects. They have plump bodies, may be winged or wingless, and are characterized by modification of the maxillae into a pair of chitinous rods or 'picks' which, together with the mandibles enable the animal to bite or rasp food from the surface of bark or leaves. They take their name from one wingless species *Liposcelis divinatorius*, found especially in old books, feeding on the flour, size and glue of the bindings and on the moulds that grow on old paper.

Most species are winged but many are wingless or short-winged and these occur naturally under bark or in nests of birds and mammals. Some have established themselves in houses, warehouses and ships' holds, thereby becoming cosmopolitan, and are classed as minor pests. FAMILY: Psocidae, ORDER: Psocoptera, CLASS: Insecta, PHYLUM: Arthropoda.

BOOMSLANG *Dispholidus typus*, large African Tree snake with three enlarged grooved fangs in the upper jaw below the eye. It is the most venomous of the back-fanged snakes and its bite can prove fatal to man. 'Boomslang' is Afrikaans for 'Tree snake'.

The boomslang averages 4½ ft (1·4 m) in length. It has a short head with very large eyes and a slender body and tail covered above with narrow, oblique, strongly keeled scales. It is common throughout Africa south of the Sahara in well-wooded country.

The female lays 5–10 elongated eggs about 1 in (25 mm) in length. The newly hatched young are about 15 in (38 cm) in length.

The boomslang hunts by day and may stay in a tree or group of trees for several days if food is plentiful. Its diet consists largely of chamaeleons, but during the nesting season many fledgling birds and eggs are eaten; adult birds are rarely caught. Lizards, frogs and rats are also devoured but other snakes are rarely attacked.

If disturbed, the boomslang will always try to escape at speed, but when cornered it inflates its throat with air, giving the impression of an enormous head, then makes savage lunges at its aggressor with gaping jaws. Its venom is extremely toxic, destroying the fibrinogen in the blood and causing extensive internal bleeding. Because the amount of venom produced by a boomslang is very small, the specific anti-venom is in short supply. FAMILY: Colubridae, ORDER: Squamata, CLASS: Reptilia.

BOT FLY, a fly, the larvae of which are better known than the fly and are parasitic in warm-blooded animals. The larvae are the 'bots' and are generally less pointed than maggots and covered with rows of strong spines which help them to move about in the tissues of their host. The hind spiracles have many small pores, which make them less liable to become clogged.

The Sheep nostril fly *Oestrus ovis* lives in the head sinuses of sheep, feeding mostly on mucus. *Cephenomyia* similarly infests deer, *Tracheomyia* the throats of kangaroos, *Cephalopina titillator* the head-cavities of camels and *Pharyngobolus africanus* the gullet of African elephants. *Hypoderma bovis* and *H. lineatum* are the common Warble flies of cattle in Europe and are more directly parasitic. Their larvae migrate through the body until they come to rest under the skin of the back where they form boils with an opening to the exterior for breathing purposes. *Oedemagena tarandi* is a Warble fly of reindeer. Bots do not normally attack man, but infrequently the eggs of *Oestrus* or *Hypoderma* may get into the eyes of shepherds or herdsmen and the small first-stage larvae can cause irritation or even more serious damage to the eye. FAMILY: Oestridae, ORDER: Diptera, CLASS: Insecta, PHYLUM: Arthropoda.

BOWERBIRDS vary from 9–15 in (23–38 cm) long and show a wide range of colours and patterns in their plumage. Bold patterns of green, orange, lavender, and yellow with grey or black are found in many species;

some have a plain grey or brown plumage and a few are spotted. In the more brightly coloured species the male is much brighter than the female, but the sexes are alike in the dull-coloured forms. Some have a crest of elongated feathers, often brilliantly coloured. In a few it forms an elaborate ruff or a mane hanging over the upper back. The bill is slightly hooked at the tip in all of the bowerbirds, but in some it is slightly down-curved, in others straight, in some it is thin and weak, in others heavy, and in a few species the upper mandible has some small tooth-like notches along its cutting edge.

Bowerbirds are most numerous in New Guinea. The stagemaker or Tooth-billed bowerbird *Scenopoeetes dentirostris* is found only in Australia. It is an olive-brown bird, about 11 in (28 cm) long, with prominent pale stripes on the underparts. The Golden bowerbird *P. newtoniana*, which is found only in the mountain forests of northern Queensland, Australia, is about 9 in (23 cm) long, rather short-billed, with different plumages in the male and female birds. The male is bright olive-green with yellow underparts, head, neck and tail, while the female is dull yellow-green with grey underparts. The Satin bowerbird *Ptilonorhynchus violaceus* is confined to eastern Australia. About 1 ft (30 cm) long, it is long-billed, the bill also being heavy and straight. The plumage is glossy black in the male and grey-green in the female.

Bowerbirds are so-called for the complicated, and often highly decorated, structures the males of some species use when displaying. These sometimes take the form of cleared areas the size of a table-top, containing a domed tunnel of sticks, decorated with brightly coloured stones, fresh flowers, spiders' webs and coloured insects' skeletons. Some of these bowers are so impressive that, when they were first discovered, the explorers believed they could only be the product of human skill and artistry.

The male stagemaker defends a perch from which it sings, above a cleared patch of ground amongst slender young trees. It decorates its private lawn with large leaves laid upside down and a few snail shells. In display the male flicks its wings open, bobs its head from side to side with its bill gaping, hops about erratically, fluffs its breast feathers and holds a leaf in the bill for long periods. The males only see the females at mating time and take no part in rearing the young.

Each adult male Satin bowerbird defends a separate court and bower inside a traditional courtship area. The bower consists of a solid mat of small sticks with a wall of sticks on each side. The whole is painted with vegetable juices and is brilliantly decorated by the male with shells, flowers, leaves and dead insects. In display the male spends most of its time at the bower, uttering scraping, grating, cackling, churring and squeaking notes. It dances about with its tail raised over its back, jumps right over the bower, points the bill to the ground and becomes so excited that its eyes bulge outwards. The female bird enters the bower and may crouch down as a signal to the male that she is ready to mate. The female remains at the bower with the male for several days, but after this they separate and the female builds a nest and raises the young alone.

The complexity of bowerbirds' plumage patterns bears a fairly close relationship to the complexity of the bower that is built. In the species that build no bowers, or only clear a ground court, the plumage is often coloured with red, orange, yellow, green or black in varying combinations of brilliance, but in the species that build the most elaborate and brilliantly decorated bowers the birds are disappointingly dull in colour, with the exception sometimes of the crest.

So far as is known all of the bowerbirds live mainly on the fruits of trees and bushes, supplementing this diet with insects, larvae, spiders, and sometimes small snakes and lizards, Tree frogs and seeds.

Usually the female bird builds the nest alone, lays the clutch of from two to five eggs, incubates them and then feeds the young until they fledge and for a week or two afterwards. Incubation periods of between 12–15 days have been recorded and approximate fledging periods of from 13–20 days. FAMILY: Ptilonorhynchidae, ORDER: Passeriformes, CLASS: Aves.

BOWFIN *Amia calva*, a member of one of the two surviving groups of Holostei, primitive ray-finned fishes that gave rise to bony fishes. Fossil bowfins have been found in Europe but the only surviving species is now confined to the eastern side of North America. It is a cylindrical, solid-looking fish with a long dorsal fin and a heavy armour of scales. The body is dull brownish-green in colour, lighter underneath, with several dark vertical stripes. A black spot is found near the base of the tail, margined in males with yellow.

There are certain anatomical features which are of interest in the bowfin. Underneath the lower jaw is a bony plate, the gular plate, a relic from its more primitive ancestors. In the intestine there are remnants of a spiral valve, a device found in many primitive fishes increasing considerably the digestive surface of the intestine. The swim-bladder has a cellular structure that enables the bowfin to breathe atmospheric oxygen. Whereas most fishes swim by undulations of the body, the bowfin cruises majestically by a series of waves passing along its long dorsal fin. The normal method is adopted for faster swimming.

Bowfins live in warm sluggish waters, especially in shallow and weedy areas. In the breeding season in early summer the males make a round nest on sandy or gravelly bottoms or in clearings in weed patches. They then mate with several females and after the eggs are laid guard them until the fry hatch and can swim well. They are carnivorous and seem to have a particular liking for game fishes. A large bowfin may reach almost 3 ft (91 cm) in length. FAMILY: Amiidae, ORDER: Holostei, CLASS: Pisces.

BREAMS, deep-bodied carp-like fishes of European freshwaters. They are unrelated to the Sea breams. In England there are two species, the Common bream *Abramis brama* and the *Silver bream *Blicca bjoerkna*. The Common bream has a compressed body with a very high back and short head. The upper parts are grey to black, the sides lighter, the belly silvery and the fins grey or blue-black. It is found chiefly in sluggish weedy waters throughout most of Europe north of the Pyrenees. Bream normally swim in shoals, each made up of individuals of about the same size, usually near the bottom except in hot weather when they tend to lie still near the surface. They grow to over 12 lb (5·4 kg) in weight and are cunning and difficult to catch. They feed on insect larvae, molluscs and worms which they extract from great mouthfuls of mud sucked up from the bottom. The Common bream often shoal with Silver bream and when small the two species are difficult to distinguish. FAMILY: Cyprinidae, ORDER: Cypriniformes, CLASS: Pisces.

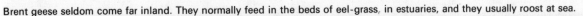

Brent geese seldom come far inland. They normally feed in the beds of eel-grass, in estuaries, and they usually roost at sea.

Brent goose

BRENT GOOSE *Branta bernicla*, a small dark goose with an arctic circumpolar distribution, breeding in the tundra. It has a black head, neck and breast, dark grey upper-parts, a white rear and an incomplete white collar. Brent geese are on the breeding grounds for three months of the year from about mid-June. They nest on the ground in large colonies, often with Eider ducks. Three to five eggs are laid and incubated by the female, with the male standing guard. The parents share in the care of the young, which are active soon after hatching and accompany the parents, feeding on the tundra plants and invertebrates.

After the breeding season, Brent geese migrate south and winter on the shallow coastlines of the more temperate regions of the Atlantic and Pacific Oceans. During this period they take a wide variety of food, mostly plant material and including some algae, but on both the European and North American coasts of the Atlantic the preferred food has long been the Greater eelgrass *Zostera maxima*. FAMILY: Anatidae, ORDER: Anseriformes, CLASS: Aves.

BRILL *Scophthalmus rhombus*, a flatfish from the Mediterranean and eastern North Atlantic. It lies on its right side and is similar to the turbot, but is more oval and has smooth scales with no tubercles. The general colour is grey, brown or greenish with darker patches or mottlings and usually speckled with white spots. The brill lives on sandy bottoms at depths of 180–240 ft (54–72 m). It grows to about 2 ft (60 cm) in length and the flesh is considered most delicately flavoured. In the North Sea spawning takes place in spring and summer, the adult female producing about 800,000 eggs. FAMILY: Pleuronectidae, ORDER: Pleuronectiformes, CLASS: Pisces.

BRISTLETAILS, wingless insects closest to the ancestral type, world-wide with 400 species, they are rarely seen because with few exceptions they are less than 1 cm long. With springtails and a few other primitive wingless types of insects they make up the subclass Apterygota ('without wings'), the rest of the insects being placed in a subclass Pterygota ('winged').

Bristletails are the only apterygote insects with compound eyes, like those found in the Pterygota. In most of them the mouthparts are of an unmodified type suitable only for biting and chewing living or dead plant material. The antennae are long and multisegmented. The abdominal segments carry a series of leg-like appendages of unknown functions. At the end of the abdomen are three long, movable, antenna-like appendages which give them their popular name. These are believed to be sense-organs. Fertilization is internal. The young are like miniature adults in appearance and although they undergo several moults with increase in size

before reaching adulthood they show no metamorphosis.

What little is known of their feeding habits suggests that most bristletails feed on decomposing plant and animal material. Perhaps the best known species is the silverfish *Lepisma saccharina* which is common in buildings all over the world, especially in damp places like kitchens and bathrooms. Its bright metallic colour is due to a covering of shiny scales.

A species of bristletail that used to be much more common than it is now is the firebrat *Thermobia domestica*. This is found in bakehouses and kitchens and other humid places where the exceptionally high temperatures the firebrat needs for the development of its young—up to 104°F (40°C)—are found. The firebrat probably feeds on food scraps dropped during cooking and, since in recent years bakeries have become much cleaner places, the species has become quite rare. ORDER: Thysanura, SUBCLASS: Apterygota, CLASS: Insecta, PHYLUM: Arthropoda.

BRITTLESTARS, mobile, star-shaped marine animals with the five-fold radial symmetry, endoskeleton of calcite plates and water vascular system characteristic of Sea urchins, Sea lilies, Sea cucumbers and starfishes, to which they are related. They resemble the starfish in appearance but may be distinguished from it in details of structure, biochemistry, larval development and mode of life. The most obvious difference is that in brittlestars there is a clear distinction between the central disc which houses the vital organs and the flexible arms.

The arms are long relative to the diameter of the central disc, narrow from base to tip, and somewhat bony in appearance since they are formed of little more than plates (ossicles) of calcite. Their snake-like form has given rise to the alternative popular name of 'Serpent stars'. The arms break easily when handled, hence the name brittlestar.

The 2,000 species are divided into two main groups. The first is the Ophiurae or brittlestars proper. Their unbranched arms have a series of calcite plates embedded in

the upper, lower and both side surfaces, with a central series of vertebra-like ossicles that articulate by ball-and-socket joints, permitting sideways movements only. The second, smaller group, is the Euryalae, including the basketstars. In these, disc and arms are covered with thick skin, sometimes with granules or tubercles. There is a central series of vertebral ossicles in each arm, and these articulate with broad hourglass-shaped surfaces, permitting all round movement of the arms which may actually coil vertically. The arms may branch and in some genera do so repeatedly. Those in which the arms branch right from the base are known as basketstars, for when the animals are alive and feeding the arms extend upwards and outwards to form an open mesh basket in which they catch their prey. CLASS: Ophiuroidea, PHYLUM: Echinodermata.

BROADBILLS, 14 species of small, squat tropical birds with short wings, outsize heads, short legs and strong feet. The bill is short and very broad, so that it appears triangular from above; the upper mandible overlaps the lower and terminates in a small hook. Many of the broadbills are brilliantly coloured and even the more sombre of them with brown plumage, usually have bright patches of colour. In addition, several species have brightly-hued eyes, bills or naked face patches. One species *Eurylaimus steerii* of the Philippines has wattles.

Broadbills construct exquisite pendant nests usually slung from a branch overhanging a stream. The main body of the nest, below the suspending 'rope', is pear-shaped, with an entrance hole at one side. A wide variety of fibrous nesting materials, roots, leaf midribs, lianas, etc. are used by different species. In many cases the outside is covered with moss or lichen and strands of these materials are left hanging below the nest as a 'beard'. This undoubtedly helps to make the nest even more inconspicuous and confuses the nest robbers such as snakes, birds of prey, monkeys and other small mammals, which abound in the humid forests. The eggs are

Bristletail *Petrobius*, showing the three movable appendages which give it its name. Members of this genus can be seen on rocks at night near the sea-shore.

The Green broadbill *Calyptomena viridis*, of Malaya, sits for much of the day among foliage.

In Australia budgerigars live in flocks throughout the arid interior regions and in dry coastal areas. They are most numerous in open country that is interspersed with belts of timber or patches of scrub. In prolonged droughts the flocks roam widely in search of food and water and are often seen in very large numbers, sometimes tens of thousands, at isolated water holes. Experiments on captive birds have, however, shown that they can live without water for up to 20 days, eating only dry seeds. Wild budgerigars feed mainly on small seeds from low-growing plants, running actively on the ground in search of food.

Budgerigars breed in colonies. No nest is built, and the clutches of 5–8 eggs are laid on detritus in the bottom of a hole in a gnarled old tree. Several pairs often breed in one tree, so that large areas of old acacia trees are often occupied by breeding colonies. The oval or rounded eggs are incubated by the female alone, but the male helps to feed the nestlings, regurgitating partly digested seeds into their open bills. The young birds remain in the nest-hole for about 20 days and they are fed by the parents for a week or so after they fledge. FAMILY: Psittacidae, ORDER: Psittaciformes, CLASS: Aves.

pale in colour, usually two to four. FAMILY: Eurylaimidae, ORDER: Passeriformes, CLASS: Aves.

BROCKETS *Mazama*, four species of small deer ranging from Mexico to Argentina. The coat colour is red or brown, the underside of the tail is white. The antlers are simple spikes 3–5 in (7–13 cm) long. The largest is the Red brocket *M. americana* 28 in (71 cm) high at the shoulder. FAMILY: Cervidae, ORDER: Artiodactyla, CLASS: Mammalia.

BRYOZOA, a phylum of quite common, though often inconspicuous, aquatic animals, alternatively known as moss-animals, which are present in freshwater but are especially numerous in the sea. There are nearly 4,000 living species of Bryozoa and perhaps four times as many preserved as fossils, the beauty of which can generally be appreciated only by the use of a microscope.

They are colonial animals constructed from repeated units called zooids. While the zooids in a colony may be few, in the Membranipora which forms lacy patterns over the fronds of large seaweeds, they may number up to 2 million. Such a colony spreads over many square inches, but bryozoans are usually smaller than this. Incrusting species rarely cover more than 1 sq in (6 cm²), although the tufted and coralline types may reach 2–3 in (5–7½ cm) in height, and one was once found in a clump 7 ft (2¼ m) in circumference.

BUDGERIGAR *Melopsittacus undulatus*, small Australian parrot commonly kept as a cage-bird. Wild budgerigars are small, 5½ in (14 cm), long-tailed parrots with green under-

parts, a yellow back with closely-spaced black barring, a bright yellow head with blue and black stripes on the cheeks, and a row of black spots on each side of the upper neck. Selective breeding in captivity has produced all-blue, all-white, all-yellow and all-green budgerigars, as well as patterned forms. Besides producing colour variations, selective breeding has favoured those with large heads and distinct face markings; because of this many captive budgerigars bear little resemblance to the neatly proportioned wild ones.

Since budgerigars were first introduced into Britain in 1840 by John Gould, the famous bird artist, they have steadily increased in popularity, and are now the commonest cage-bird, considerably outnumbering the canary, formerly the favourite.

BUFFALO, a name which in the original Greek was used for any large cloven-hoofed animal and especially for the Water buffalo *Bubalus bubalis* of southern Asia. It was later used for the Cape buffalo *Syncerus caffer* and also for the North American bison *Bison bison*.

BULBULS, tropical tree-dwelling songbirds with few distinctive characters to immediately identify them. There are about 112 species and they vary in size from sparrow to thrush-size.

Bulbuls have the body plumage soft, dense and long, tending to be noticeably thick on

Pentopora foliacea, a shallow sea bryozoan forms rigid calcified colonies.

the rump, with typically long, hair-like filo-plumes on such parts as the nape or flanks. Another typical character appears to be the relative absence of feathering on the back of the short neck which, when extended, shows a bare patch. The wings tend to be short and rounded at the tip; and the tail is usually relatively long, the shape of the tip varying from forked to rounded. The eyes are fairly large and dark. The bill is usually slender and of a type associated with insect-eating, al-though for a great many of these species the most important food item is fruit, some insects being taken as well. The rictal bristles around the base of the bill are usually well-developed. Compared with birds which move and feed in similar fashion the bulbuls have legs and feet that are relatively weak and sometimes rather small.

The plumage is for the most part dull, olive-green, yellow or brown, and grey or black on one species, the Black bulbul *Microscelis madagascariensis*. Such plumage may, however, be varied by single patches of contrasting colour, in white, red or yellow. A number of species, particularly those in Asia, have crests that vary from a loose

shaggy rounded mass of elongated crown feathers to a slender tapering conical crest. The sexes are alike in size and colour, while immature birds do not differ conspicuously from the adults.

Although nesting in scattered pairs, bul-buls are frequently gregarious at other times, travelling and feeding in small flocks, when they tend to be inquisitive and noisy. The call notes vary considerably, from the harsh or squeaky to the melodious but many species also have loud and musical songs. These usually consist of brief notes or phrases and at times some species will mimic calls of other birds. Bulbuls feed mainly on berries and other fruits which they take in quantity and where they occur in any number they are usually regarded as pests by fruit-growers. FAMILY: Pycnonotidae, ORDER: Passeriformes, CLASS: Aves.

BULLFINCH *Pyrrhula pyrrhula*, a stocky little bird, about 6 in (16 cm) long, with a short conical bill, black cap, bib, wings and tail and a white rump. In the male, the breast is pinkish-red and the back bluish, but in the female both are brownish-grey. Bullfinches extend from the British Isles, across Europe and Asia to Japan. Over most of this area, they live in conifer forests, but in western Europe they also extend south into decidu-ous woods, parks and gardens. For most of the year they eat a great variety of seeds from woody and herbaceous plants but in spring they live mainly on buds; the young are reared on a mixture of seeds and insects. Compared to other finches bullfinches eat many more seeds from fleshy fruits, like rowan and bramble.

The breeding season of the bullfinch is prolonged, up to three broods being raised each year. The nest is made of thin twigs and roots, and is placed in a thick bush in wood, hedge or garden. There are four to six eggs which are bluish white with red-brown spots.

Blackcrested yellow bulbul, one of over a hundred species of starling-sized birds.

Budgerigars usurped the popularity rating formerly held by canaries.

The beautiful bullfinch, of Europe, has a bad reputation among fruit-growers and horticulturalists for stripping flower buds from shrubs and trees.

The species has several interesting courtship displays in which both sexes participate, the male puffing up the red abdominal feathers and turning his tail sideways towards the female. FAMILY: Fringillidae, ORDER: Passeriformes, CLASS: Aves.

BULLFROGS, large frogs the males of which have a call that has been likened to the bellowing of a bull. In different parts of the world the name refers to a particular species: the American bullfrog is *Rana catesbeiana*; the African bullfrog is *Pyxicephalus adspersus* and the Indian bullfrog is *Rana tigrina*. These are only related to one another in that they are all true frogs.

The American bullfrog grows to 8 in (20 cm) the females being larger than the males. It is robust and powerful, a greenish drab colour with small tubercles on the skin, strictly aquatic preferring still pools with shallows and plenty of driftwood or roots along the banks. The jumping ability of American bullfrogs is well-known and a contest is held every year in Calaveras to commemorate Mark Twain's famous tale 'The Jumping Frog of Calaveras County'. In fact the bullfrogs' jump, about 6 ft (2 m), is easily beaten by smaller, more athletic species of frogs from South Africa.

American bullfrogs emerge from hibernation in May and breeding lasts until July, the males calling from the edges of lakes and ponds. The tadpole reaches a length of 6 in (15 cm) and it is three years before it changes into a froglet. The adults eat anything of the right size, including mice, lizards, birds, fish, salamanders and other frogs, even those of the same species. Bullfrogs are easily caught by dangling a piece of cloth on a fish hook in front of them, and the meat of the large hindlimbs is considered a delicacy.

The African bullfrog is up to 9 in (22·5 cm), the male being larger than the female, which is unusual. It is plump and olive-coloured with many longitudinal folds in the skin. The mouth is enormous, reaching back to the shoulders and there are three tooth-like projections on the lower jaw. African bullfrogs burrow, shuffling backwards into the soil and remaining buried, with only the tip of the snout exposed. FAMILY: Ranidae, ORDER: Anura, CLASS: Amphibia.

BULLHEADS, a group of fishes dealt with under Miller's Thumb.

BUMBLEBEES or humblebees, large, furry social bees, living in underground colonies founded by the mother or queen and containing her offspring, the sexually undeveloped females or workers. The queens are produced in the late summer. They hibernate and awake in the spring to begin feeding on the nectar of fruit trees until their ovaries develop. Each queen then searches for a nest-site which is frequently the disused burrow of a small mammal. Depending on the species, the site chosen will be approached by a long tunnel or may be on the surface of the ground but protected by tussocks of grass or moss. Within the nest, the queen prepares a small chamber lined with dried grass and moss and makes a shallow cup or egg-cell from the wax she produces in thin sheets from glands situated between the segments of her abdomen. At this time, the queen begins foraging for pollen which she stores in the egg-cell until there is sufficient to feed her first offspring. 8–14 eggs are laid on the pollen in the cell which is then sealed with a canopy of wax. Once the eggs have been laid, the queen makes a wax honeypot in which she stores some of the nectar she has collected and from which she feeds the growing larvae. This she does by making a hole in the egg-cell and regurgitating the honey from her stomach into the cell.

When the maggot-like larvae have completed their feeding and are full-grown, they spin silken cocoons within which they change into the adult form (pupation). After the young workers chew their way out, the vacated cocoon is used to store honey and pollen. The workers, the ovaries of which normally remain undeveloped, take over the foraging duties of the colony while the queen remains within the nest, making egg-cells on top of the cocoons, laying eggs and incubating them by stretching herself over them like a broody hen.

When the colony is mature, the number of workers may vary from 100–400, although over 2,000 have been recorded in some tropical species. The considerable variation in size of workers results in a division of labour, with the larger bees performing the

Burbot

Bumblebee on clover, its pollen baskets (the yellow mass on each hindleg) filled.

foraging duties and the smaller ones, or house-bees, restricting themselves to duties within the nest. FAMILY: Bombidae, ORDER: Hymenoptera, CLASS: Insecta, PHYLUM: Arthropoda.

BURBOT *Lota lota*, the only freshwater member of the cod family. It derives its common name from the Latin for a beard, a reference to the barbel on its chin. The

burbot lives in most European rivers except those in the extreme north and south. Its nearest relative is the ling. It has an elongated, subcylindrical body blotched with shades of brown and its general form has given rise to an alternative name, eelpout. It was formerly found in most eastward-flowing rivers in England and its great stronghold was the Norfolk Broads. In recent times draining the land and other works have led

to its becoming very rare in England. A rather secretive fish, it lurks near the bottom among weeds during the day but comes out at night to feed on frogs and small fishes. It is also found in Asia and there are two subspecies in North America. It usually grows to 24 in (60 cm) but sometimes to as much as 39 in (98 cm). FAMILY: Gadidae, ORDER: Gadiformes, CLASS: Pisces.

BURYING BEETLES, also known as Sexton beetles, strikingly marked with yellow or orange and black, are famous for burying the corpses of small birds and mammals, on which they lay their eggs, the larvae from these feeding on the decaying flesh. FAMILY: Silphidae, ORDER: Coleoptera, CLASS: Insecta, PHYLUM: Arthropoda.

BUSH-BABIES, nocturnal African mammals with forward-pointing eyes and grasping hands and feet. The Common bush-baby *Galago senegalensis* which weighs just over 1 lb (300 gm), with head and body 7 in (17 cm) and tail 10 in (25 cm) long, is the best known and is often kept as a pet. It has grey or greyish-brown fur, and the long tail is bushy. The smallest is the Dwarf bush-baby *G. demidovii* weighing only 2 oz (60 gm). The head and body measure only 6 in (15 cm) and the tail 8 in (20 cm) long. The fur is a dark rufous brown and the pointed snout is very conspicuous. The large Thick-tailed bush-baby *Galago crassicaudatus*, with a head and body length of 13 in (33 cm) and a tail 18 in (44 cm) long, is almost the size of a rabbit. There are also two less well-known species, which are about the same size as the Common bush-baby. One is Allen's bush-baby *Galago alleni* and the other is the Needle-clawed bush-baby *Galago elegantulus*. The latter species differs from all the other bush-babies in the structure of its nails. All others have flat nails on every finger and toe, whilst the Needle-clawed bush-baby has a claw-like extension in the middle of every nail except those on the thumb and big toe. The thumb and big toe are opposable in all species, and these digits are important in grasping the fine branches and trunks among which these animals live.

Insects form their main food, with fruits, gum and leaves making up the balance. Bush-babies cling to branches in a vertical position and take off and land in this posture. Most, if not all, species can build spherical leaf-nests, but some live in hollow trees as well. The nest is usually only occupied for two to three weeks; a new one is then constructed. The nest naturally acts as a centre for the home range, and bush-babies apparently defend a territory around their nest. In some species, such as the Dwarf and Common bush-babies, small social groups of up to eight individuals are formed, with each social group occupying a common nest.

The female gives birth to one offspring

The best known bushbaby *Galago senegalensis*, or Lesser galago, surprised by the photographer at its sleeping nest.

The bushbaby, halfway between monkeys and lemurs, is named for its cries heard at night resembling those of a human baby.

Bushbuck

at a time, which she leaves in the nest when she goes off to feed. If the nest is disturbed, the mother will usually carry her baby to another nest, by carrying it in the mouth. FAMILY: Galagidae, ORDER: Primates, CLASS: Mammalia.

BUSHBUCK *Tragelaphus scriptus*, red-coated antelope with a variable number of white stripes and spots on the flanks. Also known in some areas as the Harnessed antelope, it is related to the kudu and is found over most of Africa south of the Sahara. It stands 2–2½ ft (60–75 cm) at the shoulder. The young are reddish with light markings, including 4–6 white stripes and

Female bushbuck, called Harnessed antelope when it has white striped flanks.

one or two longitudinal bands. The white markings disappear with age, especially in males of races living in open country. There is a short crest on nape and back. The horns, 14–25 in (35–63 cm) long, have only one spiral turn and are black-tipped. FAMILY: Bovidae, ORDER: Artiodactyla, CLASS: Mammalia.

BUSH-CRICKETS, jumping insects of moderate to large size closely related to the crickets and also known as 'katydids' or 'Long-horned grasshoppers'. The antennae are thread-like, longer than the body and composed of more than 30 segments. Behind the head is a saddle-shaped structure, the pronotum, protecting the front part of the thorax. There are usually two pairs of fully developed wings, but these may be reduced in size or completely absent. The hindwings are membranous and fold up like a fan beneath the tougher forewings when at rest. The hindlegs are usually much enlarged for jumping, but the attachments of the jumping muscles do not form the herring-bone pattern on the hind femora found in the grasshoppers. The females usually have a conspicuous egg-laying structure or ovipositor at the tip of the abdomen.

There are about 4,000 species and the distribution is world-wide.

The eggs are sometimes laid in the ground, but more often in or on the stems or leaves of plants. They are often laid in groups but never

in a pod as in grasshoppers. The young are usually similar to the adults in appearance, though lacking wings.

Almost all male bush-crickets can produce sounds by rubbing the hind edge of the right forewing against a row of teeth on the left forewing. These 'songs' are high-pitched and often mainly ultrasonic, but most contain sounds that are audible to the human ear and some are quite deafening.

Most bush-crickets show a tendency to be nocturnal. Most feed on a mixture of plant and animal matter. FAMILY: Tettigoniidae, ORDER: Orthoptera, CLASS: Insecta, PHYLUM: Arthropoda.

BUSHDOG *Speothos venaticus*, short-legged, sausage-shaped carnivore in the same family as wild and domestic dogs, but not a close relative. In addition to its undoglike body shape, it has small ears, a short, almost naked tail, and dark brown fur with a golden ruff. It is adapted in body shape for rapid movement through the dense undergrowth which surrounds the river banks of tropical forests. The bushdog is reported to be an excellent swimmer, and its size is well-suited for this. Further features distinguishing it from other dogs are found in the thickness of its bones and in its dentition, only 36 teeth compared with the typical canid 42.

The bushdog is 22–30 in (57–75 cm) long in head and body with a 5–6 in (12–15 cm) tail, and it is 9–12 in (23–30 cm) at the shoulder. It weighs 12–15 lb (5–7 kg).

Ranging through the tropical forests of Central America and northern South America, bushdogs travel in packs, preying upon large rodents such as pacas and agoutis as well as small forest deer.

Bushdogs have two vocalizations. One call, a high-pitched squeak which sounds like a bird and is heard almost constantly, probably functions to keep pack members in touch. The second is a piercing screech given by aggressive animals after a fight. FAMILY: Canidae, ORDER: Carnivora, CLASS: Mammalia.

BUSHMASTER *Lachesis muta*, the longest of the New World venomous snakes inhabiting the northern portions of South America, Trinidad and ranging northward into Central America to Costa Rica. It can exceed 12 ft (3·6 m) in length. FAMILY: Crotalidae, ORDER: Squamata, CLASS: Reptilia.

BUSHPIG *Potamochoerus porcus*, or Water hog or Redriver hog, a large hog with reddish-brown coarse hair over its entire body. Bush-pigs are found throughout most of Africa south of the Sahara and in Madagascar. The male bushpig is larger than the female. The largest males weigh 250 lb (114 kg), the largest females only 200 lb (91 kg).

Bushpigs inhabit brushy woodland and grassy areas. They travel in bands of from 4 to 20. They are almost entirely nocturnal

except in remote areas where they move about in daylight if undisturbed. FAMILY: Suidae, SUBORDER: Suiformes, ORDER: Artiodactyla, CLASS: Mammalia.

BUSTARDS, a well-defined family of 22 species related to the seriemas, cranes and rails, some being called korhaans in South Africa or floricans in India. They are birds of deserts, grassy plains and open savannahs. They vary in size from about 14 in (35 cm) long in the Lesser florican *Sypheotides indica* of India, to more than 50 in (130 cm) long in the Kori bustard *Ardeotis kori* of Africa. Males are generally larger than females. The Kori bustard and others of the same genus are among the largest and heaviest of all flying birds attaining weights of more than 30 lb (13·5 kg). They are close to the size limit above which flight is impossible and only fly reluctantly and for short distances. Smaller species fly strongly, many performing migrations of considerable length, but even so they depend more upon running and their cryptic colouring to escape predators. All bustards have long, strong legs and a long neck. Their three forward pointing toes are short and broad, while the hind toe, or hallux, is absent as in many other cursorial species. The plumage is various shades of grey, brown and buff, beautifully vermiculated and spotted with black and white, and other shades of grey and brown. The majority of bustards have large white patches on their wings, which are usually visible only in flight. Several species have short crests, while the males of some, such as the Great bustard *Otis arda* of Eurasia and the Houbara bustard *Chlamydotis undulata* of northern Africa and southeastern Asia, have ornate bristles or plumes on the head and neck. FAMILY: Otidae, ORDER: Gruiformes, CLASS: Aves.

BUTTERFISH, or gunnel *Pholis gunnellus*, an elongated blenny-like fish commonly found hiding under stones along European and North American coasts when the tide is out. Generally it is buff-coloured with a row of black spots along the base of the long dorsal fin; the pectoral fin may be orange or yellowish. The body is covered with fine scales and is slimy; anybody trying to pick it up will be in no doubt why it is called the butterfish.

The female lays eggs in a small compact ball about 1 in (2·5 cm) in diameter, by curving her body into a loop and laying the eggs within the circle. The ball is then thrust into a hole in the rocks or into an empty shell. Both parents take turns in guarding the eggs until the young hatch after about four weeks. The young swim out to sea for several months and then return to the shore. These fishes grow to about 10–12 in (25–30 cm) in length. FAMILY: Pholididae, ORDER: Perciformes, CLASS: Pisces.

The head of a young Rough-legged buzzard, of northern Europe, a species widespread in the higher latitudes of the whole northern hemisphere.

its range it is migratory. Practically all its prey is taken on the ground, either by dropping onto it from a perch, or by diving onto it after circling or hovering briefly.

Breeding begins about February with striking aerial displays. These usually involve one or both birds circling together, interspersed with spectacular dives followed by upward swoops. The loud clear mewing note 'peee-oo' is repeatedly uttered during the display. The nest is built by both birds of the pair in a tree or on a ledge, the clutch of from two to six oval eggs being laid in late March or early April. They are a dull white, sparingly marked with red or brown. Both sexes take part in the five weeks incubation and the young are in the nest for 40–50 days. In the early stages the female remains at the nest with the young, while the male brings the food. After one or two weeks the female helps with the hunting.

The Common buzzard is replaced in the north by the Rough-legged buzzard *B. lagopus*. This holarctic species breeds between latitudes 76°N and 61°N in Europe and America. It is highly migratory, moving south in winter to southern Europe, Asia Minor and the central United States. It is slightly larger and much paler than *B. buteo* and, as its name implies, has a feathered tarsus. FAMILY: Accipitridae, ORDER: Falconiformes, CLASS: Aves.

BY-THE-WIND SAILOR *Velella*, a kind of jellyfish, known as a siphonophore, living in the warmer oceans and the Mediterranean. It has a flat almost oblong float like a miniature raft, with a transparent gas-filled triangular sail on its upper surface, which the wind catches and drives the animal along the surface of the sea. The raft is deep blue and up to 2½ in (63 mm) long and 1½ in (38 mm) broad. On the undersurface is a central mouth surrounded by rings of reproductive bodies or gonophores and, outside these, by a ring of delicate mobile tentacles round the margin of the float. These are heavily charged with stinging cells for the capture of food and for the animal's protection. The gonophores bud off small male and female medusae which lack a mouth. After release from the gonophores they produce eggs and sperm. They were named *Chrysomitra*, since they were originally thought to represent a separate genus. ORDER: Athecata, CLASS: Hydrozoa, PHYLUM: Cnidaria.

BUTTONQUAILS, small, skulking birds, very like quail but more closely related to the rails and cranes. They are terrestrial and have a generally brown plumage above, usually cryptically patterned and variegated in black, buff and white, while the underside is pale, often with a spotted pattern. In some species the female is distinguished by a bright chestnut breast patch. The bill is more slender and longer than that of a quail, but some Australian species have evolved heavy, blunt bills for seed-crushing. The feet are small, with no hind-toes; the wings are rounded, and the short tail mostly concealed by the wing coverts. Buttonquails are about 4–8 in (10–20 cm) in length.

Buttonquails occur in grassland or low cover, both dry and swampy, and open woodland with some ground cover. They keep to cover and are difficult to see. If scared into flight they tend to fly low for a short distance and drop down to land again. The food is seeds, parts of plants, and insects. In the widely distributed Striped buttonquail *Turnix sylvatica* the female has a loud booming call.

There are 14 species, 13 in the typical genus *Turnix*, six of which live in Australasia. The others occur widely over the Old World, through Africa, Asia and the Oriental region, reaching Europe in southern Spain. In most species the female is the larger and more brightly-coloured. She displays, fighting other females and courting the males. The male incubates the eggs and cares for the chicks.

The nest is a shallow scrape, lined with dry grasses and dead leaves, on the ground in a sheltered spot. Growing grasses may be pulled downwards to conceal the nest. The clutch is usually of four eggs. FAMILY: Turnicidae, ORDER: Gruiformes, CLASS: Aves.

BUZZARDS, large, broad-winged predatory birds renowned for their soaring flight, but spending much of the day perched on rocks, trees or telegraph posts. The body length is about 20 in (50·8 cm) and the wing span 3–5 ft (91·4–152·4 cm). They live in open, wooded and mountainous habitats and feed principally on ground prey of mammals and reptiles, but also take carrion and birds. Most are dark brown and superficially resemble eagles, but buzzards are smaller, have a less massive and less fierce appearance and lack the heavy bill and large claws of the eagles. There are 25 species of true buzzards included in the genus *Buteo*.

The most widely distributed is the Common buzzard *Buteo buteo*. It breeds throughout the Palearctic region. Where a suitable habitat exists it is found from sea level to 10,000 ft (3,000 m) and in the more northerly parts of

C

CADDIS FLIES, a group of moth-like flies closely related to the moths and butterflies, from which they may be distinguished by the possession to a greater or lesser extent, of hairs instead of scales on the wings. Trichoptera, the order to which Caddis flies belong, literally means 'hairy-winged'. The wings of Caddis flies are held tentwise over the body and are never held vertically upwards as are those of butterflies and, as in moths, mandibles are absent. The antennae are slender thread-like and sometimes exceptionally long, as much as three times the length of the body. Caddis flies are most often drably coloured, brown and yellows predominating, while a number are blackish. Some are green or white, a few show iridescence and one is bright blue. They are mostly small to moderate in size.

They are found throughout the world and about 3,000 species are known in 18 families. With only very few exceptions, the immature stages of Caddis flies are aquatic so that the adult flies are to be found in the vicinity of water, although many species, being attracted to light, sometimes wander a few miles.

With the exception of the very few terrestrial species, the eggs of Caddis flies are laid either above water or in it. If in the former the larvae hatch out of a jelly-like egg-mass during rain and find their way into the water.

The larval stage of Caddis flies is better known than the adults as the larvae of many species construct a case for themselves which is of such a size that when the larva is feeding or pulling itself along by its rather spidery legs, the abdomen is contained within it and, indeed, held fast to it by a pair of hooked appendages situated at the hind end. When alarmed or resting the larva can retract itself completely within its case.

The larval case is made of a wide variety of materials which can be collected by the caddis larva in the water and comes in a wide

Adult Caddis fly *Stenophylax permistus*, typically drab coloured, found near water in which eggs are laid and the larvae live.

range of patterns. In order to cement the pieces together, a silk-like secretion is produced from the mouth, and in a number of species the whole case is made of this substance which takes on a leathery or horny consistency. The case is commonly made from a number of small rectangular pieces cut from leaves, or sometimes pieces of stalk, and arranged in a spiral fashion, or it may be made of the shells of water snails or of small pebbles. ORDER: Trichoptera, CLASS: Insecta, PHYLUM: Arthropoda.

CAECILIANS, long-bodied, limbless amphibians which superficially resemble large earthworms. They are invariably blind and the eyes are covered with opaque skin, or by the bones of the skull. There is a small sensory tentacle just in front of each eye. The tentacle has two ducts which communicate with Jacobson's organ, a sensory area adjacent to the nasal cavity. There is no tympanic membrane and it is likely that caecilians 'hear' by picking up vibrations in the ground via their lower jaw. Caecilians move by sinuous lateral undulations of the body. Many are able to burrow rapidly and the majority spend most of their time below ground level. A number of species are, however, aquatic. Caecilians vary considerably in size. The largest reaches a length of 55 in (139·7 cm), the smallest 4½ in (11·2 cm).

The body of caecilians is divided by a number of folds in the skin which give a ringed appearance. Many species bear small scales in pockets just below the epidermis. In the majority the hind end is short and rounded, but a few species have a small 'tail'. Externally the sexes cannot be separated. Fertilization is internal. Some species lay eggs in cavities in the mud or among rocks close to water. The female usually coils around the developing eggs. The larvae develop within the egg capsule and although gills are present these are resorbed before hatching. Others lay eggs which develop into free-swimming larvae with external gills. In other species the eggs are retained and develop within the mother, some species producing live young which have developed outside the egg-capsule within the mother.

Caecilians feed on earthworms and insects, especially termites. They need moist surroundings and are usually drab although some have a little colour.

The 158 species are distributed throughout the warm-temperate regions of the world from sea level to around 6,000 ft (2,000 m). ORDER: Apoda (or Gymnophiona), CLASS: Amphibia.

CAIMANS, a group smaller in size than the other crocodilians but possessing the same general characteristics. Caimans occur only in the western hemisphere. South America contains most of the eight species. The powerful tail, lashing from side to side,

Young caiman showing its many pointed teeth, with mouth open ready to bite.

propels them through water at a rapid rate. The back has a tough hide reinforced by bony plates. The throat contains a fleshy flap that can be closed to permit breathing at the water's surface with only the tip of the nose showing. The nostrils have external valves and the eyes are doubly protected by eyelids and a movable, clear membrane. The teeth of the lower jaw fit into pits in the upper jaw when the jaws are closed.

The huge Black caiman *Melanosuchus niger* reaches a length of 15 ft (4·6 m) in the Amazon basin and Guiana region. Most caimans reach sexual maturity at a length of 5 or 6 ft (1·5–1·8 m). The Smooth-fronted caiman, *Paleosuchus trigonatus*, and the Dwarf caiman *Paleosuchus palpebrosus*, from the Amazon, are the smallest of the caimans. To protect their bodies from rapids in the swift waters they inhabit, the bony plates in the armour of these small creatures extend down to the belly.

Mating occurs with the male mounting the female in the water and twisting his tail beneath hers to accomplish a union. Approximately one month after conception the female builds a nest close to a stream, composed of decaying leaves and branches. The heat from the decaying vegetation keeps the eggs at a constant 90°F (32°C).

When the young in the eggs are ready to hatch they respond to any activity on the mound by making 'croaking' sounds. The female caiman hears the young and digs down to them.

Young caimans grow rapidly and eat huge quantities of crayfish, fish, insects, snails, snakes and small rodents. Within three years the 8 in (20 cm) hatchlings reach a length of 3 ft (90 cm). FAMILY: Alligatoridae, ORDER: Crocodilia, CLASS: Reptilia.

CAMEL. There are two species of camel both belonging to the Old World: the One-humped or Arabian camel *Camelus dromedarius*, of North Africa and the Near East, and the Two-humped or Bactrian camel *C. bactrianus*, of Asia. The first is not known in the wild, the second survives in the wild in the Gobi Desert. The One-humped camel is commonly referred to as the dromedary, a name which strictly speaking should be reserved for a special breed used in riding.

Camels are up to 9 ft (3 m) long and stand nearly 7 ft (2·2 m) at the shoulder. The legs are long, the neck is long and curved, the ears are small, the eyes have long lashes and the nostrils can be closed as an additional protection against blown sand. The foot consists of two toes united at the sole by a web of skin. There are horny callosities on the chest and leg joints. The dental formula is: $i\frac{1}{3} c\frac{1}{1} pm \frac{3}{2} m\frac{3}{3}$.

Because of its fleshy lips and long papillae on the inside of the mouth a camel can eat hard thorny food. It will eat almost any kind of dry vegetation and while food is abundant fat accumulates in the hump as an energy store.

The Arabian camel is more slender, with a shorter coat than the Bactrian and the colour of the coat is more variable.

Caravans cover only about 20–25 miles (30–40 km) a day, but the camel is superior to the horse in its steady trot, which if necessary it can keep up all day. Record performances of 125 miles (200 km) a day have been known, but the animals only recovered from these after months of rest. In the cool season camels can travel across 620 miles (1,000 km) of waterless desert. They have a strong homing instinct and often escape from distant areas to their original home 300 miles (500

Canary

km) or even 620 miles (1,000 km) away.

Gestation is 12–13 months and lactation lasts 1–2 years. The mares foal every second year and go apart from the herd, to give birth either lying or standing. The foal can run after 2–3 hours, first of all in a mixture of stagger and amble, and not later than the second day it can amble confidently.

A camel does not store water in its stomach and the hump is an energy store. It drinks only as much water as it has lost since the last watering through sweat, urine and faeces. This loss is unusually small, chiefly due to the high variability of the body temperature. Whereas other mammals and human beings prevent overheating of the body by perspiration, the thirsty camel can raise its temperature by 9°F (6°C) without getting feverish. The thick coat also gives protection from loss of heat. FAMILY: Camelidae, ORDER: Tylopoda, CLASS: Mammalia.

CANARY *Serinus canaria*, a finch named after the islands from which it was first brought, which has now been domesticated to become a common cage-bird. The wild bird is a subspecies of the European serin and is also found in the Azores and Madeira. The male is a streaky olive-green above and yellow-green below, while the female is duller and browner. The bird was apparently brought to Germany early in the 16th century, and the modern yellow varieties have been developed by selective breeding from chance mutations. FAMILY: Fringillidae, ORDER: Passeriformes, CLASS: Aves.

CANDIRU or carnero, a small South American catfish which becomes parasitic on larger fish. Habitually it lives in the gill cavities, and with its sharp teeth and the spines on its gill covers it induces a flow of blood on which it feeds. The species greatly feared by the peoples of Brazil is *Vandellia cirrhosa*. This enters the urinogenital apertures of men and women, particularly if they happen to urinate in the water. It seems likely that this is accidental, the fish mistaking the flow of urine for the exhalant stream of water from a fish's gills. Having penetrated, however, it is almost impossible to remove the

Cape hunting dog of the African savannah has a highly developed social system.

candiru without surgery. FAMILY: Trichomycteridae, ORDER: Cypriniformes, CLASS: Pisces.

CAPE HUNTING DOG *Lycaon pictus*, also known as the African wild dog. It ranges through Africa south of the Sahara. It weighs 60–100 lb (25–45 kg), and has a short sleek coat marked with blotches of brown, yellow and white. The patterning of the fur differs from individual to individual, the only constant markings being the white-tipped tail and dark snout. Its ears are outstandingly big and rounded and the muzzle, short and powerful-looking. The hunting dogs have also retained five digits on the forefeet, a primitive trait not found in other canids.

Cape hunting dogs typically breed once a year, cubs being born between April and June and August and November. Gestation is 70 to 71 days.

They are pack hunters, packs ranging from 3 to 50 animals, commonly 12 and 20. Hunts usually take place at dawn and dusk, when the pack will travel together towards a herd of wildebeest, zebra, buffalo, or gazelles. One or two dogs will select a single animal and begin chasing it. The remainder station themselves at various distances to ensure that any quarry circling back will be cut off. The leaders of the hunt can outrun most prey and begin to nip and bite the hind quarters of the victim when they have caught up with it.

The other pack members close in for the kill. The dogs then tear the prey apart, sometimes without killing it beforehand. Most of the carcass is eaten immediately, and soon after, the pack returns to the den or settles in a favourite rest site.

Hunting dogs have a highly developed social life, the needs of the individual being subordinated to the needs of the group. When a female is rearing cubs, the pack members all bring food back to the den. Moreover, hunting dogs have developed an unusual feeding ritual derived from the infantile pattern of begging for food. Each individual begs the others to regurgitate meat by pushing at the snout and licking its lips, and in this way, partly digested food passes from one dog to another until all are fed. Unlike wolves, this species does not have a rigid hierarchy or rank order although one male usually shows more leadership qualities than the others. Nursing females are dominant over other animals.

Among themselves, hunting dogs are extremely friendly, especially before the hunt when pack members chase each other playfully until everyone joins together in a greeting ceremony uttering a peculiar twittering sound. Despite the complexity of their social life, hunting dogs do not use specialized facial expressions to communicate with each other. FAMILY: Canidae, ORDER: Carnivora, CLASS: Mammalia.

CAPE JUMPING HARE *Pedetes capensis*, or springhare, a rodent of the short-grass plains of eastern and southern Africa, sole representative of the family Pedetidae, with uncertain relationships among the rodents, measures up to 15 in (38 cm) with a bushy tail of about equal length. It is bipedal, its hindlegs, and especially the hindfeet, are very long and the front feet disproportionally short. The long ears, large bulging eyes, prominent whiskers and deep muzzle with large protruding orange teeth combine to give the head a uniquely quaint appearance. The pelage is of uniform yellowish brown except for the brush of the tail which is black.

The front feet bear five long curved claws with which the springhare can very quickly dig a burrow. The burrows may be quite complex but are usually only inhabited by one animal or a pair. Springhares are strictly nocturnal, emerging after dark to feed on bulbs, rhizomes and other fleshy plant material. They are slow breeders. The litter consists of one, or occasionally two, young which are fairly well developed at birth and open their eyes within two days. FAMILY: Pedetidae, ORDER: Rodentia, CLASS: Mammalia.

CAPERCAILLIE *Tetrao urogallus*, a large game bird of the grouse family, found in forests, particularly of conifers, in northern Europe and Asia, with a relict population in

The characteristic attitude of the cock capercaillie during his courtship display.

Arab police patrol, Wadi Rum, Jordan.

Capuchin

the Pyrenees. The cock capercaillie is very striking, some 34 in (86 cm) long, with a basically grey plumage, brown wing-coverts and dark glossy blue-green breast. The tail coverts and belly are marked with white and there is a white wing patch. The strong bill is dull white and there is a bright red wattle above each eye. The legs are feathered. The female, 24 in (61 cm) long, is cryptically coloured like other female game birds, mottled and barred with buff, grey and black.

Capercaillies prefer dense, shady forests with substantial underbrush interspersed with glades and boggy areas. They feed on a variety of plant materials, particularly the buds and needles of pine, spruce and larch. For centuries this species has been hunted for sport and food. This, with deforestation, brought about their extermination in Britain in the 16th century but re-introductions from 1837 onwards re-established it.

Cock capercaillies have a particularly striking breeding display. In the spring small numbers of cocks gather at the lek, or display ground, each beginning its display with a peculiar clicking utterance which develops to a crescendo and terminates with a loud 'pop', followed by a short wheezy, grating sound. The characteristic attitude during this song is with the neck stretched up to display beard-like feathers beneath the chin, with wings drooping to touch the ground and with the tail fanned and almost vertical. Noisy flapping of the wings and jumps into the air also take place. Rival males are charged, with the wings drooping, but most of the attacks are ritualized and seldom result in much injury.

The nest is usually on the ground, well hidden amongst the forest vegetation or under a fallen branch, frequently at the foot of a tree. 5–8 eggs are laid and incubated by the female for about 28 days. FAMILY: Tetraonidae, ORDER: Galliformes, CLASS: Aves.

CAPUCHIN *Cebus*, perhaps the best-known of all New World monkeys, so named because the hair on the head recalls the cowl or capuche of Franciscan monks. Capuchins, one of the 'organ-grinder's monkeys', are medium-sized, brownish short-haired monkeys, 15–21 in (38–53 cm) long, the tail being longer and hairy throughout but none the less prehensile.

The most distinctive species is the Tufted capuchin *C. apella*, with tufts of hair on the forehead, usually a pair but sometimes a single ridge of hair. There is a dark brown cap on the head with a rounded border. The skull is high and vaulted, the brow-ridges weak and in old males the jaw muscles tend to meet over the top of the skull and form a sagittal crest between them. This species, with its rather cross-looking, scowling face, is common throughout the forests of South America.

The untufted group of capuchins are not found south of the Amazon. They have no

The white-throated capuchin searching among the tangled vegetation for insects.

frontal tufts but females have an eyebrow brush of hairs, or long stiff hairs radiating from the middle of the forehead. The face, throat, sides of the neck, shoulders, chest and inner surfaces of the arms are pale, while on the crown is a dark cap which is often pointed in front. There are three species: White-throated capuchin *C. capucinus* from Central America, western Columbia and the Pacific coast of Ecuador, black with the pale areas white; White-fronted capuchin *C. albifrons* from north-eastern South America, which has the black replaced by yellowish to dark brown; and Weeper capuchin *C. nigrivittatus* which replaces the last in the Guianas and extends into Venezuela, Colombia and Brazil, has a much smaller, wedge-shaped cap and a less contrasting, more restricted white area, with a coarser brownish coat. FAMILY: Cebidae, ORDER: Primates, CLASS: Mammalia.

CAPYBARA, like an overgrown Guinea pig, it is the largest of all living rodents, being the size of a sheep. The two species, found in South America, belong to the genus *Hydrochoerus*. A fully grown animal is about 4 ft (1·3 m) long with almost no tail and long legs. The unusually deep muzzle gives a very characteristic appearance and is correlated with the long, rootless, evergrowing cheek-teeth, four in each row, that are adapted for grinding tough vegetation. Capybaras are semi-aquatic and this is reflected in their

partially webbed feet, sparse coat and the thick deposit of fat in the skin.

The best known species, *H. hydrochaeris*, is found in woodland adjacent to rivers, lakes and swamps from the Parana River in Argentina northwards. A smaller species, *H. isthmius*, occurs in Panama. Capybaras sometimes damage crops of cereals and fruit, but their normal diet consists of aquatic vegetation and grasses.

They are sociable animals and it is not unusual to find a party of 10–20 feeding together in a weed-filled waterway at dawn or dusk. In the water they behave rather like hippopotamuses. On land they sit on their haunches like dogs. FAMILY: Hydrochoeridae, ORDER: Rodentia, CLASS: Mammalia.

CARACAL *Caracal caracal*, usually known as a lynx, but more closely related to the serval, one of the most beautiful of the cats, is long legged and better adapted for running than most cats, and shows remarkable leaping ability. It measures 27½ in (70 cm). Its colouring is a regular reddish brown above, with no other markings except for the ears, which are black behind, and a small dark spot above each eye. The underparts are white, with vague brownish red spots on the belly. The tail is short and the ears have distinctive tufts or plumes at their tips.

The caracal is widely distributed throughout the drier areas of southern Africa and Asia and was formerly much more common than it is now. It will also be found in mountainous areas, bush and desert. It is semi-nocturnal and lies up during the day in hollows, under tree roots or in a disused porcupine or aardvark den.

Its main food is birds, which it hunts when they are roosting, although it has been observed to catch some prey on the wing. The caracal will take a wide range of small animals such as a duiker, steinbok, sheep, goats, and young reed-buck and impala. The caracal's system of hunting involves a stalk and then a light pounce.

The one to four young resemble the adults at birth, and the majority of breeding occurs in July and August. FAMILY: Felidae, ORDER: Carnivora, CLASS: Mammalia.

CARACARAS, large, long-legged carrion-eating birds belonging to the falcon family, but looking quite unlike true falcons. Found commonly in parts of South and Central America, caracaras associate with vultures at carcasses, but some are insectivorous or omnivorous. They build their own nests, unlike true falcons, but will rob other carrion-eaters for their food. They are well adapted for walking and running and live in forests, savannah, or more open country. FAMILY: Falconidae, ORDER: Falconiformes, CLASS: Aves.

CARDINALS, finch-like birds with conical bills for crushing seeds, related in anatomy and behaviour to the American grosbeaks and tanagers. Like the latter, they are brilliantly coloured and are prized as cage-birds outside the United States and Canada (where stringent laws forbid the capture and raising of native birds).

The name is given to a mixture of birds with red plumage, and by association transferred to other similar or related forms no matter their colour. In North America it is usually applied to a large, heavy-billed bunting *Pyrrhuloxia (Richmondena) cardinalis.* The male is almost entirely red save for a black patch on the throat, and has a small spiky erectile crest. The female is similar but mostly brown, with only a little red in the plumage.

The familiar Common cardinal *P. cardinalis,* of the city suburbs of temperate eastern North America, sings a much repeated *to-wit,* a common backyard sound in spring. Closely related, with a longer crest, the Vermilion cardinal *P. phoenicea* represents it in Venezuela and Colombia. The less brightly coloured Mexican *P. sinuata* is known as the pyrrhuloxia, a former scientific name adopted as a vernacular name. Cardinals of the genera *Paroaria* and *Gubernatrix* are favourites among bird fanciers and well known in aviaries.

The cardinals include the most colourful seed-eaters in America, males being brightly coloured although the females are usually brown. The males of the genus *Passerina* are variously deep blue, light blue and buff, blue, scarlet and green, purple, red and blue and blue, green and yellow. The male is deep blue and buff in the Blue grosbeak *Guiraca caerulea* and black and white with a red breast patch in the Rose-breasted grosbeak *Pheucticus ludovicianus.* Other species are more drab. The cardinals are mostly woodland birds, usually occurring in pairs but sometimes flocking when not breeding. They have loud melodious songs. They make cup-shaped nests in trees or bushes. The eggs are variously coloured but usually spotted or blotched.

As with many familiar birds, cardinals have been the subject of some quaint observations, the most extraordinary of which being that of a male cardinal feeding some goldfish in a backyard pool for several days (photograph in the National Geographic book "Song and Garden Birds of North America," 1965, p. 324). FAMILY: Fringillidae, ORDER: Passeriformes, CLASS: Aves.

CARIBOU *Rangifer tarandus,* a large ungainly deer of the tundra and northern forest regions. It has a wide distribution in both eastern and western hemispheres, being referred to as reindeer in the east and caribou in North America.

The European reindeer *R. t. tarandus* is found in parts of Scandinavia and Russia, where it continues its range eastwards into Siberia north of about latitude 65°N.

In the western hemisphere two types of caribou—the Barren-ground and the Woodland caribou—are recognized, their range including much of Canada and adjacent northern islands and Greenland. The word 'caribou' is the North American Indian's name for this deer.

The bulls have a thick muzzle, maned neck and broad flat hooves that are concave underneath and designed for travelling over snow and boggy terrain. They are considerably larger than the cows, but both are larger than the reindeer. A full-grown caribou bull will be 42–50 in (107–127 cm) at the shoulder whilst the weight will vary from 200 lb (91 kg) to 600 lb (272 kg). A full-grown European reindeer bull will measure 44–45 in (112–114 cm) at the shoulder, the cows being some 4–6 in (10–15 cm) less.

The body colour of the males is brown, with the neck a palish grey turning white in winter. There is more variation of colour in the female, particularly in reindeer which have been domesticated.

Both reindeer and caribou cows are unique in normally possessing a pair of antlers, smaller than those of the males. The bulls generally have a palmated 'shovel' close to the face on one of the antlers. The upper points are also frequently palmated and there is a back tine about halfway up the main beam. The antlers on the older males are shed during the early part of the winter, but the new growth does not commence until the spring. The younger animals retain their antlers until the early part of the year, but not until late spring or early summer, at about the time the calves are being born, are the cows' antlers cast.

The caribou is usually found in herds which are small except during the long migrations of spring and early winter, when they may run into thousands.

Although the lichen *Cladonia rangiferina* forms the staple diet willow, mosses, grasses and sedges are eaten. FAMILY: Cervidae, ORDER: Artiodactyla, CLASS: Mammalia.

Bull Barren ground caribou of Alaska, in prime condition during summer feeding.

Carps

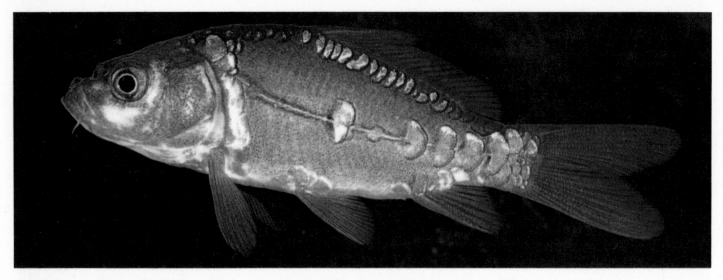

The Mirror carp, a domesticated variety of the Common carp, is named for the large mirror-like scales on its flanks.

CARPS or carp-like fishes, slender stream-lined fishes almost entirely found in fresh-water, although a few occasionally go into brackish water, as in the Baltic Sea.

They are slender, with silvery scales, a single dorsal fin set at about the midpoint of the body and a forked caudal fin. There are no teeth in the jaws, but these may develop a horny cutting edge for scraping algae or may bear disc-like lips which act as a sucker. One or two pairs of short barbels may be present at the corners of the mouth. Mastication of food, such as insects, plants, detritus, is achieved by a set of teeth in the throat, the pharyngeal teeth.

The Common carp *Cyprinus carpio*, a native of Asia, was introduced into Europe, presumably by monks who kept these fishes in monastery tanks, in about the 12th century. In Japan, the Common carp has for centuries been regarded as a symbol of fertility, but the earliest record of this fish is from China in 500 BC. FAMILY: Cyprinidae, ORDER: Cypriniformes, CLASS: Pisces.

CASSOWARIES *Casuarius*, large flightless birds living in the tropical rain-forests of New Guinea and adjacent islands and in northern Australia.

Adults of the largest, the Double-wattled cassowary *C. casuarius*, stand about 6 ft (1·8 m) high when erect, but normally the head is held about 4 ft (1·2 m) above the ground. The plumage is almost black and has a glossy texture. Each feather has two equal shafts, and as there are no barbules the barbs of the feathers do not link together to form a firm vane. The plumage hangs loosely from the body looking more like hair than feathers. The head is embellished by a casque, or flattened horny crown, projecting up to 6 in (15 cm) above the top of the skull. The skin of the head and neck is blue, and in two of the three species ornate wattles, or folds of loose skin coloured red, orange and yellow, hang from the neck over the throat. The cassowaries have three toes, flattened beneath

as in the emu, with a long sharp claw on the innermost toe of each foot. The wings are greatly reduced and the wing quills, of which only the shaft is present, are horny spines, up to 15 in (38 cm) long, which hang conspicuously at the bird's side as it stands.

The Single-wattled cassowary *C. unappen-diculatus*, 5 ft (1·6 m) tall and weighing up to 128 lb (58 kg), lives in riverine and coastal swamp forests of New Guinea and adjacent islands. Its single wattle is only about 1½ in (3 cm) long and hangs from the throat.

The Dwarf cassowary *C. bennetti* stands about 3½ ft (1 m) high, and inhabits montane forests in most parts of New Guinea and the surrounding islands.

The birds appear to live in pairs and family parties, each pair defending a territory during the breeding season. Eggs are laid from May onwards, and have been found even in September in North Queensland. Incubation probably takes about seven weeks, and the male undertakes the whole of the incubation. The clutches so far recorded range from three

Double-wattled cassowary, commonest of the three species, with its tall casque, said to be used to fend off thorns as the bird runs through undergrowth.

to eight eggs and the nest is a scrape on the forest floor in the dense vegetation of the bird's normal habitat. The chicks are striped with a dark and light longitudinal pattern and probably resemble those of the emu.

Wild cassowaries have been recorded eating the fruit of various native and cultivated plants and swallowing whole items as bulky as a large plum. Leaves have also been found in their gizzards. FAMILY: Casuariidae, ORDER: Casuariiformes, CLASS: Aves.

CATFISHES, widespread chiefly freshwater fishes with barbels round the mouth. There are 31 families from all parts of the world except the colder regions of the northern hemisphere. Some have completely naked, scaleless bodies while others have a heavy armour of bony plates. There is a single dorsal fin followed by an adipose fin which in some families (e.g. armoured catfishes) is supported by a spine. The common name for these fishes refers to the barbels round the mouth which look like whiskers and serve a sensory function in detecting food.

Europe has only two catfishes, both of which spread into Europe from Asia after the last Ice Age but which never reached the British Isles. The larger of the two, and one of the largest of the European freshwater fishes, is the wels *Silurus glanis* which is also found in Asiatic USSR. The second is *Parasilurus aristotelis*, an Asiatic species found in a few rivers in Greece. Both these belong to the family Siluridae, naked catfishes with the dorsal and adipose fins short, small or even absent. The anal fin may be very long and may be continuous with the tail. The Glass catfish *Kryptopterus bicirrhis* from Burma is familiar to aquarists. The body is completely transparent and slightly yellow, and the dorsal fin is reduced to a single ray.

The African family Mochokidae contains one of the best known of all catfishes, the famous Upside-down catfish *Synodontis nigriventris*. The body is naked, an adipose fin is present, and there is a strong spine in both dorsal and pectoral fins. This fish has the habit of swimming on its back, with the belly uppermost, a habit that is, however, shared with a few other members of this genus. In most fishes the back is much darker coloured than the belly, but in *S. nigriventris*, as its Latin name suggests, the belly is darker than the back. This species reaches 12 in (30 cm).

The family Chacidae from India and Burma contains only a few species. *Chaca chaca* grows to about 8 in (20 cm) in length and has an extremely flat body and a large head. It lives on the bottom and is beautifully camouflaged with blotchy dark browns and small protuberances to break the outline of the fish. So confident is it in its camouflage that it rarely moves even if touched, lying on the bottom like a piece of dead wood. ORDER: Siluriformes, CLASS: Pisces.

Upside-down catfish lacks the silver belly of fishes that swim the right way up.

CATS, thought to have been first domesticated by the Egyptians, have been given the scientific name of *Felis catus*. They seem to have been derived from the Cafer cat or Bush cat of Africa *F. lybica*, perhaps with some admixture from the European Wild cat *F. sylvestris*. It is possible that most of the domesticated cats of India may have had a totally independent origin from those of Europe and that the Indian Desert cat *F. ornata* may have been its original parent stock.

A typical short-haired domestic cat is about 2½ ft (76 cm) long, including a 9 in (23 cm) long tail which, unlike that of the Wild cat, is held horizontally when walking. The weight varies considerably but up to 21 lb (9 kg) has been recorded. It is a graceful animal with a well-knit, powerful body and a rounded face with a broad, well-whiskered muzzle. The whiskers are used to feel the way in the dark. The cat uses its teeth to tear and chop meat. The legs are strong and well-boned, the feet small and neat with retractile claws which are kept in good condition by scratching on a post or rough surface. They are a great help in climbing and enable a cat to shin swiftly up a tree to avoid a dog, or to rob birds' nests or just to lie on a branch basking in the sun.

The colour of the coat varies considerably. The most common, the tabby, is of two kinds. The striped tabby has narrow vertical stripes on the body, similar to those of the Bush cat and European Wild cat. The blotched tabby is nearly the same colour but has broad, mainly longitudinal dark lines and blotches on a light ground. In extreme cases the dark markings are relatively few, strongly drawn and standing out conspicuously against the lighter background. Such cats are recurrent mutants.

There are many colour varieties of the ordinary domestic cat including marmalade, ginger, tortoiseshell, blue, silver and black. All of the well-known colour variations have arisen by mutation after the cat was domesticated. The pure white cat is either a total albino with pink eyes or a dominant white usually with blue eyes. Darwin was the first scientist to note that white cats with blue eyes are usually deaf.

There are many breeds of domestic cats, not all officially recognized in every country. The long-haired Angora, said to come from Ankara in Turkey, and the smaller Persian, are now considered as one, owing to interbreeding. They have long silky fur with heavy ruffs of fur round the neck and thick tufts between the toes. The tail is long and bushy. The colour varies from pure white to grey.

Of the short-haired varieties, one of the most popular breeds today is the Siamese, said to have descended from the sacred, royal or temple cat of Thailand. It was introduced into England in 1884 and into the United States in 1894. The colour of the fur is remarkable in changing from pure white in the kitten to a pale fawn colour in the adult with the nose, mouth, ears, feet and tail dark brown. The eyes are a very bright blue and the tail is sometimes kinked. The forelimbs are relatively short and the hindquarters high. The related Burmese is seal brown with yellow or golden eyes and it lacks the dark points of the Siamese.

The Abyssinian is nearest in looks to the cats of Ancient Egypt. There seems no proof that it originated in Abyssinia. The Russian blue is also becoming popular. It has a soft seal-like coat, bright blue in colour and vivid green eyes.

One of the most familiar of the short-

There are a number of breeds of domestic cats in various parts of the world but no matter what their colour they all have much the same shape and appearance.

haired breeds is the Manx cat, remarkable for being tailless. It looks very like a lynx in outline and differs from the ordinary domestic cat in its short back, its higher hindquarters and its habit of walking with a kind of bobbing gait. Although not a good climber it is by far the fastest on the ground of all domestic cats. In general its coat is double, with long top hairs and shorter hairs forming a dense undercoat. Although it takes its name from the Isle of Man, it probably originated in the Far East.

A cat hunts by night by sound or sight and accordingly its hearing and sight are very acute. Its hearing extends beyond the range of the human ear into the higher frequencies and this is why a cat probably responds more readily to a woman's voice.

Although a cat cannot see in total darkness its eyes are so constructed as to make the fullest use of any light available when out hunting at night. During the day its eyes are protected by an iris diaphragm which helps to exclude the bright rays of full daylight making the pupils become smaller until they are mere vertical slits. As with most nocturnal animals, the cat's eye has a layer of cells behind the retina called the tapetum, that causes the cat's eyes to glow, or shine in the dark. The cat hunts by sound and sight, stalking with patience and stealth or by lying in wait and finally pouncing on its prey.

Domestic cats are sexually mature at 10 months or less, the earliest record being 3½ months. The height of the breeding season is from late December to March but the female may come on heat at intervals of 3–9 days from December to August. She is at her best for breeding purposes from 2–8 years. Males are at their highest potential from 3–8 years. Oestrus (heat) may last up to 21 days and is preceded by 2 or 3 days of excessive playfulness. Gestation is usually 65 days but may vary from 56–68 days. There may be up to eight kittens in a litter, but 13 are known. Very young mothers have only one or two

and the number drops again as the female approaches 8 years of age.

Kittens are born blind, deaf and only lightly furred. The mother will often lift and move her young one by gently grasping its body in her mouth. The eyes open between 4–10 days. Milk teeth may appear at 4 days but it may be 5 weeks before all have come through. Permanent teeth are cut between 4 and 7 months. Weaning begins at 2 months. FAMILY: Felidae, ORDER: Carnivora, CLASS: Mammalia.

CATTLE, DOMESTIC *Bos taurus*, large herbivorous mammals exclusively living in some kind of association with man, their origins shrouded in archaeological confusion and conflicting opinions, they were domesticated over 6,000 years ago from the wild aurochs.

Modern Western Cattle. These stand about 5 ft (1·5 m) high and weigh 1,000–2,200 lb (450–1,000 kg) or more, the bulls being heavier than the cows. They are grazing animals, nibbling grass with their lower incisor teeth biting against the hard pad of the upper lip. Cattle eat about 150 lb (70 kg) of grass in an eight hour day, and spend the rest of their time resting and chewing the cud.

Cows are mature when 18 months to three years old, depending on the breed and feeding. They are referred to as heifers before producing their first calf, and can continue breeding for over ten years. Usually only one calf is born, after a gestation of nine months.

Cattle products include fat, glue, fertilizers, soap and leather, but their main uses in western society are for meat and milk.

Notable meat producing breeds; Shorthorn. A stocky breed with a level back and a deep body boldly marked in reddish brown and white; the horns are very short and sharply curved inwards. Modern bulls weigh up to 2,000 lb (1,000 kg); the cows are smaller. They are sturdy beef-producing animals which will also give a good milk yield.

Hereford. This breed originated in Herefordshire (western England) and was formerly much used as a draught animal. Herefords are very solidly built and their markings (red-brown body, white head and belly) are highly characteristic. They are reared for beef production.

Aberdeen Angus. Angus cattle are short with a heavy build and straight back. They are black all over and hornless. They produce very high quality beef.

Notable breeds of Dairy Cattle. These are bred specially for the quantity or quality of their milk.

Ayrshire. A large brown and white blotched animal, which is able to produce plenty of milk without needing high quality fodder.

Friesian. Tall and robust with variable markings, usually a pattern of black and white, which originated in the Netherlands. Friesians are famous for their generous milk production. They hold all the world records for sheer quantity of milk and butterfat: the record is 42,805 lb (19,262 kg) of milk (4,280 gall/19,454 lt), plus 1,246·4 lb (560·9 kg) of butterfat per year.

Jersey. This breed are kept on good pasture-land as producers of high quality milk rather than large quantities. The milk is very fatty and Jersey cows thus hold the records for buttermilk production.

Guernsey. Fawn or brown and white cattle developed in the Channel Islands. They are hardy and adaptable and can be used for quality production under severe conditions. FAMILY: Bovidae, ORDER: Artiodactyla, CLASS: Mammalia.

Above: Chartley bull, ancient Park cattle.

Below: Highland x Hereford cow.

CENTIPEDES, swift-moving invertebrate predators with a long, thin segmented body, each segment bearing a single pair of legs. The first pair of legs are modified into a pair of robust pincer-like claws which meet horizontally beneath the head. The head carries a pair of thread-like antennae and three pairs of jaws, the mandibles and two pairs of maxillae. CLASS: Chilopoda, PHYLUM: Arthropoda.

CHAFFINCH *Fringilla coelebs*, a bird about 6 in (16 cm) long and weighing around 1 oz (20–30 gm). The male has a bluish head, pink breast, chestnut back and green rump, with white on the wings and tail, while the female is mainly a pale greenish-brown, also with white on the wings and tail. The chaffinch extends over most of Europe and is spreading east into Siberia. It breeds anywhere where there are trees, including deciduous and coniferous woods, parks, hedges and gardens. The compact nest is made of moss and lichens and lined with hair; and the eggs, which number three or four, are blue-grey with purple-brown spots. In summer the bird feeds largely on caterpillars from trees and in winter on seeds from farmland, including spilled grain and weed seeds. Over most of its range, it is migratory, but the females tend to move farther than the males. The Latin name *coelebs* (bachelor), which Linnaeus gave to the chaffinch, was inspired by the fact that on the whole males remained to winter in his homeland (Sweden).

The Canary Islands chaffinch, *F. teydea* is also known simply as chaffinch. FAMILY: Fringillidae, ORDER: Passeriformes, CLASS: Aves.

CHALCID WASPS, sometimes called Chalcid flies, include some of the smallest of all insects with bodies only 0·25 mm in length. Chalcids can be distinguished from typical wasps, for their body has no "waist' between the thorax and abdomen. Another distinguishing character of the chalcids can be found in the structure of the hindlegs, in which the femur is greatly enlarged and, as a rule, very conspicuous. Many chalcids lay their eggs in the eggs of other insects and when the larval wasp hatches it eats the tissues of its host. In this way, these wasps can inflict heavy mortality on insect pests. FAMILY: Chalcididae, ORDER: Hymenoptera, CLASS: Insecta, PHYLUM: Arthropoda.

CHAMELEONS, Old World lizards especially noted for their adaptation to life in the branches of trees and shrubs. There are 90 species; the genus *Chamaeleo* alone has about 70 species. Most chameleon species are to be found in tropical Africa and Madagascar. The Common chameleon *C. chamaeleon* is the most northern representative of the family and can be found in North Africa, southern Spain and Portugal, Malta, Krete in the north of the Arabian peninsula and in India and Ceylon. Most chameleons are about 6–12 in (15–30 cm) long, but there are some just a few centimetres in length

Front view of a chameleon: one eye is looking forwards, the other backwards.

(e.g. species of *Brookesia*) and some giants that reportedly reached a length of 32 in (80 cm).

The chameleon's body is usually flattened from side to side; the head often has a showy crest, horns or skinfolds. The eyes can be moved independently. The chameleon's tongue is built like a catapult with a club-like tip and can be shot out at high speed to a length greater than the chameleon's body. The prey is hit by the tip of the tongue, glued to it and drawn back to the mouth at the same speed. Small to medium-sized chameleons will catch mainly insects; the large ones will also capture other lizards, small mammals and birds.

While at rest the muscular tongue is curled around the tongue bone. The circular muscles at the back end of the tongue contract violently, the longitudinal muscles relax and the tongue shoots out of the mouth under the resulting pressure, rather as one would shoot an orange pip by squeezing it with the fingertips. It is withdrawn through the contraction of the longitudinal muscles.

The limbs of a chameleon are long, thin and carry the body high. The toes are united into two opposing bundles on each foot: two toes on the outside and three on the inside on the front feet and three on the outside and two on the inside on the hind feet. This has changed each foot into a pair of clasping tongs that enable the chameleon to get a firm grip on a perch. In addition the species of *Chamaeleo* have a prehensile tail.

The chameleon's ability to change colour is well known but it cannot always match its surroundings. The body colouration of the day-active arboreal chameleons is green or bark-coloured. Very often, however, colouration and markings play a part in disputes with another member of the same species. A surprising number of chameleons have a pale whitish sleeping colouration and with the help of a torch can easily be found in the dark foliage. Male and sometimes also female chameleons hold territories which they will defend jealously against others. When the

two rivals are at viewing distance they threaten each other by displaying their brilliant colours, always showing the side of the inflated body to the enemy in order to look more impressive. Sometimes the mouth is opened wide to show the contrasting colouration of the mucous membrane.

Most chameleons lay eggs which the female deposits in holes in the ground which she has previously dug herself. Some species, mainly in southern Africa are viviparous. FAMILY: Chamaeleonidae, ORDER: Squamata, CLASS: Reptilia.

CHAMOIS *Rupicapra rupicapra*, one of the 'goat-antelopes', mountain-living and closely related to the goats; famous for its agility. 30–32 in (75–80 cm) high, both sexes are of approximately equal size. Most individuals weigh 77–100 lb (35–45 kg), but members of the largest race, from the Carpathians, may weigh as much as 130 lb (60 kg). Chamois have stiff coarse hair, fawn or brown in summer and dark, nearly black, in winter; there is a black dorsal stripe and flank-band and the legs are black; the under-parts are white and so is the face, except for a thick black line from the base of the horns through the eye to the muzzle. The hoof pad is somewhat elastic, giving the animal an enviable sure-footedness. The horns are upright, thin and hooked back at the tip.

Chamois are found on all the major mountain-ranges of Europe and Asia Minor. They live in herds of 15–30, consisting of females and young; the males are solitary for most of the year, some being attached to the herds, following slowly behind as the herd moves along, single file. In the rutting season, August to October, big bisexual herds are formed and the actual rut takes place at the end of October and beginning of November, when the males fight for possession of harems. The male has glands behind the horns, which enlarge in the rutting season. Gestation is from 153 to 210 days. In the Caucasus the young, usually single but sometimes two or three, are born in early or mid-May; in the Alps, one month later. Females mature at two years, males at three to four. A chamois may live as long as 22 years. They have been recorded as high as 15,430 ft (4,750 m) on Mt. Blanc. In winter they descend to feed on pine shoots and moss in the forest. Each herd has a sentinel, which whistles and stamps when alarmed. FAMILY: Bovidae, ORDER: Artiodactyla, CLASS: Mammalia.

CHEECHAK *Hemidactylus frenatus*, or Common house gecko. It gets its name from the call it makes when prowling about at night for food. It prefers native huts and some city buildings as its habitat. Its origin was mainland Asia, but by hitching a ride on boats and in cargo, it has spread to most of the Pacific Islands. In the daytime, the

Cheese mites

cheechak is dark brown to nearly black as it hides in crevices. At night, when on the prowl, it becomes almost ghostly white. FAMILY: Gekkonidae, ORDER: Squamata, CLASS: Reptilia.

CHEESE MITES, tiny animals related to spiders, living on cheese, its high content of fat and protein, and the moulds, on ripe cheese, being attractive to mites, which are detritus feeders. CLASS: Arachnida, PHYLUM: Arthropoda.

CHEETAH *Acinonyx jubatus,* shows many dog-like characteristics not found in other cats. It has long legs and is built for great turns of speed, from which it gets the reputation of being the fastest mammal. There are two records of a cheetah attaining 71 mph (114 kph). The feet are similar in construction to the dog: they have hard pads with sharp edges, rather than the soft elastic pads found in the rest of the cats. These pads, and the blunt, non-retractile claws give this very fast moving animal the additional grip required for sudden stops and turns. The dew claws, more developed than in other cats, play a big part in gripping prey. The head is small in comparison to the rest of the body and the eyes are set high upon it which helps the animal when peering over low cover and hillocks. The ears are small and flattened, reducing the silhouette still further. The nasal passages are larger than in the other cats to allow the intake of the extra oxygen required for the final sprint to the prey.

The cheetah is further distinguished by its very distinctive markings. The ground colour of the coat is a reddish shade of yellow and is broken by spots of solid black. The face is marked by the very noticeable 'tear stripes' running from the corner of the eyes down the sides of the nose. There is another form, called the King cheetah, but this appears to be no more than a recurrent mutation. The male measures 7 ft (2·1 m) overall, of which the tail, a very effective aid to turning, measures 2½ ft (0·8 m). The height at the shoulder is about 2 ft 9 in (0·83 m) and the total weight is about 130 lb (59 kg). The female is usually about three quarters of the size and weight of the male.

Cheetahs range from Algeria and Morocco to the Transvaal, through Egypt, Ethiopia, Arabia, Syria, Persia and India, and throughout much of its range it has been captured and trained as a hunting leopard, which is one of its names. When trained, it is used in much the same way as a coursing greyhound. In the wild, the cheetah will hunt either with a partner, or as a member of a group and it lives mainly on the smaller antelopes or the young of some of the larger species, although it has been observed taking quite small mammals. When the kill has been made, the cheetah eats the heart and kidneys first, and it also drinks the blood. After that the head

A baby chimpanzee stays with its mother for a long time but also learns to play.

is eaten and only then is the muscle meat attacked. It is not usual for a cheetah to return to a kill after the first feed. This difference in feeding habits is reflected in the teeth which are neither as large, nor as sharp as those of the leopard.

There appears to be no regular breeding season, and two to four kittens may arrive at any time of the year. At birth, the coat is a blue grey colour on the back and the rest of the animal is brown with dark spots. The eyes open after about two weeks. The kittens, unlike the adults, are good climbers.

The African race is still fairly plentiful, although not as widespread as it used to be, but the Asian race is in danger of extinction. FAMILY: Felidae, ORDER: Carnivora, CLASS: Mammalia.

CHIMAERAS, ratfishes or rabbitfishes, cartilaginous fishes related to sharks. They are characterized by the presence of a curious appendage or 'clasper' on the head in front of the eyes. It is found only in males. Like sharks, these fishes have a skeleton of cartilage and the males have one pair of claspers or more modified from the pelvic fins which are used for internal fertilization. They differ from sharks, however, in that the gill openings are covered by an operculum (resembling the gill cover of bony fishes). The majority of species belong to the genera *Chimaera* and *Hydrolagus* in which the snout is fairly blunt, the mouth ventral, the tail elongated and rat-like, and the first dorsal fin provided with a serrated spine capable of injecting a painful venom into wounds. *Chimaera monstrosa* is found along European shores and in the Mediterranean and grows to a length of 5 ft (1·5 m). Its scientific name

recalls the chimaera of Greek myth. The most monstrous of all the chimaeras is *Callorhinchus* in which the snout is not only long but curls down and back towards the mouth. FAMILIES: Chimaeridae, Rhinochimaeridae, Callorhinchidae, ORDER: Chimaeriformes, SUB-CLASS: Bradyodonti, CLASS: Chondrichthyes.

CHIMPANZEE *Pan troglodytes.* Adult chimpanzees weigh 80–110 lb (36–50 kg); males are larger than females. The long sparse hair is black and the skin changes from flesh-colour in juveniles to bronze then black in adults. The face is long and prognathous and the lips thin and mobile. The brow ridges are marked and the ears are very large, often remaining light coloured long after the face has gone black. Nearly half their time is spent on the ground, walking quadrupedally on the backs of their knuckles, and when they go into the trees they climb and move with all four limbs equally, as often as swinging from their arms alone.

Chimpanzees are found throughout the African lowland forest belt, from Senegal in the west to Uganda and Tanzania. They ascend mountains to quite high altitudes, reaching 7,000 ft (2,100 m) in the Itombwe Mts (Congo) and 11,000 ft (3,300 m) on Mt Ruwenzori.

Throughout their wide range, there is only one species of chimpanzee, *Pan troglodytes,* but there are four well-marked subspecies, which differ in size, colour, head shape and development.

Chimpanzees are highly promiscuous. Females in oestrus develop huge pink genital swellings which serve as signals to males; a female at the height of oestrus may be served by half a dozen males in fairly rapid succession. The female's sexual cycle lasts 35 days; gestation is 225 days. An infant chimpanzee is carried on its mother's belly at first, clinging tight. Sometimes she places the infant on her back. Mothers and infants continue to associate even after the young have become independent, and up to a year after birth of a second infant. The juveniles continue to build their nests near the mother's but at this stage they are associating more with their peers, playing amongst themselves—wrestling, chasing and swinging around: as they play they make little panting noises . . . laughter?

Chimpanzees feed mainly on fruit, but also eat leaves, nuts, bark, ants, termites and even meat. They have been observed co-operatively stalking and killing prey, such as Colobus monkeys or young antelope, killing the prey by swinging it high and slamming it on the ground. They live in large societies of as many as 60 or 80 individuals, occupying a home range of 2·6 per sq mile to 10 per sq mile (2·7 km²). The whole society splits up into smaller bands of varying size during daily movement when they go around in four types of association: adult bisexual bands, all-male bands, 'nursery groups' (females with their young) and mixed bands. Males sometimes move around on their own. The discovery by one of the wandering bands of a prolific food source is announced with hooting, screaming and drumming on trees, bringing other members of the local group to the spot.

At times when there is a sudden abundance of insects, such as termites, the chimpanzees spend a long time feeding on them .At other times they will break off a twig or grass stem, removing the side twigs to straighten it, and push it into a termite mound; termites crawl all over it, and the chimp then pulls it out and eats the termites.

At night chimpanzees make nests in the trees wherever they happen to be. These are made by bringing together, interlacing and patting down branches to make a platform with a rim, in which the chimpanzee lies with his legs drawn up and goes to sleep. The nests take only one to five minutes to make; usually a new one is made each night. All adults and youngsters over about three years of age make separate nests, but an infant sleeps with its mother. Nests are always built high in the trees.

Chimpanzees are thoroughly noisy: they call loudly throughout the day and even sometimes during the night. Their calls can carry up to two miles, and the drumming that accompanies it carries even farther. When two groups meet, especially if there is a mature male in each, there is loud calling, increasing in intensity with the number of males in each group; not only calling, but drumming, shaking of branches and slapping the ground. When a group reaches a fruiting tree, it calls for ten minutes or more, and other bands respond by calling back and

moving towards the source of the calls. Nesting, and waking up in the morning, are the occasions for vocal celebration, especially if a large group is nesting together.

Within the local society there are no leaders and there is very little trace of the 'rank order' seen in monkey societies. Quarrels, which last only a few seconds and involve stamping and branch shaking as a kind of threat, often break out. Sudden attacks, never serious, may occur. When two individuals meet after a separation, there is some form of greeting ceremony between them: the subordinate animal will approach the dominant one, a male, and touch the top of his head, his shoulder, thigh, groin or genitals; two males may greet each other by standing up with one arm held high, one running towards the other. They then fling their arms round each other.

Psychological tests have indicated a high level of intelligence, and experts have sometimes been puzzled why this should be so, since the species does not appear to use its exceptional mental powers much in the wild. FAMILY: Pongidae (or Hominidae), ORDER: Primates, CLASS: Mammalia.

CHINCHILLA *Chinchilla laniger*, a rodent; rabbit-like in appearance but with a bushy tail and a body 10 in (25 cm) long. It is best known for its long, soft, bluish-grey fur.

Wild chinchillas have been hunted almost to extinction since the value of their pelts was first appreciated in the 18th century. The South American governments saved the species from complete extinction by banning their hunting and export in the early 1900's. Later, government farms were set up and, eventually, successful chinchilla farms were established outside South America, for example in California. As a result the price of chinchilla fur dropped sufficiently to protect the remaining wild populations. In their natural habitat on the Andes the only food available is coarse grass and herbs. Chinchillas live a communal life among rocks or in burrows in the mountains. Although nocturnal they will bask in the morning and evening sun. Pairs mate for life. FAMILY: Chinchillidae, ORDER: Rodentia, CLASS: Mammalia.

CHINESE WATER DEER *Hydropotes inermis*, of eastern and central China and Korea, inhabits reed swamps and grasslands close to rivers. It stands 21 in (about 52 cm) at the shoulder, has an extremely short tail and a summer coat of reddish brown which, as winter advances, becomes a dull brown faintly flecked with grey. Twins and triplets are common and up to five or six fawns have been recorded. When fighting, the bucks often make a 'chittering noise', perhaps produced by clicking the tusks. FAMILY: Cervidae, ORDER: Artiodactyla, CLASS: Mammalia.

CHITAL *Axis axis*, or Spotted deer of India, standing 36 in (91 cm) at the shoulder, rufous brown profusely covered with white spots in winter and summer. Chital are comparatively common and herds of 100 or more can be seen. This deer has been successfully introduced to other parts of the world including the Hawaiian Islands.

Related to it is the Hog deer or para *A. porcinus* of southern Asia, slightly smaller than the chital.

Two other related species are the bawean or Kuhl's deer *A. kuhlii*, restricted to Bawean Island in the Java Sea and the Kalamian deer *A. kalamianensis*, restricted to the Kalamian group of islands in the Philippines. FAMILY: Cervidae, ORDER: Artiodactyla, CLASS: Mammalia.

CHITONS, about 600 species of primitive marine molluscs, deriving their name from the Greek word for a coat of mail, as the shell is formed from eight overlapping plates. They are generally oval in shape, mostly rather small, between $\frac{1}{2}$–2 in (1·5–5 cm) long, although some may reach 13 in (34 cm). The eight overlapping shell plates run along the centre of the back, surrounded by a fleshy girdle of tough, scaly or bristly mantle tissue, which secretes the shell.

Between foot and mantle is a deep groove, the mantle cavity, which contains the gills of which there are between six and 88 pairs. Water currents flow over the head into the mantle cavity, carrying oxygen to the gills and passing backwards to carry away excretory and genital products. The head, with the mouth on the ventral surface, is not well developed and has neither eyes nor tentacles, though its posterior corners may be extended into sensory processes. Unspecialized sensory cells are scattered all over the body. There may be large numbers of these, for example a total of about 11,500 in *Acanthopleura echinata* concentrated at the anterior end.

Chitons are world-wide with particularly large numbers on the North American shores of the Pacific and in Australia, especially in intertidal regions where they cling tightly to rocks.

Chitons move slowly, by muscular waves passing along the foot from front to back. If detached from a rock, they roll up protecting the ventral surface, like a woodlouse. Most chitons avoid light and only move at night.

Underside of a chiton showing the foot.

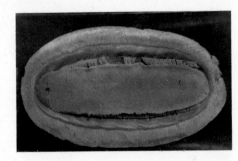

Choughs

They are herbivorous, feeding by rasping any small plant or animal growth from the surface of the rocks with the long radula. ORDER: Chitonida, CLASS: Polyplacophora, PHYLUM: Mollusca.

CHOUGHS, black, crow-like birds of Europe and Asia or Australia. In Europe and Asia there are two species of chough of the crow family, Corvidae; in Australia there is one species of chough in the mud-nest building family, Grallinidae.

The Cornish chough, *Pyrrhocorax pyrrhocorax*, was formerly much more common. Apart from its rarity in the Alps, its European distribution is the same as that of the Alpine chough *P. graculus*, that is the mountainous regions from the Iberian Peninsula and the Atlas in the west to China in the east.

Both species are about 15 in (38 cm) long and have red legs, but the bill of the chough is long, curved and red, while that of the Alpine chough is shorter, less curved and yellow. Both are aerial experts able to take full advantage of the updraughts and other air movements so typical of their habitat. They breed in cliffs, caves and rock crevices (including those in large stone buildings) and feed on insects and other invertebrates.

The Australian bird, also called chough, is the White-winged chough *Corcorax melanorhampus*, 17–18 in (43–45 cm) long. Its English name derives from its similarity to the European choughs—black plumage (but with a white patch on the wing) and strong, though slender decurved bill. FAMILIES: Corvidae and Grallinidae respectively, ORDER: Passeriformes, CLASS: Aves.

CHUCKWALLA *Sauromalus obesus,* one of the iguanas, New World equivalents of the Old World lizards. The chuckwalla is a heavy-bodied reptile which attains a length of 1½ ft (46 cm). Its robust head, powerful legs, coat of small scales and long tail are typical of many iguanas. The chuckwalla feeds on the flowers and fruits of cacti living in desert areas of the southwestern United States, Northern Mexico and Lower California. It can inflate its lungs so that the body becomes almost globular. When threatened, it runs into a rock crevice, inflates itself and is virtually impossible to remove by force. FAMILY: Iguanidae, ORDER: Squamata, CLASS: Reptilia.

CICADAS, large plant sucking insects well known for their shrill monotonous song. They are characterized by three bead-like simple eyes, ocelli, between the main eyes and two pairs of membranous wings.

There are 1,500 known species, most of which live in the warmer regions of the world, only one *Cicadetta montana* occurring in Britain, being extremely local in the New Forest.

One of the best known species is the Periodical cicada or 17-year locust *Magicicada septendecim*, of the United States, remarkable for the long time required for development. The adults are about 1–1½ in (25–40 mm) long. The female lays eggs in slits she makes in the branches of trees. The young emerge in about six weeks, drop to the ground and bury themselves. They then live below the surface, sucking sap from the fine roots of trees. They come to the surface again after 13 or 17 years.

Cicadas are famous for their sound-producing powers, the shrill noise the males make in tropical forest being almost deafening. The sound-producing organs consist of a pair of shell-like drums at the base of the abdomen, vibrated by the action of powerful muscles, the sound produced varying greatly in note and intensity in different species. The function is almost certainly to attract females. FAMILY: Cicadidae, SUB-ORDER: Homoptera, ORDER: Hemiptera, CLASS: Insecta, PHYLUM: Arthropoda.

CICHLIDS, perch-like fishes found chiefly in freshwaters (rarely brackish waters) in Africa and South America, but with one genus in India and Ceylon. There are over 600 species and more are being discovered every year. Cichlids have a fairly deep and compressed body, a single long dorsal fin (the first part having spines) and a shorter anal fin beginning with one spine or more. The body bears fairly large scales which in some genera are smooth (cycloid) but in others are rough-edged (ctenoid). The cichlids have a single nostril on each side.

Cichlids are usually found in lakes or sluggish waters although some live in rivers and streams. Many are carnivorous and all have a set of teeth in the throat, the pharyngeal teeth. In those that feed on fishes or large invertebrates, the pharyngeal teeth are fairly large and coarse, but in filter-feeders that live on algae or other small organisms, the teeth are fine and close-set. In mollusc-eaters, the teeth form flat pads for crushing and grinding.

In the nest-building forms, such as the species of *Tilapia*, the male usually excavates a circular hollow in the sandy or muddy bottom and goes through a fairly elaborate display of fin movements and swimming antics when a female arrives. When the female has deposited the eggs the male sheds its sperm and in the mouth-brooding species the female (occasionally the male) sucks the eggs into her mouth where they remain for the incubation period and even after they hatch the fry remain there until they are able to fend for themselves. In other species the eggs may stay where they are laid or be scooped up and deposited at another site where they are aerated by fanning movements of the fins by one or both parents.

The angelfishes (*Pterophyllum* sp.) from the Amazon are graceful, deep-bodied fishes with elongated fins.

The Fire-mouth cichlid *Cichlasoma meeki* from Central America grows to about 6 in (15 cm) and takes its name from the brilliant red colour of the inside of the mouth. The genus *Cichlasoma* contains many South

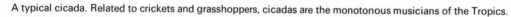

A typical cicada. Related to crickets and grasshoppers, cicadas are the monotonous musicians of the Tropics.

American species of interest to the aquarist, including the Jack Dempsey *C. biocellatum*, the Flag cichlid *C. festivum*, the Chameleon cichlid *C. facetum* (which shows remarkable colour changes), the Banded cichlid *C. severum*, and Cutter's cichlid *C. cutteri* notable for having eggs that have stalks. Other South American cichlids are the discusfish and the acaras.

The Orange chromide *Etroplus maculatus* of India and Ceylon grows to about 3 in (8 cm) in length and has a gold to grey body with rows of red spots. As in the discusfish, the young often attach themselves to the body of the parent.

The African genus *Haplochromis* provides some insight into the speed at which evolution has occurred. Where it has been possible to date the age of a lake the time taken for species endemic to that lake to evolve is thus known. One case is Lake Nabugabo in Uganda, a small arm of Lake Victoria that was cut off from the main lake only 4,000 years ago. Of the seven species of *Haplochromis* in Lake Nabugabo, five are endemic to the lake and must therefore have evolved, not in millions of years, but in only a few thousand.

The jewelfish *Hemichromis bimaculata* is one of the most colourful of African cichlids. The underparts are a brilliant red, the top of the head and the back are olive green with a red sheen and there are rows of blue spots between dark bars on the flanks. The dorsal fin is of two shades of red separated by brilliant blue spots. FAMILY: Cichlidae, ORDER: Perciformes, CLASS: Pisces.

CIVETS, related to mongooses and genets, are long-bodied with long tails and sharp muzzles. They have ten more teeth than the cats and the face is generally longer. In habits and pattern of coat, however, they resemble the small cats. They are generally striped or spotted over a solid ground colour and the claws are sometimes retractile. They differ from the cats in having a fifth toe on the hindfeet. They have large musk glands, from which a substance known as 'civet' has been extracted from earliest times and used as a base for perfume and in some forms of medicine.

Civets are found in tropical Asia and Africa. The African civet *Civettictis civetta*, of Africa south of the Sahara, is the best-known. It is stout-bodied with short legs, 30 in (76 cm) head and body with 18 in (46 cm) of tail. It weighs 15–24 lb (6·8–10·8 kg). The fur is coarse with a ground colour of ash grey, broken by black spots and stripes. The tail is ringed black and white. The Large Indian civet *Viverra zibetha* of India, Burma and southern China, is very similar in size and appearance, except for the ridge of erectile hairs down the spine, the distinctive black and white throat markings and its thick and soft fur. The Small Indian civet *Viverricula indica*, which ranges through southern China

to Ceylon and to Bali in the Malayan Archipelago, is similar but smaller.

All three are usually solitary and nocturnal and very seldom seen as they keep in dense cover. They rest by day in abandoned burrows and come out to hunt at night. They can climb and swim well. Their food is mainly animal including insects, crabs, frogs, snakes and birds and their eggs. The African civet is said to assist reafforestation. Although a carnivore it also eats a large amount of fruit and berries, the seeds from which are passed undigested in the excreta. It has, however, a bad reputation for its liking for young domestic stock and poultry and its marked preference for maize.

The six species of Palm civets in southern Asia and one in Africa differ from true civets in anatomical details. Their teeth are weaker and most species have naked soles and sharp curved claws which aid their tree climbing. One of the best-known is the Common Indian palm civet or Toddy cat *Paradoxurus hermaphroditus*, ranging from Ceylon and India through southern China and Southeast Asia to the Philippines. It is just over 4 ft (1·2 m) total length of which about a half is tail. The fur is grey to brown broken by dark stripes on the back, spots on the flanks and white patches on the head. It uses the obnoxious secretion from its anal gland as a form of defence in the same way as skunks. The Toddy cat often makes its home near houses, in the gardens or in the thatched roofs. It gets its name from its fondness for fermenting palm sap the local people collect for winemaking. The African palm civet *Nandinia binotata*, or Two-spotted civet, ranges from Senegal to the Sudan and southwards to Rhodesia and Angola. Its fur is grey to brown tinged with buff or chestnut with lighter underparts, and two large white indistinct spots on the shoulders. Palm civets usually have two to four young in a litter born in a hollow tree or among rocks. FAMILY: Viverridae, ORDER: Carnivora, CLASS: Mammalia.

CLAWED FROG *Xenopus laevis*, a purely aquatic frog, 5 in (12·5 cm) long, limited to southern Africa where it is found in pools or streams that dry up in summer causing the animals to aestivate. Claws on the inner three toes of each foot give this frog its common name. The Clawed frog is best known to doctors as the 'pregnancy frog' as it was once used extensively to test suspected pregnancy in women. FAMILY: Pipidae, ORDER: Anura, CLASS: Amphibia.

CLICK BEETLES, or skipjacks, elongated dull brown insects having the ability to spring upwards when placed on their back. The leap, accompanied by a noticeable click, is achieved by a sudden movement of the joint between the first and second segments of the thorax. This behaviour allows the beetle to right itself when it falls on its back and also to

A Click beetle falling on its back can right itself with a jackknife leap.

escape some of its enemies. Their larvae, the familiar wire-worm, are among the most destructive agricultural pests. FAMILY: Elateridae, ORDER: Coleoptera, CLASS: Insecta, PHYLUM: Arthropoda.

CLIMBING PERCH *Anabas testudinosus*, a labyrinthfish reputedly able to climb trees and suck their juices. It is found in Southeast Asia and the first specimen to be seen by someone from the West, at the end of the 18th century, was found in a crack in a tree. Recent research has shown, however, that these fishes arrive in the trees after being dropped struggling by birds. The Climbing perch has an accessory breathing organ, a series of plates in the upper part of the gill chamber richly supplied with blood vessels. It frequently moves from one pool to another and it is probably during these overland journeys that it is seized by birds and later dropped. The gill covers are used as an extra pair of 'legs' while it is moving overland. They are spiny and are spread out to anchor the fish while the pectoral fins and tail push forward. The Climbing perch can survive out of water for some time and is carried about by local people as a fresh fish supply. FAMILY: Anabantidae, ORDER: Perciformes, CLASS: Pisces.

CLOTHES MOTHS, term including several species of small brown moths, ½ in (1·5 cm) or a little more in wing-span, which appear periodically in houses, the most important is *Tineola bisselliella*. They are called Clothes moths because their whitish larvae, up to ½ in (1·5 cm) long with pale brown heads, attack woollen fabrics, such as clothes, carpets and blankets. In a survey carried out in Britain in 1948 a quarter of the houses investigated had harboured Clothes moths in the previous few months and loss through moth damage was estimated at £1,500,000.

Clothes moth larvae are unusual in being able to digest keratin, the very resistant protein of hair and wool, but this alone is not adequate for their survival and most infestations of clothes moths begin in parts which are soiled with sweat or urine. The soiling

Clownfishes

apparently adds traces of essential substances to the diet. But damage far exceeds the amount eaten because the larvae tend to bite through strands of wool, take a few bites, and then move on elsewhere. Very often they spin tunnels of silk over themselves and construct cases in which to moult and pupate. These are made of fragments of wool bound with silk.

Adult Clothes moths cannot feed and live little more than a week. The males fly fairly readily, but the females mostly move by running from place to place. They may lay up to 100 tiny white eggs which hatch in about a month. FAMILY: Tinaeidae, ORDER: Lepidoptera, CLASS: Insecta, PHYLUM: Arthropoda.

CLOWNFISHES, small damselfishes of the Indo-Pacific region which have a remarkable association with species of Sea anemone and for this reason are often called anemonefishes. About 12 species are known, all very brightly coloured. *Amphiprion percula* grows to a few inches and has a bright orange body with three intensely white vertical bars, the fins being edged in black. Similar patterns are found in the other species. They spend their lives amongst the waving tentacles of large Sea anemones, which eat fish caught by means of the many hundreds of thousands of stinging cells along the tentacles, and the question arises how the clownfish manages to escape being stung. At first it was thought that the clownfish was agile enough to avoid the tentacles, but observation of the Australian clownfish *Stoichactis* has shown that these fishes actually rub against the tentacles to encourage the Sea anemone to open. When inside, the fish often rests with its head poking out of the Sea anemone's mouth. If danger threatens, it dives back into the Sea anemone and remains there even if the latter is removed from the water.

If the clownfish is deprived of its host it usually falls an easy prey to predators. It is difficult to see what the anemone gains from this curious association since the fish not only takes shelter but may feed on the tentacles and on any food that the anemone traps. The anemone can live quite well without its guest but one species, *Amphiprion polymnus*, feeds the anemone by placing on its tentacles pieces of food from the sea floor. FAMILY: Pomacentridae, ORDER: Perciformes, CLASS: Pisces.

COALFISH *Pollachius virens*, also known as the coley or saithe, a cod-like fish found from the Arctic to the Mediterranean. It resembles the cod but has only a rudimentary barbel under the chin, no speckling on the body and a dark green or almost black upper surface. It is a fairly deep-water fish usually found at 300–600 ft (100–200 m). One of the largest rod-caught specimens weighed nearly 24 lb (11 kg). FAMILY: Gadidae, ORDER: Gadiformes, CLASS: Pisces.

The coati usually holds its tail erect when walking, as a signal to its fellows.

COATI, three species of raccoon-like animals extending from Oklahoma through South America. The most conspicuous features of the coati are its long, ringed tail which is carried erect and the thin muzzle with the extremely mobile nose. The colour ranges from red to black-brown. The males are larger than the females, measuring 38·6–47·2 in (98–120 cm), the tail accounting for at least half the total length. Weights vary between 12 lb (5·5 kg) to 23 lb (10·4 kg). Black or brown markings are present on the face with white patches below the eyes. The chin and chest may be light buff or whitish and the coarse fur of the back has a reddish brown hue. Coatis are diurnal and social, living in bands of 5–30 individuals. During the day they forage on the jungle floor, softly grunting to each other, pausing frequently to investigate logs or vegetation. Although small invertebrates nosed out of the leaf litter are their main food items, coatis have powerful claws and dig out lizards, tarantulas and crabs. Should one of them become suddenly frightened and bark or chitter, all the others immediately scamper up the nearest tree. At sunset, the group climbs into its roosting tree and makeshift nests of lianas and leaves are used. After a ten week gestation, the female leaves the troop and three to five young are born in a tree-nest where they remain for five weeks. The eyes and ears open a week later and the cubs then begin to walk clumsily and hold their tails erect. They descend and join the band at six weeks, keeping close to their mother. When the males reach sexual maturity two years later, they leave the band and become solitary during the non-breeding season. FAMILY: Procyonidae, ORDER: Carnivora, CLASS: Mammalia.

COBRAS, snakes capable of spreading a 'hood' when alarmed: the long anterior ribs swing upward and forward, stretching the skin like the fabric of an umbrella.

The true cobras may reach 8–9 ft (c. 260 cm) in length. Their bodies are covered with smooth scales which may be dull as in the Egyptian cobra, or very shiny as in the Forest cobra. The head is broad and flat and the hollow fangs are set well forward in the upper jaw.

The Egyptian cobra *Naja haje* appears on ancient Egyptian royal headdresses, rearing up with hood spread. It has a wide distribution in Africa and Arabia, but is absent from rain-forest and desert regions. It reaches a length of over 8 ft (2·4 m) and is a relatively thick and heavy snake. It is usually brown to black, often with lighter speckling.

The Cape cobra *Naja nivea* is restricted to South Africa, the Kalahari and South West Africa. It may be bright yellow, golden-brown or speckled yellow and brown.

The Forest cobra *Naja melanoleuca* occurs in evergreen forests of West, central and southeastern Africa, reaching its southern limit in Zululand. It reaches 9 ft (2·7 m), but it is more slender than the Egyptian cobra. It may be black or yellow-brown, heavily speckled with black, while a banded variety is found in West Africa.

The 8 ft (2·4 m) Black-necked spitting cobra *Naja nigricollis* occurs in the savannah regions bordering the rain-forests from West Africa to the Western Cape Province. Adults are usually uniform black above. There is a single broad black band on the throat.

The Mozambique spitting cobra *Naja mossambica* of southeastern Africa rarely exceeds 5 ft (1·5 m) in length and is pale grey to olive above and salmon-pink below, with a series of irregular black bands and blotches on the throat. A subspecies *N. m. pallida*, from southern Egypt to north Kenya is pink with one or two black bands on the neck.

A cobra makes a great show to intimidate by spreading its hood.

The Indian cobra *Naja naja* has a wide range from West Pakistan east to southern China and the Philippines. The body is usually brown, often with narrow light rings. On the back of the neck is often a dark-edged pale marking that may take the form of a pair of spectacles or a dark-centred ring.

Other cobras include the King cobra, the ringhals and the Water cobras *Boulengerina* of central Africa.

Female cobras lay between eight and 25 eggs in a hole. The newly hatched young are about 10 in (25 cm) in length.

Cobras are active at night. During the day a cobra may often be found basking in the sun close to its refuge, which may be a termitarium, rodent burrow or a rock crevice. Cobras' diets include rodents, birds and their eggs, lizards, other snakes, amphibians, and fishes, even locusts are occasionally devoured. Cobras are notorious poultry raiders, taking eggs and young birds.

A cobra will usually try to escape when disturbed by man, but if surprised or cornered, it will raise its head and neck, at the same time spreading the hood. If approached it will strike, or may even glide forward to attack. When a cobra bites successfully, it will often hang on and chew, injecting large quantities of venom. A full bite will cause death in man in about six hours, respiratory failure being the usual cause of death.

Four species of cobra spray venom into the eyes of an enemy, causing temporary blindness. 'Spitting cobras' are the Black-necked and Mozambique cobras, the ringhals and the Southeast Asian populations of the Indian cobra. FAMILY: Elapidae, ORDER: Squamata, CLASS: Reptilia.

COCKATOOS, medium-sized to large parrots, mostly short-tailed with white, grey or black plumage. They are found from the Philippines to Australia and Tasmania, some species being commonly kept in captivity. Apart from anatomical characters, cockatoos have no features to distinguish them from other parrots, but the combination of black, grey or white colouring, large size, square-ended tail and robust build serve to distinguish most of them.

There are 17 species. The Palm cockatoo *Probosciger aterrimus*, a large, short-tailed parrot with dark grey plumage, and a crest of long feathers on the nape, is a bird of woodland and jungle on the Cape York peninsula of Australia and in the New Guinea region. It has a huge, curved bill which enables it to crack open palm nuts.

The four Black cockatoos *Calyptorhynchus* are rather similar and long-tailed. They are found in different parts of Australia, distinguished from each other in the shape of the bill and the colour of the tail. Except for the tail, the males of all species are completely black, but the females have narrow bars of pale yellow on their underparts. They are

Sulphur-crested cockatoo *Cacatua galerita*, best known of the cockatoos.

found in lightly wooded country, often in flocks. They feed on seeds, nuts, and insect grubs excavated from dead wood.

The Gang-gang cockatoo *Callocephalon fimbriatum* is found only in wooded areas of eastern Australia. It is medium-sized with a short tail and grey plumage. The male has a crest of red-tipped feathers on the crown and the female has narrow pale yellow bars on its underparts. The bill is very stout.

The 10 species of *Cacatua* are distributed from Tasmania to the Philippines. Most are predominantly white with erectile crests coloured white, yellow, orange, red or pink, and some have large pale yellow patches on the wing linings. The galah *C. roseicapilla* of Australia has grey upperparts, a pale pink cap and bright pink underparts. They are sociable and inhabit open or lightly wooded country. They feed mainly on nuts, fruit, seeds and the roots of low plants. With a few other cockatoos, those of the genus *Cacatua* differ from other parrots in that the eggs are incubated by both sexes rather than the female alone.

The cockatiel *Nymphicus hollandicus* is a distinctive small cockatoo with long, pointed tail feathers, grey plumage, a slender crest and yellow and orange markings on the cheeks, found in the arid interior regions of Australia, mainly in open country with scattered trees, where it feeds predominantly on small seeds collected on the ground. FAMILY: Psittacidae, ORDER: Psittaciformes, CLASS: Aves.

COCKCHAFER, common name for *Melolontha melolontha*, a scarabaeid beetle of economic importance in Europe because its larvae feed on the roots of potatoes, cereals and grasses. The adult is a relatively large beetle, coppery brown in colour, with prominent club-shaped antennae. The wing covers are longitudinally striped and the abdomen terminates behind in a narrow, cylindrical 'tail-piece'. Chafers can often be collected at night in large numbers around lights, particularly in early summer. An alternative name is June bug. FAMILY: Scarabaeidae, ORDER: Coleoptera, CLASS: Insecta, PHYLUM: Arthropoda.

COCKLES, marine bivalve molluscs. The best-known species is the intertidal Common or Edible cockle *Cerastoderma (Cardium) edule*. It lives just beneath the surface of slightly muddy sands, although it often occurs in coarse sands and sometimes also in gravels. The shell is whitish yellow and globular with an obvious ligament and is crossed by 24–28 conspicuous ribs. When covered by the tide the cockle filters plankton from the overlying water, using two very short siphons. When uncovered, however, the cockle retreats to about ¾ in (2 cm) below the surface. Sometimes the population of cockles is so dense that the shells touch one another and growth is inhibited. More usually, a commercially-exploited cockle bed may have several hundred cockles per sq yd (sq m). The method of collection varies. In some areas a

Cockroaches

large rake is used to bring the cockles to the surface, while elsewhere the deposits are passed through a coarse sieve, principally on the lower part of the shore where they are uncovered for a relatively short time. Cockles can also be dredged from a boat when the tide is high.

The fertilized egg of the Common cockle gives rise to a ciliated veliger larva which spends two to three weeks, from March on through the summer, in the plankton before coming to rest. FAMILY: Cardiidae, ORDER: Eulamellibranchia, CLASS: Bivalvia, PHYLUM: Mollusca.

COCKROACHES, largely nocturnal insects commonly thought of as domestic pests but the vast majority of the 3,500 species are independent of the domestic environment. They are found mainly in tropical regions. In temperate countries, they usually occur indoors in places artificially heated. A few species occur naturally in temperate regions and in England there are three species of a small brown cockroach called *Ectobius*. The best known domestic pests are *Periplaneta americana*, *Blatta orientalis*, sometimes known as the Black beetle, and *Blattella germanica*.

Cockroaches were very common during the Carboniferous period, 350–270 million years ago. They have jaws for biting and chewing, legs all rather similar and the thorax weakly armoured and not very well adapted for flying. Apart from *Blatta*, the commoner species have wings but rarely fly, unless it is very hot. The forewings, leathery in appearance, protect the large, delicate hindwings, while a large shield-like plate covers the front part of the body often including the head. Cockroaches typically have very long antennae.

They are fast running insects with soft, almost slippery, bodies which make them difficult and slightly unpleasant to handle and these features, added to the fact that they spoil food and have a peculiar smell, probably account for the general distaste with which they are viewed. Many species will eat almost anything, although some tropical species are wood-eaters.

Their eggs are coated with a secretion as they are laid, which is moulded and hardens into a purse-like structure or ootheca. This protects the eggs, especially from drying out. The young emerging from the eggs escape from the ootheca when it splits open. They look like miniature versions of the adult except they have no wings. ORDER: Dictyoptera, CLASS: Insecta, PHYLUM: Arthropoda.

COCKS OF THE ROCK, bizarre birds of tropical America. The bulk of our knowledge concerns the more common of the two species, the Orange cock of the rock *Rupicola rupicola*, the male of which is bright orange and the female brown. Some 12 in (30 cm)

long, with a short tail and rounded wings, and particularly strong, though short, feet and legs, these birds are unusual in some of their display features. The male has a peculiar crest in the form of a laterally compressed disc-shaped helmet which, during the breeding displays, is erected in a fan which covers the top of the head and bill. The second species, the Peruvian cock of the rock *R. peruviana* is very similar but has red and grey plumage. The cock of the rock spends most of its time near or on the forest floor where the displays are performed in small cleared areas or 'courts'. These are social affairs involving several males, but very little is known about the participation of the females. One unusual feature of the displays is the adoption of immobile trance-like postures which may last several minutes. Prodigious leaps may also be performed.

R. rupicola breeds semi-socially, several nests of mud and vegetable fibres being attached to a rock face within a few yards of each other. Two eggs seem to form the usual clutch. FAMILY: Cotingidae, ORDER: Passeriformes, CLASS: Aves.

Female of the bizarre Cock of the rock.

Common cockle half buried in sand with siphons out, feeding.

CODS, marine fishes typified by the Atlantic cod *Gadus morhua* but also including the coalfish, pollack, haddock, ling, pouting and whiting, as well as the rocklings and the freshwater burbot. These fishes have softrayed fins, either one, two or three dorsal fins and one or two anal fins, the scales are small, the pelvic fins are set far forward in front of the pectoral fin base and under the throat, and there is a large and oily liver. The cod-like fishes are one of the largest and most important of all the commercially exploited groups of fishes.

The Atlantic cod is an olive green to brown with darker spots on the flanks and a silvery belly. It can be recognized by the small barbel under the chin, the pointed snout, the white lateral line and the presence of three dorsal fins. Large cod can reach 5 ft (1·5 m) in length and weigh up to 210 lb (95 kg). The cod is tolerant of a wide range of temperatures and is found in both temperate waters and in the Arctic. It is omnivorous and voracious, feeding chiefly on crustaceans (especially Norway lobster *Nephrops* in European waters), molluscs, echinoderms, worms and fishes. Cod are extremely prolific and a large female may produce up to 7 million eggs, although only a very small percentage ever reach maturity. FAMILY: Gadidae, ORDER: Gadiformes, CLASS: Pisces.

COELACANTHS, primitive fishes once thought to be long extinct but now known to be represented by a single living species *Latimeria chalumnae*. They are related to the rhipidistian fishes, which gave rise to the first land vertebrates. Coelacanths first appear in the rocks of the Devonian period 400 million years ago and the group finally disappears from the fossil record in the Cretaceous period 90 million years ago. During all that time they altered remarkably little. They had heavily-built bodies covered by thick, rough scales made up of four distinct layers and known as cosmoid scales (as found also in the fossil lungfishes). The vertebral column was poorly ossified and represented only by the cartilaginous notochord and the fin spines were also hollow cartilage, hence the name 'coelacanth' or 'hollow spine'. One of the most striking features of these fishes were the leg-like lobes that supported the pectoral, anal, pelvic and second dorsal fins and the curious central lobe in the tail. The skull was hinged in the middle as in the earliest of the land vertebrates. ORDER: Crossopterygii, CLASS: Pisces.

COLLARED DOVE *Streptopelia decaocto*, 11 in (28 cm) long, noteworthy for the speed with which it has spread northwestwards across Europe from Asia Minor during the 20th century. Sometimes called Collared turtle dove, it is greyish fawn above, paler beneath with a pinkish flush on the breast. The tail is rather long, white-edged when seen from above and with the terminal half white when seen from below. There is a narrow black, white-edged half-collar on the back of the neck and the eyes are red.

Originally a native of India, it was introduced into China and Korea and possibly the Middle East, and from China into Japan where it still occurs in a limited area. It has spread westwards into some parts of Africa, but its main expansion has been into Europe, probably as a result of the development of feeding habits which take advantage of human cultivation. It was probably a common bird in Constantinople during the sixteenth century, but it is not recorded farther east until 1835 when it reached Bulgaria. Around 1912 it appeared in Hungary and about 1943 it was breeding near Vienna, near Venice and in Rumania. It was nesting in Germany in 1946 and had reached the Netherlands, Denmark and Sweden by 1949. In 1950 it bred in Poland and appeared in France, and by 1955 it was breeding in England and Switzerland. It first bred in Scotland in 1958 and now breeds over much of the British Isles. FAMILY: Columbidae, ORDER: Columbiformes, CLASS: Aves.

Collared dove, Europe's latest invader. It has spread across Europe from Asia.

COLOBUS, the only leaf-eating monkeys in Africa, distinguished from their Asiatic relatives, the langurs by their lack of a thumb—the most that is present is a little nubbin. By and large, they are more compactly built and less rangy than langurs but rival them in their bright colours and variety of hair-patterns. Colobus monkeys are 20–27 in (50–70 cm) long in head and body, with a tail of about the same length. There are three groups, the Black-and-white, the Red and the Olive colobus restricted to a belt of forest along the West African coast.

The Mantled guereza *Colobus guereza* is the best-known of the Black-and-white group. It is deep shining black in colour with a white ring round the face, a long white 'veil' of hair on the flanks which meets its fellow over the base of the tail, and a full white tuft on the tail.

Guerezas live in troops of up to 20, with a single male in each. The surplus males live alone or in small bachelor bands. Each troop has its own territory, which is very small, only 20 acres on average.

The King colobus *C. polykomos* is found in West Africa, from the Niger delta west to Gambia. It is also black, with whitish fringes on the cheeks and shoulders, and the whole tail is white, without any long 'brush' of hair. The Black colobus *C. satanas* is entirely black, but with long hair fringes on the cheeks and shoulders. It occurs in Cameroun, Gabon and parts of the Congo (Brazzaville). Finally the Angolan colobus *C. angolensis* has long shoulder-tufts but no white on the brows, and the white does not extend along the whole of the tail. It is found in the Congo (Kinshasa) and isolated forests in Rwanda, Tanzania and Uganda.

The Red colobus is more slenderly built and lacks the long hair tufts or the convex nose of the Black-and-white. The Bay colobus *C. badius badius* of Ghana is black on the back with sharply distinct maroon-red limbs; the Brown colobus *C. b. tephrosceles* from the northeastern Congo and Uganda, is brown above with straw-coloured limbs; Thollon's colobus *C. b. tholloni* from the forests south of the Congo river is bright red in colour; and the Zanzibar colobus *C. b. kirkii*, has a brick-red back and head, a black area on the forepart of the back, extending down the outside of the forelimbs, and the underside and the rest of the limb-hair white. The face varies from blue in the Bay colobus to black, with a flesh-coloured mouth and nasal septum, in the Zanzibar form.

Red colobus live in the tops of the trees, often in the emergent crowns. On Zanzibar the average troop size is said to be 15, but on the mainland 50 or more seems to be the rule.

The Olive colobus *Procolobus verus* is very small, with a head and body length under 20 in (50 cm), olive green, the hairs being green-yellow at the base and black at the tip. The only adornment is a small crest on the crown. The head is small and rounded; the

Colorado beetle on a potato leaf. Its larvae can ruin a potato crop.

face is flesh-coloured except round the eyes, where it is bluish. The nose is small and the face straight. It haunts the shrub and lower layers of the forest, not being usually found above 30 ft (10 m). It lives even in dry scrubby areas where there are no other colobus. The troops of 10–15 constantly associate with troops of guenons. SUBFAMILY: Colobinae, FAMILY: Cercopithecidae, ORDER: Primates, CLASS: Mammalia.

COLORADO BEETLE *Leptinotarsa decemlineata*, a leaf-eating beetle easily recognized, being about $\frac{3}{8}$ in (1 cm) long, very convex above and with longitudinal black and yellow stripes on the wing-cases. The fat, hump-backed, red and black larvae are also easy to identify.

The Colorado beetle was originally native to the eastern slopes of the Rocky Mountains where it fed on a weed called the Buffalo bur *Solanum rostratum*. The cultivated potato *Solanum tuberosum* was first planted in the United States near the Atlantic seaboard and as its cultivation spread westwards it eventually reached the home of the Colorado beetle which, in 1850, took to it and spread eastwards across the potato fields, completing its conquest by about 1874. In the early 1920's the Colorado beetle became established in France and soon spread to most areas of western Europe wherever potatoes were grown.

The female Colorado beetle lays batches of orange eggs on the early potato leaves and these hatch in about one week into reddish larvae which feed on the foliage. When large numbers of larvae and adults are present, most of the foliage may be devoured so that the potato plants die, or the tuber yield is reduced. FAMILY: Chrysomelidae, ORDER: Coleoptera, CLASS: Insecta, PHYLUM: Arthropoda.

CONCH SHELLS (pronounced konk), marine operculate snails found in the shallow waters of the tropics. The shells, widely collected as they are large, well coloured and

Condors

ornamental, are spirally coiled, often armed with processes (as in the Spider conch, *Pterocera lambis*) or with a huge reflected lip (as in the Queen conch *Strombus gigas*) or with both these features (as in the West Indian Fighting conch *Strombus pugilis*). The outside of the shell is often well marked and in some species, such as the Queen conch, the inside of the reflected shell mouth is a delicate pink colour. These animals are a staple food in the West Indies and the shells are sold for the manufacture of cameo brooches. Conch shells were used as currency by the inhabitants of the islands of the western Pacific, and also for medicinal purposes, but there is no scientific evidence that these, or any other molluscs (cf. oysters), act as aphrodisiacs. FAMILY: Strombidae, ORDER: Mesogastropoda, CLASS: Gastropoda, PHYLUM: Mollusca.

CONDORS, very large birds comprising two species of New World vultures: the California condor *Gymnogyps californianus* and the Andean condor *Vultur gryphus*. The former is one of the rarest of living birds of prey, found only in a small area of California, and reduced to about 40 individuals. The Andean condor is more numerous and widespread, inhabiting the whole Andean chain from Venezuela to Patagonia, but even this bird is much reduced from former times.

The Andean condor is the largest of living Falconiformes. In contrast to most diurnal raptors the males are as large as, or larger than the females. California condors weigh 18–31 lb (8–14 kg) and recorded wingspans vary from 8 ft 2 in–9 ft 7 in (2½–3 m). In the Andean condor males weigh about 25 lb (11 kg), females 17–22 lbs (7½–10 kg), and wing-spans of up to 10½ ft (3·2 m) have been recorded. If wing area and weight are taken together the Andean condor is the world's largest flying bird, exceeding the largest swans and bustards in wing area if not in weight.

The California condor is mainly black, with white underwing coverts and edges to the secondaries. The bare skin of the head and neck is orange, sometimes yellowish or grey. The Andean condor is more variegated, mainly glossy black, but with white upper wing coverts, inner primaries and secondaries, and a snowy-white neck-ruff. The bare skin is red or blackish red, there is a large comb-like fleshy caruncle on the head, loose folds of skin on the sides of the neck, and a 2 in (5 cm) pendent wattle. The sexes in this species are distinguishable by eye colour—grey in the male, red in the female.

It has not been proved that either species kill live animals, though ranchers accuse the Andean condor of taking many live lambs and calves. Both have relatively weak feet, with blunt claws and a rudimentary hind toe, adapted to walking on the ground but not to grasping and killing. Despite their great size and weight they probably could not kill anything but an animal already weakly or

A West Indian conch pulling itself across the sand with its muscular foot.

moribund. On the whole they seem to be beneficial, since their main food is unquestionably carrion that would otherwise become noxious. FAMILY: Cathartidae, ORDER: Falconiformes, CLASS: Aves.

CONE SHELLS, prosobranch molluscs of the genus *Conus*, with cone-shaped shells that are beautifully patterned. They live mostly in the warm waters of the Indo-Pacific, often on coral reefs. They have been classified as toxiglossans, or poison-tongues, on account of their highly modified feeding apparatus with its associated poison gland. The radula has only a few elongated and specialized marginal teeth which are hollow, harpoon-shaped and connected by the pharynx to a poison gland consisting of a long, thin secretory tube with a muscular pumping organ at one end. All are carnivorous, able, it seems, to locate food at a distance by a chemical sense. The poison acts like curare, causing a total inhibition of nerve impulses to muscles. All Cone shells should be regarded as dangerous and their 'bite' has been known to have caused at least six deaths of humans. Cone shells are widely collected and some, like the *C. gloriamaris*, the Glory of the Sea, are exceedingly rare and known from less than 40 specimens. The record price paid for a Glory of the Sea was $2,000 in 1964. FAMILY: Conidae, ORDER: Stenoglossa, CLASS: Gastropoda, PHYLUM: Mollusca.

CONGER EEL *Conger conger*, a very elongated fish with no pelvic fins. This is a large marine eel widely distributed in the North and South Atlantic, in the Mediterranean and in the Indo-Pacific region. It is not found off the west coast of America. The conger, like the freshwater eels, makes a spawning migration. The population of the North Atlantic migrates to an area between latitudes 30° and 40° N and spawns at depths of 4,800 ft (1,500 m). The Mediterranean population spawns in the deeper parts of that sea. The eggs float at that depth until the small, ribbon-like leptocephalus or larva hatches. It metamorphoses into the adult form near coasts but remains pinkish in colour until it is about 12 in (30 cm) long, after which it assumes the grey-brown of the adult. A large female may lay up to 8 million eggs.

Both the Conger and the Common freshwater eel lack pelvic fins but in the Conger eel the dorsal fin, which extends to the tip of the body, begins over the pectoral fins whereas in the Common eel the dorsal begins much further back. There are no scales on the body. Congers are large, voracious fishes of nocturnal habits, feeding on molluscs, crabs and fishes and often haunting wrecks. Females grow larger than the males and may reach a length of 9 ft (2·7 m); one of the largest rod-caught specimens weighed 84 lb (38 kg). FAMILY: Congridae, ORDER: Anguilliformes, CLASS: Pisces.

COOTS, small to medium-sized birds, the commoner species being about 14 in (35 cm) long, with dark plumage and living in ponds, lakes or marshy areas.

They are like other rails in having a back and forth bobbing motion of the head when walking or swimming, but unlike them in commonly staying on open water where they are conspicuous.

Coots have a short neck and tail and therefore appear squat. Their wings are proportionally short, but their legs are long. They are noteworthy for the large size of their feet and the lobes on the toes which act as 'mud-boards' enabling the bird to walk over soft mud and floating vegetation. Coots must patter along the surface to become airborne, but when in the air they are strong fliers. The lobes on the feet also act as swimming aids and coots feed much in the water, diving with ease and bringing up various vegetable materials for sorting at the surface.

A distinctive feature of coots is the frontal shield which continues the soft horny material of the bill up and over the front of the head. In the European species this is wholly whitish, like the bill, hence the phrase 'as bald as a coot'. In other species the shield may be wholly or partly pigmented. The function of this rather noticeable feature seems to be to assist the orientation of the young to the bill of the adult during feeding in the tangled undergrowth of the water's edge.

The European coot *Fulica atra* is found through much of Europe and in Asia and Australia. In New Guinea it is found up to 11,000 ft (3,350 m). The Common coot of North America *F. americana* is found from southern Canada to northern South America; it is very closely related to the European species and, like it, is widespread and common.

Another closely related species is the Crested coot *F. cristata* of South and East Africa, Madagascar, a relatively small area of

The European coot with its white head shield, a recognition badge between coots.

northwest Africa, and a small part of southern Spain. This is distinguished by two prominent red knobs on the head—one above each side of the bluish-white frontal shield. It is more secretive than the previous species and found less often in open water.

The greatest development of the coot subfamily has been in South America where the other seven species are found. One species, *F. caribea*, is found in the West Indies, and two species are found on the high lakes of the Andes. One of these is the large *F. gigantea* and the other the rare Horned coot *F. cornuta*, so called because of the large horn-like projection on the frontal shield.

Coots nest around the edges of ponds and lakes, building large nests of reeds, sedges and other materials, sometimes floating amongst the aquatic vegetation. They usually lay up to ten eggs. The young have brightly coloured head-patches, presumably to show the adult where the chick's head is, to put

food into its beak. After the eggs are hatched extra nests may be built for brooding the young. FAMILY: Rallidae, ORDER: Gruiformes, CLASS: Aves.

COPEPODA, small crustaceans mostly microscopic, the larger being pin-head size, abundant in fresh water and sea. Some are free-living in offshore waters, some are more sedentary on or near the bottom or live a semi-parasitic life, while others are wholly parasitic. Copepods form an important constituent of the plankton and the main source of food for some important food fishes. CLASS: Crustacea, PHYLUM: Arthropoda.

CORALS, may be Soft corals, Horny corals, Thorny corals or True or Stony corals, the last being builders of reefs and atolls. They can be most easily thought of as small polyps, similar in structure to Sea anemones each of which lays down a skeleton, usually calcareous, in the form of a cup. Most corals are colonial and the polyps are connected to one another by extensions of the body wall that lie above the level of the skeleton. So the colony generally sits on its massive skeleton.

The colonial or reef-building corals range from solid spherical masses to those with delicate branches. At the other extreme are the solitary corals such as the Mushroom coral *Fungia* and the Devonshire cup coral *Caryophyllia*.

The Soft corals have an eight-rayed symmetry in contrast to the six-rayed symmetry of the True corals and they differ also in having a skeleton of small rods of varying shapes composed of calcium carbonate and known as spicules. These may be scattered in the tissues of the polyp or massed together to form an internal axis. Included among the Soft corals are the colonies of polyps known as Sea pens which are shaped like a quill feather, the

Conger eels rest in crevices among rocks. Their food is mainly crabs and fishes.

base of the quill being embedded in the mud of the sea floor and the vane of the feather being composed of rows of polyps.

The Horny corals which include the Precious coral *Corallium rubrum* of the Mediterranean, are colonies of polyps with a central axis of horn-like material known as gorgonin or of a solid mass of spicules. Horny corals are variously known as Sea fans, Sea whips and Sea feathers.

Thorny corals also called Black corals are slender branching corals resembling the Horny corals but with an axis at the centre of each branch made up of a horn-like material, brown or black, which bears numerous projections or thorns. CLASS: Anthozoa, PHYLUM: Cnidaria.

CORAL SNAKES, highly venomous snakes with hollow or grooved fangs fixed to the front of the upper jaw, related to the cobras, mambas and kraits. They are characterized by the head being only slightly defined from the neck, the slender body having an oval cross-section and the eye having a vertical, elliptical pupil. The vertical pupil is associated with twilight or nocturnal activity and indicates that these snakes hunt their prey mostly at night.

Coral snakes are restricted to the New World, from the United States southwards into the tropical forests of South America. The Eastern coral snake *Micrurus fulvius*, renowned as a snake-eater and up to 3 ft (90 cm) long, is one of the few very dangerous snakes in the United States. The Arizona or Sonoran coral snake *Micruroides euryxanthus*, of southeastern Arizona, western New Mexico and Mexico, is about half the size but several other species, found in Mexico and the tropics of South America, may attain a length of 5 ft (150 cm).

Coral snakes usually have a striking colour

pattern of broad, alternating orange or pink and black bands separated by narrow yellow rings. This is probably a warning colouration, indicating to other animals that the snake is dangerous and best left alone. Several harmless snakes, for example, the Milk snakes, *Lampropeltis doliata* and *Atractus latifrons*, which live in the same habitats as Coral snakes mimic their warning colouration and presumably derive some benefit from doing so. In general, Coral snakes are secretive burrowers and spend the day hidden in grass tussocks or other dense vegetation or in runs under stones and rocks. FAMILY: Elapidae, ORDER: Squamata, CLASS: Reptilia.

CORMORANTS, long-necked long-billed diving birds, sometimes known as 'shags'. There are some 30 species around the sea coasts and larger lakes and rivers of the world, excepting parts of northern Canada and northern Asia and certain islands in the Pacific. They vary in length from 19–40 in (48–101 cm).

Above left: Solitary coral of the genus *Fungia*.
Above right: Piece of a branch of Stag's-horn coral.
Below: A Sea fan, one of the Horny corals.

In most species the plumage is black, or black with a green or blue metallic sheen. In the southern hemisphere a few species are grey and others white on the throat or underparts. The eyes, bill and facial skin are often brightly coloured. In the breeding season many species have crests, or patches of white on the head, neck or flanks. The bill is long, though strong, and is hooked. The feet are large and fully webbed, and the legs are short and strong.

On the whole, cormorants only enter the water for fishing. This may be due to the plumage becoming wettened easily as a result of its general looseness. After fishing, cormorants stand for long periods with wings outstretched, presumably to dry them. Even the Galapagos Flightless cormorant *Nannopterum harrisi* has this habit. The wings are used to a certain extent under water, particularly for steering and braking.

Most cormorants are gregarious and breed colonially on rocky shores or cliff ledges or in trees. Some species are strictly marine, others restricted to fresh water. Some may be found anywhere where there is enough

The strikingly patterned and highly venomous Arizona or Sonoran coral snake. The conspicuous colours probably serve as a warning to predators not to touch.

water to harbour fishes, Crustacea or Amphibia. The Common cormorant *Phalacrocorax carbo* (the Great cormorant of eastern North America, and the Black cormorant of Australasia) for example is almost cosmopolitan in its distribution, from the tundra to the tropics and from Canada eastwards to Japan and Australasia. In many countries it is found on both fresh and salt water, and will nest in trees or on rocks. It takes a wide variety of animal food but feeds largely on fishes.

Cormorants' nests are commonly quite bulky structures, built of sticks, seaweed or other vegetation, or simply of rubbish from the shore, on rocks or in trees. In a few species, which nest together in very large numbers in rainless regions where the droppings, or guano, accumulate in thick layers, the nest is little more than a depression in this material. The eggs are basically a pale blue or green colour but typically are more or less covered with a chalky encrustation. They are elongated and vary in number from two to six, according to species. Both sexes normally incubate the eggs, which hatch in the order in which they are laid. Thus in times of food scarcity the strongest young survive at the expense of the weakest. In the Flightless cormorant, although three eggs are laid, only two hatch.

The young cormorants are fed largely by regurgitation, both parents bringing partly digested fish into the mouth and gullet and allowing the young to insert their heads to feed. Sometimes the adults present food from the bill tip, and sometimes they disgorge onto the nest. In the Double-crested cormorant *P. auritus* pebbles have been noted to be given incidentally with food and have been accumulated by the young until they were old enough to disgorge. FAMILY: Phalocrocoracidae, ORDER: Pelecaniformes, CLASS: Aves.

CORN BUNTING *Emberiza calandra*, one of the largest of the buntings, 7 in (18 cm) long with a sombre brown plumage and no striking features. Corn buntings have the conical bill of seed-eaters and they are found especially on agricultural land. The only distinctive feature is the male's song which is like a bunch of keys being rattled. FAMILY: Emberizidae, ORDER: Passeriformes, CLASS: Aves.

COTINGAS, a family of 90 species of heterogeneous tropical American birds. Cotingas vary in size from that of a sparrow to that of a crow. Practically all are birds of the forest and for this reason the life-histories of a great number, possibly the majority, remain wholly unknown. This even applies to quite common species. As they live in high trees in the rain-forests their nests are extremely difficult to locate. Some are dull coloured, but a great number have brilliant colours, with strangely modified wing feathers, fleshy wattles around the bill or

Common cormorants with their nests, usually of seaweed and dead vegetation, on a rocky cliff. The species is widely spread in the northern hemisphere and also Australia.

brightly coloured naked skin on their heads. FAMILY: Cotingidae, ORDER: Passeriformes, CLASS: Aves.

COTTONTAIL, seven species of rabbits are known by this common name because of the characteristic fluffy appearance of their tails. All belong to the genus *Sylvilagus* (Latin, *sylva*=wood; Greek, *lagos*=hare). The Eastern cottontail is the only true cottontail but the other six species of the same genus are given this name by some authors.

The Eastern cottontail *Sylvilagus floridanus*, is the most abundant and best studied of the group. The upper parts of the body and tail are brownish or grey, and the underparts white; ears are dark greyish tan bordered with black. Adults weigh up to 3½ lb (1·6 kg). There are three moults annually. During the spring and summer months the pelage is replaced in spots and in autumn in sheets. All cottontails are confined to North America apart from the Eastern cottontail which has also invaded part of South America. FAMILY: Leporidae, ORDER: Lagomorpha, CLASS: Mammalia.

COUCALS, 27 species of large, non-parasitic cuckoos. They are absent from the Americas but widespread in tropical regions elsewhere. They are heavily-built, mainly terrestrial birds; pheasant-like, with heavy, slightly curved bills, large rounded heads, squat bodies with short rounded wings, long tails and long strong legs. Their gait varies from a sedate stride to rapid running. They tend to be skulkers, keeping to low cover and occurring in grassland with tall grasses, in thick vegetation on the edges of swamps and forests, and in secondary growth in forests and clearings.

The plumage has a loose and hairy texture and is coarse and glossy. Immature birds, and hens of some species, may have a plumage cryptically coloured in brown and black, whereas the adults tend to have boldly coloured plumage in black, dark blue, chestnut and white, striated at times. Often there is a strong contrast between the dark head and tail and the chestnut and white body and wings.

The songs of coucals sound like air bubbling up through water, often descending the scale during repetition. During calling the neck is inflated and the bill-tip lowered.

The nest is a crudely-made, domed structure with little evidence of an internal cup for the eggs. It may be on the ground, where it is concealed in long grass and very difficult to find or, if above ground, low down in a thick twiggy shrub. The eggs are more spherical than the typical birds' eggs, white with a matt surface. The young have blackish skins and are not naked but have down, although

Coursers

this is sparse and remains in a sheath, appearing like distinct coarse white hairs.

Coucals are predators on small animals. Large insects are the principal item in the diet, but amphibians, reptiles, including snakes, and small mammals and birds may also be included. Although coucals are poor flyers, and will flutter up into trees only with apparent difficulty, they show more agility in planing down from perches and may descend on their prey in this manner. FAMILY: Cuculidae, ORDER: Cuculiformes, CLASS: Aves.

COURSERS, ten species of wading birds, one Australian, two Indian and the rest African. These include the Australian dotterel *Peltohyas australis* and the Egyptian plover *Pluvianus aegyptius* (neither of which are true plovers) and four species of each of the genera *Cursorius* and *Rhinoptilus*. Coursers resemble plovers in size, body shape, locomotory behaviour and call, but they have pointed and sometimes downcurved bills (rather than blunt and straight) and longer legs in proportion to body size. All, apart from the Egyptian plover, are predominantly pale brown (though often with dark brown or black and white eye-stripes), as befits their chosen habitat of semi-desert and open ground; the leg colour is also pale. The sexes are alike. The Egyptian plover, a bird of river margins and sandbanks, has grey upperparts, a characteristic head pattern of dark green crown- and eye-stripes and a black wing bar. It associates with basking crocodiles.

Of the primarily African species, the Cream-coloured courser *C. cursorius*, which breeds on both borders of the Sahara desert belt (north and east to Persia, south and east to Kenya), is the only one which reaches Europe at all frequently. When approached, it runs swiftly for short distances with head lowered, then pauses to stand erect, in the same way as many plovers. Sometimes it crouches to escape detection, again like young plover chicks.

All these coursers must be able to withstand very high temperatures in their chosen breeding areas, and they have certain behavioural adaptations related to this. For example, the Egyptian plover part buries its eggs in the sand, which it may moisten from time to time with water, apparently by regurgitation. Other species lay their eggs on open ground and shade them from the sun, rather than incubate them. The air temperature is usually high enough, and extra heat can be provided if necessary by brief exposure to the sun. Most species lay a clutch of two or three eggs. Courser chicks may also be shaded from the direct sun by their parents, and it has been reported that Egyptian plover chicks may be buried temporarily in the sand by their parents if danger approaches. FAMILY: Glareolidae, ORDER: Charadriiformes, CLASS: Aves.

COWBIRDS, small to medium-sized perching birds of generalized form remarkable for the variety of adaptations shown by the different species. One of the most remarkable is the habit of parasitizing other birds for the rearing of young, which is shown by all but one species.

Cowbirds are so-called because of their association with cattle. It is very likely that they benefit from the disturbance of insects and other small animals caused by the cattle as they walk through the vegetation. It has been shown that the Groove-billed ani *Crotophaga sulcirostris*, a tropical American cuckoo, feeds about three times as efficiently when with cattle. The Brown-headed cowbird *Molothrus ater* was previously associated closely with bison.

The cowbirds are noteworthy for the wide range of stages of development of the parasitic habit. The Bay-winged cowbird *Molothrus badius* is non-parasitic and sometimes builds its own nest, though usually it appropriates the nest of another species in which to lay its eggs and rear its young. Some are selective in their 'choice' of host. The Screaming cowbird *Molothrus rufoaxillaris* apparently only parasitizes the Bay-winged cowbird, and the Giant cowbird *Scaphidura oryzivorus* limits itself to certain other icterids —the oropendolas and caciques. The Brown-headed cowbird on the other hand is known to parasitize over 250 other species of birds.

The parasitic cowbirds lay large numbers of eggs. The reason for this would seem to be that many eggs never produce young because the parasitic habit is imperfectly developed. For example, up to 37 eggs of the Shiny cowbird *Molothrus bonariensis* have been found in one host nest, and large numbers of eggs are found on the ground. FAMILY: Icteridae, ORDER: Passeriformes, CLASS: Aves.

COWRIES, well-known marine gastropods the shells of which are highly polished, often beautifully coloured, and formerly much collected. The shells are globular on one side, flattened on the other, with an aperture showing as a long slit on the flattened side. This unusual shape is due to the last whorl of the shell being very large and rolled round the rest of the shell. Cowries are typically tropical and in parts of the world have served as currency. FAMILY: Cypraeidae, ORDER: Mesogastropoda, CLASS: Gastropoda, PHYLUM: Mollusca.

COYOTE *Canis latrans*, or Prairie wolf, a North American wild dog closely related to the wolf *Canis lupus*, but smaller. Weighing between 25–30 lb (11·5–13·5 kg), the coyote has grizzled black and yellow fur with black markings on the tail and shoulders. Although originally an inhabitant of the Western Plains of the United States, it has expanded its range in recent years, largely due to its cunning and opportunism, and is now found as far east as the New England states. The coyote takes advantage of numerous food sources, including young ungulates, small

The coyote has suffered less than the Timber wolf largely because it is smaller.

86

rodents and rabbits, carrion, insects, fruits, and even rubbish from garbage dumps. Its ability to hunt in packs composed of family groups, in pairs, or alone and to alter its habits as external conditions change is reminiscent of the jackals which occupy a similar ecological niche in Africa and southern Asia. Both the coyotes and jackals are constantly hunted by man who believes that they prey upon domestic livestock, but their cleverness in evading traps and snares has so far prevented their extermination.

The male aids in rearing the young which are born in March or April after a 63 day gestation. While the cubs are helpless and need constant tending, he does most of the hunting. Later, both parents hunt and, during weaning, they regurgitate partly digested meat to the litter to ease the transition from a milk to meat diet. FAMILY: Canidae, ORDER: Carnivora, CLASS: Mammalia.

COYPU *Myocastor coypus*, a South American aquatic rodent superficially resembling a large musk-rat or small beaver.

Coypus have a head and body length of almost 2 ft (60 cm) when fully grown and weigh up to about 15 lb (7 kg). The tail, which is about two-thirds the length of the head and body, is round in section, not flattened as in most aquatic animals. The fur is yellowish-brown above and grey below. The underfur, especially on the underside of the body, is dense and soft, and coypu pelts, known in the trade as 'nutria', are prepared by cutting along the upper surface of the body to leave the underside intact and by removing the longer bristly guard hairs. An unusual adaptation to an aquatic life is the very high position of the teats on the female's flanks, allowing the young to suckle while the mother is swimming.

Coypus are found throughout the southern half of South America wherever there is water. However, they have been kept all over the world on fur farms from which they have frequently escaped.

Although primarily herbivorous, coypus are known to vary their diet with shellfish. Breeding appears to continue all year, and the young, usually about five in a litter, are very well developed at birth and are very soon accomplished swimmers. FAMILY: Capromyidae, ORDER: Rodentia, CLASS: Mammalia.

CRABS, 4,000 or more species of decapod crustaceans having a reduced abdomen carried tucked forward underneath a broad carapace, which is often wider than long. The insertions of the legs are widely separated on the underside. When walking or running many crabs move sideways or obliquely, but the most skilled runners can move forwards, backwards or sideways with great facility. A typical crab has a pair of well developed pincers and four pairs of walking legs, making

The coypu, a large South American rodent which can be both a pest or profit-making according to circumstances.

10 legs in all (Gk: *deka*, ten, *podos*, foot). One or two of the hind pairs of legs are reduced or absent in certain families. Some of the fast running crabs appear to use only two pairs of legs when travelling at high speed.

A crab's gills are housed in chambers on each side of the thorax. These open near the bases of the legs, and also have a forwardly directed opening near the bases of the antennae. Water is moved in and out of the gill chamber by a flap, the scaphognathite, which is attached to the outer edge of one of the mouthparts, and projects back into the gill chamber. Normally the water is drawn in at the bases of the limbs and passed out over the bases of the antennae. But the current can also be reversed, and frequently is in forms such as the Masked crab. Another remarkable adaptation is seen in some of the crabs that spend much of their time out of water. *Aratus pisoni* climbs in mangrove trees and passes water from the gill chambers out of the front openings. When the crab is

in air the water flows as a thin film down the front of the underside to the bases of the limbs where it regains entry to the gill chamber.

The eyes of crabs are borne on stalks which vary greatly in length.

Crabs are often scavengers, but their pincers are capable of killing small fish and breaking open shells.

Crabs vary greatly in size and shape. The smallest species measure only $\frac{1}{4}$ in (6 mm) across the carapace, but the largest have a carapace over 1 ft (30 cm) in width, and the legs of the giant Japanese Spider crab may span nearly 9 ft (3 m). See Fiddler, Ghost, Hermit, Horseshoe, Land, Pea, Shore and Spider crabs. CLASS: Crustacea, PHYLUM: Arthropoda.

CRAB-EATING MONKEY *Macaca fascicularis*, sometimes known as the Irus macaque, Java monkey or cynomolgus, smaller than the Rhesus, not more than 20 in (50 cm) long,

A Northern stone crab *Lithodes maia* looks like a spiny Spider crab but is more nearly related to a Hermit crab.

with a tail ·1–1½ times the head and body length. It lacks the bright hindparts of the Rhesus, but sometimes has a little peak of hair on the crown or grey cheek-whiskers. It replaces the Rhesus from Thailand and South Vietnam, south through Malaya to the Philippine Islands. FAMILY: Cercopithecidae, ORDER: Primates, CLASS: Mammalia.

CRANEFLIES, flies with slender bodies, narrow wings and extremely long legs which break off easily. Thus, Daddy long legs has become a common name. They tend to settle in cool damp places, under leaves and between grass stems. They are slow flying and vulnerable to predators. Many of them bob up and down when they are perched, by bending and straightening their legs. Others hang upside-down holding on by the forelegs and rhythmically waving the hindlegs. Some of these movements are probably involved in sexual attraction and are seen mainly in larger species. Some of the smaller gnat-like species form mating swarms of males, seen just before sunset or sunrise monotonously dancing up and down. At intervals a female enters the swarm and is captured by a male. They then both drop to the ground.

Craneflies feed little as adults and then take

Cranefly or Daddy long legs, female.

only nectar. It is the growing larvae which consume the most food. They are tough-skinned, known as leatherjackets, and have biting mouthparts. They live just under the surface of the soil, attacking roots and stems of a wide range of plants including crops of various kinds. FAMILY: Tipulidae, ORDER: Diptera, CLASS: Insecta, PHYLUM: Arthropoda.

CRANES, large, long-legged birds with a superficial resemblance to herons and storks, but hardly ever perching in trees.

They stand from 30–60 in (76–150 cm) tall. The plumage varies from white to slate grey and brown, and the inner secondary feathers of the wing are curled or elongated to form a mass of plumes that droop over the hind end of the body when the wings are folded. The head is ornamented with plumes or has areas of red featherless skin and the tail is rather short.

The bill is strong and straight; the legs and feet are also strong, with the toes connected at the base by a membrane. The hind toe is elevated. The voice is loud and resonant—typically trumpeting but in others more whistling—aided by the unusual formation of the trachea which, in the males of most species, is coiled upon itself. These tracheal coils occupy part of the sternum and in some species even penetrate the breast muscles.

Cranes are world-wide, being absent only from South America, Madagascar, the Malayan Archipelago, New Zealand and Polynesia. Typically they are found in open country: marshes, plains, prairies, lakes and seashores. In the breeding season they are particularly shy and nest in wild remote areas. Most species are migratory.

Outside the breeding season most cranes are strongly gregarious, migrating and wintering in large flocks.

They will take most kinds of small animal and perhaps even more vegetable material, particularly fruits and roots. They forage in

cultivated fields whenever possible and the understandable antagonism of farmers in an increasingly competitive and demanding market has been one of the reasons for the decline in numbers of cranes. In certain countries where cranes are partial pests there are governmental schemes for protecting crops and indemnifying farmers. In Canada for example, insurance against damage to crops by wildlife, including cranes, was instituted in Saskatchewan in 1953 and in Alberta in 1962. Also, exploders are used to scare cranes off the standing crops on which they feed and alternative 'lure crops' are provided.

One of the most outstanding characteristics of cranes is their habit of dancing. This may occur at any time of year, in winter as well as the breeding season, and may involve single birds or groups of either or both of the sexes. It is probably seen, however, in its most highly developed form in the dancing displays of a mated pair. Typically, the birds walk around each other with rapid steps and partly spread wings, bowing, or bobbing their heads, and alternately jumping into the air in a manner which is graceful in spite of their bulk. From time to time they stop suddenly, erect. They also throw a stick or other pieces of vegetation into the air, either catching it or stabbing at it as it falls. Prodigious jumps may be performed during the dance.

Cranes nest on the ground or in shallow water, and the nest varies from a shallow scrape in the soil to a bulky collection of vegetable material. Occasionally one, normally two and rarely three eggs are laid. They are incubated by both sexes.

The Common crane *Grus grus* breeds from northern and eastern Europe across most of Asia. It was a regular breeder in Britain until around 1600, but it dislikes interference and human cultivation and has gradually been pushed eastwards. It stands about 44 in (112 cm) tall and is slate grey with a white streak from the eye down the neck. There is a red patch on the back of the crown. It breeds in wet or damp open countryside such as swamps and marshes with or without scattered trees or scrub. In winter it prefers more open country, including dry grassland and steppe.

It has been estimated that 100 acres (40 ha) can produce enough grain for 18,000 cranes, but this does not allow for wastage. In practice there are never more than 4,000 birds feeding in 100 acres, although 30,000 cranes may occupy one roost.

The other American species of crane, the Whooping crane *G. americana*, is far from being a nuisance because of the depredations of large flocks. On the contrary, this species, endemic to North America, has become famous among conservationists and ornithologists through the effort made to save the few remaining birds from extinction.

The Manchurian crane *G. japonensis* breeds in a few areas of Manchuria and in Hokkaido, Japan. This is a largely white species with black wings and red crown, but it also has a large grey streak running down each side of the neck. It seems that most of the birds winter in Japan, where they are strictly protected, but the breeding population in Hokkaido in 1962 was no more than 200.

Demoiselle crane of Europe, Asia and northern Africa, with white head plumes.

The Hooded crane *G. monacha*, is another species which previously was a common winter visitor in Japan. The bare head-patch in this species is red and black. The breeding area again covers parts of Japan and Man-

A group of Sarus cranes.

churia, but the winter flock consists of only a few hundred birds.

The White-necked crane *G. vipio* is grey with white throat and hind neck and white secondary wing feathers. It has a red face and forehead. It breeds in eastern Siberia and winters in Japan and also, like several other cranes, in parts of China and Korea. In Japan and Korea at least the various species of cranes have been protected for well over 50 years, but the depredations of the occupation forces after the Second World War and the havoc caused to cranes' wintering grounds in the Korean war have had a very serious effect upon a number of species.

The Sarus crane *G. antigone*, is a very impressive bird, even for a crane, standing some 5 ft ($1\frac{1}{2}$ m) tall. It is blue-grey with a bare red head and upper neck and breeds in northern India and adjacent regions. The little-known Black-necked crane *G. nigricollis* lives in central Siberia. The remaining species of the genus is the Australian crane *G. rubicunda*, also called the 'native companion'. It is a silver-grey bird with a green crown and red on the face and back of the head and neck, and is found in southern New Guinea as well as Australia.

In eastern Europe and through much of central Asia to the south of the forest belt inhabited by the Common crane is found the Demoiselle crane *Anthropoides virgo*. This is only about 3 ft (1 m) tall and has soft grey plumage with black flight feathers, face and front of neck, and white plumes curving back and down from behind the eye. It winters in northeastern Africa and southern Asia.

On the South African plateau the Blue, or Stanley, crane, *Tetrapteryx paradisea*, is still quite common. It is basically similar to the Demoiselle but has black secondary wing feathers extending far beyond the tail.

Another South African species is the Wattled crane *Bugeranus carunculatus*, which is found in East Africa also. This is a large dark bird, grey above, black beneath and with the upper breast, neck and much of the head white. The face bears red warts, or carunculations, and below it hang two white-feathered wattles, or lappets. This seems to be another species which is on the decline.

Finally, one of the most striking of all the cranes: the Crowned crane *Balearica pavonina*, which is a widely-distributed species, found over much of Africa from Abyssinia and the Sudan southwards. It is 38 in (96 cm) tall.

The Crowned crane is a dark-plumaged bird, with rufous on the hind part and white on the wings, but its most striking feature is its head with the crown which gives it its name. This is composed of a tuft of stiff straw-coloured feathers standing up in a fan from the back of the head. The head is otherwise covered with short black plumes and the bare cheeks are white. The bill is

Crayfishes

Sarus cranes of southern Asia are the biggest cranes, said to be as tall as a man, but usually up to 5 feet high.

proportionally shorter than in other cranes.

The striking appearance of the Crowned crane is enhanced by the dances which it performs, the crown being displayed to full effect in the bobbing and bowing. This is one of a number of species of birds which have provided models for the dances of local tribes in West Africa. FAMILY: Gruidae, ORDER: Gruiformes, CLASS: Aves.

CRAYFISHES, freshwater decapod crustaceans, having five pairs of walking legs, with the first pair enlarged and modified to form characteristic stout pincers. The second and third pairs also bear small pincers. The body is elongated and the tail is large, bearing a fan formed by an enlarged and flattened pad of abdominal appendages. A characteristic escape movement of a crayfish is to shoot backwards using a violent flexing of the fan.

The Common European crayfish *Astacus astacus* lives in streams and ponds where it takes a varied diet, including snails, insects and plants. It respires by means of gills which are housed in a branchial cavity on either side of the thorax. In November the female lays a batch of relatively large eggs. These are attached to the underside of the abdomen and carried for six months until they hatch. The young emerging from the eggs have the same general structure as the adult, but the form is more rounded and the limbs are not fully developed. Crayfish are most commonly found in streams with a high calcium content as they have heavy chalky exoskeletons. FAMILIES: Astacidae, Parastacidae, ORDER: Decapoda, CLASS: Crustacea, PHYLUM: Arthropoda.

CRESTED SWIFTS, or tree-swifts, related to true swifts. They differ in the males being brightly coloured, and in their habit of perching, and building their nests, in trees.

The three species of *Hemiprocne* are re-stricted to tropical Asia where they live in open woodland, secondary forest and gardens. Their food is gathered on the wing and includes wasps and bees.

The nest is a tiny cup of saliva, bark and feathers glued to the top of a slender branch. The single egg is glued into the nest which only just accommodates it. The mottled-brown nestling sits still on the branch, protected by its general resemblance to a knot or piece of lichen. FAMILY: Hemiprocnidae, ORDER: Apodiformes, CLASS: Aves.

CRICKETS, jumping insects of small to moderate size closely related to the bush-crickets. There are 1,000 species, mainly tropical but many are temperate.

The antennae are thread-like and composed of more than 30 segments. Behind the head is a saddle-shaped structure, the pronotum, protecting the front part of the thorax. There are usually two pairs of fully developed wings, but in some species these are reduced in size or completely absent. The hindwings are membranous and fold up like a fan when at rest, forming two 'spikes' that protrude from beneath the shorter and tougher fore-wings. The females have a rod- or needle-like ovipositor and both sexes have a pair of long and conspicuous cerci.

The eggs are usually laid in the ground, but in the tree-crickets they are laid on bark, in the pith of twigs or in the stems of various plants. The young are similar to the adults in appearance, but lack wings. They reach maturity after moulting from eight to 11 or more times, an unusually large number for insects of this size. The young stages often pass through a resting phase during the winter or, in the tropics, the dry season, and so may take as long as a year to become adult.

Most male crickets can 'sing' by rubbing the hind edge of the left forewing against a row of teeth on the right forewing. The sounds produced are often quite musical and in some parts of the world crickets are sold in cages, to be kept as singing pets. The females are unable to sing but both sexes have a hearing organ in each foreleg.

A few species of crickets have become associated with man and have been spread by him to many parts of the world. The best known example is the European house-cricket *Acheta domesticus* which now occurs in indoor situations throughout the world and is sometimes sufficiently numerous to be a pest.

Crickets are usually nocturnal, often living in burrows during the day and feeding on a wide variety of both plant and animal matter.

The closely related mole-crickets live almost entirely in burrows, which they dig with their mole-like forelegs. Both sexes, when alarmed, can eject an evil-smelling liquid from the tip of the abdomen. The females can produce sounds, differing from the males' song but produced in a similar way. In warm countries mole-crickets are sometimes sufficiently abundant to cause damage to crops. FAMILY: Gryllidae, ORDER: Orthoptera, CLASS: Insecta, PHYLUM: Arthropoda.

CROCODILES, 13 species differing from alligators and caimans in that the large fourth tooth in the lower jaw which fits into a notch in the upper jaw remains visible even when the mouth is closed. Moreover, the teeth of the upper and lower jaw are more or less in line, those of the lower jaw engaging between the teeth of the upper jaw.

The best known is the Nile crocodile *Crocodylus niloticus* which occurs all over Africa south of the Sahara, as well as Madagascar and the Seychelles Islands. At one time this species reached lengths of up to 33 ft (10 m) but nowadays it is hard to find specimens more than 20 ft (6 m) long. In western and central Africa, as well as in

Ujiji on Lake Tanganyika, lives the 13 ft (4 m) Long-snouted crocodile *C. cataphractus*, the snout of which is up to 3½ times as long as it is wide at the base. In contrast, the Broad-nosed crocodile *Osteolaemus tetraspis*, of western and central Africa, has an extremely short snout and is rarely more than 6 ft (1·8 m) long. It has brown eyes and is said to spend more time in the jungle than in water. It feeds mainly on freshwater crabs and soft turtles using its comparatively blunt teeth.

In Asia lives the 13 ft (4 m) long mugger or Swamp crocodile *Crocodylus palustris*, mainly in India and Ceylon, perhaps also in Burma. It differs from the very similar Nile crocodile by its somewhat shorter snout and the less regular arrangement of the scutes on the back. The Siam crocodile *C. siamensis*, which has somewhat the same length, is restricted to Thailand and Indo-China and the islands of Java and Borneo. It is characterized by a triangular raised portion in front of the eyes. The somewhat longer Sunda gavial *Tomistoma schlegeli* does not belong to the gavials but to the true crocodiles. Its snout is extremely long, and up to five times as long as its width at the base. It is found in Malaya, Sumatra and Borneo.

The Estuarine crocodile *Crocodylus porosus* ranges from Ceylon to the Fiji Islands, including northern Australia. It reaches 33 ft (10 m) in length, lives at the mouths of rivers and in salt water and can be seen swimming many miles from the coast.

Apart from the Estuarine crocodile, in northern Australia we find the Australian crocodile *C. johnsoni* which is only 8 ft (2·5 m) long and is recognized by its long narrow snout.

The most northern species of true crocodile in the New World is the light olive coloured American or Sharp-nosed crocodile *C. acutus* in the south of Florida, on the islands of Cuba, Jamaica and Hispaniola, as well as Mexico and Central America to Venezuela, Colombia, Ecuador and Northern Peru. It is characterized by its narrow and long snout having a bulbous dome in front of the eyes. Whilst this species reaches almost 12 ft (3·5 m), the Bulbous crocodile *C. moreletii*, found in British Honduras and Guatemala, is only a little more than 8 ft (2·5 m) long and is almost black when aged. Here, too, the snout carries a lump in front of the eyes but has a much broader and shorter effect than in the previous species. Restricted to Cuba there is the barely 7 ft (2 m) long Cuba crocodile *C. rhombifer* which has a triangular raised portion in front of the eyes similar to that in the Siam crocodile. The older individuals are almost black and exhibit light yellow spots on the back legs. The only wholly South American species is the Orinoco crocodile *C. intermedius* which reaches a length of up to 15 ft (4·5 m). It differs clearly from all other American species of crocodile by its extremely narrow and very elongated snout. FAMILY:

Crocodilidae, ORDER: Crocodilia, CLASS: Reptilia.

CROSSBILLS, finches with peculiar crossed mandibles for extracting seeds from cones which provide almost their entire food. They also have large feet for gripping the cones and are adept at climbing among the branches, using feet and bill to pull themselves along parrot-fashion. They are found in northern regions throughout the world. The three species differ in body size, size of bill and preferred food. The largest, the Parrot crossbill *Loxia pytyopsittacus* has a heavy bill and feeds from the hard cones of pine; the medium-sized Common crossbill *L. curvirostrus* has a medium bill and feeds from the softer cones of spruce; while the smallest Two-barred crossbill *L. leucoptera* has a slender bill and feeds from the delicate cones of larch. In all three species, the males are coloured brick-red, with brownish wings and tail, and the females and young are greenish; but the two-barred has white bars across its wings.

Crossbills nest high on the branches of conifers, laying three to four bluish-white spotted eggs. So that the young can be raised while seeds are still plentiful, all three species nest early in the year before the seeds have fallen. The main breeding season of the Common crossbill lasts from January to March. In the winter of 1940/41, some nests were found near Moscow when temperatures were down to 0°F (−18°C); but inside the nests, while the female brooded, they reached 100°F (38°C). It is perhaps because the young are often raised in cold snowy weather that they develop more slowly than other finches and stay in the nest for up to 30 days.

The migrations of crossbills are also unusual, being adapted to their special food-

supply. Cone-crops vary enormously in size, both from place to place in the same year and from year to year in the same place, a good crop usually being followed by a poor one. The birds therefore move around every summer, settling wherever cones are plentiful. Here they will remain for a year, but will move on at the end of the year in search of new areas rich in seed. Thus the crossbills differ from other migratory birds in making only a single movement each year. In addition, these movements sometimes develop into 'irruptions', in which the birds leave their home range in enormous numbers and appear in regions quite unsuited to their needs. This is supposedly caused by widespread crop-failure or 'overpopulation'. FAMILY: Fringillidae, ORDER: Passeriformes, CLASS: Aves.

CROWS, 100 or so species of perching birds, usually sombre-coloured of the family Corvidae, probably the most advanced of all birds. They include the largest of the perching birds and the most advanced psychologically. Certain species have a fairly complex social organization, or perform activities which in mammals would probably be labelled 'play'. The family is cosmopolitan, being entirely absent only from New Zealand and certain Pacific islands.

Corvids range in length from 7–28 in (17–71 cm). The typical crows are usually entirely black, or black with white, grey or brown. At close quarters the black plumage can usually be seen to have a blue, green or purple metallic sheen. The jays and magpies are more variable in colour, often showing much blue or green, and they are frequently crested or have long tails. Bright wing or tail bars are seen in some. The bills are stout

The crossbill has what must be the most extraordinary bill of all, the mandibles being crossed as if damaged but used for taking seeds out of pine cones.

Cuckoos

and moderately long, very strong in some such as the ravens, which can open carcasses and skulls with relative ease. The nostrils are protected by forwardly-directed bristles which presumably help to exclude foreign material during feeding. Some species, such as the raven *Corvus corax* and the chough *Pyrrhocorax pyrrhocorax*, show a highly developed mastery of the air exceeded by few other animals. The sexes are similar in appearance.

Most species are omnivorous, taking a wide variety of food, often opportunistically. Many feed on dead or dying animals as well as on garbage. Most will take the eggs or young of other animals, as well as weak adults or anything small enough which they catch unawares.

The breeding of corvids is, in many species, colonial, though other species, e.g. the Carrion crow *Corvus corone*, are gregarious only outside the breeding season. Several species pair for life and both sexes take part in rearing the young. The nest is large, made of stout twigs and placed in a tree or bush or on cliffs or buildings. In a few species, such as the magpie *Pica pica*, the nest is domed, and in the jackdaw *Corvus monedula* it is less bulky and placed in a hole in a tree, building, or cliff face or in the ground. Eggs vary from two to ten in number and are usually cryptically coloured varying from cream to blue with dark markings. Incubation takes two to three weeks and the nestling period is five to six weeks, according to the size of the bird and other factors.

The raven is solitary for much of the year. The rook *C. frugilegus*, on the other hand, is common wherever there are large trees in which to build its groups of nests or 'rookeries' and suitable land on which to forage. It is both gregarious and colonial and is 18 in (46 cm) long. The jackdaw, another colonial species, is only 13 in (33 cm) long. The two species are frequently found together, particularly when feeding. The Carrion crow and Hooded crow, both probably *C. corone*, are found through most of the Palearctic region. They are 18½ in (47 cm) long, the Hooded crow being distinguished by a grey back and belly. In North America these two species are replaced by the Common crow *C. brachyrhynchos*, a very similar species and also, to a certain extent, by the slightly smaller Fish crow *C. ossifragus*, which feeds particularly along rivers and tide-lines.

Another typical species of *Corvus* is the Pied crow *C. albus*, which is common through much of tropical and southern Africa and is the only corvid of any kind found in Madagascar. FAMILY: Corvidae, ORDER: Passeriformes, CLASS: Aves.

CUCKOOS, show a considerable range of variation in size, shape, colour and behaviour, although the name is, for most people, associated with birds that leave their eggs in the nests of other birds which then rear the

A male Common cuckoo looks like a hawk except for the bill and the longer neck.

young. In fact only 47 of the 127 species in this family are brood-parasites.

Most cuckoos have zygodactyl feet, the outermost toe being reversed so that two are directed forwards and two backwards; relatively short legs, causing the bird to squat close to a perch; an elongated shape, a longish tail and a relatively large head and heavy bill. Some tropical species have bare, and often conspicuously coloured, skin around the eyes, and some have noticeable eyelashes. Some have a small, usually tapering crest on the back of the head and this can be erected to some extent. As a group they tend to be skulkers, keeping to the concealment of foliage, better known for their voices than for their appearance. A number of them are mainly terrestrial, usually larger, longer-legged and capable of running strongly, but with wings reduced in size and with poor flying power.

The songs of cuckoos are usually a monotonous repetition of a single call or of several notes. While the repetitive disyllabic call of the Common cuckoo *Cuculus canorus*, which has given the whole family its name, is hailed as a welcome sign of summer, the incessant calling of the Brain-fever bird *Cuculus varius* of the Orient, combined with a hot climate, is reputed to drive men nearly mad.

The principal food of cuckoos ranges from insects and small invertebrates in the case of smaller species to snakes, lizards, small rodents and birds taken by the larger terrestrial forms. A few species also eat fruit. The cuckoos are among the few birds that regularly eat hairy caterpillars.

The typical parasitic cuckoos occur throughout the Old World. They vary from tiny sparrow-sized Glossy cuckoos to the giant Channel-billed cuckoo *Scythrops novae-hollandiae* of northern Australasia, which is over 2 ft (60 cm) long. They have fairly long tails and long narrow wings and are strong

flyers. Some migrate, the Common cuckoo of northern Europe travelling south to Africa in winter, while in the southern hemisphere the little Shining cuckoo *Chalcites lucidus* breeds in Australia and migrates north as far as the Solomon Islands. The smallest species have plumages with vivid iridescent green tints, and in one case a glossy violet colour.

These cuckoos exploit a wide range of host species. The koel *Eudynamys scolopacea* parasitizes crows, the Great spotted cuckoo *Clamator glandarius* uses magpies, other cuckoos of the genus *Clamator* use babblers, typical cuckoos of the genus *Cuculus* exploit a range of small songbirds, and the smallest of the Glossy cuckoos, the Violet cuckoo *Chalcites xanthorhynchus*, lays eggs in the tiny pendent nests of sunbirds. They lay an egg directly into the nest of the host. Where the nest is domed or partially inaccessible the cuckoo forces its way in or clings to the outside of the nest and lays the egg so that it falls into the nest. Only two or three seconds are required to lay the egg. Usually only a single egg is laid in a nest by any one cuckoo, and one of the host's eggs is removed and often eaten. The cuckoo will have observed the nest for a period prior to laying and will usually deposit its egg during the time the host is laying its own clutch. The cuckoo's egg has a shorter incubation period than that of the host. The young cuckoo grows much faster than the young of the host and may simply supplant them by taking almost all available food, so starving them, forcing them out of the nest as it grows. The young of the genus *Cuculus* have a more certain method. For the first few days after hatching the young cuckoo appears to be physically irritated by the presence of an egg or nestling touching it and will wriggle underneath it until it rests on its back. It then rears up against the side of the nest and heaves the egg or nestling out, continuing this until it has the nest to itself. The host parents appear indifferent to their ejected nestlings. The young cuckoo may grow to such a size that it bursts the nest apart.

In many instances cuckoos lay eggs that closely mimic those of the host in colour, pattern and, to some extent, in size. The eggs of the Black-and-white cuckoo *Clamator jacobinus* and some of those of the Violet cuckoo may so closely resemble those of the host that it is very difficult to distinguish them with certainty. This is aided by the tendency for a female cuckoo to lay in the nests of the same host species as that in which she was reared. Some young cuckoos reared in nests of crow species which could harm intruding nestlings have a superficial resemblance to the young of their host. While the advantage of this to the cuckoo is obvious, the fact that several adult cuckoos have a strong superficial resemblance to birds in other families is less obviously advantageous. Some cuckoos closely resemble hawks and in some of these species the immature cuckoos also resemble the immature raptors. The Drongo cuckoo *Surniculus lugubris* resembles the drongo, whose nest it parasitizes, both in its black plumage and its shape.

The non-parasitic cuckoos of the subfamily Phaenicophaeinae are widespread, with a few species on each continent with the exception of Australia. They are slenderly-built skulking birds of forest and thickets. They build shallow cup-shaped nests in trees and incubate their own eggs and rear their own young. The Oriental forms tend to have boldly-coloured bills, bare facial skin and long tails. See also anis and coucals. FAMILY: Cuculidae, ORDER: Cuculiformes, CLASS: Aves.

CUCKOO-SHRIKES, probably most closely related to the bulbuls, have no affinity with either cuckoos or shrikes. There are 70 species in this exclusively Old World family, ranging from about 5–14 in (13–35 cm) long. The family includes the brilliantly coloured black and scarlet or yellow minivets *Pericrocotus*. Otherwise it consists of about 60 species, usually sombrely coloured in various shades of grey or patterned in black and white. Most species have long graduated tails which, combined with their colouring, gives them a shrike-like appearance. This is reflected in several of their numerous vernacular names, e.g. cuckoo-shrike, wood-shrike and fly-catcher-shrike. The scientific name of the family, Campephagidae, means 'caterpillar-eaters', an appropriate description that is also recognized in the vernacular names caterpillar-shrike and caterpillar-bird. Other common names by which some species are known are greybird and triller. In most species the lower back and rump are characteristically covered with a densely matted patch of loosely attached feathers with stiff spine-like shafts. FAMILY: Campephagidae, ORDER: Passeriformes, CLASS: Aves.

CUCUMBERFISHES, also known as pearl-fishes, elongated marine fishes related to the cods that live inside Sea cucumbers. In England they are often called fierasfers, derived from their former scientific name meaning 'shining beasts'. The most striking feature of these fishes is their habit of entering any small crevice tail first. Some species are very particular and *Carapus bermudensis* will only live in one species of Sea cucumber, while others, such as *C. homei*, will live in any shell or Sea cucumber. Although Sea cucumbers are hollow a certain strategy is required in converting the animal into living quarters. When a young cucumberfish finds its host it searches for the anus and pushes its way in. As the fish becomes larger it tends to enter the Sea cucumber tail first. Some cucumberfishes are not above nibbling at their hosts while inside. *Carapus apus* from the Mediterranean is believed to spend its entire life inside the Sea cucumber, presumably feeding on its host. This may not do as much damage as might be thought since the Sea cucumbers have great powers of regeneration. FAMILY: Carapidae, ORDER: Gadiformes, CLASS: Pisces.

CURASSOWS, common name for a family of forest-dwelling birds ranging from southern Texas to Uruguay and Argentina. There are 44 species but only one, the Plain chachalaca *Ortalis vetula* goes as far north as southern Texas. They are large birds, the largest being almost of the size of a turkey. The smallest are the chachalacas of the genus *Ortalis* of which there are ten species. In many features they resemble pheasants. Their plumage is mostly glossy and either black, brown or olive-brown and in most of the species the sexes are alike. Some, such as the seven species of *Crax* have a crest of curly feathers, while others like *Mitu* and *Pauxi* have bizarre looking and colourful helmets on the base of their bills or skulls. Their bills are short, often with a brightly coloured cere, their wings are rounded, the tails are long and flat and they have strong feet. Their flight is heavy but fast and direct even through a dense forest.

All curassows live in forests partly on the ground, partly in the trees, running fast over thick branches. They feed on leaves and fruits.

The nests of curassows are small in comparison to the size of the birds. They make open cup nests of dead sticks, often lined with fresh leaves, in trees and shrubbery frequently quite near the ground and seldom at a great height. FAMILY: Cracidae, ORDER: Galliformes, CLASS: Aves.

CURLEWS, eight species of wading birds of the genus *Numenius* distinguished by long downcurved bills and characteristic call-notes. Their plumage is largely cryptic, with mottled brown upperparts, but most have a white rump, conspicuous in flight. In the Palearctic, the large curlew *N. arquata* breeds in wet meadows and on moorlands in the temperate zone, while the smaller whimbrel *N. phaeopus* replaces it at higher latitudes

Crested curassow *Crax alector* of the forests of the Amazon Basin.

Cuscus

(and altitudes), where it has a discontinuous circumpolar distribution. Whimbrel are absent from north central Siberia, where the Little or Pygmy curlew *N. minutus* breeds, and from northeastern Canada, where the now almost extinct Eskimo curlew *N. borealis* occurs. Further south, in the temperate zone of North America, the whimbrel is replaced by the Long-billed curlew *N. americanus.*

Curlews feed on a variety of small organisms living on or close to the surface of the soil, including insects and crustaceans, but also take many seeds and berries. The significance of the curved bill in obtaining food is not known. FAMILY: Scolopacidae, ORDER: Charadriiformes, CLASS: Aves.

CUSCUS, six species of marsupials, genus *Phalanger*, resembling monkeys in appearance. They have a tropical distribution from the Celebes east to the Solomon Islands. Cuscuses are arboreal, with rounded heads, small ears, large eyes, dense soft fur and a long prehensile tail, the terminal portion of which is without fur. The head and body of the larger species is over 2 ft (60 cm) in length and the tail is only a little shorter.

The Bear cuscuses (*P. celebensis, ursinus*) are large, brown to black animals found only in the Celebes and adjacent islands. The Grey cuscuses include a multiplicity of colour phases ranging from pure white, through various shades of grey, to chocolate-brown or even distinctly reddish (*P. orientalis, gymnotis, vestitus*). The pure white phase is restricted to the male only. This, the most generalized and widest ranging group, extends from the Celebes and Timor, through New Guinea, eastward to most of the Solomon Islands and southwards to Cape York on the Australian mainland.

The Spotted cuscuses (*P. maculatus, atrimaculatus*) include forms in which both sexes may be pure white. Other forms are brightly coloured and spotted in a variable and irregular, nonsymmetrical fashion; a rarity amongst wild animals. The Spotted cuscuses range from New Guinea to Cape York, the Moluccas and other islands near New Guinea but not to the Celebes or Solomon Islands. Except on certain islands northwest of New Guinea, female cuscuses appear to lack the spotted pattern. FAMILY: Phalangeridae, ORDER: Marsupialia, CLASS: Mammalia.

CUTTLEFISH *Sepia officinalis*, marine mollusc related to the squid and octopus, having a well-defined head with two large eyes, and eight arms and two retractile tentacles encircling the mouth. The head is attached by a short neck to the body which is supported internally by the cuttlebone. This not only acts as a support, it is also a buoyancy mechanism enabling the cuttlefish to remain on the bottom or swim freely at any depth. The cuttlefish is a coastal animal and, like all known cephalopods, is a predator.

Cuttlefish swimming and showing a striped colour pattern assumed when among seaweed (protective) and when courting.

The family Sepiidae is confined to the Old World. The cuttlefish is found in the northeast Atlantic, the Mediterranean, the North Sea and the English Channel. The 100 species of Sepiidae are found in tropical and temperate seas, rarely in colder waters. The cuttlefish inhabits coastal regions in water of 16–390 ft (5–120 m) depth. In summer it generally remains in water of 32–65 ft (10–20 m) depth.

Along the length of each of the eight arms are four rows of stalked suckers. The long retractile tentacles when fully extended capture prey on a terminal pad bearing several rows of suckers, the central row having five particularly large ones. These tentacles are normally retracted into two pockets which lie close to the mouth between the base of the third and fourth arms. They are used for capturing prawns and shrimps. The eyes are situated on either side of the head so that the animal can see both in front and behind, with a horizontal visual field of 360°.

The mouth found at the centre of the arms has an upper and a lower beak surrounded by a circular lip. The beaks are chitinous and resemble those of parrots, except that in the cuttlefish the upper one fits into the lower one. Inside the mouth is a tooth-bearing ribbon, the radula, used in the transport of food particles to the oesophagus.

Below the cuttlebone, the visceral mass is enclosed by the muscular mantle which forms a cavity, open at the front. The gills are suspended within the mantle cavity and water is drawn in and then expelled through a median funnel. Contraction of the mantle muscle forces a jet of water through the funnel, strong enough to use for rapid swimming. A cuttlefish also swims more slowly by means of an undulatory movement of the lateral fins. The current of water is also used to expel the produce of the ink sac.

During the courtship both male and female

display a zebra-like pattern, less brilliant in the female, produced by the chromatophores or colour cells of the skin. When the male approaches another cuttlefish the pattern intensifies and the left fourth arm, which is more prominently marked, is extended towards the other. If the other cuttlefish is a female the display is not returned and the arm will touch. The female may accept the male immediately, or swim away in which case the male will follow. The animals then face each other with their arms interwoven. They remain in this position for at least two minutes during which time the spermatophores, or packets of sperm, are transferred to the female by the fourth left arm of the male, which has a reduced number of suckers near the base.

The female lays her eggs a few days after mating. Each in a bluish-black capsule the whole looking like a bunch of grapes. Hatching occurs about 50 days after laying. The young cuttlefish measure about ⅜ in (10 mm).

The cuttlebone consists of numerous thin plates each supported by pillars. Each of the chambers contains gas spaces. The density of the cuttlebone can be changed by pumping liquid in and out of these chambers thereby altering the volume of the gas-filled space.

Changes in the chromatophores occur quickly in response to the environment. A cuttlefish swimming amongst seaweed in a lighted aquarium has a striped pattern which breaks up its outline making it difficult to see. On a sandy bottom the cuttlefish will adopt the pattern of its background and then almost bury itself using the jets of water from the funnel and the undulatory movement of the fins to excavate the sand.

Another protective device is the ejection of ink, the cloud of ink distracting the attention of a predator as the cuttlefish escapes from behind it. FAMILY: Sepiidae, ORDER: Sepioidea, CLASS: Cephalopoda, PHYLUM: Mollusca.

D

DAB *Limanda limanda*, a small flatfish living in sandy bays along the coasts of northern Europe. The dab, which reaches 17 in (43 cm) in length, can be recognized by the sharp curve of the lateral line near the pectoral fin and the spiny margins of the scales on the eyed side of the fish. The colour of the eyed side is sandy brown, flecked with orange and black, while the blind side is white. Occasionally specimens are found which are coloured on both sides and the scales are spiny on the two sides as well. These fishes are inactive during the day but feed at night and are more easily caught then. The breeding season is from March to May, the eggs being pelagic and amongst the smallest of the European flatfishes (0·8 mm in diameter). FAMILY: Pleuronectidae, ORDER: Pleuronectiformes, CLASS: Pisces.

Dab, enormously abundant European flatfish, feeds on marine bristleworms.

DAMSELFLIES, slender dragonflies with fore- and hind-wings similar and stalked at the base. Their larvae have external gills. SUBORDER: Zygoptera, ORDER: Odonata, CLASS: Insecta, PHYLUM: Arthropoda.

DARTERS, aquatic birds related to cormorants. The body is elongated and the neck very markedly so, the wings and tail are long, the head is small and the bill is long and thin but with no terminal hook. Including bill, neck and tail the birds are nearly 3 ft (1 m) long. All four toes are connected by a web. The plumage is for the most part black or dark brown, with a few lighter markings and with pale areas below. The sexes are only slightly dissimilar, but in the breeding season the male has white tufts on the sides of the head and neck.

They live near lakes, slow-flowing rivers and calm estuaries. They often swim on the surface with the body deeply submerged, and they go under without any jump. The food consists mainly of fishes, caught by underwater pursuit. A kink in the neck is due to a conformation of the cervical vertebrae by which the bill becomes a 'triggered spear', the head being suddenly thrust forward as the neck is straightened. Indeed fishes seem to be speared on occasion, but commonly the prey is brought to the surface between the mandibles, tossed in the air, caught in the gape and swallowed.

The nest, in a tree or bush near and often overhanging the water, is a platform of sticks, sometimes bulky. The three to six eggs are pale blue or green under a chalky outer layer. The young are hatched naked but grow a pale down plumage while in the nest. Both parents incubate the eggs and tend the young. FAMILY: Anhingidae, ORDER: Pelecaniformes, CLASS: Aves.

One of the darters, *Anhinga sp,* underwater javelin-thrower with a trigger in its neck.

Geospiza, one of the Ground finches of the 14 species of Darwin's finches.

DARWIN'S FINCHES, a group of sparrow-like birds confined to the Galapagos archipelago (13 species) and Cocos Island, 600 miles (960 km) northwest of the Galapagos (a single endemic species). Although the original stock is unknown, they probably arose by speciation within the islands after their colonization by a single species.

Historically they are important for the impression they made on Darwin during his short visit to the islands. To quote him, 'the most curious fact is the perfect graduation in size of the beaks in the different species of *Geospiza*, from one as large as that of a hawfinch to that of a chaffinch'.

The *Geospiza* species feed on the ground and the different bills enable each to deal efficiently with a different range of seeds so that on the larger islands, which have a range of different habitats, the various species can co-exist. The exceptions are the two species of cactus-finch, *G. scandens* and *G. conirostris*. These two are restricted to islands with the Prickly pear cactus *Opuntia*, and as only one species is found on any one island, the slight differences in the bills may be insufficient to prevent severe competition between them, so that one species will always oust the other.

The other large group are the tree-finches *Camarhynchus*, the six species of which can be conveniently divided into three sub-genera: *Camarhynchus* of three species which feed on largish insects and soft seeds, *Platyspiza* with a single species eating buds, leaves and fleshy fruits and *Cactospiza* of two insect-eating species. Again there are marked differences in bill size and shape correlated with the different diets. The wood- and mangrove-finches *Cactospiza pallida* and *C. heliobates* regularly use small twigs and cactus spines to prod out insects which they would otherwise be unable to reach. The two remaining finches, the warbler-finch *Certhidea olivacea* and the Cocos-finch *Pinarolaxias inornata* have thin bills and eat mainly insects, although the latter species may also eat some nectar. FAMILY: Fringillidae, ORDER: Passeriformes, CLASS: Aves.

DASSIES, short-tailed mammals the size of a rabbit yet showing links with elephants, rhinoceroses and tapirs. In size and general form they appear to have much in common

with rodents, yet their skeleton and nervous system place them between the rhinoceroses and the elephants. The forefeet have four functional toes and a rudimentary first toe, all of which have short nails in the manner of the rhinoceros. The hindfeet have only three toes, of which the inner has a curved claw. The other toes are similar to those on the front feet. The incisors of the upper jaw grow from persistent pulps and are curved as in rodents. They do not follow the rodent plan of ending in a chisel-like edge, but are prismatic and end in fine points. There is one pair of incisors in the top jaw, but those in the lower jaw number four and differ in being rooted. The outermost pair tend to lie flat and have trilobate crowns. The grinding or cheekteeth, separated from the incisors by a considerable gap, are seven in number and resemble those of a rhinoceros.

The dassie, Rock hyrax, Rock rabbit or coney, *Procavia capensis* is about the size of a rabbit, has a blunt head with small ears and is covered with soft brown fur. In the middle of the back is a yellowish white patch of hair that marks the site of the dorsal gland.

The dassie is found throughout Africa, southern Arabia and Syria. Dassies live in groups of 60 and more, making their homes in cliffs and rocky hilltops. They are experts at climbing rocks and boulders.

They feed mainly on plants and fruits. Their feeding times are rigid and they will appear for this purpose in the early morning and the late afternoon. They also have the habit of using a communal latrine in their dens, and the excrement that collects here has a commercial value, as it contains an ingredient used in the manufacture of perfumes. They spend a large part of their day basking in the sun, but they also have to keep at least one eye open for predators such as leopards, hawks and eagles. When alarmed they either utter a whistling note or make a chattering noise. The litter of two or three young are born after a gestation period of $7\frac{1}{2}$ months (225 days). At the time of their birth the young are able to see and very soon after they are born they can follow the mother.

The Syrian hyrax *Procavia syriaca* is very similar. This is the 'coney' of the Bible. The Tree dassie, or bosdas *Dendrohyrax arboreus*

is a tree-dwelling hyrax which differs slightly from the dassie in that the fur is often longer, the coat may vary from a rich brown to a grizzled grey and the soles of the feet are entirely naked, allowing it to move with ease in the trees. It is found from South Africa northwards into the Belgian Congo, Tanzania and Kenya. The cry differs in that it starts with a series of groans and culminates in a screaming wail. FAMILY: Procaviidae, ORDER: Hyracoidea, CLASS: Mammalia.

DASYURE *Dasyurus quoll*, alternative name for the *Native cat of southeast Australia and Tasmania. See Marsupial cat.

DEAD MAN'S FINGERS *Alcyonium digitatum*, a Soft coral, drab yellowish-white and shaped rather like a human hand. It is a colony of octocoralline polyps found in temperate waters, although most Soft corals live in warm seas. The colony is a mass of mesogloea in which the polyps are embedded. Each polyp bears eight feathery tentacles and is very much elongated, the cylindrical tube-like body extending through the mesogloea to the base of the colony. It is connected to other polyps in the colony by tube-like extensions of the body wall. The skeleton consists of a mass of spicules, elongated spindles of calcium carbonate secreted by ectodermal cells and generally distributed through the mesogloea. The polyps catch their prey by means of nematocysts on the feathery tentacles. FAMILY: Alcyoniidae, ORDER: Alcyonacea, CLASS: Anthozoa, PHYLUM: Cnidaria.

DEALFISHES, a family of ribbon-like oceanic fishes related to the oarfish and the opah and usually found in deep water in all oceans. Although quite large, dealfishes are very fragile and it is often difficult to determine the exact form of the fins. In some species there are two dorsal fins, the first one consisting of a few elongated rays narrowly separated from the second long dorsal fin; in other species the two dorsal fins are united. The anal fin is missing, the pectoral fins are very small and the pelvic fins are reduced or absent. The most curious feature is the tail. Only the upper half is present and this sticks up like a fan at right angles to the body.

The dealfish is found everywhere in the Atlantic and has even been recorded from New Zealand. It lives at depths down to 1,800 ft (600 m). The largest specimen washed ashore was 8 ft (2·4 m) in length. A related species, *T. iris*, is found in the Mediterranean and the tropical southern Atlantic. FAMILY: Trachipteridae, ORDER: Lampridiformes, CLASS: Pisces.

DEATH WATCH BEETLE *Xestobium rufovillosum*, a small wood-boring beetle related to the wood-worm, about $\frac{1}{4}$ in (5–7 mm) long, dark chocolate-brown with patches of yellowish scales which soon wear off. Although under favourable circumstances out-of-doors the length of its life-cycle may be as little as one year, when infesting interior woodwork this may take ten years or longer, depending on the state of fungal decay of the wood it is eating. The presence of wood-rotting fungi appears to be obligatory for the development of the beetle which usually emerges in April or May. It is seldom seen to fly. Perhaps the best-known feature of the Death watch beetle, however, is the tapping noise it makes, by both sexes striking the head, usually against the wood on which the insect is standing, and appears to act as a sexual call. Infestations by this species are almost entirely confined to buildings where large dimensional timbers were installed at least 100 years ago and it seems virtually certain that Death watch larvae went into the buildings with the timber in the first place. There are no new infestations of Death watch beetle so that with progressive control, the number of viable infestations is decreasing. FAMILY: Anobiidae, ORDER: Coleoptera, CLASS: Insecta, PHYLUM: Arthropoda.

DESMAN, aquatic insectivore resembling a very large shrew. Formerly widely distributed in Europe they are now represented by two localized relict species: *Galemys pyrenaicus* in the Pyrenees and northern Portugal and *Desmana moschata* in the rivers north of the Caspian Sea. They are 8 in (20 cm) and 4–5 in (11–13 cm) long respectively.

The desman's hindfeet are powerful and have webbed toes, the forefeet are also wholly or partly webbed. All four feet bear fringes of bristles to increase their effectiveness as paddles.

The snout projects well beyond the teeth and lower lip and is so long that it may be bent back on itself and licked with the tongue. It is flattened, tubular, has two grooves along its length and is only sparsely covered with short bristly hairs. It is very mobile and is frequently waved about in scenting the air. It is also used to investigate food by touch and smell. The nostrils, situated at the end of this snout, can be closed by small skin flap-valves. Eyes and ears are very tiny, and the desman relies very much on its snout and whiskers for investigating its environment.

Desmans live in burrows beside streams and rivers. An entrance tunnel is dug from water level up into the bank, often under tree roots. Their food is insects and their larvae, crustaceans and fish together with some worms. The snout is used for winkling out smaller creatures from under stones and other hiding places. FAMILY: Talpidae, ORDER: Insectivora, CLASS: Mammalia.

DEVIL RAYS, large ray-like cartilaginous fishes whose 'devilish' reputation stems more from their size and curious appearance than from their supposedly ferocious behaviour.

They have the wing-like pectoral fins of the ordinary skate or ray and closely resemble the Eagle rays except that the mouth is much wider and has a pair of appendages on either side, used as scoops in feeding. They are surface-living and feed on small crustaceans and plankton. The mouth, terminal in most of the species, is kept open as the fish cruises along and food is collected by fine sieve-like rakers before the water passes to the gills. Some species grow to an enormous size and there is a record of a specimen that measured 22 ft (6·6 m) from tip to tip of the pectoral fins. There are many records of these fishes leaving the water and sailing through the air, the resounding noise of their return to water having been compared with the sound of a cannon. A single species of the genus *Manta* is known from the warmer parts of the Atlantic and it is possible that it is this same species, *M. birostris*, that occurs throughout the Indo-Pacific region. FAMILY: Mobulidae, ORDER: Hypotremata, CLASS: Chondrichthyes,

DHOLE *Cuon alpinus*, Asiatic wild dog, a fierce hunter of great stamina. It weighs from 25–35 lb (11–15½ kg) and has a head and body length of 38 in (96 cm) and a tail length of 18 in (45 cm). It differs from most canids in having a reduced number of molar teeth in its lower jaw and a thick muzzle. Distributed throughout the Oriental tropical and mountain forests, in Nepal, India, Malaysia and Sumatra, the dhole has rufous fur with a darker-coloured tail ending in a black tail tip. It lives in groups of 5–20 although large packs of several families and their young may have up to 40 members.

When hunting, dholes display a degree of teamwork, with different individuals alternately chasing the prey and then resting. Favourite victims are Wild pigs, chital, Spotted deer, and muntjac which are attacked mainly on the muzzle and face or rump region and then pulled down.

Dholes are mainly active during the day, but the preferred time for a hunt is the early

morning. While travelling through the forest, individuals communicate with one another by a whistling call, but they also howl, bark and whine, the latter especially when they are distressed. FAMILY: Canidae, ORDER: Carnivora, CLASS: Mammalia.

DIBATAG *Ammodorcas clarkei*, a long-necked, long-legged antelope superficially resembling the gerenuk. However, although it has gazelline face-stripes, it lacks facial or carpal glands, has a large bare muzzle, and has a tufted tail. The horns are short, forwardly concave.

A dibatag stands 31–36 in (79–92 cm) high, and weighs 60–75 lb (27–34 kg). The build is slender. The colour is dark cinnamon, white below; the face is marked with white longitudinal streaks, with dark median and lateral stripes.

The dibatag is found in Somalia, east of the Webi Shebeli river, and in eastern Ethiopia as far as 9° or 10°N. It lives in arid, thornbush country, in small groups of three to five individuals, or solitarily. When disturbed it bounds away with its head arched back and its tail swung forward above the rump. FAMILY: Bovidae, ORDER, Artiodactyla, CLASS: Mammalia.

DIK-DIK, six species of small antelope (*Madoqua, Rhynchotragus*) found from Ethiopia to northern Kenya with one species in southwest Africa. They are 21–27 in (53–69 cm) in head and body length, stand 12–16 in (30–40 cm) at the shoulder and weigh 7–11 lb (3–5 kg). The males have short horns often partly hidden by a tuft of hair. They live solitary or in pairs, sometimes in small family parties, in dense undergrowth from which they race away, when flushed, on a zigzag course. FAMILY: Bovidae, ORDER: Artiodactyla, CLASS: Mammalia.

DINGO, Australian wild dog, probably descendant of a domesticated dog, introduced 3,000 years ago, gone feral.

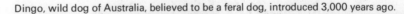

Dingo, wild dog of Australia, believed to be a feral dog, introduced 3,000 years ago.

Dippers

Dipper feeding nestling. Dippers may build their nests in crevices in rocks or in holes in bridges, often under waterfalls.

DIPPERS, wren-like songbirds of western North and South America, northwest Africa, Europe and the temperate parts of Asia. They resemble wrens in their short wings and tail, copious plumage and type of nest, but are specialized for feeding in or under running water, with the tarsus long and sturdy and with stout claws for gripping the river bed.

Dippers vary in size between a sparrow and a Song thrush, have thin bills and are predominantly grey or brown. Although the sexes look alike (and both sing), the dipper *Cinclus cinclus* of Europe can be distinguished in the hand by the greater wing length of the male, 87–95 mm compared with 84–92 of the female.

Dippers are confined to hilly and mountainous regions. The European dipper ranges from Britain eastwards to northwest Africa and central Asia, reaching 16,000 ft (4,920 m) in the Himalayas and nearly 17,000 ft (5,230 m) in Tibet.

Nests are usually built on rock faces (including waterfalls), on sluices, mills, culverts and bridges, and under overhanging banks and against tree trunks. The entrance is normally over water. Most nests are built at heights of 4–5 ft (1·2–1·5 m).

The large nest usually fits into a roofed cavity, its outer shell made of mosses. The material, collected by both cock and hen, is dipped into the river before use, presumably to make it work more easily into the shell of the nest. An inner nest of dried grasses is added and finally a lined cup of leaves.

Nest-building begins as early as February and proceeds slowly. Eggs may be laid in mid-March but more usually in April. Four or five thin-shelled white eggs are laid. They hatch in about 16 days and the young are fed by both parents for about three weeks.

There were early controversies as to whether a dipper could walk under water and, if so, whether it could do so only against the current. More recently dippers have been filmed swimming under water using their wings, not their legs. It is also quite easy to watch dippers walking upstream in shallow water searching for prey on the river bed. Their food mainly consists of the larvae of aquatic insects, and small aquatic molluscs and crustaceans. Small fishes are also taken but not very expertly dealt with, together with worms and tadpoles. FAMILY: Cinclidae, ORDER: Passeriformes, CLASS: Aves.

DISCUSFISHES *Symphysodon*, flattened disc-shaped freshwater fishes of South America. They are remarkable for their parental care and also because the fry feed for the first weeks on a secretion from the parental skin. They feed on the body of one parent, who after a while flicks them skilfully onto the flanks of the other parent. FAMILY: Cichlidae, ORDER: Perciformes, CLASS: Pisces.

Black-throated diver, also called Arctic loon, nests near the water's edge. It has difficulty in walking on land.

Lesser spotted dogfish swimming in the aquarium of the Plymouth Biological Station.

DIVERS, fish-eating diving birds, also known as loons. They are quite large, from the weight of a large duck to a small goose, with a long body and thick, strong neck. The tail is short, the legs and feet strong, with webs between the three front toes and the bill is stout, long and pointed. The only externally visible part of the leg is the so-called 'tarsal' or lower segment, and the foot. The leg emerges from the body at the rear which allows great propulsive efficiency in water. But this also means that loons have great difficulty in standing on land and their mode of progression out of the water is by pushing themselves along on the belly.

The plumage is of a hard, harsh texture, except on the neck where it is soft. The young have two successive coats of down. Adult loons are strikingly marked, with white stripes or spots contrasting with the basic colour of black, grey or brown. The sexes are externally similar. They have a distinctive appearance in flight with head and legs hanging down somewhat and the feet projecting beyond the tail. In the Red-throated diver *Gavia stellata*, this attitude is seen in its most definite form giving the appearance of a flying banana! Because of their swimming adaptations, particularly the small wings, loons have difficulty in taking flight and need to taxi for a considerable distance to pick up speed before becoming airborne. Once aloft they fly strongly.

Loons have a wide distribution throughout the Arctic, though the Common loon is almost exclusively a nearctic breeder. During the breeding season all species are essentially freshwater birds, frequenting lakes, ponds, streams and slow-moving rivers. However, enormous tracts of land fulfilling these requirements in the Arctic are found near the sea, and loons in such areas may divide their time between fresh and salt water even in the breeding season. Outside that season their habitat is essentially the maritime one, particularly estuaries and inshore waters.

The distribution of these birds is largely determined by their food, which consists almost entirely of fishes, which they pursue and capture beneath the surface of the water. They dive effortlessly from the surface in a smooth forward plunge, and stay beneath the surface for up to a minute or more, mostly in water of a depth of 6–18 ft (2–6 m) thus swimming with only the head above water.

The Common loon or Great northern diver *Gavia immer* breeds throughout arctic North America and in Greenland and Iceland and some smaller islands. It is one of the larger species, up to some 36 in (91 cm) long. The Yellow-billed loon (White-billed diver) *G. adamsii*, replaces the Common loon in the far north and west of North America and also breeds around the European and Asian coasts of the Arctic Ocean. The Arctic loon or Black-throated diver *G. arctica* has a circumpolar distribution in arctic and subarctic habitats. It is 24 in (60 cm) long.

The Red-throated loon or Red-throated diver *G. stellata* is another circumpolar species and is the most widely distributed of all the loons. FAMILY: Gaviidae, ORDER: Gaviiformes, CLASS: Aves.

DOG, a general term referring to members of the Canidae, including the wolf, coyote, jackals, foxes and the domestic dog. All have an acute sense of smell and hearing and specialize in hunting, usually relying on speed and endurance to wear down their prey. They show, for mammals, an unusual variability in size, shape and colouring. This has been used to produce the wide range of domestic dogs, including sporting breeds, hounds, working dogs, terriers and toy dogs, from the chihuahua 3–5 lb (1.5–2.5 kg) to the St Bernard up to 200 lb (90 kg). Domestication began 10,000 to 15,000 years ago. By 3000BC the Egyptians already had mastiffs, terriers, pointers and greyhounds. FAMILY: Canidae, ORDER: Carnivora, CLASS: Mammalia.

DOGFISHES, are small sharks characterized by having two dorsal fins, which lack a spine in front, and one anal fin. A spiracle is present but there is no nictitating membrane or 'third eyelid'. The two most common European species are the Greater spotted dogfish *Scyliorhinus stellaris* and the Lesser spotted dogfish *S. caniculus*, the former also known as the nursehound or bullhuss. In both species the body is generally light brown with a fine speckling of black on the upper surfaces, the spots being larger in the Greater spotted dogfish. They feed on worms, molluscs, crustaceans and echinoderms. Dogfishes are oviparous and produce rectangular egg cases with a spiralling tendril at each corner. The embryo does not hatch for seven months. FAMILY: Scyliorhinidae, ORDER: Pleurotremata, CLASS: Chondrichthyes.

DOLPHINS, a group of small Toothed whales difficult to define accurately. Strictly speaking, the term should be limited to the true dolphins (family Delphinidae), but it would be unreasonable not to include the closely related Long-beaked dolphins (Stenidae). Rather more dissimilar are the River dolphins (Platanistidae). In practice, therefore, the term is used for smaller Toothed whales that are not porpoises. The difficulty surrounding the name dolphin is made greater by the fact that even among the true dolphins there are whales in the generally accepted sense: large animals of over 20 ft (7 m) in length. A male Killer whale, for instance, may be 30 ft (10 m) long. Another difficulty, particularly in America, is that the word dolphin tends, in popular language, to be restricted to the game fish dolphins *Coryphaena* and hence cetacean dolphins are popularly called porpoises. But the name porpoise should more properly be restricted to the family Phocaenidae which are all fairly small animals, rarely over 6 ft (2 m) in length, with a rounded head, a mouth with spade-like teeth, a triangular dorsal fin and rather rounded fore-flippers. Dolphins on the other hand usually have conical teeth (when present), commonly a beak-like mouth and a dorsal fin with a curved trailing edge (though some have no dorsal fin).

The best known is the Bottlenosed dolphin *Tursiops truncatus*, the highly intelligent and friendly creature now so popular in many large aquaria. It is up to 12 ft (4 m) in length and has a medium-sized beak with 40 teeth in each jaw. It is usually grey on the back but may approach black; the belly, chest and throat are white or pale grey but there is no sharp line between the two shades. It is found on both sides of the North Atlantic and in the Mediterranean. A very similar Bottlenosed dolphin *T. aduncus* is found in the Red Sea, Indian Ocean and around Australia, whilst *T. gilli* is the Pacific form.

Members of the genus *Sotalia* are small, only about $3\frac{1}{2}$ ft (1 m) long. Four species are found in the Amazon and one in the harbour of Rio de Janeiro. The genus *Sousa*, also

Dolphins

long-beaked, is found in tropical waters of the eastern Atlantic, the Indian and Pacific Oceans. It includes *S. teuszii*, found in rivers in Senegal and the Cameroons, which was formerly thought to be the only whale to feed on vegetable material. *S. plumbea* is found off East Africa. The Chinese white dolphin *S. sinensis* is a truly white animal found up the Yangtze and other Chinese waters.

The Common dolphin *Delphinus delphis* is found in large schools in temperate waters throughout the world. It is slender, up to 8 ft (2·4 m) in length and has a pronounced beak, It has a dark grey to black back and a white belly with light grey or brownish stripes on the mouth. It is probably the fastest of all dolphins. When caught it has been found to be very nervous and difficult to keep in captivity as it needs to be with its fellows. At sea in freedom and company, however, it will approach boats and even swimmers.

The Irrawaddy dolphin *Orcaella breviros-tris*, a beakless dolphin about 7 ft (2·1 m) in length, with a small dorsal fin, rather long broad flippers and an overall blue-grey colour, is found in the Irrawaddy over 900 miles (1,400 km) upriver. It is traditionally adopted by the local fishing communities and, although feeding exclusively on fish itself, has the reputation for driving fish into the fishermen's nets.

There are two species of Right whale

dolphins, so called because they have no dorsal fin, like the true Right whales. *Lisso-delphis peronii* is found in southern seas around New Zealand and southern Australia. It is a strikingly patterned animal of some 6 ft (1·8 m) length, having the top of the head, back and flukes black and the rest of the body, including the flippers, white. The northern species *L. borealis*, found in the North Pacific is larger, over 8 ft (2½ m), and the black extends downwards to include the flippers.

The Dusky dolphin *Lagenorhynchus obscurus*, is the commonest dolphin around New Zealand where it is found in large schools but extends across to the Falkland Islands and to South Africa. It is black and white with black back, mouth, eye, flippers and tail but with white bands coming from the belly giving a marvellous effect.

Risso's dolphin *Grampus griseus* is a longish, beakless dolphin about 12–13 ft (4 m) in length. It is grey and may be black on the fin, flippers and tail whilst the underside is paler to lighter grey or even white. It is very widely distributed in the North Atlantic and the Mediterranean and in the south around New Zealand and South Africa. The famous Pelorus Jack was a Risso's dolphin which frequented the Pelorus Sound between Nelson and Wellington, New Zealand, where it swam at the bows of ships for 24 years. FAMILIES: Delphinidae and Stenidae, ORDER: Cetacea, CLASS: Mammalia.

Dolphin in a seaquarium, a familiar sight to visitors over the last 30 years.

Tursiops catalania, of the Indian Ocean and Australian seas, a near relative of the Bottlenosed dolphin, at play.

Common or Hazel dormouse seems most of its time to be asleep or about to fall asleep.

Common dragonets courting. The male is considerably larger than the female.

DORMICE, rodents that tend to bridge the gap between squirrels and mice. With one exception they have bushy tails but are mostly mouse- rather than squirrel-sized and, like most mice, they are nocturnal. Dormice are agile climbers living in trees or in the shrub layer of woodland. The fur is soft and dense. It varies in colour from orange-brown to grey, and many species have dark marks around the eyes, accentuating the already large eyes. The feet are well adapted for climbing, with long flexible toes, and the hindfeet can be turned outwards at right angles to the body enabling the animal to move confidently on slender twigs.

Their food is varied, including both animal and vegetable material, although it is mostly seeds and berries.

The dormice of the temperate region are noted for their hibernation, which begins in October. They become very fat in early autumn and during hibernation become torpid and cold, but may awaken occasionally. The reputation for deep sleep is well founded, since even the daily sleep is unusually profound and is accompanied by a distinct fall in body temperature.

The Hazel dormouse of Europe (the Common dormouse in Britain) *Muscardinus avellanarius* is one of the smallest and has a distinctive orange-brown coat. It lives in dense shrubby undergrowth where it constructs neat nests, only using the shredded bark of honeysuckle. The largest European species, the Fat dormouse *Glis glis*, is more arboreal, nesting in holes or in exposed positions quite high in the woodland canopy. It is also known as the Edible dormouse, since the Ancient Romans fattened it for the table in special jars.

One of the most attractive of all dormice is the Garden dormouse *Eliomys quercinus*, a European species with a conspicuous black mask and a long tail, bushy only towards the tip. It frequents rocky hillsides as well as woodland and is especially common in the Mediterranean region. By far the most isolated species of this family, geographically speaking, is the Japanese dormouse *Glirulus japonicus*, since dormice are quite absent from the mainland of temperate eastern Asia.

African dormice belong to the genus *Graphiurus* and are found throughout the forest and savannah zones of Africa. Although primarily arboreal, they are frequently found living in the thatch of houses. FAMILY: Gliridae, ORDER: Rodentia, CLASS: Mammalia.

DORCAS GAZELLE *Gazella dorcas,* known as afri in Arabia. Its horns are compressed, usually curved in at the tips and its coat is pale red-fawn with an inconspicuous flank-stripe and well-developed face-stripes. It lives on the stony desert of the Sahara into Egypt, northern Somalia, Arabia, southern Iran, Pakistan and northern India. FAMILY: Bovidae, ORDER: Artiodactyla, CLASS: Mammalia.

DRAGONETS, flattened, bottom-living fishes, the dragonets rarely grow to more than 12 in (30 cm) in length. They have flat, depressed heads and slender bodies, but many are so beautifully coloured that they resemble some of the tropical reef fishes. There are no scales on the body.

Two species are found along European shores, the Common dragonet *Callionymus lyra* and the Spotted dragonet *C. maculatus.* The female is rather dull coloured, but the male is a splendid fish, especially in the breeding season. His back is red-yellow with blue markings and the flanks and lower part of the head are orange, again with blue spots and marks. There are two blue bands along the body and the fins are marked with blue, yellow and green. The differences between the sexes are so striking that they were once thought to be quite different species, the 'sordid' and the 'gemmeous' dragonets. Spawning takes place in spring and summer, the male swimming around the female and displaying with gill covers and fins until the female is sufficiently stimulated. The two then swim together to the surface, close together and with the anal fins forming a gutter into which eggs and sperm are shed.

The Spotted dragonet is a smaller fish and can be distinguished by the three or four rows of ocellated spots instead of bands along the dorsal fin. FAMILY: Callionymidae, ORDER: Perciformes, CLASS: Pisces.

DRAGONFLIES, robust, winged carnivorous insects most often seen flying along the edges of ponds and rivers during sunny weather. They have two pairs of narrow, richly-veined wings, a long slender abdomen and prominent eyes. Features that distinguish dragonflies from other insects are the skewed thorax and forwardly directed legs, the inconspicuous antennae and the existence of accessory genitalia on the second and third abdominal segments of the male. The larvae (sometimes referred to as nymphs) are fully aquatic, and have the labium (second maxillae) highly modified for seizing prey.

Because they are large, active by day and often strikingly coloured, dragonflies have captured man's interest and imagination.

Dragonflies are primarily tropical but occur in temperate latitudes to the limit of trees. In the northern hemisphere they reach the Arctic Circle.

Dragonflies are able to reproduce in almost

Drongos

A dragonfly nymph (left) crawls up a stem, turns into a pupa (centre), the pupal skin splits, the mature dragonfly struggles out.

any kind of fresh water that is not too hot, acid or saline. There are species adapted to breeding in temporary ponds, rockpools, waterfalls, brackish marshes, and even the water that collects in the leaf-bases of certain forest plants. In Hawaii lives the only species known to have a terrestrial larva, *Megalagrion oahuense*.

The order Odonata is represented today by three suborders: Zygoptera, Anisoptera and Anisozygoptera. All but two of the 5,000 or so known species belong to the first two suborders.

Zygoptera, known as damselflies, have both pairs of wings similar in shape and stem-like at the base. The compound eyes are widely separated and project like buttons on either side of the head. In Anisoptera the hindwings are much broader than the forewings, neither pair being stem-like at the base. The compound eyes are always less than one eye-width apart and usually touch across the middle of the head. Some migrate regularly and have been known to accomplish flights of hundreds of miles over the sea.

Anisozygoptera possess characters inter-mediate between those of Zygoptera and Anisoptera.

The earliest known dragonflies occurred in the Upper Carboniferous era, about 280 million years ago, and included the largest known insect, *Meganeura monyi*, which had a wing-span of 28 in (70 cm) against the $7\frac{1}{2}$ in (19 cm) of the largest living dragonfly.

Dragonfly larvae catch their prey in an unusual way. Typically, they remain motionless until a small creature comes near enough to be detected by sight or touch. When the creature comes within range, the larva suddenly extends the labium, at the tip of which are hooks that open to grasp the prey. The labium then draws the victim back to the mandibles. When in the resting position, the labium lies folded beneath the head and thorax, sometimes hiding the lower part of the face; for this reason it is sometimes called the 'mask'.

Adult dragonflies lay eggs in or near water. The aquatic larva casts its skin 8–15 times before completing development, passing through a corresponding number of intervening stages, or instars. ORDER: Odonata, CLASS: Insecta, PHYLUM: Arthropoda.

Black drongo *Dicrurus macrocercus*, stoops like a falcon at nest predators.

DRONGOS, medium-sized songbirds with flycatcher habits. There are 20 species through Africa south of the Sahara, southern Asia from India to China, and south to Australasia. They vary from 7–15 in (18–38 cm) in length but this is due in part to a fairly long tail. The stance on a perch is upright, the legs are short, the wing long and tapering, and the tail forked. The bill is strong and stout, hooked at the tip and slightly notched to grip the prey, with long strong bristles around the base. Drongos are agile and swift in flight and can manoeuvre quickly. The feet are strong and can not only help to seize larger prey in the air but can also be used to hold an insect and raise it towards the bill parrot-fashion.

The plumage is grey in two species, flight feathers are red-brown in another, but otherwise drongos are black, with a few showing some white on the underside, wing-coverts or head. The black plumage shows glosses of blue green or purple to varying degrees, often confined to a part of the plumage. The tips of the forked tail may be greatly extended, apparently as a decoration.

The calls of drongos are very varied, consisting of whistling, chuckling, harsh or melodious notes. Some species are mimics. FAMILY: Dicruridae, ORDER: Passeriformes, CLASS: Aves.

DUCKS, 137 species of aquatic birds comprising most of the smaller members of the family Anatidae, which also includes the geese and swans. See eider, mallard, Mandarin duck, Muscovy duck, pochard and shelduck.

DUGONG *Dugong dugon*, or seacow, a large, totally aquatic, herbivorous mammal which lives in warm Indo-Pacific seas. The dugong commonly grows to a length of about 10 ft (3 m) although lengths of 16 ft (5 m) have been noted. It is heavily built, torpedo-shaped with a horizontally flattened whale-like tail. Like the whales, too, all trace of hindlegs has disappeared. The fore flippers are small and take no part in propulsion. All the bones are of exceptional density and the skull is heavy and down-turned in front. The teeth are limited to a small number of crushing teeth and there are horny pads in the front of each jaw. A pair of tusks is also present in the upper jaw. The tusks of the female never become visible.

The grey skin is immensely thick and tough and nearly hairless. The flesh is palatable.

The head is well suited to feeding on plants growing on the bottom. The bristly mask forms a flat and down-turned front to the head above the mouth. The nostrils are high on the head and are equipped with powerful muscular valves. The eyes are small and circular and the ear holes are minute.

The single pair of mammary glands are almost in the armpit. The occasional suckling of a young one held vertically by a flipper must be a reason for the mermaid myth.

The dugong is limited to the coastal waters. Today its numbers have been greatly depleted by man almost everywhere so that it has become a rare animal. On the east coast of Australia there was systematic exploitation for oil, in the last century by the European Australians, in addition to local hunting. Breathing at the surface is normally a brief soundless visit every few minutes, the tips of the nostrils only just becoming visible. One young is born at a time and it probably accompanies its mother for a long period.

Their habit is to feed, especially at night,

Banded duiker, or Zebra antelope of West Africa, only 16 in (40 cm) high.

in the shallow areas where dense patches of dugong grass (*Zostera* etc.) grow. The food is pulled off by the powerful lips, and dislodged vegetation floating to the surface informs the hunter of the creature's presence. FAMILY: Dugongidae, ORDER: Sirenia, CLASS: Mammalia.

DUIKER, a group of small African antelopes. None is more than 30 in (76 cm) tall and many are less than half that. The head is conical with a convex nose and a small bare muzzle. The horns are smooth, somewhat keeled, and placed on a backwardly-projecting eminence of the frontal bone. In front of the eyes are face-glands. Instead of being close to the eye, they are halfway between it and the muzzle. There is a line of bare skin, lying at a slight angle to the eye-muzzle axis, which is studded with a line of glandular pores. As well as face-glands, duikers have foot-glands, and sometimes inguinal (groin) glands too. The duiker's fur is short and close, often rather harsh and longer on the rump than on the neck, and there is usually a long tuft between the horns.

Duikers occur all over subsaharan Africa. They inhabit forest and savannah where there is thick ground-cover. There is only one savannah species. This has long legs, and the horns turn upwards from the base. There are at least 11 species of the forest duikers. They have horns that point straight backwards in a line with the face, and their

The mandarin, most showy of ornamental ducks, is often kept in ornamental gardens. Escapers soon go wild and settle down.

One of the many species of Dung Beetle related to the scarab.

build is wedge-shaped, with short forelegs and a high rounded rump—an obvious adaptation to pushing through thick undergrowth. The name comes from the Afrikaans word meaning 'diver', referring to the way duikers plunge into the undergrowth when disturbed. FAMILY: Bovidae, ORDER: Artiodactyla, CLASS: Mammalia.

DUNG BEETLES, dark heavy-bodied insects that feed on animal, especially mammalian, droppings. The adults of the larger Dung beetles have powerful spiny legs. The head often has a flat scoop-like projection used to push balls of dung over the ground. The beetles fashion the balls by breaking off a portion from a large mass and tumbling it to and fro until it is spherical. The beetles may also roll dung balls by holding them between their hindlegs. The ball is transported to a suitable retreat before being eaten. Some Dung beetles are unique among insects in that a male and female may co-operate in their care of the young stages. They excavate two to seven chambers in the soil and stock each with a separate store of dung. A single egg is deposited in each chamber and the female remains to guard the nest. In some species the female even remains long enough to tend her brood to maturity. The larvae develop into thick grubs with well developed legs. FAMILY; Scarabaeidae, ORDER: Coleoptera, CLASS: Insecta, PHYLUM: Arthropoda.

A Shoveler duck, widely spread round the northern hemisphere, skims a variety of small food from the surface.

E

EAGLES, powerful, rapacious, diurnal birds of prey. 'Eagle' includes many widely divergent species which divide naturally into four not very closely related groups.

1 The Sea and Fish eagles, *Haliaetus* and *Ichthyophaga*, with a worldwide range except for South America are typified by the European sea eagle *Haliaetus albicilla*. To these may be added the aberrant Vulturine fish eagle or Palm-nut vulture *Gypohierax angolensis* which feeds almost exclusively on the pericarp of oil palm nuts.

2 The Snake and Serpent eagles, confined to Africa and Asia, typified by the European serpent or Short-toed eagle *Circaetus gallicus*.

3 The Harpy and Crested eagles and relatives, an ill-defined group, mainly South American, but with representatives in the Philippines and New Guinea. Typified by the Harpy eagle *Harpya harpyja*, these are large or very large raptors, allied to buzzards.

4 The true 'Booted' or Aquiline eagles, which differ from all the others in that the tarsus is feathered to the toes. They are worldwide, but more common in the Old World, typified by the Golden eagle *Aquila chrysaetos*.

Eagles vary in size from the largest and most formidable of all birds of prey the Harpy eagle and Philippine monkey-eating eagle *Pithecophaga jefferyi* to tiny species such as the Nias Island serpent eagle *Spilornis cheela asturinus* and Ayres hawk-eagle *Hieraetus dubius*.

Two huge species are the European sea eagle or erne *Haliaetus albicilla* and Steller's sea eagle *Haliaetus pelagicus*. The latter is a huge bird, weighing 15 lb (6½ kg) or more, with a wing-span approaching 8 ft (2½ m) capable of killing a seal calf.

Sea, Fish and Vulturine fish eagles have bare tarsi and adults show much white, especially on the head and tail; immature birds are brown. They are all more or less confined to large lakes, rivers or the seashore. Some, for example, the African fish eagle *Haliaetus vocifer*, are numerous and familiar in such habitats. All these eagles except the Vulturine fish eagle, have spicules on the feet adapted to grasping fishes, but not to

such an extreme degree as the osprey. Fish is important in the diet of all, even the Vulturine fish eagle. Two species, the Bald eagle *H. leucocephalus* and Steller's sea eagle, feed much on stranded and dying Pacific salmon.

Most Snake Eagles have bare tarsi and short, powerful toes, to grasp and quickly immobilize quick-moving and venomous serpents. They are not immune to snake venom and depend upon agility, dense feathers and heavily scaled legs. All have rather large, often crested heads, with very large yellow eyes. The most unusual is the African bateleur *Terathopius ecaudatus* with exceptionally long wings and a very short tail. They spend most of the day traversing the African skies,

usually at 2–500 ft (60–150 m), at an airspeed of about 35–55 mph (56–88 kph). They hold their wings with a pronounced upward slant and, having little tail, steer by canting from side to side—hence the name 'bateleur' French for old-time tightrope walkers. Bateleurs eat snakes, but also take mammals and ground birds and will eat carrion.

The Harpy eagle is huge, females weighing about 15 lb (6½ kg) or more, males 8–10 lb (3½–4½ kg). It ranges widely in tropical South and Central American forests. Harpies are fierce and powerful predators, feeding upon large forest mammals such as monkeys, agoutis and sloths. A female Harpy has legs almost as thick as a child's wrist and massive

African Bateleur eagle, French for 'circus artist' performs somersaults in the air.

feet with huge curving talons. In addition, the Harpy has a flaring double crest which makes it look truly savage.

Nearly as large as the Harpy, the Philippine monkey-eating eagle is rare. Perhaps 50 pairs now exist, threatened especially by increasing destruction of habitat and by the prestige value of an eagle trophy.

The larger true, or Booted eagles, include the best known eagles in the world: the Golden eagle, African Verreaux's eagle *Aquila verreauxi* and the Crowned eagle *Stephanoaetus coronatus*. Booted eagles vary from very small such as Ayres hawk-eagle *Hieraetus dubius*, or Wallace's hawk-eagle *Spizaetus nanus* of Malaysia, to very large and powerful eagles such as the African Crowned and Martial eagle *Polemaetus bellicosus* and Siberian Golden eagle, sufficiently large and powerful to kill wolves.

There is doubt whether the Indian Black eagle *Ictinaetus malayensis* is an eagle or some form of kite. Superficially, the young resemble kites, but the general habits of the species resemble eagles.

The typical eagles *Aquila* vary from the small Wahlberg's eagle *A. wahlbergi* to huge Golden, Verreaux's and Wedge-tailed eagles, spanning 7–8 ft (2–2½ m) in large females, and able to kill mammals as large as a deer calf. The Tawny eagle *Aquila rapax*, widespread in open country in Asia and Africa, is probably the most common of the world's large eagles. It feeds on small mammals and carrion, and is strongly piratical, pursuing other species to obtain prey. All *Aquila* species are brown, immature and adults alike, except for Verreaux's eagle, which is a magnificent coal-black with a white patch on the back. It feeds almost exclusively on Rock hyrax.

The Martial eagle is the largest, but not the most powerful of all 'booted' eagles. A female may weigh 14 lb (6·3 kg).

A Golden eagle needs about 9 oz (250 gm) of flesh per day, about 7% of the eagle's body-weight. A pair and their offspring require about 550 lb (250 kg) of flesh a year, but must kill about 15% more, or about 660 lb (300 kg) altogether, to keep alive. Much of the winter and spring food is carrion, as then there are abundant dead deer and sheep. A pair might possibly kill two or three lambs per year at most, less than 1% of those available in an average territory of 11,000 acres (4,450 ha).

The largest animals killed by any eagles are young deer, young seals (Steller's and European sea eagles) or young antelope (Crowned eagle). The Harpy eagle, immensely powerful, can probably kill larger mammals than any, but its full range of prey is unknown. A Crowned eagle, itself weighing 9 lb (4 kg) has been known to kill a bushbuck of 35 lb (15½ kg) about four times its own weight. Very large kills are dismembered skilfully, and the portions hidden in trees until needed.

Most eagles kill prey of half their own weight, or less. Some, such as Tawny and Long-crested eagles, live like buzzards on abundant small animals.

Eagles are long-lived; several have lived 40 to 50 years in captivity, for example Golden and Imperial eagles; the oldest acceptable record is for a bateleur, alive at 55.

Eagles apparently mate for life but if one of the individuals of a pair dies, the other obtains a new mate as soon as possible. All lay small clutches, one or two, the most prolific being the kite-like Sea and Fish eagles, which often lay three eggs. Incubation is by the female, less often by the male but when two eggs are laid, the male is more likely to incubate. Incubation periods are from 43–49 days. The eggs are laid, and hatch, at intervals of several days. In many species, notably of the true or Booted eagles, the eldest hatched young is much larger than those hatched later, which it invariably kills. The nestling is at first downy and helpless. A second and thicker coat of down grows after two to three weeks, and brooding is reduced. The male often feeds the female while she is incubating, but some females leave the nest to feed. The male does most, or all of the killing until the young is partly feathered; at this stage he is killing for himself, the female and the brood. Once the young is feathered, the female can assist in providing the food. Eaglets fly of their own accord between 60–125 days after hatching. In a tree they may first jump to other branches, and on a cliff they will make a short flight to another ledge. An eaglet may still depend on its parents for food for some time longer. In the Crowned eagle the young is fed by the parents for 9–11 months after its first flight. FAMILY: Accipitridae, ORDER: Falconiformes, CLASS: Aves.

EARTHWORMS, feed mainly on decaying organic matter within the soil itself.

Earthworms overcome desiccation largely by burrowing in soil. The cuticle surrounding the worm is very thin and permeable unlike that of, for example, an insect. Consequently, it provides very little check on water loss, although it affords an efficient means of entry of oxygen for respiratory purposes and release of carbon dioxide. Earthworms have some behavioural adaptations, however, which serve to minimize water loss. Usually they confine themselves to damp soil and only come out of their burrows at night, when the drying influence of the sun is past and when the relative humidity is higher than during the day. They rarely emerge completely from their burrows. In hot or dry weather they move deeper into the soil, thereby tending to keep in moist conditions.

An earthworm has no eyes. There are, however, microscopic sense organs sensitive to light, distributed mainly near the ends of the worm, the areas most likely to receive

Earthworms pairing. Each is hermaphrodite and fertilizes the other. Mating takes place mainly at night.

light. There are also minute receptors sensitive to chemicals, touch and vibrations. There are probably taste receptors in the mouth, for an earthworm seems capable of some choice over the leaves it pulls into the burrow for food.

The earthworm feeds either on such leaves pulled into the burrow with the aid of its suctorial pharynx, or by digesting the organic matter present among the particles of soil which it swallows when burrowing in earth otherwise too firm to penetrate. Undigested matter is extruded from the anus on to the surface of the soil as the familiar worm casts.

An earthworm moves by waves of muscular contraction and relaxation which pass along the length of the body, so that a particular region is alternately thin and extended or shortened and thickened. A good grip on the walls of the burrow is aided by the spiny outgrowths of the body wall called chaetae. The nervous system consists of ganglia in the head and other ganglia at intervals on a long nerve cord, lying below the gut, which gives off a series of paired nerves, one of the functions of which is to co-ordinate movement. Circulation of the blood is maintained largely by five pairs of contractile vessels called pseudohearts, situated in the front part of the body.

Earthworms are hermaphrodite, each worm producing both sperm and eggs. During pairing, two come together, head to tail, and each exchanges sperm with the other. The sperm are stored by each recipient in pouches called spermathecae until after the worms separate. A slimy tube formed by a glandular region, the clitellum, later slips off each worm, collecting eggs and the deposited sperm as it goes, and is left in the soil as a sealed cocoon. In the cocoon the eggs are fertilized, the young worms develop, and eventually escape.

Megascolecides australis, of Australia, is enormous, growing up to 10 ft (3 m) or more in length. CLASS: Oligochaeta, PHYLUM: Annelida.

EARWIGS, slender insects, commonly $\frac{1}{2}-\frac{3}{4}$ in ($1\frac{1}{4}-2$ cm) long, with distinctive pincer-like structures at the end of the body (function unknown). If one pokes at an earwig with a finger it may curve its tail over its back and use the pincers (forceps) in a threatening manner, like a miniature scorpion, but it has no poison and the forceps are not strong enough to hurt.

The name earwig is probably derived from the fact that it occasionally gets into the ear. The ear is just another crevice to the earwig. It is also possible, although less likely, that the name comes from the appearance of the hindwing. This is semi-circular and transparent, marked with veins and folds and slightly resembles an ear. At rest the wings are folded beneath the short, leathery forewings.

Earwigs have jaws used for biting and chewing and they seem to eat almost anything. They are of little economic importance, but sometimes they are a minor horticultural pest because some flowers, like dahlias, provide ideal crevices in which to hide. When they are hungry they come out and gnaw holes in the petals.

The eggs of earwigs are laid in batches and the young look like miniature adults except that they have no wings and the forceps are straight. Female earwigs are unusual among insects in displaying parental care. Usually she rests over her brood and if the eggs become dispersed she will collect them together again. ORDER: Dermaptera, CLASS: Insecta, PHYLUM: Arthropoda.

ECHIDNAS, also known as Spiny anteaters, are four-legged terrestrial animals, rather like hedgehogs in appearance. They belong to a special subclass of the Mammalia, the Prototheria or egg-laying mammals. A large echidna is about 18 in (46 cm) long and 8 in (20 cm) wide, rounded on the back, flat ventrally, and weighs over 10 lb ($4\frac{1}{2}$ kg)—the heaviest recorded weight is 14·3 lb (6·5 kg). The back is covered with hair interspersed with long sharp spines, the underparts, however, are covered with hair only. There is no neck and two hairy holes one on each side of the head serve as ears; a true cartilaginous pinna is present in all specimens but usually is difficult to detect. The eyes are small and beady; the retina is made up of rods only. There is a short stubby tail devoid of hairs and spines but there is no scrotum, the testes being internal.

The legs are short and stout, the enormously strong forefeet furnished with long spatulate claws. The hindfeet also bear five claws, the second of which is always elongated and is used as a grooming claw. The femur is parallel to the ground and widely everted giving the hindquarters a reptilian appearance. The feet are turned out so that the strongly curved grooming claw actually points backwards. The ankle in all males and some females bears a short spur of unknown function. The stoutness and strength of the musculature of the forelimbs is an adaptation for digging in hard earth or breaking up forest litter to expose the ants and termites that comprise their main food, hence the name Spiny anteater.

Echidnas are specialized in other ways for living on ants. The snout is elongated into a beak about 3 in (7·5 cm) long which houses a long whip-like tongue that can be thrust out 6–7 in (15–18 cm) beyond the tiny mouth at the end of the snout. The tongue is smeared with a secretion, of the sub-lingual gland, that has the stickiness and consistency of treacle so that the ants and termites stick to it. In the mouth the ants are scraped off, when the tongue is thrust out again, against a series of transversely arranged spines on the very long palate. There are no teeth on the jaws, and the ants and termites are pulped by the rubbing action of a set of spines on the base of the tongue against the spines on the roof of the mouth.

There is no separate anus for the passage of the faeces; the urine, reproductive products and the faeces, all passing through a chamber called a cloaca to the exterior.

Echidnas occur only in Australia and New Guinea. In Australia they live in habitats ranging from the hottest and driest of deserts through humid rain-forests to ridges and valleys at an altitude of 5,6000–6,000 ft (1,500–1,800 m) in the Australian Alps where the mean air temperatures for the three coldest months rarely rise above freezing.

The pouch or incubatorium of the echidna appears on the ventral surface in the females at the beginning of the breeding season which lasts from early July to late September. There is equivocal evidence that the period of gestation in the uterus is 27 days. After this the egg is deposited in the pouch (no one knows how) and is incubated there. The pouch egg has diameters of about $0·75 \times 0·5$ in (16×13 mm). At hatching a little animal looking most remarkably like a newborn marsupial, breaks out of the egg by means of an egg tooth and attaches itself by clinging with its relatively enormous forearms to one of two milk patches or areolae found on the dorsal surface of the pouch. From the areola it sucks milk secreted by the paired mammary glands which have the many-chambered (alveolar) structure found in the mammary glands of other mammals.

New Guinea harbours a very large echidna growing up to 39 in (1 m) in length and a weight of about 21 lb (9·5 kg). The snout is proportionately much longer than that of the Australian species and it houses an extremely long tongue. FAMILY: Tachyglossidae, ORDER: Monotremata, SUBCLASS: Prototheria, CLASS: Mammalia.

EELS, elongated fishes which lack pelvic fins. Characteristic is the long body and the long dorsal and anal fins which are joined to the tail fin to form a single long fin. Pectoral fins are usually present but the bones supporting them have lost the connection with the skull usually found in the bony fishes. As a result, the pectorals are often distant from the head, and the gill apparatus and branchial region of the head are elongated. The long and narrow branchial or gill chamber is used as a pump to force water over the gills and out of the sometimes small gill opening. Some species have smooth, naked bodies while in others there are small but deep-set and irregularly scattered scales. There are very many vertebrae, normally 1–200 but sometimes as many as 5–600, and the sinuous body is extremely flexible. This eel-like form is nearly always associated with a bottom-living, burrowing or crevice-dwelling mode

Echidna or Spiny ant-eater of Australia, one of the primitive egg-laying mammals.

Eelworms

of life. In most of the burrowing eels the fins are reduced or lost and the tail may become hardened to form a digging tool. Eels are often rapacious feeders and the jaws and teeth are well developed. Common to all the eels is a thin, leaf-like larval form, the leptocephalus stage, from which the eel metamorphoses into the adult after a few months or even after two or three years.

The Moray eels of the Mediterranean and tropical oceans are large with naked mottled bodies, often living in holes in coral or rocks. One species, *Thyrsoidea macrura*, is reported to reach 13 ft (4 m) in length.

The family Cyemidae contains deep-sea Snipe eels. *Cyema atrum* is found in all tropical and temperate oceans at depths below 6,000 ft (2,000 m). The jaws are slender and elongated like the beak of an avocet and the dorsal and anal fins are separated at the tail. This species, which grows to 6 in (15 cm), has a short and deep-bodied leptocephalus.

The Snipe eels (Nemichthyidae) are elongated, deep-sea eels with long and slender jaws that curve away from each other at the tips. The body tapers to a point. *Nemichthys scolopaceus* grows to about 5 ft (153 cm) and lives at depths of 1,500–6,000 ft (500–2,000 m) in the tropical Atlantic. It breeds in the Sargasso Sea and the leptocephalus is worm-like. ORDER: Anguilliformes, CLASS: Pisces.

Egg-eating snake swallowing an egg larger than the width of its own head.

EELWORMS, colourless, transparent microscopic worms found wherever there is moisture and organic matter. They inhabit soils in all climates, often to a depth of 5–6 ft ($1\frac{1}{2}$–2 m) in sandy soils. They also live on sea shores, in fresh water, sewage beds, vinegar vats, cardboard beer mats, mosses in the Arctic, lichens on walls and trees, in mushroom beds and the tunnels of bark-boring beetles, while some are parasites in insects and others are parasites in plants. They are usually worm-shaped with a thick superficially ringed cuticle. Most eelworms are only $\frac{1}{100}$–$\frac{1}{25}$ in (0·2–1·0 mm) long but a few are $\frac{1}{5}$–$\frac{2}{5}$ in (5–10 mm) or longer. Some have elaborate cuticular processes on the head but never true appendages on the body. The body wall has four longitudinal muscle bands. There is a nerve ring with associated ganglia round the hind end of the muscular pharynx. The excretory system consists of longitudinal canals leading to a ventral excretory pore in the front third of the body.

For movement they need water which can be a film as thin as $\frac{1}{500}$ in (0·005 mm) such as that covering the particles of a moist soil. Some survive desiccation for long periods: coiled, quiescent larvae of the Stem and bulb eelworm *Ditylenchus dipsaci* can remain viable for 20 years in a dry cotton-wool-like mass. *Anguina tritici* forms galls or 'cockles' in ears of wheat and many survive in the dry galls for 30 years. The encysted eggs of cyst-forming eelworms *Heterodera* also survive for many years, whether in moist soil or dry in tubes. Although some eelworms die in flooded soil through lack of oxygen, some survive immersion in sea water. CLASS: Nematoda, PHYLUM: Aschelminthes.

EGG-EATING SNAKES, can eat eggs at least twice the size of the snake's gape. Modifications in their structure allowing them to engulf, swallow, pierce and crush eggs and then regurgitate the shells are to be found in the very small teeth, flexible jaws, special neck muscles and long, downward and forwardly directed spines on some of the vertebrae. These sharp spines, tipped with dense bone, penetrate the wall of the gut and form a mechanism for cracking eggs.

Five species occur in Africa south of the Sahara and in Arabia and belong to the genus *Dasypeltis*. One species, *Elachistodon westermanni*, found in northeast India is exceedingly rare; since it has grooved back fangs and a sensory nasal pit it may not feed exclusively on eggs. All true Egg-eaters lay eggs; there may be a dozen in a clutch. An adult 2 ft (60 cm) long *Dasypeltis* can eat a chicken's egg four times the diameter of its own head. Forcing the egg against a loop of its body the snake may take 20 minutes to engulf it. Once worked into the throat the egg is forced back, then as the snake arches its neck the shell is pierced by the spines on the backbone. As the snake moves its neck down

again boss-like processes on the vertebrae in front of the spiny ones flatten the egg and by means of a valve in the oesophagus the contents are squeezed towards the stomach and the shell compressed into a neat package is regurgitated. FAMILY: Colubridae, ORDER: Squamata, CLASS: Reptilia.

EGRET, name given to certain herons, usually those with an all-white plumage. The size and body shape of egrets varies considerably. The Great white egret is the largest. It has very long legs and measures about 3 ft (1 m) in length including the long sinuous neck and daggerlike bill. Among the smaller species is the Little egret *Egretta garzetta* which is only half the size of *E. alba* though with similar proportions. The Cattle egret *Ardeola ibis* differs in having a short neck giving it a somewhat hunched appearance. The long legs of the *Egretta* species are an adaptation to wading in shallow water. The Cattle egret, which normally feeds on dry land, has relatively short legs and therefore a short neck.

Egrets are widely distributed in the tropics and warmer temperate regions of the world. The Great white egret has a particularly extensive range, being found in the warmer parts of five continents. The distribution of the Cattle egret is particularly interesting and gives us a well-documented example of an animal extending its range naturally. Late in the 19th or early in the 20th century, Cattle egrets were found to have colonized part of the northern coast of South America. It is presumed that a party of these birds had crossed the Atlantic from Africa. They increased rapidly in their new home and began to spread. The Cattle egret is now abundant and widespread in southeastern North America and in the north of South America and is still spreading. At the other extreme of its range the Cattle egret is moving eastwards into Australia.

Most egrets nest colonially, either in pure colonies or in mixed colonies with other water-birds. In such a mixed colony in East Africa, over 40,000 nests of storks, cormorants, egrets and other herons were counted. These included some 10,000 nests of Cattle egrets, over 1,500 of Little egrets, and smaller numbers of Great white egrets and Yellow-billed egrets *Egretta intermedius* nests. Most egrets build a simple platform of sticks or reeds in trees, or in dense aquatic vegetation. The eggs are usually pale blue or white and both sexes incubate. During the breeding season, male and female egrets become adorned with long white plumes which grow from the nape, back or breast. The plumes are frequently erected and displayed during breeding activities and may function in species recognition. The beautiful white feathers were much sought after a few decades ago, when it was fashionable for ladies to wear ornate headgear.

Lesser Egrets *Egretta intermedia*, with, on either side, Openbill storks.

The diet of egrets varies considerably, a number of them catch fishes and frogs, but some of the smaller species are largely insectivorous. The Cattle egret is named from its habit of gathering in flocks around domestic stock. The birds walk close to the grazing animals, even perching on their backs, and catch the grasshoppers and other insects they disturb. The habit, which is simply an extension of their association with wild buffalo and other big-game animals, has brought them in close contact with man so that they are often extremely tame. FAMILY: Ardeidae, ORDER: Ciconiiformes, CLASS: Aves.

EIDER, largest of the sea-ducks, about 2 ft (60 cm) long, lives around the coasts of Arctic Canada and Siberia, spreading down the coasts of the North Pacific and North Atlantic. Of the four species three are in the genus *Somateria*. The males in these species are boldly marked in black and white with apple or emerald green on the head while the females are mottled brown. The Common eider *S. mollissima* is well-known for providing the best down for pillows and mattresses. Eiders feed in company off low rocky and sandy coasts or in estuaries, their main food being shellfish and small crabs. They

nest close together under cover or in the open, the duck incubating the 4–6 large green or cream eggs for about four weeks. The young unite in large groups and take about two months to fledge.

The King eider *S. spectabilis* resembles the Common eider in general habits but is smaller with a rounder head. The male is outstandingly handsome with soft grey on the head as well as green and with an unusual helmeted forehead formed from a continuation of the orange horn of the bill.

Steller's eider *Polysticta stelleri*, is only 18 in (45 cm) long, the drake having a chestnut breast and belly with long black and white shoulder feathers. The very dark duck has a purplish speculum. FAMILY: Anatidae, ORDER: Anseriformes, CLASS: Aves.

ELAND, the largest of the antelopes, differs from the kudu and its relatives, in lacking preorbital glands, in the presence of horns in the female, a tufted tail, a pendulous dewlap, a tuft on the forehead of bulls, and in the entirely different spiral form of the horns.

A bull eland stands 5½–6 ft (165–180 cm) at the shoulder and weighs ¾–1 ton (700–1,000 kg). There is a short mane along the back of the neck. The dewlap is very long and extends all the way from the upper part of the throat to between the forelegs and is tufted for part of its length. The shoulders are slightly hunched, the neck is longer than that of an ox and the head is held higher than the

Common eland, in East Africa, the largest antelopes. Both male and female have horns. Eland are recognizable by the heavy dewlap.

Elephant

withers. The general colour is reddish-brown to buff, becoming a smoky blue-grey in old bulls. Most races have white stripes on the body. The nose is dark, often with a white chevron between the eyes and bulls have a dark thick mat of hair on the forehead.

The Common eland *Taurotragus oryx* of East and South Africa has pointed ears. The horns are comparatively short, with two spiral twists near the base which are so close that they overlap.

The Giant eland *Taurotragus derbianus* is found from Senegal east to the Nile in Uganda and the Sudan. It has longer horns, which are as much as twice the length of the head, a large white spot on each cheek and broad, rounded ears with a dark bar on the inside. The neck is darker than the body, often bordered behind by a white stripe and the dewlap is more extensive, beginning just behind the chin.

Elands inhabit open forests and bush country, where they browse, breaking down high branches with their horns. They live in herds of 12–30, but sometimes gather into groups of 100 or more. Each herd has one or two bulls, but many bulls are solitary. The herd is continuously on the move, restlessly, moving at a fast walk, its members snatching food as they go and walking in single file. They are usually quite silent as they move, but occasionally a bull makes a low grunt to signal to the rest of the herd and calves bleat

Indian elephant with its young bathing, a favourite routine for all elephants.

to their mothers. During the dry season elands will dig up bulbs with their hoofs and eat melons, and at this time the big migrating masses are formed. When alarmed, they pause, then gallop away excitedly, often leaping over each other's backs. They have been known to clear obstacles 6 ft (2 m) high. They are placid, and rarely defend themselves.

Elands, at least the females, become sexually mature at two years. Gestation lasts nine months and calves are born at different seasons in different parts of Africa. FAMILY: Bovidae, ORDER: Artiodactyla, CLASS: Mammalia.

ELEPHANT, the largest land mammal, two species of which are known; the African and the Indian. The African elephant *Loxodonta africana*, found only on that continent, has two subspecies, the Bush elephant (subspecies *africana*) and the Forest elephant (subspecies *cyclotis*), the former being larger, more abundant and better known. The Bush elephant is the largest of the elephants, the female reaching an average mature height of 8 ft 4 in (2·5 m) and the males, owing to a post-pubertal growth spurt, 10 ft 2 in (3·1 m). Forest elephants are about 2 ft (0·6 m) smaller and the difference between the sexes

African elephants at a water-hole. The long trunk, an elongated nose, enables the elephant to drink without kneeling.

is less pronounced. The body weight of an average mature female Bush elephant is 5,900–7,700 lb (2,700–3,500 kg) and the male 10,000–11,700 lb (4,500–5,300 kg). There is a large seasonal variation as well as a variation in weight between populations according to the state of the habitat. The overall length of a large male (trunk to tail) is up to 27 ft (9 m).

In order to support this weight, the limbs are massive columns and are so constructed that the elephant cannot run or jump. The limb bones are heavy and have no marrow and the soles of the feet cover a fatty cushion, which helps to distribute the load evenly. They usually have five and four toe nails on fore- and hindfeet respectively, but they are reduced to three on all feet in some individuals. The ears are large, shaped like a map of Africa and measuring up to 3 ft × 5 ft (1 × 1½ m). They are important in thermoregulation and in aggressive behavioural displays. The ears of the Forest elephant and the Indian elephant *Elephas maximus* are very much smaller, no doubt related to their more shady habitat. The skull is huge, being modified to support the tusks, which are rooted in large sheaths formed from the premaxillary bones. The brain case is massive, with walls which are thick, but cellular in structure, to give strength with lightness.

The tusks first appear at two to three years of age. They are upper incisor teeth, composed of dentine with a very small, 2 in (5 cm), enamel cap that is quickly worn away. Their shape follows an equable spiral and they continue to grow in length at the rate of 3½–4½ in (9–11·5 cm) a year throughout life, but owing to breakage and wear they only reach about half their potential length. The average lengths of the tusks of the oldest males and females are about 8 ft (2·5 m) and 5 ft (1·6 m) respectively. Their rate of growth in weight increases progressively with age and male tusks are much more massive than female tusks, reaching an average paired weight of 240 lb (109 kg) as compared with 39 lb (18 kg) in females. The world record single tusk weight (from East Africa) is 235 lb (107 kg) for males and 56 lb (25 kg) for females. In some populations, for example in Zambia, tuskless elephants are not uncommon.

The other teeth are also unusual. Because of their longevity and continued growth in size throughout life the elephants need a series of teeth, functionally covering their life-span and increasing in size as the animal grows larger. This is achieved by having a series of six teeth in each side of each jaw (24 in all) which are formed and replace each other in succession throughout life. No more than one (or two) in each series are wholly (or partly) in wear at any one time and they are progressively larger from the first to the sixth. The teeth themselves are unique, being constructed of a series of flat vertical plates

of dentine and enamel, held together by a matrix of cementum. The average number of these plates or laminae increases from three in the first tooth to 13 in the sixth.

The grinding area of the teeth in use in each jaw in a nine-month old calf is only 1·5 sq in (9·4 cm²) and reaches a maximum of 50 sq in (320 cm²) and 40 sq in (260 cm²) in males and females respectively in their late forties. Subsequently, as no more teeth are produced wear results in a reduction of the grinding area to 16 sq in (100 cm²), they are unable to feed efficiently and death due to 'mechanical senescence' occurs. This sets a limit to the elephant life-span of 60–70 years. The replacement and wear of the teeth can be used as criteria for estimating the age of elephants with surprising accuracy.

The senses of sight and hearing are only moderately developed in contrast to the sense of smell which is acute. Smell plays an important part in their social contacts and the trunk is used to locate scents precisely.

The calf is suckled by its mother for at least four years but this is extended to six years or more in populations with low reproductive rates. The fat content of the milk increases with the age of the calf, at least over the first half of the lactation period.

About half the mature bulls are solitary and the remainder collect in bull herds usually containing 2–15 animals but occasionally over 100. Single bulls and bull herds form

temporary associations with family units and the family units may aggregate to form bigger herds, either an 'extended family' of up to 20–30 fairly closely related animals, which frequently recombine, or chance aggregations of up to 100 or more. Close ties exist between members of family units and examples of elephants supporting and assisting wounded companions are known. Large herds of as many as 1,000 elephants are found in certain situations, usually at the periphery of populations that have been displaced by human settlement or activity, or are otherwise in conflict with man. These often form spectacular tight-packed cohorts, leaving a trail of destruction in their wake.

The daily cycle is one of fairly continuous movement in search of food or water, and larger groups tend to be more mobile. In savannah regions the hot hours of the middle of the day are often spent resting in the shade —and the destruction of shade by the elephants' own activity may lead to an increase in the mortality rate, especially of young calves, from heat stress. Elephants eat food equivalent to about 4% of their body weight daily and cows with suckling calves about 6%. For a large bull this amounts to some 600 lb (270 kg). The preferred diet contains only about 30–50% grass, the greater amount being taken in the wet season.

There is much less information on the

African elephant picking fruit, demonstrating one of the many uses of the trunk.

Elephant seal

African elephants in Lake Edward. Bathing is health-giving and good elephantine fun.

biology of the Indian elephant *Elephas maximus*. It differs from the African elephant in its shape (arched back and domed head), smaller tusks, often absent in the female, and much smaller ears. The end of the trunk has only a single process as compared with the two 'fingers' of the African genus. In general it appears to be an animal of jungle or bush country, although it is found in grassland areas. Another point of interest is that, in contrast to the African elephant there is a progressive loss of pigment with age, from the trunk and ears, which consequently develop pale patches. Albinos are also probably more frequent.

This species is now found in India, Assam, Burma, Siam, Malaya, Sumatra and Ceylon, with a few also in Borneo. They seem to frequent as wide a range of habitats as the African species. FAMILY: Elephantidae, ORDER: Proboscidea, CLASS: Mammalia.

ELEPHANT SEALS, largest of the Earless seals, with two species: the Northern *Mirounga angustirostris*, and the Southern *M. leonina*.

The Northern elephant seal occurs on the islands off the coast of southern California and Mexico but breeds only on San Miguel, San Nicholas, Guadalupe and San Benito.

Breeding colonies of the Southern elephant seal are to be found on the sub-antarctic islands of South Georgia, South Orkneys, South Shetlands, Kerguelen, Heard, Macquarie, Campbell, Falkland, Gough, Marion and Crozet. The largest is on South Georgia where there are about 310,000 animals. Kerguelen and Macquarie also carry large populations, 100,000 and 95,000 respectively. The present breeding range of the Southern elephant seal is now expanding to include those places from which it was previously wiped out by commercial exploitation. Elephant seals are on their breeding grounds in spring for breeding, and in summer for moulting, but during the rest of the year they are feeding widely dispersed out at sea.

The two Elephant seals are similar. The adult male may be 16–20 ft (4·8–6 m) in nose to tail length and up to about 8,000 lb (3,628 kg) weight. The adult female is smaller, 10–12 ft (3–3·6 m) in length and weighing about 2,000 lb (907 kg). The pup at birth is about 4 ft (1·2 m) in length and 80 lb (36 kg) weight.

The hair of Elephant seals is short and stiff and the general colour is dark grey. Fighting between the bulls leads to much scar tissue about the neck and chest and the skin here gets very rough and thick.

The inflatable snout or proboscis of the adult male is an enlargement of the nose. When fully developed it overhangs the mouth so that the nostrils open downwards. During the breeding season it can be erected by inflation, muscular action and blood pressure, and may act as a resonating chamber to increase the volume of a big bull's roar.

Bulls may reach an age of 20 years. They become sexually mature at four or five years old, but they are not strong enough to hold a harem against older bulls until they are 7–12 years old. The breeding season of the Southern elephant seal starts at the beginning of September. The bulls come ashore first, followed by increasing numbers of females from about the middle of the month. By the end of the month there are enough animals present to form harems, each male eventually presiding over 30–40 females. Each harem has one dominant bull whose function is to mate with the females of that harem, and prevent other bulls from doing so. Younger mature bulls hang about the edges of the harem, sometimes managing to steal a female. A challenger to a reigning harem bull may threaten by roaring for some time. The reigning bull may then retreat without a fight or may stand his ground. If this does not deter the challenger a fight will take place, the victor taking the harem.

Most of the pups are born in October and are 4 ft (1·2 m) long and clad in black woolly hair. Their mothers feed them for about 23 days and towards the end of this period each pup will be putting on about 20 lb (9 kg) a day, while the mother, remaining on land without feeding until the pup is weaned, may lose 700 lb (317 kg). Elephant seal milk is very rich, containing 40–50% fat (compared with 9% in a dog and 3·5% in man), and enables the babies to quickly put on a thick layer of blubber as a protection against the cold. At about 35 days old the pup sheds its black coat for a silvery grey one and is ready to enter the sea. The cows mate again about 18 days after the birth of the pup and, after it is weaned, they go off to sea to feed.

After the breeding season, the next gathering of adult animals is for moulting in December, January and February. The moult takes about 30–40 days and again no food is taken during this time. At the moult large sheets of skin are shed with the old hairs embedded, pushed out by the developing new hair, instead of the more normal method of shedding single hairs.

The life history of the Northern elephant seal is similar. The pups are born in December and January and the harems are smaller, usually of only about 12 females. The females mate during lactation and go to sea to feed during lactation. The main anatomical difference between the Southern and Northern elephant seals is in the head.

The total population now of the Northern elephant seal has been estimated to be about 15,000 animals, whereas commercial sealers had by 1890, reduced it to about 100 animals. FAMILY: Phocidae, ORDER: Pinnipedia, CLASS: Mammalia.

ELEPHANT SHREWS, small mouse- or rat-sized animals confined to Africa. Their most distinctive feature is the long, pointed proboscis, adapted for nosing out ants, termites and other insects. Otherwise they have a fairly normal mouse-like build, adapted for running swiftly on the ground. The hindlegs and feet are longer than the front, hence the alternative name of Jumping shrews. This is a misnomer for they do not jump bipedally like jerboas but run with lightning dashes, using the powerful hindlegs for thrust as in a hare. The eyes are large and bright, adapted to daytime vision, for Elephant shrews are predominantly diurnal. The tail is usually as long as the head and body and almost naked.

Most of the 15 or so species of Elephant

Elephant shrews owe their common name entirely to the trunk-like snout.

shrew have rather uniform brown or grey fur on the upper side, usually closely matching the colour of the local soil. One group, the large Forest elephant shrews *Rhynchocyon*, are much more boldly patterned in black and rufous, or finely chequered to match the dappled background of the forest by day.

The litters number one or two, the young being very large and well developed at birth.

Elephant shrews are found throughout east, central and southern Africa, but one isolated species, *Elephantulus rozeti*, is found in Morocco and Algeria. FAMILY: Macroscelididae, ORDER: Insectivora, CLASS: Mammalia.

ELEPHANT-SNOUT FISHES, freshwater African fishes related to the Bony tongues. In some species, such as *Gnathonemus numenius* and *G. curvirostris*, the snout is elongated and turned downwards, much like an elephant's trunk, with the small mouth at the tip. In other species only the soft lower lip is elongated and in yet others the snout is bluntly rounded with no elongation. In spite of this, all the members of the family Mormyridae have a quite unmistakable look, with smoothly scaled bodies, dorsal and anal fins set opposite to one another, the body brownish grey or slaty grey and a rather delicate forked tail on a slender base. There are about 100 species found in the lakes and rivers of Africa, mostly feeding on invertebrates at the bottom. Most are small but some reach 5 ft (1·5 m) in length.

A number of species are found in the Nile and these seem to have fascinated the Ancient Egyptians, who depicted them in tomb drawings, mummified them and produced amulets in the form of mormyrids.

Relative to body weight, the mormyrids have very large brains, the ratio brain-weight to body-weight being about the same as in man.

Mormyrids often live in murky waters and their eyesight appears to be poor. In compensation, the muscles at the slender base of the tail are modified into electric organs which can detect obstacles or predators. A small electric field is set up round the fish which acts in the same way as radar. FAMILY: Mormyridae, ORDER: Mormyriformes, CLASS: Pisces.

ELK *Alces alces*, a large European member of the deer family closely related to the moose of North America and almost identical with it. The name is also used in North America as an alternative to wapiti, the North American equivalent of the Red deer. FAMILY: Cervidae, ORDER: Artiodactyla, CLASS: Mammalia.

EMU *Dromaius novae-hollandiae*, the largest bird inhabiting the Australian continent, it is flightless and its tiny wings are only $\frac{1}{10}$ of the length of the bird's body.

Emus are brown although when the feathers are new after the moult they may appear nearly black, fading to pale brown with age. The bases of the feathers are white. Each feather has two indentical shafts, with the barbs so widely spaced that they do not interlock to form the firm vane as in most birds. Rather they form a loose, hair-like body covering. The sexes are similar in plumage except in the period prior to egg laying, when the female's head and neck are densely covered with black feathers, whereas the male's head and neck are largely bare. Adult females weigh about 90 lb (41 kg) and males 80 lb (36 kg). The female of a pair is usually larger than the male. The legs are unfeathered and so long that a running bird can make a stride of 9 ft (2·7 m) with ease. Emus have three toes, compared with the two of the ostrich, and the underside of each toe is flattened with a broad pad. The bill is broad and soft, adapted for browsing and grazing but with muscles too weak to hold any smooth heavy object.

The birds usually breed in the winter months, May–August. The nest is a low platform of twigs or leaves, generally placed so that the sitting bird has a clear outlook, often downhill. The early eggs of the clutch are covered and left, and the male does not begin sitting until between five and nine eggs have been laid. A hen will lay from 9–12 eggs, each weighing 1–1½ lb (0·5–0·7 kg), but in very good seasons the clutch may exceed 20, and in poor seasons be as low as four or five. Once the female has laid the clutch the male carries out the whole incubation taking about eight weeks and during this time he hardly eats and does not drink. The tiny chicks leave the nest after two or three days. At first their plumage is cream with brown longitudinal stripes, and dark dots on the head.

Adult emus feed mainly on fruits, flowers, insects, seeds and green vegetation. Caterpillars are favoured whenever they are available and beetles and grasshoppers are taken in large quantities when they are abundant. FAMILY: Dromaiidae, ORDER: Casuariiformes, CLASS: Aves.

ENGRAVER BEETLES, or Bark beetles are closely related to both the weevils and the Ambrosia beetles. The females burrow through the bark of trees, such as pine or elm, and then excavate a large chamber or egg gallery. Along the edge of this chamber eggs are deposited each of which hatches into a wood eating larva. These larvae tunnel into the wood to produce a burrow of increasing diameter as the larvae are growing in size. When fully grown the larvae pupate and hatch into adult beetles which then have to burrow their way out of the timber. The adults then mate and infest a new tree.

Many of these beetles cause serious damage to timber and one species transmits the fungus disease Dutch elm disease which is fatal to those trees it infects. FAMILY: Scolytidae, ORDER: Coleoptera, CLASS: Insecta, PHYLUM: Arthropoda.

EYED LIZARD *Lacerta lepida*, also known as the Spanish or Ocellated lizard, lives in southern France and the Iberian Peninsula and grows to 2 ft (60 cm), of which 16 in (40 cm) is tail. It is brownish-green to reddish with black spots which sometimes form rosettes with black centres. On the flanks are bluish oval markings, the so-called 'eyes' or 'ocelli'. FAMILY: Lacertidae, ORDER: Squamata, CLASS: Reptilia.

FALLOW DEER *Dama dama*, the typical park deer. At the end of the last century, in England alone, over 71,000 Fallow deer were being preserved in parks. It has a wide distribution in Europe and the countries bordering the Mediterranean. About 36 in (91 cm) high at the shoulder, the typical feature of the buck is the palmated antler. There are also more colour variations in Fallow deer than in any other wild mammal, and these include black, white, menil, cream, sandy, silver-grey and the normal fallow, which is spotted in summer, but with little or no spotting in winter. The rut usually takes place during October, at which time the bucks make a husky rolling grunt.

Fallow deer have been successfully introduced to Australia, Tasmania, New Zealand, North and South America.

Another species is the Persian fallow deer *D. mesopotamica* which has always had a limited distribution and occurs only in Iran, where its total population is probably under fifty animals. Only slightly larger than the European Fallow deer and with spotted summer pelage, the antlers of the bucks are the main point of difference, the brows being very short, with a long tray point sprouting close to it. The upper points never palmate to the same extent as the European Fallow. FAMILY: Cervidae, ORDER: Artiodactyla, CLASS: Mammalia.

FEATHER MITES, several families of mites which are epizoic (that is, living on rather than parasitic) on birds and are found sitting in rows along the barbs of quill feathers or on the harder parts of contour feathers. ORDER: Acari, CLASS: Arachnida, PHYLUM: Arthropoda.

FEATHER STARS, a group of echinoderms related to the Sea lilies. In contrast to the Sea lilies, which are attached to the substratum by a stalk, the Feather stars are free-living, stalkless and can swim with the aid of their long arms, although they are sedentary forms and most often are encountered sitting inactively on the sea bottom. The common genus *Antedon* is an example of this group. See also Sea lilies. ORDER: Articulata, CLASS: Crinoidea, PHYLUM: Echinodermata.

FENNEC *Fennecus zerda*, of North African and Middle East deserts. Weighing 3–4 lb (1·5 kg), the delicate fennec is noted for its pale buff-coloured fur and unusually large pointed ears, possibly an aid in its search for food: lizards and insects, rodents, birds, eggs and vegetable matter. Deep subterranean burrows are constructed, usually with several entrances, and in some cases, the burrows of several foxes may interconnect. These dens are far deeper than those of most fox species to enable the fennec to keep cool during the day by avoiding the fierce desert heat.

Another species with unusually large ears is the Bat-eared fox *Otocyon megalotis*, of dry plains and savannahs of Africa. After its very large ears its most striking feature is the number of teeth, 46–48, compared with the normal complement of 42.

Bat-eared foxes are small and slender, weighing 7–10 lb (3–4½ kg). They have grizzled grey-brown fur with black stockings and a black stripe running down the length of the tail. There is a black mask around the eyes which appears to be important in social behaviour. They feed on a variety of small mammals, birds, lizards, eggs and insects (e.g. termites and their larvae). Fruits and other types of plant matter may occasionally be eaten.

Of all foxes, this species seems most gregarious. They play as adults, groom each other and often sleep in contact. FAMILY: Canidae, ORDER: Carnivora, CLASS: Mammalia.

FERRET *Mustella eversmanni furo*, a domesticated form of the Asian polecat, a species usually smaller and lighter in colour than the European polecat *Mustela putorius* but having similar behaviour. The ferret has now been spread throughout Europe, interbreeding with the endemic wild polecat until the one can hardly be distinguished from the other. Because of a larger cranial capacity, true polecats have more rounded heads and 'pop-eyes' than the cross-bred polecat-ferrets. FAMILY: Mustelidae, ORDER: Carnivora, CLASS: Mammalia.

FIDDLER CRABS. The male Fiddler crab *Uca* has one pincer very much larger than the other. The body is rectangular, and the eyes are borne on stalks that can be folded sideways to lie flat against the front of the

Male Fiddler crab's enormous right claw used in courtship and in warning off rivals.

head. The small pincer is used in feeding. Sand is picked up and passed to the mouth. After usually 6–16 small pincersful of sand have been passed through the mouthparts a ball of sand is formed behind the mouth. This is then removed by the small pincer and placed carefully on the sand surface. This results in the sand surface around a feeding crab being dotted with small balls of sand. Often they become arranged in a fairly regular pattern.

Fiddler crabs make burrows in intertidal sand and mud. When the tide comes in the burrows are usually plugged up. Sometimes the plug takes the form of a small dome. Some species also build sand shelters over the entrance to the burrow.

The large pincer of the male is used with various leg movements to produce a display characteristic for each species. The movement of the pincer looks like a beckoning wave, and is a signal to any passing female that the male is ready to mate. The display is also used to warn other males to keep away. SUBORDER: Brachyura, ORDER: Decapoda, CLASS: Crustacea, PHYLUM: Arthropoda.

FIGHTING FISH *Betta splendens*, a fish found in Thailand and throughout the Malayan Peninsula. Because of the pugnacity of the male, these fishes have been 'domesticated' for a considerable time in Thailand and used for sport, wagers being laid on the outcome of a fight between two contestants. In the wild, the dorsal and anal fins are short

and the colour of the body is variable but dull. However, special varieties have been bred that have long fins and vivid colours. The males are always more spectacular than the females.

During a fight between two males, the fins are spread as far as possible and the mouth and gill covers are opened wide. When full grown, these fishes are only 3 in (7·5 cm) in length. The Fighting fishes construct bubble nests. FAMILY: Anabantidae, ORDER: Perciformes, CLASS: Pisces.

FINFOOTS, three species of grebe-like birds related to the rails, one in South America, another in Africa and a third in Southern Asia. The long, but stout, bill suggests a rail, the long neck and short legs placed well back on the body with flattened lobes bordering the toes are grebe-like, while the long thin neck, low swimming position and longish graduated tail suggest a cormorant or darter. The legs give a horizontal body posture on land, but finfoots can run well and take to land when pursued. They swim with head-bobbing movements, presumably synchronized with simultaneous kicks of both legs.

They prefer still or slow-moving water at the edges or rivers, estuaries, or occasionally where thick vegetation overhangs the water's edge. They mostly keep to the cover of overhanging vegetation, and are adept at scrambling over low branches as well as swimming. When alarmed they hurry into cover, at times fluttering along the surface

with the help of the wings. Finfoots eat small aquatic animals mainly. FAMILY: Heliornithidae, ORDER: Gruiformes, CLASS: Aves.

FISH LOUSE, not a louse, but a crustacean parasitic on fishes and remarkable for its disc-like body and a pair of large adhesive suckers with which it clings to host fishes. The head bears a pair of sessile compound eyes and the underside of the front part bears numerous triangular spinules. These spinules point backwards and help the louse in adhering to the host. Members of the genus *Argulus* align themselves so that the head points in the same direction as that of the host and the spinules catch firmly in the fish's skin.

The Fish louse has four pairs of swimming legs, so that it can swim actively to seek out its host. Once on the host the louse clings by means of its suckers and spines and pierces the skin with its narrow mandibles, which are housed in a proboscis on the underside of the head. The physical damage inflicted is not great but small wounds becoming infected may kill the fish. FAMILY: Argulidae, ORDER: Branchiura, CLASS: Crustacea, PHYLUM: Arthropoda.

FLAMINGOS, large aquatic birds which inhabit alkaline and saline lakes and lagoons of the Old World (except Australia), North and South America and some Oceanic Islands, including the Galapagos. In the Andes they live on freezing alkaline lakes at 14,000 ft (4,250 m).

A flock of Lesser flamingos on Lake Nakuru, Kenya, a soda lake containing a broth of microscopic plants on which they feed.

Greater flamingo feeding chick on nest.

Flamingos are 3–6 ft (1–2 m) in length, with long sinuous necks, long legs and webbed feet. The bill is highly specialized for filter-feeding, sharply bent in the middle, with the lower mandible large and trough-like and the upper one small and lid-like. The plumage is pink, red and black, often brilliant. The enormous flocks of Lesser flamingos *Phoeniconaias minor* seen at some East African alkaline lakes, are probably the most remarkable of the world's bird spectacles.

Phoenicopterus, the Greater flamingo, differs from the others in the structure of the bill. In *Phoenicopterus* the upper mandible has a shallow internal keel, quite different from the deep triangular keel of *Phoeniconaias* and is adapted for feeding upon relatively large organisms on the bottom and in deep water, whereas the deep-keeled species are adapted for feeding on the surface or in shallow water.

The Lesser flamingo *Phoeniconaias minor* is mainly African but also occurs in Asia. It is the smallest, least brilliantly coloured, but by far the most numerous of all flamingos. There may be as many as 4–5 million of which about 3–3½ million inhabit East Africa.

All flamingos feed by filtering small animals or microscopic plant life from the mud or water. The bill is sharply bent in the middle, so that when the flamingo is walking and feeding, the upper mandible is underneath and the lower uppermost. In the James' and Andean flamingos the lower mandible is bulbous and full of cellular bone and may actually act as a float, helping the bird to feed. In all species water and mud are sucked into the bill and special structures within the bill catch the small organisms while unwanted material is rejected.

Both sexes incubate, in all observed cases. The flamingo does not incubate, as in old travellers' tales, with the long legs hanging down beside the mud mound nest, but with them doubled under the bird and projecting behind like red drumsticks.

The newly-hatched chicks are clad in soft, silky, grey down. The legs are swollen, soft and bright red. For the first few days the chick does not leave the nest mound; it may be unable to climb back onto it if disturbed. The legs harden and become blackish in four or five days and the chick then becomes more active. FAMILY: Phoenicopteridae, ORDER: Anseriformes, CLASS: Aves.

FLEAS, small wingless insects with streamlined, flattened bodies, which are hairy and shiny and vary from yellowish-brown to almost black. Those living on animals having dense fine fur are sleaker and more streamlined than those on coarse-coated hosts. Nest fleas, that spend most of their adult life in the nest of a host, might lack eyes or have reduced powers of jumping. In body fleas the eyes are usually well developed, unless these fleas are parasites of wholly nocturnal hosts such as bats, or subterranean hosts. The large antennae lie in deep grooves, one on each side of the head and are erectile in the male only, used for grasping the female during mating. The mouthparts consist of two pairs of palps while three stiletto-shaped parts together form the piercing, sucking tube. Each of the three thoracic segments bear a pair of legs. ORDER: Siphonaptera, CLASS: Insecta, PHYLUM: Arthropoda.

FLOUNDER *Platichthys flesus*, one of the best known of European flatfishes. It can be distinguished from other inshore flatfishes by the opaque, mother-of-pearl whiteness of the underside. The upperside (right) is brownish-green with some faint orange marks which are similar to those found in the plaice, but soon disappear once the fish is out of water. The body is lozenge-shaped and the scales are, for the most part, small and embedded.

Most flatfishes live their entire lives in the sea, but the flounder migrates up rivers to feed. Anglers are sometimes surprised to catch flounders 40 miles (65 km) or so from the coast. They spend most of the summer in rivers feeding and then in late autumn they make their way down the rivers, without feeding, to spawn in fairly deep water off the coast.

Flounders may reach 12–15 in (30–38 cm) and a weight of 6 lb (2·7 kg) although a 2 lb (0·9 kg) fish is considered a fair size. FAMILY: Pleuronectidae, ORDER: Pleuronectiformes, CLASS: Pisces.

FLOUR MITES, normally found in collections of debris, such as dry leaves, stubble and animals' nests, are attracted to man's food stores. The Flour mite *Acarus siro* shows a preference for the germ of wheat but can only attack damaged grain. Mechanical processes produce a good deal of this and so the protection of bulk stored grain, flour and similar substances presents a very real problem. It thrives at relative humidities of 80% at temperatures of 64–68°F (18–20°C). Consequently, the most effective preventive is storage under dry conditions. Flour and grain stored at 13% or less moisture content remains free of mites for a long time, even for years. The use of plastic sacks helps limit infection. Stringent precautions to keep stores clean are also necessary as these mites will feed in organic dust and on the moulds that grow thereon. The mites occur in the growing areas of grain and may often be on the freshly harvested material; they can also be carried on clothing and on sacks, so that their introduction into stores is all too easy. ORDER: Acari, CLASS: Arachnida, PHYLUM: Arthropoda.

Profile of a flounder, from left side. This picture shows strikingly how a flounder uses its fins to row itself on short journeys when looking for food.

FLYCATCHERS, perching birds of similar ecology but of two separate families—one in the Old World, one in the New. Some members of each capture insects by making short flights from a perch. The two groups are the Old World flycatchers, now in the subfamily Muscicapinae of the family Muscicapidae, and the New World flycatchers of the family Tyrannidae. Certain of the Tyrannidae, or 'Tyrant flycatchers', are called 'kingbird', 'tyrant', 'phoebe' or 'pewee'—the last two names arising from the bird's call.

The best-known of the Muscicapinae are the Spotted flycatcher *Muscicapa striata*, an ashy-brown bird with a creamy breast, and the Pied flycatcher *Ficedula hypoleuca*, black above and white beneath; both European and 5 in (13 cm) long. There are over 300 other species, however, spread over the whole of the eastern hemisphere, except for the extreme north of Asia, and reaching New Zealand, the Marquesas and Hawaii in the Pacific. The species are very variable, some are dull-coloured, some very bright. A few are crested, others have face wattles. And the tail may be extremely long, as in the Paradise flycatchers of the genus *Terpsiphone* found around the Indian Ocean. In these the males' central tail feathers may be elongated to give a total length of 21 in (53 cm).

The range of form in the Muscicapinae is well illustrated by the 50-odd species in New Guinea. These are extremely diverse. They vary in bill shape, behaviour and tarsal length, so that some of them are more like warblers, chats or shrikes than flycatchers. Other species from elsewhere may be as well-built as a European blackbird or an American robin, or almost as slight as a kinglet, genus *Regulus*.

The Tyrant flycatchers—over 360 species, confined to North and South America—also show a considerable range of form. They vary from 3–16 in (7½–40 cm) in length, including tail, and from the grey of the Eastern phoebe *Sayornis phoebe* of North America, to the black, white, green, orange and scarlet of the Many-coloured tyrant *Tachuris rubrigastra* of South America. They also vary considerably in feeding habits. FAMILIES: Muscicapidae, Tyrannidae, ORDER: Passeriformes, CLASS: Aves.

FLYING DRAGONS, or Flying lizards, a misnomer, for the 'wings' of these lizards are not supported by the forelimbs nor can they beat in flight. All four limbs are free for landing and for climbing on tree trunks but along the sides of the flattened body and between fore- and hindlegs are wings consisting of a thin membrane or skin stretched across greatly elongated and movable ribs. These when extended provide a taut patagium that can be opened and closed like a fan. When at rest on a tree wings are closed; they open only when the lizard is displaying or when ready to launch itself from a trunk. As it prepares to glide it turns, faces downwards, dives steeply, straightens out at an angle of about 22° and then as it is about to alight it banks to land in an upward position. FAMILY: Agamidae, ORDER: Squamata, CLASS: Reptilia.

FLYING FISHES, marine fishes with large fins for gliding out of water. Species of *Exocoetus* have large pectoral fins which can be spread like wings, and the lower lobe of the tail enlarged to provide the motive power for taxiing at the surface. The species of *Cypselurus* have both pectoral and pelvic fins enlarged and they taxi at the surface to reach speeds of 35 mph (56 kph) before lifting themselves into the air. The flight may last up to half a minute and the fishes can cover ¼ mile (400 m). Flyingfishes probably make use of updraughts of air in the troughs of waves and in a stiff breeze may be lifted 20–30 ft (6–9 m) sometimes landing on the deck of a ship. Flyingfishes are hunted by the dolphinfish and many of the tuna-like fishes, and flight offers only temporary safety.

The so-called Flying gurnard *Dactylopterus volitans* also has very large pectoral fins. It is bottom-living, in the Mediterranean and the warmer parts of the Atlantic, and no photographic evidence has been produced to show that this rather heavily-built fish ever flies. When disturbed the Flying gurnard will suddenly spread its colourful pectoral fins and this flash of colour is startling. This may be the true function of the 'wings', to scare an enemy.

Freshwater hatchetfishes of South America exhibit true flapping flight. They make little leaps out of the water while rapidly vibrating their sickle-shaped pectoral fins (causing a faint humming noise).

In Africa, the freshwater butterflyfish *Pantodon buchholtzi* flaps its large pectoral fins during flight.

FLYING FOXES, bats of the sub-order Megachiroptera, family Pteropidae, although sometimes restricted to the genus *Pteropus*. All are Old World fruit-eating bats which have fox-like faces. Some species attain a large size and may be a nuisance to agriculture by raiding plantations.

FLYING GECKO *Ptychozoon homalocephalum*, also known as Fringed gecko or Parachute gecko, of Southeast Asia, has flaps of skin on its legs, tail and sides, those on the flanks being half as wide as the trunk. It is usually assumed that these flaps help to conceal the animal when it flattens itself, at rest, on a tree. Within recent years, however, tests have shown that they act as planing surfaces enabling the gecko to parachute at a steep angle down to the ground. FAMILY: Gekkonidae, ORDER: Squamata, CLASS: Reptilia.

FLYING LEMUR *Cynocephalus variegatus*, the colugo or caguan, a cat-sized mammal of southeast Asia, eastwards to the Philippines. It is the best equipped mammal for gliding, but does not fly in the true sense. A membrane extends from the sides of the chin down either side of the body taking in the forearm and all the fingers and continuing in a broad web to take in the hindlegs and toes and beyond right up to the tip of the tail. The fur is mottled grey, fawn and buff.

The Flying lemur rests on the limbs of trees, its fur harmonizing with the bark. When disturbed it moves along the branch to the main trunk, climbs rapidly to a higher position, then takes a flying leap to the next tree, a long smooth glide up to 229 ft (70 m).

It lives in forests feeding on leaves and fruit and it has a single young at a birth, which clings to the mother while lying in the gliding membrane as in a hammock. FAMILY: Cynocephalidae, ORDER: Dermoptera, CLASS: Mammalia.

FLYING PHALANGERS or marsupial gliders, glide from tree to tree and tree to ground using a flap of skin which connects fore- and hindlimbs. They range from the mouse-like Pigmy glider *Acrobates pygmaeus* to the lightly built but much larger Greater glider *Schoinobates volans* which may reach a length of over 3 ft (1 m). Gliders have soft fur, long tails, rounded heads and large eyes. They are mainly eastern Australian. FAMILY: Phalangeridae, ORDER: Marsupialia, CLASS: Mammalia.

FLYING SNAKES, four species of Southeast Asian snakes, one of which is the oriental Golden tree snake *Chrysopelea ornata*. They live in trees and have developed a capacity to leap from branch to branch and to descend over considerable distances to ground level in an inclined glide. The leaping is achieved by the sudden straightening of the body from a strongly coiled position. When gliding the body is held straight with the broad under-surface concave to form a 'parachute' surface. FAMILY: Colubridae, ORDER: Squamata, CLASS: Reptilia.

FLYING SQUIRRELS, do not really fly but glide. There are about 30 species in the tropical forests of southeastern Asia, with one species in temperate Eurasia and two in North America. They range from mouse-sized, the Pygmy flying squirrel *Petaurillus hosei* of Borneo, to cat-sized, the Giant flying squirrel *Petaurista petaurista* found throughout southeastern Asia.

Gliding is achieved by a membrane on each side of the body, stretching from the wrist to the ankle and in some species also between the hind legs and the tail. The membrane, furred on both sides, is supported in front by a rod of cartilage attached to the wrist. Although the membrane looks like

The Sugar glider *Petaurus australis* one of the Flying phalangers of Australia.

cytoplasm passes in the form of long thin filaments or pseudopodia which join with each other to form a feeding net. Particles of food entangled in the net are drawn into the body. Foraminiferans reproduce sexually and there is a true alternation of generations between the sexual phase and an asexual phase. Gametes are formed and released to fuse in pairs and form zygotes. The first chamber of the shell forms round the zygote and the animal increases in size by simply growing and adding new chambers to its shell. The asexual form possesses a number of nuclei and eventually fragments of the parent, each containing a single nucleus, are shed and begin life on their own by secreting the first chamber of a shell.

Most foraminiferans live on the ocean floor and their skeletons accumulate to form a thick calcareous layer known as foraminiferan ooze covering a third of the ocean floor. ORDER: Foraminiferida, CLASS: Sarcodina, PHYLUM: Protozoa.

FOSSA *Cryptoprocta ferox*, Madagascan carnivore related to the civets. It measures up to 5 ft (1·5 m), of which the tail accounts for almost half. It looks like a tawny, or grey, long-bodied, short-legged cat with a long tail. Its fur is short and coarse and is found in two colour phases. The fossa is arboreal, mainly nocturnal, and is unusual in being plantigrade. Its claws are strongly hooked, sharp and retractile. Its main food is small birds and lemurs that it catches in the trees, but as the scientific name indicates, it also has a reputation of being a ferocious killer of almost anything that crosses its path. Modern observation suggests this is not entirely justified. FAMILY: Viverridae, ORDER: Carnivora, CLASS: Mammilia.

FOUR-EYED FISHES, freshwater toothcarps of Central America, characterized by appearing to have four eyes. The eyes are divided horizontally into an upper half for vision in air and a lower for vision under water. A different kind of lens is required in air than in water and although these fishes have a single lens it is through the thickest part of it that underwater objects are viewed. The Four-eyed fish *Anableps* spends its time cruising along at the surface with the upper part of the eyes exposed. This enables the fish to search for food and at the same time to keep an eye out, so to speak, for predators. The Four-eyed fish must constantly duck its head under water to prevent the eyes drying out. FAMILY: Anablepidae, ORDER: Atheriniformes, CLASS: Pisces.

FOUR-HORNED ANTELOPE *Tetracerus quadricornis*, a small antelope of the grasslands and open jungle of India, closely related to the nilgai. The male has two pairs of horns, the posterior pair 3–4 in (8–10 cm) long, in the usual place, the front pair $\frac{1}{2}$–1 in

only two layers of skin, it contains a thin layer of muscle by which its curvature can be altered to control the aerodynamic properties. The tail is generally about equal in length to the head and body and in most species the overall surface area is increased by the arrangement of hairs on the tail, which spread sideways like the vanes of a feather. Otherwise, flying squirrels closely resemble tree squirrels but being nocturnal have larger eyes.

Flying squirrels usually nest in holes in trees and only emerge after dark. They tend to live entirely in the forest canopy and glide from tree to tree, the larger species achieving glides of several hundred yards with very little loss of height. The diet of flying squirrels probably does not differ much from that of other squirrels.

Amongst the flying squirrels of southeastern Asia, one of the best known is the largest, *Petaurista petaurista*, which occurs,

especially in montane forest, from the Himalayas to Java and Borneo. It is a uniform brown and the tail is long and bushy, not flattened as in some species.

In the coniferous forests of Siberia lives a small grey flying squirrel *Pteromys volans*, and two similar species occur in North America, a northern one *Glaucomys sabrinus* mainly in coniferous forest, and a southern one *Glaucomys volans* in deciduous forest throughout eastern USA. FAMILY: Sciuridae, ORDER: Rodentia, CLASS: Mammalia.

FORAMINIFERANS, single-celled, largely marine Protozoa with calcareous shells. The shell is at first single chambered but, as the animal grows, new chambers may be added and the final shell takes a variety of forms from a long straight shell to the more common flat spiral. The shells are perforated with tiny holes, or foramina, and through these the

(1–2·5 cm) long, above or slightly in front of the eyes. The horns are straight, smooth and keeled in front. Females are, however, hornless. The animal stands 25 in (65 cm) high and weighs 37–46 lb (17–21 kg). It is dull red-brown, white below, becoming lighter and yellower with age. There is a dark stripe down the front of each limb and a naked, black slit-like gland in front of each eye. Also known as chousingha, the Four-horned antelope lives a solitary life, sheltering in the tall grass and setting up a territory near water. It is found especially in hilly country from the Himalayan foothills to Cape Comorin. FAMILY: Bovidae, ORDER: Artiodactyla, CLASS: Mammalia.

FOWL, DOMESTIC, or chicken, descended from the Red junglefowl *Gallus gallus* inhabiting southeastern Asia. The history of its domestication is lost in antiquity but chickens were probably kept in the Indus Valley in India as early as 3,200 BC and they are known to have occurred in China by 1,400 BC.

By the 5th century BC chickens were kept by most civilized countries both in the East and as far west as Greece and Italy. In Greece and Rome the fowl had a religious significance and its spread throughout western Europe by the 1st century BC was almost certainly the result of the expansion of the Roman Empire.

It seems likely that the use of the Domestic fowl as a sacrificial or religious animal together with the popularity of cock fighting were responsible for its original spread. FAMILY: Phasianidae, ORDER: Galliformes, CLASS: Aves.

FOX, general term referring to several species in the family Canidae, distinguished from dogs by their smaller size, stealth in hunting and solitary habits.

In the Red fox group, *Vulpes*, most species have black or dark stockings and black markings on the back of the large pointed ears. The thick brush can be either black- or white-tipped, and there is often a black mark near the base of the tail where the dorsal scent gland is situated. The Red foxes have slim muzzles.

The Red fox *Vulpes vulpes* is distributed throughout the northern hemisphere in Europe, Asia, Africa, and North America although the New World form is considered by some to be a separate species, *Vulpes fulva*. Living in wooded areas and plains country, this species hunts mainly at twilight and dawn when its chief prey, rabbits, voles, and rats, is most active. Although they rely largely on sound and smell to find food in the dark, Red foxes do employ vision when they switch to daytime hunting. During the summer, vixens who must feed their fast-growing cubs are often abroad in the day.

Although they prefer small mammals and birds, Red foxes supplement their diet with plant material and some have been known to survive while eating more than 50% fruits and vegetables.

Breeding is from late January through February. After a gestation of 50–56 days, four to ten cubs are born helpless and weighing 4 oz (100 gm). At eight or nine days of age, the cubs' eyes open, but the young remain relatively inactive until shortly before they emerge from the lair at five weeks.

A special form of the Red fox which has been specifically bred by man is the Silver fox. Although originally just a colour variation, modern Silver foxes, the fur of which ranges from silver to deep black, now breed true and their farming is a large and lucrative business.

Two close relatives of the Red fox, although different species, are the Kit fox *Vulpes macrotis* and Swift fox *Vulpes velox*. Both dwell in the Great Plains region of western North America, ranging from southwest Canada to Texas and New Mexico. Being inhabitants of open prairie and desert country, they are paler than the Red fox. Kit foxes are small and only weigh up to 7 lb (3 kg). FAMILY: Canidae, ORDER: Carnivora, CLASS: Mammalia.

FRANCOLINS, birds very closely related to partridges which they resemble in colour and shape. They have large coarse bills and legs with one or several spurs. Most are dull brown. There are five Asian species the best known being the Black or Common francolin *Francolinus francolinus*, from Asia Minor, Cyprus through to Assam. It inhabits grasslands or open country densely overgrown

with bushes or scrub. There are also 36 African species of francolins, genus *Francolinus*.

Francolins have always been considered first-class game birds, being comparatively large and many living in fairly open country. In the breeding season the coveys split into pairs. The female incubates the clutch of 5–12 eggs but the male assists in caring for the chicks. FAMILY: Phasianidae, ORDER: Galliformes, CLASS: Aves.

FRIGATEBIRDS *Fregata*, five species of strong-flying, non-swimming seabirds of the warm seas. Unlike most seabirds, their feathers are not water-repellent so they are unable to take off if forced to land on the sea. Also there is a shortening of the legs and a reduction of the webs which join all four toes. The species are sedentary and it is unusual to see them far from land. However, they have extraordinary powers of flight so if blown outside their normal range they can travel many thousands of miles. They do not mind flying over land and regularly fly between the Atlantic and Pacific across Panama.

Frigatebirds are about 3 ft (1 m), with long thin wings spanning some 7 ft (2·1 m), deeply forked tail and long straight bill with a hooked tip. In proportion to weight they have the largest wing area of any bird. Adults are either black (most males) or black with white underparts (females of four species); immature birds have the head white, or white tinged with buff, and spend several years in this plumage before becoming adult.

They normally nest in trees or bushes, but

A male Frigate bird, during the courtship season, develops an inflatable orange-coloured sac used in display. Once the hen has laid throat returns to normal.

they can nest on the ground. The male selects a nest-site and advertises for a mate by showing off a vivid crimson, balloon-like throat sac which is only inflated during courtship. During the display the wings are spread, the whole body quivers, bill and wing quills rattle and the bird utters a falsetto warble. The single large white egg is laid in a flimsy nest of twigs. The male then deflates his pouch and settles down for the first ten-day-long incubation period. An ugly naked chick hatches after six to seven weeks. It fledges at five or six months. Even then it is still fed while it learns to find food for itself. This 'weaning' is a critical period and many young die at this stage. The time taken to raise young is so long that adults may be unable to breed every year.

Although frigates eat the young and eggs of seabirds, their basic diet consists of fishes, taken from the surface of the water and flyingfishes caught just above the waves. They also harry boobies and tropicbirds in order to make them regurgitate their last meal, which the frigates then eat. This habit has given them the sailor's name of Man-o-war birds. FAMILY: Fregatidae, ORDER: Pelecaniformes, CLASS: Aves.

FRILLED LIZARD *Chlamydosaurus kingii*, an agamid lizard of northern Australia and New Guinea, named for the large ruff or frill of skin around its neck. This normally lies in folds back along the body; when the lizard is alarmed it opens its mouth wide and the frill is erected, supported by long extensions of the hyoid or tongue bone, which act like umbrella ribs. The Frilled lizard grows to nearly 3 ft (1 m), with spindly legs and a long tail. Its colour varies from grey or russet to almost black. Below it may be white to bright rusty-red with a shiny black chest and throat,

Using a tree trunk as a vantage point it forages for grasshoppers and other insects. The female lays about a dozen eggs in a shallow nesting chamber which she digs in soft earth. FAMILY: Agamidae, ORDER: Squamata, CLASS: Reptilia.

FRILLED SHARK *Chlamydoselachus anguineus*, primitive shark with six gill slits (five in most other sharks) of which the first is continued right across the throat. Each of the partitions between the gill slits is enlarged to cover the slit behind, thus forming a frilled collar. The body is slender, the tail is not bent upwards as in other sharks. The mouth is large and terminal, with well-developed teeth, giving the head a reptilian appearance. This rare species reaches a maximum recorded length of 6½ ft (2 m). The first was caught off Japan in 1884 but has since been found in the Atlantic (Portugal to Norway) and off California. A deep-water species, it feeds on octopuses and squids. It is ovoviviparous, the young hatching within the female and

later being born. FAMILY: Chlamydosela-chidae, ORDER: Pleurotremata, CLASS: Chondrichthyes.

FRIT FLY *Oscinella frit*, small black fly, 1–1·5 mm long, the larvae of which are serious pests of oats and other cereal crops in Europe and the New World. The eggs are laid at the bases of grasses and young oat plants in May or June and hatch into legless larvae which burrow into the young shoots and kill them.

When the larvae are fully grown pupation occurs in the soil at the base of the infected plant. The adults from these lay their eggs in the flower heads of the oats, the larvae feeding on the developing grain and then pupating inside the grain husk. A third generation from these puparia in the autumn lay their eggs on the shoots of grasses. These hatch to produce larvae which feed throughout the winter, pupate in the spring and so give rise to the adults which can then attack the young oat plants in the spring. FAMILY: Chloropidae, ORDER: Diptera, CLASS: Insecta, PHYLUM: Arthropoda.

FROGS, a name that should refer strictly only to members of the family Ranidae, the true frogs. *Rana* is the largest genus and is found all over the world except in southern South America, southern and central Australia, New Zealand and the eastern part of Polynesia. It is the only genus of true frogs to reach America or Europe. Its 200 species are all similar in shape: slim, agile frogs with a pointed head and protruding eyes. The hindlimbs are long and the toes are webbed. The skin is smooth and usually brown or green.

There are ten species of *Rana* in Europe, divisible into two fairly distinct groups: the 'brown' or 'land' frogs like the Common frog and the 'green' or 'water' frogs like the Edible frog. The Common frog *Rana temporaria* is about 4 in (10 cm) long and, although it varies greatly in colour, it is usually a shade of brown above with black-brown spots or patches. Largely terrestrial, it is usually found

Female Edible frog among water crowfoot.

Gaudy *Rana malabaricus* of West Africa. Since frogs are promiscuous their colouring can only serve as camouflage.

in damp grass. The Edible frog *Rana esculenta* by contrast, spends most of its time in water. In the male Common frog the vocal sacs which help amplify its call are situated under the skin of the throat and when the frog calls the throat swells up. In the Edible frog the vocal sacs are external and located at the sides of the mouth. During calling two small greyish balloons emerge behind the corners of the mouth. CLASS: Amphibia.

FRUIT FLIES, true two-winged flies, the larvae of which feed on fruit. They belong to two families, the larger flies to the Trypetidae, the smaller to the Drosophilidae. The large Fruit flies are about ⅖ in (1 cm) long, often with patterned wings. The end of the female's abdomen is produced to form a horny pen shaped ovipositor, used to pierce the young fleshy fruit to lay eggs. The larvae feed on the developing fruit often reaching the pupation stage when the fruit is nearly ripe. They then crawl out of the fruit, which has usually fallen, to pupate in the ground. Species of *Dacus* and *Ceratitis* are widespread and serious pests of stone fruits. The Mediterranean fruit fly *Ceratitis capitata* will attack almost all commercial fruits and now occurs in all fruit growing countries with a Mediterranean climate.

The drosophilid flies are much smaller, have a rather swollen appearance and red eyes. They are strongly attracted to fruity and fermentation odours and are commonly seen hovering rather slowly around over ripe fruit. They can be a domestic nuisance when fruit is stored or alcohol brewed. The genus *Drosophila* is the most important. Its eggs are laid in the fermenting vegetable material upon which the larva feeds and the life-cycle is completed in two weeks. *Drosophila* species have been used extensively for the study o genetics and heredity. ORDER: Diptera, CLASS. Insecta, PHYLUM: Arthropoda.

FULMARS, oceanic birds with some external resemblance to gulls to which they are not related. The name fulmar is derived from 'foul mew' (or gull) because of their

The fulmar, related to the Storm petrels, has had a spectacular spread in the North Atlantic during the last century.

habit of ejecting stomach-oil at intruders and in life and after death, their feathers retain a musty odour. Their effortless gliding on stiff, straight wings contrasts with the slower flapping flight of gulls, but on land, to which they are only attracted for breeding, they progress in an ungainly fashion, walking on the tarsus as well as the foot. The nostrils are contained within a tube on the upper mandible.

All are stocky but capable of performing well in flight. They have distensible throat pouches and all but one, the Silver-grey petrel or Antarctic fulmar *Fulmarus glacialoides*, possess lamellae on the inner edges of the mandibles. Probably all were plankton-feeders originally, but some have now assumed the role of scavenger, feeding on the offal from man's fishing and whaling activities and from ships' galley-waste. They nest in the open with little fear of predation, because they can defend themselves by spitting quantities of objectionable oil from the bill. *Fulmarus* is represented in both hemispheres, the other four genera are southern forms. The Antarctic fulmar is generally accepted as the ancestral type for the genus, and of the three northern forms the Pacific fulmar *F. glacialis rogersii* resembles it most closely. *F. g. glacialis* and *F. g. auduboni* are

found in the North Atlantic. FAMILY Procellariidae, ORDER: Procellariiformes, CLASS: Aves.

FUR SEALS, belong to the Otariidae or eared-seals, and have the two most obvious characters of this group—the small external ears and the ability to bring their hindflippers forwards underneath the body. Characters that distinguish them from sealions, the other members of the Otariidae, are their more pointed noses, the shape of their hindflippers and the quality of their fur. The hindflippers have all the digits of approximately the same length, whereas those of sealions have the outer digits longer than the inner three.

As in most mammals the coat is composed of two sorts of hair, the longer and stronger guard hairs, and the shorter finer fur hairs or underfur. The hairs grow in groups, each with a single, flattened, strong guard hair with a variable number of fur hairs underneath it. In true seals (phocids) and sealions there are less than six fur hairs to each guard hair, but in Fur seals there are 20 or more. The guard hairs help to prevent abrasion by rocks, and the fur hairs, by trapping bubbles of air provide an insulating blanket which helps to keep the animal warm in cold climates.

The Northern or Pribilof fur seal *Callorhinus ursinus*, the best known of the Fur seals, breeds on the Pribilof and Commander Islands on either side of the Bering Sea, and on Robben Island off Sakhalin, north of Japan, but although their breeding areas are restricted, they have a very wide migration route. Some cross the Pacific but most of the Commander and Robben Island herds move down the Japanese coast in winter, while the

Bull Fur seal showing the heavy neck which identifies the male.

121

Australian Fur seals *Arctocephalus doriferus*, living along the southern coast of Australia. Little is known of their habits.

Pribilof animals go down the Canadian and American coast. The southward migration takes place in winter and spring and extends to about 33° N; the Pribilof animals leave in about October, have reached their southerly limit and start to return home in April, and from June to October most animals are back on the Pribilofs.

The adult male Northern fur seal is about 7 ft (2·1 m) in length, with a peculiarly short pointed nose and long whiskers that give it a very haughty appearance. The colour is rich dark brown with a greyish tinge on the shoulders due to the presence of white hairs. The females are 5 ft (1·5 m) in length, greyer dorsally and more chestnut ventrally, and at 130 lb (59 kg) are more delicate and much slimmer than the male, weighing about 700 lb (317 kg).

When the adult males return to the rookery at the beginning of June, usually to the same place year after year, they fight and roar and establish their territories so that they are well in command by the time the females arrive in mid-June. Younger and immature bulls, known as the bachelors, hang about the edges of the territories while the harem bull keeps an eye on his 50 or so cows. He does not return to the sea for feeding for about two months. Bulls do not become harem masters until they are about 12, but they may continue until they are 20 years old.

The pups are born, 2 ft (0·6 m) in length 12 lb (5·4 kg) in weight and black in colour, between about June 20 and July 20. Each is suckled for three months, but only for the first week does the mother stay close by it. After this she goes to sea for a day at a time, feeding, and the pups gather together in groups or 'pods' in quiet areas of the rookery. Although able to swim at birth they do not normally enter the water until they are about a month old, when they spend much time playing in pools. In a rookery of many thousands of animals it is difficult to appreciate how a cow finds her own pup, yet she will feed no other in spite of advances from hungry youngsters. She recognizes her own pup by voice and smell, and by coming ashore at the right place each time she returns she does not often fail.

All the other Fur seals of the world belong to the single genus *Arctocephalus*, and all except one are restricted to the southern hemisphere. The species of the northern hemisphere, the Guadalupe fur seal *A. philippii* lives only on the island of Guadalupe off Lower California.

The remaining members of the genus live in the southern hemisphere, and their size, colour, behaviour and general life-history are very similar. Their underfur is a rich chestnut, covered by darker guard hairs. The males, with a thicker mane mixed with white

hairs, have a grizzled appearance, while the females are more grey. The South American and Kerguelen fur seals are the smallest, the males being about 6 ft (1·8 m) long, while the Australian and South African are the largest at about 7 ft 6 in (2·3 m). The females are usually about 1½–2 ft (0·45–0·6 m) shorter.

The South American fur seal *A. australis* lives round the coasts of South America from near Rio de Janeiro to north Chile, and is also present on the Falkland Islands and the Galapagos Islands.

The South African fur seal *A. pusillus* occurs on the islands off the coast of South West Africa and Cape Province from Algoa Bay to Cape Cross.

The Australian fur seal *A. doriferus* is found chiefly on the rocky islands off the coasts of Victoria and Tasmania, on islands in Bass Strait and on some of the islands off the southern New South Wales coast. The New Zealand fur seal *A. forsteri* lives round the South Island of New Zealand, on the islands to the southeast of New Zealand from Chatham to Macquarie Island, and is also found around South and Western Australia.

The Kerguelen fur seal *A. tropicalis* occurs on many of the islands in the South Atlantic and South Indian Oceans. FAMILY: Otariidae, ORDER: Pinnipedia, CLASS: Mammalia.

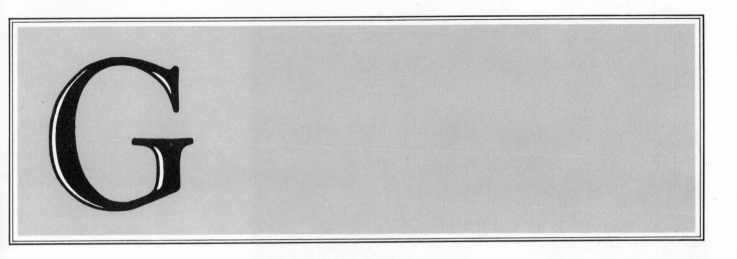

GABOON VIPER *Bitis gabonica*, of Africa south of the Sahara, the largest Puff adder, up to 6 ft (2 m) long. It has unusually long fangs, up to 2 in (5 cm) long, and is gaudily coloured yellow, purple and brown in a geometrical pattern. FAMILY: Viperidae, ORDER: Squamata, CLASS: Reptilia.

GANNETS *Morus bassanus*, large seabirds, of temperate regions, weighing nearly 7 lb (3 kg), which spend much of their time on the wing and feed by plunge-diving for fishes from the air. They have dense, white plumage with a buffish-yellow tinge on the head and upper neck, a bluish bill with the bare facial skin and feet black, as is the thin gular-stripe of skin from the base of the bill down the centre of the chin. The sexes are alike but males are slightly larger.

Gannets are streamlined for flight, with long pointed and angled wings of some 6 ft (180 cm) span and a cigar shape due to the tapering bill in front and the long, wedge-shaped tail behind. They have binocular vision. The upper breast and neck carry air-sacs below the skin which 'cushion' the impact when the birds strike the water at great speed on diving. The skull is correspondingly strong and reinforced. The bill is stout, pointed and conical and lacks external nostrils; and there are tooth-like serrations along the cutting edges which facilitate the seizure of fishes. The jaw and throat are widely distendible and the tongue is minute, allowing the birds to swallow large prey easily. The neck is moderately long, the body stoutly elongated, the legs shortish but the feet are large with long toes and webs between all four toes. On the nail of the third toe a series of notches forms a functional comb used in scratching.

When at sea, gannets often congregate over shoals of fishes in large numbers and make spectacular mass plunging dives from 50 ft (15 m) or more above the surface, falling like projectiles and raising great spurts of spray as they enter the water vertically. They are even more social when breeding and form dense colonies, often of

great size, on inaccessible headlands, cliffs and islands at traditional sites. At many gannetries, nests are spaced out over the ground at an even 3 ft (1 m).

The nest is a drum-like structure of flotsam and jetsam, often including seaweed and grass, solidified by excrement. A single white egg is laid which is incubated by both sexes, not in the conventional way but by cupping and overlapping the feet around it. Incubation lasts six weeks and the nestling is born blind and helpless with a scanty amount of down which soon develops into a thick, white fluffy coat. FAMILY: Sulidae, ORDER: Pelicaniformes, CLASS: Aves.

GARDEN SPIDER *Araneus diadematus*, also known as the Diadem or Cross spider because of a white cross on its body which caused it to be regarded as holy in Germany in the Middle Ages. It builds a round web. FAMILY: Argiopidae, ORDER: Araneae, CLASS: Arachnida, PHYLUM: Arthropoda.

GARFISHES, or needlefishes, elongated, long-jawed fishes related to the flying-fishes. The body is long and slender and slightly compressed. The most striking features are the jaws which are as long or longer than the head and bear needle-like teeth. The dorsal and anal fins are set far back on the body and the lower lobe of the tail is larger than the upper.

The garfish *Belone belone* is found in the Mediterranean and Black Sea but reaches as far north as Trondheim and the Baltic. It has an electric-blue back, silvery belly and flanks, rosy pectoral fins and a yellow eye encircled with red. Hunted by tunas, they themselves feed on herring, sardines and crustaceans and are sometimes caught by fishermen on spinners intended for mackerel. The bones of this fish are a suprising green. FAMILY: Belonidae, ORDER: Atheriniformes, CLASS: Pisces.

GARPIKES, primitive fishes from the fresh waters of the southeastern states of North America. There are several species belonging

to the genus *Lepisosteus*. All have long thin bodies covered with thick, shiny scales which are diamond-shaped and, unlike the overlapping scales of other fishes, fit together like a mosaic. The scales can be fairly easily removed and have been used in jewellery. The dorsal and anal fins are short-based and far back on the long body. This positioning of the fins is typical of fishes that need to accelerate rapidly towards their prey, all the thrust-receiving surfaces being at the rear of the fish. The gars live in weedy water and it is only when lunging towards their prey that they move swiftly. The jaws in some species are elongated and have rows of long, sharp teeth. FAMILY: Lepisosteidae, ORDER: Amiiformes, CLASS: Pisces.

GARTER SNAKES, harmless snakes of the genus *Thamnophis*. They are the most common, and among the more colourful, snakes of North America. The majority are dark with two or three vivid yellow or orange stripes. All but one of the 20 species are limited to 20–30 in (50–75 cm) in length. FAMILY: Colubridae, ORDER: Squamata, CLASS: Reptilia.

GAUR *Bos (Bibos) gaurus*, the largest wild ox. Bulls average 5 ft 8 in (175 cm) and are commonly up to 6 ft 4 in (195 cm) at the shoulder; a huge male shot in Burma was 7 ft (210 cm). Cows are smaller. A big bull may weigh 2,000 lb (900 kg). Gaurs are largely black or dark brownish-black but the legs are white from the knees and hocks to the hoofs and the forehead and arched ridge between the horns are grey-white. The face is sinuous, with a concave forehead and convex 'Roman' nose. Bulls are extraordinarily muscular, with a strongly developed dorsal ridge, a dewlap between the forelegs and another just behind the chin. In big bulls the horns are yellowish with black tips, and corrugated for about a third of their length.

Young gaurs are brownish in colour, darkening at maturity. Their horns are orange, acquiring a greenish tint and corrugations with age. In bulls the horn-tips turn

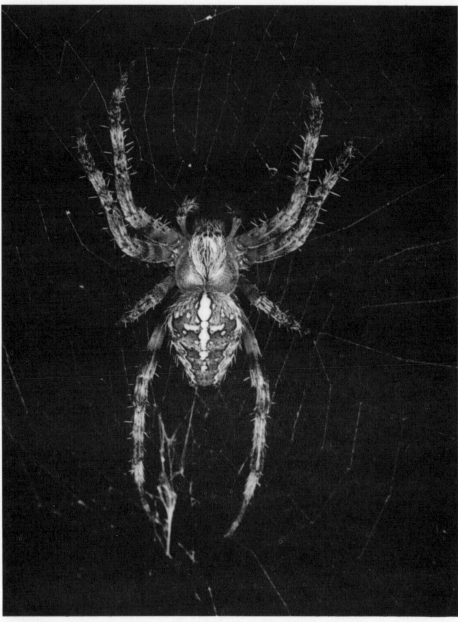

The Garden spider, on its web.

Gavial, the crocodilian of southern Asia with the long narrow snout.

upwards, but in cows they point inwards and occasionally cross. They live in hilly forests in India, Burma, Cambodia, Laos, Vietnam, Thailand and Malaya. FAMILY: Bovidae, ORDER: Artiodactyla, CLASS: Mammalia.

GAVIAL *Gavialis gangeticus*, a crocodile with a long beak-like snout. It may be up to six times longer than broad. Adult gavials may be up to 20 ft (6 m) long. There are 29 teeth on each side of the upper jaw and 26 on each side of the lower jaw, all of approximately the same size. When the gavial's mouth is closed the teeth are locked between each other and point outwards at an angle.

The end of the snout broadens into an octagonal where during the breeding season the male develops a shell-like hump. This is the only known secondary sexual characteristic in crocodiles. FAMILY: Gavialidae, ORDER: Crocodilia, CLASS: Reptilia.

GAZELLE, slenderly built, long-necked antelope with short, wagging tail. Gazelles are fawn above, white below, with an alternating pattern of dark and light face-stripes. This pattern is known as the gazelline face-pattern. On the flanks, the white of the underside is always sharply marked off from the fawn of the upperparts. Sometimes there is a dark flank-strip between the two colours. Similarly, the white of the rump may be divided from the body-colour by a dark band.

Gazelles have horns tending to be lyre-shaped from in front and S-shaped from the side. They are tightly ringed almost to the tip. The closely related blackbuck has spiral horns, and the gazelline face-pattern is altered to an eye-ring. See blackbuck, dorcas, gerenuk, Grant's gazelle, springbok, and Thomson's gazelle. FAMILY: Bovidae, ORDER: Artiodactyla, CLASS: Mammalia.

GECKOS, 675 species living mainly in the tropics, famous for their nocturnal habits and, more especially, for their climbing abilities. A few retain the conventional claw and toe, but many have retractile claws and 'snowshoe' pads for dashing across sand, but most geckos have developed 'friction' pads which enable them to climb a vertical wall or a pane of glass and to continue scampering across a ceiling upside down. They live in forests, swamps and deserts, on mountains, and on islands as long as the nights do not get too cold. They range from 2 in (5 cm) total length, to over 1 ft (30 cm), the majority being 3–6 in (7·5–15 cm) long. Roughly half the length is tail.

Their bodies are covered by a soft skin with minute scales, among which, in many species, are larger scales. A few have fish-like imbricating scales on all or some parts of the body. In most species some of the scales on the underside of each toe are specialized as broad pads, at the base, the tip

Buck Grant's gazelle, of East Africa.

Geese

or throughout the toe. Each pad resembles a miniature densely packed pincushion; every microscopic bristle is split into delicate branches, each terminating in a disk-like thickening, the free face of which is slightly concave. Recent studies show that the multitudinous tiny terminal disks adhere by suction, but on surfaces where this is not possible, the bristles act like so many miniature hooks. The peculiar wriggling gait of the gecko is due to the fact that in order to lift its foot from the wall surface, it must curl each toe upward from the front to disengage the fringes without damaging them. This must be done each time the toes are picked up as it runs.

Geckos are the only lizards that regularly vocalize. In many, usually the nocturnal species, the males utter special calls, something like 'tsak-tsak' or 'tik-tik', repeated a few times in succession. These masculine calls are different from the squeaking of either sex when seized. The social function of the male calls is not really known. The tokay *Gecko gecko* of southeastern Asia has a vocabulary of three different calls, all frighteningly loud. FAMILY: Gekkonidae, ORDER: Squamata, CLASS: Reptilia.

GEESE, water birds intermediate between ducks and swans, longer in the legs and neck than most ducks. They are not so aquatic as ducks or swans, feeding largely by grazing on land. As geese are large and their flesh highly palatable they have been important as food to the peoples of all countries where they occur regularly in appreciable numbers, the Grey lag goose *Anser anser* and the Swan goose *A. cygnoides*, having been domesticated for meat production.

There are two natural groups: the 'grey' geese, genus *Anser* and the 'black' geese, genus *Branta*, all confined to the northern hemisphere, typically breeding in arctic or subarctic regions. They are gregarious, particularly outside the breeding season, and migrate in large flocks. In flight they usually adopt a formation of wavy lines or, particularly, a 'V' shape, each bird flying slightly to one side of its neighbours, flight formations known as skeins, from their similarity to strands of wool, and during peak migration they may cover much of the sky for several days. The strength of the social bond may be seen in parties of geese on their feeding grounds, where the members of a family stay together, and groups of families form larger units. The general term for a flock or party of geese on the ground is a gaggle.

The grey geese are typified by the Grey lag, which is widespread in the Palearctic region and divided into eastern and western races. This is the largest of the grey geese, up to 35 in (89 cm) long, with a large, heavy head and a stout bill, orange in the western race, pink in the eastern. Unlike the other grey geese it has no dark markings on the bill.

Undersurface of a tokay climbing up glass, showing the sucker-like pads on the toes.

The feet and legs are pink and the forewing is pale grey. Otherwise, the plumage is grey-brown, with light tips to the body feathers which lie in such a way as to give a barred appearance on the back. The tail is grey with a white tip and the upper and lower tail coverts are white. The head and neck are no darker than the rest of the body, and the breast is generally unmarked.

The Grey lag breeds in lowland marshes, moors and often on islands. The nests may be close together, usually on the ground, hidden amongst heather or similar vegetation, with a lining of heather, mosses, and grasses, mixed with feathers. Sometimes they are built of dead reeds and similar materials among floating willow roots. Generally 4–6 creamy-white eggs are laid, incubated by the female alone for 27–28 days, while the male stays in the vicinity. The young leave the nest shortly after hatching accompanied by both parents.

The adults feed on many kinds of grasses and berries, and take readily to agricultural land, visiting cornfields at night and feeding on other crops such as peas and turnips.

The breeding range of the western Grey lag extends from Iceland and Scandinavia to Jugoslavia and Macedonia. The winter range is from Britain and Holland southwards to North Africa.

Another important palearctic grey goose is the Bean goose *A. fabalis*, almost as large as the Grey lag but of slighter build. It is more northerly, breeding in the tundra and coniferous forest regions from East Greenland to eastern Asia. In this range the Bean goose exists in a number of geographical races, of general build, shape and colour of bill, and habitat preference. The most westerly is the Pink-footed goose *A. f. brachyrhynchus*, often regarded as a distinct species. It breeds in East Greenland, Iceland, and Spitzbergen, and has a lighter coloured back than the other forms. Also the bill is shorter and the head more rounded. The bill is black and pink and the feet and legs pink. The third form is the Forest bean goose *A. f. fabalis* which has a longer, more slender bill, and breeds in a chain of at least three races.

The Bean goose tends to nest more on hummocks which provide good all-round visibility. The pink-foot may even nest on cliff edges.

The White-fronted goose *A. albifrons* also breeds in the Arctic and flies south in enormous flocks for the winter. It is smaller and darker than the Grey lag, has broad black irregular bars across the belly, a white frontal patch on the forehead above a pink bill, and orange legs. There are four forms, one of which, the Pacific white-front *A. a. frontalis*, breeds across arctic North America. Another, the Tule goose *A. a. gambelli*, is also North American, but its population is dangerously small and its breeding grounds unknown. The European white-front *A. a. albifrons* breeds on the arctic coasts of Asia and eastern Europe; and the Greenland white-front *A. a. flavirostris* breeds in a small area of West Greenland.

A similar but smaller species, not exceeding 26 in (67·6 cm) in length, is the Lesser white-front *A. erythropus*.

The Swan goose breeds in Siberia, Mongolia and Manchuria, and has been domesticated in China for at least 3,000 years. Apart from the greater bulk and a knob at the base of the bill of the domestic form, the two are similar, having the typical grey goose plumage but with a neck cream coloured at the front and sides and chestnut behind. The bill of the wild form is longer than in any other goose. The Swan goose is better able to stand heat than the Grey lag and is therefore the more common domesticated form in hot countries.

There are five species of black geese, of which one, the Canada goose *Branta canadensis*, has been divided into 12 races, one probably extinct. All Canada geese have brown body plumage, a white rump, black head and neck, and a white cheek patch. The largest race, the Giant Canada goose *B. c. maxima*, is about twice the bulk of the smallest, the Cackling goose *B. c. minima*.

The Canada goose breeds across Canada, part of the northern United States and the Aleutian Islands.

The Brent goose is the smallest and darkest of the black geese, measuring no more than 24 in (61 cm) in length. The plumage is largely black or black and brown, paler beneath and with an incomplete white collar. The Dark-bellied brent goose *Branta bernicla bernicla* breeds in arctic Europe and Asia; the Light-bellied brent *B. b. hrota* in northeastern Canada, northern Greenland, Spitzbergen and Franz Joseph Land; and the Pacific brent or Black brant *B. b. orientalis* in northwest Canada, Alaska and Siberia.

The Barnacle goose *B. leucopsis* has a handsome grey, white and black plumage; black on the neck and upper breast, grey on the back, pale grey beneath and with a white rump and face. It breeds in the tundra regions of the western Palearctic, including east Greenland and Spitzbergen, and usually makes its nest in inaccessible places such as cliff faces.

The most striking of the black geese is the Red-breasted goose *B. ruficollis* which has a bold black, white and chestnut-red plumage. The upper-parts are black, the rump and flanks white, and the neck and breast red, picked out with white. It breeds in the tundra of northern Siberia.

Finally, the né-né or Hawaiian goose is a species saved from extinction by active conservation. The plumage is barred in

Canada geese with goslings, a species introduced into Europe and New Zealand.

The gelada, a baboon-like monkey of the highlands of Ethiopia.

brown, black and white, and it has a black head with rufous neck and cheeks. The neck feathers are conspicuously pleated or furrowed. Non-migratory, it is terrestrial rather than aquatic. Its stance is upright and the webs on the feet are reduced. As a result it was at a disadvantage in competition with introduced predators and by the 1950s there were less than 50 birds left. Conservation efforts in Hawaii and in Britain have, however, built up the world population to around 900 birds in 1970.

The Magpie goose, in a subfamily to itself, seems to represent a link with the screamers with which it has a number of structural features in common. It is a large black and white bird inhabiting southern New Guinea and northern Australia, and is unusual among geese in regularly perching in trees. FAMILY: Anatidae, ORDER: Anseriformes, CLASS: Aves.

GELADA *Theropithecus gelada*, a large baboon-like monkey of the Ethiopian Highlands. Although it is as large as most baboons, has a long face and a similar type of sexual dimorphism, the gelada is not a true baboon, being as closely related to the mangabeys and macaques. Its facial elongation, so marked in baboons, is effected in a different way: instead of being lengthened into a long narrow muzzle, with the nostrils at the tip, the gelada's face is deep, with massive jaws and a snubby nose which is not at the tip of the thick, square snout. The face is grooved on either side of the snout. The fur is yellow to brown, with pink naked patches on the chest which meet in the middle. In the female there is a 'necklace' of warty eminences around the chest patch, and at the height of oestrus these become very prominent and the chest patch turns bright red, a condition likened to a 'bleeding heart'.

Gemsbok

The gelada feeds mainly on seeds, blades of grass, and shoots, which it gathers by sitting in one place and picking them up, storing them in the hand until it has a fistful, when all is transferred to the mouth. FAMILY: Cercopithecidae, ORDER: Primates, CLASS: Mammalia.

GEMSBOK *Oryx gazella*, largest and most widely distributed oryx, about 48 in (120 cm) high, it is fawn above with a black dorsal stripe and a black flank-band separating the fawn from the white underside. The forelegs have a black garter above the knees, and are white below this, as are the hocks. The ear-tips are black, as is a line down the throat and chest. The black nose-patch and eye-stripes often unite to form a girdle round the muzzle.

The gemsbok has a disjunct distribution: in the Kalahari and again in the Somali arid zone. The Kalahari race, the true gemsbok *O. g. gazella*, is scarcer than formerly, but is well protected in reserves, and in the Kalahari Gemsbok National Park. FAMILY: Bovidae, ORDER: Artiodactyla, CLASS: Mammalia.

GENETS, six species related to the civets and mongooses. The best-known is the Feline or Small spotted genet *Genetta genetta*, of Africa and also found in Spain and southern France. It is cat-like but more slender, elegant and graceful in movement, up to 40 in (1 m) in length of which nearly half is tail. Its fur is soft and spotted with brown to black on a light ground colour. The head is slender and tapers to a pointed muzzle with long whiskers and the ears are large. The tail has alternate black and white rings, while along the spine is a crest of long black hairs which is raised in moments of excitement. The legs are short with small paws and retractile claws.

The Blotched or Tigrine genet *G. tigrina*, numerous throughout Africa, is similar to the Feline genet but has larger spots on a more yellowish ground colour and the crest is missing. The Rusty spotted genet *G. rubiginosa*, found south of Tanzania, is like the Blotched genet except for its more reddish spots. The rare Abyssinian genet *G. abyssinica* of the highlands of Ethiopia is the smallest of the genets not more than 20 in (51 cm) total length. It has ash-coloured fur broken by longitudinal black stripes. The Victorian genet *G. victoriae* and the Water genet *Osbornictis piscivora* are known only from skins brought back by pygmy hunters in the Ituri Forest of the Congo.

Feline genets live in areas of bush and low scrub. They are usually solitary hunting by night and sleeping by day among the branches. They stalk their prey gliding swiftly over the ground the tail held straight out behind, finally seizing their prey with a swift pounce.

Genets feed on small rodents, birds and insects, particularly night-flying moths and

The Ghost crab of tropical beaches is best known from its shadow.

beetles. A certain amount of grass is also regularly eaten. FAMILY: Viverridae, ORDER: Carnivora, CLASS: Mammalia.

GERBILS, 50 species of mouse- and rat-sized rodents, amongst the dominant small mammals of the zone of desert, steppe and savannah, stretching from the Gobi Desert through central Asia to the Sahara and south throughout most of the drier parts of Africa. Some species are known as jirds, others as sand-rats.

The fur is sandy brown above and pure white below, the feet are white and the tail thickly haired, rarely tufted. The hindfeet are slightly longer than the forefeet but gerbils do not hop on the hindfeet alone. Many gerbils, especially those in deserts, have the bony capsule of the ear, the bulla, enormously enlarged, a feature found in many desert mammals where acute hearing over long distances and in dry air is of particular importance.

Most gerbils are nocturnal, lying up in burrows during the day, and emerging at dusk to feed mainly on seeds, bulbs and succulent plants, although some species are also partial to insects. FAMILY: Cricetidae, ORDER: Rodentia, CLASS: Mammalia.

GERENUK *Litocranius walleri*, a long-necked gazelle of Somalia and parts of East Africa. It stands 41 in (103 cm) at the shoulder and has a fox-red coat. The males have short curving horns, up to 17 in (43 cm) long. Gerenuks browse the dry thorn bushes standing vertically on their hindlegs and reaching up with their long giraffe-like neck. They move about in ones or twos or in small groups of females led by a single male. When disturbed a gerenuk runs away with its neck held horizontally, its body somewhat crouched. Gerenuks seem able, when neces-

sary, to go without water. FAMILY: Bovidae, ORDER: Artiodactyla, CLASS: Mammalia.

GHOST CRABS *Ocypode*, also known as Racing crabs, sometimes as Sand crabs. They run at speed over tropical sandy beaches; their colour is similar to that of the sand; and when they run in bright sunshine their shadows are often more conspicuous than their bodies. When they stop and lower their bodies to the sand the shadows disappear, and so apparently do the crabs.

Ghost crabs also burrow, sometimes to a depth of 3–4 ft (90–120 cm). At low tide they emerge and scavenge, sometimes catching small fish at the edge of the sea. The eye-stalks of Ghost crabs are long and mobile, and in some species they are prolonged beyond the eye to form a sort of horn. One of the pincers is always larger than the other, and in many species bears on its inner side a ridge of granules that can be rubbed against a smooth ridge on the third joint of the limb bearing the pincer to produce twittering squeaks or croaks, warning other crabs that a burrow is occupied. SUBORDER: Brachyura, ORDER: Decapoda, CLASS: Crustacea, PHYLUM: Arthropoda.

GIANT ANTEATER *Myrmecophaga tridactyla*, the largest of the three living species of anteaters. Giant anteaters are easily recognized. They are grey with a pronounced white-edged black stripe that runs diagonally from the throat across the shoulders to the back. The hair is coarse and particularly long on the bushy 2–3 ft (0·65–0·90 m) tail that resembles an enormous plume. Some of the hairs that radiate from the spine of the tail may be 16 in (40·6 cm) in length. The tube-like head, with its small rounded ears and long tapering snout, ends in a tiny mouth through which the Giant anteater can extend its pencil-slim tongue almost 2 ft (61 cm). The forefeet bear stout claws, and because of these the Giant anteater walks on its knuckles and edges of its palms. Adults weigh from 38–51 or more lb (18–23 kg) and may measure 5·5–7 ft (1·6–2·1 m) from tip of snout to tip of tail. Males are usually larger than females.

Terrestrial in habit, Giant anteaters live in swamps and humid forests, frequenting open grasslands from southern British Honduras to northern Argentina.

They give birth to a single offspring after a gestation of 190 days, and the baby may weigh 3·5 lb (1·5 kg). The mother carries it on her back, and the two remain together until the female is ready to breed again.

They feed principally on termites, ripping open the hard-walled nests with their claws, poking their snouts into the crumbled mounds. and picking up the insects with their sensitive probing tongues that are covered with a sticky saliva. FAMILY: Myrmecophagidae, ORDER: Edentata, CLASS: Mammalia.

GIANT PANDA *Ailuropoda melanoleuca*, or beishung, bear-like relative of raccoons, weighing 160–400 lb (75–180 kg) and measuring 44·5 to 63 in (1–1·6 m) including the diminutive tail, is white or yellowish, with contrasting black limbs, shoulders, ears and eye patches. It lives in the bamboo and

Giant salamander, largest living amphibian, which may be 5 ft (1·5 m) long.

rhododendron forests of Yunnan and Szechuan in an area approximately 500 m (800 km) wide. Because of these formidable odds, it was only discovered in 1869 by Père David, a French zoologist explorer. Bamboo shoots form the major part of its diet in the wild. While foraging, the Giant panda sits on its haunches, legs spread, and holds the delicate branch with one forepaw, using a remarkably strong 'pseudo-thumb' to grip it. It uses a slow, pigeon-toed, rolling shuffle,

swinging the heavy head from side to side. The fastest gait is a jog-trot.

Giant panda cubs are born after a 120–140 day gestation, weighing 5 oz (142 gm), approximately $\frac{1}{800}$ th of the adult weight. FAMILY: Procyonidae, ORDER: Carnivora, CLASS: Mammalia.

GIANT SALAMANDER *Megalobatrachus japonicus*, of Japan, the largest living amphibian, reaches a length of 5 ft (1·5 m). A smaller relative *M. davidianus* lives in China. The first Giant salamander, brought to Europe in 1829, lived over 50 years.

The head and body are flattened and skin folds are present along the sides of the body. The tail is laterally flattened and the paired limbs are small in proportion to the body. When young the head region bears three pairs of gills but later these are absorbed.

The Giant salamander lives in cool swift streams. It is carnivorous, waits till the prey is within reach and seizes it with a swift lateral movement of the head. Prey consists of fish, smaller salamanders, crayfish and other vertebrates. FAMILY: Cryptobranchidae, ORDER: Caudata, CLASS: Amphibia.

GIBBONS, the smallest of apes, have arms nearly twice as long as the trunk and more than twice as long if the hands are included; they also have long legs. The hands also, are long and slender; the fingers are long and somewhat curved into hooks; the thumb, while short, is deeply cleft from the palm so that a greater proportion, than in other apes or in man, is free.

Gibbons are almost entirely arboreal, and move through the trees by their arms alone, grasping one branch and reaching over to the next with great rapidity, and often jumping between branches. As well as for their ease of movement, gibbons are known for their remarkable voices. The most characteristic of a gibbon's vocalization is the great-call, made in some species by both sexes, in

The bear-like Giant panda, adopted as a symbol of endangered animal species.

Gibbons, long-armed tailless apes, live in the jungles of southeast Asia.

others by the female only. It is a location signal, on sighting another troop, and generally in the early morning, as the sun rises, or at any marked change in the weather. In the White-headed gibbon, the call, made by the female only, is a series of musical whoops, rising in pitch and increasing in tempo and volume, finally dying away. In the Siamang gibbon, the call is made by both sexes: there is an inflatable sac in the throat, giving the call a harsh, resonant quality which is quite deafening from close-to; it is a two-tone call, a deep boom as the sac is filled, and an unpleasant shriek as the air is let out again, and this is repeated over and over for about half a minute or even more, increasing in tempo but not in volume or pitch.

On the ground gibbons walk upright with their arms bent and held to the sides, like balancing poles. Sometimes they run along a branch in this fashion.

Most gibbons feed on fruit, with some leaves, buds, flowers, eggs and insects as well.

The hoolock or White-browed gibbon *H. hoolock* is found in Assam, northern Burma and Yunnan. A few weeks after birth, both sexes turn black with white brow-bands; then at sexual maturity the female becomes light brown, with a complete face-ring. Thus the sexes are different colours when adult. FAMILY: Hylobatidae, ORDER: Primates, CLASS: Mammalia.

GIGANTURIDS, or Telescope fishes, deep-sea fishes with tubular, forward-looking eyes inhabiting oceanic waters at depths of 1,500–6,000 ft (500–2,000 m). Like many deep-sea fishes, *Bathyleptus* from the Pacific is known from only a few specimens and *Gigantura* from the Atlantic and Indian Ocean is also rare in collections. In spite of their name, giganturids are small, slim-bodied fishes. They lack scales, pelvic fins and luminous organs but are distinctive in having the lower few rays of the caudal fin elongated into a filament. The mouth is armed with large teeth and there is a record of a 2½ in (6 cm) *Gigantura vorax* with its stomach crammed with the remains of a viperfish *Chauliodus* of 5 in (12·5 cm). FAMILY: Giganturidae, ORDER: Cetomimiformes, CLASS: Pisces.

GILA MONSTER *Heloderma suspectum,* of Mexico and the southwestern U.S.A., one of the only two known venomous lizards, the other being the Mexican beaded lizard. The Gila (pronounced Hee-la) is a relatively stocky reptile, with a thick short tail, head and body, coloured pink and black.

First mentioned in 1859, it was called *Heloderma suspectum* because it was suspected of being a venomous lizard different from the already well-known Mexican beaded lizard.

The primitive venom-conducting apparatus consists of a number of grooved teeth in the front portion of the lower jaw. When a Gila chews its victim, venom flows through ducts from glands in the lower jaw, into the mouth between the teeth and lips, then by capillary action it follows the tooth-grooves into the victim's wound. FAMILY: Helodermatidae, ORDER: Squamata, CLASS: Reptilia.

GILL MAGGOTS, small crustacean parasites living in the gills of many fishes. The gills provide an excellent habitat for parasites as there is a protective outer covering and the gills themselves are soft, thin-walled and provide an easily available supply of blood for food. It is not surprising that such a habitat has been occupied by a wide range of parasites, including trematode flatworms, leeches and copepods. CLASS: Crustacea, PHYLUM: Arthropoda.

GIRAFFE *Giraffa camelopardalis,* one of the most striking animals in existence with its extraordinarily long neck, long legs, sloping back and tufted tail. The giraffe bulls may reach a height of 18 ft (5·5 m) and the cows 16 ft (5 m). The giraffe has one living relative, the okapi. It is also related, but less closely, to deer, partly since the antlers of the deer when 'in velvet' resemble the skin-covered horns of the giraffe. However, the horns of the giraffe are permanent and present in both sexes. Those of the males are longer, about 10 in (25 cm) and thicker than those of the female. Deer and giraffes have the same number of teeth (32). The wide, lobed lower canine teeth of the giraffe are situated beside the incisors. They help to increase the width of the front teeth, which comb the leaves from trees and bushes rather than clipping them off. Many fossil giraffes lived in Europe and Asia millions of years ago but today both giraffes and okapis are only found in Africa. Even here the distribution is more restricted than it was 1,000 years ago. Then giraffes roamed south of the Orange River where drawings of them by Bushmen still exist, and throughout most of the Sahara Desert, which was much less dry then than it is now. More recently giraffes have been poached or shot out in some areas or driven back out of newly developed farmlands.

Giraffes spend much of their time eating, wandering from plant to plant pulling a few twigs from this bush, a few leaves from that

The Gila monster, a mere 20 in (50 cm) long despite its name, feeds on centipedes, insects, worms, lizards, small rodents—and snakes' eggs. It stores fat in its tail.

tree. They eat many kinds of leaves, but they prefer some to others. The preferred trees often show marked cropping downwards from a height of 18 ft (5·5 m). They often browse acacia thorn bushes, reaching around the thorns with their prehensile tongues and lips to extract the leaves. The thickness of the lips and their abundance of stiff hairs prevent them from being torn on the thorns.

When water is available, giraffes may drink daily, bending their long front legs awkwardly or straddling them apart so that they can reach the water. They can also survive where there is no free water. Apparently they can satisfy their needs from the leaves they consume.

They often spend the hottest part of an African day chewing the cud, while standing or lying with their heads erect. They continue to chew the cud and browse after nightfall, since they apparently need little sleep. Observations in zoos show that giraffes sleep deeply for less than an hour a night. To do this they lay their heads back along their bodies for a few minutes at a time.

Young are born at any time of the year, after a gestation period of about 14½ months. Only one instance of twinning is known and these were born dead prematurely. The newborn animal is about 6 ft (2 m) tall and 130 lb (59 kg) in weight. It can stand and suck within an hour of its birth, and walk or run soon afterwards. FAMILY: Giraffidae, ORDER: Artiodactyla, CLASS: Mammalia.

GLASSFISH *Chanda ranga*, a fish of fresh and brackish waters of India, Burma and Thailand, the glassfish is a small stocky fish growing to 3 in (7 cm) with two dorsal fins, the first being spiny. Its most remarkable feature is the transparent, glass-like body which is so clear that not only can the vertebrae and bones supporting the fins be seen but objects behind the fish can be viewed through it. The abdominal cavity, however, is obscured by silvery tissue, possibly preventing the growth of algae inside the gut. The head is opaque. FAMILY: Centropomidae, ORDER: Perciformes, CLASS: Pisces.

Giraffes must either straddle the front legs or bend them awkwardly to drink. The neck has not kept pace with the forelegs.

Glow-worms

A female glow-worm beckons her prospective mate with light signals. The illumination, a cold light, is in her tail.

GLOW-WORMS, beetles belonging to the same family as fireflies. In the Common European glow-worm *Lampyris noctiluca* the male is fully winged and has large compound eyes, whereas the female is wingless and has very small compound eyes and more closely resembles the larva. In many glow-worms both sexes emit a cold yellowish-green light, but in contrast to many of the fireflies, the females usually produce the greater brilliance. The production of light by adult glow-worms almost certainly enables the sexes to locate each other, but it is difficult to account for the existence of luminescence in the egg and larval stages of some species.

Adult glow-worms seem not to feed. The larvae eat snails and slugs. They have a pair of sickle-shaped mandibles with which they seize their prey and at the same time inject into its tissues a digestive fluid through a fine channel in each mandible. The digestive fluid discharges from ducts opening near the bases of the mandibles. The mandibles and glands operate in the manner of hypodermic syringes. The larva then sucks up the semi-fluid mass by a pumping action of part of the fore-gut. FAMILY: Lampyridae, ORDER: Coleoptera, CLASS: Insecta, PHYLUM: Arthropoda.

GNATS, term in everyday use which, like the word 'midge', refers indiscriminately to small, slender two-winged flies usually having relatively long delicate legs and narrow wings, and in general appearance looking rather like mosquitoes. ORDER: Diptera, CLASS: Insecta, PHYLUM: Arthropoda.

GNU, or wildebeest, an ungainly-looking antelope of the tribe Alcelaphini, related to the hartebeest and impala. Gnu have short, thick necks, and the head, which is held low, is narrow, but not as elongated as a hartebeest's, and has a convex profile. The horns are smooth with expanded bases; their general direction is downward and outward, with the tips turning up.

The two species are very different. The White-tailed gnu or Black wildebeest *Connochaetes gnou* is more slenderly built, about 4 ft (120 cm) high, short-bodied and long-legged. It is black with long fringes on the nape and throat and in the middle of the face; the tail is long, horse-like and white; and the horns turn forward rather than outward. The Brindled gnu or Blue wildebeest *C. taurinus* is shorter-legged, longer-bodied, blue-grey with brownish-black stripes on the neck; there is a short-haired mat of black in the middle of the face, a beard extended backwards into a throat- and chest-fringe; a loose floppy mane; and the tail is long-haired but black. The Brindled gnu is larger, about 4 ft 10 in (144 cm) high, and the horns are shorter, less downcurved, and point out instead of forward. FAMILY: Bovidae, ORDER: Artiodactyla, CLASS: Mammalia.

GOAT *Capra aegagrus*, closely related to sheep but distinguished by differently shaped horns which are the same shape in males and females, by the absence of face and foot glands, the presence of a beard, and the possession, in the male, of a gland beneath the tail which gives a pungent and characteristic odour.

True goats are distinguished from other members of the genus *Capra*, the ibex and markhor, by their colour-pattern and horns. Wild goats are brown-grey in winter, yellow

The White-tailed gnu or Black wildebeest no longer exists in the wild, only on farms in the Transvaal and Orange Free State.

A domestic goat, with three sheep, at a well in Umari, Jordan.

or red-fawn in summer, with a black line down the middle of the back, a cross-stripe on the shoulders, and dark brown or black face, chin, beard, throat, tail, front of the legs (except for the knees) and a stripe along the lower part of the flanks. Their horns are scimitar-shaped, with a raised keel along the front edge.

Wild goats, often known as Bezoar goats because they are one source of the 'bezoar stone', a mediaeval panacea, are found in Turkey, the Caucasus, Oman, Iran and Pakistan, extending into Iraq, Lebanon and Turkmenistan. Goats thought to be truly wild also occur on Crete and on the Aegean island of Eremomilos. They stand 26–37 in (68–95 cm) high, with horns about 45 in (1·15 m) long in males but only 12 in (30 cm) in females. Males weigh as much as 40 lb (18 kg), females only 14 lb (6 kg). They live in rocky areas with little water; unlike ibex, they are not necessarily mountain animals, some living close to sea-level. However, on Mt Ararat, wild goats may be found at 13,750 ft (4,200 m). They are agile and active, feeding in the morning and evening but resting by day. The sexes live in separate herds of 10–30, even as many as 90 together. The rut takes place during the latter half of November; the males fight for harems. Young are born from May to June, at least in Iran. One to three kids are dropped.

Goat remains have been found in the Belt Cave, Iran, dating from about 9,000 BC: according to Charles A. Reed, these were domesticated goats. The existence of cork-screw-horned domestic goats in the North-west Frontier region of Pakistan suggests that some goats at least may be descended from the markhor. FAMILY: Bovidae, ORDER: Artiodactyla, CLASS: Mammalia.

GOAT-ANTELOPES, goat-like mountain animals with short horns in both sexes. They include remarkable rock climbers such as the chamois, serow and goral.

GOBIES, small fishes of coastal waters in almost every part of the globe except the polar regions. Although the majority are marine a few species live permanently in freshwater and others are able to pass from one environment to the other. The name *Gobius* was first used by Pliny the Elder nearly 2,000 years ago. Gobies are stocky little fishes with slightly depressed bodies, having two dorsal fins (the first rather flag-like) and pelvic fins which are united partially or fully to form a sucking disc. Although there is a basic similarity between all gobies, so that a goby can be very easily recognized as such, there is considerable diversity in their habits and in the ecological niches they have exploited.

The smallest known vertebrate in the world is a goby *Pandaka pygmaea* from the fresh waters of the Philippines. It grows to just under ½ in (1·2 cm) when fully mature. FAMILY: Gobiidae, ORDER: Perciformes, CLASS: Pisces.

GODWITS *Limosa*, four species of large wading birds with long legs and bills up to at least 4 in (10 cm) in length, that of the Bar-tailed godwit *L. lapponica* being slightly upturned. Some populations of all species undertake long migrations, the Black-tailed godwit *L. limosa* from western Europe, where it breeds, to west Africa, the Bar-tailed godwit from Siberia to western Europe, the Hudsonian godwit *L. haemastica* from north-western Canada to South America and the Marbled godwit *L. fedoa* from North to

Central America. One of each geographical pair of species nests in the tundra region (the Bar-tailed and the Hudsonian godwits), the other in wet meadows in the temperate zone (the Black-tailed and the Marbled godwits). FAMILY: Scolopacidae, ORDER: Charadriiformes, CLASS: Aves.

GOLDCREST *Regulus regulus*, very small warbler-like bird of European woodland, particularly found in conifers, and also occurring very discontinuously eastwards as far as Japan. Two closely-related species known as firecrests are the European firecrest *R. ignicapillus* and the Formosan firecrest *R. goodfellowi*. There are also two Nearctic species, the Golden-crowned kinglet *R. sapatra*, which resembles the firecrests and the Ruby-crowned kinglet *R. calendula*.

The goldcrest, only 3½ in (9 cm) long, often passes unnoticed because of its small size. It is olive green above, pale buff below, with a yellow, black-bordered crown. It hunts very actively for insects in foliage and may often be detected by its shrill high-pitched 'zee-zee-zee-zee' call. The nest is a delicate ball of moss, pine needles and cobwebs, suspended under a branch, often high above the ground at the tip of a conifer bough. Seven to ten eggs are normally laid.

The firecrest is very similar but its crown is more orange and it has a noticeable pale eyebrow stripe above a dark stripe through the eye. FAMILY: Muscicapidae, ORDER: Passeriformes, CLASS: Aves.

The goldcrest, tiny woodland bird with a golden crown, weighs only ⅙ oz (5 gm).

Golden eagle

GOLDEN EAGLE *Aquila chrysaetos*, of mountainous areas in the northern hemisphere, is 30–35 in (76–89 cm) long with a wing-span of about 6 ft (1·8 m) and dark-brown. The sexes are alike, although the females are larger than the males and there is considerable individual plumage variation. The typical adult bird has dark-brown upperparts and similar brown underparts, often with a paler breast giving a general golden-brown appearance. The head is much paler, with the lanceolate feathers of the crown, nape and sides of the neck having bright tawny-buff edges and tips which become abraded to a pale golden-buff. The tail is blackish-brown, banded with dark grey and dark brown and each feather is tipped with black. The wings are brownish-black. The long feathers of the legs are yellowish-brown, with the exposed legs and feet being rich yellow and the claws black. The iris is yellowish-brown or hazel; the bill black, paler at the base and the cere rich yellow.

The immature plumage is generally darker than that of the adult. It is lost by series of moults typically extending over three or four years, although it may take up to six.

The Golden eagle occurs as far north as 70° in Norway, and it breeds in north Sweden, Finland and north Russia to the Urals. It is present in the mountain ranges of central Europe, but absent from the Low Countries. To the south it reaches as far as North Africa, Arabia and the Himalayas. In the New World it extends from Alaska to California.

The breeding season begins in late March, the first sign often being an 'advertisement' flight by the male soaring over the territory. Mutual display flighting follows with the male and female soaring together in spirals, mewing to each other. Tremendous elevations are reached in these flights, which are interrupted by successions of headlong dives with half-closed wings, ending in an upward sweep at the end of the plunge.

The nest can be on a ledge or in a tree. Incubation is by both sexes and lasts for six weeks. The typical clutch is two, the second egg not being laid until three or four days after the first. As incubation starts with the first, it hatches before the other and under conditions of stress, such as food shortage, the older chick kills the younger.

The nestlings at first are covered in thin white or pale grey down, which is gradually replaced by a second, thicker down. They remain in the nest for about ten weeks, but linger in the close vicinity for a further two or three weeks. FAMILY: Accipitridae, ORDER: Falconiformes, CLASS: Aves.

GOLDEN ORFE *Leuciscus idus*, a golden variety of orfe, a cultivated form bred in much the same way as the goldfish. The orfe is a European fish which reaches 2 ft (60 cm) in length. FAMILY: Cyprinidae, ORDER: Cypriniformes, CLASS: Pisces.

GOLDFISH *Carassius auratus*, a carp-like fish native to rivers and streams of China. The wild goldfish is a dull brown. In many carp-like species a form of albinism is known in which all the colour pigments are missing except the reds. These erythritic varieties occur as a result of chance mutations. 2,000 years or more ago the Chinese kept such mutants or sports and found that they bred true. Different varieties were bred to produce forms with telescopic eyes, long or split fins and knobbly heads. The various forms of goldfishes are frequently found in Chinese art. When China was visited by merchants from the West in the 16th and 17th centuries some goldfishes were brought back to Europe and became extremely popular.

The standard colour is now red-gold, but varieties have been bred from pure white through yellow to brown, orange, red and black and individuals with mottlings of these colours are known. The Veiltail has a three-lobed tail, the Blackmoor is velvety black, has a veiled tail and bulbous eyes. In the Celestial, the eyes are telescopic and point upwards while the dorsal fin is missing. The Lionhead goldfishes also lack the dorsal fin and the head is knobbly. FAMILY: Cyprinidae, ORDER: Cypriniformes, CLASS: Pisces.

GOPHER, name applied, in North America, to any burrowing rodent, including Ground squirrels but especially to the Pocket gophers, a group of burrowing rodents confined to the more arid areas.

Pocket gophers range from 4–10 in (10–25 cm) in length and are mostly a rather uniform sandy-brown, although the colour may vary locally in one species according to the colour of the soil. The name 'Pocket gopher' refers to the presence of large cheek pouches, opening by a slit on the outside of each cheek. FAMILY: Geomyidae, ORDER: Rodentia, CLASS: Mammalia.

The Golden eagle, persecuted in sheep-farming areas for alleged lamb-stealing.

The morose expression of a zoo gorilla suffering from boredom and loneliness.

GORILLA *Gorilla gorilla*, the largest of the apes. A male gorilla stands about 68 in (170 cm) high when bipedal, and occasional giants exceed 6 ft (180 cm); the weight of a wild male is about 350–450 lb (160–205 kg).

The gorilla differs from the closely related chimpanzee in its very large size, longer arms, shorter and broader hands and feet, and different colour pattern. The build is much heavier. The much larger teeth (especially the molars) needed to support such a huge bulk must be worked by big jaw muscles, especially the temporal muscles which in male gorillas nearly always meet in the mid-line of the skull, throwing up a tall bony crest, the sagittal crest, between them. A small sagittal crest may occur in female gorillas or in chimpanzees, but a big one, meeting a big shelf of bone (the nuchal crest) at the back of the skull, is characteristic of male gorillas only, and considerably alters the external shape of the head.

The gorilla has small ears, unlike the chimpanzee, and much broader, more expanded nasal wings, which extend down onto the upper lip (a few chimpanzees have them nearly as broad). The gorilla's skin is jet-black almost from birth; the hair is black to brown-grey, and adult males develop a broad silvery white 'saddle' on the back. Hair is short on the saddle, rather long elsewhere. Both sexes turn grey with increasing age.

One population is found in west-central Africa. The second population is found in east central Africa. The Western or Lowland gorilla *G. g. gorilla* is distinguished by its brown-grey general coloration; in males the whitish 'saddle' tends to extend onto the rump and thighs. The Eastern lowland gorilla *G. g. graueri*, found in the eastern Congo lowlands and in the Itombwe mountains, is black, the male's white saddle is restricted to the short hairs of the back, and is well-marked-off from the surrounding black colour; the jaws and teeth are larger, the face longer, and the body and chest are broader and stockier. Finally the Mountain gorilla *G. g. beringei* inhabits the Virunga volcanoes and Mt Kahuzi (west of Lake Kivu), from about 9,000–12,000 ft (2,743·2–3,657·6 m); it is similar to the Eastern lowland race, but with longer hair, especially on the arms; the jaws and teeth are still larger, but the face is shorter and broader; the arms are distinctly shorter. Eastern lowland gorillas are often confused with Mountain gorillas.

Gorillas walk on the flat soles of their feet and on their knuckles (actually the middle phalanges of the fingers) of their hands. This is called 'knuckle-walking'. They spend most of their time on the ground, but young gorillas often climb trees, where they swing about by their arms.

Gorillas live in groups, with one male, which vary in size according to habitat. The home-ranges of gorilla troops overlap, and there seems not to be much aggression

GORAL *Nemorhaedus*, with their relative, the serow, east-Asian representatives of the 'goat-antelopes'. They have coarse hair with much woolly underfur and at least a slight mane on the neck. Goral are 26–28 in (65–70 cm) high and weigh 58–63 lb (25–30 kg). The horns are 9–10 in (22–25 cm) long, slightly curved back and ridged.

The Grey goral *Nemorhaedus goral*, grey or grey-brown with white throat and chest

patches, is found in mountains at 8–12,000 ft (2,460–3,700 m) from Burma, through Tibet to the Sikhote Alin Mts, near Vladivostock. The Brown goral *N. baileyi*, entirely brown, is found in the dry country of southeastern Tibet. The Red goral *N. cranbrooki* is bright foxy-red and occurs in a small area of northern Burma and Assam. FAMILY: Bovidae, ORDER: Artiodactyla, CLASS: Mammalia.

A typical goldfish: it has been a household pet for 2,000 years.

Goshawk

between them. When gorilla troops meet normally they may mingle, or ignore one another. The adult male gorilla rises on his hindlegs, hoots and beats his chest; this acts as a spacing mechanism between troops. The chest-beating used to be construed, by big-game hunters, as signal for attack—which it is not. It is often accompanied by other activities, such as tearing at the vegetation and a sideways run, giving a wild sideways sweep with the arm. Young gorillas beat their chests from about a year.

The gorilla troop wanders over about 10–15 sq miles (17–25·5 sq km). Wherever they happen to be when dusk falls, they make their nests; these are either in the trees or on the ground. They consist of a platform of interwoven branches, or vegetation, with a rim around; ground nests often consist only of a rim, and use is made of natural objects, such as fallen tree-trunks, in their construction. A new set of nests is made every night. Gorillas under the age of about three share their mothers' nests. From the adult male's nest can be seen most or all of the others.

Gorillas eat vast quantities of vegetable matter; they have never been seen to eat meat, insects or eggs in the wild although they will accept them in captivity.

There is no special birth season. Gestation is about 260 days. Newborn infants weigh 4–5 lb (1·8–2·3 kg); they are greyish-pink in colour with hair sparsely covering the back and thick on the head. The skin turns black within a few days. The young gorilla's eyes begin to focus in the first or second week; it crawls at nine weeks, and walks upright at 35–40 weeks. There is usually only one infant, but one case of fraternal and one of identical twins has been recorded. The infants play alone at first, then among themselves; juveniles (above three years of age) try to take infants from their mother to play with. Infants also play with the adult males, which are extremely tolerant of them.

Females are sexually mature at about six years, males at seven to eight; but a male may not be full-sized until he is 14 years old.

Gorillas are not savage and will not attack unprovoked. The troop male will always prefer to lead his troop away from danger. If cornered, however, he will bite and scratch and cause terrible wounds; on occasion a female will too, but if the troop male has been killed the females and young will submit to being clubbed or speared to death without much resistance. FAMILY: Pongidae, ORDER: Primates, CLASS: Mammalia.

GOSHAWK *Accipiter gentilis*, the largest of the true hawks, nearly 2 ft (60 cm) long, dark greyish-brown above with white underparts marked with close dark bars. Goshawks are woodland birds. Their broad wings and long tails are well suited for split-second manoeuvres and they were formerly trained for falconry. They can pounce and kill prey

A young hawk from the Galapagos.

as large as a pheasant or a rabbit. The nest is usually in a tree but very occasionally on the ground. The female alone incubates the 3–4 bluish or white eggs for 36–38 days, during which time she is fed by the male. FAMILY: Accipitridae, ORDER: Falconiformes, CLASS: Aves.

GOURAMIS, tropical freshwater fishes found from India to Malaya, and members of the labyrinthfishes. They have moderately deep and compressed bodies, long dorsal fins and one ray of the pelvic fin is elongated and filamentous. They are popular with aquarists, as much for their colour as for their curious habits. The name gourami should strictly be applied only to *Osphronemus goramy*, a food fish that reaches 2 ft (60 cm) in length and has now been introduced from the East Indies to India, Thailand, the Philippines and China. It has now been applied, however, to a number of similar fishes having in common a filamentous pelvic ray.

The Dwarf gourami *Colisa lalia* 2 in (5 cm), from India, has two rows of blue-green spots on the flanks on a red background. One of the best known, the Kissing gourami *Helostoma temmincki*, from the Malay Peninsula and Thailand, reaches 10 in (25 cm) in length and is a food fish in Malaya. Two individuals may bring their mouths together in what looks like kissing but is more probably an aggressive gesture. A solitary specimen can be induced to kiss a mirror. The Lake gourami *Trichogaster leeri*, known also as the Pearl or Mosaic gourami, is found in Malaya, Thailand and Borneo. The general colour is bluish with a fine lacework of white spots over the body. The bases of the fins are red or yellowish. In Croaking gourami *Trichopsis vitattus* the males make a croaking noise when they come to the surface at night for air, for like other species, there is an accessory air-breathing organ in the gill chamber. FAMILY: Anabantidae, ORDER: Perciformes, CLASS: Pisces.

The Pearl or Mosaic gourami *Trichogaster leeri* of southeast Asia.

Grasshoppers are distinguished from Bush crickets by their herringbone pattern on the hindlegs and by their short antennae.

GRACKLES, medium to medium-large perching birds of the New World, ranging from 8–18 in (20–46 cm) in length, with all black plumage except for the Red-bellied grackle *Hypopyrrhus pyrohypogastor*. Most show a distinct iridescence of purple, green or bronze and have long tails and rather heavy crow-like bills. FAMILY: Icteridae, ORDER: Passeriformes, CLASS: Aves.

GRANT'S GAZELLE *Gazella granti*, one of the larger gazelles 33 in (83 cm) high with very long horns curved back or down to the sides, and forward at the tips. The coat is fawn with a white rump-patch. It is found from southern Somalia to north Tanzania. FAMILY: Bovidae, ORDER: Artiodactyla, CLASS: Mammalia.

GRASSHOPPERS, jumping insects distantly related to the crickets and bush-crickets. The antennae are usually not longer than the body and composed of fewer than 30 segments. Behind the head is a saddle-shaped structure, the pronotum, protecting the front part of the thorax. There are usually two pairs of fully developed wings, but these may be reduced or completely absent. The hindwings are membranous and fold like a fan when at rest beneath the tough fore-wings. The hindlegs are greatly enlarged for jumping, and the attachments of the jumping muscles to the outer wall of the hind femora form a characteristic herring-bone pattern. The females have a short four-valved ovi-positor at the tip of the abdomen.

The eggs are usually laid in the ground in batches of four to several hundred enclosed in a protective pod. The young grasshoppers or 'hoppers' are similar to the adults though lacking wings and reach maturity after moulting four to eight times during a period varying from a few weeks to several months.

Many grasshoppers can produce sounds by rubbing the hind femora against the folded forewings and these are often charac-teristic of each species. The males of some species have a special 'courtship song' which can be very complex and accompanied by rhythmic movements of the body and antennae. It is usually only the males that have a fully developed sound-producing apparatus, but the females of some species produce sounds not unlike those of the males, and both sexes have a hearing organ on each side of the abdomen.

Grasshoppers are active during the day and feed entirely on grasses and other plants. A few are able periodically to multiply into vast migrating swarms: these species are known as locusts. FAMILY: Acrididae, ORDER: Orthoptera, CLASS: Insecta, PHYLUM: Arthropoda.

GRASS SNAKE *Natrix natrix*, a harmless snake, active and slender with a long tapering tail and up to 3 ft (1 m) long although 6 ft (2 m) specimens occur. Females are larger than males. The colour pattern varies con-siderably with the locality, age and individual. There is often a yellow, orange, white or even pink crescent on the neck with dark patches in front and behind this. There are several rows of dark markings down the body on a ground colour which can be green, grey,

Grayling

brown, bluish and even black. Partial albinos are found but they are not as common as black specimens.

This snake ranges from North Africa, Britain and Scandinavia in the west, to the Caspian Sea and Lake Baikal in the USSR.

After mating in April and June, about 8–40 eggs are laid in June and July in manure heaps or decomposing vegetation. The higher temperatures in such sites assist in incubating the eggs. In 6–10 weeks the hatchlings which are 6–7½ in (16–19 cm) long escape from the parchment-like egg-shell by rupturing it in several places with the egg tooth.

The Grass snake is terrestrial but its diet being fish and amphibians it is often associated with water. It relies on speed for catching its prey and for escape. Its defensive behaviour includes hissing, striking and playing dead, as well as emitting the foul-smelling contents of the cloacal gland. FAMILY: Colubridae, ORDER: Squamata, CLASS: Reptilia.

GRAYLING *Thymallus thymallus*, a salmon-like fish of the arctic and temperate regions of the Old World; a related species *T. arcticus* being found in the New World. The scientific name records the slight smell of thyme exuded from the flesh of these fishes. The graylings resemble trout in general form but the dorsal fin is very large. The colour varies, the back being a greenish, bluish or ashy grey (hence its common name) with the flanks silver or brassy-yellow and irregularly scattered with black spots and dark yellow longitudinal

Grayling, a fish highly sensitive to the slightest environmental changes.

streaks. In the breeding season the body has a green-gold shimmer and the dorsal and anal fins and the tail become deep purple. The juveniles shoal but the adults become solitary. The grayling is essentially a river fish and avoids lakes and large ponds. It feeds on insects, worms and snails and grows to about 20 in (50 cm). FAMILY: Salmonidae, ORDER: Salmoniformes, CLASS: Pisces.

GREAT DIVING BEETLES, large water beetles of the genus *Dytiscus*. They are carnivores and both adults and larvae live and hunt in water yet their pupae occur on the moist land surrounding the pond. The larvae are astoundingly voracious and can grow up to 2 in (5 cm) long. They will feed on large freshwater animals such as newts, as well as smaller animals. The larvae breathe air through two posterior channels whilst

hanging suspended from the surface and then crawl down the stems of water plants.

The adults are large, up to 1¼ in (3 cm), are active fliers and so can colonize new habitats such as water-butts and fish ponds. They are also excellent swimmers using their powerful, flattened hindlegs for this purpose. They have to come to the surface to breathe but dive with an air bubble trapped underneath their wing-cases which is gradually used up. FAMILY: Dytiscidae, ORDER: Coleoptera, CLASS: Insecta, PHYLUM: Arthropoda.

GREAT WHITE SHARK *Carcharodon carcharias*, also known as the man-eater or White pointer, the largest of all carnivorous fishes and probably the most dangerous of all man-eating sharks. It is found in all warm seas and grows to over 20 ft (6 m) in length; the largest specimen on record was one from Port Fairey (Australia) that was 36½ ft (11 m) in length and although the weight was not recorded specimens half that length can weigh over 7,000 lb (3,000 kg). The jaws are enormous and are lined with triangular teeth, the edges of which are serrated.

These sharks are chiefly found in open waters and are usually caught near the surface although there is a record of a specimen caught off Cuba at a depth of 4,200 ft (1,260 m). FAMILY: Isuridae, ORDER: Pleurotremata, CLASS: Chondrichthyes.

GREBES, highly specialized aquatic birds grey, blackish or brown above and paler below. The feathering is dense and water-proof, particularly on the satiny underparts. The nuptial plumage is usually quite distinct from the eclipse plumage, both sexes developing special plumes, colours or markings, particularly on the head, which are primarily associated with the courtship ceremonies.

The Great crested grebe *Podiceps cristatus*, in addition to the elongated, double crest on its crown, grows a long, beautiful, chestnut and black 'tippet' on each side of the head framing its white face; the foreneck and underparts remain white but the flanks become chestnut. The Slavonian or Horned grebe *P. auritus* has a black head and tippets with a small central crest on the crown and a golden-chestnut, wedge-shaped 'horn' projecting from above and behind each eye and meeting on the nape. The neck, upper breast and flanks are chestnut and the belly white. The Black-necked or Eared grebe *P. nigricollis* has a black head, neck and upper breast, with highly erectile, 'peaked' crown feathers and a long 'fan' of golden plumes extending from behind the eye; its flanks are chestnut and belly white.

Grebes are 9–30 in (23–76 cm) in length. Among the largest are the Western, Great and Great crested grebes; among the smallest, the dabchicks and the Least grebe. Grebes are highly adapted for diving from the surface and for underwater swimming. Their legs are

The Great diving beetle is particularly voracious and destructive.

A Great crested grebe on its nest with one of its chicks. The parent grebe habitually transports its chicks in this way.

strong and situated at the rear of a rotund or somewhat elongated body. The large feet are partly webbed with well-developed, paddle-like lobes on each of the three main toes. These are used to propel the bird at speed underwater with a powerful, figure-of-eight movement.

Grebes' nests are usually built in the water, either tethered to aquatic vegetation or anchored to the bottom. They are simple structures of piled-up weeds, reeds and the like. The eggs are pale and unmarked but become stained brownish during incubation. This lasts from three to just over four weeks, according to species. Both sexes take turns in incubating the eggs, which are covered by material when the sitting bird is disturbed from the nest, this habit serving both to conceal the clutch and reduce chilling. FAMILY: Podicipedidae, ORDER: Podicipediformes, CLASS: Aves.

GREENFINCH *Carduelis chloris*, is nearly 15 cm long, the male being olive-green with yellow on the wings and tail, and the female duller and brownish-green. This species is found over most of Europe feeding on the seeds of weeds and spilled grain. The nest, built in thick bushes in parks, large gardens and cultivated land, is made of moss, twigs and wool and lined with soft material. The four to six whitish eggs have reddish-brown or violet markings. FAMILY: Fringillidae, ORDER: Passeriformes, CLASS: Aves.

GREEN TURTLE *Chelonia mydas*, a Marine turtle occurring in all tropical and sub-tropical seas, with a carapace which may reach

a length of 55 in (1·4 m). It has four pairs of costals and a single pair of prefrontal shields on the snout. It is this species that is used for preparing turtle soup. The Green turtle is mainly vegetarian, with a preference for sea grass, but the hatchlings are carnivorous. The most important nesting beaches are on the islands of the Great Barrier Reef, small islands off Sarawak, in the Seychelles, on Ascension Island and on the coast of Costa Rica. The populations have declined due to the unlimited harvesting of eggs and to a lesser extent to the killing of the adults. FAMILY: Dermochelidae, ORDER: Testudines, CLASS: Reptilia.

GREY FOX *Urocyon cinereoargenteus*, one of several related species in the Americas. This species, of eastern and Pacific U.S.A., is 44 in (110 cm) long of which 14 in (35 cm) is tail and weighs 6–15 lb (2·7–7 kg). It has a grey back, rufous sides and a white belly. Preferring woody or bush country, Grey foxes are unusual in that they frequently climb trees, both for food and shelter. Rest sites may be in tree trunks or caves, but the Grey fox is not choosy about the location of its den. Most burrows, however, are near a water source and under dense cover.

The breeding season falls in February and March. There are 1–5 cubs after a gestation of about 50 days. FAMILY: Canidae, ORDER: Carnivora, CLASS: Mammalia.

GREY MULLETS, shoaling fishes with long, sturdy bodies, almost cylindrical in cross section. The weakly spinous first dorsal fin is followed by a soft-rayed second dorsal fin.

The mouth is soft and weak and directed downwards since these fishes feed on algae growing on sand, mud or rocks. The Grey mullet has a very long intestine and muscular stomach divided into two parts.

Grey mullets are almost world-wide in their distribution in coastal and estuarine waters. One of the commonest of the European species *Mugil cephalus*, extends as far south as South Africa. FAMILY: Mugilidae, ORDER: Perciformes, CLASS: Pisces.

GREY WHALE *Eschrichtius gibbosus*, a whalebone whale which grows to some 45 ft (14 m), the females being slightly larger than the males. It has about 150 thick yellowish plates of baleen on each side, the largest of which are only 15 in (38 cm) long. There are two or three short grooves in the throat. The body is grey but there is marked variation in shade and most show lighter markings. It carries heavy skin infestations of barnacles as well as Whale lice.

The Grey whale is a shallow-water, inshore species and as such has been easy prey to inshore fishermen. It is now found only in the North Pacific, though from fossil records it once lived in the North Atlantic. In the Pacific there are two groups, the Korean, which spends the summer in the Okhotsk Sea and then moves south and the Californian which spends the summer off Alaska as far north as Point Barrow and then moves south inshore into Californian and Mexican waters to breed. The two populations appear not to mix. The migrations follow a remarkably accurate timetable each year and the arrival of the whales in Californian

Gribble

waters has become an important tourist attraction. They are protected and numbers are increasing. FAMILY: Eschrichtidae, ORDER: Cetacea, CLASS: Mammalia.

GRIBBLE *Limnoria lignorum*, a marine wood-boring crustacean which causes extensive damage to piers and breakwaters resulting in the complete disintegration of the wooden piles. No completely successful way of impregnating wood against gribble has yet been found. FAMILY: Limnoridae, ORDER: Isopoda, CLASS: Crustacea, PHYLUM: Arthropoda.

GROUND BEETLES, fast running predatory beetles. The smaller members feed on mites and springtails, the larger on prey such as moth caterpillars. They will also attack other beetles. A few species also eat plant material and *Pseudophonus rufipes* has been recorded as a pest on strawberry beds.

The majority of Ground beetles are dull in colour, but some have brilliant metallic colours. *Calosoma sycophanta* is among the most splendid, with green and gold wing cases and a purple head.

Violet ground beetle *Carabus violaceus*.

The Bombardier beetles *Brachinus* produce minute explosions in their anal regions. This remarkable effect is produced by the discharge of a fluid which immediately vapourizes with a distinct cracking sound. If these beetles are handled the discharged fluid can burn and stain the skin, producing marks which last for several days.

The larvae of Ground beetles have long well armoured bodies and powerful jaws; like their parents they are active predators. FAMILY: Carabidae, ORDER: Coleoptera, CLASS: Insecta, PHYLUM: Arthropoda.

GROUND SQUIRRELS. These include chipmunks, Prairie dogs, marmots and woodchucks, in addition to many less well known species variously known as Ground squirrels, sousliks or gophers, found in open country throughout much of North America, Eurasia and Africa.

Ground squirrels do not differ much from Tree squirrels but they tend to have shorter ears, shorter legs and shorter, less bushy tails. They tend to be light in colour and many species have a longitudinal white line on

Ground squirrels rest in burrows.

the flank, serving to disrupt the outline of the animal when it freezes motionless on the approach of danger. Most make extensive burrows, and they are accordingly equipped with powerful feet and strong claws in contrast to the more delicate and flexible digits of the Tree squirrels.

Ground squirrels feed on vegetable matter, especially seeds, and most species have internal cheek-pouches to carry seeds for storage in the burrows. FAMILY: Sciuridae, ORDER: Rodentia, CLASS: Mammalia.

GROUPERS, large perch-like fishes of temperate and tropical seas with slightly compressed bodies and enormous mouths. Many have remarkable colour-patterns, of regular spots or mottlings but usually involving sombre colours. Colour variations between adults and juveniles, or between adults of the same species from different regions, are sometimes so great that identification is difficult. Some species, such as the Nassau grouper *Epinephelus striatus*, can change colour with chameleon-like rapidity. The Estuary rock cod *E. tauvina* is found through-

out the Indo-Pacific region. So variable is its coloration that what were described as 24 distinct species are now all recognized as one. Like most groupers, it lives amongst coral reefs, but it also enters estuaries. It reaches a length of 7 ft (2·1 m) and a weight of 500 lb (220 kg). It has a reputation for being dangerous. An Australian grouper *E. lanceolatus* attains 10 ft (3·5 m) and has been known to stalk divers. Pearl fishermen in the Torres Straits are occasionally killed by these fishes. FAMILY: Serranidae, ORDER: Perciformes, CLASS: Pisces.

GROUSE, game-birds usually brown, grey or black in plumage, often patterned and so camouflaged. In some the male is conspicuous with black plumage glossed with iridescent blues and greens, and three species moult into a white winter plumage. They are ground birds with short and strong bill and legs, short neck and wings, strong feet and usually a large tail. The legs are completely feathered and most grouse develop 'snowshoes' in winter by the growth of closely-packed feathers or extensions of the horny covering of the toes. Feathers also cover the nostrils. Grouse vary in length from 12–35 in (30·5–89 cm).

They feed largely on shoots, buds and fruits. They also take grain and some invertebrates, largely insects, particularly when they are young. They usually nest on the ground and the clutch is large, up to 16 eggs in some species; white, brown or buff, unmarked or speckled or blotched with brown or black. The young move from the nest shortly after hatching. As the young have food reserves, in un-absorbed yolk, for only 2–3 days, a spell of bad weather after hatching may result in death, for at this early age they must be kept warm under the female during adverse conditions.

The breeding displays of grouse are among the most spectacular in birds. In several species the males perform social displays collecting together at established display grounds, or leks, which are used from day to day or from season to season. Here they adopt ritualized postures and give special calls, often charging their rivals in mock attacks.

The circumpolar genus *Lagopus* includes the Rock ptarmigan *L. mutus* and the Willow grouse *L. lagopus*. The Red grouse of Britain is sometimes regarded as a subspecies of the Willow grouse, or it may be given specific rank as *L. scoticus*. Both Rock ptarmigan and the typical Willow grouse turn white in winter, but the Red grouse lives in more temperate areas and retains its brown colour throughout the year. The Rock ptarmigan is the smaller and is confined to the tundra. In Britain it does not nest below 2,500 ft (765 m). The Red grouse is replaced ecologically in western North America by the White-tailed ptarmigan *L. leucurus*.

Groupers derive their name from a Portuguese word of doubtful origin.

The Black grouse *Lyrurus tetrix* and *L. mlokosiewiczi* of Eurasian heaths, moors, bogs, and forest edges are two of the lek species. FAMILY: Tetraonidae, ORDER: Galliformes, CLASS: Aves.

GRYSBOK *Raphicerus melanotis*, a medium-sized antelope related to the steinbok. There is a second species, Sharpe's grysbok *R. sharpei*. Both are up to 22 in (55 cm) at the shoulder, with large eyes and ears, the males with straight erect horns, 5 in (12·5 cm) long. The coat is reddish stippled with white. The grysbok ranges from South Africa to the Zambezi, Sharpe's grysbok from Tanzania to the Transvaal. They are mainly reported from reserves. FAMILY: Bovidae, ORDER: Artiodactyla, CLASS: Mammalia.

GUAN, 13 species of birds of the genus *Penelope* which range from Mexico through Central America to northern Argentina.

They are about the size of a turkey and similar in colour, brownish to dark olive-green. They have short crest feathers and the chin and the throat are naked. The habits of guans are similar to those of other curassows.

In the Marail guan *P. marail*, which occurs from southern Venezuela and the Guianas to the north bank of the Amazon, the upperparts are dark glossy olive-green with whitish spots on the hind neck and mantle. Its lower throat and breast feathers are edged with white giving a speckled appearance. The wings and tail are uniform brown and the legs are red. It is the most numerous of the curassows in the forests of the Guianas. FAMILY: Cracidae, ORDER: Galliformes, CLASS: Aves.

GUANACO *Lama guanicoe*, a wild form of the llama, slightly smaller and more delicately built, with a reddish-brown coat, blackish-grey muzzle and ears, and belly and insides of the legs white. It stands about 3½ ft (1·1 m) at the shoulder. It is the only one of the four types of llama which thrives at high altitudes and also on the plains. It ranges from southern Peru to Tierra del Fuego.

Guanacos usually live in family groups forming herds of up to 20 led by a stallion. These cuadrillas sometimes join up into larger herds, but do not mix. The stallion gives warning of danger by penetrating 'neighing' and guards the rear when the herd is in flight, in close formation. FAMILY: Camelidae, ORDER: Tylopoda, CLASS: Mammalia.

GUENONS, 20 species of common monkeys found over most of Africa, south of the Sahara, especially in tropical rain forests. They all have long hind-limbs, long tails, small faces, round skulls and small teeth. Their fur is finely grizzled with alternating light and dark bands. Some species are strikingly coloured and most have white and coloured brow-bands, ruffs, whiskers, beards and nose-patches. They have keen sight and

Hamlyn's guenon *Cercopithecus hamlyni*.

hearing and are able to travel through the forest canopy faster than man moves on the ground. They are adept at hiding in the foliage and rest on a horizontal bough with their four legs and tail dangling.

The Vervet, Green or Grivet monkey *Cercopithecus aethiops*, is a large monkey with grizzled greyish-green fur with a black face surrounded by a white brow-band and cheek-whiskers. It lives in savannah and woodland savannah of West, East and South Africa.

The Mona monkey *C. mona*, is a small monkey with reddish fur on the back with a yellow crown and a black stripe from eye to ear. It has pure white undersides and a white thigh-stripe. It lives in all types of forest but prefers secondary growth and mangroves, usually at low levels from Ghana to Cameroun.

The Diana monkey *C. diana*, is small, with deep purple fur with a red 'saddle' on the hindparts and a long white beard curving backwards, from West Africa.

The Blue, Sykes or Pluto monkey *C. mitis*, is a large sedate monkey with blue-black fur and commonly with a white brow-band and black undersides, hands and feet. The East African races have a white throat. It lives in mature forest in East and Central Africa, where it is most at home in the upper layers of the trees.

The Moustached monkey *C. cephus*, has grey-red fur with a white 'moustache' and light undersides and a black stripe from eye to ear. One race has red ear-tufts, another has a red tail. It is found from Nigeria to Gabon.

The talapoin *Miopithecus talapoin*, is much the smallest of the guenons, rarely above 12 in (30 cm) long in head and body. It is light-green with fan-shaped cheek-whiskers and lives in swamp forests, mangroves and thick secondary growth, from Cameroun to the Congo River.

The Patas or Hussar monkey *Erythrocebus patas* is tall and rangy, built like a greyhound with long legs and long tail. The male weighs as much as 30 lb (13½ kg) and has a bright red coat with white undersides and a blue scrotum. The female is only half the male's size and more drably coloured. It lives in open country in long grass regions of West Africa, as far east as the Rift Valley in Kenya. FAMILY: Cercopithecidae, ORDER: Primates, CLASS: Mammalia.

GUILLEMOTS, two closely related fish-eating seabirds. The Common guillemot or Common murre *Uria aalge* and Brünnich's guillemot or Thick-billed murre *U. lomvia* are very similar in appearance, both being about 16 in (40 cm) long and weighing about 2 lb (900 gm). They are black above with black heads, and white beneath, with black bills and black and yellow feet. In the Common guillemot the bill is long and

Guineafowl

pointed, in Brünnich's guillemot it is shorter, thicker and has a white line extending along the basal half of the upper mandible. Both guillemots are well adapted to swimming underwater. The body is highly streamlined, the large webbed feet are placed far back and the wings are short and narrow forming efficient paddles. Guillemots in fact 'fly' underwater, beating half open wings and using the webbed feet for steering and as auxiliary propellors. As a result of these adaptations guillemots are rather clumsy on land and have to stand upright.

Guillemots are restricted to the northern hemisphere and are circumpolar in distribution. Only the Common guillemot nests on European coasts. They are highly social and breed, sometimes in enormous numbers, in colonies, also known as loomeries or bazaars. The nests are usually on ledges of steep cliffs, sometimes hundreds of feet above the water.

They make little or no nest, the one egg being placed on the bare rock, sometimes with a few stones which the bird has accumulated, but the irregularities of the rock surface are usually enough to prevent the egg from rolling away. The egg is pear-shaped, but this does not seem to be an adaptation to prevent the egg rolling away as has often been thought. In fact, many guillemot eggs are lost through being knocked off by the adults. FAMILY: Alcidae, ORDER: Charadriiformes, CLASS: Aves.

GUINEAFOWL, African game birds, about the size of domestic fowl and characterized by mainly featherless or ornamented heads and usually spotted plumage. The plumage is thick and smooth, the rounded wings and a tail partly concealed by long coverts are not conspicuous. The body is rounded and topped by a bare head which, from lack of feathers, seems disproportionally small.

The plumage pattern frequently consists of slanting rows of small black-edged white spots on a grey ground, in some plumages tinted blue. On the Vulturine guineafowl *Acryllium vulturinum* the rows of spots coalesce to form streaks and the neck feathers are white-striped. This species also has vivid blue and violet on parts of the plumage. The patterned plumage is lost in the West African forest species, the Black guineafowl *Agelestes niger* having black feathers, the White-breasted guineafowl *A. meleagrides* being white on the breast and mantle and otherwise black.

The head ornamentation is diverse. *Agelestes* species have bare red heads. The Vulturine guineafowl has a grey-blue head and neck, ornamented with a narrow strip of fluffy brown feathering round the back of the cranium like a monk's tonsure, and a crimson iris. The Crested guineafowl *Guttera edouardi* is like a parody of a fashion plate with a bare grey head arising from a collar of black feathers and topped with a cluster of curly black feathers on the crown, while a related species has a head-tuft of straight feathers. FAMILY: Numididae, ORDER: Galliformes, CLASS: Aves.

GUINEA PIG *Cavia porcellus*, one of the most familiar of all rodents. The plump body, absence of tail and extremely short legs are distinctive. Guinea pigs were domesticated by the Incas in Peru before the European conquest, but the reason at that time was purely culinary. Like many other South American rodents, they are quite palatable. The Guinea pig lends itself well to captivity: it needs little space, can tolerate the company of its fellows better than most other rodents and breeds quickly, although in the last respect it falls far short of the capability of rats and mice. The gestation period is long, about nine weeks and the litter size is small, rarely over three. However, this is balanced

to some extent by the female's ability to mate and conceive again immediately after the birth of a litter, and by the advanced stage of development at birth. New-born Guinea pigs can run within a few hours and the females are capable of breeding at an age of little over a month.

Guinea pigs feed on most vegetable food, and can be kept on a mixture of roots and greens. They will crop grass industriously if kept on a lawn, and when kept caged it is necessary to provide them with hay, whatever else they are given to eat. FAMILY: Caviidae, ORDER: Rodentia, CLASS: Mammalia.

GULLS, medium to large birds with moderately long wings and tail, the adult plumage white with darker wings and back. The outermost wing feathers are black or have black tips (black feathers are stronger than white and these outer feathers become very worn). All gulls can fly and swim strongly.

The distribution of the Herring and Lesser black-backed gulls, the *L. argentatus-fuscus* group, provides a classical example of geographic speciation and of a ring species. Between them the subspecies of the two species encircle the globe in Europe, north Asia and northern North America. In Britain the ends of the chain overlap and there are two species which are very different in plumage and habits and which breed side-by-side without interbreeding. Therefore they can be considered separate species. Even though there are several well marked geographical forms of both species in other areas, it is difficult to draw a line separating the two species because there is a perfect series of forms linking the two extremes. Although climatic changes have altered the distribution of some forms, it is possible to piece together the likely development of this ring species. In geologically very recent times there was probably a single species of this type of gull in eastern Siberia or the Bering Sea. This spread eastwards and westwards, and as birds colonized new areas, they altered slightly. Gradually these new populations stabilized as separate races and in due course the two ends of the chain developed into what we now know as the Herring gull (with a pale grey back, flesh-coloured legs, yellow eye-ring) on the Atlantic seaboard of Canada and the Lesser black-backed gull (yellow legs, dark grey back, red eye-ring) in western Europe and Britain. By the time the Herring gull colonized Europe the two forms had become so distinct that they co-existed as separate species without interbreeding.

The nest is normally an untidy mass of vegetation, usually on the ground, less commonly on a cliff or tussock of vegetation, and rarely in a tree or on a building. The normal clutch of three eggs is incubated for about 28 days. On hatching the downy young are quite mobile, but must be protected and fed by the parents. Fledging

The Helmeted guineafowl *Numida mitrata*, widely distributed over Africa.

A guenon mother with half-grown young.

Black-headed gull at nest on a marsh.

Kittiwake at nest on a cliff ledge.

Lesser black-backed gull *Larus fuscus*.

normally takes six to eight weeks.

Behaviour of animals can be modified by natural selection so that the best adapted individuals will leave the most offspring. Chicks of many species of gulls are fed near the nest by the parents regurgitating food onto the ground. As the young may be hiding some distance away, both the adults and young have special feeding calls so that they can contact each other. The kittiwake *Rissa tridactyla* nests on very small ledges on precipitous cliffs and the young take food from the back of the parent's throat since if food was regurgitated both it and the young, would be in danger of falling from the nest. As the chicks cannot move from the nest, no

feeding calls have been developed, and unlike most gulls, adults do not learn to recognize their own chicks. FAMILY: Laridae, ORDER: Charadriiformes, CLASS: Aves.

GUNDIS, a group of about six species of rodents forming the family Ctenodactylidae which is not very closely related to any other family of rodents. They are confined to rocky hills around the Sahara Desert and look rather like Guinea pigs with remarkably soft, sandy coloured hair. They feed by daylight, although mainly at dawn and dusk, on a variety of vegetation. A peculiarity of structure from which the technical name is derived is a comb of stiff bristles on each hindfoot

with which they groom their fur. FAMILY: Ctenodactylidae, ORDER: Rodentia, CLASS: Mammalia.

GUPPY *Lebistes reticulatus*, or millionsfish, a small live-bearing tooth-carp from the fresh waters of the southern West Indies and parts of northwest South America. Its common name records its discoverer, the Rev Robert Guppy, who found this little fish on Trinidad in 1866. Guppies grow to about $2\frac{1}{2}$ in (6 cm). The female is a dull olive, but the males, which are smaller and slimmer, are brightly coloured with all kinds of variable spots and patterns (in orange, blues, green-blues, white, etc). In the male, as in all the live-bearing tooth-carps, the anal fin is modified into a copulatory organ or gonopodium, with hooks and spines, for the transfer of sperm to the female. Guppies are surface-feeders and this has led to their introduction into tropical countries to control mosquito larvae. It is possible, however, that they also eat the eggs and small larvae of other fishes. This has certainly been found to be the case in the related species *Gambusia affinis* (often called guppy but better known as the mosquitofish). FAMILY: Poeciliidae, ORDER: Atheriniformes, CLASS: Pisces.

GYR FALCON *Falco rusticolus*, larger than the peregrine, 20–22 in (50–55 cm) long, frequenting open country in the vicinity of cliffs and forested regions. The typical race of northern Europe has the upper parts blotched and barred with dark and light grey and the underparts whitish with blackish streaks. The flanks are barred. Its habits are similar to those of the peregrine. It nests on ledges of cliffs, the nest being a few sticks lined with moss, down or grass. Usually four yellowish or light brown eggs spotted with reddish-brown are laid. The typical race is replaced by other forms in Siberia, Iceland, Greenland and North America. FAMILY: Falconidae, ORDER: Falconiformes, CLASS: Aves.

One of the many colourful varieties of the millionsfish, better known as the guppy.

HADDOCK *Melanogrammus aeglefinus*, a cod-like fish of the North Atlantic and economically one of the most important of all the species caught by the countries fishing the North Sea. It resembles the cod in having three dorsal fins and two anal fins but can be easily distinguished by the presence of a black blotch above the pectoral fins, the lack of other spots on the flanks and the black lateral line. There is a small barbel under the chin. The haddock grows to about 24 lb (11 kg) in weight but is generally much smaller.

It spawns early in the year, the female producing half a million small pelagic eggs. After hatching, the young live in the upper waters for the first year or so and then migrate towards the bottom in shallow waters, finally making for deeper waters. They are shoaling fishes that prefer sandy bottoms where they feed on shellfish, Sea urchins and small fishes. They are often marketed smoked.

The black spot on the side of the haddock is said to represent the thumb-mark of St Peter left when he held the fish and found the tribute money. FAMILY: Gadidae, ORDER: Gadiformes, CLASS: Pisces.

HAGFISHES, marine putty-coloured, eel-shaped fishes, up to 30 in (76 cm) in length, one of the two surviving groups of jawless fishes. There are 25 species all found in colder seas at depths of 60–2,000 ft (20–650 m). Hagfishes have a small and fleshy fin around the tail and barbels round the mouth. The eyes are in some species merely small pigmented cups capable only of distinguishing between light and dark. They find their food by smell.

Hagfishes feed on dead and dying fishes into which they burrow with the aid of their rasping tongue covered with horny teeth. They usually live burrowed in muddy areas and are very sluggish. One striking characteristic of the hagfishes is their ability to produce copious secretions of slime. The skeleton is composed of cartilage and the fish is able to tie itself into a knot and then to flow through the knot to clean off the slime. FAMILY: Myxinidae, ORDER: Cyclostomata, CLASS: Agnatha.

HAIRWORMS, very slender worms, about $\frac{1}{32}$ in (1 mm) in diameter, and varying in length from 1 ft (30 cm) to 3 ft (90 cm). They range from light brown to almost black and look like a length of horse-hair, hence hairworm and Horsehair worm; also Gordian worms because they tangle themselves in knots when kept together in a dish.

These worms are free-living, as adults, and occur in freshwater ponds, ditches, streams, lakes and the sea. They are often found in drinking troughs for horses and this gave rise to the belief that they were horsehair come to life. The sexes are separate and the males are shorter than the females, except in *Nectonema* where the males are larger. CLASS: Nematomorpha, PHYLUM: Aschelminthes.

HAKE *Merluccius merluccius*, an elongated deep-water fish of the cod family found in the eastern North Atlantic. It differs from the other cod-like fishes in that the second dorsal fin and the anal fins are single and not split into two. The back is greyish, the belly white and the lateral line scales are black. The hake is found at depths down to 2,400 ft (700 m) and occurs in the Mediterranean and northwards to Trondheim and Iceland. Hake feed chiefly on other fishes. Large commercially caught fishes can weigh as much as 40 lb (18 kg). FAMILY: Merlucciidae, ORDER: Gadiformes, CLASS: Pisces.

HALF-BEAKS, small fishes rarely attaining more than 12 in (30 cm), found in marine and fresh waters in most of the tropical and temperate regions of the world. They derive their common name from their jaws. The lower jaw is elongated and beak-like, but the upper jaw is much shorter; teeth only occur in the lower jaw where it is in contact with the upper.

Half-beaks are surface-living, the elongated lower jaw being used to catch food at the surface.

Half-beaks are clearly closely related to flyingfishes and they not only skitter along the surface but sometimes leap into the air. FAMILY: Exocoetidae, ORDER: Atheriniformes, CLASS: Pisces.

HAMMERHEAD SHARK, most easily recognized of all sharks, it was known to early writers as the balancefish because of the resemblance of the head to balance scales. Hammerheads are found in all warm seas throughout the world and show a tendency to move into temperate waters during the summer. In the Common hammerhead *Sphyrna zygaena* the flattened head is almost rectangular. It is virtually world-wide in its distribution, occasionally wandering as far north as Great Britain. It reaches 13 ft (3·9 m) in length and feeds on fishes, but like many other sharks is a scavenger and has also been known to attack men. The Great hammerhead, *S. mokarran*, also having a world-wide distribution, is the largest of the nine species, reaching 15 ft (4·5 m). In the Bonnet shark or shovelhead, *S. tiburo*, the head is rounded in front giving the appearance of a shovel. This is common in the western Atlantic and grows to about 6 ft (1·8 m). The function of the flattened head is uncertain, and suggestions that it may act as a hydroplane are unconvincing. FAMILY: Sphyrnidae, ORDER: Pleurotremata, CLASS: Chondrichthyes.

HAMMERKOP *Scopus umbretta*, a duck-sized brown bird, resembling an ibis in general appearance, but distinguished by the shorter straight bill and the crest which sticks out backwards and downwards 'balancing' the bill and producing the effect that earned it its common name. Cowles more accurately said it looked like a 'much blunted almost worn out pickaxe'. In flight the head is partly retracted over the body like a heron's, but the legs do not project beyond the tail. The broad rounded wings and shallow wingbeats make the bird appear rather owl-like, especially at dusk. It is the only large bird to build a roofed nest. FAMILY: Scopidae, ORDER: Ciconiiformes, CLASS: Aves.

HAMMOCK-WEB SPIDERS, spiders of several families that spin sheet webs. The Linyphiidae spiders run upside down below the platform. Scaffolding threads above this platform cause flying insects to fall on the platform where they are bitten from beneath

Hamsters

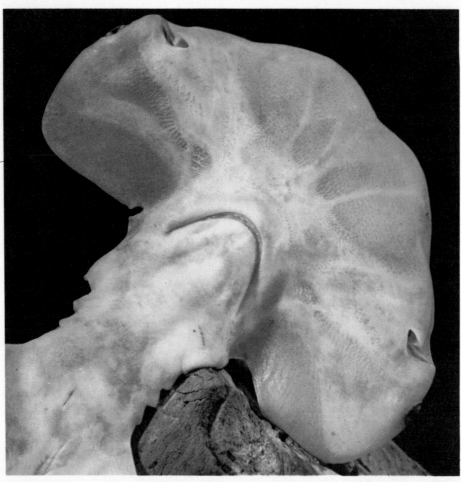

The Bonnet shark in common with the other hammerheads has its eyes singularly placed.

It is a striking fact that the millions of Golden hamsters kept as pets should have resulted from the chance finding of a female and twelve young deep in the sand.

through the fabric. The platform is not always hammock-shaped. Sometimes it is dome-shaped, as in the American and European *Linyphia marginata*, and sometimes flat as in *Floronia bucculenta*. The Linyphiidae are the dominant family in temperate and arctic regions. They include the Money spiders which cause gossamer and all are small. The hammocks are so fine that few are noticed in shrubs or on the ground until dew or frost displays their fragile beauty. ORDER: Araneae, CLASS: Arachnida, PHYLUM: Arthropoda.

HAMSTERS, short-tailed rodents, the most familiar, the Golden hamster *Mesocricetus auratus*, makes an attractive, easily cared-for pet whose only drawback is that it is most active at night. It is only one of about 14 species. The largest of these is the Common or Black-bellied hamster *Cricetus cricetus*, unusual in having black fur on its underparts with lighter, brown fur above, and white patches on its sides. About the size of a Guinea pig it is found in Europe and Asia over a wide area between Belgium and Lake Baikal. The range of the Golden hamster is from Rumania and Bulgaria through the Caucasus and Asia Minor to Iran. Its coat is a light reddish brown above and white underneath. The skin of the body is loose, giving the hamster an extraordinary waddling look.

Hamsters are mainly vegetarian, their diet consisting chiefly of cereals; in addition they will eat fruits and roots, green leaves and other plant material. The Common hamster eats frogs and insect larvae as well. The large cheek pouches are used for carrying food back to the nest. When filled the pouches give the hamster a grotesque appearance.

The habitat of hamsters is dry steppe, among sand dunes or on the edges of deserts. The Common hamster, however, often lives in cultivated country, among crops or in ploughed fields. It can also be found along river banks and will even swim, blowing out its cheek pouches to give extra buoyancy. Pet Golden hamsters, on the other hand, may die if exposed to damp.

Common and Golden hamsters are nocturnal, and although they hibernate, their sleep is not continuous for they must wake up from time to time to eat. During hibernation, the Golden hamster breathes only twice a minute and its pulse rate drops from 400 to four beats a minute.

In captivity, Golden hamsters have to be separated once mating has taken place for the female is likely to kill the male. Gestation is 17 days, while that of the Common hamster is 19–20 days. The young are born naked and helpless, 6–12, occasionally 20, to a litter.

In 1930 a female and 12 young were dug up near Aleppo in Syria. They were taken to the Hebrew University in Jerusalem and became the ancestors of all present-day, captive Golden hamsters. FAMILY: Cricetidae, ORDER: Rodentia, CLASS: Mammalia.

HARES, include true hares and seven species of Jack rabbits, all belonging to the genus *Lepus*. True hares are medium-sized animals, adapted for swift running, characterized by their long ears, short tails, long hindlegs and feet, and slender bodies. Young hares, or leverets, are born fully-furred, with eyes open and capable of independent movement. No elaborate nest is prepared for them. The gestation period lasts 40–50 days. Hares are herbivorous, inhabiting mainly grasslands, although some species occur in timbered habitats.

The Arctic hare *Lepus arcticus* weighing up to 12 lb (5½ kg), is the largest. It is found north of the tree-line in Canada, Alaska, and Greenland. In the northern part of its range its fur is white all the year round with only the tips of the ears black. In the southern parts of its range the hair on the upper parts of the body is grey in summer. It has a characteristic habit of walking on the hindfeet.

The European hare *L. capensis*—formerly known as *L. europaeus*—weighs up to 9 lb (4 kg). It lives in open grassland and its natural range is Eurasia and Africa but it has been introduced to South America, Australia, New Zealand and parts of North America. It is solitary except in the breeding season when small groups form. Three to four litters are born between spring and autumn. Superfoetation, that is, the conception of a second litter before the first is born, may occur, the pregnant females allowing copulation 3–4 days before birth, this resulting in a normal pregnancy. Homing to the point of original capture from distances up to 290 miles (460 km) has been reported.

A Jack rabbit, one of the several hares of North America.

A young Hen harrier in aggressive display shows the contrasting small size of its beak with the width of the gape.

A pair of harlequinfish in the process of spawning on the underside of a leaf.

The Mountain hare *Lepus timidus* is stockier than the European hare, has much shorter ears and much white on the top of the tail. It weighs up to 10 lb (4½ kg). In summer and autumn the fur is dusky brown, sometimes with a bluish appearance, hence the alternative common name Blue hare. There are three annual moults, the animals changing to full white in the winter with only the tips of the ears black. The occurrence of a white pelage is controlled by temperature and intensity of light. The Mountain hare extends over the whole northern part of Eurasia and is also found in the European Alps. Its chief habitat is wooded areas, and it feeds mainly on grass and bark and twigs. FAMILY: Leporidae, ORDER: Lagomorpha, CLASS: Mammalia.

HARLEQUINFISH *Rasbora heteromorpha*, a small carp-like fish from the Malay Peninsula and Thailand, 1¾ in (4·5 cm) long with a deep body. The flanks are pinky-silver with violet tints and there is a distinctive dark triangle on the posterior half of the body. It is a shoaling fish popular with aquarists and easy to keep. FAMILY: Cyprinidae, ORDER: Cypriniformes, CLASS: Pisces.

HARRIERS, medium-sized diurnal predatory birds, with long narrow wings, a long rounded tail and an owl-like face. They occupy a wide variety of open habitats over which they hunt at low level, with a leisurely flapping and gliding flight, in search of small ground prey. There are ten species. Harriers have a slender appearance and weigh about 12 oz (350 gm). The head is relatively small, the owl-like face resulting from a facial ruff of feathers. The bill is small, compressed and sharply curved and the nostrils are large and covered with bristles. The feet are yellow and long, the toes are also long and carry sharply curved claws. The average body length is 18½ in (47 cm). The largest are the Hen harrier *Circus cyaneus* and the Spotted harrier *C. assimilis* which reach 22 in (56 cm); the smallest is the Pied harrier *C. melanoleucus* of only 15 in (38 cm). The females are larger than the males.

Their coloration is mainly brown and, with

Hartebeest

the exception of the Spotted harrier and female Marsh harrier *C. aeruginosus*, all have a conspicuous white rump. The adult males of the Hen, Pallid *C. macrourus*, Montagu's *C. pygargus* and Cinereous harrier *C. cinereus* have grey upper-parts and are light underneath, although in immature plumage they are brown and resemble the adult females. The male Pied harrier is unusual in being glossy black with white shoulders and rump and the Black-harrier *C. maurus* has a generally black appearance. The most distinctively coloured is the Spotted harrier, slate grey, spotted white above, and chestnut, spotted white below. In some species dark and light colour phases are not uncommon.

The nests are relatively small and built on the ground, with one exception, the Australian Spotted harrier which builds a large flat nest of sticks in the main fork of a stunted tree about 40 ft (12 m) above the ground. The typical clutch is four eggs. The males bring food to the sitting females. The food is exchanged in flight, the male dropping it from his claws to be caught by the female in hers. The eggs hatch after about a month and the young fly when just over five weeks old.

Their prey is small mammals, but includes amphibians, small reptiles, insects, nestling birds and small birds surprised as they dart from cover. FAMILY: Accipitridae, ORDER: Falconiformes, CLASS: Aves.

HARTEBEEST, least typical of African antelopes, include the 'true' hartebeest *Alcelaphus* and the 'bastard' hartebeest *Damaliscus*. Both have upright horns with a sharp kink in the middle, long faces, rudimentary face-glands and foot-glands in the forefeet only. The 'true' hartebeests have exaggerated long thin faces, and a high horn-pedicle which makes their appearance even more bizarre. The horns tend to be short and stout and the back slopes sharply from the shoulders to the rump. The 'bastard' hartebeests are more ordinary-looking with shorter faces, horn-pedicles that are not raised, longer and more slender horns and horizontal backs. In both kinds, females have horns as large as those of males.

There are three species of 'true' hartebeest. The most widespread is the Common hartebeest *A. buselaphus*, which formerly was distributed throughout North Africa and south to Tanzania. It is reddish or yellowish brown, varying in the different races, which are: the Bubal hartebeest *A. b. buselaphus*, now extinct, the Western hartebeest *A. b. major*, Senegal, east to northern Cameroun, 48 in (120 cm) high, red-fawn with horns forming a U, the Lelwel or Jackson's hartebeest *A. b. lelwel*, Central African Republic to south-western Ethiopia, Rwanda and western Kenya, deep foxy red, the horns forming a V from in front, the Tora hartebeest *A. b. tora*, East Sudan, northern and western Ethiopia, tawny with a light rump,

Kongoni or Coke's hartebeest on the savannah near Nairobi, Kenya.

the horns forming a high, inverted bracket, the Swayne's hartebeest *A. b. swaynei*, Central, southern and eastern Ethiopia and Somalia, similar to the Tora but with no rump patch and with dark face and limbs and white-speckled flanks, the Kongoni or Coke's hartebeest *A. b. cokii*, southern Kenya and northeastern Tanzania, with bracket-shaped horns but with the mid-portion long and horizontal instead of upwardly-directed as in the last two. The horns are also rather stout. Tawny, paler on the rump.

The second species, Lichtenstein's hartebeest *A. lichtensteini*, Tanzania to Katanga, Zambia, Rhodesia and Mozambique, has horns which are on a short, broad pedicle, are very stout and flat at the base, then bend sharply in and as sharply out again. It is tawny, with the chin and limbs blackish. The hair is reversed in the middle of the face.

The third species is the Cape, Red or Rooi hartebeest *A. caana*, from the Cape north to Botswana, western Rhodesia and southern Angola. The horns are like those of the Tora, but on a higher pedicle, the colour is red, with dark shoulders, thighs, forelegs and face, and a white buttock patch.

The male marks his territory by standing on a high point such as a termite mound, in order to be seen. When another male enters the territory, the resident male chases him at a fast gallop, continually overtaking him, turning and threatening with his horns, until the intruder has been seen off the territory.

When the young are born, they lie still in the grass; the mother watches her calf without coming too near except for suckling.

Bastard hartebeest also come in three species. The best-known are the *bontebok and *blesbok. FAMILY: Bovidae, ORDER: Artiodactyla, CLASS: Mammalia.

HARVESTMEN, differ from spiders, to which they are related, in having no 'waist' in the elliptical body. There are six pairs of appendages, a pair of chelicerae or pincers, a pair of pedipalpi and four pairs of long walking legs. The body is $\frac{1}{25}$–1 in (1–20 mm) long, whereas the legs, each with seven segments, may be from one to eight times the body length. Most harvestmen have on the front of the body a tubercle of varying shape and size with an eye on each side. They have a breathing pore on either side of the abdomen, and sometimes pores on the long legs for muscular respiration.

Certain species have a very wide distribution; for example *Mitopus morio* has been recorded throughout Europe including Spitzbergen and Iceland, much of Asia, North Africa and North America. The bulk of species inhabit tropical regions. Over 2,300 species are known. ORDER: Phalangiida, CLASS: Arachnida, PHYLUM: Arthropoda.

HARVEST MITES *Trombicula autumnalis*, free-living in the nymphal and adult stages but frequently parasitic as larvae on mammals, from man to mice, in parts of Europe. In man, they cause a form of dermatitis. The six legged larvae pierce the skin with stylet-like mouth-parts and inject saliva, which dissolves a feeding canal down to the deeper layers of the skin, up which tissue fluid and cell debris is sucked. On small mammals, the ear is a favoured site, on man the wrists, armpit, groin and ankles. The larvae appear in July and reach a peak in numbers by September. After feeding for about three days the larvae drop off and undergo a moult inside the larval skin. From this emerges the one free nymphal stage with eight legs. This stage, like the adult, lives in the soil most probably in the eggs of small arthropods. There is one generation per year. In Britain, Harvest mites are more frequent in chalk areas than on clay, the reverse is said to be true over Europe generally. Harvest mite larvae act as vectors of scrub typhus in the Far East and in Australasia. FAMILY: Trombiculidae, ORDER: Acari, CLASS: Arachnida, PHYLUM: Arthropoda.

HARVEST MOUSE *Micromys minutus*, 5 in (12·5 cm) in length, including its long, scaly prehensile tail, and weighing ¼ oz (7·5 gm) or less, yellowish red with white underparts. The face has a blunt nose, black bright eyes and large rounded ears and the voice is a low chirp. The range of the Harvest mouse includes Europe and northern Asia. Its numbers are decreasing due it is thought to earlier harvesting and other modern agricultural methods.

Formerly, the Harvest mouse was considered to be mainly diurnal, but it is now known to have 3-hourly cycles of rest and activity throughout each 24 hours. During its waking period a Harvest mouse will climb about on the stalks of cereal crops and rank herbage. Its staple diet is seeds of grasses and grain, with some insects.

Breeding is from April to September and 5–9 young are born in a round nest woven from grass or wheat blades and slung between two or three stalks. FAMILY: Muridae, ORDER: Rodentia, CLASS: Mammalia.

HATCHETFISHES, small freshwater South American fishes, 4 in (10 cm) long, capable of flight. The common name refers to their slim bodies with very deep chests which resemble a hatchet in shape. The anal fin is long and the pectoral fins are large and sickleshaped. The fishes make a short dash to take off and flap their fins with a buzzing noise in the air. FAMILY: Gasteropelecidae, ORDER: Cypriniformes, CLASS: Pisces.

HATCHETFISHES, MARINE, small deepsea marine fishes equipped with light organs and bearing a superficial resemblance to the freshwater hatchetfishes. The lower part of the body is lined with light producing organs, the photophores, which shine a blue or pinkish light downwards. They form a dominant element of the bathypelagic fish fauna at depths of 800–1,600 ft (250–500 m). FAMILY: Stomiatidae, ORDER: Salmoniformes. CLASS Pisces.

HAWAIIAN GOOSE *Branta sandvicensis*, or né-né of the Hawaiian archipelago. Its plumage is sombre, with broad transverse barrings of brown or black and pale buff, the dark bars being less obvious beneath. The sides of the face and the neck are a richer buff, with conspicuous folds or pleats in the feathers arranged in a pattern diagonally backwards and downwards. The head and

Female Harvest mouse on her nest of woven grass slung between wheat stems.

back of neck are black, as are the feet, tail and bill.

The né-né, an offshoot of the migratory Canada goose stock, is a sedentary island form, adapted to the sparsely vegetated volcanic areas of the Hawaiian islands, where there is little permanent water. It shows a number of features adapting it for a terrestrial existence, such as the reduction in the webs, the strong legs and gait, and the rather upright stance. With the introduction of firearms to the region it suffered considerably, and its numbers were further reduced by its habitat being lost to agriculture and its eggs and young being taken by introduced predators such as rats, pigs, and cats. From a population of 25,000 it almost became extinct in the 1950s. Since then, captivebred birds have been released to build up the wild stocks. FAMILY: Anatidae, ORDER: Anseriformes, CLASS: Aves.

HAWFINCH *Coccothraustes coccothraustes*, the largest British finch 6½ in (16 cm) long, distinguished by its stout head, thick neck, large powerful bill and short tail. The upper plumage is ruddy-brown with paler rump, head and underparts, the throat is black and the nape grey. The hawfinch prefers to live in broad-leaved woodland, orchards or large gardens feeding on seeds on the ground and in trees. The powerful bill enables it to crack kernels and hard seeds. In winter it joins up with others to form flocks. The nest is built in a tree, often on a horizontal branch, made of twigs lined with moss or grass. 4–6 bluish or grey-green eggs, spotted and streaked with dark brown, are incubated by the female for about 10 days but the young are fed by both parents. FAMILY: Fringillidae, ORDER: Passeriformes, CLASS: Aves.

HAWKSBILL TURTLE *Eretmochelys imbricata*, the second smallest marine turtle, of tropical and subtropical seas, long persecuted by man as the source of 'tortoiseshell'. All but very old hawksbills can be distinguished from other Sea turtles by their strongly overlapping scutes on the carapace. Females nest on sandy beaches, depositing 100–200 eggs per clutch. The shell of a large hawksbill reaches about 2 ft (60 cm). Fortunately, man-made plastics have largely replaced the use of natural shell. FAMILY: Testudinidae, ORDER: Testudines, CLASS: Reptilia.

HEDGEHOG *Erinaceus europaeus*, a small, spine-covered insectivore 5–12 in (13–30 cm) long, and weighing 1–3 lb (400–1200 gm). It has a short tail, small ears and fairly prominent eyes. All feet have five toes with strong claws, and the hindfeet are laid flat on the ground when walking (i.e. plantigrade). Each spine is a modified hair, about ¾–1¼ in (2–3 cm) long, 1–2 mm in diameter and internally composed of partitions and air filled chambers; giving strength but lightness. Typically the spine is a cream colour with a broad subterminal dark brown band. The tip is sharp, but the body end of the spine forms a narrow neck, bent at an angle of about 60°, and terminating in a large round knob buried in the skin. The hedgehog has up to 6,000 spines depending on its age. The fur of the face and underside is coarse and usually pale brown.

The hedgehog's skin musculature enables the animal to roll up and become entirely enclosed by the spiny part of its skin.

The distribution of the common hedgehog is from Britain eastwards to China. Others very similar are found in Africa and Asia. There are no hedgehogs in the Americas, but

Hellbender

E. europaeus was successfully introduced to New Zealand at the end of the last century.

Hedgehogs are usually fertile from April until September. In springtime, the male accessory reproductive glands undergo a temporary but enormous growth till they occupy a large part of the abdomen, a state of flamboyant development unrivalled by any other mammal. Mating takes place after a protracted shuffling 'courtship' manoeuvre, during which the male continuously walks round the female. The gestation period is 30–35 days and the young are usually born in June or July. Some females have very early litters (April or May) and some may bear a second litter as late as October. The average litter size (in Britain) is four to five, but larger families are produced on the Continent.

All hedgehogs are nocturnal and have a keen sense of smell and acute hearing. Their eyesight is not so good. They are surprisingly agile and can run, climb and swim. Their food is mainly worms, beetles and slugs.

Hedgehogs may produce a variety of hissing and snorting noises and when alarmed they occasionally emit a loud pig-like scream. Their most remarkable behaviour is probably that of 'self-anointing', an energetic performance when stimulated to produce large amounts of frothy saliva by contact with an astringent smell or taste. The foam is then placed on the spines with the tongue. Other activities attributed to the hedgehog include suckling cows at night, now shown to be true.

The hedgehog hibernates in the colder parts of its range for four to five months in a nest, usually sited under logs or thick undergrowth. Its heart rate falls from 180 beats per minute to 20 or less, breathing almost ceases and the body temperature is greatly reduced. FAMILY: Erinaceidae, ORDER: Insectivora, CLASS: Mammalia.

HELLBENDER *Cryptobranchus alleganiensis*, largest salamander in North America is 18 in (45 cm) long, seldom seen, nocturnal and lives strictly under the water in the eastern United States. By day, it hides in cracks and crannies found around submerged rocks and logs. Its food consists of any smaller aquatic animals. Although possessing

A Night heron on its nest in India.

European hedgehog, although one of the Insectivora, feeds largely on slugs.

lungs and gills, it breathes mainly through the skin. Its fat, wrinkled, slimy, olive-coloured body is more repulsive than pretty. It reproduces by external fertilization of eggs placed in a scooped-out hole at the bottom of the pond. The male stands guard until the eggs hatch. FAMILY: Cryptobranchidae, ORDER: Caudata, CLASS Amphibia.

HERMIT CRABS small modified lobsters with a soft abdomen twisted to the right and inserted into an empty shell of a Sea snail. The legs on the right side of the abdomen do not develop, except fot the last one which forms part of a modified tail fan. This sticks out sideways from the end of the soft swollen abdomen and each branch bears special anti-skid surfaces, covered with minute spines which can be pressed against the inside of the shell. It is virtually impossible to pull a hermit out of its shell without tearing the thorax away from the abdomen.

A Hermit crab has well developed pincers and two pairs of functional walking legs. The other two pairs of walking legs are reduced and modified for use as struts against the inner wall of the shell. When danger threatens the hermit can withdraw into the shell, leaving only the tips of its pincers showing.

Hermit crabs are scavengers. The common *Pagurus bernhardus* of European shores sometimes uses its pincers to break open barnacles and Tube worms, but most of its food is collected by scraping and brushing surfaces with its outermost mouthparts. FAMILY: Paguridae, SUBORDER: Anomura, ORDER: Decapoda, CLASS: Crustacea, PHYLUM: Arthropoda.

HERONS, long billed and long legged wading birds. Most of the 64 species inhabit tropical or subtropical regions. At nesting time they are mainly gregarious, several species often living together · in mixed colonies.

Amongst Old World species the Purple heron *Ardea purpurea*, the Great white heron *Egretta alba*, the Little egret *Egretta garzetta*, the Cattle egret *Ardeola ibis* and the Squacco heron *Ardeola ralloides* breed in Europe and are very rare vagrants to Britain. Of the European herons only the Grey heron *Ardea cinerea* nests in Britain.

New World species include the American egret *Casmerodius albus egretta*, the Snowy egret *Leucophoyx thula*, the Louisiana heron *Hydranassa tricolor*, the Little blue heron *Florida caerulea* and the Green heron *Butorides virescens*.

The Green heron of North America may measure only 16 in (40 cm) while the largest herons measure up to 50 in (127 cm). The Grey heron reaches a height of 3 ft (91 cm), has a wing-span of over 5 ft (152 cm) and weighs from $3–4\frac{1}{2}$ lb (1·3–2 kg). In flight the feet extend beyond the tail and the neck is withdrawn.

Herons feed mainly on fishes and animals caught near water, including a surprising number of moles. The disruptive pattern of the Grey heron is ideal for wait-and-watch hunting. The heron stands motionless at the water's edge waiting for prey to swim within grasping distance, then uses its bill as a vice, not a spear. Occasionally in deeper water, it may swim or dive after fishes.

About the end of February the adults gather in the vicinity of the nesting trees, but do not immediately take to the tree-tops. At first only a few birds arrive, the number growing until the full complement is present. They stand all facing one direction, just waiting. Gradually, they begin to occupy the tree-tops.

At the nest a male advertises for a mate by formalized displays, vocal and visual. Gradually the female responds and, after some rebuff, is accepted and the nest is prepared for the reception of the clutch which, in Europe, averages four eggs. FAMILY: Ardeidae, ORDER: Ciconiiformes, CLASS: Aves.

HERRINGS, highly important food fishes of world-wide distribution, the best known being the herring of North Atlantic and Pacific waters. Many of the 200 species are small and confined to tropical waters but often are of great importance to fisheries. The herring-like fishes have single soft-rayed dorsal and anal fins, the former usually set near the midpoint of the body and over the pelvic fins. Typically, the belly has a serrated 'keel' made up of a series of sharp scutes running from the throat to the anus.

The herring *Clupea harengus* is found throughout the North Atlantic, reaching southwards to Cape Hatteras in the west and the Bay of Biscay in the east. There is a distinct population in the White Sea closely related to the northern Pacific herring. The herring has a cylindrical body with the belly rather smooth and the scutes barely forming a keel. Rarely it may reach a length of 17 in (43 cm) but usually the adults are about 12 in (30 cm). The herring congregates in enormous numbers for feeding or spawning at certain times of the year. It was once assumed that the successive appearance of the herring shoals down European coasts resulted from a

Head-on view of a hippopotamus emphasizes the bulk of a well fed animal.

gigantic army of these fishes in the Arctic that spread southwards in spring. It is now known that the shoals in each area are local phenomena and it is the southward spread of the shoaling behaviour and not the southward spread of the fishes that gives the impression of a vast migration.

Off European coasts there is no time of the year when spawning is not taking place. The eggs may be laid some distance from the shore and down to 600 ft (200 m), or close to the shore in bays, brackish water or in the nearly freshwater of the northern Baltic. Off the North American coasts the more northerly fishes spawn in spring while those to the south spawn in summer and autumn. The herring is unique amongst the commercially important bony fishes of European seas in that the eggs are laid in enormous numbers

at the bottom on stones, shells or weeds, either in irregular layers or clusters and are heavily preyed upon by cod, whiting and mackerel. A large female may deposit up to 30,000 eggs. The larvae hatch at the bottom and later migrate to the surface layers where they feed on plankton. FAMILY: Clupeidae, ORDER: Clupeiformes, CLASS: Pisces.

HIPPOPOTAMUS *Hippopotamus amphibius*, one of the largest living land mammals, distantly related to pigs. It has a large barrel-like body and massive head, set on short legs, each with four toes with hoof-like nails. In spite of its unwieldy appearance the hippo is fast and agile and can overtake a running man. Its life is spent largely in water, its nostrils, eyes and ears set on top of the head. All three senses are good. The nostrils can be tightly closed when it submerges, which is usually for not longer than 5 min at a time. It is a slaty copper brown, shading from very dark above to pink below the body, face and neck. Albinos are known and are coloured a brilliant pink due to the superficial blood vessels. It is hairless, except for sparse bristles on the tail, ears and muzzle. The voice is a loud repeated grunting 'moo' which carries a long way over water.

The largest recorded, a Kenya male, weighed 5,872 lb (2,664 kg) and was over 15 ft (4½ m) long, but in general they are much smaller. In a very large sample from Western Uganda fully adult males averaged 11½ ft (3½ m) from nose to tip of tail, the females

A hippopotamus nearly submerged, showing how eyes and nostrils are the last to disappear under water. In a moment later the hippo will have closed its nostrils and ears. It is a question that remains unresolved what senses it relies upon while under water.

Honeybee

being about 6 in (15 cm) shorter. The average shoulder height is 4½ ft (1½ m). Average mature weights of males and females were about 3,500 lb (1,600 kg) and 3,100 lb (1,400 kg) respectively, the heaviest recorded being 4,552 lb (2,065 kg).

The continuously growing lower canine teeth are enormously enlarged and are exclusively used for fighting, being kept razor-sharp by wear against the upper teeth. In the male the lower canines reach a combined weight of 5½ lb. (2½ kg) but they grow to only half this size in the female. Their curved length is generally about 25 in (60 cm) but less than half protrudes from the gum. The large incisors are used for digging for salt and other minerals.

The Common hippopotamus was formerly found throughout Africa, including North Africa and the Sahara, along rivers and in lakes and swamps. It is still widespread south of the Sahara, but is very vulnerable to hunting and is becoming increasingly scarce in most areas outside national parks. It is restricted to water during the day, but feeds on land at night, intensively grazing a strip extending up to 6 miles (10 km) inland. The width of this grazing zone varies seasonally, increasing in the dry season as grazing quality deteriorates. The hippo trails leading inland are punctuated by dung heaps probably serving as chemical markers in the dark.

The gestation period is about eight months, the calf weighs an average of 110 lb (50 kg) at birth and suckles for about a year. Mating has been observed to take place in the water.

Hippo schools usually consist of about ten animals but there may be over 100. They contain adult females, calves and juveniles, and a few adult males. Solitary animals, usually adult males, are found in the vicinity of the schools. Territorial fights are common and always start at the water's edge or in the water, with an aggressive 'yawning' display. If the challenger is answered by the submissive posture (a lowering of the head) fighting is averted.

Hippos are said to 'sweat blood'. In fact the hippopotamus has no sweat glands and the 'blood' is a pink sticky secretion from skin glands. This dries to form a protective lacquer over the skin when the animal is on land, and may also have antiseptic properties.

The average individual nightly consumption of grass is about 150 lb (70 kg).

The Pigmy hippopotamus *Choeropsis liberiensis*, of Liberia and Sierra Leone, frequents forest streams singly or in pairs. It closely resembles a young Common hippopotamus which, compared with the adult, has a shorter body, relatively longer legs and a small head with the eyes and nostrils not much raised. The Pigmy adult is about 5–6 ft long (1·5–1·8 m), 2 ft 6 in (76 cm) high and weighs about 400–500 lb (180–230 kg). FAMILY: Hippopotamidae, ORDER: Artiodactyla, CLASS: Mammalia.

A honeybee worker in characteristic pose disseminating scent. The scent gland, exposed, can be seen as a pale area near the hind end of the uptilted abdomen.

HONEYBEE, most widespread of the three species is *Apis mellifera*. Its ability to regulate the temperature and humidity of its nest and to survive on stored food during unfavourable periods, has played a major part in its successful colonization of most of the world.

Each honeybee colony contains three castes: the mother or fertile female known as the 'queen', the infertile females known as 'workers' and the fertile males known as 'drones'. Usually there is only one queen to a colony but up to 60,000 workers. In natural conditions the nest of a honeybee colony consists of a series of vertical wax combs in a hollow tree or cave, or under an overhanging rock or some such shelter. On either side of each wax comb are series of hexagonal cells in which the young are reared and the honey and pollen are stored. Most of the tasks of the colony are done by workers. Those born in the spring and summer generally undertake a series of duties which are dependent to some extent on the development of certain glands in their bodies. At first they clean cells and remove debris, but after a few days special brood-food glands in their heads have developed sufficiently for them to feed a protein-rich secretion to the larvae. A few days later the wax glands, which are located on the underside of the abdomen, have developed sufficiently for them to secrete wax and build a comb. Other tasks done inside the nest include packing pollen loads into cells, receiving nectar from foragers, converting it into honey and guarding the entrance to the nests. The task done by a particular worker depends not only upon its physiological condition but also on the requirements of the colony at the time. Indeed a worker spends much of its time 'patrolling' the combs and so becomes aware of current needs. A worker first leaves its nest when only a few days old to make orientation flights during which it learns the location of its home in relation to that of surrounding landmarks and when it is about two to three weeks old it begins to forage. It does so for the rest of its life, which may be only about four weeks in midsummer, but as long as six months for bees emerging in late summer.

Like solitary bees and bumblebees, worker honeybees collect nectar and pollen, but they also, on occasion, collect propolis and water. Propolis is a sticky exudate of various buds and the bees use it to cement and block gaps in the covering to their nest and to reduce the size of the entrance. Water is used for cooling the nest as well as to dilute honey. To cool the nest the bees either spread it on the surface of the wax cells or manipulate it on their tongues to hasten its evaporation. They also aid cooling by fanning a current of air through the nest with their wings.

Most foraging trips are for nectar or pollen or both. Although, unlike many solitary bees, honeybees do not restrict themselves to one or a few plant species, during any one foraging trip an individual bee tends to keep constant to one plant species only. Indeed they tend to become conditioned to make their flights at the time of day at which flowers of their particular species open or present pollen. Fixation to a particular species is temporary and should a species cease flowering, or for other reasons fail to yield nectar or pollen, the bees will forsake it for another. Although some bees may find a particular source of forage for themselves, more often they are informed about it by others. The ability of bees to communicate a favourable source of forage is one of the most remarkable biological discoveries of this century. On its return home a successful forager performs a 'dance' on the surface of the comb, features of the dance indicating the direction of the food source in relation to the direction of the sun from the nest entrance and its distance from the nest. Bees that follow the dancing bee and receive the information are further helped to locate the food by the odour of the flowers that clings to the dancing bee's body.

In turn, egg-laying and brood-production are governed to a considerable extent by the amount of pollen a colony can collect. The queen is specialized for egg laying and, unlike the queen bumblebee, is incapable of doing the tasks of worker bees. Her egg production reaches its peak in late spring or early summer when she may lay about 1,500 eggs per day. A large protein intake is then necessary and the workers feed the queen entirely with glandular secretions to enable this to occur. The queen lays two types of egg, fertile eggs giving rise to workers or queens and unfertilized eggs giving rise to drones. The worker- and drone-producing eggs are laid one per cell, the drone-producing eggs in slightly larger cells than the worker-producing cells. The worker eggs hatch to larvae in three days and after five days of feeding the larvae change into pupae and the top of the cells are covered with a cap of wax. The larvae are visited and fed a great many times (progressive feeding) in contrast to the mass provisioning practised by solitary bees. After 13 days as pupae the soft downy adults emerge, making altogether 21 days from egg to adult. The larval and pupal stages of the drone are slightly longer making a total of 24 days. Apart from their larger size drone cells can be easily recognized during the pupal stage by their much more pronounced concave wax capping.

New queens are reared in special cells that hang vertically downward from the comb. The queen larvae receive special food and attention and their total period of development is only 16 days. They are either reared to replace the queen of the colony when she is dead or failing, or because the colony is about to reproduce by swarming and a new queen is needed to replace the mother queen which will leave with the swarm. Bees that leave with the swarm each carry a supply of honey in their honeystomachs and as soon as the swarm has settled in its new home some of this is rapidly converted into wax to start building the new comb. FAMILY: Apidae, ORDER: Hymenoptera, CLASS: Insecta, PHYLUM: Arthropoda.

HONEYCREEPERS, small brightly coloured birds of the New World about the size of a tit, with thin decurved bills, ranging from Mexico through Central America and the West Indies to Argentina. One of the best known species is the bananaquit *Coereba flaveola*.

Most species live in groups often associating with other species of honeycreeper at the tops of trees in light forests, forest edges, shrubbery and gardens. They feed on nectar and also on fruits and small insects.

Only a few of the most conspicuous species can be mentioned here. Among the most brightly coloured are the Red-legged honeycreeper *Cyanerpes cyaneus* and the Purple honeycreeper *Cyanerpes caeruleus*. The former occurs from Mexico south to Bolivia while the latter is restricted to Colombia and Venezuela south to northern Bolivia. The male Red-legged honeycreeper has purplish blue under-parts, the crown of the head

A queen bee on the comb surrounded by workers laying eggs in the cells.

being turquoise blue and the back, wings and tail black. It has bright red legs. The male Purple honeycreeper is purplish blue except for the throat, wings and tail, which are black. It has bright yellow legs. The females are totally different as they lack the purple-blue coloration, being green on their upper-parts and streaked green and white on the under-parts. FAMILY: Coerebidae, ORDER: Passeriformes, CLASS: Aves.

HONEY-EATERS, small to medium sized, mainly nectar-feeding, birds. There are 167 species. Most are found in Australasia and the Pacific Islands, but one species occurs in the Bonin Islands near Japan, and the two sugarbirds *Promerops* are confined to the southern tip of Africa and isolated from the rest of the family. Honey-eaters are slenderly-built, with strong feet enabling them to cling to twigs and plants in a variety of postures, a rather elongated and often slender bill, and a specialized brush tongue for extracting nectar from flowers. This tongue is long and narrow and can be extended beyond the tip of the bill. It is curled upwards and inwards along the edges to form a double groove. The tip is brush-like, being split into a number of filaments.

Honey-eaters range from the size of small warblers or wrens to jays or magpies. Their habitats are equally diverse, ranging from moist tropical forest to dry heathland and semi-desert, although usually associated with flowering trees or shrubs, however small. In addition to nectar many species take insects and various small fruits.

The smallest, the Pygmy honeyeater *Oedistoma pygmaeum*, is olive coloured, less than 3 in (7 cm) long with a thin, decurved bill and very similar in appearance and behaviour to a sunbird.

The largest honey-eaters are the Australian wattlebirds; the Yellow wattlebird *Anthochaera paradoxa* of Tasmania being about 18 in (46 cm) long. The wattles in this species are yellow pendent vermiform structures about 2 in (5 cm) long, one on either side of the head behind the ear coverts.

The nests of honey-eaters are usually open and cup-shaped, placed in tree forks or partly slung between horizontal twigs, suspended from them by their edges. Fine strips of bark are often used for building such nests. Hair is used as a lining in many and the birds will pluck hair from live animals, even from human beings. FAMILY: Meliphagidae, ORDER: Passeriformes, CLASS: Aves.

HONEYGUIDES, small, dull birds, brown or greyish with short stout bills. Undistinguished in appearance but remarkable in their feeding and reproductive behaviour, most of the 12 species of honeyguides live in African forests and well-wooded savannah. The remaining two species are found in southern Asia.

Five of the honeyguides are known to be brood parasites and the rest probably are. The Black-throated honeyguide *Indicator indicator* of Africa lays its eggs in the nests of barbets, bee-eaters, woodpeckers, starlings and other hole-nesting birds. Most other honeyguides also select hosts which nest in holes. Honeyguide eggs are white, like those of many of their hosts which lay in dark nest-chambers. When the female honeyguide enters the nest to lay, she destroys all the hosts' eggs. Nestlings produced from eggs of the host laid subsequently are killed by the baby honeyguide which has hooked tips to its upper and lower mandibles.

Upon finding an active bees' nest, which it is unable to break into itself, a honeyguide will guide a man or Honey badger to the spot by calling insistently. The bird keeps ahead by making short flights which eventually lead to the wild honey. After the combs have been broken open, and the honey removed by the animal in attendance, the bird consumes bee-grubs and pieces of wax, which it can apparently digest. FAMILY: Indicatoridae, ORDER: Piciformes, CLASS: Aves.

HOOKWORMS, intestinal parasites of man and domestic animals which belong to the roundworms. In past times they have infected and debilitated many millions of people over wide areas of the world. Modern methods of treatment and improved standards of hygiene have greatly reduced the extent of infection.

The life-cycle of the hookworm involves free-living larval stages, which lead an independent existence in the soil, and a direct mode of infection of the final host. Because of these factors, transmission of the parasite is possible only in warm, humid regions, between latitudes 30° N and 30° S. Two species infect man: *Ancylostoma duodenale* and *Necator americanus*. Although similar, the two differ in their biology, distribution and effect upon the human host. *Ancylostoma* is primarily an Old World parasite and is probably the more harmful. *Necator*, the New World hookworm, was possibly taken to America by infected slaves. The worms of both are about $\frac{1}{2}$ in (10–12 mm) in length. The body shows a flexure at the front end, producing the 'hook' appearance. It has been estimated that *Ancylostoma* lays 10–20,000 eggs per day and *Necator* 5–10,000. The thin-shelled eggs pass out of the intestine with the faeces and, in warm, humid conditions, develop rapidly to the first larval stage. When a person walks barefoot over infected ground, the larvae penetrate rapidly through the skin of the feet by secreting digestive enzymes and dissolving the layers of the skin. Once through the skin they enter blood vessels and are carried passively to the heart and then to the lungs. Here they break out of the blood capillaries, move through the air spaces of the lungs, are carried up the trachea and swallowed. They

pass unharmed through the stomach and establish themselves in the wall of the intestine. ORDER: Strongylida, CLASS: Nematoda, PHYLUM: Aschelminthes.

HOOPOE *Upupa epops*, a pink-buff and black-and-white striped bird widely distributed in warmer parts of the Old World. It is 10–12 in (25–30 cm) long, with a slender decurved bill set on a small head, but the most diagnostic feature is a large fan-shaped crest, rich buff with a black tip, which can be sleeked down on the crown or raised fore and aft. The crest is erected when the bird is excited. Head, neck, back and breast are pinkish-buff, richer above and paler below, and the wings and tail are broadly barred black and white.

Hoopoes are not sociable and the sexes are similar. For their small size, their gait is stately as they walk over lawns, gardens and arable land probing in search of the insects, larvae, spiders and worms. Occasionally young lizards are taken too. Hoopoes roost in trees, and often nest in tree-holes.

The nest is always a natural cavity—in a tree, wall, the ground or a termite hill— and is seldom lined. Four to six or more immaculate pale blue or brown eggs are laid. The nest becomes foul as it is not cleaned in any way. FAMILY: Upupidae, ORDER: Coraciiformes, CLASS: Aves.

HORNBILLS, an Old World family of birds with large, brightly-coloured bills, divided into two subfamilies: the Bucoracinae, which includes the two mainly terrestrial African Ground hornbills (*Bucorvus*) and the Bucerotinae of rather more than 40 mainly arboreal species. Hornbills are characterized by a large bill usually surmounted by a large decorative casque. Both bill and casque are often brightly coloured while the bill itself may be ridged and grooved. The casque is sometimes enormous and reaches its extreme development in males of the Black-casqued hornbill *Ceratogymna atrata* of West Africa, the Great hornbill *Buceros bicornis* of India and much of southeast Asia and the Rhinoceros hornbill *B. rhinoceros* of Malaya, Sumatra, Java and Borneo. The general effect is of being unwieldy and top-heavy, although the casque is very light, being composed of a thin outer covering of horn filled with a sponge-like cellular tissue. An exception is the Helmeted hornbill *Rhinoplax vigil* of Malaya, Sumatra and Borneo. It has a solid casque, with the consistency of ivory, red on the outside but golden inside. After being specially processed this is known as hornbill ivory, or *ho-ting* to the Chinese who used to value it more than jade or ivory.

Many hornbills have brightly coloured patches of bare skin on the throat and around the eyes. The most common colours are blue, red and yellow and these may differ between the sexes. In addition, the Black-casqued

Male Purple honeycreeper preening. The downcurved bill is used for sipping nectar.

An unfamiliar portrait of a hoopoe which is usually pictured with its crest raised.

two to four young, are fed on insects brought one or two at a time. On the other hand, the females of many other species, for example the Silvery-cheeked hornbill *Bycanistes brevis*, remain in the nest until the young fledge. This hornbill feeds its young on fruit and the male is obviously capable of bringing sufficient to feed the female as well as the one or two young for the whole of the fledging period.

Most hornbills eat fruit when it is available but otherwise eat almost any animal which they can overpower. Even small birds and bats are readily taken, while poisonous animals make up a high proportion of the animal diet of at least a number of the Asian species. FAMILY: Bucerotidae, ORDER: Coraciiformes, CLASS, Aves.

HORNED FROGS *Ceratophrys*, bizarre frogs of South America, east of the Andes. They are almost round when sitting with their short, powerful legs tucked in. The head is large and arches high, with a blunt snout and very wide jaws. The eyes are set high and have a horizontal pupil. The 'horns' are soft extensions of the upper eyelid, pointed and even curved slightly.

The smallest Horned frogs are little larger than a bottle cap; the largest would nicely fill a large soup bowl. They have a toad-like warty skin. Many species have a bold pattern of blotches or bars and some are vividly coloured. When annoyed they may attack and bite ferociously and can inflict a painful wound with their long teeth, which inspires the belief that they are venomous. They feed on frogs and mice which they stuff into their capacious mouths with their stout forelimbs. FAMILY: Leptodactylidae, ORDER: Anura, CLASS: Amphibia.

HORNETS, name originally given to the European *Vespa crabro*, which has been introduced to America, but has been applied to many large wasps, such as the American *Dolichovespula*. Unlike many commoner wasps which nest underground, hornets build their homes in trees or in human dwellings attached to rafters or the underside of the eaves. The nest is constructed of a series of horizontal combs, each lying parallel to its neighbours above and below it, and connected by a central spindle made of toughened paper; the whole is enclosed in a paper shell. Each comb consists of a cluster of cells in which the young are reared, and the entrance to each cell is closed by a wafer-thin paper seal. The adult bites through this delicate envelope and emerges. The papery material is made from woody material chewed by the hornets and mixed with saliva until it is transformed into a pulp.

In some countries, notably the warmer parts of the Americas, hornets are treated with considerable respect on account of their painful stings and their habit of con-

hornbill and the Yellow-casqued hornbill *Ceratogymna elata*, both of West Africa, have bright, cobalt blue neck wattles. Another peculiarity of hornbills is their eyelashes which are long, thick, black and curly and quite as attractive as the false variety worn by some women. Most species also have a distinct and rather hairy crest. The plumage of hornbills tends to be boldly patterned in black or brown and white. The sexes are usually similar although the casque is often bigger and more brightly coloured in the male.

Hornbills vary greatly in size from the 15 in (38 cm) long Red-billed dwarf hornbill *Tockus camurus* of West African forests to the turkey-sized Ground hornbills of African savannahs and the 4 ft (1·3 m) Great hornbill of Asian forests. Most have rather thick tarsi while the toes are broad-soled, the three that point forwards being partially united to form a pad. The two Ground hornbills have much longer and thicker tarsi, an adaptation to their terrestrial habits. The flight of the larger species is slow and laboured, consisting

of a series of wing beats followed by a glide. In the smaller species flight is light and swooping, the tail appearing disproportionately long and cumbersome. The larger species are remarkable for the great rushing noise their wings make.

The breeding behaviour of hornbills is even more remarkable because the females of all species except the Ground hornbills are walled into the nest chamber during incubation, and are fed by the males. The wall, which blocks the entrance to the nest hole, is built by the female with her own droppings which are viscid at first but harden on exposure to air. In some species the male assists by bringing pellets of clay mixed with saliva. When the wall is completed there remains only a narrow slit just large enough to allow the male to feed the female. The female of Von der Decken's hornbill *Tockus deckeni* breaks out of the nest hole when the young are two to three weeks old and about half-grown, and thereafter helps the male to feed them. The young replaster the hole after the female has departed. The usually gregating around human dwellings. FAMILY: Vespidae, ORDER: Hymenoptera, CLASS: Insecta, PHYLUM: Arthropoda.

HORSE *Equus przewalskii*. Wild horses occurred, in prehistoric times, over most of Eurasia in immense numbers. They survived until historic times in eastern Europe and in Siberia and Mongolia but are now on the verge of extinction. They were exterminated because they damaged crops and were competitors with domestic stock for food and water.

Three subspecies are recognized: the Steppe tarpan *E. p. gmelini*, the Forest tarpan *E. p. silvaticus*, and the Eastern wild horse or Przewalski horse *E. p. przewalskii*. The domestic horse originated from these three. It is usually referred to as *E. caballus*.

The Steppe tarpan lived in the open steppe country of south-eastern Europe. It was grey with black mane and tail and with a dark line along its back. It was finally exterminated in the 19th century.

The Forest tarpan inhabited wooded areas of western, central and eastern Europe, and only in the east did it survive the Middle Ages. Small populations still existed, at the beginning of the last century, in the forests of Bialowieza and eastern Prussia. Forest tarpans were taller than the Steppe tarpan; they had a shoulder height of about 48 in (1·20 m).

The Przewalski horse inhabited the steppes and semideserts of southern Siberia, Mongolia and western China. In the wild it is now probably extinct, although occasional resightings have been reported during the

Another Horned frog—*Megophrys nasuta*, of India, belongs to the family Pelobatidae, the members of which are superficially like the Horned frogs of South America.

last few years from the Gobi desert. It is, however, doubtful that these animals are pure-blooded wild horses, as these abduct domestic horse mares and interbreed with them. FAMILY: Equidae, ORDER: Perissodaactyla, CLASS: Mammalia.

HORSE MACKERELS, also known as scads, jacks, cavallas and pompanos, are not true mackerels and are distinguished from them by two small spines before the anal fin and the absence of small finlets behind the dorsal and anal fins. They are usually fast-swimming, well streamlined, but in some species deep-bodied and compressed. The body has a line of little keeled scutes along part or the entire length of the flanks. They are found in temperate and tropical waters throughout the world.

The common Horse mackerel *Trachurus trachurus* of the Mediterranean and eastern North Atlantic grows to about 14 in (36 cm). It has a short first dorsal fin, with the first spine directed forwards, and a long second dorsal fin with soft rays. The back is grey-blue or green, the flanks silvery and there is a dark spot behind the gill opening. It feeds on fishes and invertebrates. The young take shelter in the bell of the Sombrero jellyfish *Cotylorhiza*. FAMILY: Carangidae, ORDER: Perciformes, CLASS: Pisces.

HORSESHOE CRABS, called King crabs in North America, are large marine arthropods, up to 2 ft (60 cm) in length, closely related to the extinct Water scorpions (Eurypterida). They are not crustaceans, their closest affinities being with spiders.

They are easily recognized by their horseshoe shape, the upper surface of the body being covered by a scoop-shaped carapace, fringed on the abdominal region with a series of short, stout movable spines, and ending

Male of von der Decken's hornbill, of Africa. The female's bill is all-black.

Hounds

Young of the Common horse mackerel in the Plymouth Aquarium.

locomotion is by walking, although small Horseshoe crabs can swim on their backs using the plate-like abdominal appendages as swimmerets.

These curious animals are 'living fossils'; they have remained virtually unchanged for over 300 million years. The four species living today are *Limulus polyphemus* of the Atlantic seaboard of North America and Mexico, *Tachypleus gigas, T. tridentatus*, and *Carcino-scorpius rotundicauda* of southeast Asia. All live in shallow coastal waters and are encountered frequently during springtime when they come into the intertidal zone to mate and lay their eggs which are buried in a depression in the sand. The larvae hatching from these bear a close resemblance to the extinct trilobites. ORDER: Xiphosura, CLASS: Merostomata, PHYLUM: Arthropoda.

HOUNDS, also known as Smooth hounds or Smooth dogfishes, a family of small sharks. Most sharks have triangular or pointed teeth for cutting or grasping prey, but the flat pavement of teeth in the hounds is used for grinding and crushing molluscs and crustaceans. They have a world-wide distribution but the best known species of European coasts is the Smooth hound *Mustelus mustelus*. It has a supple, streamlined body with two dorsal fins and one anal fin and grows to 6 ft (1·8 m) in length. It is extremely abundant, as is its counterpart in the western Atlantic the Smooth dogfish *M. canis*. Both frequent inshore shallow waters and mostly browse on the bottom. Hounds are viviparous the young being not only hatched within

in a long tail spine which articulates with the rear end of the abdomen. The mouth is on the underside, almost in the centre, and is surrounded by a pair of pincers and five pairs of walking legs. The abdomen carries on its underside six pairs of flattened plates, the last five pairs bearing leaf-like gills. There is a pair of compound eyes sited laterally on the carapace, in addition to a median pair of simple eyes.

Horseshoe crabs prey on worms and molluscs, burrowing into soft sand and mud for them by pushing the scoop-shaped carapace into the substratum. The cephalothorax and the abdomen are hinged so that the body can 'jack-knife', aided by the tail spine. By flexing and straightening in this way, additional thrust for burrowing can be obtained, and the animal often buries itself completely in the sand or mud. The usual method of

A Horseshoe crab crawling towards the sea having laid its eggs.

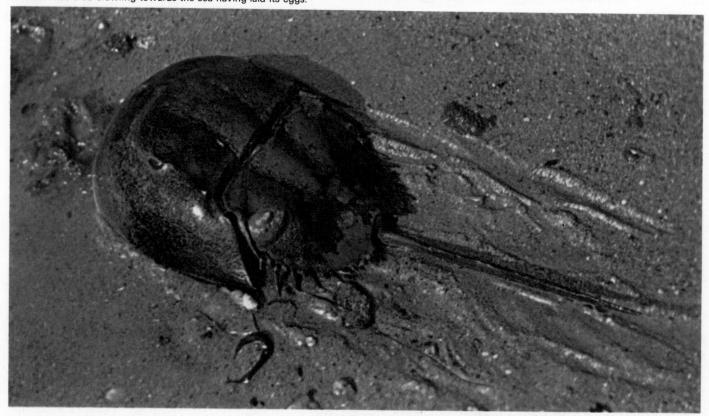

A House mouse returning to its litter of blind and helpless babies, in a nest opened up for purposes of photography.

the uterus but nourished through a placenta-like connection between the embryo and the uterine wall. There are about 30 species, none of which grows to more than 6 ft (1·8 m) in length. They are a considerable pest to commercial fishermen because of their predation on lobsters, crabs and other fishes. FAMILY: Triakidae, ORDER: Pleurotremata, CLASS: Chondrichthyes.

HOUSE FLY *Musca domestica*, unique among flies because both adult and larva like the surroundings in which man lives, and as a result it has become attached to man wherever he goes. It almost certainly originated in the tropics, but now occurs throughout the world. The House fly is small, ash brown and grey, with four thin, blackish stripes on the thorax. Indoors it is likely to be confused with the Lesser house fly *Fannia canicularis*, the males of which fly round and round in the middle of the room. The true House fly can be distinguished by the conspicuous bend in the vein at the tip of the wing.

The House fly has a spongy proboscis, with large lobes richly supplied with branching grooves and can feed only by mopping up liquids or semi-liquid food. Solid food must be softened by expelling saliva over it, as well as regurgitating liquid from the crop. These fluids contain digestive enzymes, which predigest the food until it can be sucked back into the crop. It is this alternate vomiting and sucking that makes the House fly so dangerous to health, because any disease organisms the fly has picked up with its food are likely to be voided again on to its next meal. FAMILY: Muscidae, ORDER: Diptera, CLASS: Insecta, PHYLUM: Arthropoda.

HOUSE MOUSE *Mus musculus*, a rodent that has followed man throughout the world as a pest, and is also the ancestor of the domesticated mouse, kept as a pet by children and as an experimental animal in the laboratory. Most wild House mice that infest buildings can be distinguished from other mice by their smoky greyish brown fur above and below.

The House mouse probably began its association with man soon after he first began to cultivate cereals more than 8,000 years ago. It is therefore difficult to know what was the original distribution of the species, but it seems likely that it included the grassland areas of the Near and Middle East, and probably also the Mediterranean region and the steppes of eastern Europe and southern Russia, perhaps as far as western China. In most of this area small, pale-bellied, short-tailed outdoor forms are still found, but often in company with the larger, darker, longer-tailed forms that seem to be more closely adapted to an indoor or farmyard existence. House mice occur from the Arctic to the Equator and even live and breed in frozen meat stores.

House mice, when living indoors or in corn-ricks with an abundance of food and protection from cold, continue to breed throughout the year. Under these conditions five or six litters per year of five or six young is normal and the potential rate of increase enormous. FAMILY: Muridae, ORDER: Rodentia, CLASS: Mammalia.

HOUSE SPARROW *Passer domesticus*, seed-eating bird, 5½ in (14 cm) long; brown streaked with black, with a dark grey crown and greyish-white underparts. The male has a black throat. This is the best known of the small European birds and is found wherever there is human settlement or agricultural land. House sparrows will eat almost anything, but especially grain and will damage flowers to get at the nectaries. It has been introduced to North and South America, Australia, New Zealand and South Africa. It is a member of the weaver family, one indication of which is the large untidy nest of dried grass lined with feathers built in bushes and more especially in holes or on ledges in buildings. The 3–6 eggs, white with grey or brown streaks are incubated by the female for about three weeks and both parents feed the young which fly in about 15 days. There may be three broods in a year and in the autumn young and adult birds form large flocks in rural areas especially where there are ripening cereal crops. FAMILY: Ploceidae, ORDER: Passeriformes, CLASS: Aves.

HOVERFLIES, characteristically seen hovering, especially around flowers, their wings beating so quickly they are more or less lost to sight. Some are more common in woods where they remain poised at different heights above the ground apparently motionless, but occasionally darting away in any direction to a new position, and back again. From the hovering position they can fly forwards, backwards, sideways, up or down with equal ease. Many are banded black and yellow, like bees or wasps, so are not immediately recognized as flies.

Flowers are essential for hoverflies. The constant activity requires a high intake of carbohydrate, and they feed freely on the nectar. At the same time they pollinate flowers, next in importance to bees for this.

159

Howler monkeys

A hoverfly, master of helicopter flight, at rest on a flower, which is a source of nectar essential to its well-being.

The larvae of hoverflies have varied habits. One, the rat-tailed maggot, lives in water or mud, feeding on decaying organic matter. It has a long telescopic breathing tube so that it can breathe atmospheric air while remaining submerged. The adult is the Drone fly, so called because it resembles the drone of the honeybee. Other hoverfly larvae live in ants' and wasps' nests where they feed on excreta, while a large group are actively carnivorous, feeding on aphids, which are easy prey for a blind hoverfly maggot as they move so little. Only the soft, easily digested body contents are sucked out and up to 60 may be eaten daily. FAMILY: Syrphidae, ORDER: Diptera, CLASS: Insecta, PHYLUM: Arthropoda.

HOWLER MONKEYS *Alouatta*, five species of South American monkeys. They are large, thickset and bearded, with a long prehensile tail, naked below at the tip, and well-developed thumbs. The lower jaw is expanded and the throat swollen to accommodate a sound-box of enlarged hyoid bones at the root of the tongue. The voice of the Red howler *A. seniculus* carries for three miles. All the howlers are black or very dark brown except the Red howler which is red.

Howlers usually live in groups of 15–20. They are entirely arboreal and move slowly, both quadrupedally and by arm-swinging. Howling precedes early morning movement and is initiated by the leading male. When two troops meet at the territorial boundary a noisy vocal 'battle' ensues but very rarely is there any fighting. FAMILY: Cebidae, ORDER: Primates, CLASS: Mammalia.

HUMMINGBIRDS, 319 species of tiny, fast and active nectar-drinking birds of the New World, which take their name from the noise made by their incredibly rapid wing-beats. They feed on the wing, and are related to swifts. Like them they have very small legs and feet, used only for perching and the bony structure of the wings is also very much reduced, the greater part of the visible wing consisting of a large area of elongated primary flight feathers. The head is large in relation to the body.

The largest, the Giant hummingbird *Patagona gigas* of the Andes, is a little over 8 in (20 cm) long of which half is tail. The smallest, the Bee hummingbird *Mellisuga helenae* of Cuba, is the size of an insect. The body is about 1 in (2·5 cm) long, the bill and tail adding another inch to this. In a majority of species the body size is 2 in (5 cm) or less.

The hummingbird has a problem associated with its mode of feeding. When taking nectar from blossoms there is no convenient perch nearby so it must hover while feeding then move backwards to withdraw its bill from the flower. As a result the flight is specialized. The wing-beat is highly efficient and, proportionally, the hummingbird uses fewer beats than other birds. Some of the larger hummingbirds have a rate of 20–25 beats per sec, comparable with that of the considerably larger and slower tits. In small hummingbirds the rate rises to about 70 beats per sec but in the Giant hummingbirds it is the surprisingly slow 8–10 beats per sec.

The bill is long and fine, an exceptionally short one being only about half as long again as the head, while the longest, that of the Sword-billed hummingbird *Ensifera ensifera*, is straight and as long as head, body and tail combined. Such a bill is designed for probing long tubular flowers. The tongue, slender and elongated, can be extended well beyond the tip of the bill and the edges are rolled in to form a double tube up which the nectar is sucked.

Many hummingbirds are forest-dwellers, but they may occur in a wide range of habitats, extending into open country where flowering plants are present and also to high altitudes in mountain regions. In some areas they are nomadic or subject to seasonal movements to take advantage of the flowering seasons of different plants. Several species are migratory and three move into North America to nest in the southern parts of Canada or Alaska.

The displays of the hummingbirds are relatively unspectacular in terms of movement, usually being very rapid swoops terminating in a hover in front of the female, but the brilliance of the display lies in the vivid iridescent colours of the male's plumage and the often elaborate plumage decorations such as crests, ruffs, beards and tail-streamers. Most of the more vividly iridescent plumage is on the throat and crown—brilliant shades of red, yellow, pink, purple, blue or green. In many cases this is only really conspicuous from one angle, usually from the front, so that it shows to best advantage when the male hovers before the female. The head colour may be enhanced by decoration such as the long tapering green or violet crests of the plovercrests *Stephanoxis*, the green and red paired horns of *Heliactin cornuta* or the black and white paired crest and pointed beard of *Oxypogon guerinii*. In addition to a bright crest, the coquettes *Lophornis* have erectile fan-shaped ruffs on the sides of the neck, boldly coloured and with contrasting bars or spots at the feather-tips. When the male hovers before the female the other visible parts of the plumage are the undersides of wings and tail. The body plumage of most hummingbirds is glossy green or blue and the underwings may have a contrasting chestnut-red tint. The tails of some show an overall bronze or purple iridescence on the undersides of tail feathers, visible in display but not obvious from above, while on others the feathers may be tipped, streaked or blotched with white. In addition the tails may have a variety of shapes. Broad fans are frequent, and forked tails vary from blunt forks to the long scissor-shapes of the trainbearers *Lesbia* and the slender tail streamers of the streamertail *Trochilus polytmus*. Others show different degrees of tapering and elongation of the central tail feathers, as in the hermits *Phaethornis*.

The nests are built of fibres, plant down and similar fine material and moss and lichen, bound together with spiders' webs. Some are smooth neat cups on twigs, others are domed, and some are pendent, or built onto hanging plants. They are often decorated externally with lichens. The female builds the nest, incubates and cares for the young. She lays two white eggs, which are large in proportion to her body and bluntly elliptical. Incubation takes about a fortnight and the young are born naked. The female feeds them by inserting her bill well into the chicks' gullets and regurgitating food. The young take three to four weeks to fledge, the period varying, apparently in response to the food supply available. FAMILY: Trochilidae, ORDER: Apodiformes, CLASS: Aves.

HUMPBACK WHALE *Megaptera novae-angliae*, a whale with long flippers, hence *Megaptera* (large wings), with serrated hind edges, which are about a third the total body length of some 50 ft (16 m). Nodules are present on the head and the body is usually covered with large barnacles. As the body is black dorsally and white ventrally the barnacles are very obvious on the back, giving a rough black and white spotted appearance. The humpback is bulky and appears to hunch its back on diving.

Humpbacks are widely distributed throughout the oceans and follow the rorqual migratory pattern. This follows coasts in certain parts of the world, for example, in New Zealand, where the schools move close inshore frequenting bays and inlets. In spite of this the humpback rarely becomes stranded.

In spite of the great bulk, humpbacks may be seen sporting in the sea, often leaping and rolling to fall back in the water with an enormous splash. FAMILY: Balaenopteridae, ORDER: Cetacea, CLASS: Mammalia.

HYAENAS, much reviled for their habit of eating carrion and their unlovely appearance. There are three species: the Spotted or Laughing hyaena *Crocuta crocuta* of Africa south of the Sahara, the Brown hyaena *Hyaena brunnea* of southern Africa, and the Striped hyaena *H. hyaena*, which ranges from northern Africa through Asia Minor to India. The shoulders are noticeably higher than the hindquarters, giving them an ungainly, hunchbacked appearance. They are also remarkable for their gait, known as pacing in which both limbs of one side of the body move together, instead of the normal quadrupedal action. The head is massive with large ears and powerful jaws equipped with large teeth capable of shearing through a zebra's thigh bone. The tail is short and each foot bears four toes.

The Spotted hyaena is the largest and most aggressive of the three. The male may be 5 ft (1·5 m) long in head and body with a 13 in (33 cm) long tail and 3 ft (91 cm) at the shoulders. It can weigh up to 180 lb (81 kg). The female is slightly smaller. The fur is scanty varying from grey to tawny or yellowish-buff broken by numerous brown spots. There is only a slight mane. Spotted hyaenas are nocturnal spending most of the day in holes in the ground. They live in clans of up to 100 in defined territories marked by their urine and droppings. They often hunt in packs and can run up to 40 mph (65 kmph). The usual call of the Spotted hyaena is a mournful howl, made with the head held near the ground, beginning low but becoming louder as the pitch rises. When excited it utters what can only be described as a demented cackle, which has earned it the name

Striped hyaena of Africa and Asia: now exonerated of the charge of cowardice.

of the 'Laughing hyaena'. It also appears to have the ability to project its voice, making it hard to locate the animal from its call. Spotted hyaenas eat carrion and it is believed they can detect a carcase over a range of several miles. They also kill sheep, goats, calves, young antelopes and even smaller prey. They may even eat locusts. They have been observed at night in a pack of up to 20 following a herd of wildebeest and harassing until they have slowed down one of them.

The Striped hyaena, the smallest, is 4 ft (1·2 m) long in head and body with an 18 in (46 cm) long tail. It stands 30 in (76 cm) at the shoulder and a full grown male may weigh up to 85 lb (38·2 kg). The coat is grey to yellowish-brown broken by dark, almost black stripes. Along the line of the spine there is a crest or mane of longer hairs.

The Brown hyaena is halfway in size between the Spotted and Striped hyaenas. Its coat is dark brown with indistinct stripes but with dark rings round the lower part of the legs. Like the Striped hyaena it has a long-haired erectile mane. It lives near the shore and feeds on carrion and marine refuse, eating anything from dead crabs to the carcases of stranded whales. For this reason it is also known as the strandwolf. FAMILY: Hyaenidae, ORDER: Carnivora, CLASS: Mammalia.

HYDRA, a solitary polyp, with a long cylindrical body, closed at one end and with a mouth borne on a projection or hypostome at the other. Surrounding the mouth are tentacles, generally five or six of differing lengths. The body wall is composed of two cell layers, an outer ectoderm and an inner endoderm separated by a thin, non-cellular layer, the mesogloea. It encloses a single enteron or body cavity and the body is a simple tube, there being no projections or septa dividing the enteron, as in Sea anemones.

The tentacles bear 'batteries' of nematocysts, or stinging cells, which are used to capture small Crustacea. On the capture of prey, the tentacles curve towards the mouth, which opens wide.

Hydras are noted for their power of regeneration. Almost any piece cut from the polyp will reorganize and form a complete, although small, individual. Each piece will retain its 'polarity'; a head will always be formed at the head end with respect to the original piece of tissue. Similarly, tentacles, if removed, will be replaced. Hydras when well fed will reproduce asexually, by budding. A small protuberance arises somewhere along the long axis of the polyp, the site depending on the species. This bud grows and develops mouth and tentacles at the end furthest from the parent polyp. When fully developed the new animal is constricted off the parent. FAMILY: Hydridae, ORDER: Athecata, CLASS: Hydrozoa, PHYLUM: Cnidaria.

IJK

IBEX, the name given to seven species of wild goat living in high mountains. They mostly differ from the true wild goat in the smaller amount of black in their coloration, in their flattened foreheads, and in their broad-fronted horns, although this last difference does not apply to the Pyrenean or Spanish ibex. The Alpine ibex *Capra ibex*, which is typical, is 32–34 in high (80–85 cm), with backcurved horns averaging 26 in (67·5 cm) long. The horns have a broad front surface with even-spaced knots on it; the outer angle is somewhat bevelled off, so that the knots fade towards the outer side. Alpine ibex are dark brown, darker on the underparts and face. FAMILY: Bovidae, ORDER: Artiodactyla, CLASS: Mammalia.

IBISES, stork-like birds of moderate size with long, thin and markedly decurved bills. The neck is long, as are the legs; the feet are slightly webbed, between the three forward-directed toes. There is a considerable range of plumage coloration among the species. The Wood ibises (to which the generic name *Ibis* belongs) are classed with the true storks.

The 24 species are world-wide in tropical, subtropical and some temperate countries. Their usual habitat is in the neighbourhood of fresh water and their food consists largely of small animals, aquatic and otherwise.

Ibises tend to be gregarious and breed in colonies. The nesting site is commonly in trees, bushes, or reedbeds and sometimes on cliffs, or on stony islands. There are usually three or four eggs, coloured off-white to blue, and they may be marked or plain. The sexes share parental duties.

The Glossy ibis *Plegadis falcinellus*, is found in all six continents. The distribution of its breeding colonies is, however, strangely sporadic and there seems to be a tendency to irregular population movements as well as annual migrations. The feathers show a metallic gloss of bronze and green. The

The White ibis of tropical America, best known of the New World ibises.

prevalent colour of the plumage is otherwise purplish-brown.

The Hermit ibis *Geronticus eremita*, also called Waldrapp, is now found only in the Middle East and North Africa, but until the 17th century it bred in Switzerland and other parts of Central Europe. It is peculiar in living in dry country and nesting on cliffs. It has a very disagreeable and persistent smell. The plumage is mostly bronze-green and purple, with a metallic sheen, but the face and crown are bare of feathers, the skin being dull crimson like the bill.

The best known, the Sacred ibis *Threskiornis aethiopica*, is now extinct in Egypt, but was revered there in ancient days and mummified. Farther south in Africa, it is still common feeding in flocks on the river banks or on open ground. The plumage is all white, except for dark wing-tips and dark plumes on the lower back. The head and neck are bare of feathers, with black skin, and the dark red legs may appear black from a distance. Nesting is in trees or on the ground.

The hadada *Hagedashia hagedash* is an African species with a loud yelping cry, uttered in flight or at rest and sometimes at night. The plumage is dark olive-brown, with a green metallic sheen on the wing-coverts.

The Warty-headed ibis *Pseudibis papillosa* of India, which has bare areas of strongly pigmented skin on the head and neck, also has a patch of red papillae on the bare black skin of the crown.

Of the now very rare Japanese ibis *Nipponia nippon*, a white bird with a red face, only one small colony is known to exist.

The most beautiful species is the Scarlet ibis *Eudocimus ruber* of the Caribbean area, the adults of which are bright scarlet. FAMILY: Threskiornithidae, ORDER: Ciconiiformes, CLASS: Aves.

ICEFISHES, or bloodlessfishes, Antarctic fishes that appear to lack blood. They are not, in fact, without blood but the blood contains no red cells. This is most noticeable in the gills, which are a pale cream instead of the usual red. All are slim-bodied fishes, less than 12 in (30 cm) long, and have large heads and mouths.

The only oxygen in their blood is the very small amount dissolved in the blood plasma. In active fishes in warmer waters this would not be sufficient for the normal body requirements. In icefishes, however, the environment is only a little above freezing point, and the fishes themselves are sluggish in their habits. In addition, there is an unusually large amount of blood in the body. FAMILY: Nototheniidae, ORDER: Perciformes, CLASS: Pisces.

ICHNEUMON FLIES, parasitic wasps the females of which have a spine-like ovipositor, used as an organ of penetration to lay their eggs inside or close to the bodies of their

Ichneumon fly *Rhyssa persuasoria* with her long ovipositor, used to bore into wood.

hosts, usually other insects. Ichneumons are largely parasites of caterpillars of moths but they also attack aphids and beetles. They are generally red, black or yellow and are active fliers. They have long, many segmented antennae which are not elbowed. The ovipositor protrudes from the ventral part of the abdomen some way before the tip.

Adult ichneumons are often to be found in the summer visiting flower heads, especially those of the Umbelliferae. They are quickly flying insects. When egg laying, the female unsheaths the ovipositor and thrusts it into the body of the host, thus depositing the egg hypodermically. The young ichneumon larva grows rapidly inside the host, feeding first on its blood and later on other body tissues. Eventually the host is entirely consumed from inside and the Ichneumon fly larva breaks through the now shrunken skin of the caterpillar to make its own cocoon and

Common iguana of tropical America.

to pupate. ORDER: Hymenoptera, CLASS: Insecta, PHYLUM: Arthropoda.

IGUANAS, the largest and most elaborately marked lizards in the New World, with two genera in Madagascar and one genus in Polynesia. They range from 3 in (7·5 cm) to 6 ft (2 m) in length. All are oviparous except for the Swift lizards *Sceloporus* and Horned lizards *Phrynosoma* some of which are ovoviparous. The eggs are soft-shelled and buried underground.

The Common iguana *Iguana iguana* ranges from the lowlands of central Mexico south into southern South America. It lives in the vicinity of ponds or rivers at altitudes from sea-level to the mountains. Iguanas bask on branches of trees during the day, usually over water so that if danger appears the reptile can drop (sometimes for a considerable distance) into the river or pool, dive, and remain submerged on the bottom for many minutes. These reptiles are fast runners, good climbers, swimmers and divers. FAMILY: Iguanidae, ORDER: Squamata, CLASS: Reptilia.

IMPALA *Aepyceros melampus*, one of the most abundant and graceful of African antelopes, impala are around 39 in (1 m) high, red-brown in colour with a well-marked fawn band on the flanks and a white underside. There are no lateral hoofs. Only males have horns; these are 20–30 in (50–75 cm) long, turning first up, then out and back, then up again, with long tips. The horns have well-marked, spaced-out ridges on them.

Impala are found from the northern Cape to Uganda. They live in herds of hundreds of individuals; in the wetter months these break up into small one-male units, with 15–25 females to every male. The surplus males live in bachelor bands, up to 50 or 60 strong. The male herds his females by walking around

Indian wild dog

Impala make prodigious leaps even when there are no obstacles to clear.

them with a nodding motion of his head, roaring as he does so; he has at all times to be ready to defend his possession, and fierce fights take place. FAMILY: Bovidae, ORDER: Artiodactyla, CLASS: Mammalia.

INDIAN WILD DOG *Cuon alpinus*, Red dog or dhole, a short-haired, reddish dog widely distributed throughout Asia, south to latitude 50. It is 38 in (95 cm) in head and body, with a tail 18 in (45 cm) long. It is powerfully built with great stamina and a reputation for persistence in running down deer, and has been known to force even tigers and leopards to give up their kills. FAMILY: Canidae, ORDER: Carnivora, CLASS: Mammalia.

INDRI *Indri indri*, a large, grey-and-black lemur characterized by a vertical clinging and leaping habit and a specialized diet of leaves, buds, flowers, fruit and bark. It is the largest of the Madagascar lemurs, with a head and body length of 28 in (70 cm), and is peculiar in having a very short tail, 1 in (3 cm) long. Its long back legs, used for its enormous vertical leaps, give the impression it is much bigger, and in the villages of the east coast rain-forest it is regarded as one of man's distant relatives.

Indris live in small social groups, probably family units, of 2–4 adults. The indri is most famous for its eerie howls, which carry over great distances and are answered by howls from neighbouring groups. It also utters short, intermittent grunts as a mild alarm call. There is a single offspring at birth, which is carried on the mother's fur. The indri is only found in the northern part of the east coast rain-forest and, after the aye-aye, it is probably the most threatened species at the

present time. If forest destruction continues at its present rate, it could become extinct in a decade.

The avahi *Avahi laniger* is a greyish or brownish, soft-coated, slightly smaller lemur with a head and body length of 12 in (30 cm) and a tail of 16 in (40 cm) long. It differs from the indri in being nocturnal. FAMILY: Indriidae, SUBORDER: Prosimii, ORDER: Primates, CLASS: Mammalia.

JACAMARS, tropical American birds resembling bee-eaters. There are 14 species from southern Mexico to southeastern Brazil.

Jacamars are small to medium sized, bright-plumaged hunters of air-borne insects, which the birds await sitting patiently at favourite vantage-points in savannah woodland, farmland and at the edges of forest, often near water. Most species have an iridescent dark green head and upper-parts, rufous or green under-parts, and a contrasting white patch on throat or breast. Sexes are similar. The bill is straight, sharp and pointed, and one to three times the length of the head. The legs are very short, with the toes two forwards, two backwards and the tail moderately long and graduated.

The 10 in (25 cm) long Rufous-tailed jacamar *Galbula ruficauda* is typical. A pair will perch quietly low down at the edge of gallery forest, or in the shade of a riverside shrub, and dart out after a passing insect which, despite the slender 2½ in (7 cm) bill of this species, is deftly snapped up and brought back to the perch, where it is beaten until inactive. Their diet is chiefly hard-bodied insects, with wasps and bees comprising about 80%.

All jacamars excavate their nest cavities at the end of a tunnel 1–3 ft (1 m) long in earth banks and shelving ground. In the oval terminal chamber is laid the clutch of two or more round white eggs. FAMILY: Galbulidae, ORDER: Piciformes, CLASS: Aves.

JACANAS, or lily-trotters. There are seven species, distributed as follows. The American jacana *Jacana spinosa* from Mexico through Central and most of South America. In Africa, the lily-trotter *Actophilornis africana*, the Lesser lily-trotter *Microparra capensis*; with *Actophilornis albinucha* in Madagascar. From India through South-east Asia to the

A jacana's long toes enable it to walk on waterlily leaves without sinking in.

Despite their reputation for meanness, jackals are handsome dogs and the Side-striped jackal is the most handsome. It is less often seen than the other three jackals, being more shy, more silent and more often solitary. At most it forms only small packs.

Philippines is found the Pheasant-tailed jacana *Hydrophasianus chirurgus*, while the Bronze-winged jacana *Metopidius indicus* has a similar but more restricted range. Lastly the lotus-bird *Irediparra gallinacea* inhabits Indonesia and Australia.

The jacanas form a fairly uniform group of plover-like birds inhabiting the fringes of lakes and only differing amongst themselves in relatively trivial points. In length they are 6½–12 in (17–30 cm), except for the Pheasant-tailed jacana, the name of which suggests its principle feature, an 8 in (20 cm) tail which makes the bird 21 in (53 cm) long overall. The wings are long but rounded, the tail short in most species, the bill about the same length as the head or rather shorter and straight, and the legs long and thin. In addition, the toes are very long and the nails long and straight, especially the hind toenail, so that the jacana's weight is distributed widely by the foot, enabling it to walk nimbly over lily leaves.

Lily-trotters can usually be seen picking their way along the margins of sluggish rivers, water meadows, or well out in the open water of lakes with good water-lily beds, feeding on a variety of invertebrates and seeds.

Breeding takes place during the rainy season and the sexes participate equally in building the nest, a simple platform of leaves of water plants concealed in sedges at the edge of the water or built on floating vegeta-

tion, and in incubation. The four eggs are pointed and highly polished and are brown, heavily pencilled with irregular dark lines. FAMILY: Jacanidae, ORDER: Charadriiformes, CLASS: Aves.

JACKALS, carnivores very similar to dogs and wolves. There are four species distributed throughout Africa and southern Asia which, although similar in habits, differ markedly in appearance. The Golden jackal *Canis aureus*, ranging through southern Asia and North Africa, looks like a small wolf or coyote with a tawny coat and black markings on the back and tail. The much smaller Black-backed jackal *C. mesomelas*, inhabiting the plains of central and South Africa, has a black saddle extending along the back and a black stripe along the length of the tail; its sides and legs are bright rufous and it has large pointed ears. The Side-striped jackal *C. adustus*, greyer in colour and with a thin black and white stripe extending along the sides of the body, a black stripe along the tail, and a white tail tip, inhabits the African tropical forest or woodland areas with dense vegetation. Finally, in a very limited area in the highlands of Ethiopia, is the little-known Simenian jackal *C. simensis*, bright rufous in colouring and with a cream belly and black-tipped tail.

Like most dogs and wolves, the gestation of jackals is about two months.

Although often considered to be mainly

scavengers, they will also hunt and kill birds, hares, mice, lizards, turtles and various insects. Moreover, several individuals may band together in a small pack (especially the Side-striped jackal) to prey upon larger game like sheep, goats and small antelopes. Without a steady source of live prey, jackals will turn to fruits and vegetables for nourishment and will scavenge the kills of the larger African predators, like lions and hyaenas, or frequent the outskirts of towns and cities where they gather together at garbage dumps.

In hunting small prey, jackals typically stalk and then pounce suddenly, like foxes.

On the whole, jackals are solitary or associate in pairs although occasionally small packs form for brief periods. FAMILY: Canidae, ORDER: Carnivora, CLASS: Mammalia.

JACK DEMPSEY *Cichlasoma biocellatum*, a small freshwater fish of the Middle Amazon, reaches a length of 7 in (18 cm). The body is mottled brown with bright blue spots anteriorly and pale spots towards the tail. In the larger males a curious bulge develops on the forehead. FAMILY: Cichlidae, ORDER: Perciformes, CLASS: Pisces.

JAGUAR *Panthera onca*, the only big cat of America, the jaguar is sometimes confused with the leopard because both have spots in rosettes but those of the jaguar have a black spot at the centre. The yellowish buff ground colour is similar in both, but in the jaguar the

Jaguarundi

Female jaguar (below) and kittens (above) with the characteristic rosettes.

rosettes tend to be concentrated along the back. The belly and chest are pale and have irregularly placed black spots, and the lower half of the tail is ringed. There is a black mark near the mouth on the lower jaw, and the backs of the ears are black. The variations in colour range from an almost white ground colour to black forms, in which the rosettes can only be seen as a variation in texture. Jaguars are 5½–9 ft (1·7–2·7 m) overall, the tail being one third the total length. At the shoulder, they are 2¼–2½ ft (68–76 cm) high. The weight is 125–250 lb (56·7–113·4 kg), which makes it a heavier animal than the leopard or the puma. It is a good climber.

The jaguar inhabits an area bounded to the north by the southwestern USA and to the south by Argentina. It lives in thick cover, in forests or swamps, but it is also found in desert and savannah areas in the north and south of its range. Each individual has its own territory and this usually consists of an area of 2–5 sq miles (5–13 km²) although there have been records in the past of individuals that have travelled 500 miles (800 km) on their own, and more, for no apparent reason.

Jaguars are solitary, only coming together at mating time. After mating, the female has no more to do with the male and, after a gestation period of 95–105 days, the cubs are born. The usual size of a litter is two, fully furred at birth and blind. FAMILY: Felidae, ORDER: Carnivora, CLASS: Mammalia.

JAGUARUNDI *Felis yagouaroundi*, jaguarondi or yaguarondi, a cat shaped like an otter. It has very little in common with the jaguar. The average length is about 3½ ft (107 cm), of which a third is tail, while the height at the shoulder is only 11 in (28 cm). A well grown individual will weigh about 20 lb (9 kg).

There are two colour phases and for many years they were thought to be distinct species: either a black to brownish grey coat or tawny to chestnut. Neither is spotted. The brown form is known as the eyra. The grey form becomes somewhat darker in the winter months.

The jaguarundi is found in the extreme southwest of the USA, but is far less common than it used to be, because of the thinning out of the cover along the delta of the Rio Grande. Its southern limit is Paraguay. It appears to be an animal of the swamp and forest and is an excellent swimmer, from which it derives one of its many local names of 'otter cat'. In North America its favourite habitat is the chaparral scrub near water.

They are solitary, meeting only in the mating season, in November and December, or May and June. The young are born after a gestation of 70 days and the litter usually consists of two kittens, but there can be as many as four. The den is in a hollow log or among rocks. The young are unmarked at birth and the one litter may well contain both the grey form and the brown.

Jaguarundis prey on small mammals and game birds. They often cause havoc in pens of domestic fowl. FAMILY: Felidae, ORDER: Carnivora, CLASS: Mammalia.

JAYS, a diverse group of the crow family many of which are brightly-coloured—particularly in shades of blue—and have screeching, raucous voices.

The jays are most numerous in America, particularly in the tropics. The original bearer of the name, however, is the European jay *Garrulus glandarius*, a shy species found in most of Europe and east through Asia to Japan. It is a strikingly beautiful bird some 13 in (33 cm) long, with a pinkish brown body, black, white and blue wings and a black tail. The rump is white and the erectile crown feathers are streaked in black and white. Like many other jays it is omnivorous and will take eggs and chicks of other birds. It is a woodland bird and feeds to a large extent on acorns, of which it makes stores in autumn for use in the following winter and spring. The nest is a cup of twigs in which five to seven eggs are incubated for 16–17 days.

There are nearly 30 other species of jays in America, 20 in the tropical areas. The most common is the Blue jay *Cyanocitta cristata*, widespread in North America, mostly blue, with black and white on wings and tail. There are, however, several other species which are well-known, some of limited distribution. The Florida or Scrub jay *Aphelocoma caerulescens* is restricted to the scrub oak areas of Florida. Another ecologically restricted species is the Piñon jay *Gymnorhinus cyanocephala* of the mountains of the western United States.

The Turquoise jay *Cyanolyca turcosa*, of the Andes, is almost entirely turquoise blue. The Green jay *Cyanocorax yncas*, from Texas to Peru, is green above, yellow below, with a blue crest and yellow outer tail feathers. FAMILY: Corvidae, ORDER: Passeriformes, CLASS: Aves.

European jay in the snow. Jays bury acorns singly, in autumn, but seem able to go straight to them again, even under snow.

JELLYFISH, marine animal that swims under the surface of the sea with a pulsating bell and long trailing tentacles.

The bell varies from a wide saucer to a cube and may be grooved on the upper surface. Round the edge of the bell are a varying number of tentacles and the margin is scalloped into lappets. From the under-surface hangs an extension bearing a four-cornered mouth. The bell and arms are covered with stinging cells enabling the capture of food organisms over a large surface. Prey captured on the surface is carried to the edge of the bell by cilia, removed by the arms and conveyed to the mouth. CLASS: Scyphozoa, PHYLUM: Cnidaria.

JERBOAS, about 25 species of rodents in the deserts and steppes from central Asia to the Sahara. They progress by jumping on their very long hindlegs and feet in the manner of a kangaroo. The jerboas should not be confused with the gerbils which, although adapted to similar habitats, look more like typical rodents and are more closely related to the hamsters and voles.

Jerboas range from 1½ in (4 cm) excluding tail in some of the Dwarf jerboas of central Asia to 6 in (15 cm) in, for example, the North African jerboa *Jaculus orientalis*. The tail is always very long, sometimes over twice the length of the head and body, and in most species has a tuft of long white hairs at the tip. In one group, however, the Fat-tailed jerboas, *Pygeretmus*, of Turkestan, the tail is shorter than the head and body and contains large deposits of fat. The front legs are very small. The hindfeet are enormously elongate and in the larger species they enable the jerboa to make prodigious leaps of up to 8 ft (2·4 m). They usually have only three toes, and these are supported by a single strong foot-bone which results from the fusion of the three central metatarsals.

Like most desert animals, jerboas have either large external ears or enormously inflated auditory chambers in the skull. The Long-eared jerboa *Euchoreutes naso*, of Mongolia, has ears as big as a hare's. Its whiskers reach to the base of the exceedingly long thin tail. Equally bizarre are the Dwarf jerboas, *Salpingotus*, with very short external ears but enormous tympanic chambers that dwarf the rest of the skull and make the whole head as large as the rest of the body. These Dwarf jerboas are like tiny balls of fluff with grotesquely long whiskers and tail, minute front legs, and long hindfeet on which they progress in short hops so rapid that the legs seem to vibrate.

Most jerboas are sandy coloured and they lack bold markings except for the contrasting black and white tail-tip. The fur is extremely soft and silky, and the ear opening is protected from sand by long hairs. The hair of the feet is also closely adapted to life on sand, with dense fringes of hairs on the toes.

Jerboas are predominantly nocturnal, spending the day in burrows which may be quite elaborate, with several entrances and with one or more nest chambers. These burrows provide protection, not only against predators, but against the extremes of climate. In most Asiatic species the burrows are also used for hibernation.

Jerboas feed on seeds of grass, salt-bush and other desert plants, and especially on bulbs and tubers.

One of the best known is the Desert jerboa *Jaculus jaculus*, of the Sahara and Arabia, one of the larger species, capable of living in all but the most extreme desert conditions. FAMILY: Dipodidae, ORDER: Rodentia, CLASS: Mammalia.

JOHN DORIES, grotesque fishes of temperate oceans. John appears to be a nickname bestowed by fishermen. Dory is from the French *dorée* or golden, a reference to the shining yellow of the flanks. The John dory is also called the St Peter fish because legend has it that it was in this fish the apostle found the tribute money, the dark blotch on the flank being St Peter's thumbprint. Another name, given by fishermen in northern Germany, is 'King of the herrings' since it is reputed to shepherd the herring shoals. In reality, the John dory feeds on herrings, pilchards and sand-eels.

The John dory *Zeus faber* is an almost oval, compressed fish, 3 ft (100 cm) long, with the rays of the anterior spiny dorsal fin greatly elongated into filaments. The pelvic fins are also long. The jaws are protrusile and can be thrust out a surprisingly long way. This fish is found in depths down to 600 ft (200 m) and is widely distributed in the Atlantic from Scandinavia to South Africa. FAMILY: Zeidae, ORDER: Zeiformes, CLASS: Pisces.

JUNCOS, North American species of finch-like birds, the most common of which is the Slate-coloured junco *Junco hyemalis*, a bird of coniferous woodland, about 6 in (15 cm) long, with a dark slate-grey plumage. FAMILY: Emberizidae, ORDER: Passeriformes, CLASS: Aves.

JUNGLEFOWL, ancestors of modern domestic fowl, their general appearance closely resembling that of chickens, especially leghorns. Junglefowl are found from India eastwards but are absent from Borneo. They inhabit a wide variety of country from low-altitude forest, dry scrub and bamboo groves to small woods and rough ground near villages. They are always wild and extremely wary so that they continue to survive despite persecution by man. During the breeding season they are often found in family parties consisting of one cock and several hens and they congregate in larger flocks during the winter.

All junglefowl feed chiefly upon seeds, grain, shoots and buds, as well as insects.

There are four species of junglefowl. The best known and most widespread is the Red junglefowl *Gallus gallus*. The male resembles a Brown leghorn cockerel with his fiery red and golden-brown plumage. Red junglefowl exist in the genuine wild state from north-west India through Assam and Burma, Thailand and Malaya, to Indo-China in the east and also to south China, Sumatra and Java. Males of the Red junglefowl, if of pure stock, undergo a moult into dull plumage in the summer. They have a short shrill crow which ends abruptly. FAMILY: Phasianidae, ORDER: Galliformes, CLASS: Aves.

KAKAPO *Strigops habroptilus*, nocturnal New Zealand parrot, about 2 ft (60 cm) long, chiefly greenish-yellow with darker barring. It is almost flightless, the rounded wings being used only for gliding. The bill has strong ridges on the lower part. It is also called the 'Owl parrot' because of its 'facial disc' of feathers. The call is a weird bittern-like booming.

The kakapo used to be widespread in southern beech *Nothofagus* forests throughout the country, but is now drastically reduced in numbers. It runs along paths through the forest and grassland, but occasionally climbs trees and glides for some distance. The paths are maintained by its constantly trimming the surrounding vegetation and they lead from daytime resting places in holes among tree roots and rocks to feeding areas.

Kakapos breed in natural holes or construct tunnels of their own. The female incubates two to four white eggs in a bare nest from January to May.

Their food consists mainly of the leaves of tussock plants, berries and nectar. Fibrous material is thoroughly chewed to extract the juices and then rejected as a ball. FAMILY: Psittacidae, ORDER: Psittaciformes, CLASS: Aves.

KANGAROO, a marsupial animal with large hindfeet and strong hindlimbs and tail, which adopts a bipedal method of locomotion when moving quickly. The female bears a pouch, containing the teats, in which the young is raised. In its widest sense the name kangaroo is applied to 50 kinds of animals, from the tiny Musky rat kangaroo *Hypsiprymnodon*, weighing a little over 1 lb (500 gm) to the largest Grey and Red kangaroos which approach 200 lb (90 kg) in weight and reach a height of 6 ft and occasionally 7 ft (2 m).

Kangaroos may be divided into Rat kangaroos and the true kangaroos. Of the latter, the largest are called kangaroos while the smaller are called wallabies. There is, however, no real criterion by which kangaroos and wallabies may be distinguished. Attempts have been made to do so on the

Kea

Female Red kangaroo with a Joey in her pouch, a forerunner of the carry-cot.

length of hindfoot but have proved unsuccessful. Some species fall into the kangaroo group on one criterion and the wallaby group on the other. Thus, the group generally called Tree kangaroos are wallaby-sized animals.

Kangaroos are heavily built in the hindquarters and lightly built in the forequarters; the forelimbs are thin, mobile and frequently used in bringing food to the mouth. The tail is heavily built in the largest kangaroos and serves to balance the forepart of the body, being held clear of the ground during bipedal locomotion. It is used as a prop during bipedal stance and may be the only part touching the ground during fighting when a kangaroo can kick an opponent using both hindfeet together. During quadrupedal locomotion the tail 'walks' along, behind the kangaroo, and leaves a characteristic track on soft ground. The foot is very long and bears four toes. The second and third are very small and bound together by skin, a condition known as syndactyly.

Kangaroos generally produce a single young at a time. The gestation period varies between 29 and 38 days in the large kangaroos. A female kangaroo about to give birth cleans the inside of her pouch by licking it, and then assumes a resting position with her back supported, hind legs extended forwards and tail passed forwards between them. The baby climbs through the mother's fur and into the pouch where it attaches itself to one of the teats. Rates of development of young in the pouch vary from species to species. Red kangaroo young leave the pouch when seven to eight months old but Grey kangaroo *Macropus giganteus* young occupy the pouch for almost a year.

The Hill kangaroos *Osphranter robustus*, are distinguished from most kangaroos by having a hairless area around the nostrils. The Red kangaroo *Megaleia rufa* inhabits plains country with scattered trees.

The Tree kangaroos *Dendrolagus* consist of six species of animals of stocky build which retain the non-prehensile tail and general hindlimb structure of their terrestrial kangaroo ancestors. In returning to the trees they have redeveloped the ability to move their hindfeet independently; terrestrial kangaroos are able only to move them together. Tree kangaroos weigh up to about 25 lb (11 kg) and have a head and body length of 27 in (70 cm), the tail being about as long as the head and body. FAMILY: Macropodidae, ORDER: Marsupialia, CLASS: Mammalia.

KEA *Nestor notabilis*, a New Zealand mountain parrot, largely olive-green with dark edges to the feathers, with wing and tail quills bluish-green. Keas are now found only in the South Island of New Zealand.

The nest is usually placed in a rock crevice or a hollow log. The two to four white eggs are usually laid between July and January.

Keas are not popular with sheep farmers, because around 1870 it was suspected they were attacking sheep and they rapidly acquired a reputation as killers. Since then thousands of keas have been shot. However, a recent analysis showed that the keas' bad reputation was ill founded. FAMILY: Psittacidae, ORDER: Psittaciformes, CLASS: Aves.

KESTRELS, falcons that hover for ground prey, rather than taking prey in flight. There are about ten species of true kestrel, with four others regarded as aberrant kestrels.

New Zealand mountain parrot, with its long, only slightly curved beak, which distinguishes it from other parrots.

The European kestrel always lands on the ground to seize its prey.

The Pygmy kingfisher *Ispidina pictus*, recognizable by its violet collar.

The average size is 11½ in (29 cm), the largest being the Fox kestrel *F. alopex* of Africa reaching 15 in (38 cm) and the smallest the Seychelles kestrel *F. araea* of 8–9 in (20–23 cm). Females are usually larger than males. The coloration of the upper-parts is typically reddish-brown spotted black; underneath they are more buff, streaked and barred black. Males are often distinguished by the inclusion of grey on the upper-parts.

The Common kestrel *F. tinnunculus*, of Europe, Asia and Africa, replaced in the New World by the similar American kestrel *F. sparverius*, commonly known as the sparrow-hawk in America. Other species occupy the islands in the Indian and Pacific oceans: the Australian or Nankeen kestrel *F. cenchroides* is the kestrel of Australia and New Guinea. Throughout their range kestrels occupy open habitat, but this can be desert, savannah, cultivated, partially wooded or mountainous. They also now occur commonly in cities and suburbs.

Kestrels lay their eggs on ledges, in holes and in the old nests of other species. Incubation is by the female alone, the male hunting and bringing food to the vicinity of the nest. The principal food is small mammals, but their diet may be largely insectivorous; small reptiles, frogs, worms and birds are also taken. FAMILY: Falconidae, ORDER: Falconiformes, CLASS: Aves.

KILLER WHALE *Orcinus orca*, or grampus, a true dolphin. The males reach whale proportions of 30 ft (10 m) and it has always been said that the females are only half this size, rarely reaching 20 ft (7 m). During 1948–1957, however, Nishiwaki measured 600 Killer whales caught in Japanese waters and found the average adult lengths to be 21 ft (6·4 m) for males and 20 ft (6 m) for females. Killer whales have a black back and white belly with a large white patch behind the eye. The flippers are large and rounded; the dorsal fin is up to 6 ft (1·8 m) high.

The Killer whale eats dolphins and por-poises, seals and sealions, penguins, fish and squid. Even the largest Whalebone whales may be attacked and killed by a hunting pack of Killer whales of up to 40 or more.

Killer whales are found throughout the world but most frequently in arctic and antarctic waters.

The False killer whale *Pseudorca crassidens*, up to 16 ft (5 m), is black almost all over, slimmer than the Killer whale with a narrower flipper and smaller dorsal fin whilst the snout is rather rounded over the lower jaw. FAMILY: Delphinidae, ORDER: Cetacea, CLASS: Mammalia.

KINGFISHERS, 87 species of birds related to the bee-eaters, hornbills, motmots and others and sharing with them a syndactyl foot, the three front toes being joined for part of their length. They are divided into two subfamilies: Alcedininae and Daceloninae, the former being the fishing kingfishers with long narrow, sharp-pointed bills, and the latter the Forest kingfishers which often live far from water and whose bills are broader, flatter and sometimes hooked at the tip. The best-known is the *kookaburra.

The Common kingfisher *Alcedo atthis* is found in Europe, Africa and the Far East, eastward to the Solomon Islands. It is a dumpy bird only 6½ in (16·6 cm) long. The azure feathers of its back can also look emerald green depending upon the angle of the light. The underparts are a warm chestnut orange. It has a white throat or bib, white neck patches and orange cheek patches behind the eye. The 1½ in (3·8 cm) dagger-shaped bill is the only external indication of the sex. In an adult male it is wholly black, but the female usually has a partially or completely rose-coloured lower mandible. The small feet and legs are sealing wax red.

Kingfishers live mainly on unpolluted rivers, lakes and streams, canals and fen drains. They also inhabit tidal estuaries, salt marshes, gutters and rocky sea shores, especially in the winter when driven to the coast because fresh water has frozen over.

The chief prey is fish, which the kingfisher secures underwater by grasping the fish between its mandibles, not by stabbing as is the popular misconception. The diet also includes tadpoles, small molluscs and Crustacea.

The nest is in a tunnel in a bank, to a depth of 3 ft (0·9 m) and sloping upwards. Seven eggs are laid in a spherical chamber at the end and the parents share the incubation and the feeding of the chicks, which hatch after 19–21 days. FAMILY: Alcedinidae, ORDER: Coraciiformes, CLASS: Aves.

KINGLET, a small warbler-like bird of North America related to the European *goldcrest. There are two species, the Golden-crowned kinglet *Regulus sapatra* and the Ruby-crowned kinglet *R. calendula*.

KINKAJOU, or 'Honey bear' *Potos flavus*, South American member of the raccoon family living in forests from Mexico to Brazil. This agile climber is a long, low-bodied animal the forelegs of which are shorter than the hind ones. The most outstanding feature is the prehensile tail which serves as a fifth grip, when moving cautiously through the tree tops. Cat-sized, kinkajous measure 31½–44½ in (81–113 cm) overall, the tail being at least as long as the body, and weigh from 3–6 lb (1·4–2·7 kg). The ears are small, placed low on either side of the round head in line with the dark, sparkling eyes. General coat colour varies from golden yellow to brown and the fur's texture is soft and woolly. During their noctural forays, they travel singly or, during the breeding season, in pairs. Favourite foods include fruit, insects and nestlings. FAMILY: Procyonidae, ORDER: Carnivora, CLASS: Mammalia.

KITES, birds of prey whose smooth gliding has given its name to man-made flying devices. They include many and diverse

Koala, Australian Teddy Bear, lives in trees and is tied to a diet of eucalyptus.

species throughout the world. The Black kite *Milvus migrans* is one of the commonest in the Old World where it scavenges in thousands in towns and villages in Asia. The Red kite *M. milvus* formerly scavenged the streets of London and other European cities. The Everglade kite *Rostrhamus sociabilis*, of the United States breeds in colonies and feeds exclusively on snails. The Brahminy kite *Haliastus indus*, regarded as sacred in India, lives in swamps and feeds on frogs and offal. FAMILY: Accipitridae, ORDER: Falconiformes, CLASS: Aves.

KITTIWAKE *Rissa tridactyla*, medium-sized, lightly-built gull of the open sea. It is more oceanic than other gulls, being found over the open sea outside the breeding season rather than near the coasts. It nests on precarious cliff ledges. The average length is 16 in (40 cm). The wing tips are entirely black without the white 'mirrors' seen in many other gulls, and the legs also are black. The bill is yellow. The plumage is grey above and white beneath. Juveniles, however, have a striking plumage-pattern with a black neck band and tail tip and a long, black shallow 'V' stretching the length of each wing.

The kittiwake is widely distributed around coasts in the northern hemisphere. FAMILY: Laridae, ORDER: Charadriiformes, CLASS: Aves.

KIWI, three species of flightless New Zealand bird standing about 18 in (45 cm) high and lacking a tail and visible wings.

Their feathers are grey or brown and hair-like in texture. Their eyes seem to be rather ineffective, at least during the day, but they have prominent ear openings and a keen sense of smell. The long slender bill is remarkably adapted for probing into soil, with the tip of the upper mandible covering that

of the lower and bearing the nostrils on either side . This tip seems also to have a highly-developed sense of touch.

They are birds of the damp New Zealand forests, feeding at night on worms, insects and berries. They are rarely seen, not because of rarity, but rather because they are shy and can move nimbly through the forest at night.

The male finds or excavates a hole beneath the roots of a tree, or in a bank, and builds the nest. The female's sole task is to produce the enormous eggs (usually two), each about a quarter of her weight. The male incubates the eggs for about 75 days, and though the chicks can find their own food soon after hatching they stay with their father for a considerable time. FAMILY: Apterygidae, ORDER: Apterygiformes, CLASS: Aves.

KNIFEFISHES, three families of South American freshwater fishes related to the Electric eel. There is a very long anal fin and these fishes swim gracefully by passing a series of undulations along this. The elongated and whip-like tail is in some species used as a probe when the fish is swimming backwards. Often, the tail is bitten off by other fishes, but this does not seem to cause the owner much distress and a new tail is grown. Like the Electric eel, the knifefishes have electric organs along the flanks. Impulses are discharged intermittently at a rate of up to 1,000 per second and this system is used for the location of food or other objects around the fish.

One well-known species is the Banded knifefish *Gymnotus carapo*, often imported for aquarists. The body is light brown with vertical dark bars that coalesce on the back. It reaches 2 ft (60 cm) in length and is peaceful with other species but is liable to attack members of its own. It is best fed on meat and live foods, and may eventually take food

from the hand of its owner.

The largest of knifefishes, *Rhamphichthys rostratus*, is a food fish of the Amazon region that reaches 4 ft (1·2 m) in length. FAMILIES: Gymnotidae, Rhamphichthyidae, Apteronotidae, ORDER: Cypriniformes, CLASS: Pisces.

KOALA *Phascolarctos cinereus*, a small bearlike marsupial, 2 ft (60 cm) high and averaging 20 lb (9 kg), with tufted ears and prominent beak-like snout. Its fur is thick, ash-grey with a tinge of brown in places, yellowish-white on the hindquarters and white underneath. The tail is vestigial, as are the cheek pouches. The pouch of the female opens to the rear. The first two toes of the forefeet are opposable to the other three. The present-day range is eastern coastal Australia southwards from 20°S, with reintroductions into South Australia.

Mating is from September to January, the single young, born after a gestation of 35 days, makes its way unaided by the mother through the opening of the birth canal up through the fur to the pouch. When it leaves the pouch it is carried on the mother's back.

'Koala' is an aboriginal word meaning 'no water' and refers to an alleged lack of drinking, but koalas will drink from pools of water left after rain. FAMILY: Phascolarctidae, ORDER: Marsupialia, CLASS: Mammalia.

KOB *Kobus kob*, antelope related to the waterbuck and found from south-western Kenya through the savannah zone west to Senegal; and on the Bijagos islands. A male kob stands 34–36 in high (85–90 cm) and weighs 200–220 lb (90–100 kg), a female weighs only 137–145 lb (62–66 kg). The colour varies geographically from reddish orange to nearly black, with white round the eyes and base of the ears; there is a black line down the front of the forelegs; and the muzzle, lips, underside, insides of the thighs and a band above the hoofs are white. FAMILY: Bovidae, ORDER: Artiodactyla, CLASS: Mammalia.

KOMODO DRAGON *Varanus komodoensis*, of the small island of Komodo, east of Java, is usually regarded as the largest living lizard. It reaches at least 10 ft (3 m) long and weighs 360 lb (163 kg). However, Salvador's monitor *V. salvadorii*, although of more slender build, is believed to reach 15 ft (4·6 m) long. FAMILY: Varanidae, ORDER: Squamata, CLASS: Reptilia.

KONGONI *Alcelaphus buselaphus cokii*, or Coke's hartebeest, one of the subspecies of the Common *hartebeest.

KOOKABURRA *Dacelo gigas*, also known as the Laughing kookaburra, Laughing jackass, or simply as Jack, the largest Australian kingfisher, named for its wild laughing cry.

There is a second, slightly smaller, species the Blue-winged kookaburra *D. leachi* in northern Australia. FAMILY: Alcedinidae, ORDER: Coraciiformes, CLASS: Aves.

KORRIGUM *Damaliscus lunatus korrigum*, one of the 'bastard' *hartebeests related to the bontebok and blesbok.

KOUPREY *Bos (Bibos) sauveli*, species of wild ox closely related to the banteng, and less closely to the gaur. Kouprey bulls stand up to 6 ft 4 in (190 cm) high and are blackish in colour with white 'stockings' on the legs. FAMILY: Bovidae, ORDER: Artiodactyla, CLASS: Mammalia.

KRAITS, highly venomous southeast Asian snakes. The widely distributed Banded krait *Bungarus fasciatus* and the Indian krait *B. coeruleus* of India and Ceylon are probably the most common. The Banded krait has a warning coloration of pale yellow with glossy black bands, and grows to about 4 ft (120 cm). FAMILY: Elapidae, ORDER: Squamata, CLASS: Reptilia.

KUDU, a large striped African antelope, with preorbital glands and in which the males have keeled spiral horns.

The Greater kudu *Tragelaphus strepsiceros*, of Africa, ranging from north of the Orange River to Somalia, southern Sudan and Lake Chad, is 4 ft 2 in–4 ft 5 in (127–134 cm) high, weighs 600 lb (270 kg) and its horns average 40 in (1 m) long, with an open

spiral of at least two and a half turns. It has a long throat fringe and mane on the nuchal and dorsal mid-line, is greyish with legs rich fawn below the knees and hocks, has white spots above the hoofs and four to ten white transverse body-stripes. The Lesser kudu *T. imberbis*, of northern Tanzania to Sudan, northern Ethiopia and Somalia, is 3 ft 4 in

(1 m) high, its horns average 2 ft (61 cm) long, with a close spiral of two and a half turns or more, no throat fringe, but a white crescent on the throat instead.

Kudus are wary animals, living mostly in hilly or broken country with thorn bushes or tall grass. Lesser kudus form herds of up to six animals which remain together the year round, but Greater kudus split up into small groups of one to four in the rains, and form bigger herds up to 14 head in the dry season. Bulls are more often solitary than cows, and are always extremely shy and difficult to approach. They hide by day and browse, rather than graze, at dawn and dusk. When disturbed, kudus pause in mide-stride, then race away, leaping over bushes as high as 8½ ft (2½ m); a Lesser kudu has been recorded as jumping 30 ft 8 in (9·2 m) on the ground, while clearing a bush of 5 ft (1·5 m) high. Kudus run with their tails, which are white underneath, curled back over the rump and, after a short dash, they invariably stop to look back.

Bushbuck are found in forest and brush, and are adept at pushing their way through undergrowth. The males lay their horns back along the neck to avoid entanglements often rubbing a small bare patch on their necks. They make a characteristic barking alarm call. Both sexes have large territories, 5–7 acres (2–3 ha) in extent. They leave the territories in the evenings to graze, in clearings in groups of up to ten, or to browse on the forest edge. FAMILY: Bovidae, ORDER: Artiodactyla, CLASS: Mammalia.

Bull Greater kudu, one of the largest antelopes, alert and shy, very difficult to approach.

L

LACEWINGS, insects, 1in (2·5 cm) long with gauzy wings.

The Green lacewing is known to fishermen as the Goldeye gauzewing, for the adult is a pale green, its four translucent wings are iridescent and it has large gold-coloured eyes. The common British species, *Chrysopa flava,* is abundant as an adult in late summer and is often seen when it flies indoors to hibernate in September and October. Lacewings emerge from hibernation in the late spring and lay their stalked eggs, each like a tiny white pin, singly on leaves. The larvae are active carnivores and feed principally on aphids.

Since they are common insects and their larvae destroy large numbers of aphids, they are an important natural control of such pests. FAMILY: Chrysopidae, ORDER: Neuroptera, CLASS: Insecta, PHYLUM: Arthropoda.

LADYBIRDS, small tortoise-shaped, brightly coloured beetles, among the best-loved of all insects, although few people associate the spiny larvae with the attractive adult. Most of the 5,000 species are between $\frac{1}{10} - \frac{3}{10}$ in (2·5–7·5 mm) long. The larvae are often greyish with darker spots, but others may be dark with white or orange markings.

Ladybirds are world-wide. The Two-spot ladybird *Adalia bipunctata* is either red with two black spots or black with four or six red spots. Also common is the Seven-spot ladybird *Coccinella 7-punctata* (red with seven black spots) and the small yellow and black spotted ladybird, *Thea 22-punctata.*

The eggs of ladybirds are yellow or orange and are laid in masses on leaves with each of the elongated eggs at right angles to the surface. They hatch in a few days and the larval stage is followed by the pupa which is formed in an exposed position, often on a leaf surface. The pupa is only attached at its extreme hind end and if disturbed it can lift the whole body upwards from its point of attachment.

The female ladybird lays her eggs close to thriving aphid colonies, so when the larvae emerge their prey is close at hand. Each larval ladybird consumes 200–500 aphids and the adults eat many more. FAMILY: Coccinellidae, ORDER: Coleoptera, CLASS: Insecta, PHYLUM: Arthropoda.

LAMPREYS, primitive jawless fishes found in both fresh water and the sea. The body is eel-like and there is a round, sucking mouth lined with horny teeth with which the lampreys rasp away at their prey. An old name for lampreys is nine-eyes, a reference to the seven external gill openings, the median nostril and the eye. In Britain there are three species, the River lamprey *Lampetra fluviatilis,* the Brook or Planer's lamprey *L. planeri* and the Sea lamprey *Petromyzon marinus,* which is found on both sides of the Atlantic. Many species are parasitic when adult, feeding on the flesh of living fishes. A few fresh water species in North America are non-parasitic and do not feed at all as adults, merely breeding and dying. Lampreys lack paired fins but have either one or two dorsal fins and a tailfin. The gills are contained in muscular pouches which open to the exterior by a series of seven small apertures but are connected internally to a canal which opens in the mouth. The skeleton is of cartilage.

River lampreys move upstream to breed but the Sea lampreys make a major migration from the sea into fresh waters, using their sucker mouths to ascend rapids and waterfalls. Crude nests are made by both parents, the mouths being used to remove stones to form a hollow of about 2 ft (60 cm) in diameter. Many thousands of eggs are laid by the female but after they have been fertilized both parents die. From each egg hatches a blind, worm-like larva quite unlike the parents and known as an ammocoete or pride. FAMILY: Petromyzontidae, ORDER: Cyclostomata, CLASS: Agnatha.

LAMPSHELLS, marine mollusc-like animals, so named from the resemblance between their shells and ancient Roman oil lamps.

They are represented today by about 260 species none of which is very common. Their fossil history is, however, extensive: at least

South African ladybird *Chiomenes lunata* laying eggs. The larvae feed on aphids.

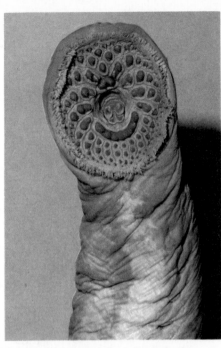

The suctorial, funnel-shaped mouth of a
Sea lamprey, armed with horny teeth.

30,000 extinct species are known and their
remains are abundant in certain deposits. The
phylum is divided into two classes: the hinged
brachiopods or Articulata, and the un-

hinged brachiopods or Inarticulata in which
the valves lack any locating mechanism.

All living forms, and most fossils, are less
than 3 in (8 cm) long, but a few extinct
species reached over a foot (37 cm) in width.
The animal is enclosed within a bivalved shell
and usually attached by a long flexible stalk.
The two valves of the shell are dorsal and
ventral, not left and right as in bivalve
molluscs. PHYLUM: Brachiopoda.

LANCELET, a small, marine fish-like animal
about 1½ in (3·7 cm) in length, with one
species on the Californian coast growing to
3 in (7·6 cm). Lancelets usually burrow in
rather coarse sand or shell-gravel at a depth of
15–90 ft (5–30 m), but they may occur in
shallower waters or even in intertidal sands in
coastal regions or brackish lagoons that are
protected from wave action. Their distribution is worldwide between latitudes 70°N and
50°S.

The animal has no head and is pointed at
both ends and was formerly known as
Amphioxus. It has a median fin down the
back, around the tail, and forward along the
ventral surface. Its anatomy suggests that it
may represent the primitive stock from which
vertebrates sprang. SUBPHYLUM: Cephalochordata, PHYLUM: Chordata.

LAND CRABS, any large crustaceans living
much of their life on land. They are mostly
true crabs, but in North America crayfish are
often known as crabs and some have left the
water to burrow in marsh or swamp. These
'Land' crabs can be a serious pest of cotton
nipping off young shoots as they push up out
of the ground.

In West Africa the species of *Sesarma* inhabit mangrove swamps and one, the West
African Land crab burrows in marshy
ground, also damaging newly planted crops.
CLASS: Crustacea, PHYLUM: Arthropoda.

LANGOUSTE *Palinurus vulgaris*, or craw-
fish, a Spiny lobster with small claws and very
long antennae, up to 10 in (25 cm) long,
reddish-brown blotched with purple, lives on
rocky bottoms offshore in the warmer eastern
Atlantic water. Famous as a French delicacy,
it has a remarkable larva, broad and flattened,
paper-thin and transparent as glass, with long
spidery legs and large black eyes on long
stalks. In warm seas the larva may be 3 in
(7·5 cm) long but usually it is ½ in (12 mm).
FAMILY: Palinuridae, ORDER: Decapoda,
CLASS: Crustacea, PHYLUM: Arthropoda.

LANGURS, leaf-eating monkeys of Asia.
They are soft-haired, with long hands and

The Spiny lobster or langouste of the Caribbean.

fingers but with only a small thumb and they lack cheek pouches. They are arboreal, almost entirely vegetarian and range from the Himalayas to Borneo. The largest, the hanuman or Entellus monkey is 30 in (75 cm) head and body with the tail 38 in (95 cm) long and weighs 50 lb (22 kg). It lives in large troops in wooded country but invades the villages, where it is held sacred by the Hindus. It feeds mainly on leaves but also eats fruit, berries and grain. Other well-known langurs are the Snub-nosed monkey *Rhinopithecus roxellanae* of the forests of Tibet, large with a thick coat, associated with the Yeti legend, the Proboscis monkey *Nasalis larvatus* of Borneo, the old males of which have a trunk-like proboscis 7 in (18 cm) long, and the Douc langur *Pygathrix remaea* of Indo-China a grizzled silvery grey with pure white arms, rump and tail, and black thighs and hands. The Proboscis monkey lives near rivers and dives and swims well. FAMILY: Cercopithecidae, ORDER: Primates, CLASS: Mammalia.

LANNER *Falco biarmicus*, 37·5 cm long in Africa to 42·5 cm in southern Europe. It is distinguished from the peregrine by its medium-sized rust-coloured head, streaked in black, and in Africa also by its larger size and different streaked or spotted underparts. Its habits are similar to those of the gyr falcon. FAMILY Falconidae, ORDER: Falconiformes, CLASS: Aves.

LAPWING *Vanellus vanellus*, also known as peewit from its distinctive call. It is a large wading plover with broad rounded wings, easily recognized by its long crest and black and white plumage. The black on the upperparts is shot with metallic green giving it an alternative name of Green plover. Lapwings live in Europe and Asia from the British Isles to Manchuria, feeding in large flocks, sometimes in the company of starlings and gulls, on pasture fields, around lakes and mudflats. They are welcomed by the farmer as they feed mainly on insects in the soil. The male has a spectacular breeding display flight after which it makes scrapes in the ground for the female to choose one for her nest. It is lined with grasses and the 3–5 eggs vary from clay-coloured to olive-green covered with dark spots and streaks. The eggs are incubated mainly by the female and the young leave the nest soon after hatching. FAMILY: Charadriidae, ORDER: Charadriiformes, CLASS: Aves.

LARKS, 75 species of small terrestrial songbirds. They are usually streaked brown above and more or less streaked below. The hind claw is often much elongated. They usually walk or run, sometimes at speed, many species preferring to do this than to take flight. They are renowned the world over for their beautiful songs, usually delivered on the

Short-toed lark *Calandrella cinerea*.

wing. They are generally regarded as the most primitive of true songbirds, and are almost entirely Old World in distribution, particularly well represented in Africa, 80% of the species occurring there. Larks live in a great variety of open habitats, from cultivated meadows and steppe country, wasteland and semi-arid sparsely vegetated areas, to sandy and rocky wastes, arctic tundra and absolute desert.

Larks are invariably ground nesters. The nest is a loose cup of dead grass and occasionally hair or wool, placed in a depression in the ground, usually in the shelter of a tuft of grass or a rock. In some species of Bush larks and Long-billed larks, the nest is a more complex structure, partially domed, and very well hidden. In several desert species a small wall of pebbles, up to ¾ in (2 cm) high, is erected on the exposed side of the nest, presumably to afford some protection from the wind. The usual clutch is three to five eggs which are generally white or whitish, heavily streaked or speckled with grey or brown.

The skylark, *Alauda arvensis* of Europe, delivers a loud and clear warbling, which may be sustained for as long as 5 min, whilst hovering in the air above its territory, sometimes at a great height. FAMILY: Alaudidae, ORDER: Passeriformes, CLASS: Aves.

Leaf-fish *Nandus nebulosus* of southeast Asia.

LEAF BEETLES, a very large group of beetles comprising 30,000 species. Many are small, often no more than a few millimetres long, but they are strikingly patterned and coloured. They feed on living leaf material and include some of the most destructive agricultural pests, such as the Colorado beetle, the Potato beetle, the Asparagus beetle, the Beet tortoise beetle and the Elm leaf beetle. See Colorado beetle. FAMILY: Chrysomelidae, ORDER: Coleoptera, CLASS: Insecta, PHYLUM: Arthropoda.

LEAF BIRDS, eight species of *Chloropsis*, related to bulbuls, living in southeast Asia from southern China to the Philippines. They are mainly pale green, with a slightly curved bill, and they feed on fruit, berries, insects, nectar and pollen. The males have more colourful markings, with more black, orange and blue on the head. The largest and most brilliantly marked is the Orange-bellied leaf bird *C. hardwickii*, 8 in (20 cm) long, which ranges from northern India to Malaya. The Golden-fronted leafbird *C. aurifrons* of India eastwards is popular as a cagebird. They are good singers and accomplished mimics. FAMILY: Irenidae, ORDER: Passeriformes, CLASS: Aves.

LEAF FISHES, tropical freshwater fishes from South America, West Africa and southeast Asia which resemble floating leaves. The most famous is the *Monocirrhus polyacanthus* from the Amazon and Rio Negro basins of South America. The body is leaf-shaped and tapers towards the snout where a small barbel increases the camouflage by resembling the stalk of the leaf. The general body colour is a mottled brown, matching dead leaves. It grows to about 4 in (10 cm) and drifts with the current, head usually downwards until it approaches a small fish on which it can feed. It can engulf fishes half its own size. FAMILY: Nandidae, ORDER: Perciformes, CLASS: Pisces.

LEAF INSECT, the name given to some large tropical insects which have the body flattened and the wings expanded in such a way that they look like leaves. Usually they are green, although some are brown, and the veins on the wings are arranged and picked out in another colour so that they resemble the veins of a leaf. FAMILY: Phasmidae, ORDERS: Orthoptera, Phasmida, CLASS: Insecta, PHYLUM: Arthropoda.

LEATHERY TURTLE *Dermochelys coriacea*, or leatherback, the largest of the Marine turtles, found in all tropical and subtropical seas, from where it wanders into temperate regions. The bony carapace, which may reach a length of 6 ft (1·8 m) is not joined to the vertebrae and ribs and consists of a mosaic of bony platelets covered with a leathery skin. The species is recognized by the seven ridges, often notched, which run lengthwise over the back. The plastron consists of four pairs of bony rods, arranged to form an oval ring; more superficially six rows of keeled platelets are present. The Leathery turtle is blackish above with numerous scattered, small irregular whitish or pinkish spots; below it is white with black markings. Its food consists mainly of jellyfish and salps. Although it breeds all through the tropics, only a few nesting beaches are known where large numbers of females come ashore to deposit their eggs. FAMILY: Dermochelidae, ORDER: Testudines, CLASS: Reptilia.

LEECHES. Some years ago the most familiar leech—at least to the wealthier classes—would have been the Medicinal leech *Hirudo medicinalis* much used by physicians in 'blood letting'. This practice was believed to be a relief for almost all imaginable ills, 'vapours' and 'humours'. Their medicinal value may be questioned, but the ability of the leeches to gorge themselves with blood in a relatively short time, and their related ability to fast for long periods between each meal, are certainly adaptations to their more normal existence in the wild. There, meals are available only at intervals and entirely in the lap of chance. The Medicinal leech has three sharp teeth which form a characteristic triradiate wound in the skin. When a leech bites, an anti-clotting saliva is poured into the wound and this prevents the blood from clotting and keeps it liquid within the leech's body.

The buccal cavity (or mouth cavity) leads into an enormous crop where the meal of blood can be stored. The crop is capable of great distention, to enable large meals to be taken as opportunity permits. Most of the gut in fact is storage crop, the part where absorption of the digested contents takes place being quite restricted.

A fully grown Medicinal leech can survive for a year on a single meal though it probably feeds more often than this. Some leeches feed on other annelids such as earthworms, or insect larvae, and may either suck their body fluids or swallow them whole. Most of the small leeches commonly found in ponds and streams in fact feed on other small invertebrates, such as worms, insect larvae or snails.

Leeches are easily recognized. Their soft bodies are annulated, usually without external projections and with a prominent often circular sucker at the posterior end. There is another sucker around the mouth, and although this may be quite prominent as in fish leeches, it frequently is not. CLASS: Hirudinea, PHYLUM: Annelida.

LEMMINGS, small rodents, about 3–6 in (7·5–15 cm) in length, closely related to voles, characteristic of the Arctic tundra. The fur is long, soft and dense, and the extremities are short, the ears being scarcely visible in the long fur and the tail just long enough to be seen. The Collared lemmings, *Dicrostonyx*, extend farther north than any other rodent, being found on the north coast of Greenland at a latitude of over 80° North, and these are the only rodents that turn white in winter. The Norway lemming *Lemmus lemmus* is boldly patterned with a black head and a large black patch on the back on a yellowish-brown background. All lemmings have strong claws by which they dig tunnels amongst the roots of the tundra heaths and grasses. In summer these are normal in shape, but in winter the Collared lemming develops two peculiar, enlarged, forked claws on the front feet, for digging in frozen snow.

Lemmings are known, above all, for their periodic mass emigrations, best known in the Norway lemming of Scandinavia, but the phenomenon occurs to some extent in all species. One reason why it appears more spectacular in Scandinavia is the mountainous nature of the country. When the mountain lemmings begin to disperse they can only move downhill and they are then concentrated in the valleys until, in the major 'lemming years', great rivers of lemmings seem to be flowing down the valleys towards the lowland fields and forests. The reasons for these periodic eruptions are still poorly

The Norwegian lemming, once believed to make suicidal migrations into the sea.

understood, but a great many of the myths that surround the subject can safely be exploded. They do not move persistently in one direction; they do not follow leaders; they do not plunge recklessly into the sea and commit suicide. Mass movements of lemmings are very aimless, although they may travel several miles each day. The animals are very aggressive, especially when they become crowded. When they come to water, they are very reluctant to swim, and it seems that they will only take to the water if it is calm and they can see the other side. They are competent swimmers but their small size makes them vulnerable and, if the water is at all rough, they drown, so that it is not uncommon for large numbers of dead lemmings to be found washed up on the shores of fjords. Others, however, survive and may settle down to form temporary breeding colonies far from the normal range. FAMILY: Cricetidae, ORDER: Rodentia, CLASS: Mammalia.

LEMURS, small relatives of monkeys found only on Madagascar and small nearby islands. They are mostly cat-sized, a few being mouse-sized, usually with a long tail and fox-like muzzle, and mainly nocturnal and arboreal. Their food may be insects to small mammals and fruit, and the incisors of the lower jaw, projecting forwards with the canines lying along each side, are comb-like and used for scooping out soft fruit as well as for combing the fur.

Mouse lemurs are among the smallest of primates, the smallest of them weighing only 2 oz (60 gm) and being 5 in (13 cm) long in both body and tail. They construct spherical leafnests wedged between fine branches, or live in hollow trees lined with a few leaves. The related Dwarf lemur is about the size of a large rat and weighs about 8 oz (250 gm).

The largest and best known lemur is the Ring-tailed lemur *Lemur catta*, grey with white underparts and black markings on the hands, face and tail. The tail has alternating rings of black and white fur. It is cat-sized, 14 in (35 cm) head and body length with a tail 16 in (40 cm) long, and one of its many vocalizations is a cat-like miaouw. The eyes are large and forward-pointing, the muzzle dog-like. There are large, canine teeth, slightly exposed when the animal is in a mildly threatening mood, this being reinforced by the glaring quality of the eyes, which have a yellow iris. This is the commonest lemur in zoos, and it seems to be one of the most dangerous. Many a zoo attendant has been badly bitten by a Ring-tailed lemur.

The Ring-tailed lemur, by contrast with all other lemurs that rarely leave the trees, seems to be equally at home on the ground and can be seen eating, playing and resting at all levels in the forest. When walking on the ground, it holds its tail erect in an S-shape, and it is a common sight to see a group

Leopard

The Fat-tailed dwarf lemur *Cheirogaleus medius* accumulates fat in its tail prior to aestivating during the dry season.

walking along the ground in the sunshine with their tails held aloft like flags.

Its basic diet is provided by a wide range of fruits, flowers and leaves.

It assembles in troops of up to two dozen, which move around, eat and sleep together. Social grooming between group members is common and the group moves, feeds and sleeps in a fairly distinct home range which is defended against neighbouring groups.

The Ring-tailed lemur has the richest vocal repertoire of all lemurs, including clicks, grunts, explosive snorts, squeaks, miaouws and howls. There is also a distinctive shriek uttered when an individual sees a hawk or other danger, and calling of this kind is most frequent in the evening, when the group is gathering for the night.

Mating takes place in April–May and births occur about $4\frac{1}{2}$ months later in September–October. There is usually a single baby, but twins are fairly frequent. At birth, the baby crawls directly onto the mother's fur and is thereafter carried by her or (later) by other adults until reaching independence. At first, the baby rides on the mother's belly, but after about two weeks it changes to riding on her back. The mother pays a lot of attention to her offspring, licking and suckling it frequently. As it grows older, the baby begins to venture away from its mother, both on the ground and in the trees, but at the slightest sign of danger it will flee back to cling on her fur.

At each breeding season, a number of females in each group will have one or two infants, and these will play and fight together as they begin to leave the mother. It is a common sight to see young *L. catta* pulling each other's ears, swinging on each other's tails and chasing. If the play of the youngsters becomes too rough or noisy, one of the adults may step in to break things up. FAMILY: Lemuridae, SUBORDER: Prosimii, ORDER: Primates, CLASS: Mammalia.

LEOPARD *Panthera pardus*, one of the smaller of the big cats, similar to the jaguar.

It is about 7 ft (2·1 m) in length, exceptionally 8 ft, of which 3 ft (1 m) is tail. The average weight is 100 lb (45 kg). The ground colour is usually a dark shade of yellow and this is marked by black rosettes on the flanks and back, the centres of the rosettes being a darker shade than the general ground colour. There is considerable variation in the spotting and the ground colour and the melanistic, or black form, known as the panther, is quite common. In extreme cases, the dark pig-

Powerful animals, leopards can carry prey as large as themselves up into trees, where lions cannot steal it.

Polyphemus moth *Telea polyphemus* of North America is 12·5 cm across spread wings.

mentation extends to the gums, tongue and palate, and the eyes may even be blue. Albinism has only been encountered on one or two occasions.

Leopards live in a variety of habitats from jungle to grassland and from semi-desert to snow covered highlands. They are found throughout Africa and much of Asia. The coat varies from the very thick rich fur of the Siberian and Chinese races to the short, coarse fur of the tropical and subtropical races. The Black panther appears to be more common where there is a heavy rainfall.

Individuals are solitary except during the breeding season. The cubs are born after a gestation period of 90–95 days fully furred and blind the eyes opening after about ten days. The number in a litter is two or three, but it may be as many as five.

Leopards are noted for their fondness for dog meat, to the point of entering bungalows to carry off dogs. Their favourite prey in India is the Spotted deer, while in Africa they even take baboons.Other prey include monkeys, dogs, pigs, deer, domestic stock, antelope, porcupines and various species of small game. The leopard is well known for its habit of dragging its kill up into a tree, out of the reach of jackals and hyaenas. Often this weighs more than the leopard.

In captivity, the leopard has lived as long as 23 years, but the life span in the wild is likely to be far less, probably a maximum of 12 or 15 years. FAMILY: Felidae, ORDER: Carnivora, CLASS: Mammalia.

LEPIDOPTERA, insect order that includes butterflies and moths. Their bodies and wings are covered with minute scales of chitin which overlap like slates upon a roof. These

The intricate antennae of a male moth are highly sensitive to odours.

White ermine moth *Spilosoma lubricipeda*, widespread across Europe.

carry the pigments that produce the colours and patterns. The mouth-parts of the adults form a proboscis, a tube for sucking up liquid, such as the nectar from flowers. When not in use it is coiled under the head like a watch spring.

The life-history includes the egg, the larva or caterpillar, the pupa or chrysalis and the, usually winged, adult or imago. The eggs may be spherical, bottle-shaped or flat, while their surface may be smooth or sculptured into complex patterns, Usually about 200 eggs are laid. The caterpillar casts its skin usually four times. When the last larval skin is shed it is found that the chrysalis has formed beneath it and on its surface can be seen cases which will contain the eye, legs, antennae and wings of the imago.

The chrysalis is inert and may take several forms. In moths it is often enclosed in a silken case, or cocoon, sometimes buried in the earth, or constructed of leaves sewn together with silk threads. In butterflies the chrysalis is generally exposed. It may be attached by the tail and held head upwards by a silken girth or it may hang head downwards by the tail alone.

Sooner or later the imago creeps forth. The wings expand by blood being pumped into them, for they are composed of a double membrane; they do not swell into bags when the blood is forced between the layers, for these are held by strands. Some hours elapse before the insect can fly, for the wings must harden. They are strengthened by struts or nervures.

In some groups, patches of scales are modified in the male to produce the scents used to stimulate the female, while in other species female scents may be perceived by, and attract, males more than a mile away. The organs of smell are in the antennae, which are branched in some moths, but never in butterflies.

Some species are capable of flying for many hundreds of miles, migrating regularly or occasionally to places where their larvae cannot survive.

Some Lepidoptera are poisonous or have an unpleasant flavour and have a 'warning coloration'. Thus they are easily recognized and avoided by insect-eating birds. An example is the Cinnabar moth *Callimorpha jacobaeae*. Its colours are brilliant red and blackish-green and the body contains poisonous alkaloids.

Much more often, the colours of the Lepidoptera are 'cryptic', or concealing, when at rest and they may match their background to perfection. Great numbers of moths resemble bark or lichen. Others resemble a piece of wood or a small stone. The Annulet moth *Gnophos obscurata* is reddish-brown on the red sandstone of Devon, white on the chalk and almost black on moors where peat is exposed.

One type of protection is 'flash coloration'

in which the forewings have a concealing pattern while the hind pair, hidden when the insect is at rest, are brilliantly coloured. Their sudden appearance when the moth flies and their disappearance when it alights is confusing and difficult to follow. Another method of protection, common in the tropics is 'mimicry'. That is, species which do not possess poisonous qualities, an unpleasant flavour or a sting, copy those that do. Some have even lost the scales on their wings and closely resemble bees and wasps.

Some moth caterpillars bore into the wood of trees and shrubs while others are common enough to defoliate forests. Perhaps the most economically important species is the Cotton boll worm, or Tomato fruit worm *Meleothis armigera*, the larva of which causes great damage to wheat, cotton, tomatoes and other crops in the USA.

The Small white butterfly *Pieris rapae* is responsible for great damage to cabbages and related species and has become widespread in the more temperate regions of the world. Originally restricted to Europe and parts of Asia, it has become one of the commonest butterflies in North America, Australia and New Zealand. The related Large white *Pieris brassicae* is similarly very destructive, but has not been introduced so extensively. The larvae of the Large white have an offensive smell and a conspicuous colour pattern, and they remain exposed on the outside of the cabbage leaves. The Small white larvae, which lack the unpleasant odour, are green, matching the cabbage leaves and they often burrow into the plants. CLASS: Insecta, PHYLUM: Arthropoda.

Linnet at nest in blackcurrant bush.

LICE, wingless parasitic insects belonging to the two orders Mallophaga (bird lice or biting lice) and Anoplura or Siphunculata (mammalian or sucking lice). Two distinct species exist on man and about 2,800 species have been described altogether. Of all insects, the lice which infest man are perhaps the most disliked throughout the world. This widespread abhorrence is justifiable as they are commonly associated with low standards of hygiene and also the transmission of several important diseases.

The 200 or more species of Anoplura are all blood-sucking parasites of mammals, having minute needle-like mouthparts (also known as stylets) that pierce the host's skin. They are very fine tubular structures that inject saliva into the host and convey blood into the insect's gut. The saliva of the louse is an anticoagulant.

The 200 or more species of Anoplura are face parasites, principally of birds, but some occur on mammals. They have biting mouthparts and feed on fragments of feathers. CLASS: Insecta, PHYLUM: Arthropoda.

LIMPET, a name usually applied to any apparently sedentary mollusc with a conical, or flattened, shell. It is applied to a wide variety of animals including many common sea-shore animals, such as the Slipper limpet *Crepidula fornicata* and the Common limpet *Patella vulgata*. PHYLUM: Mollusca.

LINNET *Acanthis cannabina*, a small finch of Europe and western Asia, generally associated with agricultural areas and particularly fond of waste land where it feeds on weed seeds. The breeding dress of the male is brown above, buff beneath, with crimson breast and crown and white edges to wings and tail. The female is duller. There is a tendency to breed socially, the nests being usually placed in gorse bushes or hedges. At one time the linnet was a popular cagebird, its song being considered second only to that of the nightingale.

The name has also been applied to other finches, the greenfinch *Chloris chloris* being called the Green linnet and the North American siskin *Spinus spinus* the Pine linnet. FAMILY: Fringillidae, ORDER: Passeriformes, CLASS: Aves.

LINSANG *Prionodon*, two species of carnivore related to mongooses, civets and genets. The Banded linsang *Prionodon linsang* ranges from Tenasserim, Burma, through Malaya to Borneo, and the Spotted linsang *P. pardicolor* is found from Nepal to Vietnam.

The Banded linsang, about 2½ ft (76 cm) long of which nearly half is tail, weighs just over 1½ lb (0·7 kg). Its body is long and slender, its legs short and its head slender with a sharp snout, containing distinctive saw teeth. The claws are retractile, those on the forepaws being sheathed as in a cat, those on the hindfeet being protected by lobes of skin. The eyes are large and the big ears are delicate and sensitive. The fur is short and velvety, whitish to brownish grey with six brownish-black bands across the back. The outsides of the legs are marked with dark spots. The tail is marked with alternating light and dark rings.

Linsangs are solitary and nocturnal resting most of the day in hollows in trees. They are expert tree climbers, hunting lizards, small mammals and birds, frogs and insects, either amongst the trees or on the ground. FAMILY: Viverridae, ORDER: Carnivora, CLASS: Mammalia.

LION *Panthera leo*, one of the 'big five roaring cats', closely related to the tiger, leopard, Snow leopard and jaguar. Lions are stockily built. Living on open plains they do not need the slender sinuous form for gliding through cover. Males stand about 36 in (0·9 m) at the shoulder, having an overall length of between nine and ten ft (2·8 m) and weighing up to 450 lb (204 kg). The female is 6 in (15 cm) shorter at the shoulder and weighs 50–75 lb (22·7–34 kg) less. The male bears a mane. The eyes are yellowish and have round pupils, whereas most cats have slits or at least oval pupils. The jaws are massive and powerful and the tongue has the usual papillae for rasping meat.

Lions are a uniform sandy buff, shading to a paler cream on the belly. The ears are black and often give the animal away when it is otherwise hidden. The tail is long, lightly furred and ends in a tuft of black hair, which sometimes conceals a spur or bony spike, the deformed last few tail bones.

The forelegs are enormously powerful. A lion can break the neck of a zebra with one blow of a paw. Although the lion is not specialized as a leaper it can perform some remarkable jumps. It is on record that lions have jumped as much as 12 ft (3·7 m) vertically and 36 ft (10·8 m) horizontally. Lions can, and the young animals frequently do, climb trees, mainly using the pulling power of the front legs.

The gestation period is about 105 days, and two or three cubs are born, each 1 ft (30 cm) long and weighing 1 lb (0·45 kg). They are fully furred and have grey spots and rosettes. It would seem that the cubs do not have full sight until about two weeks old. The teeth start to appear at about three weeks. As soon as the cubs are able to leave the den, they go back to their mother's pride, and by the time they are six months old, they join in the hunt under their mother's guidance. They become independent when one and a half to two years old. They reach maturity at three to four years old.

The first part of a kill to be eaten is the intestine, but the paunch is dragged off and buried. The feeding lion then starts at the hindquarters and eats forward. In killing

A lioness with kill in Africa.

prey the lion usually breaks the neck with a blow from the forepaw, or hooks a foreleg about the animal's neck, gripping the nose with the claws, and pulling the head back and round, throwing the prey. The much talked of leap onto the victim's back happens much less often than is usually supposed. The younger members of the pride often act as beaters for an ambush formed by the older lionesses. The favourite food is zebra, antelope and waterbuck, but if these are not available practically anything else that is handy will be taken, from carrion to fish.

Lions live in groups called 'prides' which can vary in size from three or four individuals to 30. The pride is not strictly a family group, although the nucleus is typically formed of the leader, or king, several lionesses and their young.

There are still a few surviving Asiatic lions *Panthera leo persica* in the Gir Forest Reserve on the Kathiawar Peninsula of western India, where they are maintained at a constant level of about 300. Apart from these, the lion is now confined to Africa.

The lion roars more than the other four 'roaring cats', but it does so to announce possession of a territory.

When moving normally they travel at about 3½ mph (5 kph), but they can also cover as much as 30 miles (48 km) in the course of one night. They have also been credited with fantastic turns of speed when charging, but it is unlikely that any lion can manage more than about 30 mph (48 kph) and that only over about 50 yd (46 m). FAMILY: Felidae, ORDER: Carnivora, CLASS: Mammalia.

LIVER FLUKE *Fasciola hepatica*, a parasitic flatworm which causes 'liver rot' or fascioliasis especially in sheep and cattle. It can infect dogs, horses, deer, rabbits and man. The rabbit may act as a reservoir host for the disease. Besides making the liver unfit for human consumption, the infestation causes loss of condition in the host and reduces the amount and quality of meat and milk produced. In severe cases infection may cause death, either directly or by facilitating secondary bacterial infections as in the case of 'black disease' caused by the bacterium *Clostridium oedematiens*.

Adult *F. hepatica* are leaf-shaped just over 1 in (3 cm) long and occur in the bile duct. They have an oral and ventral sucker, a bifurcate gut giving off many branching diverticula and a well developed excretory network which has flame cells in the terminal ducts and is concentrated into a median duct which opens by a single posterior excretory pore. It is hermaphrodite and produces a large number of eggs which reach the host gut with the bile and are shed to the outside with the faeces. The egg hatches to release a ciliated miracidium larva which is chemotactically attracted to its host, the small Mud snail *Limnaea truncatula*, and bores into the

pulmonary chamber or foot, loses its ciliated coat and transforms into a sporocyst which becomes mobile and produces rediae $\frac{1}{25}$ in (1 mm) long which penetrate into the digestive gland. Germ balls within the rediae produce daughter rediae and cercariae. At about the 40th day after infection cercariae, which have a roundish body and straight, unforked tail, are shed at a rate of several hundred a day. The cercaria encysts on grass around the pools formed by hoof marks, wheel ruts or ditches, is then eaten by a cow or sheep and the young flukes bore through the gut wall and migrate along the peritoneum to the liver into which they bore. About five to eight weeks after infection the flukes reach the bile ducts. FAMILY: Fasciolidae, CLASS: Digenea, PHYLUM: Platyhelminthes.

LLAMA *Lama glama*, domestic form of the guanaco, 4 ft (1·2 m) at the shoulder, its coat varying from white to black. From southern Peru through western Bolivia as far as Catamaca in Argentina and the tableland of Atacama in Chile it is the principal beast of burden of the Indians at altitudes of 7,600–13,000 ft (2,300–4,000 m). Of all domestic animals it is the most suitable for the steep mountain paths and the hard ground and can go without food and water longer than any other. Only the stallions are made to carry loads and they can do a day's march of 19 miles (30 km) with a maximum load of 110–176 lb (50–80 kg). If the weight is more than that they obstinately refuse to go on. A llama will also only allow itself to be loaded when it is one of a group. On the march the animals go in single file, like camels, and are driven by the Indians by means of calls and whistles. The wool is only of interest to the Indians, but the leather is highly valued for its durability. The dung is also used as fuel. FAMILY: Camelidae, SUBORDER: Tylopoda, ORDER: Artiodactyla, CLASS: Mammalia.

LOACHES, freshwater fishes, related to carps, of Asia and Europe, with a few species found in northern Africa. They are elongated and compressed, bottom-living, and many

are nocturnal. Most species have barbels round the mouth and the dorsal and anal fins are usually short and placed in the rear half of the body. The swimbladder is reduced and encased, either partially or totally, in bone. Some loaches use the intestine as an accessory breathing organ.

The Stone loach *Noemachilus barbatulus* is common in most clear brooks of Europe and eastwards to China and Japan. It hides in cracks or under stones during the day, coming out to feed at night. Although it only grows to 5 in (13 cm) it makes excellent eating. The Spined loach *Cobitis taenia*, with a small spine below the eye, also ranges across Asia to China. It is 4 in (10 cm) in length, and has horizontal rows of spots along the flanks.

The weatherfish *Misgurnus fossilis*, a European loach, 20 in (51 cm) long, becomes highly agitated when atmospheric pressure rises, as for example before a thunderstorm and constantly comes to the surface. This unusual behaviour arises from the great sensitivity of the bone-encased swimbladder. FAMILY: Cobitidae, ORDER: Cypriniformes, CLASS: Pisces.

LOBSTERS, large marine crustaceans with ten legs, the first pair bearing large claws. The true lobsters belong to the genus *Homarus*. The best known are the European lobster *H. vulgaris* and the lobster of the Atlantic coast of North America *H. americanus*. True lobsters live in shallow waters amongst rocks, in holes and crannies, only venturing out to feed.

The dark blue pigment of the living lobster is a complex compound closely related to the pigment of carrots. When a lobster is boiled this is broken down and the colour changes from blue to red. The two large claws of the lobster, much larger in the male than in the female, are not alike either in structure or in function. One of them is always used as a crushing claw, the other as a fine picking or scraping claw. There is no uniformity, from one lobster to another, as to which is which. Lobsters feed on carrion, small crabs, worms, fishes, or indeed any animal matter dead or alive which they

In foul water a Stone loach gulps air and uses its intestine as a gill.

can pick up. Shells are crushed in the large claw and the finer claw serves to scrape the flesh off the bones or shell of the prey. FAMILY: Homaridae, ORDER: Decapoda, CLASS: Crustacea, PHYLUM: Arthropoda.

LOCUSTS, term restricted to the swarming gregarious stage of about 50 species of tropical grasshoppers which take advantage of good conditions for breeding and then fly in large swarms to areas where food may be available. Grasshoppers in temperate latitudes feed chiefly on grasses, but many of their long-legged tropical relatives feed on all kinds of other plants, even on some like the Sodom apple which are highly poisonous to other creatures. FAMILY: Acrididae, ORDER: Orthoptera, CLASS: Insecta, PHYLUM: Arthropoda.

LOGGERHEAD TURTLE *Caretta caretta*, a Marine turtle occurring in all oceans but more commonly in the subtropics, where it breeds. It is a fairly regular visitor to the Atlantic coasts of Europe. Its general colour is reddish brown above, yellowish below. It has five pairs of costal scutes and the snout is covered with two pairs of prefrontals which often have one or more scales wedged in between them. The carapace is up to 40 in (101 cm) long. The loggerhead feeds on a variety of marine invertebrates such as shellfish, squids, Goose barnacles and jellyfish. FAMILY: Dermochelidae, ORDER: Testudines, CLASS: Reptilia.

LONGHORN BEETLES, a large group of elongate, brightly coloured beetles with long antennae. The majority are tropical and all have larvae which burrow into plant tissues, often wood. In Europe the larvae of these beetles are an important part of the diet of woodpeckers and some species are pests as their extensive tunnelling spoils timber. Some beetles of this group, like the Titan beetle *Titanus giganteus*, are among the largest insects, reaching a body length of 6 in (15 cm) with antennae as long again. FAMILY: Cerambycidae, ORDER: Coleoptera, CLASS: Insecta, PHYLUM: Arthropoda.

LONG-TAILED TIT *Aegithalos caudatus*, of Europe and Asia, a striking bird with a pink and white body with black wings and a black tail with white edgings to the feathers. It weighs only about ¼ oz (6–8 gm), but has a tail 3½ in (9 cm). Long-tailed tits are usually seen in parties of 6–10. They feed on insects from the thin outer twigs of trees and tall bushes and often join with mixed parties of other tits.

The Long-tailed tits build a complex and striking domed nest and, although not suspended, it is woven into the branches of a gorse bush or bramble clump, or built into the fork of a tree high off the ground. The nest is made mainly of feathers and moss which are woven together with cobwebs—over 2,000 feathers have been counted in a single nest. The outside is usually camouflaged with a covering of lichens. Eight to twelve eggs are laid in the frail structure and when the young are large the nest expands to hold them all and bulges when they move.

Another striking feature of this species is its roosting habit. Each party roosts together in a little ball. At dusk they fly onto a selected small branch and cluster together, tails outwards. Doubtless this helps them to keep warm during the long winter nights. FAMILY: Paridae, ORDER: Passeriformes, CLASS: Aves.

LORIKEETS, name given to the smaller species of lory, and the Hanging parrots or Bat parrots *Loriculus*. The division into lories and lorikeets, based on size, is one of convenience and does not reflect real relationships.

The plumage is predominantly green, with red and blue patches.

The three lorikeets of the Australian genus *Glossopsitta* are 5½–8 in (14–20 cm) long and have predominantly green plumage with short tails. All three have red and yellow plumage markings, and the Purple-crowned lorikeet *G. porphyrocephala* has a dark blue patch on the crown. They feed mainly on nectar and pollen, sometimes on fruit.

The Hanging parrots or Bat parrots are most commonly called lorikeets. They are small to very small, green-plumaged parrots which feed mainly on the nectar and pollen of flowering trees, some species also eating fruit and are distributed from northern India to New Guinea and the Moluccas. They hang upside down to sleep. FAMILY: Psittacidae, ORDER: Psittaciformes, CLASS: Aves.

LORISES, nocturnal mammals related to lemurs with large, forward-oriented eyes and well-developed grasping hands. The large eyes are emphasized by black, pear-shaped

A pair of Rainbow lorikeets.

Hand of a loris showing reduced index finger, giving the hand a wide grasp.

markings which almost give the impression of a pair of spectacles. There are two kinds: the Slender loris *Loris tardigradus* and the Slow loris *Nycticebus cougang*. The Slender loris owes its name to its long, thin limbs. Both lorises are normally very slow-moving, though they can move fast when threatened. The slow-moving gait is dependent upon the deliberate, powerful grasp of the hands and feet. In association with this, the index finger is reduced to a small stub in both species, and in the Slender loris there is also reduction of the second toe. Neither species has a tail long enough to show through the fur. The Slow loris has mainly dark brown fur and the head and body measure 13 in (33 cm). The Slender loris is somewhat smaller, with a head and body of 9 in (23 cm), and ranges in colour from greyish-brown to rufous. There is a white stripe between the eyes.

The Slender loris, confined to Ceylon and southern India, is completely arboreal, occurring in both wet and fairly dry tropical forest. The Slow loris is also completely arboreal and is found in wet forests from Assam to the Philippines. Both species eat insects, fruit, leaves, birds' eggs and small lizards and mammals.

There is only one offspring at birth after a gestation period of about five months. The baby climbs on to its mother's fur at birth and is afterwards carried around by her until becoming independent. Both species are solitary or pair-living. FAMILY: Lorisidae, SUBORDER: Prosimii, ORDER: Primates, CLASS: Mammalia.

LORY, 65 species of parrots all of which have a brush-like tip to the tongue. The smaller species, along with some unrelated small parrots, are called lorikeets.

The lories are probably the most brilliantly coloured of all parrots. Bright red, yellow, green and blue figures prominently in the plumage, although some are predominantly red, green, blue or black. They are 5–20 in (12·5–50 cm) long, and have tails of long, short or medium length. The central tail feathers of three species of the genus *Charmosyna* form long wispy plumes. The distribution of the lories is centred on New Guinea and the central Moluccas, with smaller

Louse

numbers of species in Australia, the Solomon Islands, and small islands from the southwest to the central Pacific Ocean. FAMILY: Psittacidae, ORDER: Psittaciformes, CLASS: Aves.

LOUSE, strictly the name singular for wingless parasitic insects but also used popularly for other types of parasites, for example, the crustacean known as a Fish louse. See lice.

LOVEBIRDS, 8–9 species of African parrots. The name is used sometimes for the budgerigar and other small parrots. The 'true' lovebirds are small, about 4 in (10 cm), short-tailed parrots found from Ethiopia to the Congo and Madagascar. The Grey-headed or Madagascar lovebird *Agapomis cana* is a small parrot found in woodland and scrub. The male is mainly green, with a white bill and a pale grey head and neck; in the female the head is pale yellow-green.

The Black-winged or Abyssinian lovebird *A. taranta* is found only in Ethiopia and Somalia. It is one of the largest lovebirds predominantly green, with black wings, and red markings on the head of the male.

Lovebirds are so-called because of the close pair-bond and the frequency with which paired birds preen each other. In some species this preening is mutual, but in other species it is only the male which preens the female. FAMILY: Psittacidae, ORDER: Psittaciformes, CLASS: Aves.

LUGWORMS, fairly large polychaete worms the coiled casts of which are a very familiar

Fischer's lovebird *Agaponis fischeri* of Africa and Madagascar. Lovebird pairs sit huddled together for hours.

The lumpsucker, also known as the sea-hen, from its devotion to its clutch of eggs.

sight on sandy shores. The worms are much used as bait by fishermen in all parts of the world. Most species never attain more than 2¾–3 in (7–8 cm), though some are much larger than this, and most have a fat cylindrical body with a narrower tail. FAMILY: Arenicolidae, ORDER: Polychaeta, CLASS: Annelida.

LUMPSUCKER *Cyclopterus lumpus*, derives its name from the warty lumps on its body and the presence of a ventral sucker. It is bulky and ungainly looking and is commonly found stranded in rock pools around British and European coasts, especially in spring when it comes into shallow waters to breed. It is also found on the western side of the Atlantic.

The lumpsucker grows to a maximum of 2 ft (60 cm) in length. The body is rounded and rather flaccid with warty tubercles, the largest arranged in three distinct rows down the flanks. The pelvic fins are greatly reduced and contribute to the sucker which is formed on the chest. During the breeding season the male and female differ somewhat in colour. The male has a dark, almost black back and a red belly, while the female is brown on the back and has a yellow belly.

The females produce a large number of eggs (up to 100,000) laid in a loose ball with gaps between the eggs so that water can percolate through the mass. They are laid just above the low water mark and are guarded by the male, even though the eggs may be exposed at low tide. The males will continue to guard them even during attacks by seabirds and in one case even while seagulls were pecking his liver. If rough weather scatters the eggs, the males search frantically for them. This behaviour has earned the lumpsucker the name henfish. FAMILY: Cyclopteridae, ORDER: Scorpaeniformes, CLASS: Pisces.

LUNGFISHES, primitive bony fishes that were world-wide in their distribution in Devonian and Triassic times but are now restricted to South America, Africa and Australia. They are characterized by the presence of one lung or a pair which are used for breathing air. ORDER: Dipnoi, CLASS: Pisces.

LYNX, bobtailed members of the cat family.

The one species, Northern lynx *Felis Lynx* gives the appearance of being larger than it really is, because of the heavy fur. The total length is 3–4 ft (0·9–1·2 m) and the height at the shoulder about 2 ft (0·6 m). A fully grown male weighs about 20 lb (9 kg) but may go as high as 40 lb (18 kg). The coat is a mixture of black, dark brown and a tawny yellow, with a silvery frosted appearance due to the fact that the long guard hairs are tipped with a silvery white shade. The underparts are cinnamon, the cheek ruffs white marked with black stripes and the tip of the tail entirely black.

Formerly three species were recognized, the Canadian, Spanish and European Lynx. These are now regarded as one species.

Lynxes live in forests, especially of pine, usually leading solitary lives, hunting by night using sight and smell. Indeed, their keen sight has become proverbial. Although they run very little they are tireless walkers, following a scent trail for miles in pursuit of prey. They are good climbers and swim well and their large paws have a snowshoe effect to carry them easily over deep snow. The voice is a caterwauling like that of a domestic tomcat but louder and like a cat the lynx uses its claws and teeth in a fight. The natural food of the lynx includes small deer, badgers foxes, hares, rabbits, squirrels, small rodents, fish, beetles and occasionally ground living birds. It will eat carrion but it prefers fresh prey. It has often been persecuted because of its alleged raids on livestock. The Snowshoe rabbit, a North American hare, is the main prey of the Canadian lynx. FAMILY: Felidae, ORDER: Carnivora, CLASS: Mammalia.

LYREBIRDS, Australian birds, pheasant-like in appearance, of especial interest because of the spectacular nature of their song and display and their use of mimicry.

They were commonly known to the early settlers as pheasants and many were shot for their beautiful tail feathers. The colour above is brown, the under-parts being a lighter brown. The throat and tail coverts are rufous. Adult males can be distinguished by the tail, which grows up to 30 in (76 cm) in length and consists of two large outer feathers which have brown crescent-shaped

Male lyrebird in full display, its tail plumes laid horizontally over its back, not vertically as so often depicted.

markings on the upper side, two black wire-like feathers and 12 filamentary feathers which are dark on top and silver underneath, as are the outer tail feathers. This combination of feathers can be erected to give the shape of a lyre.

Lyrebirds are still plentiful from southern Queensland to southern Victoria. Although they are now strictly protected, numbers are decreasing as further areas of forestland are cleared.

In June and July the single egg is laid. The female builds the nest, incubates the egg and feeds the young unaided. The egg is remarkably resistant to cold and in the early stages of incubation can be left for 24 hours or more without damage. Although the nest is large and may measure up to 24 in (61 cm) in width, nesting females can be distinguished by their bent tail feathers, which are curled round the body when in the nest. Incubation takes about six weeks and the

chick spends a further six weeks in the nest which may be on the ground, in an old tree stump, on a cliff ledge, or even at times in a tall tree. Nesting areas are established by the females in the thickly vegetated damp gullies of the forest, near a pool or running stream into which they place the droppings collected from the nestlings.

Males occupy territories on the slopes of the gullies and each will defend an area of 2–10 acres (0.8–4 ha). They make small clearings from which all vegetation is removed and scratch earth up into the form of a low mound some 6 in (15 cm) high and 36 in (90 cm) in diameter on which they sing and display. Usually from four to six such mounds, at various vantage points in the territory, are in use at any one time but several more may be built and discarded during the breeding season. These mounds are kept well tended and before a male commences to sing he carefully scratches the surface of the mound until any accumulated litter has been removed. Much of the song and display takes place in the early morning. As the male bird pours out his continuous song, which incorporates the calls of many of the forest birds, he slowly gyrates on his mound.

Lyrebirds are said to mimic sounds such as the noise of axe blows, cross-cut saws, barking dogs and a variety of other bushland noises. FAMILY: Menuridae, ORDER: Passeriformes, CLASS: Aves.

Tufted ears and cheek ruffs distinguish the lynx from other cats.

183

M

MACAQUES, the common omnivorous monkeys of Asia, related to the baboons. They are smaller than baboons with shorter faces, smaller teeth, no facial fossae; and in the male the ischial callosities do not fuse across the midline. Some are largely terrestrial, others at least partially arboreal; the dominant colour is brown, and instead of the bright and contrasted colours of the large African genus *Cercopithecus* there are flamboyant hair-patterns in the form of facial fringes and crown tufts. The brow ridges are well developed, and the canines of the adult males are large and sharp. Macaques of one kind or another are the most familiar monkeys to the general public, both in zoos and in medical research institutes: the Rhesus, Crab-eating and Pigtailed monkeys being the commonest.

Macaques are mainly tropical and subtropical, living in Indonesia, the Philippines, Southeast Asia, India, Ceylon, and southern China; but also in the Szechwan mountains, near Pekin, on Taiwan, Japan and North Africa. See Barbary ape, Crab-eating monkey, Pigtailed monkey, Rhesus monkey. FAMILY: Cercopithecidae, ORDER: Primates, CLASS: Mammalia.

MACAWS, 15 species of large gaudily coloured parrots living in the tropical rain-forests of Mexico and Central and South America. They include the largest members of the family, a number of them approaching 40 in (100 cm) in length, a large proportion of which is made up of the long, graduated tail. As in other parrots, the bill is very large—in bulk about half that of the head—and is strong, stout and much curved. It is capable of some movement at its articulation with the skull, and this, with the strong, muscular tongue, gives macaws a considerable degree of manipulative ability, of use to them in climbing about the branches as well as in feeding. In climbing they are also aided by the feet, which are zygodactyl, that is they have two toes pointing forward and two back.

Many species display the brightest yellow, green, blue, and red, often with the most striking contrast, and with a bare, white face. The plumage has long been prized by South American Indians for decorating head-dresses and other clothes, and also by Europeans for the tying of fishing flies.

The largest is the Scarlet macaw *Ara macao*, which may be over 36 in (92 cm) in length and is found from Mexico to Bolivia. Its scarlet plumage is enhanced by blue in the wings and tail and yellow and green on the wings. This and the Blue-and-yellow macaw *Ara ararauna* are the most commonly kept in zoos. The latter species may be over 32 in (82 cm) in length, and is found from eastern Panama to Argentina. It is rich sky-blue above and bright golden-yellow beneath, and has been kept in captivity in Europe since the 16th century.

The Hyacinthine macaw *Anodorhynchus hyacinthinus* is separated from the other large species by the full feathering of the face. It may reach 35 in (89 cm) in length, and is found from the mouth of the Amazon into Brazil. The plumage is a deep but rich, bright and glossy blue. A small area of skin at the base of the lower jaw is devoid of feathers and coloured bright yellow, as is a ring around the eye. FAMILY: Psittacidae, ORDER: Psittaciformes, CLASS: Aves.

MACKERELS, streamlined fish with pointed jaws and a body tapering to the slender base of the forked tail. The best known and

Blue-and-yellow macaws mutual preening. One bird nibbles the feathers which the other bird cannot itself reach.

economically the most important are members of the genus *Scomber*. The Common mackerel *S. scombrus* has two dorsal fins well separated from each other and a series of small finlets behind both the dorsal and anal fins. The back is dark green-blue with dark wavy lines on the upper part of the flanks and the undersurface is pearly white shot with rosy tints. It occasionally reaches 6 lb (2·7 kg) and is found on both sides of the North Atlantic. The mackerel is a pelagic fish forming enormous shoals at the surface near coasts in summer and feeding on small crustaceans and other planktonic animals (fish and fish larvae). In winter the shoals disband and move into deeper water where they remain in a state approaching hibernation. Off the Atlantic coasts of North America shoals 20 miles long and ½ mile broad (32 km by 0·8 km) have been seen. Spawning takes place in coastal waters, large females laying about half a million minute eggs each. FAMILY: Scombridae, ORDER: Perciformes, CLASS: Pisces.

MACKEREL SHARKS, or Mako sharks, large and dangerous fishes of all warm seas. They are fast-swimming with streamlined bodies, two dorsal fins (the second very small) and a tail that is almost symmetrical. The teeth are awl-shaped, not triangular. Two species are now recognized, *Isurus oxyrinchus* of the Atlantic and *I. paucus* of the Indo-Pacific, both of which may reach a length of 13 ft (3·9 m). Mackerel sharks have been known to catch and eat swordfishes which gives some indication of their speed. They have also been implicated in attacks on swimmers. They are live-bearers, the young hatching within the uterus and, after their own yolk is exhausted, feeding on the yolk contained in unfertilized eggs. FAMILY: Isuridae, ORDER: Pleurotremata, CLASS: Chondrichthyes.

MAGPIE-LARK *Grallina cyanoleuca*, a pied ground-feeding songbird, about 1 ft (30 cm) in length of Australia. A similar smaller species haunts New Guinea rivers. The plumage is mainly black, the male having white on the underside, base of the tail, shoulders, sides of the neck and eyebrows; the female having a white throat and no white eyebrows. The iris is staring white.

The magpie-lark is a bird of open country, found particularly by water, occurring in open grassland and pastures, roadsides and the larger lawns of gardens and sportsfields in suburban areas. It feeds on insects and other invertebrates and snails are taken from freshwater margins.

The voice is striking. A frequent 'pee-wit' call is uttered, with shriller alarm and mob-

Rhesus macaque, the best known monkey of southern Asia, taking a chew at a twig.

bing calls. Pairs have an antiphonal call: a trisyllabic utterance given by one bird being immediately answered by a bisyllabic response, variously written as 'pee-o-wit, te-he' or 'dillipot, peewit'.

The nest is a well-shaped bowl of mud, strengthened with grass strands mixed in during building; hence the species' alternative name of 'mudlark'. It is about 6 in (15 cm) across and more than half as deep, with walls $\frac{3}{4}$ in (2 cm) thick. It is placed well up in a tree, preferably a high one, and built directly onto a bare horizontal branch or a bare fork. Three to four eggs, blotched purple and brown on a white ground, are laid. Both parents co-operate in incubating and rearing the young, which resemble the parents. FAMILY: Grallinidae, ORDER: Passeriformes, CLASS: Aves.

MAGPIES, birds of the crow family, most of which have long tails and many of which are brightly-coloured or are strikingly patterned in black and white. The Common magpie *Pica pica* is widely distributed in Eurasia and in western North America in a wide variety of wooded habitats. It is black with metallic sheens of green, blue and purple, with white on the belly and flanks and a white flash on the shoulder region. It is omnivorous. Its nest of sticks is lined with fine roots and earth. There are usually five to eight eggs, incubated by the female only.

The Yellow-billed blue magpie *Urocissa flavirostris* of the Himalayas has a tail more than twice as long as the body. Another striking species is the Green magpie *Cissa chinensis* of Southeast Asia, which is light green with brown and white on the wings and a narrow black mask setting off the red bill and irides. The feet and legs are also red.

In Southeast Asia, which is particularly rich in magpie species, are found the 'treepies' and the Racquet-tailed magpies, in which the tips of the central tail feathers are expanded to form 'racquets'. A number of species are scavengers, feeding on carrion as well as eggs, baby birds, fruit and insects. FAMILY: Corvidae, ORDER: Passeriformes, CLASS: Aves.

MALARIA PARASITE, a protozoan, or single-celled animal, of microscopic size but with a complicated life-cycle, responsible for the disease after which it is named. Two hosts are involved in the life-cycle, a vertebrate and a blood-sucking insect, such as the mosquito. The cycle in the vertebrate begins when the infective stages, or sporozoites, are injected into the host by the bite of the insect. These make their way to various cells of the body where they undergo one or more cycles of division which give rise to many minute invasive stages, or merozoites. The merozoites may invade further cells or infect red blood cells. In the red blood cells sexual stages, or gametocytes, are formed and

these are taken up by the insect host when it bites. Cycles of division in the blood occur and the merozoites produced invade fresh red cells. In the insect the gametocytes mature into male and female micro- and macrogametes which fuse to produce zygotes. The zygotes become motile and pass through the gut wall of the insect to form an oocyst within which a further stage of division occurs, resulting in the production of sporozoites which make their way to the salivary glands.

In the case of the malaria parasites of man the first stage of multiplication takes place in the liver; the merozoites then invade further liver cells and also red blood cells where the second stage of multiplication occurs. The gametocytes occur in red blood cells and the invertebrate hosts are mosquitoes. Man is not the only animal to be infected by malaria parasites, and the 85 or so recorded species are distributed through reptiles, birds and mammals, especially rodents and primates. Only the species living in mammals multiply in the liver. ORDER: Haemosporidia, CLASS: Sporozoa, PHYLUM: Protozoa.

MALLARD *Anas platyrhynchos*, a well-known Dabbling duck which, in various races, breeds across most of the northern half of the world and has given rise to most of the domesticated forms of duck. About 2 ft (60 cm) long, the male or drake is brightly coloured from September to June with a dark glossy green head and neck and a white ring at the base of the neck. The breast is brown and belly and back grey. After moulting the drake changes to a mottled brown plumage similar to that of the duck. This is the eclipse plumage. Both sexes have purplish-blue specula.

Mallards spend much time on land usually near water feeding mainly on leaves and seeds, grain and berries but also take small animal life such as tadpoles from the water. They form pairs in autumn after a ritualized courtship. The nest is a shallow saucer of grass and dry leaves lined with down, either

on the ground or sometimes quite high up in a tree. Usually 10–12 greenish-white eggs are laid and incubated by the duck alone for 22–28 days. The ducklings leave the nest directly after hatching and fledge in two months. FAMILY: Anatidae, ORDER: Anseriformes, CLASS: Aves.

MALLEE FOWL *Leipoa ocellata*, a large chicken-like ground bird, also known as the lowan, the best known of the megapodes or Incubator birds. It is unusual among Incubator birds in inhabiting semi-arid regions where vegetable ground litter is sparse. It is found largely in the inland scrub country in Australia which consists of dwarf eucalyptus, known as mallee scrub. The Mallee fowl incubates its eggs by the heat generated by the fermentation of dead leaves and other plant materials.

In the habitat of the Mallee fowl suitable material with which to build a mound of fermentable vegetation is scarce, added to which the temperature fluctuates widely and the air is very dry for most of the year, so that dead plant material tends to wither rather than ferment. The Mallee fowl overcomes this by digging a hole in the ground which may be 15 ft (4·5 m) in diameter and 4 ft (1·2 m) deep. Over the winter it collects plant material from a radius of up to 150 ft (45 m) and deposits it in the hole. Then, after it has been dampened by rain, it is covered with a 2 ft (0·6 m) thick layer of sandy soil which enables fermentation to take place, generating heat.

Fluctuations in the temperature of the egg-chamber at the top of the mound are checked by the male bird which tends the mound throughout the breeding season. He tests its temperature with the bill and regulates the gain or loss of heat. In the spring there is rapid fermentation and the male cools the eggs when necessary by digging into the top of the mound in the early morning to allow the heat to escape. In summer there is overheating from the sun also and the male adds more insulating soil,

The Mallee fowl lays its eggs in an incubator, uses its tongue like a thermometer.

sometimes also scattering the covering soil very early in the morning and returning it when the mound has cooled and before the sun is too hot. In autumn there is not enough heat and the bird scoops out the centre of the mound allowing the sun to reach the eggs. He also turns the soil over in the sun to warm it and scatters it, returning the heated soil to the mound. By these various means the egg temperature is maintained very close to the required 92°F (33°C) for the whole of the incubation period from September to April. The male is busy building or maintaining the mound for 11 months of the year.

The young dig themselves out of the mound and fend for themselves entirely, never seeing the parents and being able to fly within 24 hours. FAMILY: Megapodidae, ORDER: Galliformes, CLASS: Aves.

MAMBAS, large snakes belonging to the genus *Dendroaspis*. Mamba venom is a nerve poison and bites from the Black mamba *D. polylepis* are particularly dangerous. This is the largest of the mambas, reaching a length of 14 ft (4·3 m). When disturbed, it will rear up, spreading a narrow hood and gaping the jaws to show the blackish interior of the mouth. Any sudden movement will provoke a strike, which tends to be delivered on the head or body and will, therefore, prove fatal in a short time unless mamba serum is immediately available.

The Eastern green mamba *D. angusticeps* rarely exceeds 7 ft (2·1 m) in length. It is brilliant emerald-green to yellow-green above, greenish-white below, and extends along the East African coastal plain.

The Western green mamba *D. viridis* is restricted to West Africa and is usually speckled green and yellow.

Mambas lay 9–14 elongate eggs at the beginning of the rains, a termitarium being a favourite nesting site. Newly hatched young are about 20 in (50 cm) in length.

The two Green mambas and Jameson's mamba *D. jamesonii* are arboreal and found in forested regions. The Black mamba inhabits dry savannah and, although frequently found in big trees along rivers, it is equally at home on the ground and is particularly common on rocky hills covered with thick bush. FAMILY: Elapidae, ORDER: Squamata, CLASS: Reptilia.

MANAKINS, small New World birds with a short bill and short wings. In most of the 59 species the tail is also small. Usually the males differ from the females.

Manakins are confined to Central and South America. They live in dark forests but are also found in secondary growth. They feed mainly on berries, which are snapped off in flight, but some species also eat small insects.

One of the main characteristics of the manakins is their complicated courtship in which the male makes a small clearing on the forest floor by removing all leaves and twigs. In this small court a few vertical twigs are used as display perches on which the males jump and make strange sounds. FAMILY: Pipridae, ORDER: Passeriformes, CLASS: Aves.

MANATEES, large and fully aquatic herbivorous mammals of the tropical and subtropical Atlantic coasts, estuaries and great rivers, of the genus *Trichechus* which has three species: *T. senegalensis* of the coast and certain large rivers of West Africa, *T. inunguis* of the Amazon and Orinoco, and *T. manatus* of the western Atlantic and Caribbean coasts.

T. manatus grows to a length of around 12 ft (4 m); *T. inunguis* is smaller. Manatees are heavily built, torpedo-shaped with powerful rounded tails, flattened horizontally. The tail provides the main propulsion, hindlimbs being absent and the forelimbs small. The

20 to 30 crushing molars are like those of elephants. New teeth are formed posteriorly while the front teeth are lost successively by a progressive forward movement of the whole series. The manatee is exceptional, too, in having six, instead of the standard seven, neck vertebrae. The grey-brown skin is tough, almost hairless.

The flattened pig-like bristly snout has a much enlarged and muscular upper lip and it is with the corners of this lip acting like mandibles that the animal plucks the vegetation on which it feeds. The nostrils are high on the snout and equipped with powerful valves which only open when, for a few seconds, they break the surface for air. The eyes are circular and the earholes minute.

The present distribution of the manatee is probably little different from the past, but its numbers have been greatly reduced by deliberate exploitation for meat. This quest in the Caribbean area, where labour on sugar

Eastern green mamba going along a branch and turning back at the end.

Longtailed manakins *Chiroxipha linearis* from South America.

The unlovely face of the manatee—the seacow mistaken by Columbus for a mermaid.

plantations was supplied with this meat, has probably removed the manatee completely in parts of that area.

Manatee breeding habits are little known in detail. Gestation is known to be more than 152 days and the normal birth is a single calf to which much maternal care is given. FAMILY: Trichechidae, ORDER: Sirenia, CLASS: Mammalia.

MANDARIN DUCK *Aix galericulata*, one of the Perching ducks, a familiar sight on ornamental ponds in Britain where it has been successfully naturalized, although its real home is China. Its counterpart in North America is the Carolina or Wood duck *A. sponsa*. In both species the males have a striking multi-coloured plumage, including a very handsome backward-sweeping crest, purple and green with white markings. The mandarin's crest is erectile and this duck can also be recognized by its orange hackles and by a pair of 'sails' on the back formed from a pair of chestnut coloured feathers. The females of both species have a small crest and are mainly grey above with a blue speculum and brown with white spots underneath. In their eclipse plumage the males resemble the females but have more white under the chin.

Both species are exclusively freshwater, feeding on plants and small animal food from the surface of ponds and streams but also grazing on land on acorns and other vegetable matter. They nest in holes in trees, the eggs being laid on a bed of down and the chicks fluttering to the ground soon after hatching. FAMILY: Anatidae, ORDER: Anseriformes, CLASS: Aves.

MANDRILL *Papio sphinx*, a large *baboon closely related to the drill.

MANED WOLF *Chrysocyon brachyurus*, resembles a long-legged fox. Its native South American name is the 'fox-on-stilts'. Its thin muzzle, narrow chest, long ears and very long legs are combined with a beautiful colouring of bright reddish-brown contrasting with a pure white throat patch and tail and black hackles, stockings and ears.

Maned wolves are found throughout the plains region of South America, in Brazil, Paraguay and Argentina. They feed on small animals like wild Guinea pigs, birds, lizards and frogs, which they catch either by a swift pounce or by digging into burrows or banks, supplemented by fruits such as figs, and even sugar cane. FAMILY: Canidae, ORDER: Carnivora, CLASS: Mammalia.

MANGABEYS *Cercocebus*, Old World monkeys closely related to baboons, from which they differ by their long tails, shorter faces with deep fossae under the eyes, and white eyelids. They are 18–24 in (45–61 cm) long with a tail as much as half as long again.

Mangabeys fall into two groups: crested and uncrested. The uncrested include those with short, speckled coats, blackish hands and feet, striking white eyelids, and white or yellow underparts. The species are the grey-black Sooty mangabey *Cercocebus atys* from West Africa; the White-collared mangabey *Cercocebus torquatus*, with its white neckband and maroon-red crown, from the lower Niger River to Equatorial Guinea; the brown Golden-bellied mangabey *C. chrysogaster*

with its bright golden-yellow underparts, from south of the Congo River; and the smaller, grey-speckled Agile mangabey *C. galeritus* from Gabon, Equatorial Guinea and the forests north of the Congo River, and the gallery forests of the Tana River, in Kenya. The more distinctive crested group includes just two species: the Grey-cheeked mangabey *C. albigena* which has a long black coat, grey underneath, and an untidy floppy crest on the head; and the Black mangabey *C. aterrimus* which is jet-black with an upright, pointed coconut-like crest on the head and fan-shaped cheek-whiskers which are either grey or black. The Grey-cheeked is found from Cameroun and Gabon east to Uganda, always north of the Congo River, while the Black mangabey is found south of the Congo River.

Mangabey troops occupy home ranges which overlap, but the troops rarely meet because of the males' loud spacing calls. They feed on tough, hard fruits which they crack and peel with their incisors. They are active at dawn, midday and dusk.

Mangabeys have quite a tight-knit troop, especially between the females who groom one another frequently. Males are rather aggressive towards one another. Females also groom males, but rarely vice versa: a baboon-like characteristic of mangabeys. FAMILY: Cercopithecidae, ORDER: Primates, CLASS: Mammalia.

MANGE MITES, certain skin parasites of mammals which cause irritation leading to scratching, rubbing, loss of coat and, often, the formation of scabs, beneath which the parasites pursue their activities.

MARABOU *Leptoptilos crumeniferus*, a very large stork with a massive pointed bill, its almost featherless head and neck (the latter with a long distensible pouch of pink skin), slaty upperparts and long legs. It is confined to Africa, although the adjutant *L. dubius* of southern Asia is similar. It breeds in colonies, building bulky nests in large trees, often in villages. It feeds on carrion and offal but will also catch small animals. Marabou soar majestically, with a wing-span of up to 8½ ft (2·6 m), stalk on open ground and also perch, rather grotesquely, on the topmost boughs of trees. They stand about 4 ft (1·2 m) high. FAMILY: Ciconiidae, ORDER: Ciconiiformes, CLASS: Aves.

MARKHOR *Capra falconeri*, a wild goat with compressed spiral horns. Males stand 38–41 in (95–104 cm) high and weigh 80–100 lb (35–45 kg). The colour is grey-brown, old males becoming nearly white. Females, less than half the weight of males, are dark fawn. In winter, males develop long fringes and both sexes are clothed in long silky hair.

Markhor inhabit precipitous crags and steep slopes. They range from Kashmir south to the trans-Indus hill ranges and westwards through Afghanistan to hills in the USSR. In Astor and Pir Panjal, the horns have an open corkscrew 65 in (165 cm) long; in the Suleiman range they are tightly twisted like a stick of liquorice, 48½ in (123 cm) long; around Kabul the spiral is again more open, but the horns are only 39½ in (100 cm) long; in the Soviet Union they are similar but rarely above 28 in (70 cm) long. FAMILY: Bovidae, ORDER: Artiodactyla, CLASS: Mammalia.

MARLINS, large tropical oceanic fishes related to the sailfish and the swordfish. The bony snout is often as long as, or longer than, that in the sailfish but does not reach the length of the 'sword' in the swordfish. Marlins are great sporting fishes. They are cunning and wily when hooked and are tremendous fighters.

The Black marlin *Istiompax marlina*, or Silver or White marlin, widespread in the tropical Indo-Pacific, grows to 11½ ft (3·5 m) and can weigh up to half a ton (500 kg). The Blue marlin *Makaira ampla* of the Pacific, also known as the Black marlin, grows to 1,400 lb (630 kg) and often has stripes on the body causing confusion with the Striped marlin *M. audax*, a solidly built fish with definite vertical stripes on the body. It grows to 500 lb (225 kg). A related species in Australian waters *M. zelandica* is also referred to as the Striped marlin while *M. australis* is called the Black marlin in Australia. FAMILY: Scombridae, ORDER: Perciformes, CLASS: Pisces.

MARMOSETS, New World monkeys, all very small with claws instead of flat nails on their hands and feet (except for the great toe). They have simple brains. Marmosets live in tropical forests and the south-Brazilian hardwood forests, keeping to larger branches where their claws can dig in and provide a firm hold. They tend to eat insects, leaves and fruit, but the Black tamarin *Saguinus midas* is said to eat fruit only, and the pinché feeds on seeds.

Marmosets move by scurrying, rather like a squirrel, and most species frequently jump from branch to branch or from tree to tree in the wild, but the Pied tamarin *Saguinus bicolor*, which is longer legged than other species and more lankily built, does not jump. The Pinché tamarin or Cottontop tamarin *S. oedipus* often stands bipedally when excited. Marmosets sleep curled into a ball.

Marmosets squeak and also make ultrasonic vocalizations, which have been measured at 10–50 kc per second.

Goeldi's marmoset *Callimico goeldii* is rare, being restricted to the upper Amazon region. It is 8½–10 in (22–25 cm) long with a tail of 13 in (33 cm); black in colour with a cape of hair swept back from the face, covering the ears and bushing out to the sides. The hair is soft and silky in texture.

The most familiar types of marmosets are small weighing 3–6 oz (85–170 gm). The head and body length is 6–8½ in (16–22 cm), with a tail of 10–14 in (25–36 cm). The Common marmoset *Callithrix jacchus* is marbled black and grey or black and brown;

the tail is ringed with black and grey; the ears have white, yellow or black tufts growing either in front of the pinna (and usually above and behind it too) or from its inner surface. The face is pale and hairy and there is a white blaze on the forehead. It is found along the Brazil coast.

Young marmosets are a different colour from adults, being brown with yellowish subterminal bands on the hairs, giving a tawny grizzled effect. This is precisely the colour pattern of the Pygmy marmoset *Cebuella pygmaea*, 5–5½ in (13–14 cm) long with a tail of about 8 in (20–21 cm). It has a rounded skull with a small face and is found on the upper Amazon. FAMILY: Callithricidae, ORDER: Primates, CLASS: Mammalia.

MARMOTS, ground-living, burrowing rodents found throughout the north temperate region, especially on mountains and open plains. Only one is a woodland animal, the woodchuck *Marmota monax* of North America. They are large, heavily built and ponderous by comparison with other squirrels, measuring 1–2 ft (30–60 cm) in length and weighing up to 15 lb (7 kg). The legs are short but powerful, and the tail is usually about a third the length of the body and only moderately bushy. The colour is of various shades of brown without any conspicuous pattern.

Whether living on mountains or plains, marmots are sociable, living in colonies based on a system of deep burrows that may extend for several yards underground. They spend the day feeding or just sunning themselves, but never far from an entrance to the burrow. Any individual that suspects danger emits a sharp whistle that sends the whole colony scuttling into their burrows with a remarkable turn of speed.

Marmots hibernate, probably more completely than any other Ground squirrels. They feed on green vegetation but lack cheek pouches. They do not store food but they become very fat in autumn. A new nest of dry grass is made deep in a burrow and an entire family may sleep together for up to six months, depending on the region. When they emerge in spring breeding soon begins, the litter of two or four being born after a gestation of about six weeks. The young grow slowly and are not mature until they are two or three years old.

The Alpine marmot *M. marmota* of Europe is familiar on pastures above the tree-line in the Alps, and the same, or very similar, species is found throughout northern Asia and western North America.

Three species of marmots are found in western North America, the best known being the Yellow-bellied marmot *M. flaviventris*. The Hoary marmot *M. caligata* extends north to the arctic coast of Alaska and is much prized for its dense fur. FAMILY: Sciuridae, ORDER: Rodentia, CLASS: Mammalia.

The unlovely marabou, African stork, a scavenger and associate of vultures.

MARSH DEER *Blastocerus dichotomus*, of southern Brazil to northeastern Argentina, stands 44 in (112 cm) at the shoulder and has a rich red coat. It lives near water, usually on marshy ground. The antlers usually have eight points, but 10, 12 or more are by no means rare. FAMILY: Cervidae, ORDER: Artiodactyla, CLASS: Mammalia.

MARSUPIAL 'CAT', carnivorous marsupials of Australia superficially resembling the true cats. The Little northern marsupial cat *Dasyurus hallucatus*, the Black-tailed marsupial cat *D. geoffroyi* and the Tiger cat *D. maculatus* have five toes on the hindfoot but the Eastern marsupial cat *D. viverrinus* has only four toes on the hindfoot. The smallest Marsupial cat is the Little northern, which has a head and body length of about 11 in (28 cm), the largest is the Tiger cat which is about 2 ft (61 cm) long excluding the tail. In all species the tail is about ¾ of head and body length and is hairy. The characteristic spotted pattern of the pelage is only continued onto the tail in the Tiger cat.

The newborn Eastern marsupial cat weighs but 0·015 grains (12·5 mg), that is less than the weight of a single drop of water. It is born with deciduous claws on the forelimbs which aid the journey over the hairs to the teat and are then shed. The pouch in all Marsupial cats is restricted to a flap of skin, developed only in the breeding season, which only partly covers the developing young attached to the teats.

The smaller Marsupial cats are largely insect-feeders but they also feed on small birds, mammals and reptiles. The Tiger cat feeds largely on mammals and birds. FAMILY: Dasyuridae, ORDER: Marsupialia, CLASS: Mammalia.

MARSUPIAL 'MICE', small, generally insectivorous, Australian marsupials with shrew-like snouts and ranging in size from that of a small mouse to a rat. *Planigale ingrami* has an adult body weight of only about ⅛ oz (4 gm) while Byrne's marsupial mouse *Dasyuroides byrnei* is about the size of a house rat. FAMILY: Dasyuridae, ORDER: Marsupialia, CLASS: Mammalia.

MARSUPIAL 'WOLF' *Thylacinus cynocephalus*, dog-like in appearance and size, it is the largest of the carnivorous marsupials and may now be extinct. A general tawny yellow-brown animal, with 16–18 dark brown bars across the back, its overall length is about 5 ft (1·7 m), the head and body being about 3 ft (1 m) long. In historical times the Marsupial wolf was confined to Tasmania but it inhabited New Guinea 10,000 years ago and parts of the Australian continent 3,000 years ago. It has not been positively identified in Tasmania for more than 30 years. FAMILY: Dasyuridae, ORDER: Marsupialia, CLASS: Mammalia.

MARTENS, cat-sized carnivores, among the world's most valuable fur-bearers. They are widely distributed in the forested areas of North America and Eurasia south to Malaya, dividing into six species along the way. Members of this genus (*Martes*) have a darkly coloured, lustrous fur with a white, yellow or orange neck-patch or chest-bib.

The Pine marten *M. martes*, of Europe to the Caucasus mountains, measures 24·8–31·5 in (63–80 cm) and weighs from 1·5–3·8 lb (0·8–1·6 kg). Typically found in dense pine forests, it avoids populated areas. The breeding season is in June or July and, after an eight month gestation, two to five cubs are born the following April. Consequently females only have a litter every two years. The young are naked and blind at birth, opening their eyes two weeks later. The bulk of their omnivorous diet consists in squirrels, rodents, birds, insects, fruit and eggs.

The Stone marten *M. foina* is smaller than the Pine marten, rarely exceeding 20½–29½ in (52–75 cm) in total length. It has a shorter neck with a pure white chin and chest-patch. It can usually be found on rocky slopes. This marten often lives in close proximity to man, settling in empty barns or attics, quite unafraid.

The sable *M. zibellina*, famous for its silky-soft fur, lives in Russia. Mainly terrestrial, it can be recognized by its stouter limbs and larger ears.

The fisher or pekan *M. pennanti* is the largest measuring 32·7–40·7 in (83–103 cm) and weighing 14–18 lb (6½–8½ kg). The name is derived from its reported habit of raiding baited traps and 'fishing-out' the contents, rather than a predilection for fishes. Porcupines seem to be a favoured food. It also feeds on squirrels, carrion and fruit. Two or three cubs are born in the spring after an almost year-long gestation. FAMILY: Mustelidae, ORDER: Carnivora, CLASS: Mammalia.

MATAMATA *Chelys fimbriata*, South American side-neck turtle with a broad, flattened head and neck covered with fringes of skin giving it a 'mossy' appearance. A fish wandering too close to its jaws may be engulfed by a sudden forward lunge. An elaborate hydraulic-action by use of a powerful hyoid apparatus not only pulls water into the throat but snaps the head forward to engulf the prey. FAMILY: Chelidae, ORDER: Testudines, CLASS: Reptilia.

MAYFLIES, aquatic insects of river banks and lake shores, familiar because of their summer swarms. The 1,300 living species are related to the dragonflies. Mayflies rest with the wings raised vertically above the body and at right angles to its main axis. Adult mayflies have very short lives. Their mouthparts are vestigial so they cannot feed and live only long enough to mate and lay eggs. They are soft-bodied insects with short bristle-like antennae, two pairs of wings—the hind pair being very much the smaller—and three long bristle-like 'tails' projecting from the end of the abdomen. They have aquatic larvae and are therefore never found far from freshwater. They are widely distributed throughout the world. ORDER: Ephemeroptera, CLASS: Insecta, PHYLUM: Arthropoda.

MEALWORMS, larvae of many Flour beetles *Tribolium* occurring as pests in flour and associated products. The beetles are reddish-brown or black ⅛–¼ in (3–6 mm) long, somewhat flattened, and their larvae

The American marten or sable is as agile as a squirrel in the trees. It is no less agile on the ground.

Giant millipede of Kenya, coiled at rest, with scavenging mites running over it.

is also largely black and white, but has rufous brown sides. Its most outstanding feature is its crest which extends upwards from the top and back of the head in a black-bordered white fan. FAMILY: Anatidae, ORDER: Anseriformes, CLASS: Aves.

MIDWIFE TOAD *Alytes obstetricans*, of western Europe, in which the male collects the eggs, as they are laid in strings by the female, around his legs. Thereafter he takes care of them, visiting water periodically to keep the eggs moist and finally entering water as the tadpoles hatch. FAMILY: Discoglossidae, ORDER: Anura, CLASS: Amphibia.

MILLER'S THUMB *Cottus gobio*, or bull-head, a freshwater fish of clear, fast-running and shallow streams in Europe. The head is broad and flat, the body round and lacking scales except along the lateral line. The pectoral fins are large. The colour varies to accord with the bottom on which the fish rests. It spends most of its time under stones, only darting out to catch a passing fish or insect larva. The eggs are guarded by the male which will display by expanding its gill covers to an intruder. Its common name derives from the shape of a miller's thumb which, used in testing flour by rubbing it between the thumb and forefinger, often became spatulate. FAMILY: Cottidae, ORDER: Scorpaeniformes, CLASS: Pisces.

MILLIPEDES, slow-moving arthropods well armoured. When disturbed they 'freeze' or curl-up into a tight spiral or sphere and many have a row of stink glands down both sides of the body. Millipedes, therefore, contrast markedly with centipedes which are adapted for swift running and offence.

There are over 8,000 species. The Flat-backed millipede *Platyrrhacus pictus* of South America is 5 in (13 cm) long and ¾ in (2 cm) broad. The African Snake millipede *Graphidostreptus gigas* is 11 in (28 cm) long and nearly ¾ in (2 cm) in diameter. The European *Macrosternodesmus palicola* is probably one of the smallest species ³⁄₁₆ in (3·5 mm) long.

The trunk consists of many articulating rings, most of which carry two pairs of legs, hence the name Diplopoda. The rings are similar, most of them having two pairs of legs, two pairs of swellings or ganglia on the ventral nerve cord and two pairs of openings (ostia) into the dorsal tubular heart. However, the first few rings have only one pair of legs and a few of the posterior rings are without legs.

Most millipedes tend their eggs. In the Snake and the Flat-backed millipedes an elaborate dome-shaped nest is built with moistened soil and excrement. They usually stay around their nests guarding them until the young have hatched.

Most millipedes living in temperate regions are nocturnal and secretive. They live in

are yellowish mobile grubs that burrow into flour, cereals, dried fruits and spices. FAMILY: Tenebrionidae, ORDER: Coleoptera, CLASS: Insecta, PHYLUM: Arthropoda.

MEERKAT *Suricata suricatta*, or suricate, one of the smallest mongooses, confined to the dry, sandy plains of southern Africa where it lives in colonial burrows. The meerkat's long soft coat is light grizzled grey with black transverse bars across the back and thick reddish underfur. The head is white, the ears black and the tail yellowish with a black tip. Meerkats particularly enjoy sitting on their haunches basking in the sun and make attractive pets. FAMILY: Viverridae, ORDER: Carnivora, CLASS: Mammalia.

MERGANSER, six species of saltwater diving ducks or sea-ducks with a long slim bill with serrations for gripping slippery prey, spread over Europe, Asia and South and North America. The rare Brazilian merganser *Mergus octosetaceus*, lives on streams in virgin forests. The Red-breasted merganser *Mergus serrator*, widely distributed through northern North America, northern Europe and northern Asia, lives on lakes, rivers, estuaries and sea coasts, wherever fishes live in fairly clear water. The prey is captured beneath the surface, mergansers being specialized for under-water swimming. They are highly

streamlined and have legs placed well back. The drake has a green-black double-crested head separated from a cinnamon breast by a broad white collar. The back is black, the belly cream and the sides vermiculated in black and white. The bill and legs are red. There is also much white in the wing which, when the bird is in post-breeding eclipse plumage, distinguishes it from the female which has a much more sombre plumage. She is grey with a brown head as are all female mergansers.

Another well-known species is the closely-related American merganser *M. merganser*. The European race is known as the goosander. This has the green-black head but the crest is a single backward sweep changing the apparent shape of the head. The back is black but the underparts are entirely cream. It is found much more frequently in wooded areas.

Two smaller species are the smew *M. albellus* and Hooded merganser *M. cucullatus* of Eurasia and North America respectively. Both live on inland waters bordered with good woodland cover. They nest in tree holes and crevices and take fishes, frogs and invertebrates.

The drake smew is largely white with a black face patch and a black band from the side of the head to the nape. In flight the bird appears boldly pied. The Hooded merganser

leaf-litter and soil, under loose bark, under fallen logs or in dead wood. Millipedes eat dead and decaying vegetation playing a role equivalent to that of the earthworm. Some are suspected of damaging young seedlings but probably they merely aggravate damage to living plants initiated by some other agent. CLASS: Diplopoda, PHYLUM: Arthropoda.

MINK, semi-aquatic mustelids like martens in size and appearance, except for the small ears, dark fur and bushy tails. New World mink *Mustela vison*, distributed from Alaska south to the northern United States, are more widespread than the smaller European species, *M. lutreola*. Deep chestnut in colour, the fur has long soft guard hairs, responsible for its lustrous quality. White patches may sometimes be present on the lips, chin and underparts of the European species. Males are usually larger than females, measuring from 17–29 in (43–73 cm), the tail accounting for nearly half the length, and weighing up to 3·8 lb (1·6 kg). Even though the coat is not water-repellant and the small paws with naked soles and semi-retractile claws are only partially webbed, minks were once known as 'marsh-otters' because of their amphibious habits. Exploiting both streams and woodland habitats, this versatile carnivore is both a proficient swimmer and terrestrial hunter.

Mink catch small fishes all the year round, sometimes hoarding and killing more than they can eat. They also kill rabbits and waterfowl. FAMILY: Mustelidae, ORDER: Carnivora, CLASS: Mammalia.

MISTLE THRUSH *Turdus viscivorus*, European bird, 10¼ in (26 cm) long, grey-brown above, with the breast marked with prominent diamond-shaped black spots. Its food is insects, worms and berries, and its presence is indicated by the rattling alarm call when the bird is disturbed, like the sound of a miniature, old-time police rattle. The nest may be up to 52½ ft (16 m), in a tree, and in it 3–5 pale blue eggs, spotted with brown are laid and incubated by the female for about two weeks. A remarkable feature of the Mistle thrush is that the male sings loudly and continuously in the worst weather and can sometimes be seen singing at the top of a sapling in a blizzard which whips the sapling backwards and forwards, the bird keeping its grip and singing all the time. FAMILY: Muscicapidae, ORDER: Passeriformes, CLASS: Aves.

MOCKINGBIRDS, 34 species of song-birds found in the Americas. They are mainly thrush-sized and have loud, prolonged and varied songs. They are fairly long-tailed, with short rounded wings, a slender bill of the insect-eating type and well developed legs. They are mainly terrestrial or skulk in low shrubby vegetation, either growing along or with taller forest growth. The plumage is usually a dull grey or brown, darker on wings and tail, but may be variegated with white markings on head, wings and tail.

The name originates from the Northern mockingbird, *Mimus polyglottos*. It implies that these birds are regular mimics, but this has been somewhat exaggerated for, although mimicry of other birds does occur, it only forms a minor part of the repertoire of the Northern mockingbird and seems to be even less apparent in other species.

The Northern mockingbird feeds extensively on insects taken from the surface of the ground but mockingbirds as a whole also take fruit. It has a habit of flicking its long tail and may also momentarily spread its wings. FAMILY: Mimidae, ORDER: Passeriformes, CLASS: Aves.

MOLE, COMMON, *Talpa europaea*, a small insectivore adapted to an underground life. It is glossy black with very large 'hands' projecting sideways from the body. The muzzle is long, mobile, sparsely covered with hair and pink at its tip. The eyes are extremely small and usually hidden in the fur. There is no external ear. The neck is short so that the head is hunched back into the shoulder region. The tail is short and bristly. The head and body together usually total about 5½ in (14 cm), the tail is 1–1½ in (3–3·5 cm) and the animal weighs 2–2¼ oz (80–120 g). Males are bigger than females.

Its forelimbs are massive and operated by enormous muscles. The humerus is a short, very solid bone of peculiar shape and points upwards. The forefeet are large, flat and turned outwards from the body and the wrist contains a bony modification that broadens and strengthens the hand. The shoulder blade and pelvis are long and thin and the latter is solidly fused to the vertebral column. The skull is flat and narrow.

The mole's snout is extremely sensitive, being studded with numerous tiny sensory capsules called Eimer's organs. Moles are not blind since they can be taught to perform tests involving discrimination between light and dark, but the eyes are very small, simple in structure and usually hidden in the fur of the face.

Digging is done with the forefeet, loose soil being collected together and pushed upwards to form a heap on the surface (the 'molehill' or 'tump'). The mole can push upwards a mass of earth 20 times its own weight using the forelimbs. In spring 'mole fortresses', which are very large molehills

The American mink has escaped from mink farms in Britain and become feral.

overlaying the breeding nest, are built. The nest itself is made of leaves and grass collected from the surface and in it the young are born in April or May. Litter sizes average four and second litters are rare. Newborn young are pink and naked; they leave the nest when about five weeks old to lead solitary lives.

Moles feed on soil invertebrates, mainly worms (about 90% of their diet) collected underground. They often store worms which have been immobilized by mutilation of the front end; one such store contained 1,280 worms. FAMILY: Talpidae, ORDER: Insectivora, CLASS: Mammalia.

MOLOCH *Moloch horridus*, or 'Thorny devil', of the arid regions of Australia. Slow-moving and harmless, this lizard forms a complete antithesis of its name. About 8 in (20 cm) long, coloured orange and brown and covered with spines it feeds almost exclusively on ants. Another lizard, the Horned lizard or 'Horned toad' of the American southwestern deserts, although of an entirely different family, has evolved along parallel lines both in diet and in its spiny appearance. FAMILY: Agamidae, ORDER: Squamata, CLASS: Reptilia.

MONGOOSES, carnivores with a reputation for killing snakes and stealing eggs. There are 48 species in the Mediterranean region, Africa, Madagascar and southern and Southeast Asia, all much alike in form and most of them similar in habits. They are long-bodied with short legs, a sharp muzzle and a long tapering bushy tail. Their short ears are almost hidden in their long, coarse fur, which is usually a speckled grey or brown but sometimes striped or banded as in the Banded or Zebra mongoose *Mungos mungo*, and the Broad-striped mongoose of Madagascar *Galidictis striata*. Most species have five well clawed toes on each foot. The largest are 3½–4 ft (1–1·2 m) long of which just under half is tail.

One of the larger and best known is the Common or Egyptian mongoose, or ichneumon *Herpestes ichneumon* 2 ft (60 cm) long with a tail of 18 in (46 cm), ranging from the Cape to Egypt, and in southern France and Spain. Its body is a grizzled iron-grey with a black tip to the tail. The Ancient Egyptians regarded it as sacred. Another large species, the Crab-eating mongoose *Herpestes urva*, of southeast Asia, 4 ft (1·2 m) long, is grey with a longitudinal white stripe on either side of the neck. The smallest is the Dwarf mongoose *Helogale parvula*, of Africa, south of the Sahara, which is not more than 18 in (46 cm) long. The Small Indian mongoose *Herpestes auropunctatus* is one of the most widespread of mongooses. It is grey and about 2 ft (60 cm) long and ranges through Persia, Nepal, northern India, Assam, Burma, Siam and Malaya. It has been introduced also into the West Indies and Hawaii to keep

The Small mongoose of India, one of the most widespread of mongooses.

down the snakes and rats. Wherever it has been introduced it has become a pest, attacking small native animals and poultry.

The various species occupy a variety of habitats; forest, bush, reed-beds, savannah and semi-desert, at low and high altitudes. Most of them are active by day, but a few seem to be active for parts of both day and night. The White-tailed mongoose *Ichneumia albicauda* is active at night only. Most species are ground living but a few, such as the Madagascar ringtailed mongoose *Galidia elegans*, climb trees, while the Water mongoose *Atilax paludinosus* is aquatic. They are usually solitary but the Dwarf mongoose is usually seen about in the daytime in groups of up to a dozen, sheltering by night in burrows or termite mounds. The cusimanse *Crossarchus obscurus* lives in groups of 10–24, while the Yellow mongoose *Cynictis penicillata* lives in large colonies of up to 50 in burrows. See meerkat. FAMILY: Viverridae, ORDER: Carnivora, CLASS: Mammalia.

MONITORS *Varanus*, 25 species of lizard the biggest being the Komodo dragon. Monitors have slender bodies and long necks and tails, and a forked tongue.

Monitors resemble snakes in their ability to swallow large prey. The bones of the jaws are movable on each other and give a wide

gape and the two halves of the lower jaw are joined by a ligament. No monitor has poison fangs.

Monitors are found in Africa, southern Asia and, more especially, the islands of the East Indies and Australia. *V. griseus* lives in the deserts of North Africa, whereas *V. niloticus* readily takes to the rivers in its search for food, while *V. prasinus* is at home in the treetops in the tropical rain-forests of New Guinea. Monitors may either dig their own burrows or use the abandoned burrows of mammals or they may sleep in crevices in rocks or in hollow trees.

All monitors are predators on any animals they can overpower. The smaller kinds eat mainly insects, the larger species catch lizards, small mammals and birds. Some are egg-eaters and the Nile monitor is famous for its ability to find the nests of crocodiles and gorge itself on the eggs. FAMILY: Varanidae, ORDER: Squamata, CLASS: Reptilia.

MOORHEN *Gallinula chloropus*, otherwise known as the waterhen or, in America, the Common gallinule, a cosmopolitan species except for the extreme northern and southern latitudes and Australasia. In Australia it is represented by *G. tenebrosa*, the very closely related Dusky moorhen.

The moorhen is brownish-black, some 13 in

Yellow monitor *Varanus flavescens*, a large lizard of southern Asia.

The moorhen is almost world-wide; in America it is called the Common gallinule.

MOSQUITOES, two-winged flies of the family Culicidae, with 3,000 known species. The females of many species feed on vertebrate blood. Their mouthparts are drawn out into slender stylets which, except when feeding, are enclosed in a sheath forming a long proboscis. During blood-feeding the sheath is drawn back and the bundle of stylets is inserted through the skin into a small blood vessel.

Four larval stages and a pupal stage are passed through in the course of development. The larvae are found in water of almost every kind. Besides absorbing oxygen through the body surface they take in air at the surface of the water through a pair of breathing pores or spiracles situated at the tip of the abdomen. The pupae breathe by means of paired respiratory trumpets situated on top of the thorax.

The eggs may be laid singly or compacted into a floating ribbon or raft or, in some cases, a more or less symmetrical egg mass attached to the underside of floating vegetation.

One species of *Aedes* breeds in volcanic pools hot enough and alkaline enough to take the skin off a foot incautiously inserted into them. Organic pollution is lethal to many species but favourable to some. Huge increases in *Culex fatigans*, the urban carrier of the disease known as Bancroftian filariasis, have occurred in recent years in consequence of the pollution of tropical cities by domestic and industrial waste.

Only the females feed on blood. Male mosquitoes feed on sugary substances such as the nectar secreted by flowers. Such substances also form an important part of the diet of the females of many species, the blood meal serving mainly to provide additional resources for developing the eggs.

Many birds and mammals harbour blood

(33 cm) long, with a pattern of white streaks on the flanks and a short tail which is frequently 'flirted' to display the white undertail coverts separated by a black central band. The underparts are greyer in tone than the back, the legs are green with a red garter above the tarsal joint, the frontal shield on the head and the base of the bill is red and the bill tip is yellow. As in other rails the head is jerked back and forth when the bird is walking or swimming.

Moorhens frequent a considerable variety of freshwater habitats, as long as there is cover close at hand. They eat many kinds of small animals and a larger proportion of leaves and fruits. Flight is strong once the bird is on the wing, with the feet trailing behind the tail.

The nests of moorhens are on or near the edge of still or slowly moving fresh water from swampy rain-forests to isolated desert pools, and from sea level to over 13,000 ft (3,900 m) in the Andes. The nest is made of dead reeds, sedges and similar plants, though sometimes the birds will build above ground or water level, occasionally using old nests of other species. Usually 5–11 eggs are laid, and normally there are two broods in a season, frequently three. FAMILY: Rallidae, ORDER: Gruiformes, CLASS: Aves.

MOOSE *Alces alces*, a very large long-legged deer of cold climates. It is known as elk in northern Europe and Asia and moose in North America and has a wide distribution in both eastern and western hemispheres. The moose, deep brown up to 7 ft 9 in (2·3 m) at the shoulder, has a short tail and broad,

overhanging muzzle, the nose of which is covered with short hair except for a small bare. triangular patch between the nostrils. Its rump is noticeably lower than its shoulders. The neck is comparatively short, and from it hangs a dewlap or 'bell', which is well developed in the North American form, but short in the elk. Adult males, particularly of the Alaskan moose, develop extremely large palmate antlers which may measure up to 6 ft (1·8 m) in span. Outstanding bulls from Alaska may weigh as much as 1,700–1,800 lb (733–816 kg). FAMILY: Cervidae, ORDER: Artiodactyla, CLASS: Mammalia.

Female mosquito *Aedes aegypti,* its blood-sucking mouthparts can puncture human skin.

The Blue-crowned motmot, noted for perching for long periods, calling monotonously.

hind and front legs. The underwool tends to be greasy to the touch. Males and females are almost identical in appearance and both have large chin beards, narrow pointed ears and short, recurved, black horns. The males carry large glands behind the horns, which swell during the rutting season. FAMILY: Bovidae, ORDER: Artiodactyla, CLASS: Mammalia.

MOUSEBIRDS, small, long-tailed and crested arboreal birds. They are found only in Africa south of the Sahara and in Abyssinia, in the more open tree savannahs and forest edge habitats. The six species are finch-sized and all have tufted crests and long, slender graduated tails. The plumage, particularly that of the head and neck, is soft and lax. It is generally brown or grey, at times with some fine transverse barring. The only distinctive colouring is on the head, which is red-cheeked on *Colius indicus*, white on *C. leucocephalus*, and blue-naped on *C. macrourus*. There is bare skin around the eyes and nostrils which may be red, blue or grey; and the bill may be black-and-white or red in different species.

In general appearance mousebirds are squat and large-headed, with a stout, short and curved bill. The legs are short and the feet are strong, with long sharp claws. The hindtoe can be reversed so that all four toes

Mousebird of Africa south of the Sahara, eating flowers of the Kaffirboom.

parasites, ranging from viruses to single-celled Protozoa, such as the Malaria parasites, and parasitic worms, such as those causing filariasis. FAMILY: Culicidae, ORDER: Diptera, CLASS: Insecta, PHYLUM: Arthropoda.

MOTMOT, common name for the eight tropical, forest-dwelling birds, from Mexico south to northeastern Argentina. Motmots vary in length from $6\frac{1}{2}$–$19\frac{3}{4}$ in ($16\frac{1}{2}$–50 cm) and have short and rounded wings, a long tail and a large bill, which is broad and somewhat decurved with serrated edges. In most species the tail is graduated and in typical motmots the two central tail-feathers are much longer than the others and in the subterminal parts the barbs are loosely attached and fall off when the bird preens them. This results in part of the vane becoming naked while at the end of the vane the barbs remain intact leaving a racquet tip.

Most motmots are greenish, olive- or rufous-brown with some bright colours on the head and a dark spot on the breast. They live in dark forests and are difficult to locate even when they call constantly. They feed on insects and berries snapped off in flight.

Motmots nest in holes which they dig with their strong bills, either in a bank or in the level ground of the forest floor. The entrance pipe can be long and even curved and at the end is a chamber where are laid three or four round, pure white eggs. Both sexes share the incubation of 21–22 days. FAMILY: Momotidae, ORDER: Coraciiformes, CLASS: Aves.

MOUNTAIN GOAT *Oreamnos americanus*, one of the most peculiar hoofed mammals; not a goat, but a goat-antelope and a distant relative of the European chamois. It is an animal specialized to live on steep, wet, and usually snowcovered mountains, where chilling snowstorms are not absent even in summer and where winter reigns for up to eight months of the year. The Mountain goat has massive, muscular legs which terminate in large, broad hooves. It is a methodical climber, not a jumper, and resembles a bear when moving. Only exceptionally is it found away from steep, broken cliffs. Its white coat is made up of thick, long underwool and long guard hairs. There is a hair ridge on the neck, withers, and rump, and long hair parts on

Mudskippers

may point forwards, and the bird will frequently hang from a twig, tail downwards, with the toes hooked over the perch; but on a flat surface both the outer toe and hind toe may point back to give a zygodactyl foot. The birds tend to rest back on the whole tarsus when moving or resting, but can shuffle and clamber about the branches of trees in a variety of acrobatic postures, and hop or run on level surfaces. The shafts of the tail feathers are stiff and lend some support. The birds clamber rapidly about on trees and bushes, feeding mainly on fruit, but also eat other parts such as leaves, and occasionally take insects. FAMILY: Coliidae, ORDER: Coliiformes, CLASS: Aves.

MUDSKIPPERS, a family of small goby-like fishes living in brackish waters and mangrove swamps of the Indo-Pacific region. Their common name refers to their habit of leaving the water and skipping across the exposed sand or mudflats at low tide. The eyes bulge from the top of the head and the pectoral fins have become modified with a fleshy base so that they can support the body. In some species the pelvic fins are also modified in this way; in others they are joined to form a sucker.

One of the most widespread species is *Periophthalmus koelreuteri* of the Indian Ocean. It spends a great deal of its time, at low tide, perched on the edges of small pools in mangrove swamps with the tip of its tail just in the water. When disturbed it will skip to the next pool, often with jumps of 2 ft (60 cm), rarely missing its target. These leaps are made by curling the body and then straightening it suddenly. It can also leap along the surface of the water. This species grows to about 5 in (12 cm) in length but certain of the Indo-Malayan species grow to about 12 in (30 cm) and are dug up from holes in the mud by local fishermen. FAMILY: Gobiidae, ORDER: Perciformes, CLASS: Pisces.

Male Reeve's muntjac.

MULE DEER *Odocoileus hemionus*, which is found over a vast expanse of western North America and in a variety of habitats, from high mountains to plains and deserts, from central Mexico to southern Alaska. 11 subspecies are recognized of which the typical deer *O. h. hemionus* has the greatest range. The type inhabiting the Northwest Pacific coastal areas, *O. h. sitkensis*, is generally referred to as the Black-tailed deer or Sitka deer. The smallest Mule deer is *O. h. peninsulae*, found in lower Baja California.

The Mule deer is fairly uniform in colour throughout its range, and distinctions between subspecies are not too well defined. Generally speaking, the winter coat is a brownish-grey which changes to a rusty-tan or red in summer. FAMILY: Cervidae, ORDER: Artiodactyla, CLASS: Mammalia.

MUNTJAC *Muntiacus*, a small deer ranging from India to southeastern China and Formosa, and to Indonesia. It includes five species and 17 subspecies. Other names are Barking deer and Rib-faced deer, the latter because the antlers, which consist of a short brow tine and an unbranched beam measuring about 3–7 in (7·6–17 cm) in length, are supported on long skin-covered pedicles which continue down the forehead as converging ridges. The cry of this deer is a loud, short bark, similar to that of a dog, and this is often repeated many times, hence Barking deer.

Both sexes have canine teeth in the upper jaw, those of the bucks extending to about 1 in (2·5 cm), used for fighting.

An adult male Indian muntjac *Muntiacus muntjak* measures 22–23 in (56–58 cm) high at the shoulder, the body colour being a deep chestnut in summer, slightly darker in winter.

Reeve's muntjac *M. reevesi* is sometimes referred to as the Chinese muntjac. It measures only 16–18 in (40–45 cm) at the shoulder. One of the rarest of the Chinese deer is the Black or Hairy-fronted muntjac *M. crinifrons* which occurs in Chekiang Province. It is a large muntjac, with a shoulder height of about 24 in (61 cm). FAMILY: Cervidae, ORDER: Artiodactyla, CLASS: Mammalia.

MUSCOVY DUCK *Cairini moschata*, an ugly Perching duck which breeds in tropical America and is the ancestor of the domestic muscovy. The plumage of the wild muscovy is usually greenish-black with patches of white with lead-blue legs. The naked skin of the face is bright-red thrown into a knob-like carbuncle more developed in the male than the female and the male also has a mane-like crest. In captivity several colour varieties have been bred, one being white with a black crest. The domestic muscovies are larger and heavier than the wild bird and are popular as ornamental waterfowl. They are also kept for their flesh particularly in America where they are fairly common farmyard birds.

In their native home muscovies are found on streams, lakes and marshes near woods and forests. They feed mainly on plants but also take small fish, crabs and insects. Outside the breeding season they live in flocks of 50 or more, roosting in the trees. The males are promiscuous and very fierce, fighting with their bills and the claws on their feet. The nest is built in a hole in a tree, the female doing all the incubating. FAMILY: Anatidae, ORDER: Anseriformes, CLASS: Aves.

MUSK DEER *Moschus*, three species of small solitary deer of central southern Asia. The males are completely devoid of antlers. Instead, they are armed with long upper canine tusks, $2\frac{3}{4}$–3 in (7–7·6 cm) in length. On the does they are much shorter.

An adult Musk deer stands 20–22 in (53 cm) high at the shoulder, and generally is a rich dark-brown, mottled and speckled with light-grey above, and paler beneath. Its principal habitat is forest and scrubland at elevations of about 7,000–11,000 ft (about 2,120–3,350 m).

This deer is much hunted for its musk, a brownish wax-like secretion from a gland on the abdomen of the bucks, used in the manu-

Mudskippers *Periophthalmus chrysospilos*, Malaya, on a muddy beach at low tide.

facture of perfume and soap. About 1 oz (28 gm) of it can be obtained from a single male. Unlike all other species of deer, the Musk deer possesses a gall bladder. FAMILY: Cervidae, ORDER: Artiodactyla, CLASS: Mammalia.

MUSK-OX *Ovibos moschatus*, heavily-built, from the Arctic of North America; not a true ox, but more closely related to sheep and goats. It is 44–60 in (110–150 cm) high, weighing at least half a ton (500 kg). The long guard hairs are blackish and the soft light brown underfur is dense, and is shed in patches in the summer. The stocky legs are white. There is a hump on the shoulder. For all their clumsy appearance, musk-oxen are agile. They are highly aggressive and during the rut the bulls even chase birds!

For most of the year, musk-oxen form herds of four or five or up to 100 or more; adult bulls are often solitary, young bulls herd together. The cow is sexually mature at four years, the bull at five or six. The rutting season may start as early as mid-July, but does not reach its peak until September. The bulls give off a strong odour at this season, butt each other, bellow and try to mate with the cows. Finally a few dominant bulls emerge; each of these stands with his forefeet on a rock or mound, preparing to defend his cows. Calves are born in April or May, a single calf to each cow; it weighs on average 15½ lb (7 kg), and stands 18 in (46 cm) high. The mother protects her calf fiercely. Suckling continues for nine months; hence a female will calve only every other year. The calf moves along with the herd from its first day. Calves are heavily predated by wolves, and the herd's defence mechanism is to form a circle of adults around the calves, facing outwards showing a well-nigh impenetrable array of horns. Musk-oxen live for twenty years. FAMILY: Bovidae, ORDER: Artiodactyla, CLASS: Mammalia.

MUSK RAT *Ondatra zibethica*, or musquash, the largest of the voles, found throughout North America wherever the habitat is suitable. There is a second species *O. obscura* restricted to Newfoundland. Its total length is up to 25 in (63 cm) including a scaly rudder-like tail up to 10 in (25 cm) long. It weighs about 2 lb (0·9 kg). Its coat ranges in colour from silvery-brown to almost black and is composed of a thick waterproof underfur overlaid with long glistening guard-hairs. Its feet are broad and flat, the hindfeet webbed.

The Musk rat is aquatic, living in freshwater or salt marshes, or by streams and rivers. In summer it lives among the water plants and in the winter it builds a house of stems and other vegetation which projects above the water-line. Sometimes it tunnels into the river banks and builds its nest there. It feeds mainly on water plants but will also take fish, frogs and freshwater mussels. It mates in the water and has 3–5 litters a year with an average of 5–7 young in each. The gestation is 19–42 days.

The Musk rat is valued for its fur and also because it helps to keep waterways clear of water plants. It has been introduced into Europe where it is kept on ranches. Many, however, have escaped and gone wild and caused damage to river banks. FAMILY: Cricetidae, ORDER: Rodentia, CLASS: Mammalia.

MUSSELS, bivalve molluscs mainly living in the sea but with a few freshwater species. The best-known of the marine mussels is the Edible mussel *Mytilus edulis* which often occurs in dense communities near the mouths of estuaries or elsewhere on the shore where there is a suitable surface for attachment. The tissues are completely enclosed by the black-blue shell which may reach 3 in (7·7 cm) in length, and which is attached by means of a series of threads, the byssus threads, to the substratum. Each of the shell valves is the mirror-image of the other and can be closed very tightly by an anterior and a posterior adductor muscle which join the two valves transversely. CLASS: Bivalvia, PHYLUM: Mollusca.

MYNAH, Indian word for birds of the starling family. The common mynah *Acridotheres tristis* and the Hill mynah *Gracula religiosa* are the best known.

The Common mynah was originally found only in Afghanistan, India, Pakistan, Nepal and Indochina but it has been successfully introduced into Malaya, Natal, Australia, Hawaii, Seychelles, New Zealand and many other islands. It is a little larger than a Common starling, with a black head and neck, brown body and white underparts. The bill, legs and a patch of bare skin on the face are yellow and conspicuous white patches on the wings and tip of the tail show in flight.

Mynahs are well known because they live in association with man and make plenty of noise. They are as common a sight on the roadside of pastoral New Zealand as they are in the dry hills of India. The food consists of fruit as well as insects, which makes them unpopular with fruit growers, though they are certainly blamed for a good deal of the damage done by less conspicuous birds.

In autumn and winter mynahs return at night to communal roosts, much in the manner of starlings, but apart from this they are very territorial. Both members of a pair can be found on the territory for most of the year. The song and calls consist of a variety of rather loud raucous, chattering and whistling notes, some parts of which are quite melodious. The nest is an untidy cup placed in a niche in a tree or building, and from four to seven pale blue eggs are laid. Incubation takes about a fortnight and the young spend as long again in the nest before fledging.

The Hill mynah or 'grackle' (not to be confused with the New World grackles, family Icteridae) is best known as a cage-bird and is perhaps the best mimic of them all. It is similar to the Common mynah, but has prominent yellow wattles pointing backwards from behind the eye. Its natural habitat is the forests of India, Ceylon, Pakistan, Burma, the Malay peninsula and Indonesia, where it feeds in noisy flocks in the canopy of trees. FAMILY: Sturnidae, ORDER: Passeriformes, CLASS: Aves.

Indian hill mynah, a pet favoured for its ability to mimic sounds and speech.

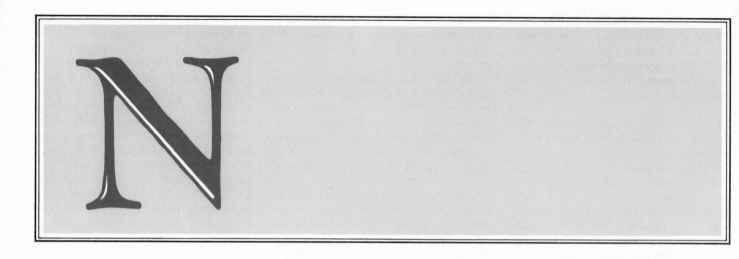

N

NARWHAL *Monodon monoceros*, a Toothed whale, probably the prototype of the fabulous unicorn. Its name, of Scandinavian origin, means corpse-whale. The teeth are completely absent in both sexes except for the single specialized left-sided tusk in the male. Sometimes the tusk may be on the right side and rarely there are two tusks, one on each side of the head, but the spiral always turns the same way regardless of which side of the head it is on. The body may be some 15 ft (5 m) and the tusk half as long. The function of the tusk is unknown. The narwhal is an arctic species that feeds on a wide variety of food which it catches effectively in spite of its toothless mouth. All the Toothed whales have asymmetrical skulls and that of the narwhal shows this feature to a considerable extent. This is not only on account of its tusk but is particularly associated with asymmetry in its nasal passages, probably related to needs of sonar sound production. FAMILY: Monodontidae, ORDER: Cetacea, CLASS: Mammalia.

NATIVE CAT *Dasyurus quoll*, one of the few living carnivorous marsupials, so called because it is about the size of a domestic cat to which is it unrelated. See Marsupial cat.

NEWTS, tailed amphibians which constitute the family Salamandridae. In Europe newt refers solely to the genus *Triturus*. Newts have a life history very similar to that of frogs and toads, the adults spending most of the year on land and only returning to the water to breed. They feed on small animals such as worms, snails and insects when on land, and on tadpoles, insect larvae and crustaceans while living in the water. The jaws of newts are lined with tiny teeth and there are two rows of teeth on the roof of the mouth. These are used for holding slippery prey. Newts hibernate in the autumn on land in crevices in the ground or under stones or logs. When they come out of hibernation in the spring they make their way to ponds for breeding. When in water they can breathe through their skins but rise to the surface every now and then to gulp air. During the breeding season the male

The Night heron *Nycticorax nycticorax* is inactive by day sheltering in trees near water or marsh and moves out as dusk spreads to feed mainly on small fishes.

develops a prominent crest on the back and tail which is used to attract the female during courtship displays. After courtship the male's sperm is deposited in the water in a spermotaphore. This is picked up by the female with her cloaca. The female usually lays 200–450 eggs which are fertilized inside her by the sperm. The eggs are attached to the stem or leaf of a water plant or to a small rock. Metamorphosis from the tadpole is usually complete by the end of the summer when the young adults leave the water. They remain on land until they become sexually mature three or four years later.

There are three European newts which are native to Britain. The most common is the Smooth or Common newt *T. vulgaris*. The length of the body is up to 4 in (10 cm) and the colour is usually olive-brown with darker spots on the upperparts and streaks on the head. The underside is vermilion or orange with round black spots. The throat is white

or yellow. The female is usually paler on the underside and sometimes without spots. The male's breeding crest is wavy.

The Palmate newt *T. helveticus* is very similar to the Smooth newt but only 3 in (7·5 cm) long and with a square-sided body. During the breeding season the males of the two species can be distinguished because black webs form between the toes of the hindfeet of the Palmate newts and the crest is not wavy.

The Crested or Warty newt *T. cristatus* is the largest European newt, growing up to 6 in (15 cm) long. The skin on the upperparts is dark-grey or blackish-brown and is covered with small warts. The underside is orange or yellow, spotted with black. The male's breeding crest starts from the head as a low frill, becomes higher between the shoulders and thighs and ends as a tail fin. FAMILY: Salamandridae, ORDER: Caudata, CLASS: Amphibia.

NIGHT HERONS, wading birds closely related to, but smaller than, other herons, mainly active at night. The Black-crowned night heron *Nycticorax nycticorax* ranges across southern Europe, Asia and Africa. It is replaced in the Americas by geographical races making it one of the most cosmopolitan of birds. Three other species are American and a fourth, the Nankeen night heron *N. caledonius*, is found in Australia, the Philippines and Polynesia.

The Black-crowned night heron is about 24 in (60 cm) long. The crown and back are black with a greenish gloss, the forehead and throat are pure white and the rest of the plumage is dove-grey or white tinged with grey. The sexes are similar in appearance. The adult plumage includes pale cream plumes, usually three, which fall from the nape and may measure 8 in (20 cm). Except when windblown, or at a nest, these are held together and resemble a single plume. The large eyes have crimson irises. The bill is black and shorter than that of a typical heron while the yellow legs, which may redden at nesting time, are comparatively short giving the bird a hunched appearance when perching.

Throughout the daylight hours the birds perch gregariously in trees, becoming active soon after sundown, when they fly to the marshes to feed on small fishes, amphibians and a variety of other animals, including small mammals.

The nests of sticks are small compared with the size of the bird and are sometimes so flimsy that the contents are visible from below. Pair-formation follows the general pattern of the Grey heron, the male taking up a position in a potential site and advertising for a mate. The plumes are raised in an 'appeasement ceremony' admitting the female to the nesting-site. Four eggs are an average clutch, incubated by both parents for three weeks. Feeding the young by regurgitation is also shared. FAMILY: Ardeidae, ORDER: Ciconiiformes, CLASS: Aves.

NIGHTINGALE *Luscinia megarhynchos*, bird renowned for its beautiful song. The nightingale is ordinary-looking, 6½ in (16·5 cm) long, warm-brown in colour, lighter beneath, and with a chestnut-brown tail. It has a southwestern palearctic distribution, including much of Europe, and its preferred habitat is deciduous woodland with dense undergrowth and a rich humus layer on the ground in which it searches for insects and other invertebrate food. It is frequently found in damp places. It nests near the ground, usually laying four or five eggs which are incubated for 13–14 days. FAMILY: Muscicapidae, ORDER: Passeriformes, CLASS: Aves.

NIGHTJARS, known as goatsuckers, from a myth that these birds drank milk from nanny goats. There are some 67 species, usually nocturnal, insectivorous and well-camouflaged,

covering most of the world excepting high latitudes, New Zealand and some oceanic islands.

North American species known from their calls are the whip-poor-will *Caprimulgus vociferus*, chuck-will's-widow *C. carolinensis* and the poorwill *Phalaenoptilus nuttallii*.

The word 'nightjar' is derived from the churring or jarring song, particularly of the European nightjar *C. europaeus*. This is 10½ in (26 cm) long with a grey-brown plumage which is mottled and barred and provides extremely good camouflage. Nightjars nest on the ground and rest on the ground or on branches, typically along the branch rather than across it. The rapid churring of the European nightjar is normally heard only at night.

Nighthawks are restricted to the New World. The Common nighthawk *Chordeiles minor*, 9 in (23 cm) long, is widespread in North America and is one of the few species which habitually flies by day.

The nightjars are almost entirely insectivorous. Most of them have large eyes, being nocturnal or crepuscular, 'hawking' for insects on the wing. The mouth has a very broad gape and most species have a fringe of stiff, bristle-like feathers around the mouth to increase the catchment area. The eggs are highly cryptic, marbled and blotched with shades of brown, grey and purple, on a pale background. Eggs and young are cared for by both sexes.

The poorwill is apparently unique in hibernating. FAMILY: Caprimulgidae, ORDER: Caprimulgiformes, CLASS: Aves.

NILE PERCH *Lates niloticus*, the largest African freshwater fish. It is found in the Nile, in some of the African lakes and in the larger West African rivers such as the Congo and the Niger. Most Nile perch are 4–5 ft (1·2–1·5 m) in length, but giants of

6 ft (1·8 m) and weighing more than 250 lb (113 kg) are not rare.

The Nile perch was well-known to the ancient Egyptians, who drew accurate pictures of it on the walls of their tombs. These fishes were not infrequently embalmed and placed in tombs.

They spawn in relatively sheltered conditions in water of about 10 ft (3 m). The eggs are pelagic and contain a large oil globule which gives them buoyancy. The adults are fish-eaters and are sometimes cannibalistic. FAMILY: Centropomidae, ORDER: Perciformes, CLASS: Pisces.

NILGAI *Boselaphus tragocamelus*, a large antelope of the hilly grasslands of peninsular India. Its closest living relative is the Four-horned antelope. Bull nilgai reach 52–56 in (130–140 cm) at the shoulder and may weigh 600 lb (270 kg); females are much smaller. The horns are short, smooth and keeled, averaging 8 in (20 cm) in length; they are found only in males. The build is robust, and the withers are higher than the rump. Males are iron-grey, looking blue in some lights (hence the alternative name of 'Blue bull'), but females and young are tawny. Both sexes have a white ring above each hoof, two white spots on each cheek, and white lips, chin, inner surfaces of ears, and underside of the tail. There is a dark mane on the neck and the male has a tuft of stiff black hair on the throat.

Small groups of four to ten are seen together (sometimes more) consisting of cows, calves and young bulls. Adult bulls live alone or associate in bachelor groups. In the rutting season the bulls fight, dropping to their knees and locking their foreheads, pressing down with their necks. The gestation period usually varies between eight and nine months. FAMILY: Bovidae, ORDER: Artiodactyla, CLASS: Mammalia.

Nilgai or Blue bulls showing the characteristic white ring above the hoof.

Old World nutcracker whose strong bill is used for opening nuts and digging for seeds and insects.

NOCTILUCA, marine protozoan of relatively large size (up to 2 mm), remarkable for being highly luminescent. It often occurs in enormous numbers in surface waters and is responsible for the 'phosporescence' of the sea at night and its reddish tint by day. FAMILY: Noctilucidae, ORDER: Dinoflagellata, CLASS: Mastigophora, PHYLUM: Protozoa.

NODDIES, five species of small terns restricted to tropical seas. Two are dark coloured, two are intermediate and one, the Fairy tern *Gygis alba*, is pure white. Some lay their single egg in an untidy nest in bushes or on the smallest of rock protuberances. The Fairy tern lays its egg in a crevice or depression on a bare tree branch. The Common noddy *Anous stolidus* is one of the few sea birds to breed and moult at the same time. FAMILY: Laridae, ORDER: Charadriiformes, CLASS: Aves.

NORWAY HADDOCK *Sebastes marinus*, or redfish of the North Atlantic, deep bodied with a perch-like appearance. The head is spiny, and scaled as far forward as the eyes, there is a single dorsal fin which is notched between the spiny and soft portions, and the general body colour is a bright red. The Norway haddock is found along both American and European coasts, at depths of 300–700 ft (90–200 m). It is of some commercial importance, particularly to the Norwegians but also along the American coasts, where it is known as the Rosefish. The Norway haddock is viviparous and a female of about 13 in (33 cm) has been known to bear as many as 20,000 young. FAMILY: Scorpaenidae, ORDER: Scorpaeniformes, CLASS: Pisces.

NORWAY LOBSTER *Nephrops norvegicus*, or Dublin Bay prawn, is lobster-like, 3 in (7·5 cm) long in the body with claws of nearly equal length, and is a beautiful orange-red. It lives in depths of 60–300 ft (20–100 m) on a soft mud bottom, and is commonly taken in the North Sea and exported to Italy where it is eaten as scampi. ORDER: Decapoda, CLASS: Crustacea, PHYLUM: Arthropoda.

NUTCRACKER, two crow-like birds, the Old World nutcracker *Nucifraga caryocatactes*, found at high altitudes and latitudes in coniferous forest throughout the Palearctic region (with eastern thin-billed and western thick-billed forms) and Clarke's nutcracker *N. columbiana*, which occupies similar habitats in western North America.

The Old World nutcracker is 12½ in (32 cm) long, dark-brown with noticeable white spots, white under-tail coverts, a white tail tip and white beneath the tail at the edges. The tail is otherwise very dark, as are the wings. The flight is rather heavy and undulating. On the ground progress is by strong bounding hops. The bill is black, long and strong and is used for digging in the ground for a variety of food —particularly fruits, seeds and invertebrate animals—and for opening nuts or pine cones.

The nutcrackers are outstanding examples of birds which store food. During the autumn almost all the daylight hours are spent in finding, carrying and storing the nuts. Journeys of up to 4 miles (6·5 km) are made from the spruce forests where the birds

European nuthatch bringing insect food to its nestlings. The nest is built in a ready-made hole.

have their stores to the hazel coppices where they forage. The exact position of the stores is remembered and the birds will dig down to them with accuracy even through snow.

Nutcrackers nest in conifers, the nest being made of twigs, moss, lichens and earth, lined with grass and hairy lichen, and typically placed near the main trunk, 15–30 ft (4·5–9 m) from the ground. Three or four eggs are laid and incubated by the female who is fed on the nest by the male from his throat pouch. The young are fed by both parents, largely from this pouch. FAMILY: Corvidae, ORDER: Passeriformes, CLASS: Aves.

NUTHATCHES, small, dumpy birds that forage on tree trunks for insects and spiders. They are found almost throughout the forested regions of Asia, Europe and North America. The true nuthatches are all placed in the genus *Sitta* and number about 18 species.

All but two nuthatches nest in trees, some of the small species excavating the hole themselves. Many of the Old World species reduce the size of the entrance hole by plastering it with mud which may deter some of the larger potential nest-site competitors. Two species of *Sitta*, the Rock nuthatch *S. tephronota* and *S. neumayer*, have left the forest environment and inhabit rocky hillsides of south-western Asia. These are the most industrious plasterers, walling up a rock cavity and constructing an entrance entirely of mud which may project 6 or 8 inches (15–20 cm) from the rock face. None of the New World species uses mud though the Red-breasted nuthatch *S. canadensis* smears the edge of its hole with pine resin. Four to ten eggs, white with reddish spots, are laid in the nest, which may consist simply of bark flakes or be lined with moss or hair. Incubation lasts a fortnight and is carried out solely by the female, but the male assists in feeding the young which remain in the nest for a further three weeks before fledging.

Most members of the family are about 5 in (12 cm) long, though the largest, the Giant nuthatch *Sitta magna* of Burma is about 9 in (23 cm) long. Apart from three very brightly coloured southern Asian species, the upperparts are normally grey-blue with the underparts white, grey, red-brown or chestnut, often more richly coloured in the male. The wallcreeper *Tichodroma muraria* resembles the nuthatches in build but the bill is slender and curved and the feet are weaker. FAMILY: Sittidae, ORDER: Passeriformes, CLASS: Aves.

NUTRIA, an alternative name, used especially in the fur trade, for the *coypu.

NYALA *Tragelaphus angasi*, an antelope of southeast Africa, related to the *kudu. The Mountain nyala *T. buxtoni*, is confined to the mountains of South Abyssinia. FAMILY: Bovidae, ORDER: Artiodactyla, CLASS: Mammalia.

OARFISH *Regalecus glesne*, a long, ribbon-like fish, which may reach 20 ft (6 m) in length. It is thin and the colour of polished silver. The dorsal fin is almost as long as the body. Starting just over the eye, the anterior rays are elongated into long plumes and these and the rest of the dorsal fins are bright red. The name of the fish derives from the scarlet pelvic fins, which are thin and elongated but expanded at their tips like the blades of an oar. The anal and caudal fins are lacking in the adult. The body is naked and the shining silver colour comes from guanine crystals deposited in the skin. Very few have been seen alive but it is said that when one swims at the surface it lies on its side and undulates its body. Since the snout is short and the face a little horse-like, there are all the ingredients for a real sea serpent—a bright red mane, shining body, large size and humps (undulations when swimming).

In some areas this fish is known as the 'King of the herrings' (a name also given to the John dory). FAMILY: Regalecidae, ORDER: Lampridiformes, CLASS: Pisces.

OCEAN SUNFISHES, five species of large, disc-shaped oceanic fishes apparently lacking a tail which has earned them the alternative name of headfishes. The body is greatly compressed, the head large and the dorsal and anal fins prolonged into paddle-like structures. The most striking feature is the abrupt termination of the body behind the dorsal and anal fins so that they seem to be all head. The Ocean sunfish *Mola mola*, found in all oceans, is the largest in the family up to 11 ft (3·6 cm) in length and weighing up to a ton. FAMILY: Molidae, ORDER: Tetraodontiformes, CLASS: Pisces.

OCELOT or Painted leopard *Panthera pardalis*, a medium sized South American cat, small but highly patterned, of the general leopard type. It has a shoulder height of 20 in (50·8 cm) and an overall length of 4½ ft (1·4 m) including the tail, which accounts for one third of the total length.

The ocelot is found from southern Texas through the Isthmus of Panama to Brazil and Bolivia. It subsists mainly on small mammals and birds.

Ocelots in Texas produce their young in the autumn, while those in Mexico breed in January. The gestation is approximately 115 days, at the end of which two kittens are born. The den usually consists of a small cave in the rocks or of a hollow log. The young are fully marked at birth, but are somewhat darker than their parents. Food is supplied by both the parents, and the pairs do not separate after the litter has been born. The adults communicate with mewing sounds. FAMILY: Felidae, ORDER: Carnivora, CLASS: Mammalia.

OCTOPUS, a mollusc whose most striking feature is the eight arms which encircle the mouth at the front of the head. On either side of the head are two large eyes enabling the animal to see all around. Behind the head is a sac-like body containing the viscera. Movement is either by 'walking' on the arms or by jet propulsion.

The Common octopus *Octopus vulgaris* is bottom-living. Each of its eight arms, of about equal length, bears two rows of suckers. The arms are joined together for about half their length by the interbrachial web.

At the centre of the bases of the arms is the mouth. There is a circular lip surrounding the chitinous beak, the upper half fitting into the lower one. Inside the mouth is a tooth-bearing ribbon, the radula.

Opening just below the head is the mantle cavity into which the gills project. A locking mechanism, which consists of a cartilaginous stud or ridge fitting into a socket on each side of the mantle, seals the mantle cavity while the exhalant jet of water is expelled through the funnel.

The Common octopus is widely distributed, being found in tropical and temperate seas throughout the world.

A male matures at a weight of about 7 oz (200 g); the female at about 4½ lb (2 kg). The male is recognizable by the hectocotylus or

Boldly masked ocelot. The name is from the Mexican thaloceloti or field tiger.

The Common octopus is eaten as seafood and is also used widely as a laboratory animal.

black and white that reminded him of a zebra. He realized it was a relative of the giraffe when he obtained several skulls. These possessed the lobed canine teeth and permanent horns partly covered by skin characteristic of the Giraffidae. In the okapi, the pointed horns are present only in the males.

When people see the few captive okapi near giraffe in zoos, they seldom appreciate their close relationship as superficially there are striking differences. The okapi's coat is a rich black with white markings on the thighs, legs and throat. This coloration serves to camouflage it in the dark forest. Its ears are large, enabling it to detect danger that may be close but unseen in the thick vegetation. It lives a relatively solitary life. Like the giraffe the okapi is not mute, but it seldom makes any vocal noises, at least in captivity. Like the giraffe too, the okapi is entirely a browser. FAMILY: Giraffidae, ORDER: Artiodactyla, CLASS: Mammalia.

OPOSSUMS, North and South American, generally carnivorous and arboreal, marsupials of the Family Didelphidae. The name 'opossum' has also been applied to Australian marsupial phalangers which are herbivorous and arboreal. The latter are now usually called possums to distinguish them from American forms. The opossums are the most primitive living marsupials.

All opossums are quadrupedal with five digits on each foot, the first toe of the hindfoot usually being opposable to the remainder. The tail is usually prehensile. In size they range from mouse-like to forms a little larger than domestic cats. They are crepuscular and nocturnal, occurring from northern USA to Patagonia and on some West Indian Islands.

specialized third right arm on the underside of which there is a groove. The spermatophores, or bundles of sperm, pass along the groove and are deposited in the mantle cavity of the female. Mating occurs close inshore from March until October in different parts of the world. As many as 50,000–180,000 eggs are laid in long strings and attached to rocks. The eggs are guarded and cared for by the female for up to nine weeks and once the eggs hatch she dies.

The octopus moves by jet propulsion, by the expulsion of water through the funnel by contraction of the mantle muscles. Movement by this means is usually backwards, the arms close together and streamlined behind the head. Forward movement is possible by ejecting the water towards the hind end of the body.

An important protective mechanism is the ability of the octopus to change its colour, by means of its chromatophores.

The octopus can alter its bodily form and outline and make the skin appear rough. These variations in colour, body form and outline make it almost impossible to discern amongst the rocks and seaweed.

The octopus will eject ink into the sea when disturbed, perhaps by a predator. The ink forms a black suspension from behind which the octopus can escape. FAMILY: Octopodidae, ORDER: Dibranchia, CLASS: Cephalopoda, PHYLUM: Mollusca.

OKAPI *Okapia johnstoni*, of the dense rainforest of west central Africa, was unknown to zoologists until 1901. Sir Harry Johnston, its discoverer, at first believed this animal, with a 6 ft (2 m) head and body length and a tail of 17 in (43 cm), must be a type of horse, as he had seen pieces of its hide striped with

Okapi, a relative of the giraffe, made known to science in 1901 and originally thought to be a kind of horse.

Opossum shrimps

Virginian opossum.

Opossum shrimp showing the marsupium or brood pouch and the statocysts.

The pouch, or marsupium, is well developed in some, but vestigial or absent in others. The Virginian opossum *Didelphis marsupialis virginiana* has a well developed pouch usually containing thirteen teats although there may be as few as nine or as many as seventeen. The Mouse opossums *Marmosa* of South America are pouchless and with seven to fifteen teats.

The Virginian opossum breeds at least twice in each year throughout its extensive range. After conception the fertilized eggs, often 25 or more in number, develop for 13 days in the uterus. There they are nourished by a placenta. The young at birth are minute and weigh 2½ ozs (0·16 gm). They are suckled in the pouch for about 80 days before they emerge to ride the mother's back.

The Virginian opossum is the only form occurring in North America to which it migrated from South and Central America in comparatively recent geological times. Within recorded history the Virginian opossum has rapidly extended its range and is now found in parts of southern Canada. It is about the size of a house cat with grizzled grey pelage, white head, black legs, unhaired ears and scaly, naked, prehensile tail. The clawless great toe of the hindfoot is held at right angles to the other toes. Opossums live in woodchuck burrows, natural cavities in rock piles, tangles of low vines and, more rarely, in natural cavities in trees. Climbing is the opossum's first means of escape but it has a remarkable facility for 'playing possum' or appearing to be dead. The nest is made of dried leaves and grasses gathered by mouth and passed under the body to be grasped by the curved tail and carried to the nest site. FAMILY: Didelphidae, ORDER: Marsupialia, CLASS: Mammalia.

OPOSSUM SHRIMPS, small transparent crustaceans mostly less than 1 in (2·5 cm) long, with some oceanic species attaining a length of about 6 in (15 cm) and coloured red. All live in marine or estuarine (brackish) water except *Mysis relicta*, which lives in freshwater lakes, and two species of *Antromysis*. The body is similar in many ways to that of the crayfish and lobster.

Opossum shrimps occur in most sandy bays and among the seaweeds on rocky shores throughout the world, often in large shoals in brackish water areas and are most easily found at the water's edge at low tide.

Most mysids live close to the bottom. Their food is varied, many feeding on fragments of seaweed and small animals found on the seabed but they also eat organic material carried by rivers or streams from the land into the sea. Some feed almost exclusively on small copepods.

The shoals of mysids are eaten by fish, birds and marine mammals. They are also harvested by fishermen in certain areas and used as bait, and in India and parts of Asia they are used for human food. ORDER: Mysidacea, SUBCLASS: Malacostraca, CLASS: Crustacea, PHYLUM: Arthropoda.

ORANG-UTAN *Pongo pygmaeus*, large anthropoid ape related to the chimpanzee, gorilla and man. The name is derived from two Malay words: 'orang', meaning 'man', and 'utan', meaning 'jungle'. In west Borneo, the native term 'Maias' is nearly always used, as it is by Malays.

The orang-utan is large, males growing to double the weight of females. The coat has coarse, long and shaggy hair, especially over the shoulders and arms, where it may grow up to 18 in (45 cm) long. It comes in shades of orange to purplish- or blackish-brown and is generally darker with increasing age. Infants and sub-adults have a shock of hair standing up from the crown of their heads which becomes short and flattened in adults, falling in a slight fringe over the forehead. The face and the gular pouch are bare, except for a fringe of hair on the upper lip and chin, growing strongly orange-coloured, in adult males. The skin is tough and papillated, dark brownish to black with irregular, wide patches of blue and black shining through the hair, especially on the abdomen. A large gular pouch and prominent cheek flanges of fat and tissue placed at the side of the face are the most striking features of heavy, adult males. The face is concave, like a dish, with projecting mighty jaws and slightly pronounced eyebrow ridges. The eyes and ears are small, the latter pressed close the the skull. The arms are extremely

The female orang-utan has a gular pouch like a monstrous double chin.

long with spans ranging between 7 ft and 8 ft (2·1–2·4 m). Similarly the hands are longer than those of either the gorilla or chimpanzee and are extremely powerful, except for the thumb which is small. The legs are relatively short and weak. Nails on hands and feet are strongly curved. The nail of the first or big toe is frequently missing in Bornean orang-utans. There is no tail.

The impression of huge size is gained mainly when an adult male is seen with arms extended, moving arboreally. However, owing to its short legs, when standing up the animal may only reach about 4 ft 6 in (1·3 m) in height; a female is about 3 ft 6 in (1·1 m). Males may weigh between 165–220 lb (75–100 kg); females between 75–100 lb (35–45 kg), depending on their age and state of health, and the food supply in their range, which varies with the seasons.

Orangs live in tropical rain-forest, usually within river boundaries or mountain ranges over 6,500 ft (2,000 m). Free-ranging orang-utans number approximately 5,000 at present, with little more than half of that number distributed in Bornean areas, mostly as scattered, smallish groups.

The infant is born weighing between $2\frac{1}{4}$–$3\frac{1}{8}$ lb (1·1–1·6 kg) and clings to mother's fur from the start. But it is necessary for the mother to carry and hold the infant as well, which she usually does over her hip with one arm, leaving three limbs free for locomotion and feeding in trees. She nurses her baby with gradually decreasing quantities of her milk for two or three years, but already during the first year, she starts feeding it supplementary food in the form of masti-

cated fruits and vegetables which she pushes with her lips right into the baby's mouth.

The orang-utan walks quadrupedally along branches or bipedally with arms holding on above, its powerful, far-reaching 'hook grip' bearing it main weight. It progresses, balancing and swinging slowly, using its body weight on trees and branches to bend them in a desired direction. It does not jump. Descending a tree is a reversed climb or a jerky glide.

The normal ground gait is quadrupedal, the weight being borne by the clenched fists and inverted, clenched feet. The walk is similar to that of dogs, that is two diagonally opposing limbs advance while the other pair carries and propels the body forward. Quadrupedal locomotion is sometimes alternated with rolling head over heels—especially if the animal speeds to a near gallop on sloping ground free of vegetation. It may also playfully roll over from a squatting position, to cover a few feet of ground.

Fruits, buds and leaves are stored in the mouth and chewed at intervals. Lips sweep the tongue clear, sometimes after inspection of the debris on tongue and lower lips. For this purpose the jaw juts forward so that the eyes may glance right down onto the tongue.

Honey of wild bees, the eggs of birds and occasionally soil, are also eaten by orang-utans. Their favourite fruit is the durian, a spiky, smelly fruit with soft, pulpy flesh the size of a football. This particular fruit has brought the animal into conflict with man as in many areas it is cultivated in orchards.

The nests of the orang-utan are conspicuous tangles of branches and they are constructed in a few minutes at any place where

there is sufficient support and a suitable quantity of small branches, especially in crowns and forks. Branches are bent or broken towards the animal, assembled and laid across each other and finally lined with additional, smaller twigs. All is then patted down with hands and feet into a rough circle of about 2–3 ft (0·6–1 m) diameter. Nests may be placed at between 10 and 100 ft (3 and 30 m) above ground and sometimes even higher. FAMILY: Pongidae, SUBORDER: Anthropoidea, ORDER: Primates, CLASS: Mammalia.

ORB-WEAVING SPIDERS. The crowning achievement of spiders' engineering triumph is the orb-web. A circular design was encouraged by the habit of random wandering from one fixed base while trailing a silk thread.

Space can be bridged by a drifting thread, and a centre is established by hauling downwards and fixing a loose horizontal thread thus forming a triangle with a vertical thread from its apex. Radial threads like spokes are followed by spirals which alone are coated with gum.

The Argiopidae do not repair webs but they normally remove the viscous spirals every night and spin new ones.

The thick golden threads of the largest tropical species of *Nephila* were once used for making silk garments, but the spiders ate each other and were too difficult to rear to make the experiment a success. *Araneus quadratus* lays nearly 1,000 eggs which weigh twice as much as the female laying them. FAMILY: Argiopidae, ORDER: Araneae, CLASS: Arachnida, PHYLUM: Arthropoda.

Orb-web spider. Female Garden spider *Araneus diadematus* and (on right) male.

Orioles

ORIOLES, medium-sized songbirds, often brightly coloured. In several species the males have bold yellow and black patterns. The true orioles occur only in the Old World but the name is sometimes given to some species of troupials of the genus *Icterus* which have similar yellow and black plumages but which occur in the Americas. There are 26 species, comprising the genus *Oriolus*. Orioles occur through Africa and southern Asia, south through the Philippines and Indonesia to Australasia, while one species, the Golden oriole *O. oriolus* extends up into the Palearctic as far as Northern Europe.

Oriolus are starling- to thrush-sized but tend to be more slender-bodied, like the former. The bill is slender and a little elongated. The wings are long and pointed. The legs are somewhat short, but legs and feet are strong. The males are mostly brightly-coloured; yellow, red or maroon combined with varying amounts of black, or more rarely green. The females are usually duller, olive-green and often streaked beneath, and the young resemble them. These are birds of the tree-tops. They usually occur singly or in pairs, feeding on insects and fruits.

The two figbirds of Australasia are larger and more heavily built. The males are yellow and green with black on the head and bare red skin around the eyes. The females are brown, streaked on the underside. The bill is heavier than in the typical orioles. Figbirds are more sociable than other orioles, often occurring in parties or small flocks. They are fruit-eaters and feed extensively on wild figs. They have harsh calls. The nests are similar to those of other orioles but the eggs are greenish and heavily marked in red-brown and purple. FAMILY: Oriolidae, ORDER: Passeriformes, CLASS: Aves.

Female Golden oriole of Europe at her nest.

OROPENDOLA, 12 species of social birds of New World orioles, from Mexico, to northern Argentina. Oropendolas are large birds and in all species the male has brighter plumage and is considerably larger than the female. They live the whole year round in flocks, feeding, nesting and roosting in groups in forests and groups of trees in open country.

Among the best known is the Crested oropendola *Psarocolius decumanus* which occurs from Panama south to northern Argentina. It is glossy black, the lower back, rump and lower underparts are chestnut and in the rather long tail the middle feathers are black and the outer ones, yellow. The strong bill is pale yellow and the eyes a pale blue. Males weigh 10–10½ oz (280–290 gm), but females are only 5–6 oz (145–170 gm). The male has a few long and narrow feathers on the head forming a crest. It feeds partly on fruits and can do a lot of damage in cultivated areas. Insects also form a large part of its diet.

Crested oropendolas nest in colonies, usually in trees that tower over the surrounding vegetation. The nest is a long, pendent purse about 3 ft (1 m) in length with the entrance at the top. The nest-chamber is at the end and is lined with dry leaves. It is constructed of long stripped leaf-fibres and fastened at the very end of a branch. Nest-building, incubation and the feeding of the nestlings is confined to the female. Many of the colonies of oropendolas, especially the Crested and the Green *Psarocolius viridis* species, are parasitized by another member of the Icteridae, the Giant cowbird. FAMILY: Icteridae, ORDER: Passeriformes, CLASS: Aves.

ORYX, medium- to large-sized antelope of the Afro-Arabian desert. Oryx are distinguished by their straight or slightly back-curved horns, which are slender and closely ridged, and placed immediately behind the eyes; by their predominantly light colouration; and by their face-pattern, there being a dark eye-stripe, a dark nose-patch and often a separate dark forehead-patch. The three may unite to form a bridle pattern.

Beisa oryx, an antelope of the gemsbok group, found in the open parts of East Africa, from Eritrea to the Tana river.

The largest and most widely distributed is the gemsbok *Oryx gazella*, about 48 in (120 cm) high. It is fawn above with a black dorsal stripe and a black flank-band separating the fawn from the white underside. The forelegs have a black garter above the knees, and are white below this, as are the hocks. The ear-tips are black, as is a line down the throat and chest. The black nose-patch and eye-stripes often unite to form a girdle round the muzzle.

The second species is the Arabian or Beatrix oryx *O. leucoryx*, smaller than the previous species, only 40 in (1 m) high. It is white with brown limbs, blackish frontal and nasal patches and eye-stripes which expand below and unite under the lower jaw, being continued back as a throat-stripe. The horns in this species are often at least as long as the animal is tall. Formerly found all over the Arabian peninsula and north into Syria and Iraq, this species has been drastically reduced in numbers and in range. It has always been hunted because of the believed connection between killing an oryx and virility.

The third species of oryx is predominantly red and white, and its horns curved. This is the Scimitar oryx *O. dammah*. It is 4 ft (120 cm) high, weighs 440 lb (200 kg) and has horns up to 40 in (1 m) long, which are lightly backcurved, but more strongly so than in the other two species. It lives in the southern Sahara, east of the Nile to as far west as Senegal and Rio de Oro.

A recent investigation has shown that oryx can tolerate unusually high temperatures—104°F (40°C) and above—without significantly increased water loss; moreover it feeds at night when the dry desert plants on which it lives, containing only 1–2% water by day, absorb moisture so that they then contain 40%. FAMILY: Bovidae, ORDER: Artiodactyla, CLASS: Mammalia.

OSPREY *Pandion haliaetus*, a large fish-eating bird of prey, found regularly throughout the world except for South America. In North America it is known also as the Fish hawk. Measuring up to 24 in (61 cm) long, the osprey is unusual among birds of prey in being almost wholly dark above and white beneath. It has a white head with a dark streak through the eye, a barred tail, and angled wings with a dark patch beneath at the angle.

The osprey feeds very largely on fish and occupies both freshwater and marine areas where there is sufficient food. It hunts by cruising above the water at heights up to 200 ft (60 m) and take its prey by plunging in a shallow dive.

Ospreys usually nest in trees or on cliffs, though they also nest on the ground. In some regions, particularly eastern North America and northeast Africa, they nest in large colonies. The nests usually command a clear view of the fishing grounds, and are built of sticks, grasses or any other available material. FAMILY: Pandionidae, ORDER: Falconiformes, CLASS: Aves.

OSTRICH *Struthio camelus*, the largest living bird, is flightless. At one time found in large numbers in many parts of Africa and southwest Asia, the ostrich is now common in the wild only in parts of East Africa. There are also considerable numbers in ostrich farms in South Africa and domesticated birds have become feral in South Australia.

The ostrich is able to run well. The legs are very long and strong and with the long neck make up a considerable part of the ostrich's height, which in a large male may be 8 ft (2·5 m). Such a bird would weigh up to 300 lb (135 kg). Typically the colour of the male is black with white wings and tail and that of the female grey-brown. The female is smaller but in both sexes the head appears small in proportion to the rest of the bird.

The ostrich has only two toes on each foot —the original third and fourth digits. The third is much the larger.

Ostriches are omnivorous, though the bulk of their food is usually of plant origin. They take a variety of fruits and seeds and also the leaves and shoots of shrubs, creepers and succulent plants. A variety of invertebrates and smaller vertebrates, such as lizards, are also eaten. Quantities of grit and stones are swallowed, aiding digestion by assisting in the grinding of resistant foods.

All ostriches are polygamous. The nest is a shallow pit dug in sandy soil and in this the eggs of all the females of a particular male

Left: Ostrich in typical habitat, the dry plains. Right: Almost naked head and neck of an ostrich. Below: Ostriches do not put their heads in the sand, as legend has it, but at times they seem to be doing something near it.

Short-clawed otter eating a fish. This is the smallest otter.

are laid. Varying clutch sizes are recorded, from 15–60 eggs. It seems that each female lays from six to eight eggs, usually one every other day. The average egg is around 6 in (15 cm) long and 5 in (13 cm) wide, with a weight only 1·4% of that of the laying female.

Ostriches have been farmed for their plumes in Cape Province in South Africa since the 1850's. In the early part of this century there were over 700,000 birds in captivity and ostrich farming enterprises had also been started in North Africa, the USA and various European countries, as well as South Australia. But the First World War almost eliminated the industry and now there are only about 25,000 birds in captivity in South Africa, principally for the production of high-quality leather. FAMILY: Struthionidae, ORDER: Struthioniformes, CLASS: Aves.

OTTER, a carnivore belonging to the weasel family and living a semi-aquatic existence. Otters are absent only from large oceanic islands, Australasia, Madagascar and the polar regions.

Covered with a close, waterproof underfur and long guard hairs, otters are muscular and lithe, built for vigorous swimming. The limbs are short and the trunk cylindrical. The paws, each with five digits and non-retractile claws, are generally webbed and the forefeet are shorter than the hind ones. The fully-haired tail, thick at the base but quite flexible, tapers to a point and is flattened on its under surface. Below its base are situated two scent glands (except for the Sea otter) which give the otter a characteristic odour, sweet and pungent. Adults may use these glands when suddenly frightened. Tropical species are usually lighter than their northern counterparts and in all, the fur is paler before the moulting season, ranging from black-brown to a pale-grey hue. Stiff vibrissae, or whiskers, are numerous around the snout, and smaller ones appear in tufts on the elbows.

The European otter *Lutra lutra* extends from the British Isles to Japan, south to Sumatra and is also found in North Africa. It measures 36–48 in (91–122 cm) and weighs 10–25 lb (4·3–11·4 kg). The male's home

range covers approximately 10 miles (16 km) of stream or lake. Generally solitary and nocturnal, European otters rarely vocalize. Pairs or small family groups can be found only at certain times of the year. One to five cubs, but more usually two or three, are born at any season after a nine week gestation.

The Canadian otter *L. canadensis* ranges America south to Texas.

The Indian 'Smooth-coated' otter *Lutrogale perspicillata*, is heavier-set and larger than the European otter. It can be found in marsh areas from Iraq to Borneo. Characterized by its short, dense fur, the Smooth-coated otter also has a flattened tail and thickly webbed paws with thick nails which enable the animal to be remarkably agile in manipulating and retrieving small objects.

Southeast Asia possesses the smallest of all otters, the Asian Small-clawed otter *Amblonyx cinerea*. Adult males may not exceed 30 in (75 cm) in total length or weigh more than 11 lb (5 kg). The forefeet have long agile fingers, only partially webbed, with tiny spike-like claws. Aptly called 'Finger otter' in German, these otters use their sensitive fingertips to search for prey under stones and pebbles in shallow water or mud.

The Clawless otter *Aonyx capensis*, is found from Ethiopia down to the Cape. Usually it prefers the slow, shallow streams of the rain-forests. These large otters measure 64 in (160 cm) and can weigh over 50 lb (23 kg).

The Giant Brazilian otter *Pteronura braziliensis*, can measure up to 8 ft (2·3 m) and weigh 75 lb (34 kg). It is found from the upper reaches of the Amazon south to

Argentina. Yellowish-white patches on the chin, neck and chest contrast sharply with the dark-brown body fur. Its wide tail is flattened and fer-de-lance shaped. FAMILY: Mustelidae, ORDER: Carnivora, CLASS: Mammalia.

OVENBIRD, small to medium-sized South American perching bird, usually with brown or chestnut-brown plumage. The true ovenbird or Pale-legged hornero *Furnarius leucopus* is one of the more brightly coloured species, being a bright chestnut-brown above and white below. Ovenbirds vary from about 4–9 in (10–23 cm) in length. Most remarkable, however, are the huge domed mud nests built by the true ovenbirds, the name ovenbird having originated in the resemblance that these nests bear to an oldfashioned stone oven. FAMILY: Furnariidae, ORDER: Passeriformes, CLASS: Aves.

OWLS, soft-plumaged, short-tailed, big-headed, usually nocturnal, birds of prey. They have large eyes directed forwards surrounded by facial discs. The bill is hooked and the claws sharp. Owls vary in size from the sparrow-sized Pigmy owl to the huge Eagle owls.

When most other birds are roosting the owl must find food and defend its territory against competitors. The success of owls under these conditions depends upon the efficiency of their sense organs, which are adapted to work in the dark. Their vision is estimated to be 35–100 times more sensitive than our own. Their eyes are relatively enormous with very wide corneas that allow the maximum of light through to the retina. The sense of hearing is also extremely well developed, particularly in the Barn owls. Their ears, though completely hidden under their feathers, are large and partly covered by flaps of skin. The part of the medulla of the brain concerned with hearing is also well developed, containing 95,000 nerve cells in the Barn owl compared with only 27,000 in a crow twice the weight.

Many owls, including the 6 lb (2·7 kg) Eagle owl, fly with hardly a whisper. Silent flight doubtless helps them to pounce on unsuspecting prey, and ensures that their sensitive hearing is not 'jammed' by noisy pinions.

Not all ovenbirds build an oven. *Seiurus aurocapillus,* of North America, builds a domed nest.

Left: The White-faced scops owl *Otus leucotis*, 9 in (22 cm) long, is common in the African bush and also penetrates far into the Sahara and other desert areas. Right: The Oriental hawk owl *Ninox scutulata* of eastern and southern Asia, 9 in (22 cm) long, hunts insects in forest edges and in jungle.

Owls are vociferous and their hoots and screams make up a well developed language. The majority have low frequency voices, giving them a human-like quality. Owls need to proclaim their hunting territories and communicate with their mates over large areas and the carrying power of low pitched notes is much greater than that of high pitched or squeaky ones. Hoots then act rather like foghorns, as sound beacons in the darkness.

Owls are basically hole-nesters, laying their eggs in crevices, open cavities or inside the vacated homes of woodpeckers. A few like the Snowy owl *Nyctea scandiaca* nest on the ground. Like the eggs of other hole-nesting birds, those of owls are white.

Clutches vary from 1–7 or more and usually both sexes incubate and in all both parents feed the young.

The main diet is mice, voles and rats and the Snowy owl and Short-eared owls take also lemmings and hares. Owls usually swallow their prey whole, the indigestible bones, feathers and fur afterwards being regurgitated as pellets.

There are about 132 species of owls divided into two families, the Barn owls, Tytonidae and the typical owls, Strigidae.

Barn owls are characterized by big heart-shaped facial discs and long tarsi and by having the middle claws on each foot expanded into serrated 'combs'. They are 13–18 in (33–45 cm) long, the females usually being larger than the males. They are not migratory. The Common Barn owl *Tyto alba* has an almost world-wide range. It is golden-brown above and lighter below, barred with white, black and grey. It nests in hollow trees or on buildings. It is nocturnal and hunts its prey of rats and mice by sound more than by sight. It is believed that the facial disc has an acoustical function, gathering and concentrating the sound waves. It has been discovered in recent years that a Barn owl can catch living rodents in complete darkness provided the prey makes some sound.

In the genus *Bubo* are 12 kinds of large Eagle owls occurring in the New World and across to the Philippines. The Hawk owls *Ninox* replace the Eagle owls in Australasia, as they do the Eared, Scops and Screech owls *Otus* which stretch from the Americas through Eurasia and Africa to the southwest Pacific islands. Lacking ear tufts are the three similar Eurasian Little owls *Athene*. Tropical genera include the curiously marked Spectacled owls *Pulsatrix*, Wood owls *Ciccaba* and the Afro-Asian Fishing owls *Ketupa* and *Scotopelia*.

The best known are the 'earless', chiefly black-eyed Wood owls, *Strix*, most of which have feathered feet and rounded wings. They are chiefly found in temperate woodlands in the New and Old Worlds, excepting Australia and New Zealand. The Tawny owl *Strix aluco* is found over most of Europe and parts of Asia and North Africa. It is the owl most often seen in Britain. Also known as the Brown owl, it has two colour phases, grey and brown.

Six *Asio* owls are all 'eared' and the Long- and Short-eared owls, *A. otus* and *A. flammeus* are both widely distributed circumpolar species. The second of these being found even in temperate South America, must be one of the most southerly of all owls. Four members of the genus *Aegolius* are rather like miniature *Strix* owls and lack ear tufts. There are three mono-specific strigine genera, the eared *Pseudoscops grammicus* and *Rhinotynx clamator* of the Caribbean and South America respectively and the non-eared but large Fearful owl *Nesario solomonensis* from the southwest Pacific. ORDER: Strigiformes, CLASS: Aves.

OXPECKERS, starlings adapted for feeding on hides of large grazing animals, found only in Africa. The Yellow-billed oxpecker *Buphagus africanus* is widespread over western and central Africa except in the Sahara and the Congo Basin, while the Red-billed oxpecker *B. erythrorhynchus* is confined to eastern Africa from the Red Sea to Natal.

Oxpeckers scramble over the bodies of

Oystercatchers

large animals woodpecker-fashion. They are about 7–8 in (18–20 cm) long, with a rather slender body. The longish, pointed tail is well-developed, with stiff-shafted tapering feathers which can help to prop the bird as it clings upright to a vertical surface. The legs are fairly short and stout with strong feet equipped with large sharp claws to give a firm grip. The bill is heavy, and broad at the base. Both species are a dull coffee-brown above, with a duller, paler brown on the head. The belly is light-buff, grading into a dull olive-brown on the breast.

Oxpeckers tend to live and feed entirely on the skin of animals such as buffalo, rhinoceros, giraffes, zebras and various antelopes. They shuffle over the bodies of the animals with considerable agility, but prefer to perch woodpecker-fashion, with head uppermost, and in this posture will move sideways or drop back or downwards in short jerky hops. The principal activity of the birds is feeding on the blood-gorged ticks which they remove from the animals' bodies.

Oxpeckers spend most of their time on the animals. Some even roost on the bodies of their hosts. This association is not without other advantage to the animal host. The birds are alert to danger and will react to the approach of a potential predator by ascending to the back of the host and uttering hissing and rattling warning calls. FAMILY: Sturnidae, ORDER: Passeriformes, CLASS: Aves.

OYSTERCATCHERS, sea-shore wading birds, about the size of a pigeon found on the shores of every continent except Antarctica. There are four species and 21 subspecies of which seven are completely black while the remainder have pied plumage. The pied forms are very distinctive, having a black head and upperparts, white belly and rump, white tips to the primary wing feathers and patches on the secondary wing feathers forming a broad wing bar. The feet and legs of all species are stout with three toes and the

colour varies from bright orange-pink to a pale-pink depending on age and subspecies. The bill is long, laterally compressed and about 3½ in (9 cm) long. It is bright orange in the breeding season, but becomes duller during the rest of the year.

They feed on marine shellfish and worms and are hence restricted to coastal areas in winter. Most of them remain on coasts to breed on sanddunes, among rocks and shingle or on small islands, but some move inland to breed, notably in parts of Europe, USSR and New Zealand.

Oystercatchers are noisy birds, particularly in the breeding season, and much of this noise results from their 'piping'. The birds strut around, shoulders hunched forward with their bills pointing almost vertically downwards and a continuous, loud, rapid trilling accompanies these movements. FAMILY: Haematopididae, ORDER: Charadriiformes, CLASS: Aves.

OYSTERS, the Edible oysters, as distinct from the Pearl oysters and other so-called 'oysters', are bivalve molluscs belonging to the family Ostreidae.

Structure and life history can best be described with reference to the European flat oyster, including the British 'native', *Ostrea edulis*. The body, exposed after removal of the flat upper valve and the mantle flap which forms this, is organized around the central adductor muscle. This consists of a 'catch' muscle of smooth fibres which closes the shell for, if necessary, prolonged periods if exposed to the air or to unfavourable conditions in the sea, and a 'quick' muscle of striated fibres responsible for repeated sudden contractions needed for the ejection of sediment and other waste which collects within.

The pair of extremely voluminous gills, the 'beard' of the oyster, lies in a half circle around the adductor muscle. Each consists of two flaps, or lamellae, made up of great numbers of parallel filaments, attached from

place to place and so forming a highly complex lattice-work covered with different series of highly active ciliary hairs. Those that line the sides of the filaments create a powerful inhalant current of water which passes through the lattice-work to emerge above and behind the gills and then leave the shell as a posteriorly directed out-flowing current. It carries with it waste products from the anus and from the kidneys.

Particles contained in the inflowing water are retained on the surface of the gills where, under the action of frontal cilia on these surfaces, mixed with mucus, they collect into streams along the base and free margins of each half gill (demibranch) where a further series of ciliary currents convey them to the mouth. The food of oysters, like that of other bivalves, consists essentially of the largely microscopic plant life of the surrounding sea water.

Although at any one time an individual is either male or female, there is an alternation of sex, the speed of succession depending on temperature. Thus, at the northern end of its range, *Ostrea edulis* may function as male and then female in alternate years. In British waters it may often spawn in both capacities in the one year while in southern France oysters may spawn as females with intervening activity as males several times in the same season. Spawning begins when the sea temperature reaches about 59°F (15°C). Only in the male phase are the sexual products, the spermatozoa, released. In countless numbers they are carried out in the exhalant current and almost immediately drawn in by the inflowing current of individuals in the female phase, the eggs of which are fertilized as they issue from the oviducts. Surprisingly, the fertilized eggs then pass through the meshwork of the gills, that is against the flow created by the cilia lining the sides of the filaments, to be incubated in the mantle cavity, forming first a creamy mass, when the oyster is said to be 'white sick' and then, as pigment accumulates in the digestive organs, becoming grey or 'black sick'.

Up to one million larvae may be incubated for a period of up to two weeks depending on temperature. When liberated, during the 'swarming' process, they are shelled and have a velum or ciliated sail used for swimming and for the collection of the most minute members of the plant plankton for food. For anything from one to two-and-a-half weeks these active larvae are members of the animal plankton at the mercy of water movements. Settlement involves change in both habits and structure with the loss of the velum and the temporary appearance of a foot and sense organs, including an eye spot. These enable the larva to find a suitable substrate, when it turns over on the left side and attaches itself by a spot of cement. FAMILY: Ostreidae, ORDER: Eulamellibranchia, CLASS: Bivalvia, PHYLUM: Mollusca.

The cosmopolitan oystercatcher at its nest where it lays three well-camouflaged eggs.

PACA *Cuniculus paca*, a rodent found in tropical America, from Mexico to southern Brazil. It is up to 2 ft (60 cm) in length. It has almost no tail, but it is distinguished by a pattern of bold white spots and lines on the back and sides. The skull of the paca is unique in having the cheek-bones grossly enlarged and inflated, with a peculiar honeycombed texture, perhaps acting as resonating chambers. Pacas are vegetarians and sometimes damage crops. FAMILY: Dasyproctidae, ORDER: Rodentia, CLASS: Mammalia.

PACARANA *Dinomys branicki*, a South American rodent superficially resembling the *paca. It is heavily built about 22 in (56 cm) long and it has a similar pattern of rows of white spots on a background of dark brown. It differs from the paca, however, in having a conspicuous tail, about 8 in (20 cm) long. The pacarana is confined to the lower slopes of the Andes from Colombia to Bolivia. It is a poorly known animal and appears to be becoming very rare. Its survival is not helped by its temperament, being unusually docile and slow-moving for a rodent. FAMILY: Dinomyidae, ORDER: Rodentia, CLASS: Mammalia.

PADDLEFISHES, primitive fishes related to sturgeons and sharing with them a skeleton of cartilage and a spiral valve in the intestine. There are only two species, one from the Yangtse in China (*Polyodon gladius*) and one from the Mississippi basin (*P. spathula*). The body, although naked, resembles that of the sturgeons except for the prolonged snout which is extended into a flat sword. This 'paddle' is sensitive and easily damaged and is not used, as might be expected, as a probe or digger in feeding, since these fishes tend to swim with their mouths open and gather their food (small planktonic organisms) in that way. The barbels characteristic of the mouth of sturgeons are reduced to small protuberances under the paddle. The Mississippi paddlefish rarely grows to more than 150 lb (68 kg). The Chinese paddlefish is reported to reach 20 ft (6 m) in length. Paddle-

fishes spawn in turbulent waters and it is only in recent years that their larvae have been identified and studied. Like the sturgeons, the paddlefishes have become rarer owing to pollution of rivers. FAMILY: Polyodontidae, ORDER: Acipenseriformes, CLASS: Pisces.

PAINTED SNIPE, a family of marsh-frequenting snipe-like birds one species of which is found from Japan to Australia and west to Africa and the other in South America. The first is the Painted snipe *Rostratula benghalensis*, with the Australian population subspecifically differentiated from that in Africa, southern Turkey, India, China and Japan, and the second is the American painted snipe *Nycticryphes semicollaris*, found from southeastern Brazil to northern Argentina. The two species differ in a few minor characters such as the amount of webbing between the toes, and the conformation of bill and tail. Resemblances with the true snipe are superficial. Painted snipe are more closely related to *jacanas and have some features in common with the cranes.

In size and shape Painted snipe are comparable with true snipe, but have shorter legs and a shorter bill, only slightly longer than the head, and a little decurved towards the tip. Like snipe, the tip of the bill is pitted and sensitive to the movement of the worms, insects, crustaceans and molluscs for which the bird probes in mud. The eyes are set at the sides of the head so that Painted snipe have monocular vision through the entire 360° field, and probably have binocular vision in front of and behind the head. Like snipe, the plumage is cryptically patterned, olive above with creamy lines over the forehead and crown, through the eyes and over the shoulders, and buff spots and bars on the wings and tail. But here the similarity ends, for Painted snipe are more richly coloured, especially the female, which is a little longer than the male and takes the initiative in courtship although playing a minor role in nesting.

In the Old World Painted snipe it is the female who displays towards the male, and

she may be polyandrous. The wings are spread and brought forward to display to best advantage to the male their rich pattern of buff circles on an olive ground, and to offset the cinnamon breast and face with its white spectacles. The male builds a simple nest on marshy ground, concealed by tall sedges or a tangle of thorny shrubs, and incubates the clutch of four or more glossy whitish eggs with handsome black or purple blotches. He rears the downy young, while the more aggressive female defends the territory. In the American painted snipe the reversal of the roles of the sexes has not proceeded so far, and the female incubates.

They tend to be crepuscular and solitary. When flushed, they fly weakly on rounded wings, with legs trailing like a rail, to drop down into cover again as soon as possible, where they stand guardedly bobbing the body up and down like a sandpiper. FAMILY: Rostratulidae, ORDER: Charadriiformes, CLASS: Aves.

PALOLO, the South Sea Islanders' name for a marine bristleworm *Eunice viridis* which swarms at the surface of the sea at certain times of the year. The adult worm lives on the sea bottom in muddy sand, amongst rocks or in crevices in coral. The body is long with many segments and with gills arched over the back. As the worm becomes sexually mature the rear half of the body becomes loaded with ova or sperm, and it looks then quite different from the front half. At the spawning season the worms leave their shelters on the sea-bed, the rear half of their body breaks away and swims to the surface where it splits shedding its ova or sperm into the water. This mass of eggs is netted by the people of Fiji and Samoa, taken ashore and cooked. The season of spawning is precisely determined, the worms maturing under hormonal influences governed by a combination of factors related to the lunar cycle and to light. This ensures that all the worms which normally live independent lives on the sea bottom release their genital products at the surface at the same time, giving maximum

Pampas deer

opportunity for the ova to be fertilized.

The average date of the appearance of the great swarms was November 27th in data gathered up to 1921. In fact swarming occurs seven, eight or nine days after the full moon.

Swarmings of other kinds of worms, in the warmer parts of the Atlantic as well as other parts of the Pacific, are sometimes called palolo, although wrongly, as for example Japanese palolo. FAMILY: Eunicidae, CLASS: Polychaeta, PHYLUM: Annelida.

PAMPAS DEER *Ozotoceros bezoarticus*, the most elegant South American deer, 27 in (69 cm) at the shoulder. It is yellowish-brown with the underparts and insides of the ears white. The upper side of the tail is dark-brown to black. The antlers usually bear six points. Pampas deer are generally in groups of 5–15 except in the fawning season when the does become solitary. They avoid woodlands. There are three subspecies: *O. b. bezoarticus* of Brazil, *O. b. leucogaster* of Paraguay and adjacent areas and *O. b. celer* of the pampas of Argentina. FAMILY: Cervidae, ORDER: Artiodactyla, CLASS: Mammalia.

PANGOLINS, or Scaly anteaters, mammals with the body covered with scales that overlap like roof-tiles. Only the abdomen, the inner sides of the extremities, the throat and part of the head are free from scales. These are covered with hair. The head is conical, the eyes and outer ear small. The very long tongue is wormlike and extensile. The legs are short and sturdy and the front paws have claws. The terrestrial species have a strong muscular tail, about the same length as the body, which is completely scaly. In arboreal species the slender tail is longer than the body with a bare patch at the tip and is used as a prehensile limb when climbing, or used for hanging from a branch. All pangolins are active mainly at night, the ground-living forms resting in burrows dug by other animals, the tree-dwellers resting in cavities in trees. They all roll up in a ball for sleeping or as a defence measure. They feed mainly on ants and termites. The termites' nest is torn open with the long front claws and the termites picked up by the sticky tongue. Since pangolins are toothless, the ants and termites are ground up by means of horny protuberances on the wall of the stomach. Pangolins usually have only one young at a birth. In the arboreal pangolins the baby rides on the mother's back clinging to her tail.

There are seven living species. The three Asiatic species are: the Indian pangolin *Manis crassicaudata*, with a head and body length of 2 ft (60 cm) and a tail 18–20 in (45–50 cm) long, and with pale yellowish-brown scales and a brownish skin; the Chinese pangolin *M. pentadactyla*, with a head and body length of 20–24 in (50–60 cm) and a tail 12–16 in (30–40 cm) long, and with blackish-brown

A golden-headed South American parakeet, *Aratinga* sp., of the kind sometimes referred to as conures.

scales and a greyish-white skin; the Malayan pangolin *M. javanica*, with a head and body length of 20–24 in (50–60 cm) and a tail 20–32 in (50–80 cm) long, and with amber to blackish-brown scales and a whitish skin. These three Asiatic species are at home on the ground but are also good climbers.

The three species living in African rain forests are: the Small-scaled tree pangolin *M. tricuspis*, an arboreal species, with a head and body length of 14–18 in (35–45 cm) and a tail 16–20 in (40–50 cm) long, with brownish-grey to dark-brown scales and a white skin; the Long-tailed pangolin *M. tetradactyla*, another arboreal species, with a head and body length of 12–14 in (30–35 cm) and a tail 24–28 in (60–70 cm), and with dark-brown scales with yellowish edges and a dark-brown to blackish skin; the Giant pangolin *M. gigantea*, a terrestrial species, with a head and body length of 30–32 in (75–80 cm) and a tail 22–26 in (55–65 cm) long and with greyish-brown scales and a whitish skin. The Temminck's pangolin *M. temmincki*, a terrestrial species, lives in the East African savannahs and has a head and body length of 20 in (50 cm) and a tail 14 in (35 cm) long and with dark-brown scales and a light skin with dark hairs. FAMILY: Manidae, ORDER: Pholidota, CLASS: Mammalia.

PANTHER, a black or melanistic variety of the *leopard. The name was in use in medieval England for the leopard itself but was later used by sportsmen in India for the black variety. It has also been applied to the puma or cougar, in North America, and to

the jaguar of South America.

PARADISE FISH *Macropodus opercularis*, one of the labyrinth fishes found in China and Southeast Asia. It grows to about 4 in (10 cm) long and has a browny-blue body with a dozen vertical, thin orange-red stripes. The tail fin is also red and there is a red edged black spot on the gill cover. FAMILY: Anabantidae, ORDER: Perciformes, CLASS: Pisces.

PARAKEETS, loose name for small or medium-sized parrots, usually with long tails. There is no natural group of parakeets, the name being given to many species not closely related to one another. Examples are: the Green parakeet *Myiopsitta monachus* of Argentina, the Rose-ringed parakeet *Psittacula krameri* of the Old World Tropics, the Ground parakeets *Pezoporus* of Australia and the Crested parakeets *Cyanoramphus* of New Zealand. To add to the confusion, the familiar budgerigar is sometimes called a Grass parakeet, and the diminutive lorikeets, which have quite short tails, are alternatively called Hanging parakeets.

Here only the members of the genus *Psittacula* are described. All have long, finely-pointed tails and have vernacular names ending in 'parakeet'. Most have a distinctive and colourful pattern on the head which relieves the overall green of the body and wings. One of the most beautiful is the Alexandrine parakeet *P. eupatria*. The head of the male is banded with red, purple, black and turquoise. The body and wings are bright green with a red flash on each shoulder and the long tail is azure-blue.

Indo-Malaya is the home of most of the species, but one of them, the Rose-ringed parakeet *P. krameri* has a wide distribution: from Senegal in West Africa to Indo-China. Like most of its relatives, the Rose-ringed parakeet lives in semi-arid country where it keeps largely to the trees. Only a few species inhabit heavily forested regions and these prefer the more open parts.

For much of the year parakeets fly around in noisy flocks, but when the breeding season begins they pair off and nest singly or in small colonies. Mating is preceded by elaborate courtship displays in which the male struts along a branch towards the female and the pair engage in rhythmic swaying and 'necking'. Like most other parrots, parakeets nest in a hole in a dead tree or branch, but where they live in towns and villages, as in India, temples, bridges and other man-made constructions provide many good nest sites. Two or three dull white eggs form the usual clutch and are laid at the bottom of the cavity with scant or no nesting material.

The natural food of parakeets is largely fruits, nuts, buds and flowers. FAMILY: Psittacidae, ORDER: Psittaciformes, CLASS: Aves.

PARAMECIUM, or Slipper animalcule, a single-celled animal with its body covered with cilia, studied intensively in schools and universities. It lives in fresh or stagnant water and is elongate and round in cross section. To one side is the conspicuous mouth lying in a deep groove called an oral groove. It swims by revolving about its axis and does not feed while swimming. When stationary the cilia in the oral region create a vortex and this actively draws bacteria and particles of plant material into the oral groove and thence into the mouth. FAMILY: Parameciidae, ORDER: Hymenostomatida, CLASS: Ciliatea, PHYLUM: Protozoa.

PARROTFISHES, colourful tropical marine fishes related to the wrasses. They are moderately deep-bodied and have a fairly long dorsal fin but shorter anal fin. The fin spines are rather weak. The teeth in the jaws are fused to form a 'beak' and this, together with their very bright colours, earns them their common name. Parrotfishes feed on coral, biting off pieces and grinding them with the pharyngeal teeth. This is then swallowed, the food extracted and the calcareous matter excreted, often in regular places where small piles of coral debris accumulate. Parrotfishes are responsible for most of the erosion that occurs on reefs. Many show strong homing instincts, returning to the same spot after foraging for food. At night, some species, such as the Rainbow parrotfish *Pseudoscarus guacamaia*, secrete a tent of mucus around themselves. This may take up to half an hour to produce and as long to break out of in the morning. Parrotfishes usually reach 2–3 ft (60–90 cm) in length, but a Tahitian species

has been reported to attain 12 ft (3·6 m). FAMILY: Scaridae, ORDER: Perciformes, CLASS: Pisces.

PARROTS, a family of about 320 species, widely distributed in the tropics and southern temperate regions. Parrots are 4–50 in (10–130 cm) in length and mostly brightly coloured, although there are some drab grey, brown, green or black species. The hooked bill, bulging cere at the base of the bill, more or less rounded wings, short legs, zygodactyl feet and other characters, as well as general appearances enable all parrots to be easily recognized as such.

The family is divided into four subfamilies of very unequal size. The first, the Strigopinae, includes only the peculiar *kakapo or Owl parrot *Strigops habroptilus* of New Zealand.

The 17 or so species of *cockatoo in the subfamily Cacatuinae are distributed from Australia to the Philippines.

Over 200 species of parrot form the subfamily Psittacinae, birds 4½–40 in (11–100 cm) or more long, found in the Americas, Africa, Asia and Australasia, as well as on many islands in the Pacific and Indian Oceans and the Caribbean. All American parrots belong to this subfamily, and the total of approximately 130 species is greater than the total number of parrot species inhabiting any other continent. American parrots vary in size from the huge, long-tailed *macaws to the sparrow-sized Andean *parakeets. Many of the larger American parrots, for example the genera *Ara, Anodorhynchus* and *Amazona*, including the macaws and Amazons, feed mainly on fruit and seeds from forest trees. Some of the smaller species eat fruit pulp, small seeds and nectar and pollen collected from flowering trees.

All American parrots nest in holes in trees, cacti, ants' nests, rocks or buildings. The Hooded parakeet *Myiopsitta monachus* is unique among parrots in building huge

communal nests of sticks in the branches of trees.

Africa has surprisingly few species of parrot. The African grey parrot *Psittacus erithacus*, a medium-sized species, is found throughout tropical Africa. The *lovebirds *Agapornis* are also peculiar to Africa.

Many species of the subfamily Psittacinae are found in southern Asia, in Australia and on the islands of the Indo-Malayan, Moluccan and Papuan regions.

Several are found in Australia, including *Aprosmictus*, of which the Red-winged parrot *A. erythropterus* is a familiar Australian bird.

The fourth subfamily Loriinae includes the lories and *lorikeets, the Pygmy parrots, the Fig parrots, the kaka *Nestor meridionalis* and *kea *N. notabilis* of New Zealand and the Australian Broadtailed parrots.

The six species of Pygmy parrot *Micropsitta* are 4–4½ in (10–11 cm) long, so that they are the smallest of all parrots. They are found from New Guinea to the Bismarck Archipelago and the Solomon Islands. All six are forest birds. They are probably unique among birds in feeding on fungi. They scrape slime-like fungi from decaying wood with their stumpy, weak bills and suck it into their throats through a tube-like tongue. Termites, lichen and seeds are also eaten at times.

The Australian Broad-tailed parrots are a group of about 31 species, most of them confined to the Australian mainland, but some occurring in New Zealand, New Caledonia and even the Society Islands. They include the *budgerigar.

The other Broad-tailed parrots are all long-tailed, and most of them have bright plumage with contrasting shades of red, yellow and blue predominating. They nearly all inhabit open areas with scattered trees or patches of scrub, and feed on the seeds of low-growing plants, sometimes fruit or flowers. FAMILY: Psittacidae, ORDER: Psittaciformes, CLASS: Aves.

Green-cheeked Amazon parrot *Amazona viridigenalis* of northeastern Mexico.

Partridges

PARTRIDGES, game birds of Europe, Asia and Africa. They include the little Stone partridge *Ptilopachus petrosus* which is found in the rocky parts of West and East Africa and the even smaller 'Bush quails' *Perdicula* of India which are really dwarf partridges.

Most well-known is the Grey or Common partridge *Perdix perdix*, of Europe, 12 in (30 cm) long, with a chestnut horseshoe on its breast. This famous game bird is monogamous and coveys usually consist of one pair with their offspring from the previous summer. The coveys break up early in the new year when the birds pair off and take up their breeding territories.

The Red-legged partridge *Alectoris rufa*, of Europe, is more colourful than the Grey. It is more at home in wooded and rocky country as well as in mountains. The chukar *Alectoris graca* is very similar to it. It is found from the Alps eastwards to Manchuria.

Most beautiful of all the partridges is the roulroul *Rollulus roulroul* from Malaysia. The plumage of the male is predominantly green with blue and red markings and a vivid crimson crest. FAMILY: Phasianidae, ORDER: Galliformes, CLASS: Aves.

PATAGONIAN HARE, or Patagonian cavy, two species of which *Dolichotis patagonum* and *D. salinicolum* are found in Argentina and Patagonia. These short-tailed rodents look like long-legged rabbits or hares, the hindlimbs being long each with three toes bearing hoof-like claws. *D. patagonum* is much larger than *D. salinicolum* having a head and body length of 27–29½ in (69–75 cm) with large individuals weighing 20–35 lb (9–16 kg). The upperparts are greyish and the underparts whitish, with some yellow-brown on the legs and feet. FAMILY: Caviidae, ORDER: Rodentia, CLASS: Mammalia.

PEA CRABS, so called for their smooth rounded bodies and because the males of many species are no larger than a pea. They readily form associations with other animals, and the best known species are those that live inside the mantle cavities of bivalve molluscs. The female of such a species may grow to such a size that she can no longer escape from the interior of the mollusc shell, but the males remain small and so can enter the shells and mate with the trapped females.

Pinnotheres pisum, which lives inside the mantle cavities of the mussels *Mytilus* and *Modiolus*, obtains its food from that collected by the host. The crab positions itself at the edge of the gills where a large ciliary tract conveys food towards the bivalve's mouth. The pincers of the crab are hairy, and are used to remove mucus and entrapped food from the ciliary current. The pincers are then wiped across the mouthparts, and these work the food backwards into the mouth. FAMILY: Pinnotheridae, SUBORDER: Brachyura, ORDER: Decapoda, CLASS: Crustacea.

Peacock displaying to a peahen. Although it is customary to speak of a peacock's magnificent tail, the brilliant feathers are in fact the tail coverts.

PEAFOWL, relatives of pheasants, the males having a long train of up to 150 feathers formed from the tail coverts, which can be erected to make a showy fan. For centuries peacocks have been admired for their beauty and hunted for their flesh, while in more recent times, they have become a graceful addition to parks and gardens. There are two species, the Indian peafowl *Pavo cristatus*, of Ceylon and India and the Green peafowl *Pavo muticus*, of Burma, Thailand, Indo-China, the Malay Peninsula and Java.

The Congo peacock *Afropavo* is the only pheasant originating outside Asia, being found in the rain-forests of the east-central Congo Basin. FAMILY: Phasianidae, ORDER: Galliformes, CLASS: Aves.

PECCARY, a pig-like mammal with long slender legs. The Collared peccary *Pecari tajacu* is greyish to black, paler underneath than on the back, and with white annulations on the bristles. An erectile mane extends from the head to the scent gland on the rump at the dorsal midline. An incomplete whitish collar crosses the neck and extends obliquely upward and backward. The young are reddish-brown with a lighter collar and usually a blackish dorsal band. There is a puffy scent gland, devoid of hair and about 4 in (10 cm) in front of the base of the abortive tail which is only about 1–1.5 in (2.5–3.8 cm) long. Males and females are of a similar size, the length of the head and body of the male averaging 36.9 in (93.7 cm) and of the

Common mussel gaping, exposing a Pea crab living within its mantle cavity.

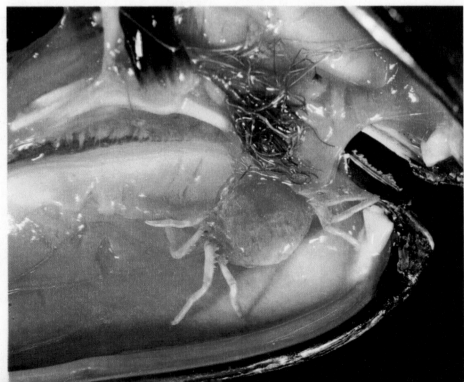

female 36·1 in (91·7 cm). The height at shoulders of 20 males measured averaged 19·8 in (50·3 cm). For females this height was 20·5 in (52 cm). The weight averages 44 lb (20 kg).

Collared peccaries range from southwestern USA to Argentina.

The White-lipped peccary *Tayassu pecari* is larger than the Collared peccary having a head and body length of 43–47 in (109–120 cm). It has long bristly hair and a scent gland on its back like the Collared peccary but unlike the latter its cheeks, nose and lips are white. FAMILY: Tayassuidae, ORDER: Artiodactyla, CLASS: Mammalia.

PELICANS, large aquatic birds with all four toes webbed. Pelicans have long bills provided with an expandible pouch attached to the flexible lower mandible. The short powerful legs are set far back on the body, ideally suited to rapid swimming, but making the traversing of land difficult. They are magnificent fliers, capable of sustained soaring flight over great distances. The whole body, beneath the skin, and even in the bones, is permeated with air spaces, probably assisting buoyant flight.

Pelicans weigh 10–25 lb (4½–11 kg) with wing-spans of 9 ft (2·7 m). They are usually white or mainly white, with areas of grey, brown or black plumage. The American brown pelican *Pelecanus occidentalis* is mainly brown. In the breeding season the colours of areas of bare skin, beak, pouch and legs, are intensified and several species grow crests at this time. In the American white pelican *P. erythrorynchos* a strange horn-like growth develops on the bill and in the Great white pelican *P. onocrotalus* the forehead becomes swollen.

All seven species of pelicans belong to one genus, *Pelecanus*, which divides conveniently into two, perhaps three, super-species or groups. In the first group there are four very large species, the American white pelican, the Great white pelican, the Dalmatian pelican *P. crispus* and the Australian pelican *P. conspicillatus*. All these breed in large colonies on the ground, roost on the ground and rarely perch in trees or bushes. The second group consists of three smaller species, the Brown pelican, the African Pink-backed pelican *P. rufescens* and the Asian spotted-billed pelican *P. philippensis*. These all breed in smaller, looser colonies in trees, but occasionally on the ground. They readily perch and roost in trees.

Contrary to general belief the bill is not used for storage or holding fish, but is simply a catching apparatus, resembling a scoop-net in function. The pouch is highly elastic. When the pelican plunges its bill into the water the flexible lower mandible automatically expands to a broad oval shape. As the pelican raises its head again fishes are scooped into the extensible pouch, the lower

The Collared peccary of tropical and subtropical America, named for its neck band.

mandible contracts again and the upper mandible closes over the pouch like a lid.

The Brown pelican alone regularly dives. Flying above the water it sights a fish and at once plunges vertically.

Pink-backed and Spotted-billed pelicans usually fish singly. They swim slowly along, or often remain stationary for some moments. On sighting a fish they dart out the head and neck and catch it in the pouch.

The 'scare line' method is used by the Great white pelican. A group of 8–12 swim rapidly forward in a horseshoe formation, with the open end of the horseshoe pointing forwards. At intervals of half a minute or so, as if at a given signal, all plunge their bills into the open centre of the horseshoe, where presumably fishes have collected.

While it is undeniable that a large number of pelicans eat great quantities of fish in a year recent work in the Danube Delta has shown that they take a higher proportion of diseased fishes than occurs in the fish population as a whole.

When travelling pelicans take off in flocks

as thermals begin to form. They locate a rising current and mount spirally upon it for several thousand feet. They then 'peel off' from the thermal, forming into long lines and V formations, alternately flapping and gliding until they reach their destination or find another thermal on which to gain more height. In this way they are able to cover hundreds of miles with little effort.

All pelicans breed in colonies of 50 to tens of thousands. The largest are those of the Great white pelican in southern Tanzania, where up to 40,000 pairs have been sighted. The smaller pelicans normally breed in trees. The four larger species breed on the ground.

Two to three, occasionally more, eggs are laid and are large, rather elongated and chalky-white. The yolk is often red. Both sexes incubate.

Newly-hatched young are ugly, being naked and pink at first, turning black or grey, then growing a coat of grey or blackish down. In ground-breeding species they collect in groups or 'pods' when they can walk after about three weeks. Even so each parent

Brown pelican, a coastal and marine species of America, preening.

Penguins

recognizes and feeds only its own young in these pods. FAMILY: Pelicanidae, ORDER: Pelicaniformes, CLASS: Aves.

PENGUINS, the most highly specialized of all aquatic birds, with 17 species restricted to the southern hemisphere.

Penguins can propel themselves through the water at a steady 10 knots, and can reach twice that speed in bursts. Their normal method of travel, when they are not pursuing prey or being pursued, is by 'porpoising', that is by leaping from the water at intervals to breathe and re-entering in a smooth curve. The plumage of penguins is a continuous covering of densely-packed feathers. In the Emperor penguin, for example, there are 38 rows of scale-like feathers from the anterior to the posterior borders of the wing, giving 3,800 feathers on the dorsal surface of the forearm alone. In a 25 mm square of the back of the Gentoo penguin *Pygoscelis papua* there were approximately 300 feathers.

Only two of the 17 species actually cross the Antarctic Circle. Five more nest in regions with a varying ice cover; six species belong to the south-temperate zone; and four species are tropical or subtropical. The size of penguins seems to have become reduced the farther they have spread from their original centre of dispersal. Thus the largest species is the Emperor *Aptenodytes forsteri* of Antarctica and the smallest the Galapagos penguin *Spheniscus mendiculus* and the Little blue penguin *Eudyptula minor* of Australia. The Peruvian penguin *Spheniscus humboldti* which extends northwards along the coast of Peru seems to be an exception for it is larger than the Little blue penguin but extends farther north.

Penguins nest on the ground, usually on the surface but some, such as the Little blue penguin, nest in burrows or crevices. An exception is the Emperor which breeds on floating sea ice and is, therefore, the only bird never to touch land. The nest is usually made of pebbles, grass, sticks or bones, depending on what is available. The Emperor and King penguin *Aptenodytes patagonica* carry their single eggs on their feet, covered with a flap of skin. Most species nest in colonies or 'rookeries', sometimes with hundreds of thousands of nests packed together, each sitting bird

being just out of pecking range of its neighbours. The clutch consists of two, sometimes three, eggs, except in the King and Emperor penguins which lay a single egg.

Penguins are long-lived and they are usually faithful to mate and nest site throughout life. The more southerly species undergo a long fast during the incubation period. and feed only their own chicks. Their food consists of crustaceans, such as krill, fish and squid.

Most rookeries are near the sea but rookeries of the Emperor penguin and Adélie penguin *Pygoscelis adeliae* may be many miles from the open sea when the birds take up territory, for unbroken sea ice extends a considerable distance from the land.

The problem facing the two large species, the King and Emperor penguins is to raise a very large chick within the short space of the Antarctic summer. The Emperor penguin has overcome this problem by laying during the winter so that the egg hatches in early spring. The male incubates the egg for 64 days and feeds the young chick on a secretion from its crop. The King penguin has a different solution. Eggs are laid in the summer and the chicks lay down a large supply of fat then stay in the nest throughout the winter, when they lose about half their weight. The following spring brings plentiful food and their development is completed. It is then too late for their parents to lay again that season, so King penguins are only able to lay in alternate years.

Another species which differs from the more 'typical' penguins in a number of ways is the Yellow-eyed penguin *Megadyptes antipodes* which breeds only in New Zealand and neighbouring islands. First, it is sedentary and may be found in the breeding area at any time of the year; secondly, it does not breed in large colonies and the nests are somewhat isolated from each other; and thirdly, it breeds in forest areas.

One of the problems which penguins have to face is the moult, which in these birds is unusual in that sizeable patches of feathers come away in one piece, rather as in a reptile sloughing its skin. During this period, which may last for a month or more, the birds are very lethargic. As they are no longer waterproof they cannot feed, and they therefore

may lose 40% of their body weight. FAMILY: Spheniscidae, ORDER: Sphenisciformes, CLASS: Aves.

PERCHES, loose name for many kinds of spiny-finned fishes.

The European perch *Perca fluviatilis*, for which the name was first used, is widespread in England and Ireland but rare in Scotland and Norway. It is common throughout the rest of Europe as far as the Soviet Union, a deep-bodied fish with two barely separated dorsal fins, the first spiny with a prominent black spot near the rear. The back is olive-brown, the flanks yellowish (often brassy) with about six, dark vertical bars, and the belly white. The tail and the lower fins are often tinged with red. The perch prefers slow and sluggish waters but can live almost everywhere. When in fairly fast streams, these fishes form small shoals in the eddies. Perches are predators, feeding throughout life on small fishes and invertebrates. Beloved of anglers, because of the ease with which they take the bait, perches have been caught up to 6 lb (2·7 kg) in England and up to 10 lb (4·5 kg) on the continent of Europe. They spawn amongst weeds in shallow waters in late spring. The males first congregate at the spawning grounds and when the females arrive several males will accompany one female as she lays long strings of eggs entwined in weeds. FAMILY: Percidae, ORDER: Perciformes, CLASS: Pisces.

PÈRE DAVID'S DEER *Elaphurus davidianus*, the most remarkable of all Chinese deer, a species which no man, living or dead, has ever recorded seeing in the wild state. In 1865 the French explorer, Armand David, first saw it inside the walled Imperial Hunting Park of Nan-Hai-Tsue near Peking. Before the close of the century, specimens of this rare deer had reached some of the European zoos, as well as Woburn Park in England. About 1900, due to flooding in the Imperial Park, the wall was breached and the escaping animals were either killed off by the starving peasantry or by troops during the Boxer rising. By 1910, not only was it extinct in China, but also in European zoos, the only survivors were at Woburn. From these a thriving herd of over 300 has been built up.

The Gentoo penguin lives on the South Shetlands and other antarctic islands.

Adélie penguins, restricted to the shores of Antarctica and neighbouring islands.

White pelicans at nest. They breed in large colonies, on the ground.

The European perch has given its name to a large order of spiny-finned fishes.

Standing about 48 in (122 cm) high at the shoulder, it has an extremely long tail, wide splayed hooves and strange-looking antlers which appear to be worn back to front. FAMILY: Cervidae, ORDER: Artiodactyla, CLASS: Mammalia.

PEREGRINE FALCON *Falco peregrinus*, most widespread of the large falcons, found on all continents but Antarctica and on many oceanic islands.

Peregrine falcons are the most valued of all falcons used in falconry. Relatively easily obtained and trained, they are docile but large enough to kill gamebirds in spectacular style. Their speed in the diving attack (stoop), variously estimated at 100–275 mph (160–440 kph), coupled with their readiness to 'wait on' above the falconer until he flushes the quarry, makes them superior to larger falcons such as gyrs or sakers.

Peregrines usually inhabit mountains or sea cliffs, but some live in tundras or in boggy areas among conifer forests. They normally feed on birds up to the size of wild duck, caught in the air and, either struck dead with the foot, or seized and carried to the ground. Their favourite prey is pigeons.

Peregrines probably pair for life and return annually to the same cliff to breed. They lay between three and six eggs in a scrape on a ledge, or sometimes in an old nest of a crow or other raptor. The smaller male (tiercel) feeds the female (falcon) during courtship and incubation and provides for the whole brood until they are half-grown. FAMILY: Falconidae, ORDER: Falconiformes, CLASS: Aves.

PERIWINKLES, small sea snails living mainly on the shore and possessing a horny operculum and breathing by means of a single gill. They feed on seaweeds, rasping these with their horny tongue, or radula. Common European species include the crevice-dwelling Small periwinkle *Littorina neritoides* which occurs at high tide mark on exposed rocky coasts. The shell rarely exceeds 0·2 in (5 mm)

in length and is dark black-brown in colour. A larger species is the Rough periwinkle *Littorina saxatilis* which occurs from the middle to the upper shore throughout much of northwest Europe and on both east and west coasts of North America. Its shell commonly reaches 0·5 in (12·5 mm) in length and is marked with fine spiral lines. It is easily confused with small specimens of the Common or Edible periwinkle *Littorina littorea* but may be distinguished by the tentacles having longitudinal dark stripes in the Rough periwinkle and transverse concentric stripes in the Edible periwinkle. The latter is a widespread intertidal and estuarine winkle which is commonest on the middle shore and below. It occurs throughout northwest Europe and on the east coast of North America. FAMILY: Littorinidae, ORDER: Mesogastropoda, CLASS: Gastropoda, PHYLUM: Mollusca.

PETRELS, seabirds which include the Storm petrels. The name is derived from the habit of some of the smaller species of fluttering so close to the surface of the water that they appear to be walking on it—as St. Peter is said to have done. ORDER: Procellariiformes, CLASS: Aves.

PHALANGERS (Possums), Australian herbivorous marsupials often called possums or, more rarely, opossums because of their superficial resemblance to the true opossums of North and South America. The group, collectively the family Phalangeridae, includes the cuscuses, Flying phalangers and Pigmy possums. FAMILY: Phalangeridae, ORDER: Marsupialia, CLASS: Mammalia.

PHALAROPES, three species of small semi-aquatic wading birds, with long, thin necks and small heads. All three swim a great deal. They have dense plumage on their breast, belly and underparts, to provide both waterproofing and buoyancy; legs with an oval cross-section so that the width of bone is much smaller in the direction of movement; and toes broadened or lobed and slightly webbed at the base. They have different plumages in summer and winter. In the

Flat periwinkles, small sea snails common on European shores, derive their name from the obliquely flattened apex of the shell.

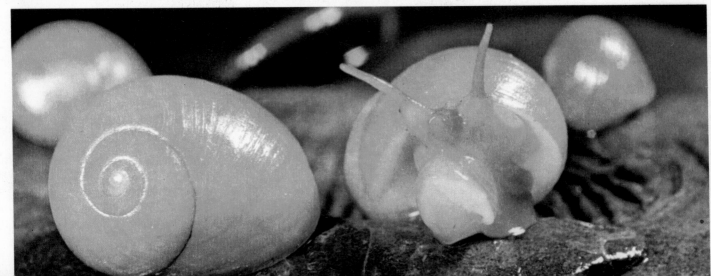

breeding plumage females are more brightly coloured than males.

In their grey and white winter plumage the Grey phalarope *Phalaropus fulicarius* and the Red-necked phalarope *P. lobatus* are very similar. The Grey phalarope is slightly larger than the Red-necked, but the main difference in winter is in bill proportions, that of the Red-necked being fine and delicate while that of the Grey is shorter and broader. In summer plumage the Grey phalarope is, confusingly, the more richly coloured of the two. This is reflected in its American common name, Red phalarope. The Red-necked phalarope is known as the Northern phalarope in North America, and this also is confusing, as the Red-necked has the more southerly distribution of the two. The third species, Wilson's phalarope *Steganopus tricolor*, is slightly larger than the other two, with longer legs and a long needle-like bill. It differs at all seasons in the possession of a white rump.

Phalaropes spend more time swimming than any other species of waders. In freshwater habitats, they take aquatic insect larvae (chiefly mosquitoes) and small crustaceans from the surface layers of the water. They stir up these food items from lower levels, or at least cause them to move so that they become conspicuous, by rapid swimming movements with their feet. At the same time they spin their bodies round and round on the water, making many revolutions per minute. FAMILY: Phalaropididae, ORDER: Charadriiformes, CLASS: Aves.

PHEASANTS, a well-defined group of game birds. In nearly all pheasants the male is more brightly coloured than the female. The sombre, cryptic colouration of the females must have considerable survival value during the long weeks of incubation and brooding.

All pheasants spend a great deal of time on the ground searching for food. They scratch the earth with their feet like domestic chickens in search of seeds, worms and insects. They have long and powerful legs and can run far and fast, so much so that many pheasants prefer to run into cover rather than take to the air when alarmed. When they do fly up, they rise almost vertically on their short but broad wings.

Most pheasants nest on the ground, making a scrape under cover of a bush, tussock of grass, or even among dead leaves on the forest floor.

No group of birds can claim to have made such an impact on the social and economic history of mankind as have the pheasants. As sporting birds they have been widely introduced throughout the Old and New Worlds and they have often indirectly affected the lives of other creatures, for whenever the pheasant is regarded as an important game bird, legislation has been passed to protect it. In his concern for the introduced pheasant man has frequently, and needlessly destroyed other forms of wildlife.

The Common pheasant was taken from Asia Minor across Europe, and has since been taken to other parts of the world, as a sporting bird.

It is probable that the first pheasants to arrive in Britain were brought by the Romans during their 400 years' occupation but the first historical evidence does not appear until the 11th century when pheasant figured on the menu at various banquets and monastic feasts. By the 12th century pheasant was a regular item on the bill of fare and by the 16th century it was established as a wild bird. This pheasant was almost certainly the Southern Caucasus pheasant or what is more popularly, if inaccurately, called the Old English blackneck.

The Great argus *Argusianus argus* is one of the most highly specialized of the pheasants and though the male's plumage may look less colourful than that of some species, his display, which is one of the most remarkable in the bird world, more than compensates. The secondary wing feathers are very broad and of tremendous length with a line of beautiful ocelli running the length of each feather while the two central tail feathers are even longer and twisted towards the tip. During his display the male argus faces the hen, bends forwards and spreads his wings, twisting them so that they meet in front of his head. The tips of the two central tail feathers project above the circle of feathers. The Great argus lives in the tropical forests of the Malay Peninsula, Sumatra and Borneo. FAMILY: Phasianidae, ORDER: Galliformes, CLASS: Aves.

PICHICIAGO *Chlamyphorus truncatus*, or Fairy armadillo. It measures 6 in (15 cm) in length and its spatula-shaped tail is less than 1 in (25 mm) long. In this smallest armadillo the many-banded head and body armour is scanty and is anchored only in two places, on the skull over the eyes and by a narrow ridge of flesh down the animal's back. It is the only armadillo in which the dorsal armour is almost separate from the body. The squared-off rump, however, is covered securely with a large plate attached firmly to the pelvic bones. Pichiciagos are said to use this rear plate to plug their burrow entrances. The tail projects from a notch at the bottom of the plate and cannot be raised because of it. The shell is pale pink and the rest of the body is covered with soft, fine white hair that hangs down over the legs and feet.

Fairy armadillos are found only in the sandy arid plains of west-central Argentina where they burrow in the hot dry earth where cactus and thorn bushes grow in abundance. They emerge from their burrows to feed principally on ants and occasionally on worms, plant tops and roots.

Burmeister's armadillo *Burmeisteria retusa* is only slightly larger. Its shell is whitish and yellowish-brown in colour and is completely attached to the skin of the back. The rear shield is made up of small individual plates scattered over the blunt rump and separated by naked skin. FAMILY: Dasypodidae, ORDER: Edentata, CLASS: Mammalia.

PIG, DOMESTIC, hog or swine, has been used by man for the last 5,000 years, since the Neolithic Period. Probably Asiatic pigs were first domesticated and there is evidence that these were first brought to Europe, although the European wild boar was later domesticated.

Although primarily a source of meat and cooking fat, pigs were put to other uses. They have been employed as draught animals and in Ancient Egypt were used to tread corn, their hoofs making an imprint in the ground of just the right depth at which wheat should be sown. Individual pigs have at various times

Wild boar, ancestor of the domestic pig. Little is known of its habits except that it will turn with ferocity on an intruder.

been used for rounding up cattle, for retrieving game and for detecting truffles, the fungus delicacy which grows 1–2 ft (30–60 cm) below ground. Their main use, apart from being suppliers of meat, was in clearing the ground. Pigs root for food, turning over the soil with their snout, feeding on acorns, beechmast and other fallen fruits, roots and tubers, and in the process destroying seedlings, even uprooting small saplings. From Neolithic times onwards they have been used to convert open woodland into arable and pasture land.

There are two kinds of pigs: herd pigs and sty- or house-pigs. Herd pigs tend to be long-legged and long-snouted and these were the kind generally used in Europe until nearly 200 years ago when Chinese house-pigs were imported and crossed with the European to give the thick-set Berkshire. FAMILY: Suidae, ORDER: Artiodactyla, CLASS: Mammalia.

PIGEONS, a term used to designate the larger species of doves. They vary in size from that of a lark to that of a hen turkey, from 6–33 in (15–84 cm) in length. They also vary considerably in plumage, some of them being amongst the most brightly coloured of birds, others rather drab. The most typical plumage is some pastel shade of grey, brown or pink, with contrasting patches of brighter colours. The legs are usually short, being rather long only in some of the terrestrial species. The body is compact, the neck rather short and the head small. The bill is usually small, soft at the base but hard at the tip, and at the base of the upper mandible is a fleshy 'cere', a naked area of skin which in some species is much swollen.

Most species of pigeons perch readily and

regularly in trees, but some are terrestrial, others cliff-dwelling and some have taken to nesting on buildings in towns and cities. The feral pigeons which are so common in towns are all 'escapes', or descendants of such, from stocks of domestic pigeons. All domestic pigeons are derived from the Rock dove *Columba livia*, of Europe, which in the wild form nests on rock ledges, so feral pigeons take naturally to breeding on buildings. Most species are gregarious, at least outside the breeding season, and some of them may be seen in large flocks.

The food of pigeons is very varied, including berries, nuts, acorns, apples, seeds

of many kinds, for example weed seeds and cultivated grain, and also buds and leaves. Food is stored temporarily in a crop which may be capacious. The distended crop of a Wood pigeon *Columba palumbus*, for example, after a successful day's feeding may be seen clearly as the bird flies home to roost. Most pigeons have a large, muscular gizzard which, with the enclosed grit deliberately swallowed, grinds up even the most intractable food.

Pigeons drink in a manner unusual for a bird. They immerse the bill and then, instead of lifting the head and tipping the water down the throat, they suck.

Pigeons build an unsubstantial, usually

Feral pigeons in Trafalgar Square, descendants of Rock doves once kept in dovecotes.

The Golden pheasant came originally from the mountains of Central Asia.

platform-like nest of twigs, stems or roots, in a tree or bush, on a cliff or building ledge. Two pale unmarked eggs form the usual clutch, and both sexes incubate. The young are helpless when first hatched and sparsely covered with a filamentous down. They are fed by both parents for the first few days on 'pigeons' milk', a curd-like material secreted by special cells lining the crop. FAMILY: Columbidae, ORDER: Columbiformes, CLASS: Aves.

PIGMY POSSUMS, dormouse-like insectivorous marsupials with prehensile tails found in Australia, New Guinea and Tasmania. They give birth to up to six young at one time. The Pigmy possums are the most primitive of the phalangers and are perhaps like the stock from which the phalangers arose. Broom's pigmy possum *Burramys parvus*, previously known only as a Pleistocene fossil, was found alive in Victoria, Australia in 1966. FAMILY: Phalangeridae, ORDER: Marsupialia, CLASS: Mammalia.

PIGTAILED MONKEY *Macaca nemestrina*, has a short tail which is held up in a loop. It is robust and long-legged, with a long snout; the crown hairs are dark brown and diverge from a parting, meeting the somewhat elongated grey cheek fringe. Big males weigh up to 14 lb (6 kg). It is found from Burma south to Sumatra, Borneo and Bangka, and also occurs on the Mentawei islands and the Andaman islands. FAMILY: Cercopithecidae, ORDER: Primates, CLASS: Mammalia.

PIKA, small, short-eared tailless rabbit-like animal, also known as Calling hare, coney, mousehare, haymaker, Slide rat. The adult weight of some species is 5 oz (140 gm). The body is short and cylindrical, the ears short and rounded, the tail not apparent externally, and the hindlegs not much longer than the front ones, permitting only a scampering run. The colour varies from dark brown or dark slaty-grey to pale sandy or ash. 12 species are distributed from eastern Europe to Japan and from the Himalayas to Siberia. Two North American species range from Alaska southwards down the Rocky Mountains. Although predominantly a high altitude animal living above the tree line among the rocks and crevices of mountain slopes, a few species inhabit plateaux and open grasslands down to sea-level. All live in a cold climate and all dig in the soil.

Pikas live in colonies spaced at distances from one another in accordance with the availability of food. They use characteristic sounds frequently and loudly, presumably for intraspecific communication, hence one of their names, Calling hare. They do not hibernate but have the habit of food-hoarding, involving not only storing it under rocky ledges but also preliminary drying and turning it as in haymaking. They feed on a variety of vegetation, the 'haypiles' often being brush piles consisting of grass, wood-twigs, and also pine cones, clumps of moss and sprigs of conifer needles. In some countries the pikas' enterprise is exploited by herdsmen who feed their sheep on the 'haystacks' in

winter. The Mt Everest pika *Ochotona wollastoni*, lives at altitudes up to 20,000 ft (6,000 m), thus having one of the highest vertical distributions among the mammals. FAMILY: Ochotonidae, ORDER: Lagomorpha, CLASS: Mammalia.

PIKE, freshwater fishes of the northern hemisphere. The European pike *Esox lucius*, is a mottled yellow-green fish with an elongate body, the short and soft-rayed dorsal and anal fins being set far back towards the tail. The position of the dorsal and anal fins is characteristic of predatory species that lie in wait for their prey and then make a sudden dash. FAMILY: Esocidae, ORDER: Salmoniformes, CLASS: Pisces.

PILOTFISH *Naucrates ductor*, a small fish habitually associated with sharks and large fishes, related to the mackerels and tunas. It is found all over the world in tropical and temperate oceans. The name comes from its alleged habit of not only accompanying sharks and sometimes other large fishes but of actually leading them to their prey. The pilotfish feeds on the scraps of food left by its host and thus deserves the name commensal (literally 'feeding from the same table'). Pilotfishes swim round sharks, making brief sorties and returning, but it is doubtful if they act as pilots. V. V. Shuleikin calculated that sharks swim three times as fast as a pilotfish. He suggested the pilotfishes are carried along by the shark's boundary layer, that is, the layer of water over its surface which travels at the same speed as the shark. FAMILY: Carangidae, ORDER: Perciformes, CLASS: Pisces.

PILOT WHALES, several species of large dolphins with a worldwide distribution. The North Atlantic species, *Globicephala melaena*, is also called the Ca'aing whale or blackfish. Adults are about 25 ft (8 m) in length and they are found in schools of several hundreds. As the scientific name implies Pilot whales have a rounded forehead which bulges forward of the lower jaw. They are black overall but for a white patch below the jaw. The flippers are distinctive being relatively long and narrow, about one-fifth of the body length.

Pilot whales are highly social, yet nervous, and as a result of this fall an easy prey particularly in the Faroes where the economy of the Faroese has been to a considerable extent dependent upon them. FAMILY: Delphinidae, ORDER: Cetacea, CLASS: Mammalia.

PIPEFISHES, elongated and rather specialized fishes related to the trumpetfishes, shrimpfishes and Sea horses. They have a world-wide distribution and although mainly marine include some freshwater species. The long, thin body is completely encased in bony rings but it is surprisingly flexible and

Pika *Ochotona pusilla*, one of the mousehares, a short-eared tailless rabbit.

prehensile. The fish is well camouflaged for a secretive life amongst weeds. The pelvic fins and the tail are lacking in some species.

In the most primitive pipefishes the male carries the fertilized eggs on his underside. In the next and more advanced group the eggs are embedded singly in a spongy layer that develops along the belly of the male. Finally, in forms like *Doryrhamphus* the bony plates encasing the body are enlarged to form a groove in which the eggs are carried.

The Great pipefish *Syngnathus acus*, reaches 18 in (45 cm) in length. It has a small anal fin and a small tail. As in all pipefishes the rays of the dorsal fin are soft and flexible and each ray can be moved independently. This is important because like the Sea horses, the pipefishes swim by undulations of the dorsal fin.

Most pipefishes are drab in colour, but the male of the Straight-nosed pipefish *Nerophis ophidion* has a greenish body with blue lines along the abdomen. Some of the pipefishes are quite small. *Doryrhamphus melanopleura* from coral reefs of the Pacific region reaches only 2½ in (6·5 cm) in length. It is bright orange-red with a longitudinal bright blue band from the snout to the tail, the latter being orange at its base, followed by blue with a white margin. FAMILY: Syngnathidae, ORDER: Gasterosteiformes, CLASS: Pisces.

PIPITS, small, sombrely-coloured terrestrial birds related to the wagtails. They are generally brown, streaked with black above, and buffish white or yellow, with or without streaks, below. The sexes are usually alike. The tail is relatively long and is often bobbed up and down wagtail fashion. The bill is fine and pointed, the legs long and slender and the hind claw often very long.

Golden pipit *Tmetothylacus tenellus* of the dry bush of East Africa.

They are birds of open ground, inhabiting grassland, steppe and savannah country, usually in well-watered areas, alpine meadows in mountainous regions and arctic tundra, although a few prefer areas with scattered bushes or trees. They walk or run but never hop. Most pipits occasionally perch on trees, particularly when disturbed, but few species do so habitually.

One of the most widespread, Richard's pipit *Anthus novaezeelandiae*, occurs from New Zealand and the neighbouring sub-antarctic islands through Australia and Southeast Asia to India and also over much of Africa. Although absent from the Middle East and Europe as a breeding species, it has occurred irregularly on migration as far west

as Britain. The Tawny pipit *A. campestris* prefers drier habitats than most pipits, occurring on sandy wastes, arid pastures, and barren rocky ground in southwest Asia, southern Europe and north Africa. Two of the commonest pipits in Europe, the Tree pipit *A. trivialis* and the Meadow pipit *A. pratensis*, although similar in appearance, show different habitat preferences. The Tree pipit is a bird of wood edges, forest clearings and heaths with scattered trees. It seems that elevated perches are essential to Tree pipits during the breeding season as the erection of a line of telegraph poles across an otherwise bare heath may lead to their colonizing the area. The Meadow pipit prefers rough grassland, moors and grassy tundra. FAMILY: Motacillidae, ORDER: Passeriformes, CLASS: Aves.

PIRANHAS or caribes, small but very ferocious freshwater fishes from South America renowned for their carnivorous habits and amongst the most infamous of all fishes. Travellers' tales relate cases where large animals and even men have been attacked and the flesh picked off their bones in a very short space of time. There are several species involved, the largest growing to about 15 in (38 cm). The jaws are short and powerful and are armed with sharp cutting teeth. Their main diet is fish or mammals but they are reputed to be strongly attracted to the smell of blood so that a single bite will draw hundreds of other members of the shoal to the same spot.

The White piranha *Serrasalmus rhombeus*, one of the largest, is olive to silver with irregular dark blotches. The Red piranha *Rooseveltiella nattereri* grows to 12 in (30 cm) and has an olive-brown back, light brown flanks and numerous bright silver spots on

Most pipefishes are marine. *Syngnathus pulchellus,* of the Congo, lives in freshwater.

Despite its bad reputation the Red piranha is sometimes kept as an aquarium fish.

the body. The belly and the fin bases are, appropriately enough, blood red. FAMILY: Characidae, ORDER: Cypriniformes, CLASS: Pisces.

PITTAS, beautifully coloured ground-living birds, very plump, with short wings and tail, and powerful legs and feet. Because of their gorgeous coloration, they have been called 'jewel-thrushes', among the most beautiful birds in the world. The male Green-breasted pitta *Pitta sordida* of southeast Asia, for example, has a brown and black head, green back and breast, red under-tail coverts, blue

rump and wings patterned boldly with blue, black and white. The females of most species are much duller than the males, and a few are quite drab-looking.

The group is centred around tropical southeast Asia where most of the 23 species live. Two species occur in Africa and a few in New Guinea, tropical Australia and adjacent Pacific Islands.

Pittas are characteristically birds of the forest. When feeding, they move about quickly on the forest floor by hopping, but can fly rapidly if they have to. Their food is spiders, ants and other insects, snails and

seeds. Generally speaking, pittas are shy birds, more often heard than seen, despite their showy appearance.

Their nests are large, untidy constructions of sticks, dead leaves and roots, built on, or near, the ground. The young remain in the nest for several weeks and are fed by both parents. FAMILY: Pittidae, ORDER: Passeriformes, CLASS: Aves.

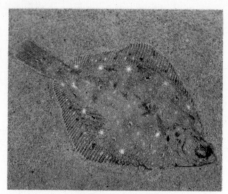

The plaice, a favourite food fish.

PLAICE *Pleuronectes platessa*, perhaps the most popular of all the edible European flatfishes. The name derives from an Old French word for flat. It is one of the most easily identified species because of the irregular orange spots on the upper surface which persist after death (similar spots in the flounder soon disappear when the fish is out of water). The blind side is a translucent white. Unlike the flounder, there are no rough scales on the head but there are small tubercles between the eyes. In contrast to most flatfishes, the plaice is sedentary, found mainly over sand or gravel. Plaice grow to 33 in (83 cm) and may reach 15 lb (6·7 kg) in weight. FAMILY: Pleuronectidae, ORDER: Pleuronectiformes, CLASS: Pisces.

PLAINS WANDERER *Pedionomus torquatus*, small quail-like bird related to buttonquails, confined to open grasslands of southeastern Australia. The role of the sexes is reversed, the female being bigger, more brightly-coloured, the male incubating the eggs and caring for the young. The bird tends to move in an upright posture, raised on the toes, unlike the crouching postures of buttonquails, FAMILY: Pedionomidae, ORDER: Gruiformes, CLASS: Aves.

PLATYPUS *Ornithorhynchus anatinus*, four-legged amphibious animal which, with the echidnas, comprises a distinct sub-class of the Mammalia, the Prototheria or egg-laying mammals. Known also as the duckbill, water-mole or duckmole, an adult male platypus is about 20 in (51 cm) long with a 6 in (15 cm) beaver-like tail, and weighs 4·2 lb (1·9 kg). The females are smaller. The duck-like bill is a sensitive elongated snout and is soft, not horny, as is usually supposed. The platypus is well-adapted for a semi-aquatic life with short legs and webbed feet with strong

Blue-winged pitta, of south and east Asia. Pittas are among the most beautiful of birds.

Platypus, the duckbill, most famous of the Australian egg-laying mammals, swimming.

claws on the toes. The webbing on the fore-feet projects beyond the ends of the claws but this can be folded back when on land, leaving the claws free for walking or digging. Adult males have a hollow curved spur on the ankles about 0·75 in (1·9 cm) long, which connects to a gland secreting a poison in the breeding season. The tail is thick, short and very fat. The coat varies from sepia-brown to almost black above, the underparts being silver, tinged with pink or yellow. There is a thick woolly undercoat with long shiny guard hairs.

The eyes are situated dorsally on the broad flattened head and immediately posterior to the eye is the external opening of the ear. There is no external pinna, and both the eye and ear are situated in a groove or fold of fur which can be closed under water. The duck-billed muzzle is covered by darkly pigmented soft naked skin, which contains innumerable sense organs. The sense of touch of the muzzle is presumably the only means of locating food.

Very young platypuses have molariform teeth, at least two in the upper jaw and three in the lower. In the adult the teeth are replaced by horny plates. These serve to crush the food some of which is then stored temporarily in cheek-pouches.

The platypus is found in fresh waters throughout Tasmania and the eastern parts of Australia and just within the borders of South Australia, in freezing waters of the Australian Alps to the warm rivers and lagoons of tropical Queensland. It spends little of its time in the water. Most of its time is spent in burrows which it digs in the soft earth of the banks, or in sunning itself

in the open. There are two types of burrow: one used for shelter and another for breeding; the latter is constructed and inhabited by a pregnant female only and is not shared with any other platypus.

Copulation takes place in the water and fertilization is followed by an unknown period of gestation in the left uterus only. The female then retires to the complicated nesting burrow where she has excavated a brood chamber containing a nest of grass, leaves, reeds and so on. Generally two eggs are laid, sometimes three; the eggs adhere to one another their shells being sticky when laid. After hatching the tiny young about 0·65 in (17 mm) long, are suckled by paired mammary glands which open at a pair of milk patches or areolae on the ventral surface hidden by thick fur. As the young grow the mammary glands become very large reaching almost from the armpits to the pelvis longitudinally and up around the flanks laterally. FAMILY: Ornithorhynchidae, ORDER: Monotremata, SUB-CLASS: Prototheria, CLASS: Mammalia.

POCHARD, a group of freshwater diving ducks. The male is usually grey on the body, black on the tail and upper breast and chest-nut-brown on the head, the female being brown. The species in the genus *Aythya* are well adapted for an aquatic life with a short, heavy body, large head and long neck and with their legs placed well back on their body. In North America the canvasback *A. valisineria* is a famous sporting duck as is the redhead *A. americana*. The canvasback has a longer bill and is a paler grey than most pochards. The European pochard *A. ferina*

is only 18 in (45 cm) long and is found on quiet lakes and ponds. Most pochards feed on vegetable matter with some animal food.

Also included in the genus *Aythya* are the four species of white-eye, brown above and paler below in both sexes. The best known is the Tufted duck *A. fuligula*, which breeds across Europe and Asia from Iceland to the Pacific. The drake is black above and white beneath, with a pendant crest from the back of his head. The female is brown with a hint of a crest.

The scaups form the rest of this genus, the sturdiest being the Greater scaup *A. marila* ranging across the whole of the northern hemisphere and spending much of its time at sea. FAMILY: Anatidae, ORDER: Anseriformes, CLASS: Aves.

POLECATS, terrestrial carnivores, larger than a stoat and smaller than a marten, best known for the pungent odour secreted by their anal scent glands. They measure 17·3–25·2 in (44–64 cm) and weigh 1 lb 7 oz–2 lb 11 oz (0·65–1·2 kg). Females are much smaller and lighter than males. Certain individuals of the European polecat *Mustela putorius* are very dark, almost black, in fact, since the thick yellowish underfur is more or less masked by the guard hairs which may be either completely black or black-tipped. A dark brown band across the eyes contrasts with the creamy white of the throat, forehead and edges of the ears.

Polecats are found in a variety of habitats in the northern hemisphere, from open grass-land to woods or thickets. The non-retractile claws are used to excavate the animal's den, but empty rabbit warrens or fox holes are

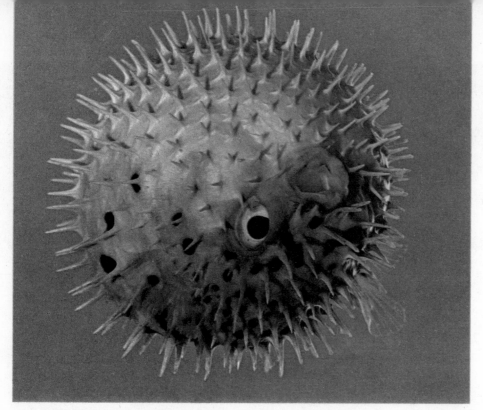

The defensive reaction of the porcupinefish is to inflate, so erecting its spines.

also used. They climb less readily than stoats or weasels and swim only when the need arises. Hunting more by smell than by sight, the polecat traverses obstacles or high grass in short leaps, stopping now and then to rear up on its hind-paws like so many other short-limbed mustelids. Rodents, insects, eggs and fruit are eaten. The thick, closely knit fur with the underlying layer of fibro-elastic tissue makes polecats almost impervious to the bite of enemies, whether fox, dog, or snake. They possess such a loose-limbed lithe muscularity that they often give the impression of being able to bound backwards as well as forwards. If suddenly alarmed, they will snort and constrict the scent glands, sending a jet of milky white fluid 20 in (50 cm) backwards, which acts as a pungent deterrent. By contrast, when attacking, the polecat hisses and keeps its head low, the back humped into an inverted U-shape, lunging forward to bite the prey on the neck. The victim is then shaken violently from side to side.

Neck grasping also occurs during mating. Females come into oestrus in March. Gestation lasts 40 to 45 days, although some authors claim 63 days. The four to eight cubs are blind and naked at birth and weigh no more than 0.3 oz (10 gm). Their eyes open after 20 days and a grey, downy fur with white muzzle and ear tips appears. FAMILY: Mustelidae, ORDER: Carnivora, CLASS: Mammalia.

POLLACK *Pollachius pollachius*, a cod-like fish found in the eastern Atlantic as far north as Norway, but absent from the Mediterranean. It resembles the cod but lacks a barbel on the chin, has smaller pelvic fins and has elongated, light-coloured smudges on the flanks. The pollack feeds on small

fishes, especially sand-eels, as well as worms and crustaceans. It reaches 24 lb (11 kg) in weight and is of some commercial value. FAMILY: Gadidae, ORDER: Gadiformes, CLASS: Pisces.

PORCUPINEFISHES, tropical marine fishes in which the teeth in each jaw are fused completely together to form a beak. They are best described as pufferfishes with well-developed spines on the body. The spines, which are modified scales, normally lie against the body. Porcupinefishes can inflate the body with air or water and erect the spines.

The most frequently illustrated species is *Diodon histrix*, one of the several forms commonly sold to tourists dried and inflated as a curio or even as a lampshade. FAMILY: Diodontidae, ORDER: Tetraodontiformes, CLASS: Pisces.

PORCUPINES, large, spiny rodents belonging to two families, one confined to the Americas (Erithizontidae) and the other to the tropics of the Old World (Hystricidae).

Old World porcupines include about a dozen species found throughout Africa and southern Asia. They are amongst the largest of rodents and the entire body is covered with quills although these vary greatly in length and thickness in different parts of the body and in different species. On the bodies of some species, and on the feet of the others, the spines are no more than rather stiff bristly hairs, whereas in the Crested porcupines the spines of the back may reach 14 in (35 cm) in length.

The Crested porcupines, *Hystrix*, occupy the savannah and steppe zones from southern Africa to India. These weigh up to 55 lb (25 kg) and measure up to 34 in (86 cm) long. The black and white banded quills on the back are very long and when erected, along with the enormous crest on the head, greatly

The North American porcupine, a tree climber, has long hair concealing its quills.

increase the apparent size of the animal as well as providing a formidable weapon of defence. The quills on the tip of the tail are modified to form a rattle. Each is hollow and the end breaks off as soon as the quill is fully grown, forming an elongated goblet-shaped structure. These clash together with considerable noise when the tail is shaken.

Hystrix cristata occurs all around the edge of the Sahara and south through East Africa to Tanzania. It is also found in Italy, perhaps an introduction dating back to Roman times. Similar species occur in southern Africa (*Hystrix africaeaustralis*) and from Turkey and Arabia to India and Ceylon (*Hystrix indica*).

The mating position is not unorthodox as is often suggested. The gestation period is about four months and the two or three young are well developed at birth.

Crested porcupines are nocturnal, spending the day in deep burrows excavated in a bank, or in caves or crevices in rock. Several may share an earth or den. They are strictly terrestrial, feeding mainly on roots, tubers and bark. They can do considerable damage to crops, especially root-crops and melons.

From southern China through Malaya to the Indonesian islands are found other porcupines of the genera *Acanthion* and *Thecurus*, closely related to the Crested porcupines. These lack the crest and in general are smaller and shorter-spined.

Brush-tailed porcupines, *Atherurus*, replace *Hystrix* in the rain-forests of Africa (*A. africana*) and southeast Asia (*A. macrourus*). These are smaller and more slender than the Crested porcupines, with longer tails. The rattle quills are quite different, being long and ribbon-like, with a number of segments flattened alternately in different planes. Brush-tailed porcupines can and do climb trees to some extent, but are nevertheless predominantly terrestrial.

The American porcupines comprise about a dozen species. Most of them live in South and Central America. By far the best known, *Erithizon dorsatum*, occurs from Mexico to Canada and Alaska. The North American porcupine is about the same size as the larger Old World species but is not so heavy. It is covered with an armour of formidable spines, but when they are relaxed they are almost concealed in a coat of long brown hair (especially well developed in the animals in eastern Canada). There is also a dense woolly underfur. The spines have finely barbed points and are readily detached when they penetrate an adversary, but they cannot be shot at an attacker as is often said. This is a woodland species.

The male sprays the female with urine before mating. The gestation period is about seven months, and a single, very well developed youngster is born in the spring.

Although the North American porcupine is less arboreal than the more southern species, it can climb well and spends a considerable time in trees. It spends the day in a hollow tree, rocky den or burrow. In summer a variety of vegetation is eaten, but in winter the porcupine feeds largely on bark and to a lesser extent on the needles of conifers. The removal of bark, both at ground level and amongst the upper branches, can cause serious damage in forests. Porcupines are also unpopular with farmers. A field of sweet corn adjacent to woodland is liable to be raided just as the ears are ripening.

The North American porcupine, when threatened, crouches low with the head drawn down between its legs and it gnashes its teeth. If the attacker persists, the porcupine leaps round to present a bristling and thrashing rear which can very quickly plant hundreds of quills in a predator's nose. In spite of these tactics the fisher *Martes pennanti*, a large member of the weasel family, can dart in to attack the unprotected underside of the porcupine and at the same time it is agile enough to avoid the porcupine's attack.

The Central and South American porcupines mostly belong to the genus *Coendou* and are much more strictly arboreal than the North American species. *Coendou prehensilis* is the best known. The spines are short but are not concealed by hair. The tail is very long with the terminal part naked and prehensile like that of the cebid monkeys found in the same habitat. This species is found in rain-forest throughout Brazil. They are slow-moving and feed on fruit, buds and leaves. FAMILIES: Hystricidae, Erithizontidae, ORDER: Rodentia, CLASS: Mammalia.

PORPOISES, small Toothed whales usually under 6 ft (2 m) in length, tubby in appearance and having a rounded head and no projecting beak-like mouth. The teeth, which are found in both jaws, are spade-like instead of being conical as in the other Toothed whales. The dorsal fin is characteristically triangular whereas in many of the dolphins it is sickle-shaped. The foreflippers are quite small and spade-like.

Unfortunately it has become customary in the United States for the name porpoise to be given to the various dolphins kept in captivity and the habit has spread with American influence to other parts of the world, particularly New Zealand.

The Common porpoise *Phocaena phocaena* is the common porpoise of the North Atlantic and neighbouring seas. It is also numerous along the Pacific coast of North America from Alaska to California, where it is known as the Harbor porpoise.

It is a very fast swimmer, black on the back shading to white on the belly. The flippers and tail flukes are always black. The small rounded black flipper is attached to the white part of the trunk but a black line runs from the angle of the jaw to its root.

It feeds mainly on such fishes as herring, whiting, sole, pilchards and mackerel. FAMILY: Phocaenidae, ORDER: Cetacea, CLASS: Mammalia.

PORTUGUESE MAN-O'-WAR *Physalia physalis*, a colourful jellyfish of the kind known as siphonophores. It consists of a colony of four kinds of polyps, the most obvious of which is a gas-filled bladder 12 in (30 cm) long and 6 in (15 cm) in diameter which carries a high crest and is coloured blue to purple. This normally floats on the surface and on its underside hanging down in the water are many polyps of three kinds, those concerned with feeding, those concerned with reproduction, and the long trailing tentacles armed with stinging cells that may be up to 40 ft (12 m) long.

Normally an inhabitant of the warmer seas, the Portuguese man-o'-war may be carried into temperate latitudes by persistent winds and there cast up on the shore in thousands. The tentacles can inflict severe stings on man. FAMILY: Physalidae, ORDER: Siphonophora, CLASS: Hydrozoa, PHYLUM: Cnidaria.

POTTO *Perodicticus potto*, a clumsy-looking, stoutly built mammal with forward-facing eyes and powerful, grasping hands and feet. It has thick, woolly fur which is brownish-grey to rufous-brown on the back and paler on the belly. It weighs about 3 lb (1·2 kg). The head and body measure 16 in (40 cm) and there is a very short tail reaching only 3 in (8 cm) long.

The potto is completely arboreal and nocturnal, occurring at medium height in the trees of the west Central African rain-forest. Its diet probably consists of insects, with fruit and other animal food. The canines are large and stout and seem to be used both in killing fairly large prey and in defence against predators. Another striking device which is used against predators and in butting members of the same species is a row of prominences along the back of the neck, formed by spiny processes of the vertebrae. Using its stout limbs and powerful grasping hands and feet, the potto can cling tightly to a branch and butt a predator until it falls off or moves on. As an adaptation for powerful branch-grasping, the index finger is reduced to a small knob, and the thumb is widely opposed to the remaining fingers.

There is normally one baby at birth, and this crawls straight on to the mother's fur. It is then carried around most of the time on the mother. FAMILY: Lorisidae, ORDER: Primates, CLASS: Mammalia.

PRAIRIE CHICKEN, name given to two species of North American grouse, *Tympanuchus cupido* and *T. pallidicinctus*, weighing about 2 lb (1 kg). They were once widespread in eastern and mid-western North America but are now uncommon and only

The pratincole, or swallow-plover, a tern-like wader of southern Asia and Africa, hawks insects over or near water.

locally distributed in areas of virgin grasslands and prairie. Initially they were reduced by overhunting by the early settlers and the decline continues, despite some protection, due to the pressures of farming and ranching. FAMILY: Tetraonidae, ORDER: Galliformes, CLASS: Aves.

PRAIRIE DOGS, in spite of the name, Ground squirrels of the genus *Cynomys.* They are social animals, very characteristic of the open plains of North America. FAMILY: Sciuridae, ORDER: Rodentia, CLASS: Mammalia.

PRATINCOLES, widely distributed, small, elegant birds living near water. The genus *Galachrysia* has two species in Africa and one in Asia, and *Glareola* has one species in Madagascar and another, the pratincole *G. pratincola*, breeding from the Mediterranean to China, India and parts of Africa.

At rest they resemble small plovers, 7–9 in (17–23 cm) long, with small heads and short bills, long wings and rather long legs. But in the air they are like large swallows, the wings being pointed and the tail deeply forked, the flight buoyant and graceful. Despite the diminutive bill, the gape is very wide enabling them to catch small insects on the wing. Pratincoles will also pursue locusts, and sometimes pick insects from the ground. The plumage matches the earth on which they nest, being grey or dun-brown. The rump, the base of the tail and the belly are white.

There is a whitish wing bar and generally some chestnut in the plumage. In all species the bill is black with a carmine base and the legs are brown or red.

A depression on the ground serves as a nest and the two to four eggs are laid on sun-baked mud in *Glareola pratincola*, on sand in the West African Grey pratincole *Galachrysia cinerea*, and the Indian Little pratincole *G. lactea* of southeast Asia, or even on bare rock in the Collared pratincole *G. nuchalis*, which inhabits rock-strewn rivers in Africa. FAMILY: Glareolidae, ORDER: Charadriiformes, CLASS: Aves.

PRAYING MANTIS, long narrow carnivorous insect, usually found in the tropics or subtropics. The name stems from its habit of sitting motionless with the forelegs raised and held together as if praying. In fact, it is waiting for its prey. Mantids feed on other insects which they seize in their long spined forelegs and eat alive. A male will sometimes have his head bitten off by the female as he mates with her. About 1,800 species are known, the most familiar being the European mantis *Mantis religiosa* of the Mediterranean region. FAMILY: Mantidae, ORDER: Dictyoptera, CLASS: Insecta, PHYLUM: Arthropoda.

PRONGHORN ANTELOPE *Antilocapra americana*, the only horned animal that sheds its horn sheath (this it does every year), and the only one with branched horns.

It differs from the true antelopes in this shedding of the outer sheath. Males can be distinguished from females by their larger horns and by a conspicuous black spot beneath the ear. They are larger than females. The height at the shoulder varies from 32–41 in (81–104 cm), head and body length from 39–59 in (99–150 cm), tail length 3–4 in (7·5–10 cm), and weight from 79–134 lb (36–60 kg). The long white hairs of a large rump patch can be erected to form a heliographic disk that may flash for several miles in bright sunlight, sending warning signals from one group to another across open grassland and semidesert shrubland habitats. The brown coat is interrupted by white on the undersides extending half way up the sides and up the ventral side of the neck.

The pronghorn's range extends through the semi-arid lands of western North America from southern Canada to northern Mexico, usually at elevations of 3,000–8,000 ft (1,000–2,500 m). FAMILY: Antilocapridae, ORDER: Artiodactyla, CLASS: Mammalia.

PTARMIGAN, game bird of the grouse family, typically of the Arctic and subarctic. The Rock ptarmigan—in Britain known simply as ptarmigan—*Lagopus mutus* and the Willow ptarmigan or Willow grouse *L. lagopus* are circumpolar in distribution. In northern Britain the Willow ptarmigan is represented by the Red grouse, sometimes given specific rank as *L. scoticus*. It is adapted to less extreme environmental conditions and does not moult

Ptarmigan have a summer russet plumage and a winter white, with autumnal tints.

The Atlantic puffin nests in colonies on grassy cliff slopes on or near the edge of the sea, often on offshore islands. It is the only Atlantic auk which digs a burrow for its nest, but it will appropriate the burrow of a rabbit or shearwater or use a natural cavity. One large whitish egg is laid and incubated largely by the female. The young are fed by both parents on fish, which is first presented in a partly-digested state. FAMILY: Alcidae, ORDER: Charadriiformes, CLASS: Aves.

PUMA *Felis concolor*, often known as the cougar, Mountain lion, catamount and painter. The puma ranges over practically the whole of America from western Canada to Patagonia. It can live in mountains, swamps, savannah and forest from sea level to as high as 13,000 ft (4,000 m).

It resembles a very slender and sinuous lioness although the size varies considerably from region to region. The maximum length recorded for a male was 9½ ft (3 m) of which about a third was tail and 260 lb (120 kg) weight, but it may be as little as 4 ft (1·2 m) and 46 lb (21 kg). The females are generally smaller than the males. The head is much rounder than is usual in cats and the ears are more rounded. The colour of the short close fur varies considerably from yellowish-brown to red sometimes being darker in the winter. The throat, chest and belly are white. The ridge of the back and the tail is usually marked by a darker line and the tail is tipped

into a white plumage in winter. FAMILY: Tetraonidae, ORDER: Galliformes, CLASS: Aves.

PUDU *Pudu*, the smallest of the deer family living in the lower Andes in South America. FAMILY: Cervidae, ORDER: Artiodactyla, CLASS: Mammalia.

PUFF ADDERS, African snakes of the genus *Bitis*, highly venomous, so called because of their loud hissing or blowing air from the lungs, that is, they puff. FAMILY: Viperidae, ORDER: Squamata, CLASS: Reptilia.

PUFFERFISHES, fishes principally of tropical waters, related to the porcupinefishes and capable, like them, of inflating their bodies with air or water as a means of defence. These are clumsy looking fishes with scales often modified into spines. The head and chest are bulky but the body narrows thereafter.

Some species are poisonous to eat and they advertise this by their much brighter colours. The poison in pufferfishes is known as tetrodoxin and it is frequently fatal. Nevertheless, a dish called *fugu* is prepared from puffers and is considered to be a great delicacy in Japan. FAMILY: Tetraodontidae, ORDER: Tetraodontiformes, CLASS: Pisces.

PUFFINS, stubby, large-headed seabirds of the auk family. The best-known is the Atlantic puffin *Fratercula arctica* which breeds on most coasts around the North Atlantic. It is 12 in (30·5 cm) long, black above and white beneath, with a white face and a much enlarged laterally-compressed bill. At the beginning of the breeding season this bill is enlarged by the development of a sheath striped in red, blue-grey, and yellow. Also

the skin at the angle of the mouth is enlarged and develops a yellow hue, as does the inside of the mouth, and a small triangular blue-grey plate is developed above the eye. The total effect is somewhat clown-like, but the function of these features is connected with the breeding displays. The feet and legs of the adults are coloured vermilion in the summer, fading to yellow in winter.

The North Atlantic puffin has a brilliantly coloured bill during the breeding season.

Not a lioness but the puma or cougar, also known as the Mountain lion, of the Americas, a graceful medium-sized cat.

with black, but has no tuft.

The puma leads a solitary life, keeping very much out of sight. It is outstanding for its stamina and strength. It is able to cover up to 20 ft (6 m) in one bound and a leap of 40 ft (12 m) has been recorded. It can also leap upwards to a height of 15 ft (4½ m) and has been seen to drop to the ground from a height of 60 ft (18 m). It will travel 30–50 miles (48–80 km) when hunting but its usual range is restricted to an area of 12 sq miles (40 km²).

There are differences of opinion on how much the puma's voice is used. It is generally accepted that a puma screams in a blood-curdling manner but some game wardens working in puma country assert that they have never heard one scream. Normally a puma will purr when contented. Its screaming may have contributed to an undeserved reputation for ferocity but records show that attacks on human beings are very rare. Its habit of stalking people seems to arise from an overwhelming curiosity.

The favourite food of the puma is deer, although an amazing variety of food has been recorded from slugs and snails to porcupines and very rarely moose and buffalo. It sometimes attacks domestic stock such as sheep and goats, as well as horses and cattle.

1–6 kittens are born in a den among rocks or dense thicket at any time of the year after a gestation of 90–96 days. At birth the kittens are blind but well furred, spotted and with a ringed tail. They are up to 1 ft (30 cm) long and weigh up to 1 lb (0·4 kg). Their eyes open in 7–14 days and they are weaned between 1–3 months. FAMILY: Felidae, ORDER: Carnivora, CLASS: Mammalia.

PYTHONS, Old World equivalent of the New World boas, and like them bearing small spurs that represent the vestiges of hindlimbs. The largest and best-known, the true pythons, belong to the genus *Python*. They all have bold colour patterns mainly in browns and yellow. Three live in Africa, the African python *P. sebae*, which reaches a length of 32 ft (9·9 m), the Ball python *P. regius*, which, when molested, rolls itself into a tight ball with its head inside, and the Angolan python *P. anchietae*. Several other species are found from India to China and the East Indies. The largest species, the Reticulate python *P. reticulatus*, reaching a length of 33 ft (10 m), ranges from Burma to the Philippine Islands and Timor. Although so large it has been found to be remarkably

inoffensive in the wild and most accounts of its attacks on humans are exaggerated or invented. The Indian python *P. molurus* with a length up to 20 ft (6 m) is found from India to China and on some of the islands of the East Indies.

There are several other genera of pythons found in the East Indies and Australia. The Rock pythons *Liasis* are all found in the Australasian region. The largest of these is the Amethystine rock python *L. amethystinus* which are known to reach a length of 20 ft (6 m).

A large python can swallow prey weighing up to 120 lb (54 kg) and one 18 ft (5·5 m) African python is known to have eaten a leopard but this is exceptional. FAMILY: Boidae, ORDER: Squamata, CLASS: Reptilia.

The Ball python of Africa has the habit of coiling itself into a ball.

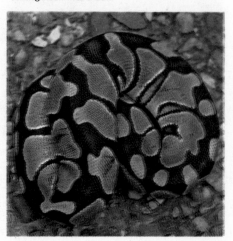

The African rock python, often kept in zoos, may attain 20 ft or more.

QR

QUAILS, two distinct groups of gamebirds, the Old World quails and the New World quails.

Old World quails are small, rounded birds with dainty bill and legs and no visible tail. They vary in size from the comparatively large Mountain quail *Anurophasis*, which is only a little smaller than the Common partridge *Perdix perdix*, down to the Painted quail *Coturnix chinensis* which is no bigger than a finch.

The most widespread and well known species is the Common quail *C. coturnix* which is found throughout most of Europe, Asia, parts of Africa and the Atlantic islands. A Japanese race *C. c. japonica* has been domesticated for centuries, being kept in small cages to produce both eggs and meat.

By means of selective breeding these birds now mature very quickly and females have been known to lay eggs only 12 weeks after they themselves were hatched.

The Common quail may be found in any open country provided there is enough cover. When disturbed quail prefer to run and hide rather than fly and for this reason they are difficult to see in the wild.

The American quails are usually larger and more colourful. The best known is the bobwhite *Colinus virginianus* one of the most popular gamebirds in the United States. There are a number of races found from southern Canada to the border of Guatemala. It lives on open plains and gets its name from the male's loud call which sounds like the words 'bob-white'. FAMILY: Phasianidae, ORDER: Galliformes, CLASS: Aves.

QUETZAL *Pharomachrus mocino*, a large bird distinguished by the dazzling beauty of the male. The breast and upperparts of the plumage are of shimmering, iridescent green, contrasting vividly with the crimson and white belly. The female is much duller in appearance. When the male comes into breeding condition, four of the upper-tail coverts grow into gorgeous metallic-green plumes, the central pair extending 2 ft (0·6 m) beyond the tail.

The quetzal is found in the dense mountain forests of Central America, from southern Mexico to Costa Rica. FAMILY: Trogonidae, ORDER: Trogoniformes, CLASS: Aves.

QUOKKA *Setonix brachyurus*, or Short-tailed scrub wallaby living in thickets and freshwater swamps in remnant colonies in Western Australia. These coarse-haired marsupials are brownish-grey in colour with a total length of $28\frac{1}{2}$–$37\frac{1}{2}$ in (72–95 cm). When moving quickly they hop on their hindlegs. They feed mainly at night on grasses and other plants. FAMILY: Macropopidae, ORDER: Marsupialia, CLASS: Mammalia.

RABBIT, a small to medium sized terrestrial herbivore, usually having long ears and a very short tail. The European wild rabbit

The quetzal, national emblem of Guatemala, has been described as a leading contender for the title of the most beautiful bird in the world.

Raccoon

The European rabbit is a good servant and a bad master, yielding a good fur and good meat, but a plague when it becomes numerous.

Oryctolagus cuniculus is the most widely distributed. Although originally confined to the western Mediterranean region, it has spread with the advance of agriculture over western and central Europe. It has been introduced to most parts of the world, notably Australia and New Zealand and numerous islands where it has attained plague proportions. The normal colour in the wild state is agouti, but occasional sandy, black, grey, white, and piebald individuals are found. Bucks and does do not vary greatly in size having a head and body length of about 18 in (45 cm) and weighing up to 5 lb (2·2 kg).

It attains maturity at three months of age and is capable of breeding at monthly intervals practically all the year round. Gestation occupies 28 days. Litters are deposited in separate breeding chambers lined with grass and the mother's fur. The entrance to the nest-chamber is sealed with an earth plug and is marked with urine and faeces to discourage other rabbits from entering. The young are born naked and are blind for the first ten days. They are suckled once a day for three weeks.

Shooting, ferreting, trapping, snaring, digging out, poisoning and gassing, as well as biological control methods, are used to reduce numbers. Myxomatosis, an epidemic disease caused by a virus, was introduced into Australia and later England and France to control rabbit numbers. The disease, endemic in the South American Forest rabbit *Sylvilagus brasiliensis*, in which it causes only local tumours, produces up to 99·8% mortality in fully susceptible European rabbits, within two weeks. FAMILY: Leporidae, ORDER: Lagomorpha, CLASS: Mammalia.

RACCOON, the best known American mammal. The stout body is roly-poly and bear-like, an impression enhanced by the short forepaws and pigeon-toed gait. The famous black 'mask' across eyes and cheeks and the five to eight black bands on the tail immediately identify it. Although the overall coloration is greyish, the long guard-hairs are buff, tipped in black, and the thick underfur is creamy white. 'Coons, as they are familiarly known, measure from 24–40 in (60–100 cm) and weigh from 4·4–44 lb (2–20 kg).

No webbing is present between the elongated, spindly fingers, which can therefore be spread widely apart and are capable of an almost monkey-like dexterity. The claws are non-retractile and the digit extremities have a well-developed network of sensitive touch nerve fibres. Appropriately called 'waschbären' (wash-bear) in German, the raccoon has the habit of 'washing' any object or food item between its forepaws. While this is a common behaviour pattern in captivity, it probably does not occur in the wild where raccoons usually search for crayfish, turtles, mussels, frogs or small fish in shallow pools, using both forepaws simultaneously, and then swallow the prey forthwith without such meticulous preamble. Raccoons are omnivorous, feeding on almost any vegetable or animal they happen to come across and also scavenging in rubbish heaps.

Descending from their tree perches at nightfall, raccoons forage alone or in small family groups over their restricted, 1 sq mile (2·2 sq km) home range. In the colder regions they sleep for most of the winter in hollow logs or underground dens, living on stored

The raccoon of North America in characteristic pose, feeling in water for its food.

body fat until February when the thaw heralds the start of the breeding season. The young are born after a 60–70 day gestation in a tree-nest. Litter size varies from one to six cubs, more usually four, which are blind and small, 2·5 oz (70 gm) at birth. FAMILY: Procyonidae, ORDER: Carnivora, CLASS: Mammalia.

RACCOON DOG *Nyctereutes procyonoides*, so called for the patch of black around and under each eye resembling the 'robber mask' of the raccoon. It is a short-legged wild dog with a total length of about 2 ft (61 cm). Its long fur is yellowish-brown with dark hair on the shoulders, the tip of the bushy tail and on the legs. Raccoon dogs are native to the forested areas of eastern Asia where they are hunted for their valuable pelt. They have been introduced into parts of eastern Europe and are rapidly spreading west. FAMILY: Canidae, ORDER: Carnivora, CLASS: Mammalia.

RADIOLARIANS, single-celled animals possessing a skeleton usually siliceous but sometimes of strontium sulphate. They are all marine and the majority of them are pelagic and occur in large numbers in the plankton. The cytoplasm is divided into an ectoplasm and an endoplasm and the two layers are separated by a membrane called a central capsule which is characteristic of the group. The form of the skeleton varies within the different suborders. In some species it is absent or very much reduced but in the majority it is spherical and possesses numerous spike-like outgrowths. The elaborations on this simple theme are many and radiolarian skeletons possess an amazing variety of spines and hooks embedded in some kind of lattice work. When these animals die their skeletons sink to the bottom and there, over the years, build up into thick oozes covering large areas of the ocean bed. ORDER: Radiolarida, CLASS: Sarcodina, PHYLUM: Protozoa.

RAILS, water or marsh-dwelling, small-to-medium-sized birds, 5–20 in (12–50 cm) long, closely related to the cranes. They are secretive, crepuscular, sombre-coloured birds living largely at ground level in marshes and similar damp areas with dense vegetation. Adaptations to this environment are seen in their long legs and feet and their laterally compressed bodies which enable them to pass easily between growing plant stems. Some species have become secondarily adapted to drier situations, while the gallinules, and especially the coots, are more aquatic.

The crakes and rails are typically grey or brown, streaked above and barred below—a plumage-pattern which is highly cryptic. The bill varies in the different species from short and stout to long and curved according to the particular feeding habits of the species. The wings and tail are short and the sexes are externally similar.

The coots and gallinules have a darker plumage and a white or brightly coloured frontal shield on the head.

All species flirt the tail and bob the head back and forth as they walk and all are omnivorous.

The Water rail *Rallus aquaticus* is 11 in (28 cm) long and has darkly streaked olive-brown upperparts, flanks barred with white and near black, and slate grey underparts from the breast forwards and up onto the sides of the head. It has long brownish feet and legs and a long red bill. It is discontinuously spread from Iceland to Japan, wintering around the Mediterranean and in southern Asia. FAMILY: Rallidae, ORDER: Gruiformes, CLASS: Aves.

RATEL *Mellivora capensis*, or honey-badger, a badger-like mammal, heavy-set and powerful. It is grey or white above and black on the limbs and ventral surface. Completely black individuals are found in certain forest areas. Males may reach 32 in (80 cm) in length and weigh over 30 lb (13 kg). It is widely distributed from Southeast Asia, throughout most of Africa down to Cape Province.

A strange association has developed between the ratel and the honey-guide bird *Indicator*. If a ratel is in the vicinity when the honey-guide gives a series of call notes, it will follow the bird to the bee's nest, rip it open, and both will then feast on the combs and larvae. Usually crepuscular or nocturnal, the ratel can be found in the open steppe of arid regions or in humid primary forests. It is omnivorous, feeding on berries, lizards, snakes, eggs and even carrion. Ratels will hunt singly or in pairs, covering up to 20 miles in a single night's foraging with a tireless jog trot.

Strong claws used for digging, nauseating scent glands and muscular jaws, serve its reputation as a fearless fighter. Its thick skin, hanging like a loose coating of rubber, makes it apparently impervious to tooth, fang or sting and no adversary seems formidable enough for it. Rushing from its burrow, a ratel will charge an intruder as large as an antelope or buffalo. Once it has bitten, it never relaxes its grip, snarling and shaking its head, until the victim drops from exhaustion. FAMILY: Mustelidae, ORDER: Carnivora, CLASS: Mammalia.

RAT KANGAROOS, small members of the kangaroo family ranging from the Musky rat kangaroo *Hypsiprymnodon* weighing ½ lb (1 kg) to the Rufous rat kangaroo *Aepyprymnus rufescens* 6½ lb (3 kg). Rat kangaroos live among low vegetation in hot rain forests, with a rainfall exceeding 50 in (125 cm) per annum to sand-ridge spinifex desert. They are less built for leaping than kangaroos. At best they hop, otherwise they proceed on all fours. They make nests of grass which they carry by wrapping the tail around it. FAMILY: Macropodidae, ORDER: Marsupialia, CLASS: Mammalia.

RATS, a vast number of species of rodents belonging to several distinct families. The smaller members of all these groups tend to be called mice and there is no sharp

Purple gallinule *Porphyrio porphyrio*, one of the rails, on a marshy lake in Kenya.

The ratel or Honey badger will eat almost anything animal and will fearlessly attack anything up to the size of a buffalo.

distinction between mice and rats. The best known rat is the Brown rat *Rattus norvegicus*, which is equally familiar as a farmyard and warehouse pest or, in its albino form, as the white rat that is so widely used for experimental work in laboratories.

Although the Brown rat is the predominant pest of Europe and temperate America, on a world-wide basis the dominant villain is the Black rat *Rattus rattus*. This occurs in a number of races and varieties, few of them black, especially in tropical Asia. This group of rats originated in southeastern Asia. The spread of rats from this ancestral area probably began as soon as man began to use vehicles for transport. The Black rat was dominant in European towns until the 16th century when it began to be replaced by the Brown rat, which arrived in North America towards the end of the 18th century. In these temperate areas the Brown rat can live outdoors, on farms, in field-side ditches, on the sea-shore and in rubbish dumps, whereas the Black rat is now almost completely confined to cities, especially sea-ports. Even in the tropics most forms of Black rat are found in and around houses and tend to be replaced by other species in the fields.

The tail is about the same length as the head and body and almost naked, and the fur tends to be harsh. The Black rat has a more slender build than the Brown rat, with a longer tail and more prehensile feet, and it

is a much more able climber, being commonly found in the upper storeys of buildings, while the Brown rat is much more at home burrowing in the foundations or in the drains.

The gestation period in both species is 21–24 days, the litters may be 12, although six or seven is more usual, and litters may follow one another in rapid succession. Rats have a strong exploratory urge and this, combined with their ability to feed on almost anything edible, makes them versatile and persistent pests. They are major pests to stored food and their ability to transmit a disease makes their control of major economic and medical importance. Black rats, by way of their fleas, were responsible for transmitting the outbreaks of plague that decimated the population of Europe during the Middle Ages, and rats also transmit typhus, tularaemia and *Salmonella* food poisoning.

The ability of rats to take advantage of man's transport is shown vividly by the Polynesian rat *Rattus exulans*, which has successfully colonized almost every island in the Pacific. In Africa the most ubiquitous and most closely associated with man is the Multimammate rat *Praomys natalensis* (formerly *Mastomys coucha*), almost mouse-sized, distinguished by its very soft fur and, in the female, by the unusually large number of teats. Cultivated fields throughout Africa usually harbour rats of the genus *Aethomys* or Grass rats *Arvicanthis niloticus*, distinguished

by speckled fur and a relatively short tail.

The largest rats in Africa are the giant Pouched rats, *Cricetomys*. These measure up to 18 in (45 cm) long without the tail and the terminal half of the tail is white. In spite of their size they are docile, inoffensive animals.

The Australian Water rat *Hydromys chrysogaster* is a large rat with the terminal half of the tail white and the fur closely resembling that of an otter.

The Wood rats, *Neotoma*, of North America are about the size and shape of a Brown rat, but can be distinguished by the well haired tail. They are inoffensive animals living in wooded country and on rocky hillsides, where they build their nests in large heaps of twigs resembling a badly made beaver lodge. FAMILIES: Cricetidae, Echimyidae, Muridae, Thryonomyidae, ORDER: Rodentia, CLASS: Mammalia.

RATTLESNAKES, named for the rattle on their tail, are unique to the Americas, from Canada southwards through South America.

Most rattlesnakes belong to the genus *Crotalus* characterized by many small scales on the top of the head.

The rattle is the most outstanding feature of these snakes. The baby rattlesnake is born with a button at the end of the tail and the first time it sheds its skin the piece next to the button remains. Each time the skin is shed a new segment is added to this, so building up the rattle, which is vibrated so fast it may appear as no more than a blur.

The Timber or Banded rattlesnake *Crotalus horridus* averages 4 ft (120 cm) in length and may attain 6 ft (182 cm). The black or brown bands on a brown or yellowish body camouflages it too well on the forest floor. It is found throughout much of the eastern half of the United States. The Eastern diamondback rattlesnake. *C. adamanteus* is one of the truly dangerous snakes of the world and inhabits the southeastern area of the United States. Although accounts vary, 8 ft (2·4 m) specimens have been captured. Such a snake would weigh well over 15 lb (6·8 kg) and be 15 in (38 cm) in circumference. An adult Diamondback could have fangs ¾ in (19 mm) long, capable of being driven through almost any boot and of injecting well over a lethal dose of venom into a victim. FAMILY: Crotalidae, ORDER: Squamata, CLASS: Reptilia.

RAVENS, several large crows including the Common raven *Corvus corax*, the African white-necked raven *C. albicollis* and the Australian raven *C. coronoides*. They are all mainly black. The African white-necked raven has a white half-collar on the back of the neck. The Australian raven has a black nape, but the feather bases are white. The Common raven is found in North America, Europe and Asia, most commonly in open or rather wild country. The Australian raven is confined to Australia.

All ravens are omnivorous, eating animal carrion, other birds' eggs, seeds, fruit, fishes, insects, small reptiles and amphibians. Some species catch small mammals and even fully-grown birds at times. All species usually nest either in tall trees or on ledges of cliffs or rocky crags. The nests are substantial cups or baskets of sticks, lined with grass, hair, dead leaves or feathers. FAMILY: Corvidae, ORDER: Passeriformes, CLASS: Aves.

RAYS, flattened fishes related to sharks. The gill slits lie on the underside of the head and not along the sides of the head as in sharks; the pectoral fins are almost always greatly expanded and wing-like and the leading edge joins smoothly onto the head. The highly flattened body and large pectoral fins enable these fishes to lie unnoticed on the bottom or cruise close to the bottom by undulatory movements of the pectoral fins. Since the mouth is also underneath the head, sand and mud would normally be taken in with the respiratory current, but in rays this problem has been solved by drawing water in through the two large spiracles behind the eyes. Certain rays, however, are pelagic (e.g. the huge Manta rays) and these breathe normally, the water being drawn in through the mouth.

The Electric rays have a round, disc-like body and rather short tail, but their most striking feature is the pair of electrical organs

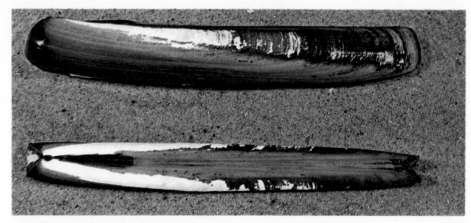

Razor shells normally burrow vertically into the sand.

on either side of the disc (muscle modified into a honeycomb of tiny plates to form 'batteries' capable of delivering up to 220 volts). The skates have a body that is more pointed in front, often diamond-shaped or almost triangular and the tail is rather longer and more slender without a well-developed tail fin. The group also includes the Sting-rays of both marine and freshwaters, the Eagle rays and the Cow-nosed rays, in which the tail is slender, often whip-like, and armed with one or more sharp spines on top and near the base

The White-necked raven scavenges throughout most of subsaharan Africa.

capable of injecting venom into a wound. The Devil rays or mantas are often huge fishes, over 20 ft (6 m) in width. The sawfishes have a large blade-like snout edged with teeth and the body more closely resembles that of a shark than a ray. ORDER: Hypotremata, CLASS: Chondrichthyes.

RAZORBILL *Alca torda*, black and white sea-bird of the North Atlantic, named from the shape of its laterally compressed bill. It breeds in colonies in crevices and clefts on rocky coasts, principally in the Old World. Its food consists largely of fish which it catches underwater, using its wings as flippers for swimming. FAMILY: Alcidae, ORDER: Charadriiformes, CLASS: Aves.

RAZOR SHELLS, known as Jack-knife clams in America, are bivalve molluscs with elongated shells and a large powerful foot specialized for deep burrowing into sand. The slightly curved, oblong shell is shaped like an old-fashioned cut-throat razor. It gapes at both ends. At the front end the large powerful foot may be protruded. At the hind end the siphons always protrude. These are rather short and stout, and water enters by one and leaves through the other after passing over the gills within the mantle cavity. When undisturbed, particularly when covered by water, a Razor shell will lie near the top of its burrow with the siphons just protruding from the key-hole shaped aperture. At the slightest disturbance the powerful foot is distended and anchors in the sand. Then the shell is

pulled down after it by the contraction of the foot retractor muscles. In seconds the mollusc lies safely at a depth of well over a foot (0·4 m). FAMILY: Solenidae, ORDER: Eulamellibranchia, CLASS: Bivalvia. PHYLUM: Mollusca.

RED DEER *Cervus elaphus* or wapiti, a deer with a rich red-brown summer coat widely distributed in the northern hemisphere north of about latitude 30°N in North America, where it is known as the wapiti, and 25°N in Europe and Asia. In Britain the name Red deer is used.

In continental Europe five subspecies are recognized, with a sixth present in small numbers in north Africa. Farther east, between the Carpathians and Manchuria a further 12 subspecies occur and these include the maral of Asia Minor, the hangul of Kashmir, the shou and Mcneil's deer of Tibet, and the wapiti types of Manchuria and the Far East. In North America are four subspecies of wapiti, erroneously referred to as elk.

In Europe the largest deer are found in the Carpathians in the eastern part of their range, where a good stag will stand about 54 in (137 cm) at the shoulder, which is some 12 in (30 cm) higher than the average stag from Scotland.

The general colour of the European Red deer is a rich reddish-brown in summer which becomes greyish-brown in winter. Colour abnormalities include white, cream and albino animals.

During the autumn rut, when each stag collects a harem of hinds, all challengers are greeted by a lion-like roar, fights between rival males often occur, and on occasions will end fatally for one of the contestants. On rare occasions antlers have become locked together, which has resulted in the death of both participants due to starvation. FAMILY: Cervidae, ORDER: Artiodactyla, CLASS: Mammalia.

RED FOX *Vulpes vulpes* is distributed throughout the northern hemisphere in Europe, Asia, Africa and North America, although the New World form is considered by some to be a separate species, *V. fulva*. The average head and body length is 24 in (61 cm) with a 16 in (40 cm) tail. The colour of the fur varies in individuals and in different habitats but it is usually sandy, russet or red-brown above and white on the underparts. Usually the backs of the ears and the fronts of the legs are black. The thick brush can be either black- or white-tipped. The Red fox lives in wooded areas and plains country hunting mainly at twilight and dawn when its chief prey, rabbits, voles and rats are most active. It relies mainly on sound and smell to find its food. Usually four cubs a year are born in a well-concealed den or burrow. When old enough the cubs are taught by the parents to hunt and the family stays together until the cubs leave their parents at about 3–4 months old. FAMILY: Canidae, ORDER: Carnivora, CLASS: Mammalia.

REDSHANK *Tringa totanus*, common wading bird of Europe and Asia, named for its red legs. The Spotted redshank *T. erythropus*, of northern Eurasia, is closely related. FAMILY: Scolopacidae, ORDER: Charadriiformes, CLASS: Aves.

REEDBUCK, a delicate, medium-sized antelope related to the waterbuck. It has slender, ridged horns which are simply curved back and then up, 8–10 in (20–25 cm) long. It is further characterized by its stiff grey coat, and the large bare patch, possibly glandular, below each ear.

There are three species. The Common reedbuck *Redunca arundinum* is 30–36 in (76–91 cm) high, with a large bare muzzle. It is light grey-fawn, becoming tawny on the neck and whitish below. The horns are simple and concave forwards. The Bohor reedbuck *R. redunca* is smaller, 27–31 in (67–78 cm) high, with a smaller bare area on the muzzle. The horns are strongly hooked at the tips and longer than the head. The colour is yellowish, white below as before, but with the head and neck colouration not contrasting with that of the body. Finally the Mountain or Rooi reedbuck *R. fulvorufula* is the same size as the Bohor, but the horns are only slightly hooked at the tips, and shorter than the head. The tail is more bushy and there are

The onset of the rut, or breeding season, is heralded by the roaring of the mature Red deer stags.

Does of the reedbuck, antelopes that spend the heat of the day in reed beds or tall grass usually near water.

distinct reddish tones on the head and neck.

The Common reedbuck is found from Cape Province north to Lake Victoria in the east, and Southern Gabon in the west, in savannah areas. The Bohor reedbuck is found in northern savannahs, from Senegal to the northeastern Congo, and as far north as 15°N in the Sudan and central Ethiopia. Its range overlaps that of the Common reedbuck throughout Tanzania.

The Common reedbuck is usually found in pairs, or solitary and never in numbers above six. When alarmed, the group runs off, its members staying together with tails held bolt upright. This contrasts with other reedbuck which scatter when alarmed. Bohor reedbuck hold their tails pressed down between their legs when running, bounding along with their limbs extended. All species have a shrill alarm whistle.

Mountain reedbuck are found in three areas: Cape Province to Natal, northeastern Tanzania to Ethiopia and the Cameroun. They are much more gregarious, associating in herds of up to 20. They occur on mountainsides amongst bushes and dry grass. When alarmed they run off, down the mountain or round it obliquely, going for 3–400 yd (275–365 m) before stopping to look back. They come down from the hillsides at night to drink, returning in the morning.

Bohor reedbuck travel in small groups, usually one buck with three or four does.

They favour swampy valley bottoms with dense grass. Young males live together in small groups. When disturbed, the reedbucks stand with one hindfoot in advance of the other, broadside on to the intruder with the heads turned, sniffing the air and watching. Then suddenly they bound away with great leaps, the females first while the male initially stands gazing. FAMILY: Bovidae, ORDER: Artiodactyla, CLASS: Mammalia.

REED BUNTING *Emberiza schoeniclus*, widely-distributed over Europe and parts of Asia and Africa. The male, about 6 in (15 cm) long, is easily recognized by its black head and throat and wide white collar. The wings are rufous-brown with black streaks and the undersides whitish. The female is inconspicuous with mainly brown plumage but with a chestnut crown and a pale stripe over the eye. The Reed bunting prefers to live on wet ground near rivers and lakes feeding on seeds and grain but taking insects in summer. In the winter it often joins other buntings and finches in flocks for feeding and roosting. The nest is made of grass lined with hair either built in a tussock of grass or in reeds or sedges over water. 4–6 dull brown eggs with dark spots and markings are incubated mostly by the female for two weeks but both parents feed the young. There are usually two broods. FAMILY: Emberizidae, ORDER: Passeriformes, CLASS: Aves.

REINDEER *Rangifer tarandus*, a large ungainly looking deer, the males and females both bearing antlers. It has a wide distribution in both eastern and western hemispheres, being referred to as reindeer in the east and *caribou in North America. FAMILY: Cervidae, ORDER: Artiodactyla, CLASS: Mammalia.

REMORAS or Shark suckers, fishes in which the first dorsal fin has become modified into a sucking disc by which the fish attaches itself to sharks, other large marine creatures or even to ships. The body is elongated and flattened on top and the sucker lies over the head. The finrays have become flattened and deflected alternately to the left and to the right to form a series of ridges, sometimes with serrated edges. The rim of the sucker is raised

The sucker on the head of a remora, a fish that hitch-hikes on sharks.

Rhea

and the plate-like finrays can be adjusted to form a strong vacuum. The grip of a remora is remarkably strong, especially on a slightly rough surface, and it is possible to tear the disc from the fish before the latter will relinquish its hold.

It is not certain what advantage is derived by the remora from attachment to another animal. The arrangement may simply be one of transport of one organism on the body of another. It is also possible that the remora feeds on the scraps left by a shark. There have been many records of remoras entering the mouths of Manta rays and several species of large sharks, as well as some of the larger billfishes. Remoras are good swimmers and often leave their host to forage and then return.

Pliny recorded that the remora attached itself to the hulls of ships and was able to bring them to a sudden halt, a legend that persisted right through the Middle Ages and was only finally explained when Sven Ekman, the great oceanographer, demonstrated how sailing ships could indeed be brought to a sudden stop by the phenomenon of dödvand or 'dead water' (the retarding action of underwater waves at the interface between fresh and salt water off river mouths).

In several parts of the world fishermen have evolved an ingenious method of fishing with the remora. A line is attached at the base of the tail and the fish is then released into the water. When the remora has fixed itself to some large fish or turtle, the line is then hauled back to the boat. FAMILY: Echeneidae, ORDER: Perciformes, CLASS: Pisces.

RHEA, two species of large, flightless, running birds of South America, related to the ostrich. Rheas stand up to 5 ft (1·5 m) tall and weigh up to 55 lb (25 kg), the biggest birds in the New World. They have a floppy loose-webbed plumage and rather larger wings than the ostrich. The legs are long and powerful and the feet bear three toes only. They run very swiftly and frequently keep company with Bush deer *Dorcelaphus bezoarticus* or even cattle. The larger species, the Common rhea *Rhea americana* is grey-brown with white tail feathers, but a white variant is not uncommon. It breeds from northeastern Brazil to central Argentina. Farther west it is replaced by Darwin's rhea *Pterocnemia pennata*, smaller and spotted with white. The sexes are similar.

Rheas live in grassland and open bush country, often near rivers or swamps. They feed on seeds, roots, grasses and other leaves, and also take insects, particularly grasshoppers, molluscs, and small vertebrates. They live in flocks of 20–30 or more. They crouch, or run to escape danger, and they also swim well.

Rheas have quite well-developed voices and the males utter mammal-like roars in

A group of rheas, the South American equivalent of the ostrich.

their breeding displays. They also posture with wings spread. They are polygamous and successful males will acquire harems of 6–8 females. The hens lay up to 20 eggs each but many are wasted, several being deposited by most females before a nest has been built to receive them. The nest is a scrape in the ground made by the male who also adds a lining of some dry vegetable material. The nest site is usually a concealed one. though he seems to clear a small area surrounding the nest by biting off the herbage. All females of a particular harem lay in the same nest. The eggs are a golden-yellow or deep-green and are incubated by the male, the full clutch being very variable in size, frequently of 20–30 eggs. Incubation takes 35–40 days and the young are grey with dark stripes. They are able to run soon after they are dry and they leave the nest with the male. FAMILY: Rheidae, ORDER: Rheiformes, CLASS: Aves.

RHEBOK *Pelea capreolus*, small South African antelope, related to the reedbuck, 28–32 in (70–80 cm) high, weighing 44–50 lb (20–23 kg), distinguished by their woolly, soft, rabbit-like fur which is brown-grey. The face and lower parts of the legs are yellowish and the underparts white. The build is very slender with long legs, and long pointed ears. The muzzle is bare and slightly swollen, glandular. The lateral hoofs are jointed across the midline. The horns are short, nearly straight but slightly back-curved. FAMILY: Bovidae, ORDER: Artiodactyla, CLASS: Mammalia.

RHESUS MONKEY *Macaca mulatta*, medium sized macaque with a head and body length of 20–24 in (50–60 cm) and a tail

8–12 in (20–30 cm) long. It has simple hair patterns, with the hair on the crown directed backwards from the brows. It is brown with brighter, orange-red hindparts, a pink face and reddish perineal-genital skin which in the female turns red at the height of oestrus. Oestrus females also tend to go blotchy red on the face. The Rhesus monkey is found in India north of the Godavari river, west to Afghanistan, north to the Himalaya foothills which it follows, reaching the banks of the Yangtze in China, with an isolated population near Pekin. A related form, *M. cyclopis* lives in Formosa, and may be a subspecies of *M. mulatta*. FAMILY: Cercopithecidae, ORDER: Primates, CLASS: Mammalia.

RHINOCEROS, five species of land mammal characterized by their nasal horn or horns. They are *Ceratotherium simum*, the White or Square-lipped rhinoceros of Africa, *Diceros bicornis*, the Black or Hook-lipped rhinoceros of Africa, *Rhinoceros unicornis*, the Great Indian rhinoceros, *Rhinoceros sondaicus*, the Javan rhinoceros and *Dicerorhinus sumatrensis*, the Sumatran rhinoceros, which is found in Sumatra, Malaysia, Burma and perhaps still in Borneo.

The horns consist of a tight mass of horny fibres continuously built up by a special tissue covering a hump on the nasal bones. *Ceratotherium*, *Diceros* and *Dicerorhinus* have two horns, both species of *Rhinoceros* only one. The African rhino have no other weapon but their horns while in the Asian species the almost tusk-like incisors (known as tushes) are also used in fighting and can inflict deep wounds.

Rhinos have poor eyesight, their sense of smell is very keen and their hearing quite acute. Weight reached by large bulls: Square-lipped rhino, over 3 tons (3,000 kg); Great Indian rhino, 2½ tons (2,500 kg); Black rhino, 1½ tons (1,500 kg); Javan rhino, 1½ tons (1,500 kg); Sumatran rhino, ½ ton (500 kg).

The skin of all rhinos but the Sumatran, is hairless, only the tip of the tail has a hairy brush and the ears have fringes of hair in all species. Rough, long and scanty hair grows on the body of the Sumatran rhino. In adults it may be rubbed off on the back and the sides.

All five rhino species are on the verge of extinction, the Asian are in a worse position than those in Africa.

Both African species inhabit more or less arid regions with pronounced dry seasons. They need bush and tree vegetation to protect them from wind, sun and their main enemy, man. They cannot exist without surface water. In regions where good feeding areas are far from water, they visit watering places at intervals of four to six days. They often bathe in pools and wallow in mud which helps to protect their skin against biting flies and to regulate their body temperature. In many regions, mud wallows are only available during the wet season; during the dry season the animals wallow in dusty places which they form for themselves. But obviously the dust film is much more quickly removed and therefore less protective than mud.

The White rhino is a grazer, it mows the grass by seizing it with its wide lips and pulling it off. The Black rhino is a browser, feeding on many bush and shrub species typical of the arid savannah. Locally it may also feed on low growing herbs and creepers. It seizes a small branch or twig with its prehensile upper lip, cuts it off with its premolars and then chews it slowly.

In contrast to the African rhinos, the Asian species are adapted to a swampy habitat. FAMILY: Rhinocerotidae, ORDER: Perissodactyla, CLASS: Mammalia.

RHINOCEROS VIPER *Bitis nasicornis*, a species of Puff adder, up to 4 ft (1·3 m) long, gaudily coloured and with large pointed and erectile scales on the tip of the snout. It is sometimes called the Nose-horned viper but, in fact, its near relative, the *Gaboon viper, has similar hornlike scales on the snout. FAMILY: Viperidae, ORDER: Squamata, CLASS: Reptilia.

RIBBONWORMS, elongated, soft-bodied invertebrates, also known as Proboscis worms, or nemertineans. There are nearly 600 species, mainly marine although there are freshwater species and a few living on land. Some are commensal in Sea squirts, sponges and bivalve molluscs, taking their food from their hosts' feeding currents. Those living in the sea may shelter under rocks or among seaweeds on or near the shore although some live as deep as 4,500 ft (1,500 m) burrowing in mud and many are free-swimming or free-floating, from surface waters down to 9,000 ft (3,000 m), the swimmers having fins on the sides or hind end, the floating forms being gelatinous. Most ribbonworms are around 8 in (20 cm) long but some are only 2 in (5 cm) or less while the Bootlace worm *Lineus longissima* may extend several yards, a length of 60 yd (55 m) having been recorded. The head is broad and flat.

The most distinctive feature is the proboscis, an extensile tube which can be shot out with force, to catch prey. This may be twice the length of the body, or more, and in *Gorgonorhynchus* it is divided into as many as 32 branches. PHYLUM: Nemertina.

RIFLEMAN *Acanthisitta chloris*, the smallest New Zealand bird, one of the 'New Zealand wrens'. It is only 3 in (7·5 cm) long, and is greenish-brown, the male having a green back and the female a brown one, a forest bird that feeds like a treecreeper. The members of a pair or family group call continually with a high-pitched 'zit zit'.

The loosely-woven nest is constructed in a hole or crevice and four to five white eggs are laid. Both sexes incubate and feed the young and there are usually two broods a year. FAMILY: Acanthisittidae, ORDER: Passeriformes, CLASS: Aves.

RIGHT WHALES, so-called because in the early days of whaling they were literally the right whales to catch. They are relatively slow and timid and so were more easy prey for the rowing boats equipped with hand harpoons of the early whalers. When killed they floated and hence were easy to handle. Then their large plates of baleen, as well as the oil, offered great financial reward. The Greenland right whale *Balaena mysticetus* was once abundant around the coasts of Greenland but the activities of whalers reduced it almost to extinction. FAMILY: Balaenidae, ORDER: Cetacea, CLASS: Mammalia.

RINGHALS *Hemachatus haemachatus*, a 'spitting' cobra with strong keeled scales. It rarely exceeds 4 ft (1·2 m) in length. It is restricted to South Africa except for an isolated population in northeastern Rhodesia. Unlike other *cobras it bears live young. FAMILY: Elapidae, ORDER: Squamata, CLASS: Reptilia.

RING OUZEL *Turdus torquatus*, a member of the thrush family, 9½ in (24 cm) long, which tends to live on uplands in Europe. The male is dark-brown with a white half collar in front and the wings paler than the rest of the body. The female is more brown, somewhat scaly-looking, and the half collar is a duller white. Ring ouzels feed on insects and small invertebrates and on berries. They build their nests on steep banks or low rock faces. The 3–5 eggs are incubated for two weeks and are fed by both parents for another two weeks. FAMILY: Muscicapidae, ORDER: Passeriformes, CLASS: Aves.

ROACH *Rutilus rutilus*, one of the commonest of carp-like fishes of Europe but also found across Asia to the Amur basin. It is fairly high-backed but slender, the upperparts being grey or blue-green fading to silvery on the flanks and belly and the fins red. It is found in both rivers and lakes, the young fishes shoaling and readily taking any bait offered but the larger adults becoming more solitary and difficult to catch. Roach grow to 16 in (40 cm) and weigh over 3 lb (1·4 kg). The young feed on algae and plankton but later turn to worms, insects, crus-

Black rhinoceroses should more properly be called hook-lipped rhinoceros.

Roan antelope

taceans, small fishes and fish eggs, as well as aquatic plants and molluscs. FAMILY: Cyprinidae, ORDER: Cypriniformes, CLASS: Pisces.

ROAN ANTELOPE *Hippotragus equinus*, a large-sized African antelope congeneric with the Sable antelope and the blaauwbok. Like these, it has strongly curved, ridged horns set on a slightly elevated pedicle just behind the eyes, and rising vertically at first. Roan are 56–60 in (143–153 cm) high and the horns are 20–38 in (50–95 cm) long with 20–50 rings, shorter and less curved than Sable antelope's horns and egg-shaped in section (oval, but blunt posteriorly). The ears are almost as long as the head, their tips sagging and usually tufted. There is a high mane along the neck, black with a light 'seam', and a noticeable throat-mane. The colour is grey-roan, with brownish limbs. FAMILY: Bovidae, ORDER: Artiodactyla, CLASS: Mammalia.

ROBBER FLY, so called because the adults of both sexes feed exclusively by catching other insects and sucking them dry. Usually the prey is chased and captured while it is in flight, and Robber flies have become highly adapted to this predatory habit. The eyes are large, the proboscis is powerful and sharp, and the head and legs are equipped with exceptionally strong bristles, which both help to hold the prey and protect the Robber fly from counter-attack. The flies are quick to notice movement, but do not see detail well, and often chase anything that moves. In the tropics some Robber flies are huge, up to 3 in (7·5 cm) or more in length, and may capture and eat the largest and fiercest bees and wasps. FAMILY: Asilidae, ORDER: Diptera, CLASS: Insecta, PHYLUM: Arthropoda.

ROBINS, several species of the bird family Muscicapidae, sharing the common characters of rather small size and a red breast. The better known species are *Erithacus rubecula* of Europe, the familiar American robin *Turdus migratorius* of North America, the Pekin robin *Leiothrix lutea* of Asia (a common cage-bird) and the Indian robin *Saxicoloides fulicata*.

The common European robin is a small brown thrush with the upper breast orange-red and the lower breast light grey. A dumpy little bird, it is a familiar sight in gardens in Britain, but shyer and more confined to its natural woodland habitats on the Continent. It feeds on insects, worms, spiders, food scraps provided by man and sometimes small seeds. Both sexes defend territories in the autumn and winter with a sweet, mellow song. The male alone defends the breeding territory in the spring and early summer. The nest is most often built in a hollow in a bank, but also in a variety of other sites. Clutches of two to six eggs are usually laid and incubated by the female, but both

parents bring food to the young. The incubation period is about 13–14 days and the fledgling period about 12–14 days. Young robins have a spotted breast, showing their relationships with thrushes. FAMILY: Muscicapidae, ORDER: Passeriformes, CLASS: Aves.

ROCKLINGS, small and elongated cod-like fishes of shallow waters and especially rock pools, from which they derive their common name. They are found off the coasts of Europe. The Three-bearded rockling *Gaidropsarus vulgaris*, with two barbels near the nostrils and one under the chin, is the largest of the eastern Atlantic species, growing to 20 in (51 cm). The Four-bearded rockling *Rhinonemus cimbrius* has an additional barbel near the upper lip and the Five-bearded rockling *Ciliata mustelus* has a total of five barbels. FAMILY: Gadidae, ORDER: Gadiformes, CLASS: Pisces.

ROE DEER *Capreolus capreolus*, of Europe, the Middle East and northern Asia, stands 25–29 in (64–74 cm) at the shoulder, and an adult buck may weigh 38–50 lb (17–23 kg), with exceptional beasts from Poland weighing as much as 80 or 90 lb (about 38 kg). The full head of a buck should be six-pointed, though multipointed heads occur. The small tail is not readily visible.

The rut takes place during late July and early August. The young, frequently twins and occasionally triplets, are born from late April to early June. FAMILY: Cervidae, ORDER: Artiodactyla, CLASS: Mammalia.

ROLLERS, solitary jay-sized birds mainly of the Old World tropics, deriving their common name from their tumbling courtship flights.

Some species extend to temperate Eurasia and these, together with a few of the African and Oriental forms, are well-known because of their tendency to breed around human habitations.

The typical rollers of the genus *Coracias* are handsome thick-set birds, with shining azure-blue wings and chestnut shoulders. The body is blue, olive, pink and brown in delicate combination. The bill is stout, the shape of a jackdaw's and the head is rather large and flat, the neck thick, legs short but strong and the wings and tail moderately long. In the single European species, the roller *Coracias garrulus*, the outer tail feather is a little attenuated and lengthened and the Abyssinian roller *C. abyssinica* of northern tropical Africa has these outer feathers elongated into 6 in (15 cm) streamers, while they are long and racquet shaped in the African *C. spatulata*. FAMILY: Coraciidae, ORDER: Coraciiformes, CLASS: Aves.

ROOK *Corvus frugilegus*, a member of the crow family widespread in Europe and parts of Asia. Adult rooks have a bare patch of skin at the base of the bill and nest in colonies of several thousands in the tops of tall trees, hence the term 'rookery'. FAMILY: Corvidae, ORDER: Passeriformes, CLASS: Aves.

RORQUALS or Fin whales, whales with triangular dorsal fins and parallel pleats along the throat. They have smaller heads and shorter baleen plates than the *Right whales and it has been postulated that the throat pleating allows them to take in more water for filtration to compensate for this smaller baleen filtration area. They are faster swimmers than the Right whales and

The Robin redbreast, one of the most familiar and most favoured of European birds.

240

The Five-bearded rockling, a small fish common between tide-marks on the rocky coasts of Europe, feeding on shrimps, crabs and other crustaceans, and smaller fishes.

The minke, Lesser piked whale or Lesser rorqual *B. acutorostrata* is the smallest rorqual being about 30 ft (10 m) in length. FAMILY: Balaenopteridae, ORDER: Cetacea, CLASS: Mammalia.

ROTIFERS, minute animals that delighted the early microscopists who called them 'Wheel animalcules', as they are characterized by the possession of a crown of cilia, which, when they beat in a rhythm, do indeed give the superficial appearance of a wheel spinning round. The crown of cilia serves as a swimming and as a feeding mechanism. The mouth opens in the middle of the cilia and many rotifers feed by gathering very small particles, including algae, from the water as they swim. CLASS: Rotifera, PHYLUM: Aschelminthes.

RUDD *Scardinius erythrophthalmus*, a carp-like freshwater fish from still waters of Europe. It closely resembles the roach but has the beginning of the dorsal fin set behind a vertical line from the base of the pelvic fins. The rudd has a fairly deep, silvery body, red fins and a red eye. It reaches 4 lb (1·8 kg) in weight and feeds on most small aquatic animals. FAMILY: Cyprinidae, ORDER: Cypriniformes, CLASS: Pisces.

RUFF *Philomachus pugnax*, wading bird of freshwater marshland and meadows showing extreme sexual dimorphism, males being much larger than females (which are called 'reeves'). In breeding plumage, males acquire coloured eartufts and a 'ruff' of feathers round the neck. It is rare for two males in the same breeding area to have identical plumage. Ruffs breed throughout the north temperate zone from Britain to eastern Siberia. In autumn they migrate both west and south, some of the Siberian birds wintering in western Europe while the majority winter away from the sea coasts in Africa. On the breeding grounds communal display and mating occur at a lek, that is an open (often grassy) area on which several males display from fixed positions (residences) about 3 ft (1 m) apart. Females visit the leks and choose residences at which to be mated. Males with residences at the centre of the lek usually mate with more females than do peripheral males, but each female may visit several residences or even several leks. FAMILY: Scolopacidae, ORDER: Charadriiformes, CLASS: Aves.

RUSA DEER *Cervus timorensis*, the most widespread deer in the Indonesian Archipelago. It has a shoulder height of about 43¾ in (110 cm). Dark brown and with the largest antler seldom exceeding 27 in (68·5 cm) in length, this is a deer of the grassy plains, though persecution will make them resort to cover. FAMILY: Cervidae, ORDER: Artiodactyla, CLASS: Mammalia.

have longer and more tapering flippers. They also sink when shot and therefore need to be inflated with air for handling.

The Blue whale or Sibbald's rorqual *Balaenoptera musculus* may reach 100 ft (30 m) in length and weigh up to 130 tons. It is dark blue-grey overall, with paler markings. Blue whales have been reported to have a sustained speed of 10–12 knots while submerged and can reach 15 knots. They are known to dive to over 1,500 ft (450 m) where the water pressure is 45 atmospheres, and can stay submerged for two hours. Blue whales seldom travel in schools and are usually seen singly or in pairs. They are found both north and south of the equator.

During the winter Blue whales move towards the warmer waters for mating and calving but in summer return to the richer krill feeding-grounds of the Antarctic or Arctic.

The Common rorqual, Fin whale or finner *B. physalus* is about 80 ft (25 m). It is light- to mid-grey on the back and white on the belly but it also has marked regular asymmetry: the lower jaw is white on the right and pigmented on the left whereas the tongue shows an opposite colouring; the baleen is white on the right for about a third of its length and the remainder, on both sides, grey with yellow streaks. Having a ridge along the back Fin whales have been called 'razorbacks'. Unlike the Blue whale, they swim in schools and are rarely found singly.

Fin whales feed on krill as do Blue whales and they follow essentially the same migratory patterns between polar regions, both north and south, in summer and the warm waters in winter.

The name of the Sei whale *B. borealis* is derived from the Norwegian *Sejhval*, a whale which swims with the fish *Seje*. It reaches a length of 50–60 ft (15–18 m) and the colour varies between grey and blue-black on the back with a variably sized white area on the belly. The dorsal fin of the Sei whale is large and has a deep cut-out at the back. The baleen plates are white and have very fine hairy fringes on the inner side which, in addition to krill, allows them to filter the smaller crustacean *Calanus finmarchicus*, but Sei whales also feed on fishes. This species holds the record of 35 knots as the fastest recorded rorqual.

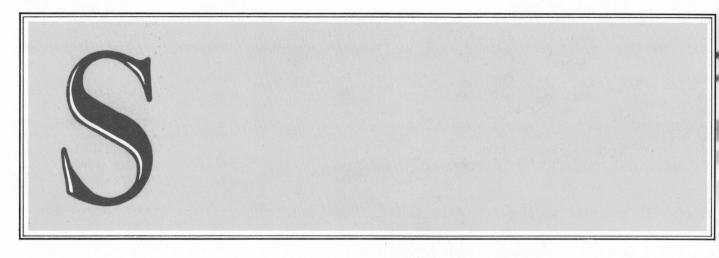

S

SABLE ANTELOPE *Hippotragus niger*, a large African antelope closely related to the Roan antelope and blaauwbok. Sable stand 51–57 in (127–144 cm) high and may weigh 500 lb (230 kg); they are shorter-bodied than Roan and blaauwbok. The horns are much longer than either, being 28–70 in (70–177 cm) with 35–59 rings. They are slender and strongly curved, elongated oval in section with the lateral side flattened. The ears are only half as long as the head. There is a mane on the neck but not on the throat and the colour is black in males, golden-brown to black in females, with lips, muzzle, upper throat, underparts and a line from eye to muzzle white. There are small white tufts below the eyes.

Sable antelope are not as widespread as Roan. They occur from western and southeastern Transvaal north to Angola, southeastern Congo, and extreme southeastern Kenya. The best-known and most beautiful race is the Giant sable antelope *H. n. variani*,

restricted to an area of Angola bounded by the rivers Luando and Dunda in the north and east and the Cuanza and Luasso in the south and west. Giant sable are slightly larger than other races, with a longer, narrower face, more vertical horn bases and much longer horns. Bulls are shining black, cows a brilliant golden-chestnut. In both sexes the white eye-stripe stops short of joining the white of the muzzle, being virtually restricted to the white eye-tufts. FAMILY: Bovidae, ORDER: Artiodactyla, CLASS: Mammalia.

SAIGA, a unique sheep-like antelope of central and western Asia. It stands 30–32 in (75–80 cm) high, and weighs 88–110 lb (40–50 kg). although females are often as little as 66 lb (30 kg). Only males have horns which are 11–15 in (28–38 cm) long, nearly straight with a very slight lyration, a pale waxy colour and semi-transparent. They bear 18–20 ridges. The coat is woolly, buff in

summer and whitish in winter. The most striking feature of the saiga is its nose, which is swollen. The nostrils are terminal, downward-looking and very mobile and in each nostril is a sac with mucous membranes which warm and moisten the inhaled air. According to Bannikov, this sac is an adaptation to fast and prolonged running in herds in a semi-desert environment. The dust is kept out of the nostrils by their low position and mobility, and by the low carriage of the head while running.

The above description applies mainly to the common species, *Saiga tatarica*, which is found in the USSR, from the Kalmyck ASSR to the Chinese border, and slightly north into Dzungaria. A second species, the Mongolian saiga *S. mongolica*, lives in the Gobi desert, being isolated from the first by the Gobi Altai range. It is small, only 24–27 in (60–67 cm) high, with delicate horns under 9 in (22 cm) long, and a duller coat, grey-sandy in summer and grey-brown in winter. The horns are poorly annulated. FAMILY: Bovidae, ORDER: Artiodactyla, CLASS: Mammalia.

SAILFISH *Istiophorus platypterus*, a large oceanic fish with a sail-like dorsal fin, up to 12 ft (3·6 m) long, world-wide in tropical and subtropical seas. It has the powerful torpedo-shaped body of fast oceanic swimmers. The dorsal finrays are enormously extended to support the 'sail' along the back. Pelvic fins are present. The tail is crescent-shaped and there are anal fins. The upper jaw is extended into a 'bill' or 'sword' which is longer than the head and is rounded in cross-section. In the juveniles the upper and lower jaws are the same length and are provided with pointed teeth, but by the time that the fish is 2 in (5 cm) long the upper jaw has outgrown the lower and the teeth have disappeared. Just in front of the tail there are two keels on the side of the body. The body and the dorsal fin are blue or blue-black, often with small dark spots.

The sailfish is an exceedingly fast swimmer, the huge dorsal fin being folded down at high speeds. It is said that they can reach 60 mph (100 kph). FAMILY: Istiophoridae, ORDER: Perciformes, CLASS: Pisces.

The magnificent sable, the most handsome of the antelopes.

SAKI *Pithecia*, several species of South American monkey living in the shrub layers of the forest, especially common on the savannah borders. FAMILY: Cebidae, ORDER: Primates, CLASS: Mammalia.

SALAMANDERS, a general term for the tailed amphibians. The family Salamandridae comprises mainly the newts but it also includes the European salamander.

Salamanders are long-bodied amphibians which retain a tail throughout life. Their limbs are usually small and in no case are they modified for jumping. The forelimb usually has four toes and the hindlimb five.

There is a tendency towards a reduction in the number of toes and in some cases limbs may also be reduced in size and even lost. For example, the Great siren *Siren lacertinia* (family Sirenidae) lacks hindlimbs, and the Mud siren *Pseudobranchus striatus* is also without hindlimbs and has only three toes on the forelimb. For rapid movement salamanders wriggle with the belly touching or close to the ground. The movement resembles that of a fish swimming and is essentially 'swimming on land'.

The Fire salamander *Salamandra salamandra*, or Spotted salamander, of Europe, also extends into North Africa. In ancient times it was thought this salamander was able to live in fire. The Fire salamander mates on land usually in July and about ten months later the female enters the water to bear live young. Each litter contains 10–15 young about 1 in (2·5 cm) long and possessing external gills which are lost during metamorphosis when the animals become terrestrial and acquire the black with orange-yellow patches characteristic of this species. The skin of the adult is kept moist by secretions of the dermal glands which also produce poisonous substances which afford some protection from predators. FAMILY: Salamandridae, ORDER: Caudata, CLASS: Amphibia.

SALMON, highly palatable anadromous fishes of the northern hemisphere belonging to the genera *Salmo* and *Onchorhynchus*.

The Atlantic salmon *Salmo salar* lives in the North Atlantic and breeds in the freshwaters of Europe and North America. In the North Pacific there are several species belonging to the related genus *Onchorhynchus*, namely the Chinook salmon *O. tschawytscha*, the coho *O. kisutch*, the sockeye *O. nerka*, the Pink or Humpback salmon *O. gorbuscha* and the Chum or Dog salmon *O. keta*. These are all confined to the western side of Canada and the United States. A further species, *O. masu*, is found on the eastern seaboard of northern Asia. The largest of these is the Chinook, which can weigh over 100 lb (45 kg) and the smallest is the Pink salmon, which rarely exceeds 10 lb (4·5 kg).

The adult Atlantic salmon is an elongated, powerfully built yet graceful fish. The fins are

The saiga, Asian antelope characterized by its inflated nostrils.

soft-rayed, the tail is slightly emarginated and a small adipose fin is present. The fishes are silvery with small black 'freckles' and a darker back, but when the breeding season approaches the male becomes suffused with a reddish tinge and its jaws become curiously hooked. The adult fishes feed in the sea for one or two years before they return to the rivers and are in good condition for the climb ahead of them. Quite often they will approach the mouth of a river but lie off it for another year before making the ascent. The salmon run up the rivers in August to September and the major spawning period is in the early winter.

The journey upstream continues into the smallest brooks and streams. Here the nest or 'redd' is built, the male making a large trough in the pebbles by lashing with its tail. Several males will often make their redds within a few feet of each other. The female then lays the eggs in the redd (about 800 eggs per lb weight of fish) and the male fertilizes them and covers them over with gravel. The time taken to hatch is directly related to the temperature of the water, and ranges from five weeks in warm waters to as long as five months in very cold water.

The newly hatched alevins are about ½ in (1·3 cm) long and they remain among the pebbles living on the food in their yolk sac. When about 1 in (2·5 cm) long they leave the nest and those that survive lead a secluded life in shallow waters feeding on small insect larvae. They reach about 4 in (10 cm) in the first year and 6 in (15 cm) in the second year. During this time they bear the parr markings of 8–10 dark oval blotches on the flanks with a red spot between each oval.

Usually in the second year a silvery pigment develops over the parr marks and the fishes are then termed smolts (if the silvery pigment is scraped away the parr markings are visible below). The smolt then migrates to the sea, spends a year or more feeding, returning as an adult to struggle back upstream to its birthplace. FAMILY: Salmonidae, ORDER: Salmoniformes, CLASS: Pisces.

SALPS, irregularly barrel-shaped transparent animals up to 8 in (20 cm) long, found near the surface in warmer seas and occasionally in temperate waters in summer. Together with the fish, reptiles and mammals they belong to the phylum Chordata. They swim by the rhythmical contractions of a series of horseshoe shaped muscle bands which are clearly seen lying to one side of the body. The action of these bands causes water which has entered the front end of the body to be forced out at the rear end, thus pushing the animal forward by jet-propulsion. Single-celled plants and small animals are filtered off from this stream of water as it passes through the body, and are consumed as food.

Salps compete with small fish in their selection of food material of small size in the plankton. Further, some of the larger species prey on small fish. When they appear, irregularly, in enormous numbers in northern waters, yields of fish may be low. SUBPHYLUM: Urochordata, PHYLUM: Chordata.

SAMBAR *Cervus unicolor*, one of the largest and most widespread deer in southern Asia. Sixteen subspecies are recognized, the largest being *C. u. niger* of India. A large sambar stag will stand 52–56 in (132–142 cm) high

243

Sand bubbler

at the shoulder and weigh about 600 lb (272 kg). With antlers normally bearing six points and measuring up to 50 in (127 cm) in length, this deer is a uniform dark brown, the calves, which are never spotted at birth, being the same colour.

Sambar occur at all altitudes from sea level up to 10,000 ft (3,000 m), their habitat ranging from coastal forest, swampland and agricultural fields to mountains. FAMILY: Cervidae, ORDER: Artiodactyla, CLASS: Mammalia.

SAND BUBBLER *Scopimera inflata*, a small crab which occurs in dense aggregations on the tropical and subtropical sandy shores of Australia. A related species *S. globulosa* extends as far north as Japan. The outline of its shell when viewed from above is semi-circular, with two distinct grooves on the front into which the eyes can be laid flat. The general colour is that of sand, with darker bands on the legs. The most interesting feature of this crab is its feeding behaviour. Most individuals emerge from their burrows 3–4 hours after being uncovered by the tide. After emerging the crab smooths the edge of the entrance to its burrow using its pincers. It then moves about ½ in (1·3 cm) away from the entrance and picks up surface sand with its pincers. This is passed to the mouthparts and scoured by special setae which scrape off any organic material, after which it is passed out at the top edge of the mouthparts. When a big enough 'bubble' has been formed it is carefully lifted off by the pincers then passed downwards and pushed backwards between the legs, finally coming to rest behind the crab. Removal of the surface sand by the pincers forms a shallow trench, and the crab moves in a straight line from the entrance to its burrow. The trench is always kept clear, so that the crab always has an escape route back to the burrow. If one of the sand pellets falls into the trench it is quickly removed. When the trench is about 8 in (20 cm) long the crab returns to the burrow and starts on a new trench. At the end of a feeding session there may be several trenches radiating from the burrow, each with a row of sand pellets alongside. SUBORDER: Brachyura, ORDER: Decapoda, CLASS: Crustacea, PHYLUM: Arthropoda.

SAND-DIVERS, perch-like fishes about 7 in (18 cm) long related to the weeverfishes. They are slim, elongated fishes found in both freshwater and saltwater throughout tropical regions. The dorsal fin is long and the first few rays are usually extended into a mane. The caudal fin is pointed. They derive their name from their habit of rapidly burrowing into the sand. Many species spend much of their time buried with only their eyes exposed and this has probably been responsible for the evolution of tubular eyes in some, giving them the added advantage of binocular

The Pin-tailed sandgrouse of southwest Europe looks like a small partridge.

vision. As in certain deep-sea fishes (telescope-eyes), binocular vision enables the fish to judge very accurately the distance to its prey so that the first attack is successful.

Sand-divers are often transparent, enabling them to remain inconspicuous against their background, but a few species are brightly splashed with colour. Members of the genus *Trichinotus* typically inhabit shallow water and as an adaptation to the glare of the sun have developed special membranes which shield the eyes, formed of radiating silvery bands. FAMILY: Trichinotidae, ORDER: Perciformes, CLASS: Pisces.

SAND DOLLARS, flattened Sea urchins known by this name in North America, whereas Cake urchin is more commonly used in Europe. They are cake- or disc-like and have a fur-like covering of dense, short spines.

The basic structural features common to all Sea urchins are found in the Sand dollars, but they have been much modified, generally as an adaptation to burrowing. Thus there is a rigid skeleton of fused calcite plates set within the tissues of the body, with a fur-like covering of short spines in life. After death the tissues decay and the spines fall off, revealing the solid skeleton (test). This follows the same pattern as that in all modern *Sea urchins. On the lower surface the mouth is central, with jaws within the test. Radiating from the mouth are usually five grooves; in the very flat disc-like Sand dollars these may branch repeatedly as they extend towards the margin of the test. It is along them that microscopic food is channelled, carried by tube-feet or brought by water currents set up by the beating action of countless minute, hair-like cilia which cover the surface of the animal in life. Minute tubercles which bear the spines in

life cover both upper and lower surfaces; both may also reveal groups of abundant small pores scattered over them, bearing in life the so-called accessory tube-feet.

One further unusual feature of the test found in some very flat species is the presence of notches in the margin or even large holes perforating the test. Their function is not fully understood.

Of the external appendages which fall away on death, both the spines and tube-feet are interesting. The spines, since they are reduced to a very short, if dense covering, that does not impede movement for burrowers yet still provides protection for the surface. The tube-feet, since there are at least two types present, with different functions; the tube-feet of the petals, which are short, broad, leaf-like structures of large surface area, used for respiration as in the Heart urchins; and the accessory tube-feet, which are smaller, denser, issuing from a single rather than a double pore, and used for dealing with particles of material for various purposes, such as concealment. Concealment is variously achieved by burrowing, by holding plant or shell fragments on to the exposed surface of the test, or by the drab coloration of the animals, which is commonly brownish to olive-green or pale grey.

The patterns of reproduction and development, as so far known, are essentially the same as those typical of Sea urchins.

Sand dollars are almost entirely shallow water forms, many of them inhabiting the intertidal zone and a few going as deep as 1,640 ft (500 m). Most species are found commonly in tropical and subtropical seas only. The only member found near British coasts is the minute *Echinocyamus pusillus*. Almost all are concentrated into American and Japanese waters: the important genera *Mellita* and *Encope* are entirely American, and the common American species *Echinarachnius parma* is the best known Sand dollar. The thicker forms, such as *Clypeaster*, have a wider distribution in that they are found on the tropical and subtropical coasts of all continents, but some such species are restricted more to the Indo-West Pacific region.

All species live on or just beneath the surface of the sea floor. Some move over the surface of the sea floor browsing seaweed. Others, and the American Pacific coast Sand dollar *Dendraster excentricus* is a good example, live with the rear edge protruding from the sediment.

Echinocyamus pusillus, the minute relative already mentioned, $\frac{2}{5}$ in (10 mm) in diameter, and ovoid rather than disc- or biscuit-shaped, nestles in the interstices of shell gravel, usually at 120–180 ft (60 m) depth, using its tube-feet and its teeth respectively to taste and then rasp off organic matter for food. So small is it that whole individuals have been found amongst the gut contents of Heart urchins. ORDER: Clypeasteroidea, CLASS: Echinoidea, PHYLUM: Echinodermata.

SANDEELS, small, silvery eel-like fishes, in no way related to true eels, found around the coasts of the Atlantic Ocean. They spend a lot of their time buried in sand. They have pointed jaws well adapted for burrowing, a long dorsal fin and no pelvic fins. Their main importance lies in their being an important item of diet for many commercially valuable fish like cod and halibut. FAMILY: Ammodytidae, ORDER: Perciformes, CLASS: Pisces.

SANDFLIES, small two-winged flies belonging to the blood-sucking genus *Phlebotomus*, but in some places this name is given to the biting midges (Ceratopogonidae) as they are also minute and blood-sucking, and may be common around estuaries and sandy river banks. In Australia, the blackflies (Simuliidae) are also known as sandflies.

True sandflies (*Phlebotomus*) are tiny, fragile flies found throughout the tropics and subtropics, generally in damp shady places and particularly at dusk and during the night. Their flight is weak and they are easily disturbed when feeding on their vertebrate hosts. It is usually only the female which sucks blood and it is therefore on account of them that sandflies are medically important as vectors of various diseases, notably 'three day fever'. They are also a considerable nuisance, not least because they are so small that they can easily get through the meshes of all but the finest mosquito nets.

The eggs are laid in damp crevices in rocks, drains and damp earth, and the larva feeds on any organic detritus in the damp environment which is essential for its survival. FAMILY: Phlebotomidae. ORDER: Diptera, CLASS: Insecta, PHYLUM: Arthropoda.

SANDGROUSE, desert-living, plump, ground birds, pigeon-like in size and shape and with a general resemblance to game birds. Sandgrouse have long been thought to drink by suction without lifting the head and to feed their young by regurgitation, as pigeons do. Recent observations have shown these ideas to be incorrect.

They have short feathered legs and toes and walk with a mincing gait. Their wings are long and pointed and their flight strong and direct. In some species the central tail-feathers are elongated to form a pin-tail. The males are brighter than the females but both have cryptic coloration, the plumage being predominantly in browns and greys, often dappled and barred on the back with chestnut, buff and black.

They inhabit deserts and steppes in Eurasia, India and Africa but they eat no succulent green or animal food, relying entirely on seeds. This means they must drink water daily which restricts their distribution to areas within about 20 miles (32 km) of water.

The nest is a simple scrape or unaltered hollow such as a dry hoof mark in which, usually three, cryptic ellipsoid eggs are laid. Both parents incubate, the male at night and the more cryptic female during the day. The nest is rarely situated in the shade which means that the female sits, without relief, in temperatures of up to 104°F (40°C) and over for several hours daily. Over-heating is prevented by rapid movements of the loose skin of the throat known as gular fluttering. The chicks leave the nest immediately after hatching (nidifugous) and feed on dry seeds. This means that they also require water daily and this is brought to them trapped in the specially adapted breast feathers of the male. The young 'strip' the water from these feathers. FAMILY: Pteroclidae, ORDER: Columbiformes, CLASS: Aves.

SANDHOPPER *Talitrus saltator*, a small crustacean which burrows in sand on European shores. It differs from other amphipods in that it does not lie on its side but rests in an upright position on the claws of the thoracic legs. The last three segments of the abdomen are shortened and partially tucked under the body. The usual method of locomotion is by jumping whence its name. It can also swim and walk. In jumping the abdomen is suddenly flexed, pushing against the substratum giving a jump of up to 3 ft (1 m) in distance, and to a height of about 1 ft (30 cm). FAMILY: Talitridae, ORDER: Amphipoda, CLASS: Crustacea, PHYLUM: Arthropoda.

SANDPIPERS, small- to medium-sized, wading birds, 5–15 in (13–38 cm) in length. Most species have long pointed wings and fairly long legs in relation to their bodies, which are rather slim and their necks thin. The bill is of moderate length. Not all bills are straight, however, some showing considerable specialization, for example the bill of the Spoon-billed sandpiper *Eurynorhynchus pygmeus* of northern Asia. Most sandpipers have inconspicuously cryptic plumage, when seen from overhead.

Most sandpipers spend at least part of the year on the sea coast, particularly on coastal mudflats. They nest chiefly on the ground, although the Green sandpiper *Tringa ochropus* often uses old nests in trees, for example those of thrushes, up to 30 ft (10 m) above the ground. The species breeding in marshland usually conceal their nests well in vegetation, which are usually not far from water. Other species, however, nesting in arctic regions rely on the cryptic colours of both the eggs and the sitting bird to provide concealment. See redshank. FAMILY: Scolopacidae, ORDER: Charadriiformes, CLASS: Aves.

SAND WASPS, brightly coloured wasps of the genus *Bembex*, the body often banded with yellow and black stripes, which live in burrows dug out of the desert soil. The nests may extend to a depth of almost 3 ft (1 m), where the wasp and its brood are well protected from the extremes of temperature occurring at the surface. The Sand wasp is a hunter, preying on small flies it stores in the nest as a food supply for the developing larva. FAMILY: Sphegidae, ORDER: Hymenoptera, CLASS: Insecta, PHYLUM: Arthropoda.

SAWFISHES, flattened cartilaginous fishes resembling the guitarfishes but with the snout greatly elongated and bearing a series of 16–32 teeth on either side. Like the guitarfishes, the sawfishes have a shark-like body, with small pectoral fins which are not used for propelling the body forward, the motive power for swimming being derived from sinuous movements of the body, as in sharks. The sawfishes, however, have the gill slits on the underside of the head and are thus clearly allied to the rays and not to the sharks. They are found in tropical marine and brackish waters but also occur in some tropical freshwaters. The Common sawfish *Pristis pectinatus* is found in the Atlantic and Mediterranean, and is known to reach a length of 18 ft (5·4 m). FAMILY: Pristidae, ORDER: Hypotremata, CLASS: Chondrichthyes.

SAWFLIES, 'tailed wasps' or 'horntails'. Some species are known by even more appropriate names, such as Giant woodwasp. There are at least 2,000 species. They have two pairs of membranous wings, often with the venation much reduced and with the fore- and hind-wings interlocked by means of a row of small hooks. The abdomen is broad and there is no constriction between it and the thorax. Sawflies have fully legged larvae which look very like caterpillars of butterflies and moths except that they generally have three pairs of thoracic legs and at least six

Scale insects

A female sawfly *Tenthredo mesomelas* photographed while laying her eggs in a grass stem.

pairs of abdominal legs, whereas true caterpillars have only four such pairs.

The name 'saw-fly' is from the serrated ovipositor of the female, adapted for sawing or boring in plant stems or wood for egg laying. The ovipositor is used solely for this purpose and cannot be used as a sting despite the ferocious appearance of some of the larger woodwasps.

Sawflies are entirely plant feeders. Their larvae have varied feeding habits. Some feed inside plant galls and stimulate their formation, while others feed in the twigs of plants or in the hard wood of trees and shrubs. The majority, however, live on the leaves of plants much in the manner of caterpillars of moths and butterflies.

The large and strikingly coloured woodwasps or horntails have wood-boring larvae. The adults can be up to 1·7 in (42 mm) long, are black or brown and yellow, or in some species a bright metallic-blue. The long ovipositor of the female projects beyond the end of the abdomen and gives the false impression of a ferocious sting. The European *Sirex gigas*, the yellow and black species, attacks coniferous wood and *S. noctilio*, the steel-blue species, is found especially in larch and silver fir plantations. ORDER: Hymenoptera, CLASS: Insecta, PHYLUM: Arthropoda.

SCALE INSECTS, plant-sucking insects, of two main kinds, the Armoured scales, small or minute and characterized by a hard waxy scale covering the adult female, and the Tortoise scales, so named because of the form of the body in many species. There are many species of Scale insects, mostly in the tropics and subtropics. They are among the most serious pests of shrubs and trees, infesting bark, leaves and fruit. Examples are the San José scale *Quadraspidiotus*

perniciosus, a pest of deciduous fruit trees in the United States and Canada, and the Black scale *Saissetia oleae* also a pest of fruit trees, especially in California. SUPER-FAMILY: Coccoidea, ORDER: Homoptera, CLASS: Insecta, PHYLUM: Arthropoda.

SCALLOPS, bivalve molluscs of which there are almost 300 species. The shells of all have a generally similar shape, one or both of the valves being convex and of rounded outline often with a series of ribs radiating across the surface. The general appearance is similar to that of a Roman comb which is why the principal genus was called *Pecten* by Pliny. Perhaps the best known of the scallops is the Great scallop or the St James's shell *Pecten maximus* which occurs on the Atlantic coast of Europe and was the emblem of pilgrims visiting the tomb of St James the Apostle in northwestern Spain.

The general form of the body in all scallops is similar. In common with other bivalves, the tissues of the scallop are enclosed on each side by a pair of calcareous shell valves which are joined dorsally in the hinge region by an elastic ligament. Inside the shell in the hinge region there is also a wedge-shaped ligament which becomes compressed as the valves are closed. This closure is brought about by a large adductor muscle whose action is thus opposed by the internal ligament.

One of the truly remarkable features of scallops is the great swimming ability shown best by the Queen scallop *Chlamys opercularis* but also exhibited by the Great scallop and by several other species. The mobility of scallops has been known for a long time. The young animals are found near the low water mark on the shore, but as they grow older, as adults, they undertake substantial migrations into deeper water. This migratory ability is thus

quite distinct from the escape reactions shown by some cockles, although scallops are also able to escape rapidly from their principal predator, the Common starfish. In effect, a scallop swims by snapping its shell. FAMILY: Pectinidae, ORDER: Filibranchia, CLASS: Bivalvia, PHYLUM: Mollusca.

SCALY-TAILS, a family of African rodents. They are superficially like flying squirrels and show the same range in size, but the tail is densely haired only at the tip. Their most striking peculiarity is the presence of a double row of strong, sharply pointed scales under the basal half of the tail. These point backwards and enable the tail to act as a supporting limb when the squirrel is clinging to the vertical surface of a tree. The extremes of size are represented by the large *Anomalurus peli*, found in Ghana and the Ivory Coast, which measures about 18 in (45 cm) without the tail, and the tiny species of *Idiurus* of the Congo forest, measuring only 3 in (8 cm). FAMILY: Anomaluridae, ORDER: Rodentia, CLASS: Mammalia.

SCAMPI *Nephrops norvegicus*, also known as the *Norway Lobster and as the Dublin Bay prawn. It resembles a small lobster with long claws. Scampi has a wide distribution from Norway to the Mediterranean. Its typical habitat is a soft muddy bottom at a depth of 60–300 ft (20–100 m). Here the scampi make burrows open at both ends. They can be caught with a trawl that disturbs the animals from their shallow lairs. The muscles of the abdomen are esteemed as food and are the basis of an increasingly important fishery. Abdomens of the Mantis shrimp are also sold as scampi in Italy. ORDER: Decapoda, CLASS: Crustacea, PHYLUM: Arthropoda.

SCARABS, beetles more or less convex, with the abdomen projecting from under the end of the wing cases. For breeding some scarabs come together in pairs, each pair combining to mould a ball of dung which they then roll to a selected site and bury. The female, working underground now moulds it into a pear-shaped mass, tamping it hard except for the neck of the pear which is left hollow. In this one egg is laid, the robust, whitish, C-shaped larva feeding on the rest. Each female lays 2–4 eggs in one season.

The Sacred scarab *Scarabaeus sacer*, of the Ancient Egyptians, is of special interest. The notched protuberances on the front of the scarab's head and the spiny projections on the legs were regarded by the early Nile civilizations as symbols of the sun's rays, and the spherical dung balls made by the beetle were symbols of the Earth itself. It seems the Egyptians took the view that just as the Scarab beetle made its ball of dung revolve so some gigantic celestial scarab kept the Earth revolving. The Sacred scarab was also considered symbolic of the Moon, as it was believed that the beetles did not start to feed on their hidden treasure (the buried dung balls) until the 28 days of a lunar month had passed. FAMILY: Scarabaeidae, ORDER: Coleoptera, CLASS: Insecta, PHYLUM: Arthropoda.

SCHELTOPUSIK *Ophisaurus apodus*, with a length of about 3 ft (90 cm) is the most impressive of the Anguid lizards and can be found from the northern part of the Balkan peninsula through Asia Minor and the Caucasus to Turkestan. The Scheltopusik is legless, snakelike and its body well armoured with a great number of bony scales. There is a furrow on each side of the body enabling the lizard to move its otherwise rather rigid body sideways. Insects alone are not enough to feed a strong Scheltopusik; it also eats snails and small rodents, crushing these with its powerful jaws. A lot of people fear the Scheltopusik more than any snake and even believe it, incorrectly, to be poisonous. FAMILY: Anguidae, ORDER: Squamata, CLASS: Reptilia.

SCORPIONFISHES, heavily built, often poisonous fishes, many from temperate waters, usually living in rocky areas, but some, like the bizarre lionfish, found in tropical seas. They are chiefly bottom-living with large mouths and in some species an ornamentation of bony and fleshy spines and appendages on the head camouflage them against a background of rocks, corals and marine plants. Many have pungent or even poisonous spines in their fins which has given them their common name. The most poisonous and perhaps the most poisonous of all venomous fish is the stonefish, the camouflage of which is so perfect that it is almost indistinguishable from its background. FAMILY: Scorpaenidae, ORDER: Scorpaeniformes, CLASS: Pisces.

SCORPIONS, with spiders, among the best known of the terrestrial arachnids, although their distribution is limited to the warmer parts of the world. They represent one of the oldest arthropod groups, with a fossil history dating back over 300 million years to the Silurian. They appear to have evolved very little during this period of time for the fossil record reveals that the scorpions of that early age were very similar in general structure to those living today.

The Scorpiones is a remarkably homogeneous group of over 600 species. In general appearance each of the 600 species of scorpion much resembles any other, although there are variations in size, colour, the number of eyes, the development of the limbs and certain minor characters. The largest, the West African *Pandinus imperator*, is just under 8 in (20 cm) in length. In most the body is brown occasionally green, bluish or black. The division of the body into an anterior prosoma and a posterior opisthosoma is well marked, for the upper surface of the prosoma is covered with a single large, rectangular shield, or carapace, whereas the opisthosoma is clearly segmented. This posterior part of the body is sub-divided into a broad 'pre-abdomen', consisting of seven segments, and a much narrower, cylindrical tail, or 'post-abdomen' of five segments, terminating in a curved and sharply pointed sting. In the normal posture, the tail is reflexed over the rest of the body so that the sting is directed forwards. This menacing attitude is enhanced by the formidable palps, two massive claw-like limbs inserted on either side of the mouth and held extended in predatory fashion. These two claws are used for capturing prey and in this they are sometimes assisted by the stinging tail. The scorpion's diet consists mainly of other arthropods, such as grasshoppers, crickets, moths, flies, ants, termites, beetles and spiders, although small vertebrates, such as lizards and mice, are sometimes taken. Once secured in the firm grip of the palps, the prey is held against the mouth where the chelate jaws, or chelicerae, tear it to pieces.

The four pairs of walking legs on the underside of the prosoma enable scorpions to move rapidly if disturbed, but normally they are sedentary, preferring to let their prey come to them. When they venture abroad, they usually move slowly and cautiously. Apart from a few blind cave-dwelling forms, simple eyes are present on the carapace, one

Scorpions *Euscorpius flavicaudis* on the isle of Elba, face to face, about to take partners for a courtship dance.

Screamers

on each side of the midline, and a group of three to five on each of the lateral margins. Sight is unlikely to be important, for scorpions are most active at dusk and they rely more on sensory hairs carried mainly on the palps.

Scorpions are mainly confined to warm, dry regions, such as the deserts of North Africa, the Middle East, Asia, Australia and the Americas; a few species, such as *Pandinus imperator*, prefer the humid conditions of West African bush and forest, while members of the genus *Euscorpius* live in the cooler Mediterranean climate. Most scorpions become lethargic during cold weather, and the group is generally absent from temperate regions; notable exceptions to this are *Euscorpius germanus* of the European Alps and *Vejovis boreus* of British Columbia.

The mating habits of scorpions have attracted considerable attention, particularly since they include a courtship 'dance'.

Scorpions give birth to living young; the fertilized eggs develop within brood chambers in the mother's body. Each embryo is attached by a tubular umbilicus to the maternal intestine from which nutrients are obtained. Immediately after birth, the young scorpions climb onto the mother's back and adhere by means of suckers at the tips of their legs. Here they remain for several days or weeks, relying for sustenance on their own supply of embryonic yolk. Shortly after their first moult, they disperse, maturing to the adult stage through six or seven moults over the period of a year.

All scorpions are furnished with a poisonous sting but most, if not all, only use it in defence. The greatest danger to humans comes from inadvertently stepping on a scorpion or from having one crawl into clothing, beds or sleeping bags. ORDER: Scorpiones, CLASS: Arachnida, PHYLUM: Arthropoda.

SCREAMERS, three species of South American, long-legged, goose-like birds with unwebbed feet.

The Crested or Southern screamer *Chauna torquata* is found from central Argentina and southern Brazil to Paraguay and eastern Bolivia, the closely related Black-necked or Northern screamer *C. chaviara* is found in western Venezuela and north Colombia and the Horned screamer *Anhima cornuta* in tropical South America from Colombia to Venezuela, southern and central Brazil and eastern Bolivia.

On the leading edge of the long, rounded wings are two spurs 1 in (2½ cm) or more long, used in fighting. Screamers rise heavily from the ground, but fly well, frequently soaring and gliding like eagles. The Crested and Black-necked screamers are both about 28–32 in (71–81 cm) long and are mainly grey, but with a ruff of grey or black feathers, a paler head and a crest of elongated feathers on the back of the crown. The Horned screamer is about 30–36 in (76–91 cm) long

The Snake-locks anemone *Anemonia sulcata* cannot fully withdraw its tentacles.

and its plumage is mainly black, with white on the neck, head, wings and breast. A 'horn' of cartilage about 3 in (7½ cm) long projects from the bird's forehead, bending forwards over the base of the bill.

Screamers are so-called because of their loud bisyllabic trumpeting call. This is audible up to 1 mile (1·6 km) away. They are mainly ground-living birds that live near water and marshes, sometimes walking on floating mats of vegetation to collect food and occasionally swimming. FAMILY: Anhimidae, ORDER: Anseriformes, CLASS: Aves.

SEA ANEMONES, probably the most familiar animals of rocky shores, they are world-wide but more abundant in warmer seas. They are all solitary and do not form a skeleton. The polyp has a relatively short, cylindrical body, attached to a rock or other substrate at the basal region or pedal disc, and flattened at the oral region to give a wide disc with numerous tentacles arranged in rings or cycles around the mouth which opens into a deep throat or pharynx, which then opens into the enteron. The enteron, or 'stomach', is subdivided by mesenteries or septa which project from the body wall. These partitions are composed of a central axis of mesogloea surrounded by endoderm, and bearing at their free ends digestive filaments. In some families these can be pushed through the body wall when the anemone is disturbed. At the oral end the mesenteries fuse into the throat, making pocket-like regions. These

mesenteries are known as digestive mesenteries and always occur in pairs. Anemones may be hermaphrodite or dioecious and gonads develop in the mesenteries near their lower ends.

Sea anemones will catch any suitable living animals for food, using nematocysts or stinging cells.

Fertilization of eggs may be external, when a ciliated planula larva develops in the plankton, or it may be internal and the young anemones develop in the enteron of the parent.

Although Sea anemones are normally sessile, they can move slowly over the substratum, but some species lack a pedal disc and there are others that float. Some anemones can swim by feebly lashing the tentacles. ORDER: Actiniaria, CLASS: Anthozoa, PHYLUM: Cnidaria.

SEA BREAMS, marine perch-like fishes not closely related to the freshwater breams, found mainly in warm and tropical waters. The body is usually deep with a single long dorsal fin, the first part of which has spines, and three spines in the anal fin. There are well-developed teeth in the jaws, sharp in front, often rounded and molar-like behind. Many species are known from the eastern Atlantic and the Mediterranean. The Common or Red sea bream *Pagellus bogaraveo*, a reddish fish with a black blotch on the shoulder, is the most frequently caught around British coasts, although Neolithic sites in Scotland have shown that the fish was evidently much more common in those times.

In South African waters the species *Rhabdosargus globiceps* has a variety of common names including that of 'Go-home fish'. In Plattenberg Bay, South Africa, the fishermen say that when this species is caught there are no other fishes around—they have all gone home. FAMILY: Sparidae, ORDER: Perciformes, CLASS: Pisces.

SEA BUTTERFLIES, marine molluscs that have two large flap-like extensions to their mantle called parapodia, which are used to propel them through the water. They are mostly carnivorous and are only found in offshore surface waters. ORDER: Thecosomata, CLASS: Gastropoda, PHYLUM: Mollusca.

SEA CUCUMBERS, small, slimy, sausage-shaped marine animals related to starfish and Sea urchins. On the front of the body is a mouth surrounded by a ring of tentacles. The skin is leathery and strengthened by variously shaped calcite spicules, such as rods, crosses, hooks, anchors or wheels. The colour of Sea cucumbers is usually dull: grey, brown, black or purple, only rarely red or orange.

Most Sea cucumbers crawl slug-like on their lower surface using two double rows of tube feet the ends of which are sucker-like. There are five double rows of tube feet altogether but those of the sides and upper surfaces have bluntly rounded tips and are mainly sensory.

Most Sea cucumbers are bottom dwellers, some concealing themselves in crevices or under stones, or among seaweed, others lying in burrows in sand or under mud. They may form very dense populations especially in the deep seas. In one deep sea trench they formed 50% of the living forms at 13,123 ft (4,000 m) and 90% at 27,786 ft (8,500 m).

A more unusual adaptation is found in those Sea cucumbers which have structures called Cuvierian organs branching from the bases of the respiratory trees. When the animal is irritated these are extruded from the arms, and since they are very sticky any attacker is likely to become trapped amongst them.

Those Sea cucumbers without Cuvierian organs may defend themselves by evisceration. When irritated they simply split the body wall and eject the gut and respiratory trees. These, it seems, provide a meal for any attacking predator, whilst the animal itself moves away and later regrows the missing parts. ORDER: Holothuria, CLASS: Echinodermata.

SEA FANS, relatives of Sea anemones but made up of colonies of polyps. Each colony forms a plant-like growth with a short main stem and lateral branches in one plant, the whole strengthened by a central axis of horn or gorgonin. They are found mainly in tropical and subtropical seas and classified with Horny corals. ORDER: Gorgonacea, CLASS: Anthozoa, PHYLUM: Cnidaria.

SEA FIRS, small tree-like colonies of polyps living in shallow waters and the tidal zones of the seashore. Each colony arises from a single planula larva which settles on a suitable substratum, often the fronds of large oarweeds. CLASS: Hydrozoa, PHYLUM: Cnidaria.

SEA GOOSEBERRIES *Pleurobrachia*, the most well known and also the most typical of the Ctenophora or comb jellies. They are pelagic and often occur as swarms in the plankton. They are globular, gelatinous animals shaped rather like a hen's egg with a mouth at the narrower end. Two long, retractile tentacles armed with adhesive cells or colloblasts are spread out either side rather like fishing lines. Sea gooseberries are carnivores, and planktonic crab and oyster larvae and fish eggs are caught by the sticky tentacles and conveyed to the mouth. A rapid digestion of the prey takes place in the long pharynx. Sea gooseberries swim using the eight rows of comb plates of fused cilia, which 'flap' in an orderly fashion from the mouth backwards. ORDER: Cydippida, CLASS: Tentaculata, PHYLUM: Ctenophora.

The Sea cucumber *Cucumaria saxicola* hides in burrows bored in rocks by other animals.

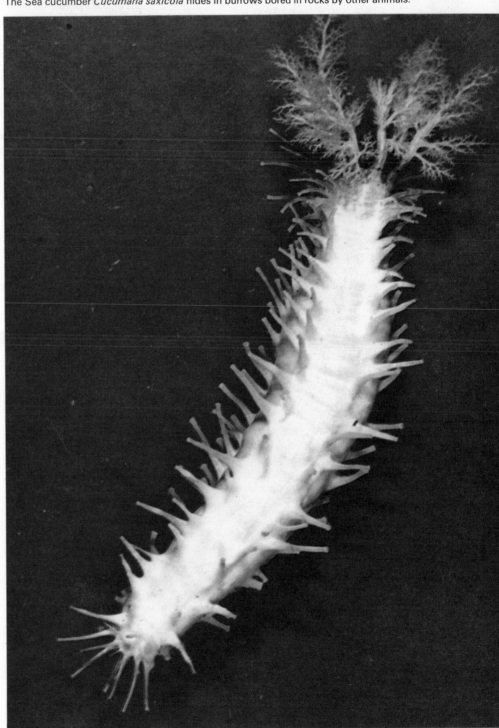

Bull sealion of the Galapagos, closely related to the better-known Californian sealion.

SEA HARE, a slug-like marine mollusc with a pair of tentacles at the front end and, behind these, a pair of tentacles called rhinophores which carry many sensory organs and are rolled inwards and shaped like hare's ears, whence the common name. A reduced plate-like shell is present, but concealed by mantle lobes which fuse along the back of the animal leaving only a small opening to the mantle cavity. Flaps, known as the parapodia, are developed at the sides of the foot, with which the animal can swim clumsily. The common European Sea hare, *Aplysia punctata* may have been the species described by Pliny who was the first to record its common name and some of its habits.

The Sea hares of the genus *Aplysia* are world-wide but particularly abundant in subtropical and tropical waters. FAMILY: Aplysiidae, ORDER: Pleurocoela, SUBCLASS: Opisthobranchia, CLASS: Gastropoda, PHYLUM: Mollusca.

SEA HORSES, small highly specialized marine fishes related to the pipefishes. They are unique amongst fishes in having the head set at right angles to the body. The body is entirely encased in an armour of bony plates or rings but the tail fin is absent and the hind part of the body is prehensile and can be twined round seaweeds to anchor the fish. Swimming is accomplished by wave-like vibrations in the dorsal fin, the fish progressing in a characteristic upright position. Care of the young by the male has reached a point where an enclosed pouch is present, formed by the bony plates of the body. Camouflage reaches bizarre proportions in such members as the Australian Leafy sea horse *Phyllopteryx foliatus*, in which fleshy leaf-like appendages decorate the body simulating seaweed. This grows to 12 in (30 cm) which is large for a Sea Horse.

Because of its unfish-like appearance and the ease with which dried specimens could be brought back to Europe, the Sea horses have long excited interest. The head is surprisingly horse-like and in the *Hortus Sanitatis* of J. von Cube, published in the 15th century there is an illustration of a Sea horse complete with hoofed forelegs and hair on the body. Sea horses were used as talismans and in potions against a variety of illnesses. The ashes of the Sea horse, however, were deemed fatal if mixed in wine, and in cases where the victim survived he was said to be plagued with a permanent desire to bathe. Mixed with pitch, the ashes of these little fishes were believed to be efficacious for restoring hair, but taken alone they were also a wise remedy for the bite of a mad dog. FAMILY: Syngnathidae, ORDER: Gasterosteiformes, CLASS: Pisces.

SEA LILIES, marine animals related to starfish and Sea urchins but attached to the sea bottom by a stem or stalk. The body, at the top of the stem, bears long feather-like food-gathering arms held upwards so that they form a sort of 'begging bowl' with the mouth at the centre, catching the bodies of small dead animals raining down from above. The stem is flexible and is made up of serially arranged ossicles bonded together by short ligament fibres. Sea lilies vary from 1–24 in (2–61 cm) high. They are probably anchored to the seabed most of the time although one kind of Sea lily is known to break free and swim trailing its stem behind it. Most Sea lilies taken in the dredge, however, have damaged stems or lower parts missing but at least some species are known to be fastened to the seabed by cement and others have root-like branches at the base of the stem.

Most Sea lilies live at depths between 656–16,404 ft (200–5,000 m) and one lives as deep as 26,247 ft (8,000 m). They are mostly anchored to the substrate. ORDER: Articulata, CLASS: Crinoidea, PHYLUM: Echinodermata.

SEALIONS, eared seals differing from the Fur seals in having blunter, heavier snouts, a coat with a very small number of underfur hairs and hindflippers with the outer digits longer than the three inner ones.

The males range in length from 7 ft (2·1 m) to 10 ft (3 m), the smallest and best known being the Californian sealion *Zalophus californianus*, seen in most zoos, and in many circuses. Sealions live along the coast of California and Lower California, on the offshore islands and there are also populations on the Galapagos Islands and off the coast of Japan. Not much is known about the Japanese animals, but they are thought to live in the southern parts of the Sea of Japan, possibly on Honshu. Both males and females are a deep chocolate-brown in colour, and the old adult bulls are recognizable by their very high foreheads, caused by the development of a high sagittal crest on the skull.

The other sealion of the northern hemisphere, Northern or Steller's sealion *Eumetopias jubatus* of the North Pacific, is perhaps the biggest of all, the males reaching over 10 ft (3 m) in length and up to a ton (1,016 kg) in weight. Its range is from Hokkaido in the west to California in the east, on the Kurile Islands and in the Sea of Okhotsk, off Kamchatka and the Alaskan coast, and on the islands off British Columbia and California. But the centre of abundance is on the Aleutian islands where there may be over 100,000 animals. Both males and females are light brown, and the male develops a heavy mane round his neck and shoulders. During the breeding season, in May, harems are formed and territories defended. The pups are born in June and are fed by their mothers for at least three months.

The Southern sealion *Otaria byronia* has almost the same distribution as the South American Fur seal. It occurs on the coast of South America south of Rio de Janeiro, on the Falkland Islands and round Cape Horn; it is also found along the coast of Chile and Peru.

The remaining two sealions both live in the Australia-New Zealand area. The Australian sealion *Neophoca cinerea* is found only along the southern coasts of Australia. This sealion is frequently found high up on sandy cliffs or asleep amongst sand dunes, and the greyish-yellow colour of the females and young males makes them quite hard to distinguish from their surroundings. Older males are much blacker and fully adult bulls have a conspicuous white area on the back of their heads and necks. These are inoffensive animals, only the female normally being aggressive when with her pup.

Hooker's sealion *Phocarctos hookeri*, about 9 ft (2·7 m) in length, lives and breeds on the Auckland Islands, Snares and Campbell Islands south of New Zealand. FAMILY: Otariidae, ORDER: Pinnipedia, CLASS: Mammalia.

Sea horses are fishes in which the male carries all the family burdens.

SEALS, TRUE, otherwise known as Earless seals, belong to the family Phocidae. They have no external ears, cannot bring their hindflippers forwards underneath the body, and their coat is mostly composed of guard hairs.

The classification of the True seals is almost coincident with their natural division into those of the northern and southern hemispheres. The family Phocidae is divided into two subfamilies: Phocinae and Monachinae. The Phocinae includes all the northern seals such as the Bearded seal *Erignathus barbatus*, the Hooded seal *Cystophora cristata*, the Grey seal *Halichoerus grypus*, the Common or Harbor seal *Phoca vitulina*, the Caspian seal *Pusa caspica*, the Baikal seal *Pusa sibirica*, the Ringed seal *Pusa hispida*, the Harp seal *Pagophilus groenlandicus*, and the Ribbon seal *Histriophoca fasciata*. The Monachinae includes the Monk seal *Monachus schauinslandi* and *M. tropicalis*, the Elephant seal *Mirounga angustirostris* and *M. leonina*, the Weddell seal *Leptonychotes weddelli*, the Crab-eater seal *Lobodon carcinophagus*, the Leopard seal *Hydrurga leptonyx*, and the Ross seal *Ommatophoca rossi*.

The most northerly of the northern seals is the Ringed seal which lives along the circumpolar arctic coasts and as far north as the Pole. Two forms of it live in the freshwater lakes of Saimaa and Ladoga in Finland.

Ringed seals grow to about 4 ft 10 in (1·4 m) in length and weigh about 200 lb (90·7 kg). The colouring of the fur usually consists of black spots surrounded by a light ring on a light grey background. Birth and subsequent mating occur in the spring and just before the pup is born the mother excavates a lair in the snow on the fast ice. This lair has a breathing hole opening into it from the water below, so that the mother may come and go without moving over the surface of the ice. The single pup is born about the beginning of April, is just over 2 ft (0·6 m) long, weighs 10 lb (4·5 kg), and is covered in long creamy-white fur, shed for a shorter coat after about three weeks. The pup is suckled for two months. Ringed seals eat many kinds of crustaceans and small fish and are in their turn preyed upon by Polar bears, Killer whales and Arctic foxes. Eskimos make great use of this seal, using the white pup skins as underclothes and the adult skin for outer clothes, bags, harnesses and tents. The blubber is used for lamps and the flesh is eaten.

Two other seals closely related to the Ringed seal are the Caspian seal and the Baikal seal, living in the Caspian Sea and Lake Baikal, respectively. Both are greyish-yellow, the Caspian seal being irregularly spotted with black.

Another arctic circumpolar seal, the Bearded seal, does not occur as far north as the Ringed seal and prefers shallow water near coasts. It is rarely found in large numbers in any one locality. Bearded seals are about 7 ft 6 in (2·3 m) in length and weigh about 600 lb (272 kg). They are grey with a slightly browner area down the middle of the back. The very profuse set of whiskers gives the animal its name, and these are curious in that when they dry they curl into tight spirals at their tips. The pups, 4 ft (1·2 m) long and grey in colour, are born out on the ice floes in April or May and are said to remain with their parents for some time. One pup is born every second year, an unusual occurrence amongst the phocids where one pup a year is more usual. Bearded seals eat animals living on the ocean floor, such as shrimps, crabs and Sea snails and are said to have a special liking for whelks. In spite of this, shells are never found in the stomach. In this they resemble the walrus.

The Hooded seal *Cystophora cristata* occurs from Newfoundland and Baffin Island to Greenland, Iceland and Spitzbergen. They are mostly solitary but during the breeding season in March they collect in widely scattered groups of families, the chief concentrations being in the Newfoundland area and near Jan Mayen. Before it is born the pup sheds its first coat of long hair for a very beautiful coat that is greyish-blue on the back and creamy-white ventrally. These 'bluebacks' are much in demand for making fur coats. Adult Hooded seals are about 10 ft (3 m) long and weigh about 900 lb (408 kg). They are grey with large irregular black spots on the back and smaller spots ventrally. The most characteristic feature of the Hooded seal is the large inflatable hood, an expansion of the nasal cavity found in the adult male. When not inflated it is slack and wrinkled and hangs down in front of the mouth, but when blown up it sits like a cushion on top of the head.

In slightly more temperate waters, the Grey seal *Halichoerus grypus*, lives on either side of the north Atlantic. The largest breeding colonies are on the British coasts on North Rona and the Orkneys. Grey seals reach 9 ft 6 in (2·9 m) in length and 650 lb (294 kg) in weight. All shades of dark and light grey and brown coats are seen but in males the background is darker with lighter spotting, in females the background is lighter and the spots are darker. Adult males have a pronounced 'Roman' nose.

The Baltic and St Lawrence pups are born in February and March, in Britain they are born September to December. Each is about 2 ft 6 in (0·8 m) long and is covered in long white fur which it sheds in about three weeks for a short blue-grey coat. At 3 days old a pup weighs 43 lbs (19·4 kg) increasing to 92 lbs (41·7 kg) by the time it is weaned at 18 days.

The Common or Harbor seal *Phoca vitulina* lives in estuaries and on sandbanks uncovered at low tide off the coasts of the North Atlantic and North Pacific. Common seals reach about 6 ft (1·8 m) in length and have a very variable coat pattern, basically light grey with irregular spots of black that may be sparsely or thickly distributed. The pups, 3 ft (0·9 m) long and 25 lbs (11·3 kg) weight, are born in May and June. Pups, except in the western Pacific, are usually born on a sandbank at low tide and are able to swim away with their mothers as the tide rises. Their long white coat is shed before birth. After weaning, at three weeks old, they progress to a diet of shrimps and then to the adult food of fish, squid, whelks and mussels.

There are three species of Monk seals—the Mediterranean Monk seal *Monachus monachus*, West Indian Monk seal *M. tropicalis* and the Laysan or Hawaiian Monk seal *M. schauinslandi*. It has been suggested that they are called Monk seals because of the cowl-like effect of the rolls of fat behind their heads. Formerly more abundant, Monk seals are now only found in unfrequented places in the Black Sea and Mediterranean, but greater numbers are along the western coast of Africa as far as Cap Blanc. They are about 9 ft 6 in (2·9 m) in length, greyish-brown in colour, sometimes with a white ventral patch.

The remaining phocids live in the cold waters of the Antarctic. They are all circumpolar, but living in different areas and with different food habits they do not interfere with each other. The Leopard seal *Hydrurga leptonyx* is the most northerly, living in the outer fringes of the pack ice. Most others are migratory and move north in winter. Leopard seals are solitary, 10–11 ft (3–3·3 m) in length and weighing about 600 lb (272 kg). Adult females may be up to 2 ft (0·6 m) longer than adult males. These seals are dark grey dorsally and light grey ventrally, very variably spotted on their sides and throats. They have very long slim bodies and the head seems disproportionately big, with a wide mouth armed with large three-pointed teeth. Their appearance has probably been responsible for their reputation of extreme ferocity, but unless annoyed they are normally dangerous only to penguins and the fish and squids which form its food.

The Crabeater seal *Lobodon carcinophagus* perhaps the most abundant Antarctic seal, is found on the circumpolar drifting pack ice, moving north with the ice in winter and south in summer when the heavier ice breaks up. It is gregarious, being found in large concentrations in the southern summer. Very occasionally it may reach Australia and New Zealand. Crabeater seals reach about 8 ft 6 in (2·5 m) long and are a silvery-brownish-grey in colour, but this colour fades during the year, and also with age so that older animals may be almost white. The Crabeater feeds on the shrimp-like krill.

The Ross seal *Ommatophoca rossi*, dark grey in colour, shading to a lighter grey ventrally and with paler streaks and lines

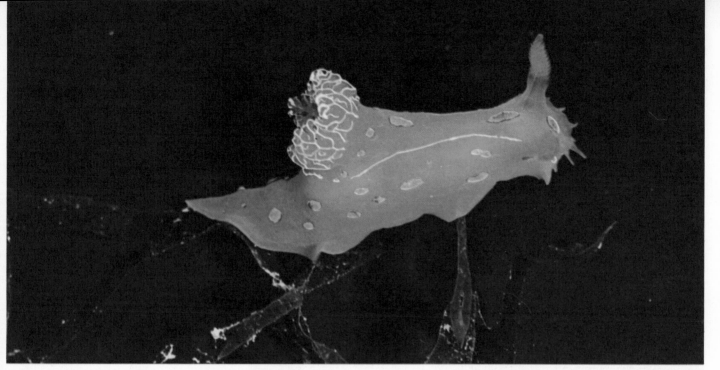

The Sea slug *Coryphelia lineata* reminds us that these marine gastropod molluscs include some of the most exquisitely coloured of lower animals.

on the sides of the neck and shoulders, occurs on the heavier pack ice round the edge of the Antarctic continent, but is only infrequently seen. Adult males reach 9 ft 6 in (2·9 m) in length.

The Weddell seal *Leptonychotes weddelli* lives farther south than the pack ice. Adults are about 9 ft (2·7 m) in length, females slightly larger than males. They are dark brown or black dorsally, fading to white ventrally with variable white streaks and splashes on the dark ground colour. See Elephant seals, Fur seals and sealions. FAMILY: Phocidae, ORDER: Pinnipedia, CLASS: Mammalia.

SEA OTTER *Enhydra lutris*, first discovered in 1751 was subsequently so persecuted for its valuable fur that by the end of the 19th century it was close to extinction. Protected in 1911, it is now making a satisfactory recovery, the entire population numbering between 30–40,000 individuals. While the Sea otter's range originally extended from the Kurile islands in Japan, across the Aleutian chain and down the west coast of America as far south as Lower California, colonies today are only local within this area. It is exclusively marine, rarely coming ashore. The massive head with a short, blunt face and large nose is much paler than the body, which varies from shades of brown to almost black, sparsely covered with guard hairs. Unlike other otters, it has a short tail, seal-like flippers and small, compact forepaws. Adults reach a little over 5 ft (1·5 m), including a 12 in (30 cm) tail and weigh up to 80 lb (36 kg). Their unique molars are broad and rounded, perfectly adapted to crushing Sea urchins, abalones and mussels. The Sea otter floats peacefully in small colonies of 10–90 animals near kelp beds. Food is eaten while the animal is on its back, and stones brought from the ocean floor serve as an 'anvil' to

break the urchin or mussel shell. The Sea otter is one of the few tool-using mammals. It lays the stone on its chest and holding a Sea urchin or a clam between its forepaws crashes it down onto the stone. It tucks its anvil under its arm while diving and uses it for several consecutive shell-breaking attempts. One young is born, rarely twins, at any time of the year after a nine month gestation. The cub is in a more advanced stage of development than any other mustelid at birth: eyes open, well furred, it also has a complete set of milk teeth and can immediately float in the water next to its mother or on her chest when nursing. FAMILY: Mustelidae, ORDER: Carnivora, CLASS: Mammalia.

SEA PENS, colonies of polyps living on a central axis and looking like quill pens. In contrast to the other Soft corals, Sea pens are mobile colonies generally living in warm coastal waters, but limited to soft muddy bottoms. The Sea pens are known for their luminescence which comes from a slime exuded on stimulation. ORDER: Pennatulacea, SUBCLASS: Octocorallia, CLASS: Anthozoa, PHYLUM: Cnidaria.

SEA SLUGS, unlike land slugs, are among the most beautiful of invertebrates. One group is exemplified by the Sea lemon *Archidoris pseudoargus*, common in European waters, and includes forms flattened in the vertical plane with a pair of sensory retractile tentacles on the front of the back which otherwise bears only small warts until the mid-dorsal anus is reached. This is surrounded by a ring of feathery gills which can be completely retracted. The Sea lemon and related Sea slugs feed mostly on sponges, swallowing large lumps. The yellowish Sea lemon feeds on the yellowish Crumb-o'-bread sponge *Halichondria panicea* and the red Sea slug *Rostanga* feeds only on red sponges,

both matching the colours of their prey.

Some Sea slugs have rows of small finger-like processes running the length of the back. They feed on Sea anemones and Sea firs and it is said that the stinging cells from these are not digested but move from the Sea slug's stomach up into the processes on the back and there are used by the Sea slug in defence. ORDER: Doridacea, CLASS: Gastropoda, PHYLUM: Mollusca.

SEA SNAKES, poisonous snakes that live permanently in the sea, having the body flattened from side to side and the tail flattened and paddle-shaped. They swim with a sculling action of the tail, keeping mainly near the surface but able to submerge, closing the valvular nostrils on the top of the snout. They are, however, fully air-breathing and must surface periodically or drown. The head is characteristically small and the front half of the body slender with the hindquarters more fully rounded. Some Sea snakes reach a length of 10 ft (3 m) but the majority are 4–5 ft (1·2–1·6 m) long. All have venom glands with cobra-like fangs, hollow and permanently erect in the front of the mouth. The 50 species are confined to the tropics, especially in the eastern Indian Ocean and western Pacific, mainly living in inshore waters. Some Sea snakes swarm in the cracks and crannies of rocks in the intertidal zone. A few are known to enter tidal rivers up to 100 miles (160 km) inland. One species only, *Hydrophis semperi*, is confined to freshwater in the Philippines. One of the commonest and most widely distributed is the Yellow-bellied sea snake *Pelamis platurus* which is black on the back and yellow or pale brown below.

Although the venom of a Sea snake is potent to small fishes there are relatively few reports of fatal accidents to fishermen. FAMILY: Hydrophidae, ORDER: Squamata, CLASS: Reptilia.

The Edible sea urchin *Echinus esculentus* of European coasts, with its tube-feet extended.

SEA URCHINS, spiny, spherical to somewhat flattened marine animals with the radial five-fold symmetry, an endoskeleton of calcite plates, and water vascular system that gives rise to avenues of tube-feet, so characteristic of the echinoderms to which Sea urchins belong, on the surface.

The basic structure of modern Sea urchins is that of a sphere made up of 20 columns of plates fused one to another to provide a rigid, usually box-like, skeleton, known as the test, pierced at the top by an opening for the anus and at the centre of the underside by the mouth. Sea urchins can, however, be divided into two groups. There are those in which the test has the original pronounced radial symmetry; there is a set of well developed jaws, the Aristotle's lantern, in the mouth. In the second group the test has a bilateral symmetry.

The body is covered with spines which vary considerably in size and shape between species. They may be large or small, long and pointed or short and club-shaped. Each spine is on a ball and socket joint, and the spines can be moved and used for protection against wave action or enemies, and they can be used for locomotion. In some species the spines are poisonous.

Among the spines are pincer-like pedicellariae which serve to keep the surface free of detritus and especially small animals, such as barnacle larvae, for instance, which would otherwise settle there. They bear jaw-like blades set on a stem. Some Sea urchins live in shallow water or even between tide marks, but the greater number live between 200 and 1,000 m, some living as deep as 4,000 m, and the species are especially numerous in the Indian Ocean and western Pacific and in the Antarctic Ocean. CLASS: Echinoidea, PHYLUM: Echinodermata.

SECRETARY BIRD *Sagittarius serpentarius*, a long-legged, diurnal, terrestrial bird of prey, confined to Africa south of the Sahara. It stands almost 4 ft (1·2 m) high, and spans 6–7 ft (1·8–2·1 m). It is mainly grey, with black wing quills and thighs, and bare orange skin on the face. The head is adorned with a black-tipped crest, the central tail-feathers are very long and the grey legs are long with short stubby toes. The name comes from the grey and black clerical livery and from a fancied resemblance of the crest to quill pens stuck behind the ear.

Secretary birds inhabit short grassland, 15–18 in (38–46 cm) high, preferably shorter. They avoid long grass and extreme desert, but sometimes adapt to cultivated areas. They roost on low thorny trees, usually in pairs, and early in the morning jump to the ground and begin hunting. They walk steadily through the grassland, nodding the head backwards and forwards like hens. Now and again one makes a quick dart to catch an insect or mouse in the bill, or breaks its pace to stamp rapidly for half a minute or so, presumably to disturb prey. The food mainly consists of rodents, insects and snakes, in that order of preference. Secretary birds kill far fewer snakes than they are usually credited with. FAMILY: Sagittariidae, ORDER: Falconiformes, CLASS: Aves.

SERIEMAS, South American birds resembling small, brown cranes. They have long, slender legs, long necks and rather long heavy bodies. The Crested seriema *Cariama cristata* stands about 30 in (76 cm) tall and is about 36 in ((91 cm) long, while Burmeister's seriema *C. burmeisteri* stands about 25 in (63 cm) tall and is about 30 in (76 cm) long. The bill is short, stout and hooked at the tip, the wings short and rounded and the tail long with dark and light bars. The Crested seriema has an orange bill and grey-brown plumage finely barred and vermiculated with dark brown and black. The wings and tail have broad, contrasting bands of black and white. Burmeister's seriema is darker in colour, with the underparts heavily streaked.

Seriemas are found on open ground, areas of open thorny woodland and scrub. Occurring in pairs and small groups, occasionally in larger flocks, they are usually seen running away in the distance as both species are shy, being hunted as game. They can run very rapidly, but the flight is weak, with the legs trailing behind. Because of their shyness they are often most easily found by their calls, which include yelping and screaming notes in the Crested seriema, and high-pitched yelpings in Burmeister's seriema.

Secretary bird playing with a tussock of grass, throwing it into the air with its feet and leaping after it.

Sheathbills *Chionis alba*, of the Antarctic, feeding on dead animals, excrement and refuse, as well as on small shore animals.

Besides eating berries, seeds and leaves, they take insects, reptiles and small mammals. Snakes are often eaten and it was considered that seriemas were immune to snake venom until recently, when an American research worker killed some by injecting snake poison into their circulatory systems. FAMILY: Cariamidae, ORDER: Gruiformes, CLASS: Aves.

SERVAL *Felis serval*, unusual looking member of the cat family because of its very long legs and large erect ears. It is entirely confined to Africa, south of the Sahara, where it lives in regions of medium cover in the broken country of the foothills.

The serval is of slender build standing some 20 in (50·8 cm) at the shoulder, with a total length of about 4 ft (1·2 m) of which about 1 ft (30 cm) is tail. It weighs about 34 lb (15·4 kg). The ears are very large for a cat, in some ways resembling the shape found in certain species of bat, and give the serval acuity of hearing beyond the normal cat's. They are so wide at the base they almost meet on the top of the head.

The serval hunts mainly at night, sometimes in pairs, lying up during the day in reeds, long grass or bush. Its long legs enable it to achieve great speed over short distances and in high grass it progresses by long, high leaps. It is a skilful and rapid climber and can swim well. Its food consists mainly of birds, such as Guinea fowl and francolins, and rodents, especially the mole-rat. FAMILY: Felidae, ORDER: Carnivora, CLASS: Mammalia.

SHEATHBILLS, aberrant birds of the subantarctic, having the appearance of heavily built white pigeons. Both *Chionis alba* and *Chionis minor* are also sometimes called Soreeyed pigeons, paddies and Kelp pigeons.

Their uniform white plumage covers a dark grey down and the stout bill has a characteristic saddle-like horny sheath covering the base of the upper mandible. There is a cluster of pink caruncles around the base of the bill and a bare patch below the eyes, which have a bald ring around them.

Sheathbills have been much maligned because of their habits of scavenging on refuse tips, stealing penguin eggs and feeding on excrement and seal afterbirths. Also, when handled, they discharge the contents of their large rectal caecae which has surprised many an unwary ornithologist. In fact, they keep their white plumage remarkably clean and should be looked upon as resourceful birds that have to take advantage of all available food supplies in their harsh environment. FAMILY: Chionididae, ORDER: Charadriiformes, CLASS: Aves.

SHEEP, DOMESTIC *Ovis aries*, short stocky animals with curly horns and a dense coat of wool. They are primarily grazers and are therefore normally kept on open grassland, often in enormous flocks. The wild sheep *Ovis vignei* of Central Asia, is probably the ancestor of our domestic forms.

The strong herd instincts of sheep make them excellent ranch animals, as they keep together in tight and easily managed flocks and do not disperse widely all over the available land, where they would be difficult to protect and almost impossible to round up.

Wool is a normal attribute of many animals, but in domestic sheep its development has been enhanced and exaggerated by selective breeding. Most mammals have two types of hair: primary hairs which are long, stiff and straight, and between these, dense masses of short curly, fuzzy secondary hairs, or 'wool'. It is the latter which is responsible for body insulation, helping maintain the mammal's high body temperature. In sheep, selective breeding has encouraged the development of animals which only grow a dense coat of secondary hairs, and this coat or 'fleece' is clipped off once or twice a year and used for spinning and weaving.

A top wool-producing breed of sheep such as the Corriedale of New Zealand may yield up to 20 lb (10 kg) of high quality fleece in a year. Some breeds have only 100 lambs per 100 ewes in a year, but others, notably the Dorset, may have many twins and triplets resulting in 140 or more lambs per 100 ewes.

'Merino' sheep, a breed developed in Spain, were, and still are, renowned as the basis of the great wool industry. They produce very fine wool with long fibres and little tendency to shrink, two features of prime importance. The breed is very adaptable and can thus be kept in a variety of different types of country. It is particularly favoured in Australia. FAMILY: Bovidae, ORDER Artiodactyla, CLASS: Mammalia.

SHEEP, MOUNTAIN. The 37 living races of wild sheep fall into the following groups: Mouflon *Ovis musimon*. The smallest most colourful sheep, native to Corsica and Sardinia, but successfully transplanted to the European mainland, the United States and Argentina. They differ from urials in having a distinct rump patch, a broad dark tail, out-curling horns and white saddle across the back. The Cyprus urial should be considered to be a mouflon.

Urial *O. orientalis*. These are small primitive sheep with long ears, long neck manes, diffuse rump patches and horns, which in the western races tend to curl inward. They live from Asia Minor to Kashmir, and Laristan in the south to Russian Turkmenistan in the north.

Argalis *O. ammon*. These include the giants among sheep. Argalis are found from the foothills of the Pamir throughout the mountain ranges of Central Asia to northern China and central Siberia south of Lake Baikal. Large Siberian argali males carry a skull and horns up to 60 lb (27 kg) in weight.

Snow sheep *O. nivicola*. Primitive Asiatic representatives of American-type sheep. The most primitive race appears to be the one in Kamchatka. They have small, thin horns and small rump patches, although in body size they almost rival the Rocky Mountain bighorn.

Thinhorn sheep *O. dalli* are intermediate in horn, skull and rump patch characteristics between Snow sheep and Bighorn sheep. Thinhorn sheep include the pure white Dall's sheep and the grey to black Stone's sheep. The distribution of the former is in Alaska, the Yukon and Northwest territories, while Stone's sheep are found from the central Yukon throughout northern British Columbia.

Bighorn sheep *O. canadensis*. This is the most diverse group of American sheep. The smallest is the Nelson's bighorn which is no larger than the urial and shows strong affinities with Thinhorn sheep, characterised by long ears, short wool, and extended breeding and lambing seasons. The largest Bighorns are the cold-adapted, short-eared, massive-horned Rocky Mountain and California bighorns from Canada. FAMILY: Bovidae, ORDER: Artiodactyla, CLASS: Mammalia.

SHELDUCK *Tadorna*, closely related to the Dabbling or Surface-feeding ducks although resembling geese in general form. Both sexes are brightly coloured, although sometimes differently, and usually there is a metallic wing speculum. The Common shelduck *T. tadorna* breeds from the coasts of western Europe eastwards through much of central Asia. Both sexes have striking white, green-black and chestnut plumage, with red bill and legs. The female is smaller.

Outside the breeding season shelduck live in pairs or parties feeding in muddy estuaries on shellfish, crustaceans and insects and some vegetable matter. They fly with slow beats and have a quacking call. The nest, lined with down, is usually made in a hollow in the ground in sand dunes or under stones and bushes. 8–16 large creamy eggs are laid and incubated by the duck for about four weeks. The young shelduck later unite in parties and fledge in about two months. FAMILY: Anatidae, ORDER: Anseriformes, CLASS: Aves.

SHIPWORM, a bivalve mollusc, despite its name, notorious for burrowing in the timbers of piers and wooden ships. The Common shipworm *Teredo navalis* makes burrows of up to 18 in (45 cm) long and $\frac{1}{4}$ in (6 mm) wide, lined with a white calcareous material given out by the shipworm. Most bivalve molluscs are entirely enclosed by the shell valves but in the shipworm these are modified to a tiny pair of abrasive plates at the head end. The body is long and worm-like and consists mainly of an elongated tubular mantle which connects the end of the burrow with the seawater outside. Water is drawn into the tube through an inhalant siphon and is pumped out through an exhalant siphon, as in many other bivalve molluscs. The siphons normally project from the surface of the timber but can be withdrawn and the hole closed by a pair of calcareous plates called pallets. The shipworm is reputed to be able to bore tunnels as long as 1 ft (30·5 cm) in one month.

Boring is by abrasion. The valves are so shaped that there is a dorsal and a ventral fulcrum upon which the two rock when the anterior and posterior adductor muscles are contracted alternately. The rasping motion is repeated 8–12 times per minute and a three month old shipworm bores up to $\frac{3}{4}$ in (19 mm) per day. FAMILY: Teredinidae, ORDER: Eulamellibranchia, CLASS: Bivalvia, PHYLUM: Mollusca.

SHOEBILL *Balaeniceps rex* or Whale-headed stork, a heavily built grey swamp bird standing nearly 4 ft (1·2 m) high. It has a long neck, long black legs and a massive head. The bill is grotesque, almost as broad as it is long and sharply hooked at the tip.

Shoebills are shy, retiring birds and spend most of their time singly, or in pairs, in the permanent swamps of eastern Africa. Large sluggish fishes feature in their diet, which also includes frogs, turtles and probably small mammals too. FAMILY: Balaenicipitidae, ORDER: Ciconiiformes, CLASS: Aves.

SHORE CRAB *Carcinus maenas*, a species common on European shores and also those of North America where the crab is known as the Green crab, or Joe Rocker. The green colour is found mainly in the males; the adult female tends to be more orange in colour. Young crabs show a very wide range in coloration and pattern. Some are almost black, others green or white with red or black patterns. This variety of coloration is lost as the animals become adult.

The Shore crab is abundant on rocky shores, but also extends a considerable distance into estuaries, and may be found in muddy areas and salt marsh pools.

The Shore crab is most active at night and at high tide. SUBORDER: Brachyura, ORDER: Decapoda, CLASS: Crustacea, PHYLUM: Arthropoda.

SHREW, small mouse-like mammal with short legs, a long pointed nose and long tail. Shrews are absent only from the polar regions, Australia, New Zealand and most of South America. Their distribution in time is equally great; fossils are known dating back

Left X-ray of a piece of shipworm-riddled wood. *Right* Shipworms and their burrows in wood exposed.

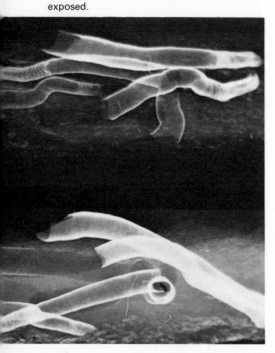

The serval, of Africa, cat with unusual build.

Shrikes

to Oligocene times. There are three kinds, the Red-toothed shrews, including the European common shrew *Sorex araneus*, and the Short-tailed shrew *Blarina brevicauda* of North America, and the White-toothed, including the Musk shrew *Crocidura russula* of southern Asia, and the Hero shrews of central Africa. The last have the spinal column so strong that they will survive a man standing on them.

Shrews all look similar with a body length of less than 8 in (20 cm) (usually less than 4 in). Shrews weigh up to 1·2 oz (35 gm) and the family includes the world's smallest mammal. the Etruscan shrew *Suncus etruscus*, which is a mere 2 gm when adult. Shrews have short dense, velvety fur which is usually grey or brown in colour. Powerful scent glands are located on the flanks. The eyes are very tiny and the shrew's eyesight is probably not very good, though it has a keen sense of smell. Hearing is very well developed and it is suggested that some shrews may use ultrasonic sounds for echolocation.

Shrews have strong neck muscles which enable them to bite and hang on to large prey and also to lift large objects in their teeth.

Some shrews are semi-aquatic and have bristle-fringed tails and feet to aid in swimming. Bristly feet are seen in certain Asiatic shrews, which enable them to run about on soft, loose sand. Many species dig small burrows or use the runs of rodents or just push through loose leaf litter, but the Shrew moles *Anourosorex* of Asia look and live like moles.

Shrews are nervous, highly active creatures, with a pulse rate sometimes nearing 1,000 beats per minute. They are on the move at all hours of the day and night resting for only brief periods. They scurry about very rapidly, often emitting a low

The ungainly looking shoebill of the African swamps.

twittering noise and stopping to sniff the air or investigate objects with the long, inquisitive nose. Shrews do not hibernate. Like most insectivores, they are usually solitary.

They are insectivorous but they also eat a variety of invertebrates and even small vertebrate animals. In addition many eat small quantities of seeds and other plant material. They are voracious feeders and soon starve if deprived of food. They may eat more than their weight of food in a day.

Most shrews breed during the summer (March–November) in the northern temperate lands, but in the tropics they often breed all the year round. The gestation period is between two and four weeks. Up to four litters may be produced in one season. The young are born naked and blind in a breeding nest, usually built under leaf litter or a log or stone for shelter. Young White-toothed shrews have the charming habit of forming 'caravans', each using its teeth to hold onto the tail of the one in front, and the whole procession, of six or more offspring, being led by the mother.

Many shrews live for only one year. FAMILY: Soricidae, ORDER: Insectivora, CLASS: Mammalia.

SHRIKES, aggressive and predatory perching birds that kill insects, birds and mammals by striking with their hooked bill. Because they impale their victims on thorns they are called butcherbirds, from the fancied resemblance to a butcher's shop.

The true shrikes are mostly between 7–10 in (18–25 cm) long and are characterized by a strong hooked bill, resembling a falcon's with a tooth-like projection behind the hook on the upper mandible and a notch on the lower; a bill unique among passerine birds. The feet are strong and the claws are sharp and are used for grasping prey. There are well-developed bristles round the mouth. The sexes are generally alike and there is a single moult in autumn.

Shrews are insect eaters and are among the most primitive of the true mammals.

One of the largest, the Great grey (Northern) shrike *Lanius excubitor* is 9½ in (24 cm) long and breeds widely in Europe, temperate Asia and North America. This, and its near relative the Loggerhead shrike *L. ludovicianus*, are the only New World species. The Great grey shrike is pale greyish with a black mask, wings and tail, and during the winter in the north feeds largely on birds and small mammals. The rather similar Lesser grey shrike *L. minor* breeds in southern Europe and Central Asia, winters in East Africa, and feeds largely on insects. Other species tend to be various shades of brown and grey. The Red-backed shrike *L. collurio* breeds in southern England, Europe and temperate Asia, wintering in tropical Africa and southern Asia.

The nest is a large deep cup of twigs, grasses, moss, flowers, wool and hair, bound with spiders' webs and placed in a bush or tree 5–20 ft (1½–6 m) up. Clutches vary from three to six eggs which are pale pink or greenish with irregular brown markings. Incubation, lasting 14–16 days, is almost exclusively by the female which is partly sustained by food brought by the male. The young leave the nest two or three weeks after hatching. Mostly living on the verges of woods and forests or among scattered shrubs, these mainly solitary shrikes are bold and aggressive especially in defence of their territories. They perch watchfully upright on high branches or telegraph poles, fanning their rather long tails. They swoop after their prey like flycatchers or small hawks, sometimes making prolonged chases after small birds, even tackling birds larger than themselves; they occasionally hover. Their flight is undulating, with glides, and is usually close to the ground so that on returning to a perch they 'zoom' upwards almost vertically. FAMILY: Laniidae, ORDER: Passeriformes, CLASS: Aves.

SHRIMPS, decapod crustaceans that swim using their abdominal limbs, instead of crawling like lobsters and crabs. A typical shrimp has five pairs of walking legs, of which at least two pairs bear pincers of some sort. These pincers may be quite large and powerful, or they may be very long and delicate. The body is usually elongated and more or less cylindrical with a distinct tail fan. The two pairs of antennae are generally very long and two-branched, at least one branch is carried reflexed over the body, reaching just beyond the tail fan. This enables the shrimp to walk backwards into crevices, and also gives warning when touched by a predator approaching from behind. A sudden flick of the abdomen is the usual response to the approach of a predator, and serves to jerk the shrimp well away from harm. The eyes are stalked, and in some deep-sea forms are very large, but in other deep-sea forms and some cave dwelling species they may be small or absent. There is great variation in the body length of shrimps, from ½ in (1 cm) to 1 ft (30 cm).

The colours of shrimps are generally cryptic, tending to conceal, and they can often change to match the background more closely. *Hippolyte varians* of Europe occurs in several colours. Some are uniform green and live on green seaweeds, others live on brown seaweeds and are a uniform brown, while yet others, living on finely divided red seaweeds, are transparent with red stripes and dots. A remarkable feature of this species is that no matter what colour the varied forms are in daylight, if placed in the dark they all change to a beautiful translucent blue. When they are returned to the light the original colours rapidly reappear. Many deep-sea shrimps are bright red in colour. This may also be a concealing coloration. Down in the depths of the sea most of the red light has been absorbed by the water above, so that a red

animal would be inconspicuous. A few shrimps, such as the Cleaner shrimps are conspicuously coloured, but this is linked with their special relationship with fish.

Some shrimps are scavengers, others are predators, and some have developed special techniques for collecting small particles.

A typical inshore shrimp, such as *Crangon vulgaris* of European shores, spends much of its time during the day buried in sand in shallow water. The sand is cleared away from under the body by movements of the limbs, so that the shrimp sinks downwards. During the night the shrimp walks or swims about and preys upon worms and any other small creatures that it can catch in its pincers. ORDER: Decapoda, CLASS: Crustacea, PHYLUM: Arthropoda.

SIFAKA, a magnificent white herbivorous lemur with orange, maroon or black markings and a terrier-like muzzle. Two species are recognized: Verreaux's sifaka *Propithecus verreauxi* and the Diademed sifaka *P. diadema*. The first is white with maroon or black patches on the head, back, belly or limbs, according to the subspecies; the second is larger, also white, but has patches of orange to deep brown and black. The name sifaka is from the Malgache name (pronounced 'shifak') for Verreaux's sifaka. The Diademed sifaka is referred to as the simpona (pronounced 'shimpoon') by local villagers. In both species, the face and ears are always black. The head and body length is 18–22 in (45–55 cm) with a tail of roughly the same length. The two species are confined to Madagascar, and are both completely arboreal and diurnal.

Their food is leaves, buds, flowers, fruits and the bark of large trees. Sifakas are vertical clinging and leaping forms, with extremely long and powerful hindlegs. When moving fast, they can make leaps of 15 ft (4·5 m) or more, taking off and landing in a vertical position. The animal pushes off with the hindlegs and lands on its feet. The thumb and big toe are opposable, so that vertical supports can be firmly grasped in squatting and leaping. Verreaux's sifaka can even leap around in the spiny forests of the south of Madagascar, characterized by tall, cactus-like trees with spiral arrays of spines. Apparently, the sifaka's leap is so accurate it can land even on these trees without injury.

The Diademed sifaka lives in the east coast rain-forest, while Verreaux's sifaka occurs in the drier forest of the northwest, west and south of the island.

Verreaux's sifaka occurs in small groups of up to eight individuals, each group occupying a home range for eating and sleeping which is vigorously defended against neighbouring groups. Each group seems to be stable for several years. FAMILY: Indriidae, SUBORDER: Prosimii, ORDER: Primates, CLASS: Mammalia.

Male Red-backed shrike, of Europe, at the nest, known as the butcher-bird from its habit of 'hanging' its meat.

Verreaux' sifaka of Madagascar remarkably matching the sun-dappled branch.

SIKA DEER *Cervus nippon*, the most adaptable of all the species of deer introduced to parts of Great Britain, Europe, New Zealand and elsewhere. 13 subspecies are recognized. In eastern Asia its range includes Japan (six subspecies), Formosa, eastern China (three subspecies), Manchuria and Korea (two subspecies) and northern Vietnam and Annam.

Sika deer vary in shoulder height from about 25½ in (65 cm) in one of the Japanese forms to about 43 in (109 cm) in Dybowski's deer from Manchuria. Antlers, usually eight-tined, seldom exceed 26 in (66 cm) in length in Manchurian specimens, considerably less in Japan.

The breeding habits are similar to the *Red deer with which this deer will interbreed on occasions. The rut call of the stags is a peculiar whistle which may change into a high pitched scream. The deer is fond of cover. FAMILY: Cervidae, ORDER: Artiodactyla, CLASS: Mammalia.

SILKWORM, the caterpillar of a moth *Bombyx mori*. Like many other caterpillars it spins itself a cocoon of silk in which it pupates and this cocoon is the source of virtually all our commercial silk. *B. mori* was

originally a native of China where the value of its silk was realised in about 1,800 BC. Since then it has been introduced to many countries and is now no longer known in the 'wild' state at all. The main silk producing countries are Japan, whence comes two-thirds of the world's silk, China, India, Russia, Italy and Brazil, but the annual production now is much less than 30 years ago because of competition from synthetic fibres such as nylon and rayon. In 1939 about 50,000 tons of silk were produced, compared with only 31,000 tons in 1963.

Most of the world's silk comes from eastern countries because the moth breeds continuously so that there may be six or more generations in a year. By contrast, in Europe there is only one generation a year and the eggs remain in a state of diapause throughout the winter. The eggs of the continuously breeding race hatch in 8–10 days.

The caterpillar feeds only on the leaves of the mulberry tree and it normally takes a month to reach full development. Then it starts to spin its cocoon. The silk is made in special glands, which in many other insects produce saliva. It is a mixture of proteins and is formed into a thread as it is forced through

a small opening just behind the mouth. The caterpillar makes a continuous thread commonly 1,000 yd (900 m) long, and sometimes as much as 2,000 yd. By unravelling this thread, in some places by hand, we obtain our silk. Normally, when the adult insect emerges from the pupa it damages the silk. To prevent this happening the pupae are killed by heating to a high temperature for a short time. FAMILY: Bombycidae, ORDER: Lepidoptera, CLASS: Insecta, PHYLUM: Arthropoda.

SITUTUNGA *Limnotragus spekei*, marsh-buck or water-koedoe, related to bushbuck, of papyrus swamps of Uganda, upper Zambesi watershed and parts of West Africa. It practically never leaves swamps and is seldom seen. The coat of the male is long and silky, chocolate-brown and that of the female fox-red with a varying amount of white striping. The female is hornless. The hoofs are long and the joints of the foot loose, thus spreading the weight of the body over soft ground. FAMILY: Bovidae, ORDER: Artiodactyla, CLASS: Mammalia.

SKIMMERS, tern-like birds of tropical rivers and shores, named for their habit of skimming low over the surface of water when feeding. There are three similar species, one each in the Americas, in Africa, and in southern Asia.

The African skimmer *Rynchops flavirostris*, is 18 in (45 cm) long. The underparts are white, the upperparts dark blackish-brown, and the forehead, sides of the tail and trailing edge of the wing are white. The tail is forked and the wings very long, the tips projecting well beyond the tail when the skimmer is at rest. The short legs and shallowly-webbed toes are vermilion. Quite the most remarkable character is the bill: both mandibles are laterally flattened, and the lower is about an inch (2–3 cm) longer than the upper. It is as thin as a penknife blade, but fairly flexible. In this species the bill is yellow, in the other two orange or red and black.

Skimmers feed by flying gracefully back and forth over still water, the bill wide open and the lower mandible slicing the surface for yards at a time, an unusual and effective means of catching small fish and crustaceans, which rise to the surface of lakes and the seas in twilight.

Skimmers are gregarious, and may be noisy during breeding, but at other times spend much of the day dozing in small flocks on seashore or river bank. In such localities nesting takes place during the hot dry season in the tropics. Because of the glaring white light of the sand, the pupils become catlike vertical slits during the day, becoming round and admitting a maximum of light at twilight, unique amongst birds. The nests are unlined scrapes in sand, and two to five buff eggs, with purple blotches, are laid. Hatching with down and well-developed legs, the chicks are concealingly coloured and semi-independent within a few hours. FAMILY: Rynchopidae, ORDER: Charadriiformes, CLASS: Aves.

SKINKS, with over 600 species, comprise one of the two largest lizard families. They are generally smooth-scaled and cylindrical, with conical heads and tapering tails, short legs or none at all, overlapping scales and a protrusible tongue. The majority are under 1 ft (30 cm) in length and most are less than 8 in (20 cm), the smallest being barely 3 in (7 cm) long. They are mostly ground-dwellers and burrowers, but many climb about in bushes or trees, although only one has a prehensile tail and thereby shows some specialization for arboreal life. This, the Solomon Islands Giant skink *Corucia zebrata*, is also the largest of the family and just exceeds 2 ft (61 cm) in length.

Skinks are the most abundant of the lizards in Africa, the East Indies and Australia. In Australia the number of species of skinks exceeds that of any other family of reptiles.

Half the species lay eggs, others give birth to living young, and one genus includes both egg-layers and live-bearers. The egg-layers may have clutches of 2–23 eggs, but live bearers seem to have smaller broods as a general rule. Some American skinks actively tend their eggs from the time they are laid in the nest until they hatch, and one species even cares for its brood after hatching.

The smaller species of the skink family feed mainly on insects, the largest skinks are wholly or partly vegetarian.

For protection from their enemies, skinks rely mainly on their retiring habits and the ability to throw off and then replace all or part of the tail. When alarmed or threatened, a skink raises its tail in the air, turns it towards its enemy and waves it slowly back and forth. The tail, once broken off, will wriggle violently for some time, diverting attention from its former owner.

The thick tail of the West African skink *Riopa fernandii* contains a store of fat.

One of the best known skinks is the Australian Blue-tongue skink *Tiliqua scincoides*, 12–15 in (30–40 cm) long, frequently kept as a pet. The name refers to the light or deep blue tongue, which is slowly but constantly flicked in and out whenever the animal is alert or on the move. Another attractive Australian skink is the Shingleback lizard *Trachysaurus rugosus* up to 18 in (45 cm) long, also known as stumpy-tail, bobtail, Double-headed lizard, boggi, and Pine-cone lizard. Unlike the other Australian skinks, the shingle-back generally has only two young at one time, only occasionally triplets. It is a sluggish animal, and feeds on flowers and fruit, as well as snails and slugs. FAMILY: Scincidae, ORDER: Squamata, CLASS: Reptilia.

SKUAS, seabirds related to the gulls and terns, which have been described as 'gulls turned into hawks'. They are best known for their piratical attacks on other birds, forcing them to disgorge their food and for the vigour with which they defend their territories against trespassers.

The shape of bill and feet are gull-like, except that the bill is strongly hooked and the feet bear curved claws. The Great skua *Catharacta skua* is about the size of a Herring gull but is heavier. The plumage appears uniformly dark brown but close-to the feathers can be seen to be streaked with rufous brown or white. The Great skua is readily identified by the white patch at the base of the primary feathers, which is conspicuous in flight and during the characteristic display with the wings raised.

The *Stercorarius* skuas or jaegers are smaller and more lightly built.

The Great skua is unusual in having a bipolar breeding distribution. In the north it is confined to the Atlantic Ocean where it breeds in Iceland, Faeroes and northern Scotland.

Skuas breed in colonies, usually near the sea, but the nests are never packed as tightly as in gull colonies. Each pair of skuas defends a territory of variable size, but the nests, which are usually near the centre of the territories, are typically about 100 ft (30 m) apart.

The nest is a depression in moss, heather or rough grass, and scantily lined with grass or moss. The usual clutch is of two greenish-olive eggs with brown blotches. Both sexes incubate, taking spells usually of less than an hour.

When a potential predator, such as a man, dog or even a penguin, approaches the nest the sitting skua and its mate give voice to raucous alarm calls and both birds swoop at the intruder, sometimes striking with their feet. The attacks are pressed home more vigorously nearer the nest and the intruder is usually effectively prevented from finding the very inconspicuous eggs.

Skuas are basically fish-eaters but are best known for their piratical and predatory habits. In many places skuas are the scourge of other seabirds. Even herons are attacked by Great skuas and its arctic subspecies feeds on small birds such as wheatears and buntings. In the tundra, lemmings are a very important food. FAMILY: Stercorariidae, ORDER: Charadriiformes, CLASS: Aves.

SKUNKS, carnivorous mammals renowned for the foul smell they produce. There are about ten species, distributed throughout the Americas, belonging to the weasel family. The best known is the Striped skunk *Mephitis mephitis* found throughout the United States and the adjacent parts of Canada and Mexico. It is about 18 in (45 cm) in length with a tail of about equal length, black with two bold white stripes on the back converging in front to meet on the crown of the head. The tail is a mixture of black and white and the hairs are several inches long, producing a great plume which is raised high in the air at the first sign of danger.

All members of the weasel family have scent glands under the root of the tail with which they mark their territory. In the skunk these are highly developed for purposes of defence: the secretion not only smells pungently but it causes severe irritation on a victim's skin and it can be shot out in fine jets to a distance of about 10 ft (3 m).

The Striped skunk is nocturnal and omnivorous. Insects constitute a large part of the diet, although mice, eggs, frogs and fruit all add variety. Activity is greatly reduced in winter, especially in the north of its range, although it does not undergo a true hibernation. Breeding takes place in early spring when a litter of about five young is born in an underground nest. The young follow their mother for much of the summer before dispersing in the autumn.

The Spotted skunk *Spilogale putorius* is smaller, boldly patterned with white lines

261

The Striped skunk, the best known of the skunks of North America.

and spots on a black background. When performing its threat display, with its long, white plumed tail held high, the Spotted skunk may make up for its smaller size by doing a hand-stand, a unique piece of behaviour amongst mammals.

In South America are found several species of Hog-nosed skunks *Conepatus* and one of these *C. leuconotus* reaches the southern states of USA. Apart from their pig-like noses, which give them their name, the Hog-nosed skunks are distinguished usually by totally white upperparts, including the whole tail, the rest of the body being black. FAMILY: Mustelidae, ORDER: Carnivora, CLASS: Mammalia.

SKYLARK *Alauda arvensis*, a small song-bird about 6 in (15 cm) long, well known for its magnificent song, characteristically delivered while hovering high in the air. The plumage is streaky brown above and white below with dark spots on the throat and breast. There is a small erectile crest on the crown. It lives in open country, never occurring near trees or in small fields with tall hedgerows. Its range extends across the whole of Europe and Asia, except for the extreme north, and into northwest Africa. Its food is seeds and insects taken from the ground. Three or four white eggs, thickly spotted with brown, are laid in a nest on the ground. Two or three broods are usual. FAMILY: Alaudidae, ORDER: Passeriformes, CLASS: Aves.

SLOTH, slow tree-dwelling mammal which, together with the anteater and armadillo, forms the order Edentata. Although the name of the group means 'without teeth', only the anteaters are completely toothless.

Tree sloths are uniquely adapted to an arboreal existence. The active part of their lives is spent upside down in trees, and this is coupled with their extreme slowness. Sloths rarely descend to the ground. They cannot stand or walk but must sprawl awkwardly on a flat surface and almost drag their bodies along. The arms are longer than the legs, and the actual digits (both fingers and toes) are closely bound together by tissue, covered with skin and hair, and terminate in long, strong, permanently curved claws. The palms of the hands and the soles of the feet are leathery pads and together with the claws form efficient hooks that can easily suspend the body from branches. Sloths can hang by all four limbs or even two, but more often they prop themselves in forks of trees or support their backs against branches while resting— always, however, with at least one foot securely hooked to a bough. A sloth climbs with a slow, deliberate (but graceful) hand-over-hand motion. Surprisingly enough sloths are good swimmers, using an over-arm stroke while in a right-side up position.

Although peaceful and inoffensive, sloths can defend themselves by biting and slashing out with their arms and formidable hooks. But perhaps their best protection is their very slowness and concealing coloration. Remaining motionless for long periods (sloths may sleep and doze 18 hours out of every 24) in a shaggy but compact mass high in a tree, a sloth is far from conspicuous to predators. During the rainy seasons, algae growing on the fur give a greenish cast to the sloth's thick wiry coat, increasing its protective camou-flage. (With its head down on its chest, a sleeping sloth can strongly resemble a bunch of dried leaves or even a wasp nest.) In addition, being able to curl into an almost impenetrable ball and having thick tough skin also helps it to weather attacks from its principal enemies—jaguars, ocelots, other carnivorous mammals that climb well, big Tree snakes and large birds of prey, such as Harpy eagles. Sloths are very tenacious of life and have been known to survive severe injuries, doses of poison, and shocks from electrical wires that would kill other mammals.

The three species are the Three-toed sloth *Bradypus tridactylus*, the Two-toed sloth *Choloepus didactylus* and Hoffmann's sloth *C. hoffmanni*. FAMILY: Brachypodidae, ORDER: Edentata, CLASS: Mammalia.

SLOW WORM *Anguis fragilis*, a limbless and smooth-scaled lizard with eyelids, without lateral grooves, rather stiffly cylindrical, the head, trunk and tail being not easily distinguishable, and with the ability to cast its tail. The young are silver-grey or light bronze, with a blackish mid-dorsal stripe and underside. Adults, up to 20 in (50 cm), are darker and duller olive-grey or bronze. The females retain the 'juvenile' stripe whereas males are usually less heavily marked and often show bluish markings dorsally.

Slow worms are found over temperate Eurasia west of the Caucasus. Their habitat is usually rocky or wooded. In Britain, pairing takes place soon after emergence from hibernation. Three to 23 or more young are born ovoviviparously, late in summer. Slow worms eat slugs, earthworms and insect larvae. FAMILY: Anguidae, ORDER: Squamata, CLASS: Reptilia.

SLUGS, shell-less, or nearly shell-less mol-luscs living mainly in the soil. They have an elongated mucus-covered body which in many species is covered at the anterior third by a loose flap of tissue, the mantle. Within this is the air breathing lung which opens to the outside by a small hole, the pneumostome. Gaseous exchange occurs in the lung and also all over the moist body surface. The head bears two pairs of tentacles and can be retracted under the mantle.

The most obvious feature that distinguishes slugs from snails is the apparent lack of a shell. In fact, in many species, a reduced internal shell is present and one rather un-usual family, the Testacellidae, have a small external shell.

Slugs are protandrous hermaphrodites, that is, the male system becomes mature, followed by the female system, the animals then being true hermaphrodites, and after this the male system becomes senescent and the animals are solely female. They mate on the soil surface after a long circuitous dance. Slugs lay their transparent eggs in the soil. These hatch into small slugs about 1·5 mm long which probably feed on fungi and decomposed plant matter before becoming large enough to feed directly on the green plant. Like snails they have a rasp-like radula and a chitinized jaw which scrapes small pieces of food into the alimentary canal. ORDER: Stylommatophora, CLASS: Gastro-poda, PHYLUM: Mollusca.

Land slug, active composter – and pest.

SMELT, small estuarine fishes related to the salmons. The European smelt *Osmerus eperlanus* is an elongated, compressed fish somewhat resembling a small trout but with a silvery body and slight blue-green tinges on the fins. A small adipose fin is present and the lateral line is short, not extending beyond the pectoral fins. The mouth is large, with fine teeth in the jaws, and there are conical teeth on the roof of the mouth and several large fang-like teeth at the front of the tongue. Smelt live in large shoals in the estuaries and coastal waters of Europe and are commonly used by fishermen for bait. They are anadromous, migrating up into fresher water to spawn. A peculiar feature of the smelt is the odour of the flesh, which resembles that of cucumbers. FAMILY: Osmeridae, ORDER: Salmoniformes, CLASS: Pisces.

SNAILS, gastropod molluscs with a spirally coiled shell. They may occur on land, in freshwater or the sea. Some snails have lost their gills and breathe air. Their mantle cavity is large and surrounded by large blood vessels and functions as a lung, which opens to the exterior on the right-hand side of the body through a variably sized opening, the pneumostome. From the lung oxygenated blood is pumped around the body by an efficient heart, the oxygen being combined with the typical invertebrate blood pigment, haemocyanin.

In Europe the widely distributed Round-mouthed snail *Pomatias elegans* lays large eggs $\frac{1}{12}$ in (2 mm) diameter in the soil between March and September. The eggs take about three months to develop into juveniles. Before copulation the animals make a series of characteristic movements or 'dances'. Some, such as the Brown-lipped snail *Cepaea nemoralis* or the White-lipped snail *C. hortensis*, use a flexible, calcified dart to stimulate its partner. This 'love-dart' which acts as a 'releaser' for successful mating, sometimes penetrates the partner's skin and works its way into its body, but it often falls to the ground after mating. Subsequently eggs are laid in moist situations often in the soil under leaf litter. They sometimes have calcified shells and in the Giant land snail *Achatina fulica* of Africa, the eggs are up to $\frac{4}{5}$ in (2 cm) diameter with chalky shells and can easily be mistaken for birds' eggs. They hatch into young snails which often live in the moist soil for some time before venturing onto the surface.

Most snails are vegetarians and feed by rasping plant material into their mouths with the radula. Some are carnivorous, feeding on earthworms or other snails. One snail, *Gonaxis kibweziensis*, of tropical islands, has been used to control the Giant African snail. CLASS: Gastropoda, PHYLUM: Mollusca.

SNAPPING TURTLES, widespread and abundant in the fresh waters of North America, and named for their aggressive disposition. Instead of retreating into its shell when approached, the Common snapping turtle *Chelydra serpentina*, a foot or more (30 cm) long, turns to face the intruder, even advancing to the attack, snapping and biting.

The head of the Snapping turtle ends in a strong, hook-shaped down-turned beak. These turtles can barely swim and usually lie quietly on the bottom of shallow pools. If they are disturbed they are extremely irascible and are even said to be capable of biting through a cane with their knife-sharp jaws.

The Common snapping turtle, also known as the Loggerhead snapper, has a carapace of up to 15 in (38 cm) long and weighs up to 85 lb (38·6 kg). It eats mainly fish, invertebrates and a large proportion of vegetation, and also carrion. FAMILY: Chelydridae, ORDER: Testudines, CLASS: Reptilia.

SNIPE, long-billed birds with flexible bill tips that can be opened below ground to grasp food items. They have large eyes, set well back in the head giving almost all-round vision. Their bodies are rather dumpy and their legs fairly short. They have cryptic plumage and keep very still until disturbed at very close quarters, when they rise sharply, often with erratic changes in flight direction.

The Common snipe *Gallinago gallinago* breeds throughout the northern hemisphere, and also in Africa and South America where the birds are chiefly sedentary. Geographical races have been named, for example Wilson's snipe of North America, which winters in Central America.

The Common snipe is able to produce a resonant drumming (or 'bleating') sound by vibrating its outer pair of spread tail feathers. FAMILY: Scolopacidae, ORDER: Charadriiformes, CLASS: Aves.

SNOW LEOPARD *Uncia uncia*, or ounce, one of the most beautiful of the big cats. It is found mainly in the Altai, the Hindu Kush and the Himalayas at heights of 6,000–18,000 ft (1,800–5,500 m), living in coniferous scrub.

The Snow leopard has thick long fur of a soft shade of grey with a pattern of dark rosettes on the upperparts. The ears are white with an edging of black and there is a thick black line down the back. Its total length is about 6 ft 5 in (1·9 m), standing about 2 ft (0·6 m) at the shoulder. It is nocturnal and shy so little is known of its habits except that it feeds on wild sheep, Mountain goats, marmots and domestic stock and usually has 2–4 young. FAMILY: Felidae, ORDER: Carnivora, CLASS: Mammalia.

SOLDIER BEETLES, beetles which often show warning coloration and are distasteful to predators. Their bright red colour being similar to that of soldiers' uniforms of the 17th and 18th century may have led to their common name. They are carnivores both as larvae, which live in the soil, and adults which can often be seen conspicuously on flower heads and leaves. FAMILIES: Cantharidae, Meloidae, ORDER: Coleoptera, CLASS: Insecta, PHYLUM: Arthropoda.

SOLE, a family of rather elongated flat-fishes of considerable economic importance. The eyes are on the left side, the mouth is small and the snout projects well beyond the mouth to give the fish its characteristic appearance. The Lemon sole *Microstomus kitt* is not a true sole but belongs to the plaice family. The Dover sole *Solea solea* has a long oval body and the dorsal fin begins over the head and reaches almost to the tail. The eyed side is dark brown with darker blotches. It

Representative of an African race of the Common snipe of Europe, by Lake Naivasha, Kenya.

lives in shallow water in the Mediterranean and along European shores as far north as the coasts of Britain, but becomes rarer in the north. It is caught by trawl, especially in the southern North Sea and the Bay of Biscay. The sole reaches 2 ft (60 cm) in length and can weigh as much as 9 lb (4 kg). The name Dover sole was coined in the last century before refrigeration when an enterprising gentleman organized a series of coach stages between Dover and London so that the fishes could be brought to the London markets with the greatest possible speed. FAMILY: Soleidae, ORDER: Pleuronectiformes, CLASS: Pisces.

SONG THRUSH *Turdus philomelos*, a familiar garden bird about 22 cm long, with brown upper parts and yellowish breast with scattered black spots. Song thrushes eat insects, worms and berries and in spring especially eat snails breaking open their shells by hammering them on a chosen flat stone, leaving the broken shells littered around the stone. The nest may be in a tree or bush, on the ground or among ivy on a wall. It is made of moss or stems and has a hard lining of mud, wood chips or dung. The 3–5 eggs are blue with black spots, incubated by the female but both parents feed the young for about two weeks. FAMILY: Muscicapidae, ORDER: Passeriformes, CLASS: Aves.

SPARROWHAWK *Accipiter nisus*, a yellow-eyed hawk in which the male is less than 1 ft (30 cm) long, bluish-grey above with brown marks on the long tail. The underparts are white barred with rusty red. The female is 15 in (37 cm) long, dark brown above with dark bars across the underparts. Sparrowhawks pursue small birds, flying low over and around hedges or among trees, often taking mice and insects. The nest of sticks is often built inside an abandoned nest of another species and in this the usual clutch is four to six greenish-white eggs with brown streaks. The female usually incubates alone for five weeks, during which time she is fed by the male. FAMILY: Accipitridae, ORDER: Falconiformes, CLASS: Aves.

SPERM WHALE *Physeter catodon*, or cachalot, largest of the Toothed whales, best known for its enormous squarish head which makes up about a third of the animal's length, some 60 ft (18 m) for a large male, the female being rather more than half that length. Moby Dick in Melville's famous novel of that name was a white Sperm whale. The front of the head contains an enormous reservoir, the 'case', filled with clear spermaceti oil and below that the junk, a lattice of fibrous and elastic tissue containing oil. Spermaceti, although fluid in the living animal, solidifies when exposed to air in cooler temperatures to form a 'wax' originally used for candles and cosmetics.

The lower jaw is much shorter than the upper. Teeth, found only in the lower jaw, number 18–28 on each side and are often different in number on the two sides. They are as much as 8 in (20 cm) in length and conical in shape. The teeth enter strong fibrous sockets in the upper jaw when the mouth is closed and so give effective grip to the food.

Sperm whales are darkish grey on the back, lightening in the flukes and belly to pale grey or white. There are often white scars and circles particularly in the head region, as a result of fights with Giant squid which form a main item of diet.

The Sperm whale is a deep water species and is rarely found in shallow or 'green' water with depths less than 330 ft (100 m). They dive deeply to 1,500 ft (500 m) and one is reported to have broken a cable at twice this depth. The deep diving is presumably associated with hunting for Giant squid. The ambergris which has considerable value as a fixer for perfumes, is found in the stomachs and intestines. It appears to be a secretion caused by irritation of the gut wall by squid beaks in the food.

The females and young and the attendant males form large schools of up to several hundreds; one count of well over 1,000 has been reported. FAMILY: Physeteridae, ORDER: Cetacea, CLASS: Mammalia.

SPIDER MITES, plant feeding mites including many serious agricultural pests occurring in orchards and greenhouses. Their common name reflects their habit of spinning a fine silk web around the leaves on which they are feeding. They use this to anchor their eggs to the leaf surface but it probably also serves as a protective canopy under which colonies of mites can feed undisturbed.

Spider mites comprise a large group of forms infesting a wide range of host species. They are not host specific; any one species may occur on a range of hosts, and it is not uncommon to find more than one species of Spider mites on the same host plant. Economically important species include the Fruit tree red spider mite *Panonychus ulmi*, which occurs on apple, pear, plum and damson, the Glasshouse red spider mite *Tetranychus urticae*, which is a pest of cucumbers and tomatoes in greenhouses and may also be found outdoors on blackcurrant and ornamental plants, the Citrus spider mite *T. telarius* of California and Florida, which may transmit a virus disease to cotton, and *Bryobia praetiosa*, the Clover mite, which is a serious pest of clover, peas, almonds, peaches and alfalfa in the United States. This last-named species often appears in large numbers in human dwellings and its wide range of distribution includes Europe where, however, it is not a serious pest. Although many of these forms are often collectively referred to as 'Red spider mites', there are complexes of related species which the experts sometimes find

difficulty in separating. Furthermore, the body colour may vary from green or yellow to brown, orange or red. The Glasshouse red spider mite is probably not one species, but a complex of related forms, some of which are green in summer and red in winter, while others are reddish-brown throughout the year. In some cases at least, it has been shown that these two colour forms can hybridize although the progeny are either sterile or all males.

The life-cycle of Spider mites varies from species to species and also with climatic conditions. In *Panonychus ulmi* two different kinds of eggs are produced, namely winter eggs which are deposited in sheltered crevices on the stems and branches of the host, and which go into a resting 'diapause' condition, and summer eggs which are laid on the leaves. Winter eggs hatch in spring and early summer; during the summer the life-cycle is completed in about a month, and there may be as many as five generations, possibly more, produced during this season. The population build-up is often staggering at this time, which is also the peak period for feeding activity. Towards the end of the summer the production of summer eggs ceases and winter eggs appear which will enable the species to survive until the following year. In northern climes, the active stages in the life-cycle are killed off by the winter cold, but in warmer latitudes adults may be active throughout the year and up to 15 generations may be produced.

The mouthparts of Spider mites are sharp stylets which puncture the leaf tissue of the host and enable the mite to feed by sucking out the cell contents. At the height of the feeding activity, the damage produced may kill the leaf and large-scale defoliation results. ORDER: Prostigmata, CLASS: Arachnida, PHYLUM: Arthropoda.

SPOONBILLS, graceful stork-like birds, related to the ibises but with long straight bills broadening to spatulate tips. The four species of *Platalea*, with mainly white plumage, between them cover most of the tropical and subtropical parts of the Old World. *P. leucoradia* has a northern outpost in the Netherlands, where it is a summer visitor. The Roseate spoonbill *Ajaia ajaja* is the New World representative. It nests in trees, bushes or reedbeds, or on the ground. Gregarious at all seasons spoonbills frequent the neighbourhood of freshwater, where they feed on small aquatic animals. FAMILY: Threskiornithidae, ORDER: Ciconiiformes, CLASS: Aves.

SPRAT *Sprattus sprattus*, a small herring-like fish found off the Atlantic coasts of Europe and in the Mediterranean. It closely resembles the herring, but is much smaller and rarely exceeds 6 in (15 cm) in length. Since sprats commonly shoal with juvenile

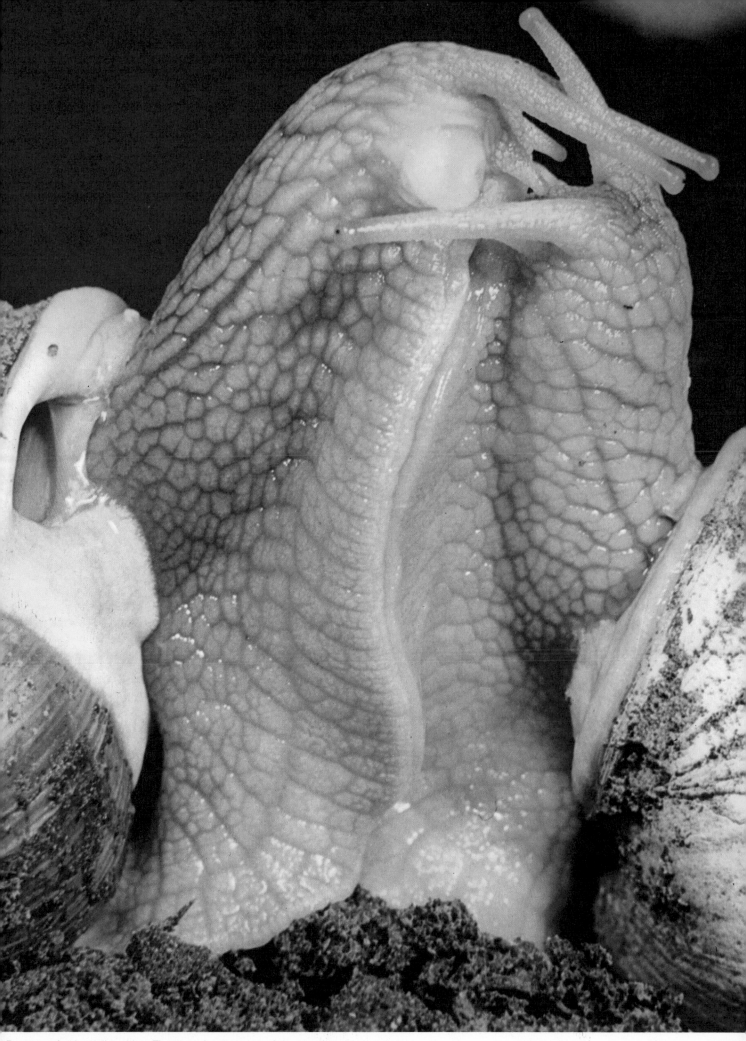

Roman or Apple snails pairing. These are the escargots of the gourmet.

Spoonbills feed by sweeping their bills from side to side, spooning up anything edible in the water.

herrings the two are often confused and at one time the sprat was thought to be the young of the herring. The sprat, however, is inclined to be greenish rather than bluish along the back and it can be fairly easily distinguished by the much stronger serrations of the scutes along the belly (this is obvious if the 'keel' of the fish is stroked from tail to head). FAMILY: Clupeidae, ORDER: Clupeiformes, CLASS: Pisces.

SPRINGBOK *Antidorcas marsupialis*, fawn gazelle with a nearly white face once abundant in South Africa and Angola, now found mainly in the Kalahari Desert. FAMILY: Bovidae, ORDER: Artiodactyla, CLASS: Mammalia.

SPRINGTAILS, also known as Collembola, are a group of insects which at no stage in their life-history have wings. The legs of the fourth abdominal segment form a furca, or springing organ. About 2,000 species of springtail are known, but there are doubtless many more to be discovered. Few are bigger than ¼ in (6–7 mm) and most are much smaller, but they are important because they occur in extremely large numbers in the soil

or at the soil surface. Populations of up to 100,000 per square metre of soil are common in temperate woodland and grassland soils; big populations are also found in the soils of extreme environments such as the polar regions. In fact it is likely that the springtails are the most numerous of all insect groups. The only environments in which they are not abundant are those with dry soils, such as deserts. Springtails cannot survive in dry places because they have little ability to withstand desiccation. Despite this, many species have very wide geographical distributions and some are known to occur in all continents; this is probably the result of their great evolutionary age which has given them plenty of time for dispersal. The oldest known fossil insects, which are about 320 million years old and come from the Devonian period, are Collembola and are very like modern species.

Sminthurus viridis, the Lucerne flea, is an important pest of clover and lucerne, especially in Australia. This is one of the few species which feed on living plant material and vast numbers may strip the vegetation completely over quite large areas. ORDER: Collembola, CLASS: Insecta, PHYLUM: Arthropoda.

SQUID, common name for a number of cephalopod molluscs related to cuttlefish but having a more streamlined, fish-like shape. The group includes the largest and fastest as well as some of the most beautiful invertebrates. All are predators, and the great majority are powerful swimmers. A few live in coastal waters, but are more typical of open waters, at the surface or down to great depths. Squid have ten arms of which two are longer than the rest. The largest squid recorded are nearly 60 ft (20 m) long, including the long arms, the smallest less than an inch (2.5 cm). Many deep water squids are jewelled with light-producing photophores (pits containing luminous bacteria), often of several colours. Some of these squids are remarkably beautiful and can justifiably be described as exquisite. ORDER: Dibranchia, CLASS: Cephalapoda, PHYLUM: Mollusca.

SQUIRRELS, a term usually meaning Tree squirrels, but the squirrel family is one of the largest families of rodents which includes a great variety of Ground squirrels, such as marmots and woodchuck, and Flying squirrels. Tree squirrels are found in most forested parts of the world and range in size from under 3 in (7·5 cm) in the pygmy African squirrel *Myosciurus pumilio* to 18 in (45 cm) in the Giant squirrels, *Ratufa*, of southeastern Asia. Tree squirrels typically have long bushy tails, usually about equal in length to the head and body, short muzzles and large, bright eyes. They are predominantly diurnal, and they tend to have bold patterns and colours. Some have longitudinal white stripes as in the common Palm squirrels, *Funambulus*, of India although this pattern is more characteristic of the Ground squirrels.

In temperate Eurasia there is only one widespread species, the Red squirrel *Sciurus vulgaris*. Most Red squirrels are indeed a rich reddish brown, with attractive tufted ears, but coloration is extremely variable. In some areas e.g. in Switzerland they are predominantly black and white.

Their food consists largely of the seeds of conifers and nuts such as acorns and beechmast. But when the seed crop is poor in coniferous woodland they will concentrate on buds, especially in winter.

Red squirrels do not hibernate, but they do store food and are less active in winter. They have been seen to collect toadstools in atutumn and to store them by jamming them in forks of twigs where they dry and provide an addition to the winter diet.

The nest is usually in a fork or on an exposed branch of a tree and it is used at all times of the year. Two litters may be produced during the summer, usually of four or five young.

North America is richer than Eurasia in squirrel species. The North American Red squirrel *Tamiasciurus hudsonicus* is smaller than its Eurasian counterpart. It, and especilly its western relative, *T. douglasi*, is often known as the chickaree on account of its chattering alarm call. The American Grey squirrel *Sciurus carolinensis* is a more southern species and lives predominantly in deciduous woodland.

Tree squirrels are much more diverse in the tropics where over 100 species are found in South America, Africa and Southeast Asia. FAMILY: Sciuridae, ORDER: Rodentia, CLASS: Mammalia.

STARFISHES, star-shaped marine animals with a radial usually five-rayed symmetry, a skeleton of mesh-like calcite plates buried within the body tissues and a water vascular system which gives rise to avenues of tube-feet on the lower surface, by which the animals move about.

A starfish consists of a central disc surrounded by five or more radiating arms. Five is the commonest number but species with up to 50 are known, as in *Heliaster*. Typically the arms are two or three times as long as the disc is broad, but there is a wide range from species with long slender arms such as *Brisinga* to the compact Cushion stars. The total size range is also large: from about $\frac{2}{3}$ in (10 mm) to 2 ft (61 cm) across. The colour varies from grey, green and blue, to vivid red or orange, sometimes mottled or with banded patterns.

One of the most remarkable features of starfishes is their ability to regenerate damaged or lost parts of the body. Whole arms when broken off by accident may be regrown again entirely. Moreover, species such as *Linckia* can actually grow a new disc and arms from a single severed arm. *Linckia*, indeed, may break off one of its arms for no apparent reason, and the resulting pieces then grow into two separate individuals. Such asexual reproduction is found in a few other starfishes, such as *Nepanthia* and *Cosciasterias*, but these split in two across the disc and then each half regenerates the arms and part of the disc that it lacks. Specimens in which such regeneration has taken place naturally show a very unequal development of the arms until the process is completed. CLASS: Asteroidea, PHYLUM: Echinodermata.

STARLINGS, a family of 105 species of medium-sized to large songbirds having, in general, slender bills, a rather upright stance and smooth, often glossy, plumage. They occur naturally in the Old World only, but a few species have been introduced into other parts of the world, where they have usually proved to be pests.

The typical starlings have slender, straight and tapering bills, and when feeding in turf, among plants or leaves, they thrust the closed bill into the ground or vegetation and open it, making a hole. The eyes are set close to the base of the bill and the bird looks along the opened bill, down into the hole, and seizes any

The Superb glossy starling *Spreo superbus* of East Africa.

food which the probing has revealed. Outside the breeding season they tend to flock together for feeding and roosting. Some of the roost-flocks are of huge size and the rapid co-ordinated manoeuvring of such flocks over the roost is typical of starling behaviour. At times the numbers may be such that the weight of the birds breaks the branches and the accumulated droppings kill trees in plantations where they roost. They have taken to flying into the centres of many cities to roost on the ledges of buildings.

The food of starlings consists of insects and invertebrates, fruits, some seeds and parts of green plants.

The Common starling *Sturnus vulgaris* has been introduced into North America and eastern Australia and has established itself and spread on both continents. The Rosy pastor *S. roseus* is a bird of the Asiatic steppes and like other species of those parts may periodically show large increases in numbers, and then in an unfavourable period spread out over wide areas, at such times often appearing in western Europe.

The Glossy starlings are the most brightly coloured group within the family. Their plumage is sleek and shiny, often with a rather oily sheen, and is coloured in strong iridescent blues, purples and greens. FAMILY: Sturnidae, ORDER: Passeriformes, CLASS: Aves.

STICK INSECTS, often called walking sticks in America, get their name from the shape of the body which is very long and slender, and usually green or brown so that they look like slender twigs. The deception is enhanced by the fact that if they are disturbed they remain quite motionless. With too much disturbance they fall to the ground without showing any sign of life, with the long thin legs held close against the body so that they look just like twigs amongst the litter of leaves under plants. The largest Stick insects may be up to 9 in (23 cm) long, but the species commonly kept in schools and laboratories, *Carausius morosus*, is not more than about 4 in (10 cm) long at most.

Stick insects are usually without wings even as adults and even in those species which have wings the forewings are usually very small. Since the forewings offer so little protection, the front edges of the hindwings are leathery and cover the membranous parts of the wings when they are folded up. Stick insect eggs are hard and rounded about an $\frac{1}{8}$ in (3 mm) across. They drop to the ground as they are being laid and often remain for a long time before hatching. The young, when they hatch, are about $\frac{1}{2}$ in (12·5 mm) long, but otherwise resemble the adults. They feed on leaves and in Australia, where Stick insects are particularly abundant, they may completely defoliate eucalyptus trees and so are

Sticklebacks

of economic importance. ORDER: Phasmida, CLASS: Insecta, PHYLUM: Arthropoda.

STICKLEBACKS, a family of common freshwater and marine fishes of the northern hemisphere, characterized by the series of sharp spines in front of the soft-rayed dorsal fin. The Three-spined stickleback *Gasterosteus aculeatus* is found in almost every brook and pond in England and is common throughout Europe, across Asia to Japan and in North America. There are, as the name suggests, three spines before the soft dorsal fin and the pelvic fins are each reduced to a single spine. The species reaches a maximum of about 4 in (10 cm) in length.

In spring, the male Three-spined stickleback changes to a bright blue with red on the chest. He then constructs a nest from plant strands which are stuck together with a sticky secretion from the kidneys. The nest is ball-like and the male enters it and makes a large central chamber. The nest may be placed in a hollow on the bottom but nests have also been found in old tins lying in the water. The male defends the nest from other males or from intruders but entices gravid females to enter and deposit their eggs. After the eggs are fertilized, the male guards the nest and aerates the eggs by fanning movements with the pectoral fins, carefully removing any dead or infertile eggs. FAMILY: Gasterosteidae, ORDER: Gasterosteiformes, CLASS: Pisces.

STILTS, wading birds distinguished by their legs which are longer in proportion to body-size than in any other wader and by their small heads and thin, dark, almost straight bills. Their plumage is chiefly black and white, but the Banded stilt *Cladorhynchus leucocephala* also has a chestnut breastband. The latter is confined to Australia while the stilt *Himantopus himantopus* has a world-wide distribution. They are catholic in choice of habitat, feeding in both salt and freshwater lagoons and flooded grassland. The Banded stilt breeds beside temporary salt lakes, feeding on the shrimps found there. FAMILY: Recurvirostridae, ORDER: Charadriiformes, CLASS: Aves.

STINGRAYS *Dasyatis*, ray-like fishes with a venomous spine at the base of the tail capable of inflicting a painful or even fatal wound. The greatly flattened body and wing-like pectoral fins vary in outline from round to triangular or diamond-shaped followed by a thin and whip-like tail that may be longer than the body. The eyes are on top of the head and close behind are the spiracles through which water is drawn to aerate the gills, the latter being on the underside behind the mouth. On the upper side and near to the base of the tail is the sting, a sharp spine with a pair of grooves down the hind edges in which lie the glandular cells that secrete the

Stick insect with every part of its anatomy elongated, giving perfect camouflage.

venom. The spine, which is usually 3–4 in (7·5–10 cm) long but may be up to 15 in (38 cm) in a large fish, is sometimes followed by one to four additional spines. The sting is used solely in defence, the fish lashing the tail from side to side or up and down, sometimes with sufficient force to drive the spine deep into a plank or through a limb. There are about 90 species of stingray, ranging in size from less than 1 ft (30 cm) across the disc of the body to 6–7 ft (1·8–2·1 m). FAMILY: Dasyatidae, ORDER: Hypotremata, CLASS: Chondrichthyes.

STOAT *Mustela erminea* or ermine, a small carnivore closely related to the weasel but slightly larger and readily distinguishable by the longer tail with the characteristic black

tip. Although the sexes are of similar appearance there is a striking size difference: while the male may measure 17·3 in (44 cm) and weigh 15·5 oz (445 gm), the female is rarely over 10·2 in (26 cm) long and may weigh less than 6 oz (170 gm). Confusingly a small female stoat may be the same size as a large male weasel but the tuft of black hair on the tail immediately indentifies the stoat. The back is brown or russet and the underside white or cream coloured with an even line separating the two.

It has a north-temperate range encompassing the forest and tundra zones of Eurasia and North America. In the northern parts of this range, ermines usually take on an overall white colour in winter, after moulting, save for the black tail tip. The ventral surface will often be much yellower than the dorsal, due to the secretions from the anal glands used to mark territorial boundaries. This change in pelage colour can be induced experimentally at any time of the year by lowering the temperature and shortening the number of daylight hours and it would appear that these are the two triggering factors concerned. The stoat lives in woods, hedges, or wherever undergrowth is thick enough to provide sufficient cover. FAMILY: Mustelidae, ORDER: Carnivora, CLASS: Mammalia.

STONE-CURLEWS, large wading birds some of which are alternatively called 'thick-knees', 14–20 in (35–51 cm) long. They are found in Europe, temperate and tropical Africa, Australia and Asia and in tropical America. The northern species migrate to warmer areas for the winter. Birds of open country, they are found on stony or sandy ground, sea-shores, along sandy river-beds and on grassy savannahs. One species, the Southern stone-curlew *Burhinus magnirostris* of Australia, is found in scrub and open woodland. There is evidence that it breeds in cover, but moves into more open areas to feed.

Stone-curlews bear a superficial resemblance to bustards, but their real relationships are with the waders, plovers and gulls. They have long unfeathered legs, long wings and large eyes. They hunt at dusk or by night and they remain crouched in concealment during the daylight hours. When disturbed they run swiftly and their flight is strong, though it is usually brief and infrequent. The plumage is of varied shades of concealing grey, brown and buff, with broad stripes on the side of the head.

The bill is short and plover-like in the seven species of the genus *Burhinus*; longer than the head, heavy and swollen in the Beach stone-curlew *Orthorhamphus magnirostris* from Australia and islands nearby, and similarly long and massive in the Great stone curlew *Esacus magnitrostris* of India, but in this species it is slightly upturned at the tip

The White stork winters in Africa and nests in Europe, choosing houses to do so.

All of the species that have been studied feed on large insects, small reptiles and amphibians, crustaceans, molluscs, worms, nesting birds and small mammals.

A clutch of one or two rounded, cryptically-marked eggs is laid either directly on the ground or in a small unlined hollow. The eggs are incubated by both parents. FAMILY: Burhinidae, ORDER: Charadriiformes, CLASS: Aves.

STORKS, large birds of heavy build, with long legs, long necks, wings that are both long and broad and long, stout, pointed bills which may be either straight or turned up or down. The plumage is commonly black and white, in a bold pattern, and some species have bright red bills and legs. They are related to the herons and ibises.

The family is widely represented in the tropics and subtropics of the Old World and two species breed in the temperate zone of Europe and Asia, performing long migrations from there. A single species is found, not exclusively, in Australia, the Black-necked stork *Xenorhynchus asiaticus*, but there is none in New Zealand. Only three species belong to the New World, and none of them to its higher latitudes.

Storks wade in shallow water or walk in marshes, the long legs and slightly webbed feet being adaptations for this. They mostly find their food in such situations, but some species feed on drier ground. The food consists largely of freshwater animals and of large insects, but three species feed mainly on carrion. Storks fly strongly, with extended neck and trailing legs in most species. Some are notably adept at soaring in thermal air-currents. They tend to be gregarious at all seasons and large flocks may be seen. Various display attitudes can be observed. In a characteristic greeting ceremony between mates at the nest, both birds bend the neck backwards until the head touches the top of the body. Most species are vocally silent, or nearly so, but a noisy clattering of the mandibles is common. FAMILY: Ciconiidae, ORDER: Ciconiiformes, CLASS: Aves.

STORM PETRELS, the smallest of all sea birds, distinct from the albatrosses, shearwaters and true petrels in having the prominent tube-nostrils fused into a single external opening. They are divided into two subfamilies, the Hydrobatinae and Oceanitinae. The former are mainly northerly breeding species which have long pointed wings, usually forked tails and short legs whereas the latter are southern hemisphere forms with shorter and more rounded wings, square tails, slimmer bills and characteristically very elongated legs. All are small being 5–10 in (12–25 cm) long. The long-legged species patter along on the surface of the water while picking up small fishes and planktonic crustaceans. This, and the belief among sailors that they herald rough weather, is responsible for their common name. The other mariners' name of Mother Cary's chickens is thought to come from Mater Cara after the Blessed Virgin Mary. Many of the species breeding in high latitudes have considerable migrations. Wilson's storm petrel *Oceanites oceanicus* breeds all round Antarctica and winters in the tropics and as far north as Britain and Newfoundland.

The chick fledges after about 8–10 weeks. FAMILY: Hydrobatidae, ORDER: Procellariiformes, CLASS: Aves.

STURGEONS, primitive, often large fishes from temperate waters of the northern hemisphere. The skeleton is of cartilage, the scales have been replaced by a series of bony plates or bucklers. The mouth is an underslung, protrusile sucking mouth. Some sturgeons reach well over 20 ft (6 m) in length. Although not related, the sturgeons have a shark-like appearance.

Sunbirds

Sturgeons are found throughout most of the cold and temperate waters of the northern hemisphere, some species living in the sea and migrating up rivers to spawn, while others live permanently in rivers or are landlocked in lakes. There are about 25 species, all slow-moving that browse on the bottom. Fleshby barbels surround the mouth and are used to detect prey (usually bottom-living invertebrates). There is a spiral valve in the intestine, a primitive feature also found in sharks.

The largest is the beluga *Huso huso* of the Volga and the Black and Caspian Seas for which a length of 28 ft (8·4 m) and a weight of 2,800 lb (1,300 kg) have been recorded. A related species, *H. dauricus* from the Amur basin and the Far East, is smaller. The Atlantic sturgeons all belong to the genus *Acipenser*. The largest from the New World is the White sturgeon *A. transmontanus* of the Pacific coasts of North America which now grows to about 300 lb (135 kg) but in the past has been known to reach over 1,200 lb (540 kg). These fishes rarely go to sea until they are almost mature.

The common Atlantic sturgeon *A. sturio* reaches a weight of 700 lb (315 kg), although the males are smaller. They live in the sea and migrate into rivers to spawn. Formerly widespread and occurring in most European rivers, Atlantic populations now survive only in the Guadalquivir in Spain, the rivers of the Gironde in France and Lake Ladoga in the Soviet Union. FAMILY: Acipenseridae, ORDER: Acipenseriformes, CLASS: Pisces.

SUNBIRDS, tiny brilliantly coloured birds, the Old World equivalent of the American hummingbirds, although they cannot match the latter in beauty, powers of flight, or minuteness, and are not related to them. The smallest of the hundred or so species is 3¾ in (10 cm) long, the largest over 8 in (21 cm). All have lightly-built bodies, slim, delicate legs and strong feet. The bill is fine and long and in many species it is strongly curved downwards. The tongue is tubular along part of its length as an adaptation to nectar-feeding, but they also eat small insects. Most male sunbirds are brilliantly coloured with green, purple or bronze metallic colours on the breast and upperparts and a non-metallic, though often colourful, belly. In a few species, such as the widespread Beautiful sunbird *Nectarinia pulchella* of Africa, the central tail feathers are greatly elongated. Female sunbirds are usually dull brown or olive. In some species, the males moult into a dull plumage outside the breeding season and then resemble the females. Many male sunbirds, and some females too, have small patches of bright red, orange, or yellow feathers (called pectoral tufts) on the sides of the breast. Though normally hidden, these tufts can be erected during display.

The greatest variety of sunbirds (66 species)

is found in Africa (Kenya alone boasts 15). There are four species in Arabia, and one reaches Palestine. Sunbirds are widely distributed in the warmer parts of Asia and a small number have reached New Guinea and northern Australia.

Sunbirds are found in many kinds of vegetation: lowland and montane tropical forests, mangrove swamps, savannah and even semi-desert, whenever there are trees or shrubs providing sufficient nectar and insect food. FAMILY: Nectariniidae, ORDER: Passeriformes, CLASS: Aves.

SUNBITTERN *Eurypyga helias*, South American wading bird resembling a small heron. It has a wide distribution, occurring from Mexico south throughout Central and South America to eastern Peru, southeastern Brazil and Bolivia.

Sunbitterns are about 18 in (45 cm) long, have long thin necks, dagger-like bills, long legs, broad tails and broad wings. The plumage is full and soft, almost like that of an owl, and is barred and mottled grey and brown. The crown is black with a distinct white streak above and below the eyes. When the bird spreads its wings a pattern of black, chestnut and yellow becomes visible. On the tail there are two bands of black and chestnut. The eyes are red. The upper mandible is black and the lower one yellow. The feet are orange-yellow.

Sunbitterns live along overgrown creeks and rivers in the tropical rain-forest and are often to be seen wading with slow movements through the shallow water of a creek, stopping suddenly, looking intensely into the water and with a quick dart of the bill seizing prey. Their food consists to a large extent of water insects and their larvae, but they also eat small snails, crabs and fishes. FAMILY: Eurypygidae, ORDER: Gruiformes, CLASS: Aves.

SURGEONFISHES, marine fishes of coral reefs. Their name derives from the little bony keels, often extremely sharp and blade-like, on either side at the base of the tail. In some species these little 'knives' are hinged at the

rear and can thus be erected to point forwards so that care should be taken when handling live specimens. FAMILY: Acanthuridae, ORDER: Perciformes, CLASS: Pisces.

SURINAM TOAD *Pipa pipa*, a tongueless frog of curiously flattened appearance and living wholly in water in the Amazon and Orinoco basins. FAMILY: Pipidae, ORDER: Anura, CLASS: Amphibia.

SWALLOWS, birds with long wings and agile flight that feed almost entirely on insects they catch in the air. They are small, from 3¾–9 in (9·5–22·8 cm) in length, and in a number of species much of this is taken up by the long, forked tail. The plumage is generally dark; black, brown, green, or blue, often with a metallic sheen. Several species show white in the spread tail, and many species are paler on the underside of the body. The neck and legs are short, and the feet small and weak. Swallows perch readily on wires, branches and other vegetation, but due to their leg and foot structure they are clumsy on the ground. In several species the whole of the legs, even the toes, are feathered.

The bill is short, broad, and flattened and can be opened to a very wide gape forming a highly efficient insect trap. It also acts as a trowel for scooping up mud for nest-building.

Swallows are found in both Old and New Worlds. Most species are gregarious and all are migratory. Some of the migrations are of very great length. The European swallow *Hirundo rustica*, for example, may fly 7,000 miles (11,000 km) from northern Europe to South Africa. And, if it survives long enough, it will undertake this journey twice a year. FAMILY: Hirundinidae, ORDER: Passeriformes, CLASS: Aves.

SWANS, large, long-necked aquatic birds closely related to geese. There are only eight species. One, the Coscoroba swan *Coscoroba coscoroba*, may not be a true swan. It is white with black wing-tips, has a shorter neck than the other swans, pink legs and feet and a bright red bill. It breeds in the southern part of South America.

Australian Black swan and a Black-necked swan of South America artificially join company.

Barn swallows winter in the tropics and nest in temperate regions, returning each year to the same nest site.

sunk into the side of the head. However, the European Common swift *Apus apus* is unable to hover and cannot fly for long in small circles. Swifts are poor at manoeuvring and need open spaces for flying. It is on the wing the year round except when nesting.

All species glue the nest structure together with their own saliva. FAMILY: Apodidae, ORDER: Apodiformes, CLASS: Aves.

SWORDFISH *Xiphias gladius*, a large oceanic fish with the snout produced into a powerful, flattened sword. Swordfishes are solitary, worldwide, mainly in tropical oceans but also entering temperate waters, occasionally as far as Iceland. They grow to a weight of 1,500 lb (675 kg). They swim often at the surface with the high but short dorsal fin cleaving the water like the dorsal fin of a shark. Where common they are exploited commercially, usually being caught by harpoon, and are also much sought after by anglers. Swordfish feed on fishes and squids and they also penetrate to depths and feed on deep-sea fishes. FAMILY: Xiphiidae, ORDER: Perciformes, CLASS: Pisces.

SWORDTAIL *Xiphophorus helleri*, a live-bearing cyprinodont fish from Mexico and Guatemala. The lower caudal fin rays in the male are prolonged into a 'sword', which is quite soft and used in sexual display. The female, having given birth to up to 100 young, may change into a male, losing her dark 'pregnancy mark' as the anal fin changes shape and the male sword develops. Such males are fully capable of fathering another 100 or so young. In some strains up to 30% of the females change sex. The change from male to female has never been recorded.

In the wild the swordtail is the 'green sword'. A cross with a reddish individual of the closely related species *X. montezumae* (the Montezuma sword) has produced the Red swordtail. A cross with a Wagtail platy produced the Wagtail sword. FAMILY: Poeciliidae, ORDER: Atheriniformes, CLASS: Pisces.

Two of the seven species of *Cygnus* are found in the southern hemisphere. The Black swan *C. atratus* is confined to Australia, though it has been introduced elsewhere and now flourishes in New Zealand. It is black with white primaries and a red bill. The Black-necked swan *C. melanocorypha* comes from southern parts of South America. It is a white bird with a black neck and head. It has a red bill and knob and is the smallest of the genus. The other five species are all white in adult plumage.

The Trumpeter swan *C. buccinator* breeds in northwestern USA and southwestern Canada. Largely resident, it has been close to extinction but strict protection has enabled it to increase in numbers to its present level of around 1,500 birds. The Whistling swan *C. columbianus* breeds in the high Arctic of western Canada and Alaska and winters largely on the eastern and western seaboard of the United States. Bewick's swan *C. bewickii* also breeds in the high Arctic, across Russia and Siberia, and migrates south for the winter, many then being seen in Europe. The Whooper swan *C. cygnus* breeds largely to the south of the Bewick's breeding areas and in Iceland. The last species, the Mute swan *C. olor*, breeds largely south of the Whooper. It is mainly resident in Europe, but in Asia and in the cooler parts of Europe it may have to leave for warmer regions for the winter.

The downy young, called cygnets, are uniform white or light grey in all species when newly hatched, except for the Coscoroba cygnets which are strongly patterned with black. FAMILY: Anatidae, ORDER: Anseriformes, CLASS: Aves.

SWIFTLET, 20 species of *Collocalia* or Cave swiftlets are distributed through Southeast Asia and parts of the western Pacific. Some nest in huge colonies in caves. The nests of some are used as the basis of 'birds-nest-soup'. Some species find the way to their nests by echolocation in a manner similar to that used by bats. FAMILY: Apodidae, ORDER: Apodiformes, CLASS: Aves.

SWIFTS, small, fast flying birds with very small feet. The wing is long and very narrow so they are extremely fast fliers and are amongst the most aerial of all birds. They catch their food on the wing and at least one species spends the night on the wing. They have small weak bills, but large wide gapes with which they catch insects. The birds are very streamlined, even the eyes being slightly

Male swordtail with young females. The male also started life as a female.

TAHR, close relative of the goat. Males have a characteristic odour, a little different from that of the 'billy-goat'. There is no beard, and the horns are short, highly compressed bilaterally and keeled in front; they are simply backcurved. The Himalayan tahr *Hemitragus jemlahicus* is 36–40 in (90-100 cm) high. Big males weigh 200 lb (90 kg), but females may weigh only 80 lb (35 kg). It has a heavy body, narrow ears and coarse shaggy hair which forms a mane on the neck and shoulders, reaching to the knees. It is brown with a dorsal stripe. It is found along the Himalayas in scrub and forest, from 10–12,000 ft (3,050–3,660 m).

The Arabian tahr *H. jayakari* is small, only 24–26 in (60–65 cm) high, slenderly built, sandy with a dorsal crest but, like the Nilgiri tahr, no mane. It has long shaggy hair, however. It is restricted to the mountains of Oman. FAMILY: Bovidae, ORDER: Artiodactyla, CLASS: Mammalia.

TAILOR-BIRDS, nine species of *Orthotomus* found from India to the Philippines. They are common garden birds named after their method of nest-building, in which leaves are stitched together with fibres to form a pouch. The Australian tailor-bird, or Golden-headed fantail-warbler *Cisticola exilis*, makes a similar nest. FAMILY: Sylviidae, ORDER: Passeriformes, CLASS: Aves.

TAIPAN *Oxyuranus scutellatus*, a slender snake and the largest and deadliest of Australasian snakes, growing to a little over 11 ft (3·4 m) in length. It has a large head distinct from its neck, a relatively slim fore-body and tapered tail. Its fangs are large and its venom one of the most potent neurotoxins known; death is usually caused by paralysis of the nerve centres controlling the lungs and heart. It is reputed to be the world's deadliest snake. Australian taipans are rich brown above and cream below, while those from New Guinea are usually blackish in colouring with a rusty-red stripe along the back.

The taipan is found in northern and northeastern Australia, from coastal rain-forests to the drier inland regions. In New Guinea it is found in the savannah woodlands along the southern coasts. About 16 eggs are laid in a clutch. The taipan is a timid, retiring snake which may become very aggressive when provoked. It may be seen in weather conditions that are too hot for other snakes, and although generally diurnal, it may move about at night if the weather has been excessively hot. It feeds upon small mammals and reptiles.

Specific and polyvalent antivenenes have been developed for the taipan, without which the chances of recovering from a bite are slender. FAMILY: Elapidae, ORDER: Squamata, CLASS: Reptilia.

TAKAHE *Notornis mantelli*, a large, flightless bird of New Zealand. Sub-fossil remains show that it was recently widely distributed, but in the 19th century European settlers found only five specimens. It was thought to be extinct until its dramatic rediscovery in a remote, high, tussock-grassland valley in 1948. It is in danger of extinction with only 300 birds left in an area of 200 sq miles (533 sq km). The takahe does not breed successfully in captivity but attempts are being made to establish it in other parts of New Zealand. FAMILY: Rallidae, ORDER: Gruiformes, CLASS: Aves.

The taipan of Australia reputed to be the most dangerous of all snakes. It is, however, said to be scarce, shy and quick to escape.

A Brazilian tapir on the bank of a stream in the Amazon basin. Tapirs are hoofed animals with a trunk-like snout.

TAKIN *Budorcas taxicolor*, an ungainly-looking goat-antelope related to the musk-ox. 42 in (110 cm) high, weighing 500–600 lb (230–275 kg), takin have a convex face, heavy muzzle, thick neck, short thick legs, humped shoulders and an arched back. The colour is golden to dark brown or black on the flanks and haunches (according to race); the withers are always lighter toned. Calves are black. The horns, found in both sexes, are thick and triangular in section. They are at first upright, then turn out, then up at the tips. Takin are found along the flanks of the mountains from Bhutan through Szechwan to Shensi. They inhabit steep, thickly wooded slopes, most characteristically the dense bamboo and rhododendron jungle at 7–10,000 ft (2,135–3,050 m). They keep in the forest by day, feeding and drinking at open springs, even at hot springs, in the morning and evening. FAMILY: Bovidae, ORDER: Artiodactyla, CLASS: Mammalia.

TAMANDUA *Tamandua tetradactyla*, Prehensile-tailed or the Collared anteater.

It has short coarse hair on the body and on top of the tail near its base, but most of the grasping tail is naked and blotched with irregular markings. Tamanduas typically have a black band encircling the middle of the body and this joins, on the back, a black ring or 'collar' around the neck. Head and legs are tan or cream-coloured. The ears are rounded. Fox-sized, the tamandua has a head and body length of 21–22·5 in (54–58 cm) with a 21 in (54 cm) tail. Tamanduas have the characteristic anteater spout-like snout and long extensile tongue, the diameter of a lead pencil. The nostrils and the tiny mouth are at the tip.

The nails of the hands are long and sharp, particularly those of the middle fingers.

The tamandua ranges from southern Mexico to Argentina and is found in tropical forests. There is a single young carried on the mother's back from birth.

Tamanduas are active mainly at night but often stir in daytime, emerging from their tree hollows in early morning and late afternoon to forage for a variety of ants, tree- and ground-nesting termites, and bees. The insects adhere to the tamandua's tongue made sticky by a coating of viscous saliva when the animal is feeding. In the tamandua part of the stomach is a muscular gizzard, presumably to compensate for the lack of teeth and to permit digestion of hard-shelled ants. FAMILY: Myrmecophagidae, ORDER: Edentata, CLASS: Mammalia.

TANAGERS, 200 species of small colourful birds of the warmer parts of the New World.

Even more colourful are some of the *Tangara*, especially the Paradise tanager *Tangara chilensis*. It is velvety black on its upperparts, while the crown and the sides of the face are green. The lower back is scarlet, the rump yellow and the underparts are mostly turquoise blue with the lower underparts black. As in most tanagers the sexes are alike. They live in groups in tree-tops at forest edges and feed on fruit.

One of the best known is the Blue-grey tanager *Thraupis episcopus*, occurring from southern Mexico south through Central America to Bolivia. It is blue-grey with sky blue wings, the sexes being alike. FAMILY: Thraupidae, ORDER: Passeriformes, CLASS: Aves.

TAPIRS, four species of plump hoofed animals with a short proboscis related to rhinoceroses. The Malay tapir *Tapirus indicus*, the largest, weighs up to 800 lb (360 kg). It is black with a white body and haunches. The white begins behind the forelegs and extends over the rest of the body except for the hindlegs and tail. It is inoffensive, rarely seen, and lives a solitary wanderer's life, following permanent and well-used trails through the forest to water. The three tapirs of Central and South America are all smaller than those of Malaya, more slenderly built, and plain brown, with white tones here and there, but no sharply defined, solid white area. Like the Malay species, however, the young are marked with spots and streaks but at a year old these fade, without being replaced by any adult pattern. FAMILY: Tapiridae, ORDER: Perissodactyla, CLASS: Mammalia.

TARPONS, powerful, silvery fishes, strong swimmers renowned for their fighting powers when hooked. There are two species, the Atlantic tarpon *Tarpon atlanticus* and the Indo-Pacific tarpon *Megalops cyprinoides*. The body is fairly compressed with large silvery scales and there is a single dorsal fin with the last ray prolonged into a thin filament.

Tarpons are not infrequently found in freshwater and sometimes even in foul waters. The Indo-Pacific tarpon reaches 3 ft (90 cm) in length, the Atlantic tarpon 8 ft (2·4 m) and weighs up to 300 lb (135 kg). Like the ladyfish and the tenpounder a tarpon begins life as a ribbon-like leptocephalus larva resembling that of the eels. FAMILY: Megalopidae, ORDER: Elopiformes, CLASS: Pisces.

Tarsier

TARSIER, nocturnal mammal related to lemurs and also to monkeys, apes and man as indicated by its large, forward-directed eyes, its opposable thumb and big toe and its relatively large brain. It is about the size of a rat, with a head and body length of about 5 in (13 cm) and a tail 8 in (20 cm) long, remarkable for being hairless apart from the tip, which has a feather-like arrangement of fine hairs. The tarsier always rests and jumps in a vertical position, typically moving around in bushes and high grass. It can rotate its head through a half-circle and, like a owl, look directly backwards over its shoulder, in order to sight a suitable landing-point for its next jump.

The tarsier ranges from Sumatra to the Philippines. There are three species: the Philippine tarsier *Tarsius syrichta*, the Spectral tarsier *T. spectrum*, of Celebes and neighbouring islands, and Horsfield's tarsier *T. bancanus*, of Sumatra and Borneo. All are mainly insectivorous, but eat some fruits. FAMILY: Tarsiidae, SUBORDER: Prosimii, ORDER: Primates, CLASS: Mammalia.

TASMANIAN DEVIL *Sarcophilus harrisii*, fox-terrier-sized carnivorous marsupial of powerful build with a widely gaping mouth and strong teeth. The muzzle is short and broad and the ears short and rounded. The head and body are about 28 in (70 cm) and the tail about 12 in (30 cm) long. There are five toes on the forefeet and four on the hindfeet each with a strong claw. The body is black with a white band across the chest and sometimes one across the rump. The jaw gape of the Tasmanian devil is wide and the teeth are large and strong.

The Tasmanian devil is now confined to Tasmania where it has been described as rare. Recent studies have, however, shown it to be very abundant over at least some of its former range and it has been implicated in the killing of some domestic animals.

The Tasmanian devil is usually solitary, terrestrial, nocturnal and feeds on mammals and birds, a variety of insects and invertebrate animals and on carrion. The litter size is up to four and the young are born in the autumn of each year. FAMILY: Dasyuridae, ORDER: Marsupialia, CLASS: Mammalia.

TAYRA *Eira barbara*, a South American forest-dwelling member of the weasel family renowned for its swiftness and climbing ability. The single species is distributed over southern Mexico south to Argentina and Paraguay. Tayras have relatively long, slender legs and tails. The very short, coarse fur is sepia or black, save for the brown head and light yellow throat or chest patch which may be speckled with white. The broad head with flat, rounded ears has such a human resemblance that Mexicans refer to the tayra as 'cabeza de viejo' (head of an old man). Adult males are markedly larger and more

Philippine tarsier, remarkable for its large eyes, one of three species of primitive relatives of monkeys, apes and man.

The Tasmanian devil is less aggressive than its name or its appearance would suggest.

The tayra, a South American member of the weasel family.

Tenrecs

muscular than females. Length varies from 38·5–45·3 in (98–115 cm), of which 16 in (40 cm) is tail, and the weight varies from 9–13 lb (4·2–5·8 kg).

Wild tayras have been frequently seen eating bananas and fallen cecropia fruit but they also prey on a variety of animals such as Tree squirrels, agoutis, Mouse opossums, snakes and birds, which are swiftly dispatched with a neck-bite and a shake of the head. When chasing a victim, a tayra may swim but does not do so willingly. Two to four cubs have been found in makeshift grass nests in May. The young, blind and helpless at birth, are covered in sparse black fur, the brown head fur appearing only six months later. FAMILY: Mustelidae, ORDER: Carnivora, CLASS: Mammalia.

TENRECS, related to moles and shrews but with many primitive characters reminiscent of certain marsupials. Half of them have spines, and *Setifer* and *Echinops* closely resemble hedgehogs. *Limnogale* is semi-aquatic and *Microgale* parallels the shrews in its way of life.

Tenrecs range from 2 in (5 cm) to 16 in (40 cm) in length. Some are tailless, but *Microgale* has a very long tail supported by 47 vertebrae, more than in any other mammal, apart from some of the pangolins.

They are found in Madagascar and the adjacent Comoro Islands, where they occupy a variety of habitats from mountain forests to marshes. Most live in burrows and are either crepuscular or nocturnal. They are terrestrial, feeding on a variety of plant and animal foods, but mainly on ground-dwelling invertebrates. *Tenrec* hibernates in the cold dry season, but *Hemicentetes*, at least, is active all the year round. Some tenrecs are among the most prolific of mammals, rivalling even the rodents in having up to 25 young per litter.

The Common tenrec *Tenrec* is 14 in (35 cm) long, with small eyes, triangular ears and no tail. The grey-brown coat consists of stiff bristles and thin spines. It lives in dry bush country and accumulates fat during the summer and hibernates in special burrows during the southern winter (May–October). It mates soon after hibernation ends, and produces 20 or more young in a litter. The young remain in a family group for several weeks during nocturnal feeding forays. FAMILY: Tenriecidae, ORDER: Insectivora, CLASS: Mammalia.

TERMITES, insects closely related to cockroaches, having similar biting mouthparts and an incomplete metamorphosis. They are the most primitive insects to have developed a social system and all termites live in well regulated communities, there being no solitary forms. Each community is made up of several distinct castes. First in importance come the reproductives, the king and queen, or in some cases several pairs together in one

Winged adults, nymphs and eggs of the termite *Neotermes*, species that bore into dry wood.

nest. Then there are the workers and soldiers and juvenile forms in various stages of development. At certain times of the year there are also present numbers of fully winged young adult termites waiting to swarm.

Winged termites vary in size according to species with wing-spans of ½–3½ in (12–87 mm). The head is round or oval with large eyes, two small ocelli, a pair of long antennae.

Worker and soldier termites are sterile individuals of either sex. Soldiers have large, hard heads with strong jaws. A large part of the community is made up of juvenile forms in various stages of growth, all white and thin

A termitarium, housing a termite colony, rising like a ruin of a building.

skinned. A queen termite develops an enlarged abdomen in order to be able to supply eggs in increasing numbers as the community grows. She may reach 7 in (17·5 cm) in length, capable of producing one egg every two seconds.

All families except the Termitidae digest their food with the aid of symbiotic Protozoa. The large mound building termites of tropical Africa and Asia have special fungus gardens in their nests where the food they collect is made palatable by special fungi.

Termites are found in all the warmer regions of the world, but their numbers and variety are greatest in the Tropics.

The mass exodus of flying termites, or swarming, takes place when the weather is suitably warm and moist. After a short time they settle down, choosing any available area of sparse vegetation where they can scurry around in search of a mate. The wings are shed and the pair move off in single file in search of a safe place to dig a simple chamber, either in the ground, or in a crack at the base of a tree, or in some dead wood, and after a few days mate. Then the female lays her first batch of eggs.

Two things in particular are commonly associated with termites—their mounds and the damage they do to woodwork. Large mounds are a feature of the tropical landscape. Some small mounds resemble large mushrooms, others are conical while others leave the ground altogether and are like footballs attached to the trunks and branches of trees. In Northern Australia the tall, slender, wedge-shaped mounds of *Amitermes meridionalis* always point north and south, giving it the common name of 'compass termite'.

Wood is the principal food of termites, and they have become pests of considerable economic importance. The kings of Ancient Egypt spent large sums of money on bringing timber from Asia Minor which was unpalatable to termites and used this for their sarcophagi. Few accounts of travels in the Tropics are without some story of the speed with which termites have eaten items of baggage left on the ground. ORDER: Isoptera, CLASS: Insecta, PHYLUM: Arthropoda.

TERNS, or Sea swallows, birds that resemble gulls, but are mostly smaller and more lightly built, often with long forked tails. They are short-legged with webbed feet and a bill that is long and tapers to a point in all but one species. They all have long, pointed wings. Most are white with a grey back and wings and a black cap on the head in the breeding season, often lost in winter. Some have black upperparts in the breeding season, a few species also having a black breast.

In Britain the Common tern *Sterna hirundo*, the Arctic tern *S. paradisaea* and the Roseate tern *S. dougallii* are mainly coastal birds that feed on small fishes caught by plunging into the water from a height. The Arctic tern is remarkable in that it probably enjoys more hours of daylight each year than any other bird. It breeds as far north as about 82°N

and migrates south in the autumn to winter in Antarctic and subantarctic waters.

Terns are very social birds and often breed in large colonies. They nest either in bare scrapes in the ground, or in flimsy nests made from seaweed and other local materials. The chicks are active and alert within a few hours of hatching and are covered with thick down that is cryptically marked in most species. FAMILY: Laridae, ORDER: Charadriiformes, CLASS: Aves.

TERRAPINS *Malaclemys terrapin*, of North America, are moderate-sized turtles with a carapace up to about 10 in (25 cm) long. The individual scutes of the dorsal carapace are often in the shape of a truncated cone and clearly concentrically grooved, so that in America they are called 'Diamondback terrapins'. They live in the sea and in salt and brackish water lakes along the Atlantic coast.

In Britain almost any small freshwater turtle is likely to be called a terrapin. In the United States many people use the word for any edible freshwater turtle. Strictly speaking it should be reserved for this one species only. FAMILY: Emyidae, ORDER: Testudines, CLASS: Reptilia.

THOMSON'S GAZELLE *Gazella cuvieri thomsoni*, a large gazelle 27–28 in (68–70 cm)

high with a bright reddish coat and a black flank stripe. It has long strongly ringed horns. It is found in Kenya, northern Tanzania and southeastern Sudan. FAMILY: Bovidae, ORDER: Artiodactyla, CLASS: Mammalia.

THREAD WORM, one of the common names used for members of the Nematoda, many of which are slender and thread-like in appearance. The name 'roundworm' is, however, more frequently employed to designate this group of invertebrates.

THRESHER SHARK *Alopias vulpinus* characterized by the enormous upper lobe of the tail, which may be equal to the length of the rest of the body. Thresher sharks are world-wide in tropical and temperate seas, living in the upper waters but with at least one other species found in deep water. It uses its tail to stun or kill fishes and birds at the surface, which it then eats. Threshers reach 20 ft (6 m) in length and may weigh up to 1,000 lb (454 kg). The young are hatched within the uterus of the female and when born are 4½–5 ft (1·2–1·5 m) long. FAMILY: Alopiidae, ORDER: Pleurotremata, CLASS: Chondrichthyes.

THRUSHES, slender-billed songbirds of small to medium size. The plumage is most

Family group of Common terns of Europe. They commonly nest on beaches and sand dunes where the chicks are inconspicuous because of their colouring.

Ticks

often grey or brown but is sometimes chestnut, blue, green, black or pale buff. Some thrushes have long pointed wings, some short rounded wings, with many intermediates. The tail is usually rounded or square, occasionally rather strongly graduated, and it is held erect in some species.

The genus *Turdus* includes about 63 species. European species include the blackbird *T. merula*, the Song thrush *T. philomelos*, the Mistle thrush *T. viscivorus* and the Ring ouzel *T. torquatus*. It also includes the American robin *T. migratorius* a common garden bird in the United States. Thrushes of the genus *Zoothera* are closely related to those in the genus *Turdus* but they have more rounded wings and white bases to the wing feathers. Most are found only in tropical Asia, but White's thrush *Z. dauma* reaches Europe and several species are found only in the New World, including the Varied thrush *Z. naevia* of the western United States and the Aztec thrush *Z. pinicola* of South America.

The female undertakes all the incubation and is given food at the nest by the male in a few species such as the European robin. Incubation is from 13–15 days and the young of most species hatch with a covering of down, which is dark-coloured in the species nesting in the open. The young are fed by both parents and leave the nest after 12–16 days.

Most of the thrushes eat insects but also take spiders, tiny reptiles, worms, snails and other animals. Many take fruit and berries in the autumn and winter. FAMILY: Muscicapidae, ORDER: Passeriformes, CLASS: Aves.

TICKS, annoying parasites of man and domestic animals the importance of which in disease transmission did not become apparent until just prior to the opening of the present century. Studies then which implicated ticks as vectors of a protozoan disease of cattle, Texas cattle fever, focused world attention on the potential danger of this group of arthropods.

The body is not divided. A true head is lacking and the thorax and abdomen are fused producing a sac-like appearance. Ticks should not be confused with the wingless insects such as the Sheep ked, often referred to as the 'Sheep tick'. Ticks differ from mites by their larger size, and in details of their anatomy.

In place of a true head, ticks have a gnathosoma bearing the mouthparts. It consists of a basal portion, a pair of four-segmented palps and a rigid holdfast organ, usually toothed, called the hypostome which serves to anchor the parasite to its host. In addition, a pair of cutting organs or chelicerae permit the tick to cut the skin for the penetration of the hypostome.

The 700 species of ticks are all blood sucking, external parasites of vertebrates including amphibians, reptiles, birds and mammals. The body of ticks is covered with a leathery cuticle capable of great distension as the blood is being forced into the diverticula of the stomach. Some species are capable of ingesting hundreds of times their weight in blood.

Ticks have four stages in their life-cycle: the egg, a 6-legged larva and an 8-legged nymph and adult. ORDER: Metastigmata, SUBCLASS: Acari, CLASS: Arachnida, PHYLUM: Arthropoda.

TIGER *Panthera tigris*, the largest of the cats, but slimmer and narrower in the body than lions. Only an expert can distinguish between the skeletons of the two species. The coat provides a natural camouflage against the patterns of light and shade in the natural surroundings, and it is said that a running tiger in the jungle looks grey against the background. The ground colour is reddish fawn, broken at intervals by dark vertical stripes. The belly is white and there are patches of white on the face. The claws are hooked and retractile.

Fossils show the tiger originated in Siberia and then spread south to occupy most of Asia and parts of the Malaysian Archipelago. Tigers shed their coats seasonally and are intolerant of great heat, indicating that they originated in a colder climate.

They become mature at three years of age, and a tigress will mate approximately every two to two and a half years. The gestation period is 105–115 days, and a litter consists of two to six young, but only one, or perhaps two of the cubs will ever reach maturity. The cubs are blind at birth, but have a fully marked coat and weigh from 2–3 lb (1–1·5 kg). By the time they are six weeks old, the cubs will have been weaned, and at the age of seven months, they will have started to kill for themselves. The males are polygamous, and play little or no part in the rearing of the young, although they may hunt with the mother, thus indirectly contributing to the supply of food.

For the most part, tigers are solitary, although they may occasionally hunt as a pair, one animal driving the prey down to the ambush formed by the hunting partner. Tigers do not roar as much as lions, doing so only briefly when charging or threatening. A surprised tiger will give a 'whoof' of alarm before making off. Another sound has been described as 'belling' because of the similarity to the noise made by the Sambar stag. This sound indicates alarm or uneasiness. Finally, there is a moaning or mewing sound made when the tiger is moving through cover. This appears to be the same as the purr of the domestic cat and may indicate contentment and satisfaction.

Tigers avoid the heat of the day, and will often lie in water to keep cool. They are

The tiger, normally thought of as tropical, originated in northern Asia. Intolerant of intense heat it keeps to the shade as much as possible.

A Tiger snake trying to eat a frog the wrong way round. The snake's eye is green as it is sloughing its skin and the cuticle is everywhere loose.

excellent swimmers. and will return to a kill a number of times. A full grown tiger will eat 40–60 lb (18–27 kg) of meat at one feed in the wild. A tiger will eat almost any animal food, alive or dead but usually kills mammals from pig to buffalo. In India it seems to have a fondness for the Durian fruit. FAMILY: Felidae, ORDER: Carnivora, CLASS: Mammalia.

TIGER SNAKES, a group of closely related Australian snakes of the genus *Notechis*. All are restricted to the coast, ranges and wetter parts of the interior of southern Australia, including Tasmania.

They are relatively heavy, thick bodied snakes with broad, rather massive heads. The Common tiger snake of southeastern Australia, *N. scutatus*, averages only a little over 4 ft (1·2 m) and varies considerably in colour and pattern. It ranges through various shades of grey, brown, reddish or olive to almost black. Typically it has numerous light yellowish cross-bands along its length, but these are often indistinct or absent.

Tiger snakes are normally shy and inoffensive, but react savagely when provoked. The neck is then flattened like that of a cobra while the first quarter or so of the flattened body is held off the ground in a long, low arc. All are highly venomous. They cause a high proportion of the average of only four deaths from snake-bite in Australia each year.

Tiger snakes produce living young, an average litter numbering about 50. The young, about 8 in (20 cm) at birth, are more strongly banded than the adults. FAMILY: Elapidae, ORDER: Squamata, CLASS: Reptilia.

TILAPIA, perch-like fishes of the genus *Tilapia*, found principally in Africa but occurring also in Lake Tiberias and other water masses connected with the northern extension of the African Rift Valley. They are found in lakes, streams and rivers, but some will penetrate into brackish waters. Typically, the body is fairly deep and compressed, with a long dorsal fin (the anterior rays being spiny) and a moderate anal fin. In some species a black spot occurs on the hind part of the dorsal fin, occasionally edged in yellow. This 'Tilapia mark' is not always retained in the adults. *Tilapia* form the basis for large local fisheries. Certain dwarfed species, such as *T. grahami* of Lake Magadi, Kenya, have become adapted to highly alkaline hot springs, while others, for example *T. spilurus*, are typically found in rivers. In good growing conditions, many species will reach at least 12 in (30 cm) and in Lake Rudolf, Kenya, specimens of *T. nilotica* weighing 14 lb (6·3 kg) have been recorded.

Many species of *Tilapia* are mouthbrooders. The male excavates a shallow circular depression 12 in (30 cm) or more in diameter, taking material in his mouth from the centre and spitting it out beyond the rim of the nest. When the nest is complete, the male guards it from intruding males or members of other species by a series of postures and swimming antics, but will go through a special ritual if a female of its own species approaches the nest. When the female has laid the eggs the male discharges sperm over them and eggs and sperm are taken into the mouth of the female. In some species

it is the male that takes up the eggs. The female mouth-brooder then leaves the nest, or is chased away, and thereafter broods the eggs until they hatch, which happens after about 5 days. Even then the fry are retained in the mouth of the parent for some days and when they venture forth in a little cloud they will swim back into the safety of the mouth if alarmed. FAMILY: Cichlidae, ORDER: Perciformes, CLASS: Pisces.

TILEFISH *Lopholatilus chamaeleonticeps*, 3 ft (90 cm) in length, is related to the Sea perches. There is a sharp crest at the back of the head. The body is fairly slender and the anal fin and single dorsal fin are fairly long. It was first discovered in 1879, at the bottom of the Gulf Stream slope of the shores of New England. Three years later, after some extremely severe gales, the course of the Gulf Stream altered and the area in which the tilefishes lived was invaded by a much colder body of water from the Labrador Current. The tilefish is exceedingly sensitive to changes in water temperatures and this sudden cooling was enough to kill off the fishes in millions. In March 1882 an area of some 15,000 sq miles (40,000 sq km) was strewn with dead tilefishes. For the next 20 years no tilefishes were caught and it was presumed that the species was extinct. Then they slowly made a reappearance. FAMILY: Pseudochromidae, ORDER: Perciformes, CLASS: Pisces.

TINAMOUS, 50 species of birds, pheasant-like in plumage and guinea-fowl-like in form. They fly weakly and with reluctance, an

Tinamous are running birds living mainly in South America. They are related to ostriches.

indication of their ancestry, for they are almost certainly related to the large flightless birds such as the ostrich. They do, however, have flight muscles attached to a keeled sternum. These are of appreciable size, but the heart and lungs are very small which accounts for the weak flight. Tinamous sometimes fly into obstacles when flushed, occasionally with serious consequences.

Tinamous are efficient running birds and have a well camouflaged plumage of browns and greys, streaked, spotted or barred. They range widely over South America from southern Mexico to Patagonia and from the tropical rain-forests to 14,000 ft (4,200 m) up in the Andes. They vary in length from 8–21 in (20–53 cm). The body is compact, with a very short tail, and the wings are short and rounded. The legs are strong, and the hind toe is elevated or missing entirely. The neck is quite long and the head is small but often strikingly marked in black and white, or crested. The bill is long, decurved and pointed for feeding on a variety of plant materials and small animals.

The nest is a depression in the ground, poorly lined. The eggs number up to 12. They are always unmarked with a surface sheen resembling polished metal or porcelain and may be green, blue, yellow, purple, black or chocolate. FAMILY: Tinamidae, ORDER: Tinamiformes, CLASS: Aves.

TITS, 50–60 species of small birds distributed throughout the northern hemisphere. The word has been misleadingly used for birds in many different families, for example Bearded tit, Tree tits, Wren tits, Shrike tit, etc. It is an abbreviation of a name 'titmouse', still used to describe one group of these birds in North America, while 'chickadee' is used for the others.

All are small, only the Sultan tit *Melanochlora sultanea* weighing much over ¾ oz (20 gm). While the North American and European species include some that are well known, the Great tit must be amongst the most studied of all wild birds. The great majority are resident, or undergo only short migratory movements. All nest either in holes or in domed nests. They have large clutches, often

of eight or more eggs, which are white with red spots.

The family is currently divided into three subfamilies, the Parinae or true tits, the Aegithalinae or Long-tailed tits and the Remizinae or Penduline tits.

The Penduline tit *Remiz pendulinus* is patchily distributed throughout southern Asia and its range extends into southern and eastern Europe, where it has been increasing in recent years. It has a longish tail, is reddish chestnut above and buff beneath and the head and neck pale grey with a black mask. It is a bird of marshy scrub and reeds. In the summer it feeds itself (and its chicks) on tiny insects. In the winter it supplements its insect diet with small seeds. Its nest, a very soft pouch-like structure with a small tubular entrance at the top, is suspended from small twigs in a bush.

There are six species of Penduline tit in Africa, all occurring south of the Sahara.

There are also eight species of Long-tailed tits. The best known is *Aegithalos caudatus*, which has a wide distribution through Europe and Asia.

The true tits are small, active, arboreal birds, usually fairly tame and easy to see, often quite noisy. The majority have a 'capped' appearance. Usually the cap is black or brown and this is enhanced by white or pale cheeks. A black or dark brown bib is also often present, though not in most of the titmice of North America. Some, including this last group and the European Crested tit *Parus cristatus*, have quite conspicuous crests. There are some 40 or more species and they range over the whole of the area described above for the family. 11 of these are found in North America and nine in Europe.

All species are hole-nesters. Both sexes help to build the nest which is basically of moss and may be lined with grass, feathers, hair, fur etc. The young usually hatch in about 13 days from the start of incubation. The nestling period is about 18–21 days. FAMILY: Paridae, ORDER: Passeriformes, CLASS: Aves.

TOAD, a name referring strictly only to members of the family Bufonidae, but the terms 'frog' and 'toad' are the only common

names available to describe the 2,000 species of the order Anura. Frog is used for those which have smooth skin and live in or near water while toad is used for those which have a warty skin or live in drier habitats. The terms are used independently of the actual relationships of the animals involved. For example, *Bombina bombina* of Europe is known as the Fire-bellied toad, but belongs to the family Discoglossidae, while *Scaphiopus holbrooki*, the Eastern spadefoot toad of America, is a member of the Pelobatidae. The term 'toad' was originally used for the genus *Bufo* which comprises the Common European toad *Bufo bufo* and the American toad *Bufo americanus* so the family Bufonidae can be referred to as the 'true toads'.

When a toad is attacked it does not rely on long rapid jumps for defence but on poison in the warts on its skin. Each wart exudes a milky fluid which acts as an irritant to the mucous membranes of the attacker. Two concentrations of these poison glands form a conspicuous oval ridge behind each eye known as parotid glands.

Toads have a marked homing instinct. Many species rest each day in a particular spot and, if taken and liberated as much as 1 ml (1·6 km) away, rapidly return to it.

Bufo bufo is the Common toad of Europe. It is usually brown in colour, sometimes spotted with dark brown, black or red, and females reach a length of about 3½ in (8·7 cm) and males 2½ in (6·2 cm) although in some warmer areas, probably because of the greater abundance of insect food, larger specimens are found, sometimes reaching a length of about 5½ in (13·7 cm). FAMILY: Bufonidae, ORDER: Anura, CLASS: Amphibia.

TORTOISES, slow-moving, heavily armoured reptiles which first appeared some 200 million years ago and have remained relatively unchanged for 150 million years. The body is enclosed in a box or shell which in many species is rigid and into which the head, tail and limbs can in many instances be withdrawn. The top of the shell, known as the carapace, is formed from overgrown, widened ribs. The lower part of the shell, called the plastron, is also made up of bony plates. Both carapace and plastron are covered with horny plates or shields known as scutes. The males are usually smaller than the females and often have a longer tail and the plastron may be concave.

The order to which tortoises belong used to be called the Chelonia but is now known as the Testudines. The order includes tortoises, turtles and terrapins, three names which tend to be given different meanings in different parts of the English-speaking world, but all have certain fundamental features in common.

For example, they have no teeth, but the jaws are covered with a horny bill which can be used for tearing food apart. They have moveable eyelids which are closed in sleep. Their external ear openings are covered with a membrane and it is doubtful if the Testudines can hear airborne sounds but like snakes they probably can pick up vibrations through ground or through water. They all lay eggs and the aquatic species must come ashore to lay them. In temperate climates land tortoises hibernate in the ground and freshwater species under mud at the bottoms of ponds. As a group they are noted for their long life-spans, the longest recorded being in excess of 158 years, for one of the Giant tortoises, but even the Garden tortoise has been recorded as living 50 years or more. ORDER: Testudines, CLASS: Reptilia.

TOUCANS, 37 species of South American birds, with heavy bodies and long and often bulky bills. They vary from 12–24 in (30–60 cm) in length, most species having a bold pattern of black, yellow, orange, red, green, blue or white plumage, in one combination or another. The most arresting feature of the larger species of toucans is the huge bill. This may be 6 in (15 cm) long, 2 in (5 cm) deep and coloured in gaudy patterns, often of orange, red or yellow. The smaller species tend to have duller plumage-patterns and smaller bills. The sexes are alike in plumage in nearly all species and both sexes of most of them have a patch of bare skin round the eye. All toucans are heavy-bodied birds with rounded wings, a rather long graduated tail and short strong legs, with stout feet of the zygodactyl pattern—that is with two toes pointing forwards and two back.

They are birds of the woodlands and forests of Central and South America, found from Vera Cruz southward to Paraguay and northern Argentina. All of them are primarily fruit-eaters, though some species have been recorded taking large insects, small snakes and the nestlings of other birds. The huge bill may serve one or more functions: it is probably used to reach fruit that is far out on thin twigs; it may help in intimidating other birds that might rob toucans' nests were it not for this defence; and it may be used in display.

Nests are in tree holes, either natural ones caused by decay, or those excavated by other birds. FAMILY: Ramphastidae, ORDER: Piciformes, CLASS: Aves.

TRAPDOOR SPIDERS, spiders which dig deep burrows the entrances to which are closed with a hinged door carefully camouflaged with moss or debris. This may be thin like a wafer or thick like cork and formed of earth and silk. Some burrows have a branch burrow closed by a second trapdoor. The doors serve as protection from rain and dust, from excessive heat and dryness and from the entrance of enemies. The spider holds the door firmly closed during the day but darts out to attack passing insects, chiefly at night.

Trapdoor spiders are found in all tropical and the warmer temperate regions including southern Europe. *Atypus affinis*, the only mygalomorph spider in Britain, has wrongly been called the Trapdoor spider. A closed silk tube extends from its burrow, which has no lid. SUBORDER: Mygalomorphae, ORDER: Araneida, CLASS: Arachnida, PHYLUM: Arthropoda.

TREECREEPERS, small, dull-coloured birds which obtain their food by climbing along the trunks and branches of trees, usually in an upward direction.

There are six typical treecreepers of the genus *Certhia*. Three are confined to Southeast Asia around the Himalayan region. The fourth and fifth together have a circumpolar range, the Common treecreeper *C. familiaris* through the temperate forests of Eurasia and *C. americana* replacing it in similar regions of North America, the two apparently differing only in voice. The sixth is the Short-toed treecreeper *C. brachydactyla* of southern Europe which overlaps the range of the Common treecreeper *C. familiaris*. They differ in both feet and voice and where they overlap the former tends to occupy deciduous forest, the latter conifers. The North American species occupies both habitats.

Typical treecreepers are small birds with large feet and fairly long, slender, decurved bills for probing in crevices for insects. The tail feathers have strong shafts and spiny tips and pressed against the tree, act as a prop to support the bird. The upper plumage is brown and streaky, the underside white.

Treecreepers roost in hollows in the bark of tree-trunks, sometimes scraping their own hollows in the spongy bark of a Sequoia. A nest of moss, twigs and bark is built in the narrow cavity behind a loose piece of bark. FAMILY: Certhiidae, ORDER: Passeriformes, CLASS: Aves.

TREEFROGS, tailless amphibians, usually living in trees, with adhesive discs at the tip of each finger and toe for clinging to vertical surfaces. *Hyla arborea*, the European treefrog, is found throughout Europe and most of Asia. It is about 1¾ in (43 mm) long, bright green with a dark stripe, edged with yellow, running along the side of the body. It spends the day sitting on leaves, relying on its coloration for protection. If approached it does not jump away but crouches lower onto the leaf. It leaps at any insect which flies within reach, catching it in its mouth. In jumping it takes no account of its height above the ground or the position of other leaves and depends on its outstretched hands and feet catching onto a leaf or twig to break its fall. Most of its hunting, however, is done at night when it is more active.

It hibernates in the mud at the bottom of ponds and breeds in April and May. About 800–1,000 eggs are laid in several lumps

attached to water plants below the surface of the water. The tadpoles reach a length of about 2 in (5 cm) and change into frogs after about three months.

There are several hundred species of *Hyla* but they are all rather similar in habits to the European treefrog. There is, however, considerable variation in the general shape and colour. About 21 species of *Hyla* occur in Australia. Several of them are able to live in the hot, dry parts. *H. caerulea* for example, can tolerate a loss of water equivalent to 45% of its body weight while *H. moorei* from the more temperate areas can only tolerate a 30% loss. FAMILY: Hylidae, ORDER: Anura, CLASS: Amphibia.

TREE HOPPERS, leaf-sucking insects related to Spittle bugs, cicadas and Leaf hoppers. The adults and nymphs are, like aphids, often attended by ants and they exude 'honey-dew'. They lay their eggs in slits which they cut in twigs and they guard their young when the eggs hatch. They are powerful jumpers. FAMILY: Membracidae, ORDER: Hemiptera, CLASS: Insecta, PHYLUM: Arthropoda.

TREE-SHREWS, small, squirrel-like mammals with a head and body length of 9 in (22 cm) and a bushy tail of 8 in (20 cm). The Malay name 'tupai' is used for both tree-shrews and squirrels, underlining their close resemblance.

The common tree-shrew is arboreal, constructing nests with leaves and mosses in hollow trees, but it also spends much time searching for fruit and insects in the leaf-litter of the forest floor. All members of the tree-shrew family are restricted to the rain-forests of southeast Asia, where they occupy different ecological niches.

The Common tree-shrew *Tupaia glis* and the Indian tree-shrew *Anathana ellioti* both have a balanced diet of fruit and insects, collected by foraging. The diet is reflected in the dentition which is of small pointed teeth at the front for trapping and killing insects, and poorly developed molar teeth at the back for grinding soft fruit and insect carcasses.

All tree-shrews have a small number of offspring (one to three) in each litter, and birth takes place in a convenient hollow in a tree or an abandoned rodent burrow, which is lined with leaves a few days beforehand.

The relationships of tree-shrews to other mammals are not yet clear. They were at first classified with the Insectivora and later with the Primates, but recent studies indicate that they should be placed in a separate order, characterized by the retention of many primitive characters. FAMILY: Tupaiidae, ORDER: Tupaioidea, CLASS: Mammalia.

TREE SNAKES, very slender snakes living in trees in Malaya and the East Indies. They are reputed to launch themselves and glide from trees to the lower bushes and are sometimes referred to as flying snakes, especially the species of *Chrysopelea*. The Golden tree snake *C. ornata* can climb a tree by forcing the sides of its body against irregularities in the bark, as if crawling up a shallow trench. In this it is helped by its belly scales being keeled at their sides. Tree snakes have only a weak venom and some species at least also constrict their prey. FAMILY: Colubridae, ORDER: Squamata, CLASS: Reptilia.

TREE SPARROW *Passer montanus*, closely related to the House sparrow but more elegant and just slightly smaller. It can be identified readily by the chestnut crown and white cheeks marked with black in both sexes. In some parts of their range Tree sparrows tend to be local and not very abundant. Their habits are similar to those of the House Sparrow and in parts of Asia Tree sparrows tend to be more numerous than the House sparrow. FAMILY: Ploceidae, ORDER: Passeriformes, CLASS: Aves.

TRIGGERFISHES, marine fishes of warm seas related to the trunkfishes and pufferfishes. The common name derives from the trigger-like action of the enlarged first dorsal spine which can be locked in the upright position by the much smaller second dorsal spine. With the spine locked, the fish is both difficult to remove from rock crevices and difficult for a predator to swallow. The body is deep and compressed, and is covered by small bony plates. The mouth is terminal and small. The triggerfishes are often brightly coloured with grotesque colour markings that contrast with their dignified movement around the reefs. There are about 30 species, the largest rarely exceeding 2 ft (60 cm) in length. They have powerful teeth with which they crush molluscs and crustaceans. FAMILY: Balistidae, ORDER: Tetraodontiformes, CLASS: Pisces.

TROGONS, brightly-coloured, arboreal birds of tropical forests. There are 34 species, all similar in appearance and 9–13 in (23-33 cm) long. They are found throughout the tropics. They are stout, heavy-bodied birds with fairly large heads and distinctive long, broad tails. Their characteristic posture is relatively upright on a perch, squatting close to it with tail hanging down vertically or at times tilted slightly forwards below the perch. This is due in part to the small legs and feet. The large dark eyes are capable of good vision in poor light. The bill is short, very broad, with serrated edges.

The colouring is usually bold. The breast, belly and under-tail coverts of males are frequently bright red, pink, orange or yellow; and these areas are similar but sometimes paler or more subdued on females. On males the rest of the plumage tends to contrast with

The triggerfish *Rhinecanthus aculeatus* is known in Hawaii as the humuhumu-nukunuku-a-puaa.

the underside; the back from head to tail, and the upper breast and head, being glossy, sometimes black, but more often glossed with purple, blue or green, the last often vivid and metallic, sometimes with gold or bronze tints.

Trogons are mainly forest birds, darting from the perch and hovering to snatch insects and other small creatures, including treefrogs, from branches or the air, while growing fruit are plucked from the stems. They are usually solitary except when nesting. Trogons nest in unlined holes in trees. The Gartered trogon *Trogon violaceus* utilizes papery arboreal wasp-nests into which the pair tunnel after eating the wasps. FAMILY: Trogonidae, ORDER: Trogoniformes, CLASS: Aves.

TROUPIALS, a diverse family of perching birds notable for its remarkable adaptive radiation. It includes the cowbirds, oropendolas, caciques, grackles, American blackbirds, American orioles or true troupials, meadowlarks, and the bobolink *Dolichonyx oryzivorus*. FAMILY: Icteridae, ORDER: Passeriformes, CLASS: Aves.

TROUT, members of the salmon family found in the freshwaters of the northern hemisphere. There is no scientific basis for the distinction between trouts and salmons and the names are merely applied by common usage. In England, the name trout refers to the Brown trout *Salmo trutta* (a member of the

same genus as the Atlantic salmon, *S. salar*), while in the United States the word trout applies to Rainbow trout *S. gairdneri*, Cutthroat trout *S. clarki* and several other species, while Brook trout, Great Lake trout and so on refer to members of the genus *Salvelinus* (otherwise termed chars).

The Brown trout is a solid, powerful fish, usually spotted but with great variability in the number, size and colour of the spots. The mouth is large and toothed. These are swift, active fishes that favour highly oxygenated and cool waters.

The breeding habits and time of spawning of Brown trout are similar to those of the Atlantic salmon. FAMILY: Salmonidae, ORDER: Salmoniformes, CLASS: Pisces.

TRUMPETFISHES, specialized warm-water fishes related to pipefishes and Sea horses and placed in the single genus *Aulostoma*. They have elongated bodies with long flat snouts and a series of isolated spines bearing membranes in front of the dorsal fin. The dorsal and anal fins are set far back on the body. These fishes rarely grow to more than 2 ft (60 cm). They use their long snouts to ferret out small fishes and crustaceans around coral reefs and are adept at camouflage, frequently hiding head down amongst the coral. Dr Hans Hass saw a trumpetfish shoot out of hiding to lay itself along the back of a parrotfish. The latter tried to dislodge its companion, but without success until they neared the next coral head, when the trumpet-fish swam quickly to safety. FAMILY: Fistulariidae, ORDER: Gasterosteiformes, CLASS: Pisces.

TRUNKFISHES or boxfishes, fishes belonging to the genus *Ostracion*, the head and body of which are enclosed in a solid box of bony plates with only the fins, jaws and the end of the tail projecting and free to move. In cross-section the box-like body is triangular, rectangular or pentagonal, the underside being flat. There are several species, growing to 20 in (50 cm) found around the coral reefs and coasts of the Indo-Pacific area. Since the body is rigid, swimming can only be accomplished by sculling movements of the paired fins, with the pectoral fins helping to stabilize what would otherwise be highly erratic movements. Many of the trunkfishes are brightly coloured with patterns and spots which probably serve to warn predatory fishes that the owner is not edible. When trunkfishes are attacked they secrete a virulent poison into the water. FAMILY: Ostraciontidae, ORDER: Tetraodontiformes, CLASS: Pisces.

TSETSE FLY, one of the greatest scourges of tropical Africa, the only important agent capable of transmitting human sleeping sickness from person to person. Tsetse flies are true, two-winged flies and in general appearance and in structure are very similar to House flies, except that the mouthparts are highly adapted for piercing the skin of man and other mammals and sucking blood. The mouthparts form a prominent, forward pointing proboscis consisting of a lower lip or labium with a tip for rasping and piercing, and which bears in its grooved surface the needle-like labrum-epipharynx and hypopharynx. The first conveys blood from the host animal into the insect's gut and the hypopharynx carries the saliva which, as in other blood sucking insects, is an anticoagulant which prevents clogging of the delicate mouthparts. When the tsetse is at rest the wings are folded one on top of the other over the back, whereas most other similar flies rest with the wings spread laterally. Tsetse fly species range in size from about the House fly up to larger than blowflies. They occur in Africa south of the Sahara and north of South Africa, within the Tropics of Cancer and Capricorn, except that a single species has a foothold in southwest Arabia.

Tsetse fly larvae are born fully grown and ready to change into pupae. The female ripens only a single egg at a time and after fertilization this comes to rest in the uterus. When the larva hatches, it is nourished by a secretion from special nutritive glands, which it imbibes directly from a papilla or nipple. The female deposits her fully developed larva (a maggot) in the shade of a tree, shrub or log, depending on the species and the climate of the area. Immediately after this, the whitish larva burrows into dry, loose soil or under ground-litter and changes into a dark brown pupa with two prominent knobs on the posterior end. The adult flies may live for upwards of 70 days but the average length of life is only about four weeks. Although a female Tsetse fly may deposit a maximum of only twelve larvae, frequently less, in the course of her life, the task of eliminating this most harmful species has, up to the present time, proved impossible in spite of massive research over half a century. FAMILY: Muscidae, ORDER: Diptera, CLASS: Insecta, PHYLUM: Arthropoda.

TUATARA *Sphenodon punctatus*, belonging to the otherwise extinct reptilian order, Rhynchocephalia, virtually extinct about 100 million years ago, now restricted to 20 islands off the coast of New Zealand. The Maori word tuatara means 'peaks on the back' and this describes the triangular folds of skin which form a conspicuous crest down the back and tail of the male. Tuataras vary in colour from black-brown to dull green, while some may have a reddish tinge. The upper part of the body is covered with small scales that may have small yellow spots. The feet have five toes each with sharp claws and are partially webbed. A vestigial third 'eye' is found on the top of the head in very young animals, but soon becomes covered over, and is invisible in adults. It may be this acts as a register of solar radiation and controls the time the creature spends in the sunlight.

The tuatara spends most of the daytime in its burrow leaving it only occasionally to sunbathe, mainly in late winter and spring. It is therefore largely nocturnal and is active at temperatures which are much lower than those favoured by lizards. Available reports indicate that the tuatara may be active at temperatures as low as 45°F (7°C) and, further, that even in winter it only hibernates lightly. Allied to its low body temperature is the very low metabolic rate. This means that it requires very little energy to keep the vital body processes, such as excretion and digestion, 'ticking over'. The tuatara is reputed to grow very slowly and probably does not breed until it is 20 years old. Growth may continue beyond the age of 50 and estimates of the life span vary from about 100 to 300 years.

Pairing usually takes place in January but the sperm is stored within the female until October-December. She then scoops out a

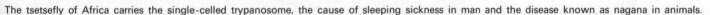

The tsetsefly of Africa carries the single-celled trypanosome, the cause of sleeping sickness in man and the disease known as nagana in animals.

Tuna fishes

Livingstone's turaco of East Africa, one of the so-called plantain-eaters.

shallow nest in the ground and lays 5–15 eggs with soft white shells. These remain in the nest for a further 13–15 months before hatching, the longest incubation period known for any reptile.

The tuatara is capable of digging its own burrow, but seems to prefer, ready-made ones, and therefore frequently shares a burrow with a seabird.

Subfossil remains show that the tuatara was originally found in a number of parts of the North and South Islands of New Zealand, but they have long since disappeared from the mainland. The species is very strictly protected by the New Zealand Government. FAMILY: Sphenodontidae, ORDER: Rhynchocephalia, CLASS: Reptilia.

TUNA FISHES or tunnies, large oceanic members of the mackerel family. Almost every feature of the tunas seems to be adapted for their life of eternal swimming. The body is powerful and torpedo-shaped, the dorsal and pectoral fins fold into grooves and the eyes are flush with the surface of the head, all of which help to reduce the drag caused by turbulent eddies as the fish cleaves the water. Behind the second dorsal and the anal fins are small finlets that may serve to control the formation of eddies, while the sides of the caudal peduncle, or base of the tail, bear little keels for further streamlining. One remarkable feature of these large fishes is that the energy expended in fast swimming warms the blood to a few degrees above that of the surrounding water. The tunas are carnivorous fishes that feed on pelagic organisms and especially on squid. They are mostly tropical in distribution. There are six species of great tuna in the world: the albacore *Thunnus alalunga*, the yellowfin *T. albacares*, the blackfin *T. atlanticus*, the bigeye *T. obesus*, the bluefin *T. thynnus* and the longtail *T. tonggol*.

The bluefin of the Mediterranean and the Atlantic, often known as the tunny, is a large species that reaches 14 ft (4·3 m) and may weigh up to 1,800 lb (816 kg). FAMILY: Scombridae, ORDER: Perciformes, CLASS: Pisces.

TURACOS, a family of 20 species of active and often highly-coloured fruit-eating arboreal birds, sometimes known as plantain-eaters or louries. They occur in Africa south of the Sahara in all habitats containing trees, from dry thornbush and gallery forest to dense evergreen forests. They are related to the cuckoos, and are fairly large, 14–18 in (35–45 cm) long, with fairly slender bodies, rather long tails and short rounded wings. The legs are rather long, with a reversible outer toe, and the birds run and leap among the branches of the trees with great agility, in contrast to the poor powers of flight. The

The turbot, large flatfish of European waters, ranked by many people as the finest flavoured of all sea fish. It feeds on many kinds of other bottom-living fishes.

head is often crested, the crest varying from hairy tufts or rounded domes to slender tapering structures rising to a point at the front, or to a coronet of feathers as in the Great blue turaco *Corythaeola cristata*. The bill is stout, somewhat broad, and slightly decurved and may be very deep, with a high arched culmen, and boldly coloured in yellow and red in some species, black in others. FAMILY: Musophagidae, ORDER: Cuculiformes, CLASS: Aves.

TURBOT *Scophthalmus maximus*, a large flatfish from the North Atlantic. The turbot is one of the flatfish species that rests on its right side, the left side being pigmented and bearing the eyes. It is a shallow water species found in the Mediterranean and all along European coasts. The body is diamond-shaped, with large symmetrical jaws lined with sharp teeth. There are no scales on the body but the 'eyed' side is covered by warty tubercles. The turbot is mostly found on sandy bottoms in water of 10–200 ft (3–60 m). Turbot are avid fish-eaters. They grow to over 40 lb (18 kg) in weight. FAMILY: Bothidae, ORDER: Pleuronectiformes, CLASS: Pisces.

TURKEYS, large game birds. The Common turkey *Meleagris gallopavo* of North America occurs in open woodland and scrub. This is the domestic turkey. Its brown, barred plumage is glossed with bronze. The head and neck are naked and coloured red and blue, with wattles and a fleshy caruncle overhanging the bill. A tuft of bristles hangs from the breast. In display the wattles swell and the colour intensifies, the tail is erected and fanned, the body feathers ruffled and the wings drooped until the tips sweep the ground. The male's call is the noisy 'gobbling' while the female has a softer sharp note. The wild turkey is a strong flyer. It feeds on a variety of seeds, nuts and small creatures. It is polygamous, females laying their eggs in shallow scrapes in well-concealed situations. FAMILY: Meleagrididae, ORDER: Galliformes, CLASS: Aves.

TURNSTONES, wading birds usually found on rocky sea-shores. They are dumpy, short-billed and fairly short-legged birds, less than 12 in (30 cm) long, and the sexes are alike. The Ruddy turnstone *Arenaria interpres* has a circumpolar breeding distribution, chiefly to the north of the Arctic Circle, while the Black turnstone *A. melanocephala* replaces it in Alaska, on the coast of the Bering Sea. The turnstone is among the world's most northerly breeding birds (to at least 83°N). The species get their name from their habit of turning over small stones and shells to search for the small insects, marine worms and shell-fishes which form their normal diet. FAMILY: Scolopacidae, ORDER: Charadriiformes, CLASS: Aves.

TURTLES, MARINE, differ from land tortoises and terrapins, in the shape of the limbs, which have developed into flat flippers. The head and neck cannot be completely withdrawn within the shell. Seven species are known, most of which are dealt with under separate entries. The genus *Chelonia* contains two species: the Green turtle *Chelonia mydas*, occurring in all tropical and subtropical seas, and the Flatbacked turtle *Chelonia depressa*, which is found only along the north and east coasts of Australia. The Green turtle is the larger of the two; the carapace may reach a length of 55 in (1·4 m). It is this species that is in demand for preparing turtle soup; for this one uses not only the meat, but also the gelatinous cartilage ('calipee'), which fills the openings between the bones of the plastron. The *Chelonia* species are mainly vegetarian.

The Loggerhead turtle *Caretta caretta* has the snout covered with two pairs of pre-frontals, which often have one or more scales wedged in between them. Its general colour is reddish brown above, yellowish below. The Loggerhead occurs in all oceans, also in the tropics, but it is more common in the sub-tropics, where it breeds. It is often found far from land in mid-ocean and on its wanderings it comes to temperate seas; it is a fairly regular visitor to the Atlantic coasts of Europe, and it even has been found at Murmansk in northern Russia. ORDER: Testudines, CLASS: Reptilia.

Hawksbill turtle, source of tortoiseshell, now happily being replaced by synthetic products.

UAKARI *Cacajao*, two species of agile, shaggy-haired monkey living in South America, related to the sakis. FAMILY: Cebidae, ORDER: Primates, CLASS: Mammalia.

UMBRELLABIRDS, crow-sized birds living in the forests of South America. There are three species: the Bare-necked umbrellabird *Cephalopterus glabricollis* living in Panama and Costa Rica, the Long-wattled umbrellabird *Cephalopterus penduliger* found in Colombia and Ecuador and the Amazonian umbrellabird *Cephalopterus ornatus* which has the widest distribution, occurring in Guyana, Venezuela, Colombia, Ecuador, Peru, Brazil and northern Bolivia.

The Amazonian umbrellabird is the best known and is largely black with a steel blue gloss on the large tuft of feathers which forms a crest on the head and on a large pendent lappet of feathers on the throat. The sexes are alike but the female is somewhat smaller. They have a strange display in which the males spread their umbrella-like crests and the glossy lappet on the breast is dilated and waved. One of the very few nests to be found was an open cup of sticks in a tree and contained a single egg which was incubated by the female alone. FAMILY: Cotingidae, ORDER: Passeriformes, CLASS: Aves.

VICUÑA *Lama vicugna*, a member of the camel family living in the western High Andes, is regarded by some people as the original form of the domesticated alpaca. It is the smallest, most graceful and most agile of the four *Lama* types, having a shoulder height of 2½ ft (75 cm). Vicuñas have a uniform, short-haired coat, reddish in colour, and a white blaze on the chest. The lower incisors, in contrast to all the others of the camel family, have an open root—as in rodents— and thus grow continuously. In captivity, for lack of wear, they often project considerably from the muzzle. FAMILY: Camelidae, SUBORDER: Tylopoda, ORDER: Artiodactyla, CLASS: Mammalia.

VIREOS, 20 or so species of small nondescript perching birds, 4–7 in (10–18 cm) long, mostly grey or brown above and white or yellow below. They have rather heavy, slightly hooked bills. Most vireos are forest dwelling birds preferring the shrub level although a number are arboreal, haunting the crowns of broad-leaved trees. The Grey vireo *Vireo vicinior* lives in scrub where there are no trees and a few others inhabit thickets with little well-grown timber.

Vireos are widespread in Central and North America, occurring as far north as subarctic Canada. The northern populations are migratory, wintering in Central and South America south to Central Argentina. Only a few vireos breed in South America and these are all widely distributed in North America.

Most vireos feed in a leisurely fashion, moving slowly through the tree or shrub and picking insects in a deliberate manner from the undersides of leaves. They often hang from a branch or stretch out to search the more inaccessible places. FAMILY: Vireonidae, ORDER: Passeriformes, CLASS: Aves.

VISCACHAS, South American rodents closely related to the chinchilla and more distantly to the Guinea pig. The two groups of viscachas, the Plains viscacha *Lagostomus maximus* and the Mountain viscachas, *Lagidium*, are superficially very different and occupy quite different habitats, as their names indicate, but they resemble each other in many details of structure and way of life.

The hanging nest of a vireo is constructed of plant materials and spiders' webs.

The single species of Plains viscacha is perhaps the most familiar rodent in Argentina. It is a large, heavily built animal, about 2 ft (60 cm) long, with a short tail about a quarter of the body length. The most striking feature is the disproportionately large head, accentuated by bold horizontal black and white lines on each cheek. The rest of the pelage is grey above and white below and the texture is coarse in contrast to the chinchilla. FAMILY: Chinchillidae, ORDER: Rodentia, CLASS: Mammalia.

VOLES, mostly small mouse-sized rodents with short tails and blunt snouts which, with the lemmings, constitute a very distinctive subfamily, Microtinae. In outward appearance voles are generally distinguished from mice by their shorter tails, less-pointed snouts and long, dense coats, but one of the most important differences is not so easily visible and concerns the molar teeth. These number three in each row, as in the majority of mice, but in most species of voles, molars, like the incisors of all rodents, grow throughout life without developing roots.

Voles are prolific breeders. Especially in the northern parts of Eurasia and America, voles tend to undergo periods of abundance and scarcity, usually with a remarkably regular cycle of four years.

The Bank voles or Red-backed voles, *Clethrionomys*, feed on soft leaves, berries and some insects and live especially in the shrubby undergrowth in woodland. The best known are the Bank vole *Clethrionomys glareolus*, in Eurasia, and the Red-backed vole *C. gapperi*, in North America.

The Field voles and Meadow voles, *Microtus*, are more specialized grassland species, and the most often reach plague densities. *Microtus arvalis* is the most common species in Europe, making conspicuous burrows in meadows. The only species in Britain, the Field vole *Microtus agrestis* lives in longer grass and burrows less. It can cause serious damage by barking young trees in plantations.

The Water vole *Arvicola terrestris* is about the size of a Brown rat. Water voles are confined to Eurasia and live especially on the banks of rivers and lakes where there is an abundance of waterside vegetation. FAMILY: Cricetidae, ORDER: Rodentia, CLASS: Mammalia.

VULTURES, two groups of large diurnal birds of prey not closely related: the New World vultures, the Cathartidae and the Old World vultures of the warmer parts of Europe, Asia and Africa. Their heads and necks are partly or wholly naked. Since, with few exceptions, they do not kill their own prey, they lack powerful grasping feet. The claws are short and blunt, more adapted to walking than to killing. Several have specialized tongues, to feed rapidly on soft flesh or perhaps extract bone marrow. All

Lammergeiers or bearded vultures, birds that tend to scavenge near human settlements.

are large, adapted for soaring. New World vultures include condors, the largest flying birds, but some of the Old World species are nearly as large, weighing more than 15 lb (6½ kg) and spanning 8 ft (2·5 m). The smallest, but not the weakest, is the Egyptian vulture *Neophron percnopterus*.

New World vultures differ from the Old World species in having 'pervious' nostrils, opening through the bill at the point. The hind toe is rudimentary, placed above the three front toes on the leg. They have large olfactory chambers and, apparently, some sense of smell, though this is not used to locate prey. In America leaks in gas pipe-lines are sometimes located by circling vultures, attracted by a small amount of vile smelling chemical added to the gas.

The seven species of New World vultures include the two huge condors, *Vultur* and *Gymnogyps*, the extraordinary King vulture *Sarcorhamphus papa*, brown and white in adult plumage, with brilliant orange, red, blue and purple bare skin on head and neck, the Turkey vulture *Cathartes aura*, widespread in North America, two other *Cathartes* species and the rather small, but locally abundant, Black vulture *Coragyps atratus*. All eat flesh, but the Black vulture is also said to eat decaying or over-ripe vegetable matter.

Old World vultures include 13 species. Two species, the Egyptian vulture and the lammergeier *Gypaetus barbatus*, have more heavily feathered heads and more powerful feet than is typical. Both are remarkable, specialized birds, the Egyptian vulture being a tool-user, using a stone to hammer open ostrich eggs, and the lammergeier, the avian equivalent of the hyaena, feeding largely on bones. The Hooded vulture *Necrosyrtes monachus*, common in most of Africa south of the Sahara, is relatively small, but still a

large bird. It is a scavenger, especially around human dwellings, and is the only African vulture found much inside forests. The typical, gregarious, carrion-feeding vultures of the genus *Gyps* include seven species occurring in open, or mountainous country throughout southern Europe, Asia and Africa. They are collectively known as White-backed vultures and griffons. Finally, there are four very large, more specialized vultures, of more solitary habits: the European Black vulture *Aegypius monachus*, the largest bird of prey in the Old World, almost as big as a condor; the African Lappet-faced and White-headed vultures, *Torgos tracheliotus* and *Trigonoceps occipitalis*; and the Asian Black vulture *Sarcogyps calvus*, black with a bright red head and neck.

New World vultures find their prey mainly or exclusively by sight, not smell. Vultures can see a large carcass, or each other, from several miles.

At a carcass gregarious griffons establish a dominance hierarchy. The hungriest thrust their way to the food with bounding, wing spreading or foot-stretching threat displays. They dominate very briefly and ability to gulp food rapidly is an advantage here. Other vultures wait their chance to replace the dominants and there are usually one or two groups of fully-fed birds resting close by. Up to a hundred vultures often feed on one carcass, and they may travel 100 miles (160 km) to reach food. They do not maintain any individual or group feeding territory.

The lammergeier feeds on bones and is known as the 'bone-breaker' in much of its range. It carries the bones to a height, approaches downwind to drop them on a chosen slab and alights upwind to pick up the fragments. FAMILIES: Cathartidae and Accipitridae, ORDER: Falconiformes, CLASS: Aves.

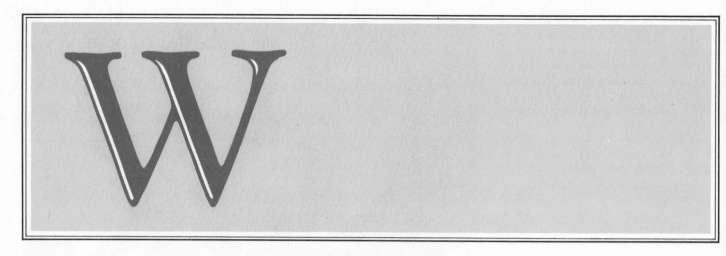

WAGTAILS, Old World group of small birds, usually found near water, deriving their name from their habit of wagging their long tails rapidly up and down (or side to side in one species—the Forest wagtail *Dendronanthus indicus*) as they stand or walk.

The White wagtail *Motacilla alba* (and the British race of this, the Pied wagtail) has a boldly patterned black and white plumage, as do the African and Indian Pied wagtails. The six or more other species have much yellow in the plumage, particularly on the underparts. The beak is finely pointed in all wagtails. FAMILY: Motacillidae, ORDER: Passeriformes, CLASS: Aves.

WALLABIES, a large and diverse assemblage of about 30 species of kangaroo-like marsupials generally smaller than true kangaroos. They have large hindfeet, strong hindlimbs and a long tapered or untapered tail. They are herbivorous and adopt a bipedal method of locomotion when moving quickly.

The Hare wallabies *Lagorchestes* (3 species) are small, swift wallabies of slender build weighing up to 9 lb (4 kg).

The pademelons *Thylogale* and Rock wallabies *Petrogale* are medium to small sized wallabies weighing 10–25 lb (4·5–11 kg). The pademelons have a tapered tail whereas the

Rock wallabies have an untapered tail. The hindfeet of Rock wallabies are equipped with pads and granulations and the claws are short, adaptations to rock haunting habits which are absent in the forest dwelling pademelons. The quokka is a stockily built grey-brown wallaby with a short tail and weighs 5–10 lb (2–4·5 kg).

The Scrub wallabies, a group of larger wallabies weighing up to 40 lb (18 kg), include Bennett's wallaby *Macropus rufogriseus fruticus* a large grey wallaby with a reddish tinge in the fur on shoulders and rump, an indistinct white cheek stripe and naked muzzle, confined to Tasmania. FAMILY: Macropodidae, ORDER: Marsupialia, CLASS: Mammalia.

WALL LIZARD, name used for several European species of lizards, the best known being *Lacerta muralis*. Their natural habitat is among rocks but when living in gardens they use walls instead. FAMILY: Lacertidae, ORDER: Squamata, CLASS: Reptilia.

WALRUS, similar to a sealion in appearance but heavier, more wrinkled and having distinctive tusks. Their hindflippers can be brought forwards underneath the body, but they lack a visible external ear. There is one species *Odobenus rosmarus*, with two subspecies, the Atlantic walrus *O. r. rosmarus* and the Pacific walrus *O. r. divergens*, the Atlantic walrus having shorter tusks and a narrower facial part of the skull. Walruses prefer the shallow water round the circumpolar arctic coasts.

Adult males are about 12 ft (3·6 m) in length and weigh up to 3,000 lb (1,360 kg), while females are slightly smaller, about 10 ft (3 m) in length and 1,800 lb (816 kg) in weight. The head looks rather square in side view and has small bloodshot eyes, rows of thick whiskers and long tusks that are present in both sexes. These tusks, the upper canine teeth, erupt at about four months old, grow to about 4 in (10 cm) long at two years, about 1 ft (30 cm) by 5–6 years, and may reach a length of over 3 ft (1 m). The skin is rough and wrinkled and adult males have

Red-necked wallaby, one of several species of wallaby killed for its fur.

many warty tubercles about their necks and shoulders. The thickness of the skin increases with age and may reach over 1 in (2.5 cm) on the body and about 2½ in (7 cm) on the neck. Under the skin is a thick layer of blubber which may also be 2½ in (7 cm) thick and weigh over 900 lb (408 kg). The hide is a light grey, but when basking in the sun the blood vessels dilate and the animals appear rust red. Young animals have a scanty coat of reddish hair, but old animals have a practically naked skin.

A single pup is born in April or May after a gestation period of almost a year, but in any one year only about half the adult females produce pups. The newborn pups are about 4 ft (1·2 m) in length, 100 lb (45·3 kg) in weight and greyish in colour, though they soon moult to become a reddish colour. They are suckled by their mothers for over a year.

Walruses have few enemies, man, Killer whales and Polar bears being their only predators. They are found chiefly in shallow waters of 40 fathoms (72 m) or less, where there is abundant gravel. Bivalve molluscs form the greater part of the food eaten, although echinoderms and fish are also taken. FAMILY: Odobenidae, ORDER: Pinnipedia, CLASS: Mammalia.

WARBLERS, small, insect-eating, perching birds related to thrushes and flycatchers. Almost all warblers have thin, pointed bills and are mainly insectivorous. They have ten primaries (flight feathers) and with a few exceptions, the sexes have similar or identical plumages.

The English name (warbler) refers to the pleasant and melodious song of many of the species. The blackcap *Sylvia atricapilla,* a common woodland warbler, for instance, has a rich warbling song rivalling, in many people's opinions, that of the nightingale.

Most are various shades of brown, green or grey and identification is often not easy, and frequently depends on behavioural differences. FAMILY: Muscicapidae: ORDER: Passeriformes, CLASS: Aves.

WARTHOG *Phacochoerus aethiopicus,* a large grey brown African hog with smooth or rough hide sparsely covered with hair, except around the neck and on the back, and warty bumps on the face beside the eyes and on the sides of the face. The lower canines are highly developed, curving to the top of the snout and being up to 24 in (61 cm) long in some specimens. The length of the head and body averages 52·3 in (133 cm), the height at the shoulder 30·5 in (77 cm), females 26·4 in (67 cm). The tail is 18 in (46 cm). Males weigh 191·4 lb (87 kg), females 132 lb (60 kg). The warthog is found over most of Africa.

Warthogs inhabit savannahs, open plains and bushy edges. Usually they form small groups but they may sometimes be solitary.

Waterbuck, African antelope typically living near but not in water.

They spend the night in burrows, usually those made by antbears or porcupines. When retreating into burrows they back in, to face any enemy. They run with tails erect. They are vegetarian, feeding largely on roots and rhizomes of grasses and other plants. FAMILY: Suidae, SUBORDER: Suiformes, ORDER: Artiodactyla, CLASS: Mammalia.

WASPS, stinging insects, banded black and yellow, related to bees and ants. The majority are solitary, male and female coming together only for mating, after which the female alone provides for her offspring. A small minority are social, which means they live in a colony of thousands of individuals, the workers, with a 'queen' that devotes most of her active life to laying eggs.

The most primitive are known as Velvet ants. The females are wingless and they look like hairy ants. They parasitize bumblebee and beetle larvae, laying their eggs in them but exercising no parental care for the offspring. The female Spider hunting wasp (Pompiloidea) excavates small cavities in the ground to store the paralyzed spiders she captures. She lays an egg on this inert prey then seals the entrance to the cavity scattering the disturbed soil to disguise the nest site. In the more specialized Sand wasps (Sphecoidea), a nest cell is prepared in sandy soil or decayed wood, and one or more paralyzed insects or spiders is placed in it before the

egg is laid, as 'living meat' for the larva.

In the Vespoidea, which include the familiar social wasps, there is progressive feeding of the larva, the tending adult chewing the prey before giving it to the larva, and, with a prolongation of adult life, the daughter wasps—all workers being sterile females, as in bees and ants—have the opportunity to co-operate in a colonial establishment with their parent and sisters. But some vespoids, such as the Heath potter wasp *Eumenes coarctata* are strictly solitary, constructing small cells of mud in which paralyzed prey are stored, the egg is laid, and the cell sealed, with no social contact between generations.

In Britain, there are seven species of social wasp including the hornet and the two most common species, *Vespula vulgaris* and *V. germanica.*

During the long winter months, queen wasps are well supplied with fat, and with a low metabolic rate, so are able to survive their six months' sleep.

When they leave their winter quarters in April they begin searching for nesting sites, often the disused burrows of small mammals, but almost any cavity will do. ORDER: Hymenoptera, CLASS: Insecta, PHYLUM: Arthropoda.

WATERBUCK, large African antelope related to the reedbuck with spreading horns, and lacking a bare patch below the ear. The true waterbuck *Kobus ellipsiprymnus* is 48–

Water buffalo

53 in (120–133 cm) high and weighs 475 lb (216 kg). The coat is long and wiry, forming a mane on the neck. The general colour is brownish, and there is a white ring or patch on the rump. The horns are long, simply divergent and forwardly concave.

For a long time waterbuck with a white ring round the buttocks, and those with a white buttock patch, were considered to be distinct species, called respectively the Common waterbuck *K. ellipsiprymnus* and the Northern, Defassa or Singsing waterbuck *K. defassa*.

They normally keep down by the banks of rivers, spending the night in the thick riverine cover, and emerging at 8–10 am onto the grassland where they remain all day, going back to the river at dusk. Where they are heavily hunted, for example in Somalia, the rhythm is reversed. FAMILY: Bovidae, ORDER: Artiodactyla, CLASS: Mammalia.

WATER BUFFALO *Bubalus (Bubalus) arnee*, the largest species of Asiatic buffalo, domesticated over very large areas of the tropics and subtropics and in the Mediterranean region. The Asiatic buffaloes can be divided into those with expanding horns, subgenus *Bubalus*, and those with straight horns, subgenus *Anoa*. To the first group belong the Water buffalo and the tamarao, while to the second group belong the two species of *Anoa*. The two groups differ in

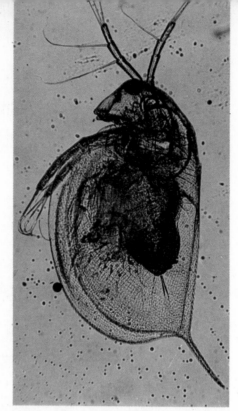

Daphnia, the Waterflea, swims by flicks of its long antennae in flea-like jerks.

their skulls and teeth as well as their horns. Asiatic buffaloes differ from African buffaloes in their skulls, and in having reversed hair along the back.

Wild buffalo are found in northern India and Nepal and from northern Burma into Indo-China, and also in Ceylon. In most parts of their range they are slaty black, with the legs white from just above the knees and hocks to the hoofs, and a white crescent on the throat.

Indian wild buffalo *Bubalus arnee arnee* are 5½ ft–6½ ft (1·7–2 m) high and some bulls may weigh 2,600 lb (1,170 kg). The horns may be as much as 6 ft (1·8 m) long round the curve, and 4½ ft (1·4 m) is not unusual.

Domestic buffalo are smaller than Indian wild buffalo, and have differently shaped, shorter and thicker horns, the tips of which are less inturned. They have been transported over most of the tropical and subtropical latitudes, and are the staple beasts of burden or milk and meat providers for much of the world's human population. There are about 78 million domestic buffalo in the world, of which 45 million are in India. FAMILY: Bovidae, ORDER: Artiodactyla, CLASS: Mammalia.

WATER FLEAS, tiny crustaceans deriving their common name from their method of swimming, which is basically a hop and drop using their branched antennae. To maintain its position in the water a Water flea has to swim continuously, otherwise it sinks slowly to the bottom. ORDER: Cladocera, SUBCLASS: Branchiopoda, CLASS: Crustacea, PHYLUM: Arthropoda.

WATER SPIDER *Argyroneta aquatica*, the only species of spider that lives more or less permanently below the surface of the water, although several spiders can run over water and some can run down plants below the surface to escape enemies or catch water insects. The Water spider is small-bodied and long legged, the front part of the body light brown with faint dark markings, the chelicerae reddish brown and the abdomen greyish, covered with short hairs. Water spiders are usually ½–⅔ in (8–15 mm) long, although females of up to just over an inch (25 mm) long have been recorded. The Water spider ranges across temperate Europe and Asia.

Although living under water the Water spider is dependent on air for breathing. It rises to the surface and entraps a bubble of air round its hairy body then descends to its silken thimble-shaped diving bell and into this releases the bubble. This is repeated until the diving bell is filled with air. FAMILY: Agelenidae, ORDER: Araneida, CLASS: Arachnida, PHYLUM: Arthropoda.

WATTLEBIRDS, a crow-like group of New Zealand forest birds, with brightly-coloured fleshy wattles at the corners of their bills.

Of the three genera, the huia is presumed extinct; the tieke or saddleback is confined to some offshore islands; and the kokako is very rare. All three began to decline in numbers

The Water spider spins a sort of silk diving bell which it fills with air.

Wasps busy on their nest composed of paper cells manufactured by the wasps from chewed wood.

soon after the arrival of European settlers in New Zealand.

The kokako *Callaeas cinerea* or 'Wattled crow' is a big bluish-grey bird with a black face. It completely lacks fear of man and can be watched as it bounds and glides through the forest, rarely flying any distance. The food is largely young leaves and fruit, but it also eats invertebrates.

The tieke *Philesturnus carunculatus* is a glossy black bird the size of a blackbird with a bright chestnut 'saddle' across its back. FAMILY: Callaeidae, ORDER: Passeriformes, CLASS: Aves.

WAXWINGS, three similar species of small forest birds the most widely distributed being *Bombycilla garrulus*, called simply waxwing or, not very happily, Bohemian waxwing. It inhabits northern latitudes in Europe, Asia and North America. Two further species exist: the so-called Japanese waxwing *B. japonica*, a native of eastern Siberia and only an irregular winter visitor to Japan, and the Cedar waxwing *B. cedrorum*, a native of northern North America and an irregular winter visitor as far south as the Caribbean.

Waxwings are about 6½–7½ in (16–19 cm) long, with short, broad and slightly hooked bills and short, stout legs. The plumage is remarkably soft and is mostly brown, greyish-brown or reddish-brown, with a black throat, wing quills and tail quills. *B. garrulus* has a yellow wing-bar, while *B. japonica* has a crimson one and also red tips to the tail-feathers where the other two have yellow. In all species (but, strangely, not in all individuals) the shafts of the secondary wing feathers are prolonged in red, drop-shaped tips like sealing-wax—hence the English name. A brown 'swept-back' crest is another conspicuous characteristic. FAMILY: Bombycillidae, ORDER: Passeriformes, CLASS: Aves.

WEASEL *Mustela nivalis*, the smallest carnivore, in the same family as the stoat and very similar in appearance to it, but smaller. The weasel can usually be recognized by the uneven line separating the cream colour of the ventral surface from the dark reddish upper side. Also, the shorter, less fluffy, tail does not have the stoat's dark tip.

A male weasel's size may vary from 6·7–11·7 in (17–29·5 cm) and the weight 2 to 4·5 oz (60–130 gm). The female, sometimes only half the size of the male, measures 6–7·5 in (15–19 cm) and weighs 1·5–2 oz (45–60 gm). FAMILY: Mustelidae, ORDER: Carnivora, CLASS: Mammalia.

WEAVERS, a large family of seed-eating birds, which includes the sparrows, best known for the pendent woven nests of some of the typical species. Their natural distribution is within the Old World, mainly in Africa.

The typical weavers, the 67 species of *Ploceus* and the ten *Malimbus*, are sparrow-like, the females, immature birds and males out of breeding plumage all having brown plumage with blackish streaking on backs, wings, and heads, and pale buffish under-parts. The males in breeding dress develop bright colour, most of the *Ploceus* species being mainly yellow with variable areas of black, and *Malimbus* species being similar but patterned in red and black, a difference apparently correlated with the moist forest habitat of the latter. These birds are normally sociable at all times and nest in colonies, sometimes of considerable size. The pendent nests are built onto the tips of twigs or palm fronds, or more rarely in lower swamp growth. The male usually makes an initial hanging ring and then builds out to form a rounded nest chamber in one direction, and in the other extends the entrance to an extent which varies considerably from one species to another but which may result in anything from a small porch to a long downward-pointing tube up which the birds will enter.

The Social weaver *Philetarius socius* of southwestern Africa is an undistinguished streaky brown bird, famous for its nest. The individual nests of a flock, with entrance holes on the lower side, are built in contact with each other to form huge masses. Each mass is roofed over with a curved roofing layer which may help to shed rain; and this roof is built first, the nests being subsequently built into the underside of it. They are not woven but consist of a tightly packed mass of grass stems, 'thatched' together by overlapping. Nests may be added around the edge later, and adjacent masses may be joined. A colony may consist of several such groups and a single mass may contain a hundred nests. See whydahs. FAMILY: Ploceidae, ORDER: Passeriformes, CLASS: Aves.

The weasel, the smallest carnivore, credited with being able to pass through a wedding ring.

Taveta Golden weaver *Ploceus castaneiceps* one of several species of sparrow-like birds of East Africa.

WEEVERFISHES, marine bottom-living, poisonous fishes related to the Red mullets. There are two species found off the coasts of northern Europe, the Greater weever *Trachinus draco* and the Lesser weever *T. vipera*. The latter grows to about 6 in (15 cm) in length and is much more abundant than the former, which reaches 20 in (51 cm). The two species are fairly similar in appearance. The body is a deep yellow-brown with grey-blue streaks and the belly is a pale yellow. The most striking feature is the first dorsal fin, which contains 5–6 spiny rays and is black in colour. The poison glands are at the bases of these rays. The spine is sheathed in skin but when this is ruptured the poison is released along the grooved spine and enters the wound. It is not fatal but can be extremely painful.

The weevers frequent shallow water, burying themselves in the sand at the bottom with only the top of the head and the black dorsal fin visible. FAMILY: Trachinidae, ORDER: Perciformes, CLASS: Pisces.

WEEVILS, form the largest family in the Animal Kingdom, with over 35,000 species, the vast majority of which are immediately recognizable by the greatly drawn out head forming a long snout, so they are also known as Snout beetles. This bears on its tip the mouthparts which are characteristically small, with short palps (sense organs), but with powerful mandibles for chewing hard

vegetable matter such as seed coats or wood. Most weevils have antennae clubbed at the tip. Such antennae are usually elbowed.

Weevils are generally oval or pear-shaped with well developed wing covers and the body wall which is very hard is often tuberculated, pitted, roughened or grooved. Frequently they are scaly, and although most species have dull colouring, some rank among the most brilliantly coloured of insects. Although weevils are particularly well represented in the tropics, they exist wherever seed producing plants occur. Their larvae, because they live surrounded by their food inside seeds, buds and stems, are fat, white legless grubs armed with a powerful pair of jaws.

Many species are injurious to crops and a considerable number are very serious pests,

A tropical weevil. These long-snouted insects form the largest family of beetles.

one of the most notorious being the Cotton boll weevil *Anthonomus grandis*, which causes damage amounting to hundreds of millions of dollars annually in the cotton belt of the United States. FAMILY: Curculionidae, ORDER: Coleoptera, CLASS: Insecta, PHYLUM: Arthropoda.

WELS *Silurus glanis*, a large catfish found in the bigger rivers of Europe. It is a naked catfish with a small dorsal fin just behind the head and a long anal fin. There are two barbels on the upper jaw and four on the lower. The jaws have rows of fine teeth and there is a patch of fine teeth in the roof of the mouth. The colour is variable.

The wels is solitary, hiding in deep pools during the day and swimming into shallower water in the evening to feed on small fishes. It will eat not only fishes but frogs, birds and small mammals. There is a record from the last century of a child being eaten by a wels, a not altogether unlikely occurrence since they can grow to about 9 ft (2·7 m) and reach a weight of 700 lb (318 kg). FAMILY: Siluridae, ORDER: Cypriniformes, CLASS: Pisces.

WHALES, name given to members of the order Cetacea, which includes the whales, porpoises and dolphins. In practice it is usual to restrict use of the word to the larger members of the order. Although there is no

A sounder of European wild boar. This species gave the western domesticated pig.

formal definition it is common to consider any of these larger than about 20 ft (6·5 m) in length as a whale. The majority of dolphins and porpoises are smaller than this but some of the larger true dolphins, the Killer whale *Orcinus orca* and the Pilot whales *Globicephala*, are called whales because of their large size. ORDER: Cetacea, CLASS: Mammalia.

WHALE SHARK *Rhincodon typus*, the largest of all fishes but harmless, found in the warm seas. It can be immediately recognized by the lines of pale spots on a greyish body and by the wide mouth at the end of the snout. The body is heavily built, with ridges down the flanks, and the snout is blunt. Like the Basking shark, the Whale shark feeds on small planktonic animals, straining them from the water with a fine mesh of rakers in the throat region. There are, however, numerous small teeth in the jaws, of which 10 or 15 rows are functional at any one time. The fish cruises through the water with its mouth open when feeding. The largest recorded Whale shark was 45 ft (13·5 m) in length but there have been reports of specimens believed to be much larger than this and a length of 60 ft (18 m) may well be reached. FAMILY: Rhincodontidae, ORDER: Pleurotremata, CLASS: Chondrichthyes.

WHELK, a common name given to a wide variety of marine molluscs. They have a thick spirally coiled shell, up to 8 in (20 cm) long in the Red whelk *Neptunea antiqua*.

Mediterranean species of the group (*Murex brandaris*, *M. trunculus* and *Thais haemastoma*) were used to produce the well known dye Tyrian purple which often coloured the clothes of important and wealthy citizens of the Roman Empire.

The Common whelk *Buccinum undatum* has a number of popular names including the White whelk and the buckie. It is usually found at extreme low tide level, or below tide level, on all types of shore. It is a voracious carnivore feeding on crabs, worms, bivalve molluscs and fresh carrion. ORDER: Stenoglossa, CLASS: Gastropoda, PHYLUM: Mollusca.

WHIRLIGIG BEETLES, small oval, black, shiny beetles, less than ½ in (1·2 cm) long as a rule, that swim rapidly in tight circles on the surfaces of pools and backwaters of streams. They can also plunge underwater if danger threatens from above. Their eyes are divided into upper and lower halves which are adapted to looking upwards into the air and downwards into the water. There are 400 species throughout the world.

Whirligigs live in swarms of several hundred and although they may all be gyrating rapidly at the same time they do not collide. Their antennae, so arranged that they lie in the surface film, perceive vibrations from an approaching neighbour so that avoiding action can be taken. The antennae also detect the movements of insects that fall from the air onto the surface film and provide the whirligigs with food. FAMILY: Gyrinidae, ORDER: Coleoptera, CLASS: Insecta, PHYLUM: Arthropoda.

WHITE-EYES, tiny, thin-billed arboreal birds, usually having a ring of white around each eye. Although there are 85 species they are mostly remarkably alike and the majority are included in the genus *Zosterops*. Typically they are green on head, back, rump and tail, and grey or yellow below, sometimes with some reddish-brown on the flanks.

The ring round the eye is formed by white feathers and differs in size and distinctness in various species. The white-eyes occur through Africa and the Oriental and Australasian regions.

White-eyes are about 3–5 in (8–13 cm) long, with a slender, pointed and often slightly decurved bill. They have strong feet which allow them to cling in a variety of postures and aid their feeding. They are gregarious, usually living in small flocks except when breeding, and are constantly active. The small flocks and parties on the move maintain contact by constant soft, shrill and plaintive notes, and when breeding the males have a rather high-pitched warbling song, but the vocabulary is not very varied. Paired birds or socially-inclined individuals will sit clumped together and frequently be seen to preen each other.

The young birds may lack the white eye rim at first. FAMILY: Zosteropidae, ORDER: Passeriformes, CLASS: Aves.

WHITE WHALE or beluga *Delphinapterus leucas*, a Toothed whale related to the narwhal and about the same size, 15 ft (5 m) long, is an arctic species largely restricted to within the Arctic Circle. It has no dorsal fin. FAMILY: Monodontidae, ORDER: Cetacea, CLASS: Mammalia.

WHYDAH, name given to long-tailed, mainly black-plumaged weaver-like birds, and as a result used for species from two different subfamilies of the *weavers. In one case it is used for some species of the genus *Euplectes*, inhabiting open country and using the long tails and dark colour of the males for advertisement, and in the other for the parasitic widow-birds of the subfamily Viduinae. FAMILY: Ploceidae, ORDER: Passeriformes, CLASS: Aves.

WIDOW-BIRDS, a small subfamily of Weaver birds with brood-parasitic habits, confined to Africa south of the Sahara. They are seed-eaters, taking their food from the ground, and differ from other weavers in the habit of scratching and turning over the ground with quick hopping, scratching movements, both feet moving together. FAMILY: Ploceidae, ORDER: Passeriformes, CLASS: Aves.

WILD BOAR *Sus scrofa*, a large woodland dwelling hog with long tusks and stiff dark grey-black or brown hair. The snout is typically pig-like with a mobile disk. There are four toes on each foot of which the middle two are used for walking. The head and body length is about 70 in (178 cm) and the height at the shoulder is about 40 in (100 cm) while the tail is 12 in (30 cm) long. The weight of males varies from 150–500 lb (68–227 kg) and that of females from 80–330 lb (36–150 kg). The upper canines turn outward and upward and these wear against the bottom canines causing sharp edges to form.

Wild boar are found throughout the deciduous wooded areas of Europe and northern Africa and throughout southern Asia to the Malay peninsula and islands of Java, Sumatra, the Philippines, Japan and Formosa.

The Wild boar is principally a vegetarian, eating a variety of green vegetation, acorns, berries, roots and tubers, but it will occasionally eat worms, insects, and even reptiles and birds' eggs. It is very destructive to gardens and farm crops where its habitat borders on agricultural land. It is generally regarded as a game animal and is hunted extensively with dogs or on horseback, and can be dangerous when wounded. FAMILY: Suidae, SUBORDER: Suiformes, ORDER: Artiodactyla, CLASS: Mammalia.

WIREWORM, the larva of the *Click beetle. Wireworms are elongated and very smooth yellow-brown grubs which live in the soil and grow to a maximum length of nearly 1 in (2·5 cm). Although different species of wireworms may be found in almost any soil, the natural habitat of the commonest species *Agriotes obscurus* is grassland. Permanent grassland may be very densely colonized by wireworms (up to eight million per acre) as there is an almost inexhaustible supply of food in the roots, crowns and lower stems of grass plants. In such situations, wireworms do little real damage as grass plants quickly regenerate damaged parts or new plants take the place of plants that have been killed. However, when permanent grass is ploughed for arable cultivation, the wireworms may become a very serious destructive force, especially if the first crop is a cereal. FAMILY: Elateridae, ORDER: Coleoptera, CLASS: Insecta, PHYLUM: Arthropoda.

WISENT *Bison bonasus*, or European bison, similar to the American bison but now nearly extinct in its truly wild form. Wisent differ from the American bison in numerous features. The hindquarters are higher and the shoulder less humped, so that the back is more nearly horizontal; the colour is uniform brown, instead of being nearly black on the foreparts; the hair on the head, limbs and tail is of the same type as on the rest of the body instead of being crisp and curled; the hair on the forehead is only 8 in (20 cm) long compared with 20 in (50 cm) in the bison, and is drawn forward and lies down, instead of forming a cap and overhanging the nose. The tail of the wisent is long, reaching below the hocks, and long-haired, not tufted as in the bison.

Formerly, wisent were spread over a great deal of Central and eastern Europe, and in the latter half of the 18th century they were still to be found in Kazakhstan. European wisent were divided into two very distinct subspecies, one in the lowlands and one in the Caucasus mountains. The Lowland wisent *Bison bonasus bonasus*, which still exists as a pure race, is the larger. Old bulls may measure 6 ft (2 m) at the shoulder and 5 ft (1·5 m) at the croup, and weigh 1,870 lb (850 kg). The hump is comparatively high, so that the line of the back is curved. The head is rather large. The hoofs also are large being 4 in (10 cm) long. The body hair is nearly smooth and the colour is brownish with ochreous tones. FAMILY: Bovidae, ORDER: Artiodactyla, CLASS: Mammalia.

WOBBEGONGS, five species of Carpet sharks, ranging from Australian seas to Japan. The largest are 8 ft (2·4 m) long. They are flattened and spend most of their time on the bottom, the marbled pattern of the skin making them inconspicuous. The broad head is ornamented with tassels of skin. They feed on fishes and crustaceans and although they snap when handled they are harmless. FAMILY: Orectolobidae, ORDER: Lamniformes, CLASS: Chondrichthyes.

WOLF *Canis lupus*, supposed ancestor of the domestic dog, ranges throughout the temperate and coniferous forests and tundra of the northern hemisphere, and is a large predator, usually weighing 60–120 lb (27–55 kg). It has a broad chest, small pointed ears and long legs adapted for a cursorial life. Although the majority are tawny with a cream chest and black markings on the shoulders, tail tip, and near the base of the tail, pure white or black individuals are occasionally found.

Wolves are pack hunters (although they can and do hunt individually) in order to take advantage of the numerous moose, deer and elk herds. Packs are large during the winter, with up to 30 members, but in the summer when there are many smaller mam-

mals available, the packs often break up into smaller groups. In addition, the spring dispersal often results from the onset of breeding. Mating occurs between January and March, and the pups are born two months later, usually in a hole dug by the mother, or in an enlarged fox den. Both the father and other adult wolves of both sexes may help in rearing the litter by guarding the cubs if the mother joins an evening hunt and by bringing meat back to the growing litter.

Packs usually have an established territory traversed over a period of weeks in the search for food. The size of the territory is partly dependent upon the size of the pack, but also upon the number of prey species available. Maximum density is probably never more than one wolf per sq mile (2·7 sq km). Territories are demarcated by scent marks placed on conspicuous trees, rocks and bushes along the wolves' trails. Howling also informs the wolves of each other's location. A pack has little tolerance for strangers, and intruders are chased away and even killed if they are too persistent in efforts to join the group. FAMILY: Canidae, ORDER: Carnivora, CLASS: Mammalia.

WOLF SPIDERS, hunters on the ground which leap on their prey. Some are entirely vagrants; others live in deep silk-lined burrows from which they pounce on passing insects. They range in body length from ¼ in (5·5 mm) in the genera *Pardosa* and *Pirata* to the largest species *Lycosa ingens*, on Deserta Grande, Madeira, which reaches 1¾ in (45 mm).

In front is a row of four small eyes with two large eyes above it looking forward. Farther back are two eyes which look upwards.

The species of *Pardosa* are small vagrants on open ground which carry an egg-sac attached to their spinnerets until the young hatch and clamber on their mothers' backs. Species of *Pirata* are small chocolate-brown spiders which frequent damp ground and can run down plants under standing water. FAMILY: Lycosidae, ORDER: Araneida, CLASS: Arachnida, PHYLUM: Arthropoda.

WOLVERINE *Gulo gulo*, or glutton, looking like an oversized, heavy-bodied marten and weighing 26–64 lb (12–29 kg), found in the Old and New World tundra. Two caramel-coloured stripes, contrasting with the long black-brown fur, run along the flanks to the rump where they overlap. The small ears are nearly concealed in the fur. The short, muscular legs have clawed feet with haired soles, usually larger than females, measuring up to 40·5 in (103 cm) in length, including the bushy tail. The male wolverine may share its vast home range, sometimes reaching over 100 sq miles (260 sq km), with two or three females. By patrolling this area, using regular trails and leaving scent and scratch marks on

Wolf spider, showing the row of four eyes with a pair of larger eyes above.

grass hummocks or tree trunks, it attempts to discourage other males.

Eskimo lore has abundantly described the wolverine's strength with the same awe Africans have for the lion. The glutton's readiness to learn, its lack of fear and especially its opportunism are all equally instrumental in tracking and successfully killing young or lame elk, an animal more than twice its size. Even lynx and bear avoid an encounter with it. Its large feet help it to race along the top of the hard snow crust where an elk will flounder and tire quickly. The glutton lives up to its name by killing more than it can eat in times of abundance and then hoarding the remains. Trappers report that after killing large prey, it will urinate on its victim then drag the carcass up a tree, being an adept climber, or into its den before abandoning it. The wolverine's diet includes berries, insects, fish, eggs, birds, lemmings, carrion and even provisions left behind in a trapper's cabin. FAMILY: Mustelidae, ORDER: Carnivora, CLASS: Mammalia.

WOMBATS, heavy, stockily built, burrowing marsupials, bear-like, with a vestigial tail and broad head, up to about 4 ft (1·2 m) in length and weighing up to 70 lb (32 kg). They are quadrupedal with short legs and with five toes on each foot, the first toe of the hindfoot lacking a claw.

The Common wombat *Vombatus hirsutus* and the Island wombat *Vombatus ursinus* have dark brown to almost black, coarse, thick fur. They are distinguished from the Hairy-nosed wombat *Lasiorhinus latifrons*

by having the muzzle between the nostrils covered with hairless granulated skin. The incisors of wombats are reduced to a single pair in each jaw separated by a long, toothless gap (diastema) from the single premolar and four molar teeth on each side of upper and lower jaws. All the teeth are rootless, but extend a long way into the bone and grow continuously throughout life from persistent pulps.

Common wombats are confined to the eucalypt forests of eastern continental Australia and Island wombats to Tasmania and Flinders Island, the Hairy nosed wombat to the drier part of South Australia.

Wombats are nocturnal and herbivorous and feed on grasses, roots and other vegetable matter. FAMILY: Vombatidae, ORDER: Marsupialia, CLASS: Mammalia.

WOODCOCK, medium-sized wading birds, related to the sandpipers, 10–13 in (25–33 cm) long, with long, straight bills and grey-brown and rufous plumage. They are solitary and live in woodland and coppices. The woodcock *Scolopax rusticola* is found throughout Europe and northern Asia and in winter reaches North Africa and India. Some six or seven other species of *Scolopax* are found in Southeast Asia, including the Celebes and New Guinea. The American woodcock *Philohela minor* occurs in the eastern United States to southern Canada.

Woodcock feed on earthworms and other insects found by probing in soft soil. The bill is sensitive at the tip and food is located by touch.

Carrying the young in flight by the female is well documented, usually between the feet and the body but also on the female's back. FAMILY: Scolopacidae, ORDER: Charadriiformes, CLASS: Aves.

WOODCREEPERS, small, solitary medium-sized American perching birds, sometimes called 'wood-hewers'. There are 50 species which range from 5–15 in (13–38 cm) long. Generally they are olive, with rufous wings and tail and light streaks on the head and underparts. The tail feathers are usually stiffened and the legs short and powerful, for climbing trees. The bill is stout, compressed and long for probing bark. The family ranges from northwestern Mexico to northern Argentina, occuring in Trinidad and Tobago, but not in the Antilles. FAMILY: Dendrocolaptidae, ORDER: Passeriformes, CLASS: Aves.

WOOD-HOOPOES, six species of slender glossy blue- or green-black birds, confined to Africa. They are 9–15 in (22–38 cm) long with long slender decurved beaks, rounded wings, long tails and short legs. Beak and legs are often red, but the black plumage is otherwise unrelieved except for bold white spots in the flight feathers of some, and a buff or chestnut head in three species. They are sociable, noisy, insectivorous, arboreal birds of forest and woodland savannah, nesting in tree holes. FAMILY: Phoeniculidae, ORDER: Coraciiformes, CLASS: Aves.

WOODLICE, also called Sow bugs, are small crustaceans. They have more or less flattened bodies and legs of more or less equal length. They are related to the Sea slaters inhabiting the seashores throughout the world. Some species, known as Pill bugs, can roll into a ball. The antennae of all woodlice are well developed; the antennules small and relatively insignificant. Woodlice are capable of rapid walking movements on land. They breathe through their abdominal legs, the first pair of which are modified to long pointed cones to assist in reproduction.

Their food is mainly vegetable but they will eat dead animals and their own cast skins, and they are cannibalistic. They are scavengers and can also cause much damage to cultivated crops in gardens and greenhouses. They are eaten by small mammals and some birds.

Woodlice are normally found in damp places such as under stones, amongst fallen leaves, under the bark of rotting trees and in crevices. ORDER: Isopoda, SUBCLASS: Malacostraca, CLASS: Crustacea, PHYLUM: Arthropoda.

WOODPECKERS, birds specialized for obtaining their food from the trunks and branches of trees. The 210 species are all, excepting the two *wrynecks, similar in appearance. They occur on all the major

European Great spotted woodpecker feeding a nestling.

continents except Australasia, but are absent from Madagascar and some oceanic islands. The majority are 6–14 in (15–35 cm) long, but the piculets are small, down to $3\frac{1}{2}$ in (8·7 cm) long, and a few are up to 22 in (55 cm) long. Their normal posture is upright clinging to a vertical surface with widely-straddled, short legs bearing large, strong feet with sharp curved claws. The feet are zygodactyl, two toes pointing forwards and upwards while the outer toe is directed backwards and outwards.

Typical woodpeckers have well-developed tails, wedge-shaped at the tip, with very strong quills which protrude beyond the tip of each pointed tail-feather and, when the tail is pressed against a trunk or branch, act as a prop, the spines of the quills resisting the abrasion which would destroy the weaker feather vane. Their habit is to fly to a low position on a trunk or branch and then move up it in a series of jerky hops; but woodpeckers can also hop backwards down a vertical surface, or sideways across it.

The wings are rounded and flight, although it may be swift, is usually undulating, with a swoop between each wing-beat, becoming more direct in the larger species. The neck is slender but muscular and the head relatively large. The bill is strong and straight, fairly thick at the base and tapering evenly to a sharp tip. It is used for chipping away wood, and the muscles and structure of the head and neck are adapted for driving the bill forward with considerable force, and absorbing the shock of the blow. The bill hacks open rotten wood and exposes the insects on which most woodpeckers feed. In addition, the tongue is long and slender, mobile and worm-like. It can be extended considerably, and this is aided by the tremendous elongation of the paired hyoid bones at its base. FAMILY: Picidae, ORDER: Piciformes, CLASS: Aves.

WOOD PIGEON *Columba palumbus*, also known as the Ring dove, a bird of both town and countryside, found in large flocks in winter. A considerable pest to farmers and therefore widely persecuted, it maintains its numbers well over most of its range. In northwest Europe it has even extended its range northwards over the last 100 years. Typically a bird of woodland and farmland, it has spread to the very edges of wooded country, even beyond the treelines, when it nests on the ground, and into towns and cities.

The Wood pigeon is 16 in (40 cm) long, bluish-grey with a mauve pink breast and cream belly. It has a white band across the wings, which is conspicuous in flight, and a white patch on each side of the neck surrounded by an iridescent area of purple-pink and green. The legs are rather short and the feet are reddish-purple.

Woodwasps

Jenny wren, of Europe, a small bird with a very loud song, at its nest.

When disturbed in trees or bushes it frequently 'explodes' from cover with loud wing-claps and crashes through twigs and foliage. The display flight consists of a series of swoops in the air in which the bird rises steeply, claps its wings loudly, and then glides down to repeat the process.

It feeds opportunistically on a wide variety of seeds and fruits, buds, and leaves; and it also takes invertebrates such as caterpillars and worms. The crop capacity is remarkable, over 50 acorns, 200 beans, or 1,000 grains of corn being recorded in one crop.

Wood pigeons make an unsubstantial platform-like nest of twigs in a bush or tree, sometimes quite near the ground. Two white eggs are laid, and the parents share incubation for about 16 days. The young are fed by both parents on 'pigeon's milk', produced in the crop and obtained by the young putting its head into the parent's gape and taking the regurgitated mixture. FAMILY: Columbidae, ORDER: Columbiformes, CLASS: Aves.

WOODWASPS, large insects with conspicuous black and yellow or metallic blue coloration, which inhabit forests. They are related to sawflies. The females have stout ovipositors used to drill through bark and into the wood. Inside the tubes thus formed, eggs are laid. Most woodwasps have an associated symbiotic fungus which females store in sacs in their abdomen, and inject into the wood during oviposition. The fungus develops in the timber, contributing to the death of the tree, and providing food for the developing larvae. The woodwasp larvae inhabit the wood for one or more years, producing long tunnels packed tight with chewed-up fragments of wood. The Giant wood-wasp or horntail *Sirex gigas*, of Europe, 1 in (2·5 cm) or so long, is often mistaken for a hornet. FAMILY: Siricidae, ORDER: Hymenoptera, CLASS: Insecta, PHYLUM: Arthropoda.

WOODWORM, the immature stage of certain wood-boring beetles found in buildings, either in furniture, structural timber or joinery, especially of *Anobium punctatum*, also known as common Furniture beetle, a $\frac{1}{6}$ in (4 mm) long, brown beetle known in New Zealand as the House borer.

Anobium punctatum causes no serious harm in the wild. Holes left by the woodworm can easily be detected in the branch scars or exposed dead sapwood of trees. These trees are almost always hardwoods, oak and orchard trees predominating. Softwood trees seldom show the results of woodworm attack out-of-doors. FAMILY: Anobiidae, ORDER: Coleoptera, CLASS: Insecta, PHYLUM: Arthropoda.

WOOLLY MONKEY *Lagothrix*, two species of South American monkey, one living in the lowland forests of the middle and upper Amazon, the other on the slopes of the Peruvian Andes. FAMILY: Cebidae, ORDER: Primates, CLASS: Mammalia.

WRASSES, perch-like fishes with elongated bodies. The lips are fleshy and in addition to strong teeth in the jaws there is a set of powerful molar teeth in the throat, the pharyngeal teeth, the lower set being fused into a triangular plate. Wrasses range from small reef-fishes of 3 in (8 cm) to large species reaching 10 ft (3 m) in length. Many of the Cleaner fishes, which remove parasites from larger fishes, are wrasses.

The tropical wrasses are usually more brightly coloured than those from temperate waters, but one of the prettiest is the Cuckoo wrasse *Labrus mixtus* of European coasts, which grows to about 12 in (30 cm) in length. Like many wrasses, the colours of the males differ from those of the females. The male has bright blue on the head and back, while the flanks, belly and dorsal and anal fins are yellow. There is a blue stripe running along the flank. The females are orange to red with three dark spots on the back. FAMILY: Labridae, ORDER: Perciformes, CLASS: Pisces.

WRECKFISH or Stone basse *Polyprion americanus*, a marine perch-like fish that derives its common name from its habit of frequenting wrecks and pieces of floating debris, reported to attain 6 ft (1·8 m) in length and to weigh up to 100 lb (45 kg). FAMILY: Serranidae, ORDER: Perciformes, CLASS: Pisces.

WREN *Troglodytes troglodytes*, a small European round-bodied bird with a short up-tilted bill, about 6 in (15 cm) long. The plumage is brown with darker bars and mottlings. The sexes are alike and the juveniles have a more mottled plumage than the adults. The wren is widely distributed from the outskirts of towns to the tops of hills up to 1000 m. It feeds mainly on insects and spiders and is noted for the remarkably large volume of the song of the male in spring, when he builds several domed nests, sometimes up to a dozen, the female selecting one and lining it to lay her 5–7 white eggs with dark markings. FAMILY: Troglodytidae, ORDER: Passeriformes, CLASS: Aves.

WRYNECKS, small slim birds about 6 in (15 cm) long, looking more like perching birds than woodpeckers. The plumage of the Common wryneck *Jynx torquilla* is grey-brown above, streaked and patterned like a nightjar, and white and pale buff below with darker bars and spots. It breeds throughout Europe, Asia and northwest Africa, and winters in Africa and India. The Red-breasted wryneck *Jynx ruficollis* inhabits Africa south of the Sahara, mainly in the east from Uganda to Cape Province but also throughout the Congo basin in the west. It is similar to the Common wryneck in general appearance but there is more red in the plumage.

The food is insects, largely ants. The wryneck does not bore into wood like a woodpecker but uses its long tongue to pick insects from bark, leaves and crevices too deep to insert the bill. Occasional flying insects are taken by flying out from a perch and occasionally it feeds on berries.

When handled wrynecks twist the head about in a most peculiar fashion. FAMILY: Picidae, ORDER: Piciformes. CLASS: Aves.

X-RAY FISH *Pristella riddlei*, of the rivers of northern South America, one of many small freshwater fishes that are semi-transparent. This particular species has been named for its almost total transparency. The swimbladder and much of the skeleton are visible through the fish's skin, the stomach and intestines are opaque, and the hind part of the body is semi-opaque. X-ray fishes are up to 2 in (5 cm) long with a fairly deep body and a forked tail. Although the body is usually described as transparent it sometimes appears silvery in reflected light. At other times it has a faint yellowish or greenish tinge and there is a black shoulder spot. A relative of the piranha, the X-ray fish feeds on small worms, insect larvae and crustaceans. FAMILY: Characidae, ORDER: Cypriniformes, CLASS: Pisces.

YAK *Bos (Bos) mutus*, the shaggy ox of the high plateau of Tibet (formerly *B. grunniens*), distinguished by the long fringe of hair on shoulders, flanks, thighs and tail, which may sweep the ground. The yak has been domesticated and is the staple beast of burden and milk-producer of the central Asian highlands. Wild yaks are larger than the domestic animals, bulls sometimes standing 6 ft 8 in (2 m) at the shoulder, and weighing 1,150 lb (525 kg). They are always black, whereas domestic yaks may be a variety of colours, from black to brown, white or piebald. The wild yak also has longer horns which turn in at the tips. In domestic yaks the tips often turn outwards and some breeds are polled.

Wild yak are found all over the Tibetan plateau and enter Indian territory in the Changechenmo valley, Ladak. Bulls travel alone or in groups of two or three; cows and calves form big herds of any number from 20 to 200. In summer, yaks ascend to 14–20,000 ft (4,270–6,100 m) where there is permanent snow and the temperature can be −40°F (−40°C). FAMILY: Bovidae, ORDER: Artiodactyla, CLASS: Mammalia.

YAPOK *Chironectes minimus*, an aquatic opossum closely related to the American *opossums and the only aquatic marsupial. The feet are broadly webbed and the tail, although prehensile, is much thicker than that of other opossums. Unlike most other marsupials the male, as well as the female, possesses a pouch into which the scrotum is pulled. The yapok is about 20 in (50 cm) long and the tail measures about 12 in (30 cm). The underparts, inner faces of the thighs, upper parts of the hindfeet and terminal portion of the tail are white. In swimming the hindfeet are used alternately, the tail streaming out behind.

The yapok is found in Central and South America. FAMILY: Didelphidae. ORDER: Marsupialia, CLASS: Mammalia.

ZAMBEZI SHARK *Carcharinus leucas*, a species probably worldwide in tropical and subtropical waters but remarkable for entering estuaries and rivers and even living permanently in freshwater. This species has many different common names: in Australia it is known as the Whaler shark, in Central America the Lake Nicaragua shark and in the United States the Bull, Cub or Ground shark. It has a broad head with short rounded snout. The body is up to 10 ft (3 m) long and weighs over 400 lb (200 kg). Wherever it occurs the Zambezi shark has a reputation for being aggressive. FAMILY: Carcharinidae, ORDER: Pleurotremata, CLASS: Chondrichthyes.

ZEBRA, three species of horse-like herbivores in Africa south of the Sahara. They have individual stripe-patterns like human fingerprints.

The living Plains zebra can be subdivided into three subspecies. In East Africa and down to the Zambezi is found the Boehm's zebra, or Grant's zebra *Equus quagga boehmi*, which has a pronounced stripe-pattern even down to the hoofs. The stripes are black or dark brown on a white background although in foals they are often light reddish-brown. Shadow stripes, that is dark stripes between the regular ones, occur in all populations of this subspecies, but are more common in the southern part of its distribution. The mane is, especially in adult stallions, often straggly and sometimes completely absent.

Rhodesia, Angola, Mozambique and Transvaal are the home of Chapman's zebra *E. quagga chapmani*, the stripe-pattern of which is somewhat reduced on the legs. Shadow stripes are common, the background colour is more cream than white, and the mane is well developed. Farther south and west, in southwest Africa, Botswana and Zululand, lives the Damara zebra *E. quagga antiquorum*, whose leg stripes are further reduced and have often disappeared. The stripe-pattern of the body is often quite irregular with large shadow stripes.

The Plains zebras are the most numerous of all wild equids and their total number has been estimated at about 300,000 of which about 200,000 live in the Serengeti-Mara area in East Africa.

Plains zebras live in small units of up to 16 members. There are two types of units: the families, consisting of one stallion, one to six mares and their young, and secondly the bachelor groups of surplus stallions, including subadult ones. Adult stallions are occasionally seen solitary.

Two subspecies of the Mountain zebra *Equus zebra* are known, the Cape mountain zebra *E. z. zebra*, which was formerly common in the Cape Province, and the Hartmann mountain zebra *E. z. hartmannae*, of southwest Africa and southern Angola. There are less than a 100 individuals left of the Cape mountain zebra. About 70 live in the Mountain Zebra National Park near Cradock, and another small population is in a reserve near Swellendam. The Hartmann zebra are more numerous. They live in the mountain ranges along the Namib Desert and even in the Namib itself. Their number has been estimated at 5–8,000. The Hartmann zebra stands about 51 in (1·3 m) at the shoulder, the Cape mountain zebra only 48 in (1·2 m). Apart from their stripe-patterns, both Mountain zebras are characterized by their dewlaps, a fold of skin under the neck. They are specialized mountain animals able to climb even steep, rocky canyons to get to water.

The Grevy's zebra *Equus grevyi* is the largest of all wild equids, measuring over 5 ft (1·5 m) at the shoulder. It inhabits the

One of the most characteristic sights of eastern and southern Africa, a herd of zebras.

semi-desert of northern Kenya and parts of Ethiopia and Somalia. FAMILY: Equidae, ORDER: Perissodactyla, CLASS: Mammalia.

ZEBRA FISH *Brachydanio rerio*, a small freshwater fish of Bengal and eastern India, less than 2 in (5 cm) long, also called Zebra danio by aquarists. A member of the large carp family it has a slim body with a fairly large single dorsal fin, and relatively large anal fin and tailfin, but with small pelvic and pectoral fins. It has two pairs of barbels and is brownish-olive on the back, Prussian blue on the flanks and has four golden stripes running from behind the head to the tail fin.

Although the name 'zebra' today conjures up a picture of the well-known member of the horse family, it is from an Amharic or Ethiopian word that first gained currency in Europe in 1600. By the early years of the 19th century its use had been extended not only to all manner of striped animals but also to materials such as striped shawls and scarves. A dozen or more fishes have received the name, including a Zebra shark, a Zebra cichlid and a Zebra salmon. Some have horizontal stripes and others vertical stripes. The foot-long marine fish *Therapon jarbuo* of the Indo-Pacific is sometimes called the Zebra fish, sometimes the Tiger fish. FAMILY: Cyprinodontidae, ORDER: Atheriniformes, CLASS: Pisces.

ZEBU *Bos indicus*, the characteristic 'native' cattle of Asia and Africa, easily recognized by the prominent hump over the shoulders and the large baggy dewlap under the throat. They usually have large drooping ears and prominent horns. The typical colour is steel grey, with the front half of the animal often a darker smoky grey, but many different colour varieties exist. The characteristic hump is a fleshy structure rising above the animal's back and supported internally by specially elongated neural spines of the thoracic vertebrae. Zebu are large, comparatively trim cattle, much less stocky than many of the western breeds, and are also noticeably longer in the face. FAMILY: Bovidae, ORDER: Artiodactyla, CLASS: Mammalia.

ZORILLA *Ictonyx striatus*, or African polecat having a black and white striped colouration reminiscent of the New World skunks. When alarmed, it erects its hair, waves its tail, hisses and sometimes feigns death. Moreover, the zorilla nearly always sprays its enemy with fluid from the anal scent glands, a secretion which has a much more foul and persistent odour than that of the African striped weasel, a species with which it is often confused. FAMILY: Mustelidae, ORDER: Carnivora, CLASS: Mammalia.

INDEX